Make the Connction

For trip planning and local activities, AAA guidebooks are just the beginning.

Open the door to a whole lot more on **AAA.com**. Get extra travel insight, more information and online booking.

Find this symbol for places to look, book and save on AAA.com.

Life Insurance Company

Have you ever stopped to think about the countless reasons why you need life insurance?

Your why isn't just about who you're protecting, it's about what you're doing to protect them.

Whether it's a new house, a new grandchild or a new life with the one we love, life insurance can cover you for the now and whatever's next.

What's your why?

Get a free quote at AAALife.com

Arkansas, Kansas, Missouri & Oklahoma

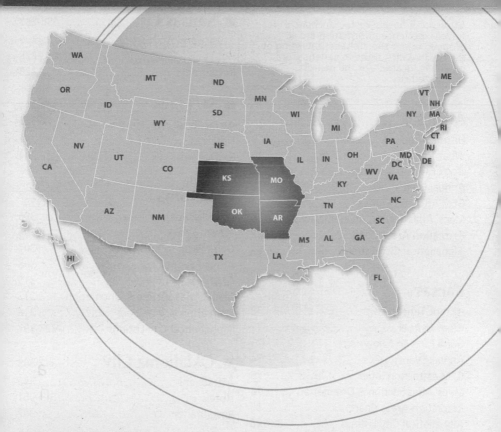

Published by AAA Publishing
1000 AAA Drive, Heathrow, FL 32746-5063
Copyright AAA 2020, All rights reserved

Advertising Rate and Circulation Information: (407) 444-8280

Printed in the USA by Quad/Graphics

This book is printed on paper certified by third-party standards for sustainably managed forestry and production.

Printed on recyclable paper.
Please recycle whenever possible.

Stock #4603

CONTENTS

Get more travel information
at AAA.com/travelguides
and AAA.com/traveltips

Attractions, hotels, restaurants and other travel experience information are all grouped under the alphabetical listing of the city in which those experiences are physically located—or the nearest recognized city.

free to
rock the boat

TripAssist travel insurance allows you to go with the flow. It can free you up to make the most of your vacation. Nothing will hold you back knowing that you and your travel plans are safe.

Talk to your AAA Travel Agent today for more information.

ESCAPE

SHOP

ENJOY

FROM EVERYDAY TO EXTRAORDINARY

APPLY TODAY!

Visit your local AAA office or AAA.com/CreditCard

Using Your Guide

AAA TourBook guides are packed with travel insights, maps and listings of places to stay, play, eat and save. For more listings, more details and online booking, visit **AAA.com/travelguides**.

Helping You Make the Connection
Look for this symbol 🔗 throughout the guides for direct links to related content.

A to Z City Listings
Cities and places are listed alphabetically within each state or province. Attractions, hotels and restaurants are listed once — under the city in which they are physically located.

Cities that are considered part of a larger destination city or area have an expanded city header. The header identifies the larger region and cross-references pages that contain shared trip-planning resources:

- Destination map – outline map of the cities that comprise a destination city or area
- Attraction spotting map – regional street map marked with attraction locations
- Hotel/restaurant spotting map and index – regional street map numbered with hotel and restaurant locations identified in an accompanying index

Cities that are not considered part of a larger destination city or area but have a significant number of listings may have these resources within the individual city section:

- Attraction spotting map
- Hotel/restaurant spotting map and index

Location Abbreviations
Directions are from the center of town unless otherwise specified, using these highway abbreviations:
Bus. Rte.=business route
CR=county road
FM=farm to market
FR=forest road
Hwy.=Canadian highway
I=interstate highway
LR=legislative route
R.R.=rural route
SR/PR=state or provincial route
US=federal highway

About Listed Establishments
Hotels and restaurants are listed on the basis of merit alone after careful evaluation by full time, professionally trained AAA inspectors. An establishment's decision to advertise in the TourBook guide has no bearing on its evaluation or designation; nor does inclusion of advertising imply AAA endorsement of products and services.

Information in this guide was believed accurate at the time of publication. However, since changes inevitably occur between annual editions, please contact your AAA travel professional, visit **AAA.com/travelguides** or download the free AAA Mobile app to confirm prices and schedules.

Attraction Listing Icons
[SAVE] AAA Discounts & Rewards® member discount

[⚡] Electric vehicle charging station on premises. Domestic station information provided by the U.S. Department of Energy. Canadian station information provided by Plug'n Drive Ontario.

[GT] Guided Tours available

[▲] Camping facilities

[🍴] Food on premises

[✖] Recreational activities

[🐾] Pet friendly (Call for restrictions/fees.)

[🎋] Picnicking allowed

In select cities only:

[🚇] Mass transit station within 1 mile. Icon is followed by station name and AAA/CAA designated station number within listing.

[GEM] AAA/CAA travel experts may designate an attraction of exceptional interest and quality as a AAA GEM — a *Great Experience for Members®*. See GEM Attraction Index (listed on CONTENTS page) for a complete list of locations.

Consult the online travel guides at **AAA.com/travelguides** or visit AAA Mobile for additional things to do if you have time.

Hotel Listing Icons
May be preceded by CALL and/or SOME UNITS.
Member Information:
[SAVE] Member rates: discounted standard room rate or lowest public rate available at time of booking for dates of stay.

ECO Eco-certified by government or private organization.

⊞ Electric vehicle charging station on premises. Domestic station information provided by the U.S. Department of Energy. Canadian station information provided by Plug'n Drive Ontario.

⊠ Smoke-free premises

In select cities only:

🚇 Mass transit station within 1 mile. Icon is followed by station name and AAA/CAA designated station number within listing.

Services:

✈ Airport transportation

🐾 Pet friendly (Call for restrictions/fees.)

🍴 Restaurant on premises

🍴+ Restaurant off premises

🍽 Room service for 2 or more meals

🍸 Full bar

👶 Child care

BIZ Business center

♿ Accessible features (Call property for available services and amenities.)

Activities:

🎰 Full-service casino

🏊 Pool

💪 Health club or exercise room on premises

In-Room Amenities:

HS High-speed Internet service

$HS High-speed Internet service (Call property for fees.)

📶 Wireless Internet service

$📶 Wireless Internet service (Call property for fees.)

📶 No wireless Internet service

🎬 Pay movies

🧊 Refrigerator

📟 Microwave

☕ Coffeemaker

🅐🅒 No air conditioning

📺 No TV

☎ No telephones

Restaurant Listing Icons

SAVE AAA Discounts & Rewards® member discount

ECO Eco-certified by government or private organization.

⊞ Electric vehicle charging station on premises. Domestic station information provided by the U.S. Department of Energy. Canadian station information provided by Plug'n Drive Ontario.

🅐🅒 No air conditioning

♿ Accessible features (Call property for available services and amenities.)

⊠ Designated smoking section

B Breakfast

L Lunch

D Dinner

24 Open 24 hours

LATE Open after 11 p.m.

🐾 Pet friendly (Call for restrictions/fees.)

In select cities only:

🚇 Mass transit station within 1 mile. Icon is followed by station name and AAA/CAA designated station number within listing.

Map Legend

For attraction and hotel/restaurant spotting maps, refer to the legend below to identify symbols and color coding.

Roads/Highways

- Interchange
- Free / Toll
- Controlled access
- Controlled access toll
- Local toll
- Primary
- Secondary
- Local unpaved
- Under construction
- Tunnel
- Pedestrian only
- Auto ferry
- Passenger ferry
- Scenic byway

Areas of Interest

- Incorporated city
- Int'l/Regional airport
- Park
- Recreation sites
- Forest
- Natural lands
- Military
- Historic
- Native American
- Beach
- Marsh

Route Shields

Interstate	95 / 95 Business	Trans-Canada
Federal	Primary 22 / Secondary 22	Provincial Autoroute
State	1 / 1	Mexico
County	1 / 1	Historic 66

Trans-Canada: Primary / Secondary
Provincial Autoroute: 22 / 22
Mexico: 1 / 1

Boundaries

- International
- State
- Time zone
- Continental Divide

Points of Interest

- **★** National capital
- **★** State/Prov capital
- **■** AAA/CAA club location
- **■** Feature of interest
- **▽** GEM attraction
- **⑫** Hotel listing
- **③** Restaurant listing
- **🏛** College/University
- o Town
- **人** Campground
- **🍷** Winery
- **⊛** Customs station
- **■** Historic
- △ Mountain peak
- Rapid transit / Stations
- Metromover

Understanding the Diamond Designations

Hotel and restaurant inspections are unscheduled to ensure our trained professionals encounter the same unbiased experience members do.

- The first step for every hotel and restaurant is to demonstrate they meet expected standards of cleanliness, comfort and hospitality.

- Only hotels and restaurants that pass AAA's rigorous on-site inspection receive a AAA Diamond designation.

Learn more at **AAA.com/Diamonds**.

Hotels

APPROVED

Noteworthy by meeting the industry-leading standards of AAA inspections.

THREE DIAMOND

Comprehensive amenities, style and comfort level.

FOUR DIAMOND

Upscale style and amenities enhanced with the right touch of service.

FIVE DIAMOND

World-class luxury, amenities and indulgence for a once-in-a-lifetime experience.

Restaurants

APPROVED

Noteworthy by meeting the industry-leading standards of AAA inspections.

THREE DIAMOND

Trendy food skillfully presented in a remarkable setting.

FOUR DIAMOND

Distinctive fine dining, well-served amid upscale ambience.

FIVE DIAMOND

Leading-edge cuisine, ingredients and preparation with extraordinary service and surroundings.

Guest Safety

Inspectors view a sampling of rooms during hotel evaluations and, therefore, AAA/CAA cannot guarantee working locks and operational fire safety equipment in every guest unit.

Contacting AAA/CAA About the TourBook Guide

Tell us what you think about the TourBook guides or your experience at a listed hotel, restaurant or attraction. If your visit doesn't meet your expectations, please contact us **during your visit or within 30 days**. Be sure to save your receipts. We also welcome your recommendations on places to inspect.

Use the easy online form at **AAA.com/MemberFeedback**, email memberrelations@national.aaa.com or mail your feedback to: AAA Member Comments, 1000 AAA Dr., Box 61, Heathrow, FL 32746.

Little Rock

Arkansas

When evaluating a diamond, it's essential to keep the four "C's" in mind: Cut, color, clarity and carat highlight the qualities of the stone and define its natural beauty.

Like the gem, Arkansas also boasts four "C's." Clear lakes and streams, caves and colorful countryside accentuate the beauty of the Diamond State. And let's not forget Bill Clinton.

Waves calmly lap the shores of Bull Shoals Lake and lakes Norfork and Ouachita. The Arkansas and White rivers meander across the state, joining with the great Mississippi.

Underground caves offer a different view of Arkansas—from the bottom up.

Arkansas' countryside adds a splash of color. Sunsets on the rivers mix shades of pinks, reds and yellows; trees among some 17 million acres of national forests don a rust-colored coat in the fall.

Monuments to William Jefferson Clinton await fans of our 42nd president in Hope,

Hot Springs National Park

Hot Springs and Little Rock. Walking tours in these cities point out numerous stops on his path to the presidency.

Come appraise the Diamond State. You'll find it full of wealth.

What's in a Name?

French explorers first started the Arkansas name game. Scouting the area now designated as the Diamond State, they met the Ugukhpah Indians, also known by the sobriquets Quapaw, Arkansas and Arkansa. One of these was adopted to identify the territory. Simple enough, right?

Well, not really. When Jacques Marquette and Louis Joliet explored the Mississippi and Arkansas rivers in 1673, the name appeared as *Akansea* in their journal. A map drawn 1718-22 by Bénard de la Harpe referred to the territory as *Arkansas.* Later, Zebulon Pike spelled it *Arkansaw.*

But how to pronounce it? Early senators were at odds; one was reputed to have introduced himself as the senator from Ar-*kansas;* the other called his home state Arkan-*saw.* To squelch any future confusion, the General Assembly passed a resolve in 1881 that the state name be spelled Arkan-sas, but pronounced Arkan*saw.*

The evolving name game was much like finding a diamond in the rough—a jewel of an idea that just needed a little polishing to reveal its brilliance. The final decision conveys a melding of its cultural origins—the pronunciation respects the heritage of the land's earliest inhabitants, while the French spelling adds a bit of panache.

Little Rock, ironically the largest city in the state, also had French origins. The same man who dubbed the state Arkansas also is credited with naming its capital. After hearing from Native Americans that a large "emerald stone" sat along the Arkansas River, de la Harpe and his party sought the treasure but found only a small rock, greenish in hue. He called it "*la petite roche*," and the name stuck.

Nowadays, the capital is anything but a small green rock. The swiftly moving waters of the Arkansas reflect both the glitter of Little Rock's contemporary skyline and its success as a primary river port.

Rising steam from more than 40 boiling springs coined the name of Hot Springs. A hot spot for centuries, Native Americans were drawn to the area for healing potions bestowed by the Great Spirit. The terrain, now a national park and health resort, still attracts visitors for its therapeutic aura, but it has a more recent claim to fame—as the boyhood home of Bill Clinton.

Funky formations in Arkansas' dark and chilly caves are named after things they resemble: Pipe organs, soda straws, frozen waterfalls and a friendly dragon are hidden in grottoes that date back almost 350 million years.

There are a few reasons why Arkansas is called the Diamond State: The 40-carat Uncle Sam, the 16-carat Amarillo Starlight and the 34-carat Star of Murfreesboro rank high on the list of sensational finds at Crater of Diamonds State Park near Murfreesboro.

The hamlet of Mount Ida in the Ouachita Mountains offers more than outstanding scenery; clear quartz crystals hide in the red clay, waiting to be unearthed by rockhounds.

Recreation

Reservoirs, natural lakes and streams lure anglers; Lake Norfork is best known for lunker bass, and nearby Bull Shoals Lake, stretching across five counties in northern Arkansas, is fantastic for catfish, crappie, bass, trout and walleye. An annual stocking program helps ensure plentiful bites in both lakes.

The White River, a world-class cold trout stream, is famous for huge cutthroat, brown and rainbow trout; for big fins, cast in the waters of the North Fork section. Check out the Missouri, Arkansas and Little Red rivers—the last holds the current world record for brown trout. Tucked into a pecan grove, Lake Chicot, the state's largest natural lake, offers crappie. At Millwood State Park, boat lanes meander through timber marshes, while crappie, summer bream and catfish swim in Millwood Lake in spring and fall.

The Buffalo River yields smallmouth bass; on its upper reaches, brave souls go canoeing on challenging white waters, while gentler souls float past limestone bluffs on the lower river. Canoes also dot the White River from Fayetteville to Brashears.

Go boating, swimming and water skiing in the waters of Lake Norfork. For scuba diving, head to limpid Lake Ouachita. Gigantic Bull Shoals Lake is called the "Caribbean of the Midwest": Its blue, crystal-clear depths provide amazing visibility for diving and scavenging.

Pinnacle Mountain State Park, within the Ouachita National Forest, offers many hiking trails. At Petit Jean State Park, trails lead past forests, canyons, streams, meadows and mountainsides to Cedar Creek Canyon, where the creek drops and becomes a waterfall.

Wander among stalagmites and stalactites in one of northern Arkansas' eight caves and shine your flashlight on subterranean lakes, mazes and otherworldly creatures like blind trout and albino crawfish.

Petit Jean State Park

Historic Timeline

1541	Exploration of the region begins under Hernando de Soto's leadership.
1686	Henri de Tonti establishes the Mississippi Valley's first permanent European settlement.
1763	Spain gains control of the area but 37 years later returns it to France.
1803	The United States acquires the region as part of the Louisiana Purchase.
1836	Arkansas enters the Union as a slave-holding state.
1921	Oil is discovered near El Dorado.
1932	Hattie Caraway of Jonesboro becomes the first woman to be elected to the U.S. Senate.
1957	Little Rock Central High School resists federally mandated public school desegregation.
1962	Sam Walton opens the first Walmart store in Rogers.
1992	Native son Bill Clinton becomes the 42nd president of the United States.
2005	The unconfirmed sighting of an ivory-billed woodpecker—long considered extinct—prompts a million-dollar search in Arkansas' Big Woods.

What To Pack

Temperature Averages Maximum/Minimum	JANUARY	FEBRUARY	MARCH	APRIL	MAY	JUNE	JULY	AUGUST	SEPTEMBER	OCTOBER	NOVEMBER	DECEMBER
Crossett	53/29	59/33	67/40	75/47	82/56	89/64	92/68	92/67	86/60	77/47	65/39	56/32
Fayetteville	44/24	51/29	59/38	69/46	76/55	84/64	89/69	89/67	81/59	70/47	57/37	48/28
Fort Smith	48/28	55/33	64/41	73/49	80/59	88/67	93/71	93/70	85/63	75/51	61/40	51/31
Jacksonport	46/28	52/33	61/42	71/51	80/60	88/68	92/72	91/70	84/62	74/50	60/42	49/33
Little Rock	50/31	56/35	64/43	73/50	81/59	89/68	93/72	92/71	85/64	75/51	62/42	53/34
Texarkana	53/36	60/39	68/46	75/54	82/62	89/69	93/73	93/72	86/65	77/55	64/45	56/38

From the records of The Weather Channel Interactive, Inc.

Good Facts To Know

ABOUT THE STATE

POPULATION: 2,959,373.

AREA: 51,945 square miles; ranks 29th.

CAPITAL: Little Rock.

HIGHEST POINT: 2,753 ft., Mount Magazine.

LOWEST POINT: 55 ft., Ouachita River.

TIME ZONE(S): Central. DST.

REGULATIONS

TEEN DRIVING LAWS: The minimum age for an unrestricted driver's license is 18. Drivers ages 16-18 holding intermediate licenses are not permitted to drive between 11 p.m. and 4 a.m., or with more than one unrelated passenger under age 21, unless accompanied by a licensed driver age 21 or older. Phone (501) 682-4692 for more information about Arkansas driver's license regulations.

SEAT BELT/CHILD RESTRAINT LAWS: Seat belts are required for driver and front-seat passengers ages 15 and over. Children ages 6-14 or at least 60 pounds are required to be in a child restraint or seat belt; child restraints are required for children under age 6 and less than 60 pounds. AAA recommends the use of seat belts and appropriate child restraints for the driver and all passengers.

CELLPHONE RESTRICTIONS: Drivers under age 18 with learner's or intermediate licenses are not permitted to use interactive communication devices while driving. Drivers ages 18-21 are prohibited from using a hand-held cell phone while driving. Text messaging while driving is prohibited for all drivers. Handheld cell phone use is prohibited for all drivers when passing a school building or school zone during school hours when children are present, or in a highway work zone when a highway worker is present.

HELMETS FOR MOTORCYCLISTS: Required for riders under 21.

RADAR DETECTORS: Permitted for passenger vehicles, prohibited for commercial vehicles.

MOVE OVER LAW: State law requires drivers approaching stationary emergency response vehicles, that are displaying flashing lights, including wreckers or tow vehicles traveling in the same direction, to move to the farthest lane from the vehicle if safe and possible to do so. Or to slow to a speed appropriate for road and weather conditions. Also included in the law are utility vehicles.

FIREARMS LAWS: Vary by state and/or county. Contact the Arkansas Attorney General's Office, 323 Center St., Suite 200, Little Rock, AR 72201; phone (501) 682-2007.

HOLIDAYS

HOLIDAYS: Jan. 1 ▪ Martin Luther King Jr. Day/Robert E. Lee's Birthday, Jan. 19 ▪ Washington's Birthday/Presidents Day, Feb. (3rd Mon.) ▪ Memorial Day, May (last Mon.) ▪ July 4 ▪ Labor Day, Sept. (1st Mon.) ▪ Veterans Day, Nov. 11 ▪ Thanksgiving, Nov. (4th Thurs.) ▪ Christmas, Dec. 25.

MONEY

TAXES: Arkansas' gross receipts tax is 6.5 percent with local options to impose additional increments. A 2 percent tourism gross receipts tax is levied on lodgings statewide; some cities may levy an additional 1 percent.

VISITOR INFORMATION

INFORMATION CENTERS: State welcome centers are 3 mi. n. of Bentonville on US 71 ▪ n. of Harrison on US 65 ▪ in Mammoth Spring on US 63N ▪ 5 mi. s. of the Missouri state line on I-55S at Blytheville ▪ 6 mi. n. of Corning on US 67N ▪ 2 mi. e. of the Oklahoma state line on I-40W at Fort Smith/Van Buren ▪ 5 mi. n. of the Louisiana state line on US 167S/SR 7 at junction with US 82 at El Dorado ▪ on US 49 Bypass at Helena ▪ 10 mi. w. of the Mississippi state line off US 82 at Lake Village ▪ on I-30 in Texarkana ▪ on US 71 on the Red River n. of Texarkana ▪ on US 412W at Siloam Springs ▪ 3 mi. w. of West Memphis on I-40 ▪ and at One Capitol Mall in Little Rock.

Most centers are open daily 8-6, Memorial Day weekend-Labor Day ▪ 8-5, rest of year. The Little Rock center is open Mon.-Fri. 8-5. Helena and Red River are open daily 8-5, Memorial Day weekend-Labor Day ▪ 8-4, rest of year. Christmas Eve hours are noon-4. Centers are closed Jan. 1, Easter, Thanksgiving and Christmas.

FURTHER INFORMATION FOR VISITORS:
Arkansas Department of Parks & Tourism
One Capitol Mall Suite 4A900
Little Rock, AR 72201
(501) 682-7777 (also TTY)
(800) 628-8725 Information
(888) 287-2757 for park information *(See ad p. 49, p. 169.)*

NATIONAL FOREST INFORMATION:
USDA Forest Service: Southern Region
1720 Peachtree Rd. N.W., Suite 700 B
Atlanta, GA 30309
(404) 347-4177
(877) 444-6777 (reservations)

FISHING AND HUNTING REGULATIONS:
Game and Fish Commission
2 Natural Resources Dr.
Little Rock, AR 72205
(501) 223-6300
(800) 364-4263 Toll-free

Arkansas Annual Events

Please call ahead to confirm event details.

Visit **AAA.com/travelguides/events** to find
AAA-listed events for every day of the year

WINTER

Dec. - Christmas and Candlelight
Washington / 870-983-2684
- The Lights of the Ozarks
Fayetteville / 479-521-5776
- Christmas Tour of Homes / Eureka
Springs / 501-253-8737

Jan. - Women's Living Expo / Springdale
203-259-3351
- Antique Alley Arkansas Antique Show
Conway / 501-230-5728

Feb. - Home & Garden Show / Pine
Bluff / 573-253-9774
- Boat, Tackle & RV Show / Hot
Springs / 501-225-6177
- Chocolate Lovers' Festival &
Emporium / Eureka
Springs / 479-253-8737

SPRING

Mar. - Daffodil Festival / Camden
870-833-2443
- Spring Bluegrass Festival / Mountain
View / 870-501-5105
- Jonquil Festival / Washington
870-983-2684

Apr. - Arkansas Scottish Festival
Batesville / 870-307-7473
- Craft Village Open House / Mountain
View / 870-269-3851

May - Arkansas Fiddlers Convention
Harrison / 870-429-6174
- International Greek Food Festival
Little Rock / 501-221-5300

SUMMER

June - Riverfront Blues Festival / Fort
Smith / 479-783-8888
- Hot Springs Music Festival / Hot
Springs / 501-623-4763

July - Fat Tire Festival / Eureka
Springs / 479-363-0625

Aug. - Old Time Fiddle Weekend / Mountain
View / 870-269-3851
- Watermelon Festival / Hope
870-777-3640

FALL

Sept. - Grandpa and Ramona Jones Banjo
Weekend / Mountain
View / 870-269-3851
- Hot Air Balloon Race State
Championship / Harrison
870-741-2659
- Jazz Fest / Hot
Springs / 501-321-2835

Oct. - Arkansas State Fair / Little
Rock / 501-372-8341
- King Biscuit Blues Festival
Helena-West Helena / 870-572-5223

Nov. - World's Championship Duck Calling
Contest / Stuttgart / 870-673-1602
- Enchanted Land of Lights and
Legends / Pine Bluff / 800-536-7660
- Caroling in the Caverns / Mountain
View / 870-269-8068

Ⓒ **Love the great outdoors? Find places**

to camp at AAA.com/campgrounds

Ozark National Forest

Hot Air Balloon Race State
Championship, Harrison

Garvan Woodland Gardens,
Hot Springs

Old State House Museum, Little Rock

Watermelon Festival, Hope

Index: Great Experience for Members

AAA editor's picks of exceptional note

Blanchard Springs
Caverns

Petit Jean State Park

Ozark Folk Center
State Park

Hot Springs National
Park

See Orientation map on p. 22 for corresponding grid coordinates, if applicable.
*Indicates the GEM is temporarily closed.

Arkansas

Atlas Section

ROADS/HIGHWAYS

- INTERSTATE
- CONTROLLED ACCESS
- CONTROLLED ACCESS TOLL
- TOLL ROAD
- PRIMARY DIVIDED
- PRIMARY UNDIVIDED
- SECONDARY DIVIDED
- SECONDARY UNDIVIDED
- LOCAL DIVIDED
- LOCAL UNDIVIDED
- UNPAVED ROAD
- UNDER CONSTRUCTION
- TUNNEL
- PEDESTRIAN ONLY
- AUTO FERRY
- PASSENGER FERRY
- SCENIC BYWAY
- DISTANCE BETWEEN MARKERS
- EXIT NUMBER-FREE/TOLL
- INTERCHANGE FULL/PARTIAL
- WELCOME/INFORMATION CENTER
- REST AREA/ SERVICE CENTER

ROAD SHIELDS

- INTERSTATE/BUSINESS
- U.S./STATE/COUNTY
- FOREST/INDIAN
- TRANS-CANADA
- PROVINCIAL AUTOROUTE/ KING'S HIGHWAY
- MEXICO
- HISTORIC ROUTE 66
- VT 41 REFERENCE PAGE INDICATOR

BOUNDARIES

- INTERNATIONAL
- STATE
- COUNTY
- TIME ZONE
- CONTINENTAL DIVIDE

POINTS OF INTEREST

- TOWN
- NATIONAL CAPITAL
- STATE/PROVINCIAL CAPITAL
- AAA/CAA CLUB LOCATION
- FEATURE OF INTEREST
- COLLEGE/UNIVERSITY
- CUSTOMS STATION
- HISTORIC
- LIGHTHOUSE
- MONUMENT/MEMORIAL
- STATE/PROVINCIAL PARK
- NATIONAL WILDLIFE REFUGE
- SKI AREA
- SPORTS COMPLEX
- DAM

AREAS OF INTEREST

- INDIAN
- MILITARY
- PARK
- FOREST
- GRASSLANDS
- HISTORIC
- INT'L/REGIONAL AIRPORT
- INCORPORATED CITY

CITIES/TOWNS are color-coded by size, showing where to find AAA Inspected and Approved lodgings or restaurants listed in the AAA TourBook guides and on AAA.com:

- Red - major destinations and capitals; many listings
- Black - destinations; some listings
- Grey - no listings

Use these detailed driving maps to plan your stops and find your way. For complete route planning, purchase the latest AAA Road Atlas at participating AAA/CAA offices, and use the free online TripTik Travel Planner at AAA.com/maps

Atlas

ROAD
2020

STAY CONNECTED

to all the things membership can do for you

- **Member discounts around you**
- **Cheapest gas nearby**
- **Diamond hotels and restaurants**
- **Travel information and reservations**
- **Roadside assistance**

**Download today.
Connect every day.
AAA.com/mobile | CAA.ca/mobile**

Recreation Areas Chart

The map location numerals in column 2 show an area's location on the preceding map.

Find thousands of places to camp at AAA.com/campgrounds

	MAP LOCATION	CAMPING	PICNICKING	HIKING TRAILS	BOATING	BOAT RAMP	BOAT RENTAL	FISHING	SWIMMING	PET FRIENDLY	BICYCLE TRAILS	NATURE PROGS.	VISITOR CENTER	LODGE/CABINS	FOOD SERVICE
NATIONAL PARKS (See place listings.)															
Hot Springs (D-2) 5,500 acres.		•	•	•						•		•	•	
NATIONAL FORESTS (See place listings.)															
Ouachita (C-1) 1.8 million acres. West-central Arkansas and southeastern Oklahoma. Horse trails.		•	•	•	•	•	•	•	•	•	•		•	•
Ozark (B-1) 1,123,079 acres. Northwestern Arkansas. Horse trails.		•	•	•	•	•	•	•	•	•			•	•
St. Francis (D-6) 22,600 acres. East-central Arkansas.		•	•	•	•	•		•		•				
NATIONAL RIVERS (See place listings.)															
Buffalo (B-3) 95,730 acres. Northwestern Arkansas.		•	•	•	•	•		•		•		•	•	•
ARMY CORPS OF ENGINEERS															
Blue Mountain Lake (C-2) 17,000 acres 1.5 mi. s.w. of Waveland on SR 10. Water skiing; playground.	1	•	•	•	•	•		•	•	•				

Recreation Areas Chart

The map location numerals in column 2 show an area's location on the preceding map.

🔗 **Find thousands of places to camp at AAA.com/campgrounds**

	MAP LOCATION	CAMPING	PICNICKING	HIKING TRAILS	BOATING	BOAT RAMP	BOAT RENTAL	FISHING	SWIMMING	PET FRIENDLY	BICYCLE TRAILS	NATURE PROGS.	VISITOR CENTER	LODGE/CABINS	FOOD SERVICE
Bull Shoals Lake (A-3) 45,440 acres 8 mi. w. of Mountain Home on SR 178. Sailing, scuba diving, water skiing.	2	•	•	•	•	•	•	•	•	•		•	•	•	•
DeGray Lake (D-2) 31,800 acres. Disc golf (nine holes), sailing, scuba diving, water skiing; fitness trail.	3	•	•	•	•	•	•	•	•	•			•	•	•
DeQueen Lake (D-1) 7,150 acres 4 mi. n.w. of DeQueen on SR 71. Canoeing, water skiing.	4	•	•		•	•		•	•	•					
Dierks Lake (D-1) 8,100 acres 5 mi. n.w. of Dierks on SR 70. Water skiing.	5	•	•		•	•		•	•	•					
Gillham Lake (D-1) 9,000 acres 6 mi. n.e. of Gillham on SR 71. Water skiing.	6	•	•	•	•	•		•	•	•					
Greers Ferry Lake (C-4) 40,914 acres. Sailing, scuba diving, water skiing.	7	•	•	•	•	•	•	•	•	•		•	•		•
Lake Dardanelle (C-2) 34,000 acres 4 mi. w. of Russellville on SR 7.	8	•	•	•	•	•	•	•	•	•		•	•		
Lake Greeson (D-2) 15,842 acres 7 mi. n. of Murfreesboro on SR 19. Sailing, scuba diving, water skiing; motorcycle trails.	9	•	•	•	•	•	•	•	•	•	•			•	
Lake Ouachita (D-3) 40,000 acres 12 mi. n. of Mountain Pine on SR 227. Canoeing, kayaking, sailing, scuba diving, water skiing; boating trail.	10	•	•	•	•	•	•	•	•	•		•	•	•	
Millwood Lake (E-2) 30,000 acres 9 mi. e. of Ashdown on SR 32. Bird-watching; playground.	11	•	•	•	•	•	•	•	•	•		•	•		
Nimrod Lake (C-2) 24,840 acres on SR 60 w. of SR 7 at Fourche Junction. Tubing, water skiing; playground.	12	•	•		•	•		•	•	•					
Norfork Lake (A-4) 22,000 acres. Sailing, scuba diving, water skiing.	13	•	•	•	•	•	•	•	•	•	•	•	•	•	•
STATE															
Bull Shoals-White River (A-3) 663 acres 6 mi. n. of Mountain Home on SR 5, then 8 mi. w. on SR 178. Sailing, scuba diving, trout fishing, water skiing; amphitheater, bicycle rentals, playground.	14	•	•	•	•	•	•	•		•	•	•	•		
Cane Creek (E-4) 2,171 acres 4 mi. e. of Star City on SR 293. Bicycle rentals, kayak trail, playground.	15	•	•	•	•	•		•			•		•		
Cossatot River (D-1) 5,401 acres 9 mi. e. of Vandervoort on SR 246. Natural area. Canoeing, kayaking, whitewater rafting; playground.	16	•	•	•	•			•	•	•		•	•		
Crater of Diamonds (D-2) 887 acres. Diamond hunting; wildlife observation blind, water park.	17	•	•	•				•		•		•	•		•
Crowley's Ridge (B-5) 270 acres. Boats with electric motors only.	18	•	•	•	•			•	•	•			•	•	•
Daisy (D-2) 272 acres .2 mi. s. of Daisy off US 70. Amphitheater, playground.	19	•	•	•	•	•		•		•			•		
Davidsonville (A-5) 173 acres. Historic. Playground.	20	•	•	•	•			•		•			•		
DeGray Lake Resort (D-2) 938 acres. Golf (18 holes), horseback riding, sailing, scuba diving, tennis, water skiing; bicycle rentals.	21	•	•	•	•	•	•	•	•	•	•	•	•	•	•
Devil's Den (B-1) 2,000 acres 17 mi. s.w. on SR 170. Scenic. Equestrian camping; canoe and pedal boat rentals, horse trails, swimming pool.	22	•	•	•	•	•		•	•	•	•	•	•	•	•
Hobbs State Park-Conservation Area (A-2) 12,056 acres 10 mi. e. of Rogers on SR 12. Hunting; firing range, horse/multi-use trails, primitive campsites.	23	•	•	•	•			•		•	•	•	•		
Jacksonport (B-4) 157 acres. Playground.	24	•	•	•	•	•		•		•	•		•		
Lake Catherine (D-3) 2,180 acres 15 mi. n.w. of Malvern on SR 171. Horseback riding; amphitheater, playground.	25	•	•	•	•	•	•	•	•	•		•	•	•	
Lake Charles (B-5) 140 acres 8 mi. n.w. of Hoxie on US 63, then 6 mi. s.w. on SR 25. Kayak boating trail, playground.	26	•	•	•	•	•		•	•	•			•		•
Lake Chicot (F-5) 132 acres 8 mi. n.e. of Lake Village on SR 144. Bird-watching; bicycle rentals, playground.	27	•	•	•	•	•	•	•	•	•		•	•	•	•

Recreation Areas Chart

The map location numerals in column 2 show an area's location on the preceding map.

Find thousands of places to camp at AAA.com/campgrounds

	MAP LOCATION	CAMPING	PICNICKING	HIKING TRAILS	BOATING	BOAT RAMP	BOAT RENTAL	FISHING	SWIMMING	PET FRIENDLY	BICYCLE TRAILS	NATURE PROGS.	VISITOR CENTER	LODGE/CABINS	FOOD SERVICE
Lake Dardanelle															
Dardanelle (C-2) 90 acres 4 mi. w. of Dardanelle. Water skiing; playground.	28	•	•	•	•	•	•		•	•	•				
Russellville (C-2) 184 acres 4 mi. s. of Russellville on SR 326. Water skiing, wildlife viewing; amphitheater, kayak rentals, playground.	29	•	•	•	•	•	•	•	•	•	•		•	•	
Lake Frierson (B-5) 114 acres 10 mi. n. of Jonesboro on SR 141. Playground.	30	•	•	•	•			•		•			•	•	
Lake Ouachita (D-2) 370 acres. Canoeing, kayaking, sailing, scuba diving, water skiing; amphitheater, boating trail, playground.	31	•	•	•	•	•	•	•		•		•	•	•	•
Lake Poinsett (B-5) 111 acres 1 mi. e. of Harrisburg on SR 14, then 3 mi. s. on SR 163. Playground.	32	•	•	•	•	•	•	•		•			•	•	
Logoly (F-3) 368 acres .7 mi. e. of McNeil on CR 47. Wildlife viewing; amphitheater, playground.	33	•	•	•				•		•		•	•		
Mammoth Spring (A-4) 62 acres. Scenic. Historic. Kayak and paddleboat rentals; playground.	34		•	•	•	•	•	•		•		•	•		
Millwood (E-1) 823 acres 9 mi. e. of Ashdown on SR 32. Bird-watching; playground, water bike rentals.	35	•	•	•	•	•	•	•		•		•	•		
Moro Bay (F-3) 117 acres 20 mi. n.e. of El Dorado on SR 15. Playground.	36	•	•	•	•	•	•	•		•		•	•	•	•
Mount Magazine (C-2) 2,200 acres 17 mi. s. of Paris on SR 309. Historic. Bird-watching, horseback riding, rock climbing; hang gliding launch.	37	•	•	•						•	•	•	•	•	•
Mount Nebo (C-2) 2,812 acres 7 mi. w. of Dardanelle on SR 155. Tennis; amphitheater, bicycle rentals, hang gliding launch, playground, pool.	38	•	•	•				•	•	•	•	•	•	•	
Petit Jean (C-3) 2,896 acres. Scenic. Tennis; amphitheater, canoe, kayak and paddleboat rentals, playground.	39	•	•	•	•	•	•	•	•	•		•	•	•	•
Pinnacle Mountain (C-3) 2,000 acres 13 mi. w. of Little Rock on SR 10, then 2 mi. n. on SR 300. Scenic. Horseback riding; arboretum, canoe, kayak and pedal boat rentals, playground.	40		•	•	•	•	•	•		•	•	•	•		
Queen Wilhelmina (D-1) 460 acres. Wildlife viewing; miniature golf, playground.	41	•	•	•						•		•		•	•
Village Creek (C-5) 6,911 acres 13 mi. n. of Forrest City on SR 284. Equestrian camping, golf (27 holes), tennis; bicycle rentals, horse trails, playground.	42	•	•	•	•	•	•	•	•	•	•	•	•	•	•
White Oak Lake (E-2) 666 acres 2 mi. s.e. of Bluff City on SR 387. Bird-watching; bicycle rentals, playground.	43	•	•	•	•	•	•	•		•		•	•		
Withrow Springs (A-2) 786 acres 5 mi. n. of Huntsville on SR 23. Tennis; baseball field, canoe rentals, playground, pool.	44	•	•	•	•	•	•	•		•		•	•		
Woolly Hollow (C-3) 399 acres 12 mi. n. of Conway on US 65, then 6 mi. e. on SR 285. Playground.	45	•	•	•	•		•	•	•	•			•		
OTHER															
Beaverfork Lake (C-3) 900 acres 3 mi. n. of Conway off US 65 or SR 25.	46		•		•	•		•	•	•					
Burns Park (C-4) 1,700 acres. Disc golf (36 holes), golf (36 holes), tennis; athletic fields, playground.	47	•	•	•	•	•		•		•	•				
Cadron Settlement (C-3) 80 acres 5 mi. w. of Conway on US 64, then 1.5 mi. s. on SR 319.	48		•	•	•	•		•		•					
Cove Lake (C-2) 160 acres s.e. of Paris on SR 309 near Mount Magazine.	49	•	•	•	•	•		•		•				•	•
Crossett Harbor (F-4) 300 acres 8 mi. w. of Crossett.	50	•	•	•	•	•		•		•					
Lake Conway (C-3) 6,700 acres 3 mi. s. of Conway on SR 365.	51	•	•	•	•	•	•	•		•					
Lake Georgia-Pacific (F-4) 1,700 acres 10 mi. n.w. of Crossett. Bird-watching.	52	•	•		•	•		•		•					

Recreation Areas Chart

The map location numerals in column 2 show an area's location on the preceding map.

Find thousands of places to camp at AAA.com/campgrounds

	MAP LOCATION	CAMPING	PICNICKING	HIKING TRAILS	BOATING	BOAT RAMP	BOAT RENTAL	FISHING	SWIMMING	PET FRIENDLY	BICYCLE TRAILS	NATURE PROGS.	VISITOR CENTER	LODGE/CABINS	FOOD SERVICE
Lake Leatherwood (A-2) 1,600 acres 2 mi. w. of Eureka Springs off US 62. Canoe and paddleboat rentals.	53	●	●	●	●	●	●	●	●	●	●	●			●
Lake Maumelle (C-3) 8,900 acres 12 mi. w. of Little Rock on SR 10.	54	●	●	●	●	●		●		●					
Lake Wedington (B-1) 139 acres 13 mi. w. of Fayetteville on SR 16. Canoeing; playground, volleyball courts.	55	●	●	●	●	●		●	●	●		●			●
Reynolds Park (A-5) 80 acres on n. edge of Paragould. Playground, volleyball court.	56	●	●		●	●		●		●					
Toad Suck Park (C-3) 78 acres 5 mi. w. of Conway on SR 60 on the Arkansas River. Playground.	57	●	●		●	●		●		●					

ALMA pop. 5,419

QUALITY INN & SUITES 479/632-4141

APPROVED
Hotel

Address: 439 Hwy 71 N 72921 **Location:** I-40 exit 13, just n. **Facility:** 61 units. 2 stories (no elevator), interior/exterior corridors. **Activities:** limited exercise equipment. **Guest Services:** coin laundry. **Featured Amenity:** full hot breakfast.

SAVE ⟦↑⟧ BIZ 🛜 🛗 🍽 ▭ / SOME UNITS 🐾

ARKADELPHIA (D-2) pop. 10,714, elev. 189'

Founded in 1839 and built along the bluffs of the Ouachita Valley, Arkadelphia was a river port during the steamboat days. The town is an agricultural and light industrial center producing aluminum, boats, clothing and wood products. It also has two colleges: Henderson State University has some 3,700 students; Ouachita Baptist College's enrollment is nearly 1,600.

Arkadelphia Alliance and Area Chamber of Commerce: 2401 Pine St., Suite B, Arkadelphia, AR 71923. **Phone:** (870) 246-5542.

DEGRAY DAM VISITOR CENTER is 7 mi. n. on SR 7, then 2 mi. w. on entrance road. Displays feature a wildlife exhibit, archeological exhibit, Caddo Indian artifacts and a 10-minute orientation video. *See Recreation Areas Chart.* **Hours:** Daily 8-4:15, Apr.-Oct.; Mon.-Fri. 8-4:15, rest of year. **Cost:** Free. **Phone:** (870) 246-5501.

QUALITY INN 870/246-5592

APPROVED Motel. **Address:** 136 Valley St 71923

WHERE TO EAT

ALLEN'S BAR-B-QUE 870/403-0331
APPROVED Barbecue. Quick Serve. **Address:** 3100 Hollywood Rd 71923

O'KEEFE'S FISH NET FAMILY RESTAURANT 870/246-7885
APPROVED Seafood Steak. Casual Dining. **Address:** 5000 Valley Hwy 7 N 71923

ARKANSAS POST NATIONAL MEMORIAL (D-5)

On SR 169, 7 miles south of Gillett along the lower Arkansas River, the Arkansas Post National Memorial occupies 389 acres. Erected as a fort by the French in 1686, Arkansas Post was the first permanent European settlement in the lower Mississippi Valley. Ownership passed to Spain 1765-1800, then briefly reverted to France. With the Louisiana Purchase, the post became a frontier village.

Arkansas Post was the home of Arkansas' first newspaper, the *Gazette,* and the first capital of the Arkansas Territory. In 1821, both the newspaper and the capital moved to Little Rock. The site continued as a river port until the Civil War, when it became the scene of one of the state's major battles.

A visitor center and museum contain historical exhibits. Visitors can tour the town site, hike nature trails and fish, as well as enjoy bird-watching opportunities available due to the memorial's location along the Mississippi Flyway. Memorial open daily 8-dusk. Visitor center daily 8-5; closed Jan. 1, Thanksgiving and Christmas. Free. Phone (870) 548-2207.

BALD KNOB pop. 2,897

WHO DAT'S CAJUN RESTAURANT 501/724-6183

APPROVED Cajun. Casual Dining. **Address:** 3209 Hwy 367 N 72010

BATESVILLE pop. 10,248, elev. 338'

COMFORT SUITES 870/698-1900

THREE DIAMOND Hotel. **Address:** 1227 N St. Louis St 72501

ECONO LODGE 870/698-1855

APPROVED Motel. **Address:** 773 Batesville Blvd 72501

HOLIDAY INN EXPRESS 870/698-2700

THREE DIAMOND Hotel. **Address:** 1130 White Dr 72501

SUPER 8-BATESVILLE 870/793-5888

APPROVED Motel. **Address:** 1287 N St. Louis St 72501

WHERE TO EAT

COLTON'S STEAKHOUSE & GRILL 870/793-7427
APPROVED Steak. Casual Dining. **Address:** 1553 S St. Louis St 72501

JOSIE'S STEAKHOUSE 870/793-7000
APPROVED American. Casual Dining. **Address:** 50 Riverbank Rd 72501

BENTON pop. 30,681, elev. 416'

BEST WESTERN BENTON INN 501/778-9695

APPROVED
Motel

🅱 Best Western.

AAA Benefit: Members save up to 15% and earn bonus points!

Address: 17036 I-30 72019 **Location:** I-30 exit 117 westbound; exit 118 eastbound; on northwest service road. **Facility:** 65 units. 2 stories (no elevator), interior/exterior corridors. **Pool:** outdoor. **Guest Services:** coin laundry. **Featured Amenity:** breakfast buffet.

SAVE ⟦↑⟧ CALL 🦽 🏊 BIZ HS 🛜 🛗 🍽 ▭ / SOME UNITS 🐾

FAIRFIELD INN & SUITES BY MARRIOTT LITTLE ROCK BENTON 501/722-6330

THREE DIAMOND SAVE Hotel. **Address:** 17320 Interstate 30 72019

AAA Benefit: Members save 5% or more!

HOLIDAY INN EXPRESS & SUITES BRYANT-BENTON AREA
501/778-8400
THREE DIAMOND Hotel. **Address:** 7224 Alcoa Rd 72015

WHERE TO EAT

CHEPE'S MEXICAN GRILL   501/794-6656
APPROVED Mexican. Casual Dining. **Address:** 17324
Interstate 30 N 72019

COLTON'S STEAKHOUSE & GRILL   501/778-6100
APPROVED Steak. Casual Dining. **Address:** 1925
Landers Dr 72015

EAT MY CATFISH   501/909-2323
APPROVED American. Casual Dining. **Address:** 1205
Military Rd 72019

TACOS 4 LIFE   501/503-2201
APPROVED Mexican. Casual Dining. **Address:** 7821
Alcoa Rd 72019

BENTONVILLE (A-1) pop. 35,301, elev. 1,280'
• Restaurants p. 28

Bentonville Convention & Visitors Bureau: 104
E. Central Ave., Bentonville, AR 72712. **Phone:**
(479) 271-9153 or (800) 410-2535.

CRYSTAL BRIDGES MUSEUM OF AMERICAN ART is at 600 Museum Way.
Housed in a Moshe Safdie-designed building, the
museum's galleries hold an impressive collection of
American art from Colonial times and the 19th century to the present. Highlights include Asher B. Du-
rand's "Kindred Spirits," Maxfield Parrish's "The
Lantern Bearers," Norman Rockwell's "Rosie the
Riveter," Mark Rothko's "No. 210/No. 211 (Orange)"
and Andy Warhol's "Dolly Parton." The building is
also impressive; its eight modern pavilions surround
two ponds and feature tall glass windows and curvaceous ceilings made of copper and Arkansas white
pine beams.

The museum's 120 acres of picturesque Ozark
countryside have more than 3.5 miles of trails highlighted by sculptures and gardens through which
visitors may stroll or ride bicycles and participate in
educational activities. Temporary exhibits and outdoor events take place throughout the year. A research library also is available.

Audio tours are available. **Time:** Allow 1 hour, 30
minutes minimum. **Hours:** Mon. 11-6, Wed.-Fri.
11-9, Sat.-Sun. 10-6. Guided tours depart daily at
2:30 and 4. Trails are open daily dawn-dusk. Phone
ahead to confirm schedule. **Cost:** Free. A fee may
be charged for temporary exhibitions. **Phone:** (479)
418-5700. *(See ad p. 49.)*

Frank Lloyd Wright Bachman-Wilson House is at
600 Museum Way on the grounds of the Crystal
Bridges Museum of American Art. The house, designed in 1954, was endangered by flooding at its
original location along the Millstone River in New
Jersey. Acquired by the Crystal Bridges Museum of
American Art in 2013, the house was disassembled
and transported to its current site overlooking

Crystal Spring, where it continues to exemplify
Wright's design principles that used horizontal lines
to blend a structure into its surrounding landscape.
Hours: Wed.-Fri. 11 to 9, Sat.-Sun. 10-6, Mon. 11-6.
Cost: Free. Reservations are required. **Phone:**
(479) 418-5700.

BEST WESTERN PLUS CASTLE ROCK INN & SUITES
479/845-7707
THREE DIAMOND
Hotel

Best Western PLUS **AAA Benefit:** Members save up to 15% and earn bonus points!

Address: 501 SE Walton Blvd 72712
Location: I-49 exit 85, 1.2 mi w. **Facility:** 83 units. 3 stories, interior corridors. **Pool:** heated indoor. **Activities:**
hot tub, exercise room. **Guest Services:**
valet and coin laundry.

COMFORT INN - BENTONVILLE   479/254-7800
THREE DIAMOND Hotel. **Address:** 3001 NE 11th St 72712

COMFORT SUITES BENTONVILLE/ROGERS   479/254-9099
THREE DIAMOND Hotel. **Address:** 2011 SE Walton Blvd
72712

COURTYARD BY MARRIOTT   479/273-3333
THREE DIAMOND
Hotel

COURTYARD **AAA Benefit:** Members save 5% or more!

Address: 1001 McClain Rd 72712 **Location:** I-49 exit 88, just e. Located in
Beau Terre Office Park. **Facility:** 90
units. 3 stories, interior corridors. **Pool:**
heated indoor. **Activities:** exercise
room. **Guest Services:** valet and coin
laundry. **Featured Amenity:** full hot
breakfast.

DAYS INN AND SUITES BENTONVILLE   479/271-7900
APPROVED Hotel. **Address:** 3408 S Moberly Ln 72712

DOUBLETREE SUITES BY HILTON BENTONVILLE
479/845-7770
THREE DIAMOND **SAVE** Hotel. **Address:** 301 SE Walton Blvd 72712

AAA Benefit: Members save up to 15%!

ELEMENT BY WESTIN BENTONVILLE   479/268-5010
THREE DIAMOND **SAVE** Hotel. **Address:** 3401 Medlin Ln 72712

AAA Benefit: Members save 5% or more!

FOUR POINTS BY SHERATON BENTONVILLE
479/715-6388

THREE DIAMOND FOUR POINTS BY SHERATON
Hotel

AAA Benefit: Members save 5% or more!

Address: 211 SE Walton Blvd 72712 **Location:** I-49 exit 85, 1.2 mi w. **Facility:** 105 units. 3 stories, interior corridors. **Amenities:** safes. **Pool:** heated indoor. **Activities:** exercise room. **Guest Services:** valet and coin laundry. *(See ad this page.)*

SAVE 🍴 🍸 CALL ♿ 🚐
📶 BIZ HS 🛜 ✕ 🛎
☕

HILTON GARDEN INN
479/464-7300
THREE DIAMOND SAVE Hotel. **Address:** 2204 SE Walton Blvd 72712

AAA Benefit: Members save up to 15%!

HOLIDAY INN EXPRESS
479/271-2222
THREE DIAMOND Hotel

Address: 2205 SE Walton Blvd 72712 **Location:** I-49 exit 85, just w. **Facility:** 84 units. 4 stories, interior corridors. **Amenities:** safes. **Activities:** exercise room. **Guest Services:** valet and coin laundry. **Featured Amenity:** breakfast buffet.

SAVE 🍴 📶 BIZ 🛜 ✕ 🛎
🖨 ☕

HOMETOWNE STUDIOS & SUITES BY RED ROOF
479/268-4400
APPROVED Extended Stay Hotel. **Address:** 200 SW Suburban Ln 72712

LA QUINTA INN & SUITES BENTONVILLE
479/271-7555
THREE DIAMOND Hotel. **Address:** 1001 SE Walton Blvd 72712

MICROTEL INN & SUITES BY WYNDHAM BENTONVILLE
479/271-6699
APPROVED Hotel. **Address:** 911 SE Walton Blvd 72712

SPRINGHILL SUITES BY MARRIOTT
479/464-4777
THREE DIAMOND SAVE Hotel. **Address:** 2304 SE Walton Blvd 72712

AAA Benefit: Members save 5% or more!

TOWNEPLACE SUITES BY MARRIOTT BENTONVILLE/ ROGERS
479/621-0202
THREE DIAMOND SAVE Extended Stay Hotel. **Address:** 3100 SE 14th St 72712

AAA Benefit: Members save 5% or more!

WINGATE BY WYNDHAM
479/418-5400
THREE DIAMOND Hotel

Address: 7400 SW Old Farm Blvd 72712 **Location:** 7.4 mi w of jct Walton and SW Regional Airport blvds. **Facility:** 102 units. 4 stories, interior corridors. **Amenities:** safes. **Pool:** heated indoor. **Activities:** hot tub, exercise room. **Guest Services:** valet and coin laundry, area transportation. **Featured Amenity:** full hot breakfast.

SAVE 🔀 🍴 CALL ♿ 🚐 📶
BIZ 🛜 ✕ 🛎 🖨 ☕
/ SOME UNITS 🐾

WHERE TO EAT

BUTCHER & PINT
479/644-9876
fyi American. Casual Dining. Under major renovation, call for details. **Last Designation:** Approved. **Address:** 1201 S Walton Blvd #105 72712

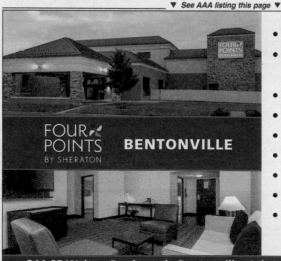

GUSANO'S   479/271-8242
APPROVED Pizza. Casual Dining. **Address:** 2905 S
Walton Blvd 72712

MELD KITCHEN + SANDWICH BAR   479/845-4640
APPROVED American. Quick Serve. **Address:** 1120 S
Walton Blvd, Ste. 152 72712

THE PREACHER'S SON   479/445-6065
THREE DIAMOND American. Casual Dining. **Address:** 201
NW A St 72712

RIVER GRILLE   479/271-4141
THREE DIAMOND Steak. Fine Dining. **Address:** 1003
McClain Rd 72712

RON'S HAMBURGERS & CHILI   479/464-4420
APPROVED American. Casual Dining. **Address:** 1702
S Walton Blvd 72712

TABLE MESA BISTRO   479/715-6706
THREE DIAMOND Latin American. Casual Dining. **Address:**
108 E Central Ave 72712

TAVOLA TRATTORIA   479/715-4738
THREE DIAMOND Italian. Casual Dining. **Address:** 108 SE
A St 72712

TUSK & TROTTER AN AMERICAN BRASSERIE   479/268-4494
APPROVED American. Gastropub. **Address:** 110 SE
A St 72712

BERRYVILLE (A-2) pop. 5,356, elev. 1,246'

Founded in 1850 by Blackburn Henderson Berry
of Alabama, most of the town was burned by military
forces from both sides during the Civil War. At one
time Union soldiers camped on what is now City
Square Park. North on US 62 is a scenic drive
through the Ozarks.

Berryville Chamber of Commerce: 506 S. Main
St., P.O. Box 402, Berryville, AR 72616. **Phone:**
(870) 423-3704.

FAIRWAY INN   870/423-3395
APPROVED   **Address:** 577 Hwy 62 W 72616 **Loca-**
Motel   **tion:** Jct SR 21, 2.5 mi w. **Facility:** 20
                   units. 2 stories (no elevator), exterior
                   corridors. **Pool:** outdoor. **Activities:**
                   lawn sports.

BLYTHEVILLE pop. 15,620

HAMPTON INN BY HILTON   870/763-5220
THREE DIAMOND **SAVE** Hotel. **Ad-**   **AAA Benefit:**
dress: 301 N Service Rd 72315   Members save up to
                                         15%!

QUALITY INN   870/763-7081
APPROVED Hotel. **Address:** 1520 E Main St 72315

WHERE TO EAT

OLYMPIA STEAK & SEAFOOD   870/838-1204
APPROVED Steak Seafood. Casual Dining. **Address:**
1700 E Main St 72315

BRINKLEY pop. 3,188

DAYS INN & SUITES   870/734-4300
APPROVED Hotel. **Address:** 1815 N Main St 72021

BRYANT (D-3) pop. 16,688, elev. 413'

Located just outside southwest Little Rock, Bryant
offers a short commute to the Arkansas state capital.

Hot Springs National Park is less than an hour's
drive west.

AMERICAS BEST VALUE INN   501/653-7800
APPROVED Motel. **Address:** 407 W Commerce St
72022

COMFORT INN & SUITES   501/653-4000
THREE DIAMOND Hotel. **Address:** 209 W Commerce St
72022

ECONO LODGE INN & SUITES   501/847-7120
APPROVED Motel. **Address:** 210 Office Park Dr 72022

HAMPTON INN BY HILTON   501/847-3200
THREE DIAMOND **SAVE** Hotel. **Ad-**   **AAA Benefit:**
dress: 307 Office Park Dr 72022   Members save up to
                                         15%!

LA QUINTA INN & SUITES BRYANT   501/847-9494
THREE DIAMOND Hotel. **Address:** 408 W Commerce St
72022

SUPER 8   501/847-7888
APPROVED Motel. **Address:** 201 Dell Dr 72022

WHERE TO EAT

DAVID'S BURGER   501/487-7024
APPROVED American. Casual Dining. **Address:**
23140 I-30 N 72022

LUIGI'S   501/847-1110
APPROVED Italian. Casual Dining. **Address:** 22000
Interstate 30 N 72022

PASTA J'S   501/847-6868
APPROVED Italian. Casual Dining. **Address:** 2900
Horizon Dr 72022

SUMO   501/943-7798
APPROVED Japanese. Casual Dining. **Address:** 5311
Highway 5 North, Suite 250 72022

TA MOLLY'S MEXICAN KITCHEN   501/653-2600
APPROVED Mexican. Casual Dining. **Address:** 206 W
Commerce St 72022

US PIZZA CO   501/943-3333
APPROVED American. Casual Dining. **Address:** 3600
Highway 5 N 72022

BUFFALO NATIONAL RIVER (B-3)

Reached via US 65 or SRs 7, 14 or 21 in northwestern Arkansas, Buffalo National River stretches through the rugged Ozark Mountains. While the Buffalo River courses 150 miles through the Ozarks, only its lower 135 miles and adjacent land are designated a national river. To protect the natural beauty of this area, Congress declared it a national river in 1972, thereby preserving it from development and population encroachment.

A variety of wildlife, including elk, bears, deer, bobcats, raccoons, opossums, beavers, armadillos, otters and minks may be found along the river. Geological resources include numerous caves, sinkholes, seasonal waterfalls and massive limestone and sandstone bluffs. A mosaic of northern, southern and prairie plant communities provide a tranquil setting for hiking, fishing, camping, kayaking, canoeing and horseback riding. The area's 19th-century farmstead, Civil War and zinc mining history is preserved in historic sites and buildings, including log houses and abandoned mines. **Note:** Some buildings are open. Visitors are not permitted to remove artifacts from the property.

Interpretive programs are offered during the summer; phone ahead for schedule. Backpacking and horseback riding are popular in the three wilderness areas. Hunting is permitted in season.

The national river is accessible daily 24 hours. There are two main visitor centers. Tyler Bend Visitor Center is 9 miles north of Marshall off US 65 and is open daily 8:30-4:30 as staffing permits, weather permitting. The Buffalo Point Ranger Station is off US 14 and is open daily 8:30-4:30 as staffing permits; winter hours may vary. Visitor centers are closed most federal holidays; phone ahead to confirm holiday schedule. There is no admission charge but camping fees are imposed at some of the site's campgrounds. For information contact the Superintendent, Buffalo National River, 402 N. Walnut St., Suite 136, Harrison, AR 72602-1173; phone (870) 439-2502. *See Recreation Areas Chart.*

CAMDEN (E-3) pop. 12,183, elev. 149'

Camden, overlooking the Ouachita River, was an ancient Native American trail crossing. Early French settlers named the town Fabre's Hill. American pioneers arrived during the 1820s, and soon a thriving cotton-growing industry was established. The proximity of the river made easy the transport of up to 40,000 bales a season. Wiped out by the Civil War, the cotton industry was replaced by timber production.

River Drive and Sandy Beach Park offer good views of the river; the latter also provides a boat ramp. In June and July, Movies on the River are offered Friday at dusk at Riverwalk Amphitheater on Washington St. Nearby White Oak Lake State Park provides camping, hiking, biking, swimming, boating and fishing *(see Recreation Areas Chart).*

Camden Area Chamber of Commerce: 314 S. Adams, P.O. Box 99, Camden, AR 71701. **Phone:** (870) 836-6426.

COMFORT INN   870/836-9000
THREE DIAMOND Hotel. **Address:** 1 Ridgecrest Dr 71701

HOLIDAY INN EXPRESS   870/836-8100
THREE DIAMOND Hotel. **Address:** 1450 US Hwy 278 SW 71701

CLARKSVILLE pop. 9,178

BEST WESTERN SHERWOOD INN   479/754-7900
APPROVED
Hotel

Best Western. **AAA Benefit:** Members save up to 15% and earn bonus points!

Address: 1207 S Rogers Ave 72830 **Location:** I-40 exit 58, just n. **Facility:** 53 units, some two bedrooms and kitchens. 2 stories (no elevator), exterior corridors. **Pool:** outdoor. **Activities:** hot tub. **Guest Services:** coin laundry. **Featured Amenity: full hot breakfast.**

HAMPTON INN BY HILTON CLARKSVILLE
479/754-4444
APPROVED
Hotel

Hampton **AAA Benefit:** Members save up to 15%!

Address: 2630 W Clark Rd 72830 **Location:** I-40 exit 55, just ne. **Facility:** 61 units. 2 stories, interior corridors. **Pool:** heated indoor. **Activities:** exercise room. **Guest Services:** coin laundry. **Featured Amenity: breakfast buffet.**

HOLIDAY INN EXPRESS   479/705-7600
THREE DIAMOND
Hotel

Address: 2502 W Clark Rd 72830 **Location:** I-40 exit 55, just ne. **Facility:** 68 units. 3 stories, interior corridors. **Pool:** outdoor. **Activities:** exercise room. **Guest Services:** coin laundry. **Featured Amenity: breakfast buffet.**

QUALITY INN & SUITES   479/754-3000
APPROVED Hotel. **Address:** 1167 S Rogers Ave 72830

CLINTON pop. 2,602

BEST WESTERN HILLSIDE INN 501/745-4700

APPROVED
Motel

Best Western.

AAA Benefit: Members save up to 15% and earn bonus points!

Address: 1025 Hwy 65 B 72031 **Location:** Jct SR 16, just s on US 65, then just sw. **Facility:** 36 units. 2 stories (no elevator), exterior corridors. **Pool:** outdoor.

SAVE 🏊 BIZ 🛜 ✕ 🍴 📷 📺 / SOME UNITS 🐾

SUPER 8 MOTEL 501/745-8810

APPROVED Motel. **Address:** 2008 Hwy 65 S 72031

CONWAY (C-3) pop. 58,908, elev. 312'

Conway, about 30 miles northwest of Little Rock, is home to the University of Central Arkansas, Hendrix College and Central Baptist College. Lake Conway is reputedly the largest man-made Game and Fish Commission lake in the United States and is a popular fishing destination. One of Conway's largest annual events, Toad Suck Daze, is a 3-day festival in early May that includes a carnival, 5K and 10K races and live music.

BEST WESTERN CONWAY 501/320-0855

APPROVED
Motel

Best Western.

AAA Benefit: Members save up to 15% and earn bonus points!

Address: 816 E Oak St 72032 **Location:** I-40 exit 127, just e on US 64. **Facility:** 50 units. 2 stories (no elevator), interior/exterior corridors. **Pool:** outdoor. **Featured Amenity:** full hot breakfast.

SAVE 🍴 🏊 BIZ 🛜 🍴 📷 📺 / SOME UNITS 🐾 HS

CANDLEWOOD SUITES 501/329-8551

APPROVED Extended Stay Hotel. **Address:** 2360 Sanders St 72032

COMFORT INN & SUITES 501/513-4989

APPROVED Hotel. **Address:** 2370 Sanders St 72032

COMFORT SUITES 501/329-8548

THREE DIAMOND Hotel. **Address:** 705 Museum Rd 72032

COUNTRY INN & SUITES BY RADISSON 501/932-0500

THREE DIAMOND Hotel. **Address:** 750 Amity Rd 72032

FAIRFIELD INN & SUITES BY MARRIOTT 501/505-8034

THREE DIAMOND SAVE Hotel. **Address:** 2260 Sanders St 72032

AAA Benefit: Members save 5% or more!

HILTON GARDEN INN CONWAY 501/329-1444

THREE DIAMOND SAVE Hotel. **Address:** 805 Amity Rd 72032

AAA Benefit: Members save up to 15%!

HOLIDAY INN EXPRESS & SUITES 501/205-1315

THREE DIAMOND Hotel. **Address:** 2330 Sanders St 72032

LA QUINTA INN & SUITES 501/328-5100

THREE DIAMOND Hotel. **Address:** 2350 Sanders St 72032

MICROTEL INN & SUITES BY WYNDHAM CONWAY 501/327-0898

APPROVED Hotel. **Address:** 2475 Sanders St 72032

QUALITY INN 501/329-0300

APPROVED Motel. **Address:** 150 Skyline Dr N 72032

SUPER 8-CONWAY 501/505-8880

APPROVED Hotel. **Address:** 2430 Sanders St 72032

WHERE TO EAT

COLTON'S STEAKHOUSE & GRILL 501/329-6454

APPROVED Steak. Casual Dining. **Address:** 120 E Oak St 72032

CROSS CREEK SANDWICH SHOP 501/764-1811

APPROVED American. Quick Serve. **Address:** 1003 Oak St 72032

EAT MY CATFISH 501/588-1867

APPROVED Seafood. Casual Dining. **Address:** 2125 Harkrider St 72032

FAT DADDY'S BAR-B-QUE 501/358-6363

APPROVED Barbecue. Casual Dining. **Address:** 1004 Oak St 72032

MARKETPLACE GRILL 501/336-0011

APPROVED American. Casual Dining. **Address:** 600 Skyline Dr 72032

MIKE'S PLACE 501/269-6453

APPROVED American. Casual Dining. **Address:** 808 Front St 72032

NEW CHINA 501/764-1888

APPROVED Chinese. Casual Dining. **Address:** 2104 Harkrider Ave 72032

THE PURPLE COW 501/205-4211

APPROVED Burgers Sandwiches. Casual Dining. **Address:** 1055 Steel Ave 72032

ZAZA FINE SALAD & WOOD OVEN PIZZA CO. 501/336-9292

APPROVED Pizza. Quick Serve. **Address:** 1050 Ellis Ave, Suite 110 72032

CROSSETT pop. 5,507, elev. 159'

TRU BY HILTON - CROSSETT 870/304-1040

APPROVED SAVE Hotel. **Address:** 920 Unity Rd 71635

AAA Benefit: Members save up to 15%!

EL DORADO (F-3) pop. 18,884, elev. 250'

Until 1921 the town of El Dorado was quiet and peaceful. In that year, however, oil was discovered, and the once tranquil city was transformed into a boomtown whose population increased tenfold in a 4-year span. Gamblers and moonshiners soon arrived, as did H.L. Hunt, who began his oil empire in El Dorado after winning an interest in an oil well in a poker game.

The oil business is still important, but it has been joined by timber, poultry production and chemical manufacturing to form a more diverse economic base.

El Dorado-Union County Chamber of Commerce: 111 W. Main St., El Dorado, AR 71730. **Phone:** (870) 863-6113.

COUNTRY INN & SUITES BY RADISSON   870/881-0455
THREE DIAMOND Hotel. **Address:** 2413 W Hillsboro St 71730

FAIRFIELD INN & SUITES BY MARRIOTT   870/862-0800
THREE DIAMOND **SAVE** Hotel. **Ad-** | **AAA Benefit:**
dress: 1800 N West Ave 71730 | Members save 5% or more!

EUREKA SPRINGS (A-2) pop. 2,073, elev. 1,130'
• Restaurants p. 34

The waters around Eureka Springs had been touted for alleged medicinal powers by Native Americans and settlers alike long before Dr. Alvah Jackson established a clinic in the area in 1850. By the late 1870s a busy resort had developed; the arrival of the railroad in 1883 made the spa more accessible, and the sick and weary came great distances to be healed.

Modern medicine caused a drastic decline in the use of the springs, but recreational and artistic businesses have kept the city alive. Eureka Springs offers a variety of activities that cater to both body and mind. Music shows abound throughout the year. The annual Eagle Watch, the third weekend in October, draws thousands of visitors from a four-state region.

Greater Eureka Springs Chamber of Commerce Visitor Center: 516 Village Cir., Eureka Springs, AR 72632. **Phone:** (479) 253-8737 or (800) 638-7352.

Self-guiding tours: Elegant Victorian houses built at the turn of the 20th century can be seen in the city's historic district. A walking trails map is available from the visitor center. Additional maps and brochures of the Eureka Springs area also are available.

Shopping: A European-style farmers market is held Tues. and Thurs. 7-noon, Apr.-Nov., in a parking lot at the Village of Pine Mountain, 1 mile north at 516 Village Circle Dr. on SR 62E. Village of Pine Mountain is a Victorian-style shopping and entertainment complex with stores that specialize in local crafts.

About 125 gift shops and restaurants are concentrated in the historic downtown district near the intersection of SRs 62 and 23N/Main Street.

BLUE SPRING HERITAGE CENTER is 5.5 mi. w. off US 62, following signs. The 33-acre complex, which features informal meadow, rock and wildflower gardens, also includes one of the largest natural springs in the Ozark Mountains. Several million gallons of water flow here each day. A 20-minute, three-screen presentation offers information about the area's history. **Time:** Allow 1 hour minimum. **Hours:** Daily 9-6, Mar. 15-second Sun. in Nov. **Cost:** $9.75; $6.50 (ages 6-17). **Phone:** (479) 253-9244.

EUREKA SPRINGS AND NORTH ARKANSAS RAILWAY departs from the town's original depot at 299 N. Main St. Narrated 1-hour rides are offered aboard a restored diesel train. Lunch and dinner trips also are available. **Hours:** Departures Tues.-Sat. at 10:30, 12:30 and 2:30, early June through July 30; Tues.-Sat. at 12:30 and 2:30 (also Sat. at 10:30) in Oct.; Tues.-Sat. at 12:30 and 2:30, mid-May to early June; Tues.-Sat. at 10:30 and 2:30 (also Sat. at 12:30), early Aug. to early Oct.; Sat. at 12:30 and 2:30, early Apr. to mid-May. **Cost:** Fare $15; $8 (ages 4-10). Reservations are suggested for meal trips. **Phone:** (479) 253-9623.

EUREKA SPRINGS HISTORICAL MUSEUM is at 95 S. Main St. Exhibits chronicling Eureka Springs' history occupy two floors of an 1889 stone house. **Time:** Allow 1 hour minimum. **Hours:** Mon.-Sat. 9:30-4. **Cost:** $5; $2.50 (students with ID); free (ages 0-11). **Phone:** (479) 253-9417.

"THE GREAT PASSION PLAY" is 1 mi. e. off US 62, following signs. This production depicts the days leading to Christ's death, followed by the resurrection and the ascension. A cast of 150 actors accompanied by live animals and birds performs in a 4,000-seat amphitheater. The 550-foot stage represents the streets of Jerusalem at the time of Christ. Prior to the play, guests may enjoy a dinner buffet and presentations, such as David the Shepherd and Parables from the Potter. A backstage tour is available. Visitors may also experience the Bible Museum, Holy Land Tour, Sacred Arts Museum and The Christ of the Ozarks.

Hours: Curtain time generally Tues. and Thurs.-Sat. at 8:30 p.m., June-July; Fri.-Sat. at 8:30 p.m. in May and Aug.; Tues. and Fri.-Sat. at 7:30 p.m., Sept.-Oct. Special performances at 8:30 p.m. Sun. before Memorial Day and Sun. before Labor Day. Dinner buffet 4:30-7:30 on performance days, May 1-Labor Day; 4-7 on performance days, day after Labor Day-Oct. 31. Backstage tour departs at 3 on performance days. Phone ahead to confirm schedule. **Cost:** Play $27; $17 (ages 12-16); $13 (ages 4-11). Dinner buffet $14.45; $13.45 (ages 12-16); $7.50 (ages 4-11). Combination ticket (includes "The Great Passion Play" and Holy Land Tour) $44; $32 (ages 12-16); $25 (ages 4-11). Backstage tour

$8. Phone ahead to confirm rates. Reservations are recommended for dinner buffet and backstage tour. **Phone:** (479) 253-9200 for information, or (800) 882-7529 for reservations. [⫟]

Bible Museum is in the Administration building of "The Great Passion Play," 1 mi. e. on US 62, then 1.2 mi. n. on Statue Rd. The museum contains more than 6,000 Bibles in 625 languages and dialects as well as a large collection of parchments and artifacts. **Hours:** Museum open 9-8 on "The Great Passion Play" performance days, 9-5 on non-performance days, May 1-Labor Day; 9-7 on performance days, 9-5 on non-performance days, day after Labor Day-Oct. 31; Mon.-Sat. 9-5, rest of year. Phone ahead to confirm schedule. **Cost:** Museum admission May-Oct. included with "The Great Passion Play" admission of $25; $15 (ages 12-16); $11 (ages 4-11). Rest of year by donation. **Phone:** (479) 253-8559 or (800) 882-7529.

Holy Land Tour is 1 mi. e. off US 62, following signs for "The Great Passion Play"; tours depart through the East Jerusalem Gate. The guided 3-hour tour covers a 50-acre tract that re-creates the features of the region where Christ lived. Re-creations of biblical scenes include Moses' Wilderness Tabernacle, the inn at Bethlehem and a "Visit with Simon Peter beside the Sea of Galilee." Visitors disembark at several stops along the route and continue on another bus.

Time: Allow 2 hours, 30 minutes minimum. **Hours:** Tours depart every 30 minutes noon-4:30 on "The Great Passion Play" performance days, May 1-Labor Day; noon-4 on performance days, day after Labor Day-Oct. 31. Visitors are advised to arrive 30 minutes before departure. **Cost:** $15; $13 (ages 12-16); $10 (ages 4-11). **Phone:** (479) 253-9200 or (800) 882-7529.

Sacred Arts Museum is 1 mi. e. on US 62, then 1.2 mi. n. on Statue Rd., on the grounds of "The Great Passion Play." The center displays more than 1,000 pieces of biblical art in 64 media, including sculptured marble, mosaics and needlepoint. **Hours:** Museum open 11-8 on "The Great Passion Play" performance days, by appointment on non-performance days, May 1-Labor Day; 11-7 on performance days, by appointment on non-performance days, day after Labor Day-Oct. 31; by appointment rest of year. **Cost:** Museum included with "The Great Passion Play" admission of $25; $15 (ages 12-16); $11 (ages 4-11). by donation. **Phone:** (479) 253-8559 or (800) 882-7529.

The Christ of the Ozarks is 1 mi. e. on US 62, then 1.5 mi. n. on Passion Play Rd. on the grounds of "The Great Passion Play." Towering seven stories above Magnetic Mountain and weighing more than 500 tons, the statue has outspread arms that measure 65 feet across, giving it the appearance of an immense cross when viewed from a distance.

Hours: Daily 8 a.m.-10 p.m. (weather permitting). **Cost:** Donations. **Phone:** (479) 253-9200 or (800) 882-7529.

ONYX CAVE PARK is 3 mi. e. on US 62, then 3.5 mi. n. on Onyx Cave Rd. Self-guiding 30-minute tours feature taped narration about the history of the cave. **Hours:** Daily 9-5, Memorial Day-Labor Day; 9-4, Mar. 1-day before Memorial Day, day after Labor Day-Nov. 30 and day after Christmas-Dec. 31 (weather permitting). Phone ahead to confirm schedule. **Cost:** $7.50; $3.50 (ages 4-13). **Phone:** (479) 253-9321.

THORNCROWN CHAPEL is just w. off US 62. This modern glass and wood chapel is noted for its innovative architecture. Woods and trails surround the chapel, which is open for Sunday services and weddings. **Hours:** Daily 9-5, Apr.-Oct.; Sun.-Fri. 9-5 in Nov; 11-4 in Mar. and Dec. Sun. services are at 9 and 11, Apr.-Oct.; at 11, Nov. 1-third week in Dec. Phone ahead to confirm schedule. **Cost:** Donations. **Phone:** (479) 253-7401.

WAR EAGLE CAVERN—see Rogers p. 62.

1886 CRESCENT HOTEL & SPA   479/253-9766
[⫸] **THREE DIAMOND** Historic Hotel. **Address:** 75 Prospect Ave 72632

ANGEL AT ROSE HALL   479/253-5405
[⫸] **FOUR DIAMOND**   **Address:** 46 Hillside Ave 72632 **Location:** Jct US 62, 1.2 mi n on SR 23, then
Bed & Breakfast   just sw. **Facility:** The spacious rooms offer a romantic retreat with Victorian décor, king-size beds, gas fireplaces, balconies and two-person jetted tubs. Enjoy breakfast at a table for two in the dining room. 5 units. 2 stories (no elevator), interior corridors. **Amenities:** safes. **Featured Amenity: full hot breakfast.**
[SAVE] [BIZ] [⊚] [✕] / SOME UNITS [⊡]

ARSENIC & OLD LACE B&B   479/253-5454
[⫸] **THREE DIAMOND** Bed & Breakfast. **Address:** 60 Hillside Ave 72632

BASIN PARK HOTEL   479/253-7837
[⫸] **APPROVED** Historic Hotel. **Address:** 12 Spring St 72632

BAVARIAN INN   479/253-8128
[⫸] **APPROVED** Motel. **Address:** 325 W Van Buren St 72632

BEST WESTERN EUREKA INN   479/253-9551
[⫸] **APPROVED**   [BW] Best Western.   **AAA Benefit:** Members save up to 15% and earn bonus points!
Hotel
Address: 101 E Van Buren St 72632 **Location:** Jct SR 23 and US 62. **Facility:** 86 units. 2 stories (no elevator), interior/exterior corridors. **Pool:** heated outdoor. **Activities:** sauna, hot tub, exercise room. **Featured Amenity: breakfast buffet.**
[SAVE] [⫟] [≈] [✦] [BIZ] [⊚] [✕]
[⊡] [▭] / SOME UNITS [☐]

BEST WESTERN INN OF THE OZARKS   479/253-9768

THREE DIAMOND
Hotel

Best Western. **AAA Benefit:** Members save up to 15% and earn bonus points!

Address: 207 W Van Buren St 72632 **Location:** Jct SR 23 N, 0.5 mi w on US 62. **Facility:** 122 units. 2 stories (no elevator), exterior corridors. **Dining:** Myrtie Mae's, see separate listing. **Pool:** heated outdoor. **Activities:** hot tub, miniature golf, game room, picnic facilities. **Guest Services:** coin laundry.

SAVE | CALL | BIZ | SOME UNITS

BRACKENRIDGE LODGE   479/253-6803
APPROVED   Motel. **Address:** 352 W Van Buren St 72632

DAYS INN   479/253-8863
APPROVED   Motel. **Address:** 120 W Van Buren St 72632

HEARTSTONE INN & COTTAGES   479/253-8916
THREE DIAMOND   Historic Bed & Breakfast. **Address:** 35 Kings Hwy 72632

RED BUD VALLEY RESORT   479/253-9028
THREE DIAMOND   Vacation Rental Cabin. **Address:** 369 CR 340 72632

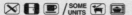
WHERE TO EAT

THE BALCONY BAR & RESTAURANT   479/253-7837
APPROVED   American. Casual Dining. **Address:** 12 Spring St 72632

BAVARIAN INN RESTAURANT   479/253-8128
APPROVED   German. Casual Dining. **Address:** 325 W Van Buren St 72632

DEVITOS   479/253-6807
APPROVED   Italian. Casual Dining. **Address:** 5 Center St 72632

ERMILIO'S   479/253-8806
APPROVED   Italian. Casual Dining. **Address:** 26 White St 72632

FOREST HILL RESTAURANT   479/253-2422
APPROVED   American. Casual Dining. **Address:** 3016 E Van Buren St 72632

LOCAL FLAVOR CAFE   479/253-9522
APPROVED   American. Casual Dining. **Address:** 71 S Main St 72632

MUD STREET CAFE   479/253-6732
APPROVED   Breakfast Sandwiches. Casual Dining. **Address:** 22 G S Main St 72632

MYRTIE MAE'S   479/253-9768
APPROVED
Regional American Casual Dining
$6-$20

AAA Inspector Notes: This locally popular restaurant features country-style cooking such as fried chicken and possum pie (chocolate cream cheese). A good-size salad bar is available for lunch and dinner. **Features:** full bar, senior menu, Sunday brunch. **Address:** 207 W Van Buren St 72632 **Location:** Jct SR 23 N, 0.5 mi w on US 62; in Best Western Inn of the Ozarks.   B L D

ROGUE'S MANOR AT SWEET SPRING   479/253-4911
THREE DIAMOND   American. Fine Dining. **Address:** 124 Spring St 72632

SPARKY'S ROADHOUSE CAFE   479/253-6001
APPROVED   American. Casual Dining. **Address:** 147 E Van Buren St 72632

FAYETTEVILLE (B-1) pop. 73,580, elev. 1,416'

Lots first were sold in Fayetteville in 1828, and the town soon became known for an interest in education. Several small colleges were founded in the 1840s and '50s. Arkansas Industrial University, established in 1871, became the University of Arkansas with an enrollment in excess of 24,000.

Walton Arts Center offers several concerts and performances throughout the year; phone (479) 443-5600.

The Washington-Willow Historic District features Victorian houses and large shade trees. The Washington County Historical Society offers living history tours of the 1853 Headquarters House Museum in this neighborhood by appointment; phone (479) 521-2970. Outdoor enthusiasts will find miles of hiking and bicycle trails throughout the city that connect to the Razorback Regional Greenway, a 36-mile, mostly off-road route that stretches from Fayetteville to Bentonville. Nearby Lake Wedington offers camping, cabins, a boat ramp and fishing *(see Recreation Areas Chart)*.

The Battle of Fayetteville Commemoration is held on a weekend close to the anniversary of the April 18, 1863, engagement; living-history demonstrations include battle camp cooking, weaving, quilting and other crafts of the Civil War period. The 4-day Bikes, Blues & BBQ Motorcycle Rally brings some 400,000 visitors into town in late September or early October; phone (479) 527-9993. The downtown square hosts First Thursday Fayetteville featuring local artisans and entertainment the first Thursday of the month.

Fayetteville Convention & Visitors Bureau: 21 S. Block Ave., Fayetteville, AR 72701. **Phone:** (479) 521-5776 or (800) 766-4626.

Self-guiding tours: A brochure outlining a walking tour Fayetteville's downtown area is available at the convention and visitors bureau.

BOTANICAL GARDEN OF THE OZARKS is at 4703 N. Crossover Rd. (SR 265), just n. of jct. Zion Rd. Visitors can experience 12 themed gardens with plantings common to the Ozarks as they progress along a circular walkway. Water features and sculptures enhance the Founders', Japanese, vegetable and herb, children's, education cottage, butterfly, four seasons, shade, sensory, Ozark native, rose and perennial, and rock and water gardens. A seasonal butterfly house also is on the grounds.

Time: Allow 45 minutes minimum. **Hours:** Daily 9-5. **Cost:** $7; $4 (ages 5-12); free to Fayetteville residents (Sat. 9-noon). **Phone:** (479) 750-2620.

BEST WESTERN WINDSOR SUITES   479/301-2882

◆ **APPROVED**
Hotel

Best Western. **AAA Benefit:** Members save up to 15% and earn bonus points!

Address: 1122 S Futrall Dr 72701 **Location:** I-49 exit 62, just se. **Facility:** 68 units. 2 stories (no elevator), exterior corridors. **Pool:** heated indoor. **Activities:** exercise room. **Guest Services:** coin laundry.

COMFORT INN & SUITES   479/571-5177
◆ **THREE DIAMOND** Hotel. **Address:** 1234 Steamboat Dr 72704

COURTYARD BY MARRIOTT   479/571-4900
◆ **THREE DIAMOND** [SAVE] Hotel. **Address:** 600 E Van Asche Dr 72703

AAA Benefit: Members save 5% or more!

GRADUATE FAYETTEVILLE   479/442-5555
◆ **THREE DIAMOND** Hotel. **Address:** 70 N East Ave 72701

HAMPTON BY HILTON   479/587-8300
◆ **THREE DIAMOND** [SAVE] Hotel. **Address:** 915 Krupa Dr 72704

AAA Benefit: Members save up to 15%!

HILTON GARDEN INN   479/856-6040
◆ **THREE DIAMOND** [SAVE] Hotel. **Address:** 1325 N Palak Dr 72704

AAA Benefit: Members save up to 15%!

HOLIDAY INN EXPRESS HOTEL & SUITES-UNIVERSITY OF ARKANSAS AREA   479/444-6006
◆ **THREE DIAMOND** Hotel. **Address:** 1251 N Shiloh Dr 72704

HOMEWOOD SUITES BY HILTON   479/442-3000
◆ **THREE DIAMOND** [SAVE] Extended Stay Hotel. **Address:** 1305 N Palak Dr 72704

AAA Benefit: Members save up to 15%!

LA QUINTA INN & SUITES FAYETTEVILLE   479/587-8600
◆ **THREE DIAMOND** Hotel. **Address:** 720 E Millsap Rd 72703

PRATT PLACE INN   479/966-4441
◆ **FOUR DIAMOND**
Bed & Breakfast

Address: 2231 W Markham Rd 72701 **Location:** 0.4 mi w of jct Razorback Rd. **Facility:** This secluded bed and breakfast is loveliest in fall as the foliage surrounding the grounds lights up in vibrant colors. The beautiful home features large wraparound porches and verandas. 7 units, some kitchens and cottages. 3 stories, interior corridors. **Amenities:** safes. **Activities:** trails, massage. **Featured Amenity:** full hot breakfast.

[SAVE] CALL [HS]

SLEEP INN BY CHOICE HOTELS   479/587-8700
◆ **APPROVED** Hotel. **Address:** 728 E Millsap Rd 72703

STAYBRIDGE SUITES   479/695-2400
◆ **THREE DIAMOND** Extended Stay Hotel. **Address:** 1577 W 15th St 72701

WHERE TO EAT

BORDINO'S RESTAURANT & WINE BAR   479/527-6795
◆ **THREE DIAMOND** Italian. Casual Dining. **Address:** 310 W Dickson St 72701

COLTON'S STEAKHOUSE & GRILL   479/973-0876
◆ **APPROVED** Steak. Casual Dining. **Address:** 642 E Milsap Rd 72703

ELLA'S RESTAURANT   479/582-1400
◆ **THREE DIAMOND** American. Fine Dining. **Address:** 465 N Arkansas Ave 72701

GUSANO'S   479/287-4000
◆ **APPROVED** Pizza. Casual Dining. **Address:** 1267 N Steamboat Dr 72704

HUGO'S   479/521-7585
◆ **APPROVED** American. Casual Dining. **Address:** 25 N Block Ave 72701

SOUTHERN FOOD COMPANY   479/313-7646
◆ **APPROVED** American. Casual Dining. **Address:** 3575 W Wedington Dr, Suite 3 72704

THEO'S AMERICAN KITCHEN   479/527-0086
◆ **THREE DIAMOND** American. Fine Dining. **Address:** 318 N Campbell Ave 72701

FORREST CITY pop. 15,371

COMFORT SUITES   870/633-2300
◆ **THREE DIAMOND** Hotel. **Address:** 320 Holiday Dr 72335

HAMPTON INN BY HILTON   870/630-9000
◆ **THREE DIAMOND** [SAVE] Hotel. **Address:** 300 Holiday Dr 72335

AAA Benefit: Members save up to 15%!

RED ROOF INN FORREST CITY   870/633-0870
◆ **APPROVED** Motel. **Address:** 2333 N Washington St 72335

WHERE TO EAT

OLE SAWMILL CAFE   870/630-2299
◆ **APPROVED** American. Casual Dining. **Address:** 2299 N Washington St 72335

FORT SMITH (C-1) pop. 86,209, elev. 439'
• Restaurants p. 40

In 1817 Maj. Stephen H. Long selected a site at the confluence of the Arkansas and Poteau rivers as the location for the region's first military fort. Named for Gen. Thomas Smith, the fort prompted settlement and the resultant town shared the fort's name. With the discovery of natural gas in nearby Mansfield, a large and diverse manufacturing industry developed; Fort Smith remains one of Arkansas' leading manufacturing cities.

A navigation channel on the Arkansas River connects Fort Smith with other ports. Fort Smith is a convenient starting point for picturesque drives through the Ozark, Ouachita and Kiamichi mountains and the Cookson Hills via two of the state's scenic highways, US 71 and I-40.

Fort Smith Regional Chamber of Commerce: 612 Garrison Ave., Fort Smith, AR 72901. **Phone:** (479) 783-3111.

ARKANSAS AND MISSOURI RAILROAD—see Van Buren p. 69.

FORT SMITH MUSEUM OF HISTORY is at 320 Rogers Ave. Chronicling the development of Fort Smith, museum collections include an early 20th-century pharmacy and soda fountain, the area's first steam-powered fire pump and memorabilia of World War II hero Brig. Gen. William O. Darby. The In the Shadow of the Gallows exhibit presents the changing perspectives of federal executions at Fort Smith from 1873-96; Judge Isaac C. Parker's original bench and chair are on display. The Boyd Gallery features changing exhibits. The Fort Smith Trolley Museum offers rides on a restored electric trolley.

Time: Allow 2 hours minimum. **Hours:** Tues.-Sat. 10-5, Sun. 1-5, first Sun. in June-Labor Day; Tues.-Sat. 10-5, rest of year. **Cost:** Museum $7; $2 (ages 6-15). **Phone:** (479) 783-7841.

FORT SMITH NATIONAL HISTORIC SITE is at 301 Parker Ave. Incorporating the remains of two successive frontier forts, the site chronicles the frontier years 1817-96. Themes include military history, westward expansion, Indian Removal along the Trail of Tears, the Indian Territory, law and order in the late 19th century and the diverse people who lived in the region.

Seventy-nine felons were hanged at the fort during Judge Isaac C. Parker's 21 years on the bench of the U.S. District Court for Western Arkansas—outlaws dubbed him the "hanging judge." The fort's visitor center in his restored courtroom features accurate furnishings and exhibits, a 15-minute DVD program about the fort's history and reproductions of the jail and barracks. A reproduction of the gallows also is at the site.

Hours: Daily 9-5. Closed Jan. 1, Thanksgiving and Christmas. Phone ahead to confirm holiday schedule. **Cost:** Site admission free. Visitor center $10; free (ages 0-15). **Phone:** (479) 783-3961. ⛫

JANET HUCKABEE ARKANSAS RIVER VALLEY NATURE CENTER is on Wells Lake at 8300 Wells Lake Rd. The nature center, on 170 acres that were part of the Fort Chaffee Army base, has interactive exhibits that provide information about the Ouachita and Ozark mountains, an aquarium with fish from the Arkansas River and a representation of a giant oak tree.

Several nature trails surround the visitor center, providing opportunities to see wildlife such as beavers, raccoons and deer. A fishing pier also is available. Educational and recreational programs are offered, including guided hikes and staff-assisted canoeing and kayaking. **Time:** Allow 45 minutes minimum. **Hours:** Tues.-Sat. 8:30-4:30, Sun. 1-5. Phone ahead to confirm program schedule. Closed major holidays. **Cost:** Free. **Phone:** (479) 452-3993. ⛫

BAYMONT INN & SUITES FORT SMITH   479/484-5770
⟦AAA⟧ **APPROVED**   Hotel. **Address:** 2123 Burnham Rd 72903

BELAND MANOR BED & BREAKFAST   479/782-3300
⟦AAA⟧ **THREE DIAMOND** Bed & Breakfast. **Address:** 1320 S Albert Pike 72903

COMFORT INN & SUITES   479/434-5400
⟦AAA⟧ **THREE DIAMOND** Hotel. **Address:** 6500 Rogers Ave 72903

COURTYARD BY MARRIOTT DOWNTOWN FORT SMITH
479/783-2100
⟦AAA⟧ **THREE DIAMOND** SAVE Hotel. **Address:** 900 Rogers Ave 72901

> **AAA Benefit:**
> Members save 5% or more!

DOUBLETREE BY HILTON FORT SMITH CITY CENTER
479/783-1000
⟦AAA⟧ **THREE DIAMOND** SAVE Hotel. **Address:** 700 Rogers Ave 72901

> **AAA Benefit:**
> Members save up to 15%!

FAIRFIELD INN & SUITES FORT SMITH   479/755-3111
⟦AAA⟧ **THREE DIAMOND** SAVE Hotel. **Address:** 7601 Phoenix Ave 72903

> **AAA Benefit:**
> Members save 5% or more!

HAMPTON INN BY HILTON   479/452-2000
⟦AAA⟧ **THREE DIAMOND** SAVE Hotel. **Address:** 6201-C Rogers Ave 72903

> **AAA Benefit:**
> Members save up to 15%!

HOLIDAY INN EXPRESS   479/452-7500
⟦AAA⟧ **THREE DIAMOND** Hotel. **Address:** 6813 Phoenix Ave 72903

HOME2 SUITES BY HILTON-FORT SMITH   479/452-2100
⟦AAA⟧ **THREE DIAMOND** SAVE Extended Stay Hotel. **Address:** 7400 Phoenix Ave 72903

> **AAA Benefit:**
> Members save up to 15%!

GOOD TIMES HAPPEN HERE

Over 900 Electronic Games • 9 Table Games • 120-Room Hotel Tower
Complimentary High-Speed Internet • 24/7 Grab & Go
Pool & Hot Tub • Meeting & Banquet Space Available

I-40 Exit 325, Roland, OK
800.256.2338 | CherokeeCasino.com

ONE★STAR

Cherokee
CASINO & HOTEL

ROLAND

Know your limits. Gambling problem? Call 800.522.4700.

HOMEWOOD SUITES BY HILTON FORT SMITH   479/452-7100
THREE DIAMOND **SAVE** Extended Stay Hotel. **Address:** 7300 Phoenix Ave 72903

> **AAA Benefit:** Members save up to 15%!

RESIDENCE INN BY MARRIOTT   479/478-8300
THREE DIAMOND **SAVE** Extended Stay Hotel. **Address:** 3005 S 74th St 72903

> **AAA Benefit:** Members save 5% or more!

WHERE TO EAT

21 WEST END   479/434-4213
THREE DIAMOND American. Casual Dining. **Address:** 21 N 2nd St 72901

CALICO COUNTY   479/452-3299
APPROVED American. Casual Dining. **Address:** 2401 S 56th St 72903

EL LORITO   479/782-3820
APPROVED Mexican. Casual Dining. **Address:** 1505 South B St 72901

EL LORITO   479/484-7018
APPROVED Mexican. Casual Dining. **Address:** 3105 S 70th St 72903

FISH CITY GRILL   479/769-2400
APPROVED Seafood. Casual Dining. **Address:** 7001 Phoenix Ave 72903

GENO'S PIZZA   479/484-9900
APPROVED Pizza. Quick Serve. **Address:** 7906 Rogers Ave 72917

MARIA'S MEXICAN RESTAURANT   479/452-2328
APPROVED Mexican. Casual Dining. **Address:** 8640 Rogers Ave 72903

TALIANO'S RESTAURANT   479/785-2292
APPROVED Italian. Casual Dining. **Address:** 201 N 14th St 72901

HARDY (A-4) pop. 772, elev. 358'

Hardy is set in the Ozark Mountain foothills along the banks of Spring River. The river provides white-water canoeing and fishing, while the town serves up its own brand of entertainment—music. Country sounds abound in musical productions and at outdoor jam sessions held at Dr. Thompson Park during the summer. The downtown district has remained virtually unchanged since the 1920s and features 43 historic buildings.

GOOD OLD DAYS VINTAGE MOTORCAR MUSEUM is at 301 W. Main St. More than 60 rare and vintage cars, trucks, motorcycles and bicycles are displayed. A large collection of cars from the 1915-29 era also is featured. Some vehicles still have all their original parts. The museum's collection is constantly changing. Vintage car jacks also are on display. **Time:** Allow 30 minutes minimum. **Hours:** Mon. and Fri.-Sat. 9:30-4:30, Sun. 12:30-4:30, June-Aug.; Sat. 9:30-4:30, Sun. 12:30-4:30, Apr.-May and

Sept.-Nov.; by appointment rest of year. Phone ahead to confirm schedule. **Cost:** $10; $5 (ages 1-12). **Phone:** (870) 856-4884.

HARRISON (A-2) pop. 12,943, elev. 1,061'

The "Gateway to the Buffalo River," Harrison is the center of a rustic resort community in the valley of Crooked Creek, one of the most scenic sections of the Arkansas Ozarks. The town is home to the two-year North Arkansas College.

Running from the state's northern border through Hot Springs National Park *(see place listing p. 43)* and ending in Arkadelphia, SR 7 encompasses lofty mountains and numerous lakes and rivers. The road is popular for leisurely drives and photographic opportunities. En route to Hot Springs, SR 7 crosses two national forests, the Ozark *(see place listing p. 61)* and the Ouachita *(see place listing p. 60)*, and the Buffalo National River *(see place listing p. 30)*. See Recreation Areas Chart.

Harrison Convention & Visitors Bureau: 200 W. Stephenson Ave., Harrison, AR 72601. **Phone:** (870) 741-1789 or (888) 283-2163.

BOONE COUNTY HERITAGE MUSEUM is at 124 S. Cherry St. This three-story museum features large collections of railroad memorabilia and antique clocks, a room devoted to medical instruments of the past, Native American artifacts and World Wars I and II memorabilia. A genealogy library also is available. Educational programs are offered. **Time:** Allow 1 hour minimum. **Hours:** Mon.-Tues. and Fri.-Sat. 10-4, Thurs. 10-7. Educational program last Mon. of the month at 6:30. Closed major holidays. **Cost:** $5; free (ages 0-11 with adult). **Phone:** (870) 741-3312.

MYSTIC CAVERNS is 8 mi. s. off SR 7 at 341 Caverns Dr. Guided 80- to 90-minute tours feature two Ozark caverns with well-lighted walkways and wide steps. Tours featuring one cavern also are available. The temperature in the caves is a constant 59 F. A jacket is advised. **Time:** Allow 30 minutes minimum. **Hours:** Tours are given every 45 minutes Mon.-Sat. 9-5:30, June-Aug.; Mon.-Sat. 9-5, Mar.-May and Sept.-Oct.; Mon.-Sat. 9-4, Nov.-Dec. **Cost:** Tour (two caverns) $16.99; $15.99 (ages 62+); $8.99 (ages 4-12). Mystic Cavern $14.99; $7.99 (ages 4-12). Crystal Dome $12.99; $6.99 (ages 4-12). **Phone:** (870) 743-1739 or (888) 743-1739. 🍴

HAMPTON INN BY HILTON   870/365-0505
THREE DIAMOND **SAVE** Hotel. **Address:** 121 Hwy 43 E 72601

> **AAA Benefit:** Members save up to 15%!

HOLIDAY INN EXPRESS HOTEL & SUITES   870/741-3636
APPROVED Hotel. **Address:** 117 Hwy 43 E 72601

QUALITY INN   870/741-7676
APPROVED Hotel. **Address:** 1210 Hwy 62/65 N 72601

COLTON'S STEAKHOUSE & GRILL   870/741-1834
APPROVED Steak. Casual Dining. **Address:** 820 Hwy 62/65 N 72601

DIAMOND HEAD CHINESE RESTAURANT   870/743-8888
APPROVED Chinese. Casual Dining. **Address:** 1408 Hwy 62/65 N 72601

NEIGHBOR'S MILL BAKERY & CAFE   870/741-6455
APPROVED Breakfast Sandwiches. Quick Serve. **Address:** 1012 Hwy 65 N 72601

HELENA-WEST HELENA (D-5) pop. 12,282, elev. 328'

Founded in 1820, Helena enacted early laws that set the speed limit at a trot or pace and required that guns be fired within town limits only with just cause. Such cause was found on July 4, 1863, during the bloody Battle of Helena, when Confederate troops tried in vain to recapture the town from occupying Union forces.

Today city sites continue to tell the story of Civil War Helena. Fort Curtis, located at the corner of York and Columbia streets, contains a nearly full-size replica of the Civil War era earth-and-wood fort and several cannons, one of which is operational. Visitors can walk through and explore the fort's interior. Battery C Park, 1298 Yorkshire Dr., is one of four earthen batteries erected during the war. Freedom Park on South Biscoe Street contains five interpretive areas showcasing the African-American experience in Civil War Helena. The park is designated as a site on the Underground Railroad Network to Freedom. The parks are open daily dawn to dusk, and admission is free; phone (800) 358-0972.

Helena is a river port; its proximity to the Mississippi River provides ample opportunities for outdoor sports including hunting, fishing and canoeing. Former Helena residents include lyric soprano Frances Greer; country singer Harold Jenkins, better known as Conway Twitty; and blues singer Sonny Boy Williamson II. A mural depicting musicians stretches for a block beginning at 95 Missouri St., on the levee walk.

The Delta Cultural Center retells the story of the Delta region and its people and hosts the Arkansas Delta Family Gospel Fest on Saturday in mid-May; phone (870) 338-4350 or (800) 358-0972. The town celebrates its musical talent again on the weekend before Columbus Day in October with the 3-day King Biscuit Blues Festival. Helena Holiday Festival rings in the holiday season in early December; phone (870) 338-8327.

An annual series of free classical and contemporary performances is offered October through May at Phillips Community College's 1,000-seat Lily Peter Auditorium and culminates with the Warfield Music Festival in early May. For more than 40 seasons, patrons of the arts have been entertained by world-renowned orchestras, opera companies, and ballet and contemporary dance troupes. For tickets and schedules, phone (870) 338-8327 or (870) 338-7602.

Cherry St. in historic downtown hosts Helena Second Saturdays featuring local artisans and entertainment the second Saturday of the month April through September. Guided tours of some of Helena's historic houses are available by appointment. For further information contact the chamber of commerce.

Phillips County Chamber of Commerce: 111 Hickory Hills Dr., Helena, AR 72342. **Phone:** (870) 338-8327.

HELENA MUSEUM OF PHILLIPS COUNTY is 2 blks. e. of US 49 Bus. Rte. at Porter and Pecan sts. The museum displays memorabilia from the Spanish-American and Civil wars as well as artworks and period costumes. Exhibits also recognize the achievements of Mark Twain and Thomas Alva Edison. **Hours:** Wed.-Sat. 10-4. Guided 1-hour tours are available. Last tour begins 1 hour, 30 minutes before closing. Closed major holidays. **Cost:** Free. **Phone:** (870) 338-7790.

BEST WESTERN INN   870/572-2592
APPROVED Motel

Best Western. **AAA Benefit:** Members save up to 15% and earn bonus points!

Address: 1053 Hwy 49 W 72390 **Location:** US 49, 3 mi w. **Facility:** 63 units. 2 stories (no elevator), exterior corridors. **Pool:** outdoor. **Activities:** exercise room. **Guest Services:** coin laundry.

PATIO MEXICAN RESTAURANT   870/228-3097
APPROVED Mexican. Casual Dining. **Address:** 1012 W Hwy 49 72390

HOPE (E-2) pop. 10,095, elev. 355'
• Hotels p. 42 • Restaurants p. 42

Known as the birthplace of Bill Clinton, Hope was settled in 1852 and named after the daughter of a railroad commissioner. Local growers began cultivating watermelons for rail shipment in the early 1900s and soon began breaking world records for giant-sized melons. Today's entries regularly tip the scales at 200 pounds. The Watermelon Festival in August features an arts and crafts show, a 5K race, a fishing tournament and watermelon-eating and seed-spitting contests.

Hope-Hempstead County Chamber of Commerce: 200 S. Main St., P.O. Box 250, Hope, AR 71802. **Phone:** (870) 777-3640.

BEST WESTERN HOPE   870/777-9222

APPROVED
Hotel

AAA Benefit: Members save up to 15% and earn bonus points!

Address: 1800 Holiday Dr 71801 **Location:** I-30 exit 30, just nw. **Facility:** 71 units. 2 stories (no elevator), exterior corridors. **Pool:** outdoor. **Guest Services:** coin laundry. **Featured Amenity: full hot breakfast.**

HAMPTON INN & SUITES BY HILTON HOPE   870/777-4567
THREE DIAMOND [SAVE] Hotel. **Address:** 2700 N Hervey St 71801

AAA Benefit: Members save up to 15%!

SUPER 8   870/777-8601
APPROVED   Motel. **Address:** 2000 Holiday Dr 71801

WHERE TO EAT

AMIGO JUAN   870/777-0006
APPROVED   Mexican. Casual Dining. **Address:** 1300 N Hervey St 71801

HOT SPRINGS (D-2) pop. 35,193, elev. 632'

Hot Springs is a year-round health and pleasure resort adjacent to Hot Springs National Park *(see place listing p. 43)*. The Hot Springs region is well-known for its three nearby lakes— Lake Hamilton, Lake Ouachita and Lake Catherine—and for being rich in quartz crystals of superior hardness and brilliance; the finest are in the veins of Crystal Mountain. Baseball enthusiasts can follow the Hot Springs Baseball Trail, a 26-marker walking and driving trail that denotes the history of the sport.

The city sponsors a variety of events, including the Miss Arkansas Pageant in July and the Hot Springs Documentary Film Festival in October. In mid-April, Arkansas Derby Day takes place at Oaklawn Park as part of its thoroughbred racing season, January through mid-April; phone (800) 625-5296. **Note:** Policies concerning admittance of children to pari-mutuel betting facilities vary. Phone for information.

Visit Hot Springs: 134 Convention Blvd., Hot Springs, AR 71901. **Phone:** (501) 321-2277 or (800) 543-2284.

Self-guiding tours: A guide book with information about driving tours is available at the visitor center.

Shopping: Temperance Hill Square, SR 7 at Central Avenue, features specialty stores including Tuesday Morning. Cornerstone Market Place, off the US 270/70 Bypass, includes Chico's, Old Navy and Pier 1.

BELLE OF HOT SPRINGS departs from 5200 Central Ave. The 200-passenger riverboat offers narrated 75-minute daytime and 2-hour evening sightseeing cruises on Lake Hamilton. Lunch and dinner cruises also are available.

Hours: Departures require a minimum of 12 people. Departures daily at 1 and 7, Memorial Day weekend-Labor Day (also daily at 3, Sat. at 5:30 and 8:30, July; Sat. at 3, 5:30 and 8:30, early Aug. to mid-Aug.; Sat. at 3, mid-Aug. to late Aug.); at 1 and 8, rest of year. **Cost:** Evening fare $19.99; $9.99 (ages 2-12). Daytime fare $18.99; $9.50 (ages 2-12). Reservations are required. **Phone:** (501) 525-4438.

GARVAN WOODLAND GARDENS is at 550 Arkridge Rd. This 210-acre botanical garden features more than 5 miles of walking trails that provide visitors access to a variety of plant collections, flower borders and a Japanese garden. A 1.5-acre children's adventure garden features a maze created with 3,200 tons of boulders, bridges, a man-made cave and a waterfall. The Perry Wildflower Overlook offers views of Lake Hamilton. A welcome center is on site. Anthony Chapel includes a carillon and meditation garden. Guided 1-hour golf cart tours are available. A holiday lights display features more than 4 million lights.

Time: Allow 1 hour, 30 minutes minimum. **Hours:** Daily 9-6, Feb. 1-Fri. before Thanksgiving. Holiday light display noon-9, Sat. before Thanksgiving-Dec. 31; holiday lights are turned on at 5. **Cost:** $15; $5 (ages 6-12). Pets on leash $5. Golf cart tour $15 (per person). **Phone:** (501) 262-9300 or (800) 366-4664.

MOUNTAIN VALLEY SPRING WATER VISITOR CENTER is at 150 Central Ave. Built in 1910, the center offers samples and self-guiding tours of the museum. **Time:** Allow 30 minutes minimum. **Hours:** Mon.-Fri. 9-6, Sun. 9-4. **Cost:** Free. **Phone:** (501) 246-8017.

BAYMONT BY WYNDHAM HOT SPRINGS   501/520-5522
APPROVED   Hotel. **Address:** 5321 Central Ave 71913

BEST WESTERN WINNERS CIRCLE INN   501/624-2531
APPROVED
Motel

AAA Benefit: Members save up to 15% and earn bonus points!

Address: 2520 Central Ave 71901 **Location:** Jct US 70/270, 1.3 mi n on SR 7. Across from Oaklawn Park. **Facility:** 120 units. 2 stories (no elevator), exterior corridors. **Amenities:** safes. **Pool:** outdoor. **Activities:** exercise room. **Guest Services:** coin laundry. **Featured Amenity:** breakfast buffet.

COMFORT INN & SUITES   501/623-1700
THREE DIAMOND Hotel. **Address:** 3627 Central Ave 71913

COMFORT SUITES   501/624-3800
THREE DIAMOND Hotel. **Address:** 320 Nash St 71913

COURTYARD BY MARRIOTT HOT SPRINGS
501/651-4366

THREE DIAMOND
Hotel

COURTYARD' **AAA Benefit:** Members save 5% or more!

Address: 200 Marriott Ct 71913 **Location:** US 70/US 270 exit 3A (3A / South/Central Ave), 0.5 mi s. **Facility:** 98 units. 4 stories, interior corridors. **Terms:** check-in 4 pm. **Pool:** heated indoor. **Activities:** exercise room. **Guest Services:** valet and coin laundry, area transportation.

[SAVE] [icons] CALL [icons]
[BIZ] [icons]

EMBASSY SUITES BY HILTON HOT SPRINGS-HOTEL & SPA
501/624-9200
THREE DIAMOND [SAVE] Hotel. **Address:** 400 Convention Blvd 71901

AAA Benefit: Members save up to 15%!

HAMPTON INN BY HILTON   501/525-7000
THREE DIAMOND [SAVE] Hotel. **Address:** 151 Temperance Hill Rd 71913

AAA Benefit: Members save up to 15%!

HOME2 SUITES BY HILTON   501/520-4444
THREE DIAMOND [SAVE] Extended Stay Hotel. **Address:** 106 Catalina Cir 71913

AAA Benefit: Members save up to 15%!

STAYBRIDGE SUITES   501/525-6500
THREE DIAMOND Extended Stay Hotel. **Address:** 103 Lookout Cir 71913

TOWNEPLACE SUITES HOT SPRINGS   501/525-7800
THREE DIAMOND [SAVE] Extended Stay Hotel. **Address:** 120 Desai-Patel Court 71913

AAA Benefit: Members save 5% or more!

WHERE TO EAT

ANGEL'S ITALIAN RESTAURANT   501/609-9323
APPROVED Italian. Casual Dining. **Address:** 600 Central Ave 71901

BACK PORCH GRILL   501/525-0885
APPROVED Steak. Casual Dining. **Address:** 4810 Central Ave 71913

BRICK HOUSE GRILL   501/321-2926
APPROVED American. Casual Dining. **Address:** 801 Central Ave, Suite 24 71901

CAFE 1217   501/318-1094
APPROVED American. Quick Serve. **Address:** 1217 Malvern Ave 71901

COLTON'S STEAKHOUSE & GRILL   501/623-2110
APPROVED Steak. Casual Dining. **Address:** 120 Crawford St 71913

CRAZY SAMURAI   501/525-0488
APPROVED Sushi. Casual Dining. **Address:** 5431 Central Ave 71901

DOLCÉ GELATO   501/525-6580
APPROVED American. Quick Serve. **Address:** 228 Cornerstone Blvd 71913

LA HACIENDA
501/525-8203
APPROVED

Traditional Mexican Casual Dining $5-$17

AAA Inspector Notes: Inside this hot pink eatery you'll find more vibrant colors in the décor and equally bold flavors on the menu, which is reminiscent of Mexican food served much farther west. Enjoy fajitas, enchiladas, tacos and specialties like carne asada and camarones al mojo de ajo, shrimp in a flavorful tomato-garlic sauce. Margaritas are served frosty and in a variety of flavors. **Features:** full bar. **Address:** 3836 Central Ave 71913 **Location:** Jct US 70/270, 0.4 mi s on SR 7. [L] [D]

MR. WHISKERS   501/262-3474
APPROVED American. Quick Serve. **Address:** 1538 Malvern Ave 71901

OHIO CLUB   501/627-0702
APPROVED Burgers. Casual Dining. **Address:** 336 Central Ave 71901

ROLANDO'S   501/318-6054
APPROVED Latin American. Casual Dining. **Address:** 210 Central Ave 71901

HOT SPRINGS NATIONAL PARK
(D-2)
• Attractions map p. 44

Elevations in the park range from 600 ft. at the corner of Central and Reserve aves. to 1,420 ft. at Music Mountain. Refer to AAA maps for additional elevation information.

Hot Springs National Park, in western Arkansas, can be reached from the north and south via scenic SR 7, as well as via US 70 from the east and US 270 from both the east and west.

In the picturesque Ouachita (WASH-i-taw) Mountains, Hot Springs differs sharply from the country's other scenic national parks in that portions of it are nearly surrounded by a sizable city. Its 5,500 acres occupy the slopes of Hot Springs, Music, North, West, Sugarloaf and Indian mountains.

The thermal water that flows from the springs is naturally sterile. It begins as rainwater, is absorbed into the mountains northeast of the park and is carried 4,000-8,000 feet underground, where the earth's extreme heat raises its temperature to 143 F. The purified water makes its way back to the surface through cracks and pores in the rock in the form of hot springs. The entire process takes about 4,000 years.

In 1832, because of tourism brought on by the water's reported medicinal properties, the federal government set aside the springs and surrounding area as the country's first park-type federal reservation. In 1921 Hot Springs became a national park, the country's eighteenth. Numerous bathhouses, eight of which still stand along a portion of Central

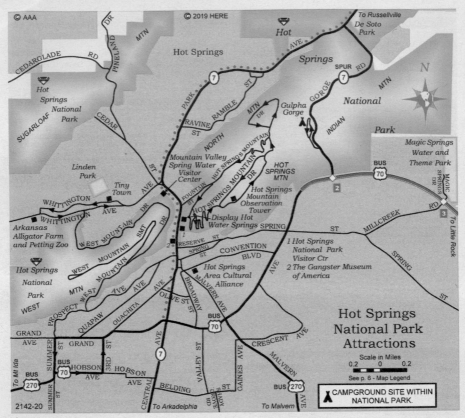

Avenue known as Bathhouse Row, catered to thousands of health seekers. The popularity of the springs began to decrease in the 1950s, but the springs still attract many visitors.

General Information and Activities

The springs are found along the west slope of Hot Springs Mountain. Within about 10 acres there are 47 springs with a daily flow of approximately 750,000 gallons. The water is collected into one central system and distributed to bathhouses and the drinking and jug fountains near the corner of Central and Reserve. The standard tub baths can be taken at the Buckstaff Bathhouse on Bathhouse Row. Options, at no extra cost, include showers, sitz tubs, vapor cabinets and hot packs. You can also experience the hot spring water in a modern day spa setting at the Quapaw Baths and Spa, the only business that uses the spring water in pools.

Other bathhouses in the city are managed in connection with hotels; prices vary according to equipment and available accommodations.

The park has 10 miles of good mountain roads for sightseeing by car, as well as 26 miles of walking and horse trails for outdoor enthusiasts; the trails are open daily year-round. Interpretive programs are presented from mid-June to mid-August; phone for schedule. **Note:** Because of sharp switchbacks, vehicles more than 30 feet long cannot negotiate Hot Springs Mountain Drive.

Fall and spring offer displays of flowering trees, shrubs and colorful foliage. Nearby Catherine, Hamilton and Ouachita lakes offer fishing. *See Recreation Areas Chart.*

ADMISSION to the park is free.

PETS are permitted in the park only if they are leashed, crated or otherwise physically restricted at all times. Pets are not permitted in park buildings.

ADDRESS inquiries to the Park Superintendent, 101 Reserve St., Hot Springs National Park, AR 71901; phone (501) 620-6715 for Fordyce Visitor Center.

DISPLAY HOT WATER SPRINGS is behind Maurice Bathhouse at 369 Central Ave. These are the two thermal springs in Hot Springs National Park from which water still issues in open view. A thermal water cascade is on the Arlington Lawn at the north end of Bathhouse Row. **Hours:** Daily 6 a.m.-10 p.m. **Cost:** Free.

HOT SPRINGS MOUNTAIN OBSERVATION TOWER is off Fountain St. at 401 Hot Springs Mountain Dr. This 216-foot tower provides scenic views of the park, city and vicinity. Several towers have stood on the site, including the original wooden fire tower that was destroyed by lightning.

Note: Because of sharp switchbacks, vehicles more than 30 feet long cannot negotiate Hot Springs Mountain Drive. **Time:** Allow 30 minutes minimum. **Hours:** Daily 9-9, mid-May through Labor Day; 9-8, May 1 to mid-May; 9-7 in April; 9-6:30 in Mar. and Oct.; 9-5 rest of year. **Cost:** $8; $7 (ages 55+); $6 (military with ID); $4.50 (ages 5-11); $4 (group of 15 or more) $2 (part of group ages 5 11). **Phone:** (501) 881-4020.

HOT SPRINGS NATIONAL PARK VISITOR CENTER is on Bathhouse Row. Housed in the historic Fordyce Bathhouse, the center offers displays about area history. The 1915 Spanish Renaissance-style building has marble and mosaic tile floors, stained-glass ceilings and ceramic fountains. Self-guiding and limited 45-minute guided tours are available. A movie is shown every 30 minutes. **Hours:** Open daily 9-5. Guided tours depart at 11 and 2 (based on staff availability), fall-spring; phone for summer tour schedule. Phone ahead to confirm schedule. **Cost:** Free. **Phone:** (501) 620-6715.

JACKSONVILLE pop. 28,364

BEST WESTERN JACKSONVILLE INN	501/982-8181

WV APPROVED

Motel

Best Western. **AAA Benefit:** Members save up to 15% and earn bonus points!

Address: 1600 John Harden Dr 72076 **Location:** US 67/167 exit 11, just s on west service road. **Facility:** 67 units. 2 stories (no elevator), exterior corridors. **Pool:** outdoor. **Activities:** exercise room. **Guest Services:** coin laundry.

QUALITY INN	501/985-4400

WV APPROVED Hotel. **Address:** 1500 John Harden Dr 72076

SUPER 8	501/982-9219

WV APPROVED Motel. **Address:** 1850 John Harden Dr 72076

WHERE TO EAT

PAPITOS MEXICAN GRILL	501/982-0611

WV APPROVED Mexican. Casual Dining. **Address:** 1700 John Harden Dr 72076

🔗 For complete hotel, dining and attraction listings:
AAA.com/travelguides

JONESBORO (B-5) pop. 67,263, elev. 302'
• Restaurants p. 46

Nearly 14,000 students attend Jonesboro's Arkansas State University. The school's 78,000-square-foot Fowler Center houses a 975-seat concert hall noted for its acoustics, a 344-seat theater and the 5,200-square-foot Bradbury Art Museum.

Jonesboro Regional Chamber of Commerce: 1709 E. Nettleton Ave., P.O. Box 789, Jonesboro, AR 72403. **Phone:** (870) 932-6691.

Shopping: The Mall at Turtle Creek, 3000 E. Highland Dr., is anchored by Dillard's and JCPenney; among its more than 70 shops are Barnes & Noble, Gap and Kay Jewelers. Boutiques, art galleries and eateries can be found along Main Street downtown.

ARKANSAS STATE UNIVERSITY MUSEUM is in the center of campus 2 mi. e. off Aggie Rd. at 320 University Loop W. Extensive displays relate to Arkansas' prehistory, native cultures, wildlife, European exploration and pioneer eras, early settlement and military history. The Tinkering Studio provides hands-on activities for children. The museum also displays changing exhibits. Guided tours are available by reservation. **Time:** Allow 1 hour, 30 minutes minimum. **Hours:** Mon.-Fri. 9-5 (also Tues. 5-7), Sat. 10-5. Closed major holidays and university holidays. **Cost:** Free. **Phone:** (870) 972-2074.

BEST WESTERN PLUS JONESBORO INN & SUITES	870/333-1419

WV THREE DIAMOND

Hotel

Best Western PLUS. **AAA Benefit:** Members save up to 15% and earn bonus points!

Address: 2911 Gilmore Dr 72401 **Location:** Just ne of jct US 63 and Caraway Rd. **Facility:** 90 units. 5 stories, interior corridors. **Pool:** outdoor. **Activities:** exercise room. **Guest Services:** valet and coin laundry.

COURTYARD BY MARRIOTT JONESBORO	870/206-9500

WV THREE DIAMOND SAVE Hotel. **Address:** 4811 E Johnson Ave 72401

AAA Benefit: Members save 5% or more!

FAIRFIELD INN & SUITES BY MARRIOTT JONESBORO	870/934-1600

WV THREE DIAMOND SAVE Hotel. **Address:** 3408 Access Rd 72401

AAA Benefit: Members save 5% or more!

HAMPTON INN BY HILTON	870/974-9500

WV THREE DIAMOND SAVE Hotel. **Address:** 2900 Phillips Dr 72401

AAA Benefit: Members save up to 15%!

HILTON GARDEN INN JONESBORO   870/931-7727
THREE DIAMOND SAVE Hotel. **Ad-**   **AAA Benefit:**
dress: 2840 S Caraway Rd 72401   Members save up to
                                          15%!

HOLIDAY INN JONESBORO   870/333-5100
THREE DIAMOND Hotel. **Address:** 2908 Gilmore Dr 72401

WHERE TO EAT

COLTON'S STEAKHOUSE & GRILL   870/802-4000
APPROVED Steak. Casual Dining. **Address:** 2309 E
Parker Rd 72401

DEMO'S BARBEQUE & SMOKEHOUSE   870/935-6633
APPROVED Barbecue. Quick Serve. **Address:** 1851
S Church St 72401

MURDOCK'S CATFISH   870/206-7822
APPROVED American. Quick Serve. **Address:** 2612
Red Wolf Blvd 72401

SUMO   870/972-8355
APPROVED Japanese. Casual Dining. **Address:** 2801
Red Wolf Blvd 72401

LITTLE ROCK (D-3) pop. 193,524, elev. 300'
* **Hotels p. 53** • **Restaurants p. 55**
* **Hotels & Restaurants map & index p. 50**

Settled in 1814 on a rocky bluff overlooking the Arkansas River, Little Rock became the seat of territorial government in 1821 when its population was less than 20. Except for a period during the Civil War when Federal troops under Gen. Fredrick Steele captured the city, it has remained the capital. It also is the state's largest city.

The oldest section of Little Rock is known as the Quapaw Quarter, a 9-square-mile area encompassing the city's central business district and adjacent residential neighborhoods. It includes many examples of Victorian and antebellum architectural styles. Of particular interest is the 1881 English-Gothic-style Cathedral of St. Andrew on the corner of Sixth and South Louisiana streets, with its stained-glass windows by the New York branch of Mayer of Munich; phone (501) 374-2794 for hours of accessibility.

The Villa Marre at 1321 Scott St. is open for special events. Built in 1881, this combination Second Empire- and Italianate-style house gained fame in the 1980s when television producers and former Arkansas residents Harry Thomason and Linda Bloodworth-Thomason used the house's exterior to portray the Sugarbaker design firm on the CBS television series "Designing Women."

Riverfront Park is part of the 17-mile-long Arkansas River Trail, and offers walkways, terraces, plazas, recreation space, a 1,200-seat amphitheater, an activity center and a historical pavilion. The "little rock" for which the city was named is marked by a bronze plaque in La Petite Roche Plaza. Murray Lock and Dam and Murray Park are among the other popular riverbank attractions. The Henry Moore bronze sculpture "Knife Edge" graces the corner of South Louisiana Street and Capitol Avenue downtown. The Big Dam Bridge, the longest bridge built specifically for pedestrians and cyclists in the world, connects Little Rock with North Little Rock via some 15 miles of scenic trails.

River Rail Streetcars connect Little Rock and North Little Rock, with numerous stops along the way, including the Historic Arkansas Museum and the Museum of Discovery (see attraction listings).

There are a variety of recreational offerings in the Little Rock area. A notable city event is Riverfest, held Friday through Sunday of Memorial Day weekend. The Quapaw Quarter Spring Tour of Homes takes place Mother's Day weekend. Little Rock's visitor information center is in a historic antebellum building, circa 1842, called the Walters-Curran-Bell home but is commonly known as Curran Hall.

Little Rock Visitor Information Center at Historic Curran Hall: 615 E. Capitol Ave., Little Rock, AR 72202. **Phone:** (501) 371-0076.

Self-guiding tours: Brochures and a driving tour map of the Quapaw Quarter are available from the visitor information center.

Shopping: Park Plaza Mall, at 6000 W. Markham Street, is anchored by Dillard's. Shackleford Crossing, at I-430 and S. Shackleford Road, is anchored by JCPenney. Pleasant Ridge Town Center, 11525 Cantrell Rd., is home to Belk as well as numerous shops and restaurants. The River Market District, 400 President Clinton Ave., with its Arcade Building at 100 River Market Ave., and The Promenade at Chenal, 17711 Chenal Parkway, offer visitors an array of diverse shops, galleries, eateries and nightlife entertainment venues. A collection of shops, including Williams-Sonoma, Pottery Barn and Ann Taylor Loft, can be found at Midtowne Little Rock at Markham Street and University Avenue. Antique buffs flock to Historic Hillcrest and Pulaski Heights for treasured finds.

ARKANSAS ARTS CENTER is in MacArthur Park at 9th and Commerce sts. The center contains nine galleries, a children's theater and a museum school. Permanent exhibits include American and European paintings, drawings and sculpture from the 16th century to the present. Temporary exhibits also are available. Food is available Tues.-Fri. 11-2, Sat.-Sun. 10-2. **Hours:** Center open Tues.-Sat. 10-5, Sun. 11-5. Closed major holidays. **Cost:** Free. A fee may be charged for special exhibits. **Phone:** (501) 372-4000 or (800) 264-2787.

Arkansas Arts Center Community Gallery is in the Arkansas Arts Center at 7th and Rock sts. Changing exhibits in the restored 1839 Terry House feature works in various styles and media by local and regional artists and students. **Time:** Allow 1 hour minimum. **Hours:** When exhibitions are mounted the gallery is open Tues.-Sat. 10-5, Sun. 11-5. Closed major holidays and between exhibitions. **Cost:** Free. A fee may be charged for traveling exhibitions. **Phone:** (501) 372-4000 to verify the gallery is open.

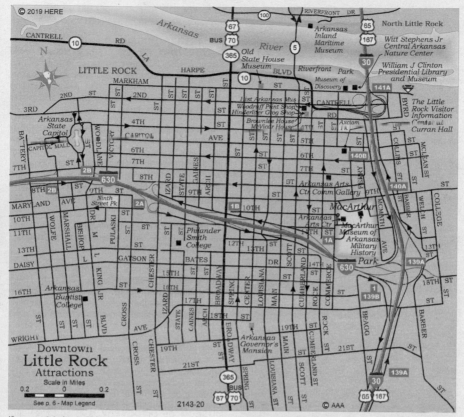

© 2019 HERE

Downtown
Little Rock
Attractions
Scale in Miles
0.2   0   0.2
See p. 6 - Map Legend

2143-20

© AAA

(See map & index p. 50.)

ARKANSAS STATE CAPITOL is at 500 Woodlane St. Made of native limestone, the building is designed in neo-classical style and took 16 years to build. A visitor center is on the first floor. Exhibits include permanent and revolving Arkansas history displays. Guided and self-guiding tours are available. **Hours:** Open Mon.-Fri. 8-5, Sat.-Sun. 10-5. Guided 1-hour tours are given on the hour Mon.-Fri. 9-3, or by appointment. Phone ahead to confirm holiday schedule. **Cost:** Free. **Phone:** (501) 682-5080.

Brownlee House is on the grounds of Historic Arkansas Museum at 200 E. 3rd St. The house was built in the 1840s by Scottish stonemason Robert Brownlee for his brother, James. The builder recuperated in the house from a mining accident before leaving for the California gold rush. The marbleized mantels are of particular interest. **Hours:** Museum Mon.-Sat. 9-5, Sun. 1-5. Historic grounds Mon.-Sat. 10-4, Sun. 1-4. **Cost:** (includes all Historic Arkansas Museum buildings) $2.50; $1.50 (ages 65+); $1 (ages 0-17); free (first Sun. of the month). Phone to confirm rates. **Phone:** (501) 324-9351.

HISTORIC ARKANSAS MUSEUM is at 200 E. 3rd St. at Cumberland St.; from I-30 take exit 141. Of the five restored early-19th-century buildings, four are open to the public. Among the offerings in the 51,000-square-foot museum are galleries devoted to a collection of items by artists and artisans of Arkansas, a Native American gallery, a contemporary Arkansas Artists' Gallery and a Children's Hands-on Gallery. This is the main center of interpretation about the state's frontier period. Changing exhibits also are offered. Special events are held throughout the year.

Hours: Museum Mon.-Sat. 9-5, Sun. 1-5. Historic grounds Mon.-Sat. 10-4, Sun. 1-4. Tours of the grounds are given Mon.-Tues. 10-4 on the hour. **Cost:** Museum free. Historic grounds $2.50; $1.50 (ages 65+); $1 (ages 0-17); free (first Sun. of the month). Phone to confirm rates. **Phone:** (501) 324-9351.

Hinderliter Grog Shop is on the grounds of Historic Arkansas Museum at 200 E. 3rd St. Built of logs in the late 1820s, the shop was an important social institution—the settlement tavern where men gathered to talk, drink and gamble. Jesse Hinderliter and his family lived upstairs until 1834 in this, the oldest house in Little Rock. **Hours:** Museum Mon.-Sat. 9-5, Sun. 1-5. Historic grounds Mon.-Sat. 10-4, Sun. 1-4. Tours of the grounds are given Mon.-Tues. 10-4 on the hour. **Cost:** (includes all Historic Arkansas Museum buildings) $2.50; $1.50 (ages 65+); $1 (ages

Make the
Connction

AAA guidebooks are
just the beginning. Open the
door to a whole lot more
on **AAA.com**. Get extra travel
insight, more information
and online booking.

Find this symbol for places
to look, book and save
on AAA.com.

iStockphoto.com_shapecharge

0-17); free (first Sun. of the month). Phone to confirm rates. **Phone:** (501) 324-9351.

MACARTHUR MUSEUM OF ARKANSAS MILITARY HISTORY is at 503 E. 9th St. Housed in the historic Arsenal Building constructed in 1840 as part of a frontier military post, the museum relates Arkansas' rich military heritage. The Arsenal Building witnessed pivotal exchanges between Federal and Confederate forces during the Civil War.

In 1880, one of the country's foremost military heroes, Gen. Douglas MacArthur, was born here while his father was stationed at the arsenal. The museum offers permanent exhibits about the Civil War, World War I and World War II, as well as an exhibit highlighting Arkansas' Medal of Honor recipients. Temporary exhibits also are offered. An audio tour by cell phone is available.

Time: Allow 30 minutes minimum. **Hours:** Mon.-Sat. 9-4, Sun. 1-4. Closed major holidays. **Cost:** Donations. **Phone:** (501) 376-4602.

McVicar House is on the grounds of Historic Arkansas Museum at 200 E. 3rd St. Built in the 1840s by James McVicar, warden of the state prison, the house exemplifies the smaller Southern house of its time. The house is held together by white oak pegs and is furnished in period. **Hours:** Museum Mon.-Sat. 9-5, Sun. 1-5. Historic grounds Mon.-Sat. 10-4, Sun. 1-4. Tours of the grounds are given Mon.-Tues. 10-4 on the hour. **Cost:** (includes all Historic Arkansas Museum buildings) $2.50; $1.50 (ages 65+); $1 (ages 0-17); free (first Sun. of the month). Phone to confirm rates. **Phone:** (501) 324-9351.

MUSEUM OF DISCOVERY is at 500 President Clinton Ave., Suite 150, in the historic River Market district. Interactive exhibits explore health, physical and earth sciences in the Amazing You, Discovery Hall and Earth Journeys galleries. Early childhood development can be explored in Room to Grow. Traveling exhibits also are offered. The Science After Dark monthly educational series is available to participants 21 years of age and older. Other educational programs also are offered. **Hours:** Mon. holidays and Tues.-Sat. 9-5, Sun. 1-5. Science After Dark last Thurs. of the month 6-9 p.m., Jan.-Oct. Phone ahead to confirm schedule. **Cost:** $10; $8 (ages 1-12, ages 60+, educators and active military with ID). **Phone:** (501) 396-7050.

OLD STATE HOUSE MUSEUM is at 300 W. Markham at Center St. One of the finest examples of Greek Revival architecture in the South, the building includes chambers once used by the state legislature and Supreme Court. Designed by Gideon Shryock, it was begun in 1833 and completed in 1842; additions were made in 1885. When Arkansas became a state in 1836, the building served as the capitol until 1911. Displayed are items of state historical interest. Temporary exhibits also are offered. **Hours:** Mon.-Sat. 9-5, Sun. 1-5. Guided 50-minute tours are given on the hour. Last tour begins 1 hour before closing. **Cost:** Free. **Phone:** (501) 324-9685.

(See map & index p. 50.)

WILLIAM J. CLINTON PRESIDENTIAL LIBRARY AND MUSEUM is at 1200 President Clinton Ave., just e. of I-30 exit 141A. This dramatic glass building cantilevers over the Arkansas River, representing a "bridge to the 21st century." State-of-the-art exhibits chronicle 8 years of the Clinton Administration.

Included in the 20,000 square feet of exhibition space are video stations, interactive displays, a collection of gifts the Clintons received in the White House and full-scale reproductions of the Oval Office and the Cabinet Room. The former president often stays in the modern penthouse suite above the museum.

Food is available Mon.-Sat. 11-2. **Time:** Allow 3 hours minimum. **Hours:** Mon.-Sat. 9-5, Sun. 1-5. **Cost:** $10; $8 (ages 62+, retired military and college students with ID); $6 (ages 6-17); free (active military with ID and on Presidents Day and July 4; veterans and family and active military family on Veterans Day). Free admission on President Clinton's birthday and library's anniversary date; phone ahead for schedule. **Phone:** (501) 374-4242.

WITT STEPHENS JR. CENTRAL ARKANSAS NATURE CENTER is at 602 President Clinton Ave. The 16,232-square-foot building beside the Arkansas River in the River Market district features aquariums, a theater, an antique fishing lure display and exhibits promoting fish and wildlife management. A self-guiding tour begins with a 10-minute video presentation about conservation. A 4-mile hiking and biking trail on the Arkansas River Trail and a wetlands boardwalk are adjacent to the center. Geocaching stations are available. **Hours:** Trail and boardwalk open daily dawn-dusk. Center open Tues.-Sat. 8:30-4:30, Sun. 1-5. Fish feeding Wed. at 2. Alligator feeding Fri. at 2. Closed major holidays. **Cost:** Free. **Phone:** (501) 907-0636.

Woodruff Print Shop is on the grounds of Historic Arkansas Museum at 200 E. 3rd St. The site includes a house built in 1824 by William E. Woodruff, founder of the *Arkansas Gazette,* the oldest newspaper west of the Mississippi River. A reconstructed 1820s print shop includes original furniture and a replica of the press Woodruff rafted up the Arkansas River. **Hours:** Museum Mon.-Sat. 9-5, Sun. 1-5. Historic grounds Mon.-Sat. 10-4, Sun. 1-4. Tours of the grounds are given Mon.-Tues. 10-4 on the hour. **Cost:** (includes all Historic Arkansas Museum buildings) $2.50; $1.50 (ages 65+); $1 (ages 0-17); free (first Sun. of the month). Phone to confirm rates. **Phone:** (501) 324-9351.

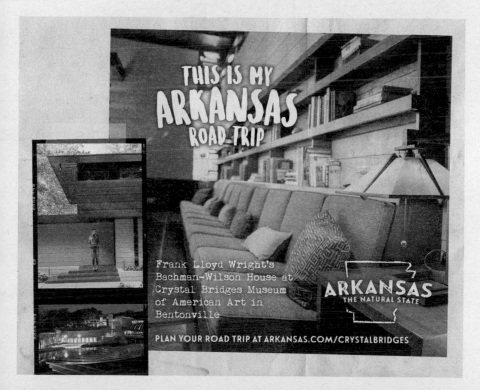

THIS IS MY ARKANSAS ROAD TRIP

Frank Lloyd Wright's Bachman-Wilson House at Crystal Bridges Museum of American Art in Bentonville

ARKANSAS
THE NATURAL STATE

PLAN YOUR ROAD TRIP AT ARKANSAS.COM/CRYSTALBRIDGES

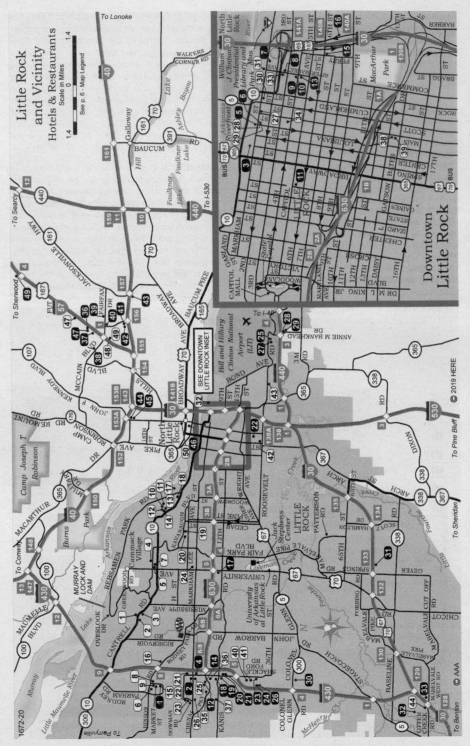

Little Rock
and Vicinity
Hotels & Restaurants
Scale in Miles

See p. 6 · Map Legend

Downtown
Little Rock

© 2019 HERE

✈ Airport Hotels

Map Page	ADAMS FIELD (Maximum driving distance from airport: 1.5 mi)	Designation	Member Savings	Page
25 p. 50	Comfort Inn & Suites Little Rock Airport, 1.1 mi	APPROVED	✔	53
27 p. 50	Fairfield Inn & Suites by Marriott Little Rock Airport, 1.3 mi	THREE DIAMOND	✔	54
28 p. 50	Holiday Inn Airport Conference Center, 1.4 mi	THREE DIAMOND		55
29 p. 50	Holiday Inn Express Airport, 1.4 mi	THREE DIAMOND		55

Little Rock and Vicinity

This index helps you "spot" where hotels and restaurants are located on the corresponding detailed maps. Restaurant price range is a combination of lunch and/or dinner. Turn to the listing page for more information and consult display ads for special promotions.

 For more details, rates and reservations: AAA.com/travelguides/hotels

LITTLE ROCK

Map Page	Hotels	Designation	Member Savings	Page
1 p. 50	The Burgundy Hotel, Tapestry Collection by Hilton	THREE DIAMOND	✔	53
2 p. 50	Ramada	APPROVED		55
3 p. 50	DoubleTree by Hilton Hotel Little Rock	THREE DIAMOND	✔	54
4 p. 50	Crowne Plaza	THREE DIAMOND		54
5 p. 50	Little Rock Marriott	THREE DIAMOND		55
6 p. 50	The Capital Hotel	FOUR DIAMOND	✔	53
7 p. 50	Courtyard by Marriott Downtown Little Rock	THREE DIAMOND	✔	53
8 p. 50	Residence Inn by Marriott -Downtown	THREE DIAMOND	✔	55
9 p. 50	Hilton Garden Inn Little Rock Downtown	THREE DIAMOND	✔	54
10 p. 50	Hampton Inn & Suites by Hilton/Downtown Little Rock at the River Market	THREE DIAMOND	✔	54
11 p. 50	Hotel Frederica, an Ascend Hotel Collection Member	THREE DIAMOND		55
12 p. 50	Holiday Inn-Financial Centre Parkway	THREE DIAMOND		55
13 p. 50	Homewood Suites by Hilton Little Rock	THREE DIAMOND	✔	55
14 p. 50	Courtyard by Marriott-Little Rock West *(See ad p. 54.)*	THREE DIAMOND	✔	54
15 p. 50	Holiday Inn Presidential	THREE DIAMOND		55
16 p. 50	Comfort Inn & Suites Presidential	THREE DIAMOND		53
17 p. 50	Staybridge Suites	THREE DIAMOND		55
18 p. 50	Hilton Garden Inn West	THREE DIAMOND	✔	55
19 p. 50	Wingate by Wyndham	THREE DIAMOND		55
20 p. 50	Hampton Inn & Suites by Hilton West Little Rock	THREE DIAMOND	✔	54
21 p. 50	Residence Inn by Marriott	THREE DIAMOND	✔	55
22 p. 50	The Empress of Little Rock	FOUR DIAMOND		54
23 p. 50	Home2 Suites by Hilton	THREE DIAMOND	✔	55
24 p. 50	TownePlace Suites by Marriott-Little Rock	THREE DIAMOND	✔	55
25 p. 50	Comfort Inn & Suites Little Rock Airport	APPROVED	✔	53
26 p. 50	Comfort Suites	THREE DIAMOND		53
27 p. 50	Fairfield Inn & Suites by Marriott Little Rock Airport	THREE DIAMOND	✔	54
28 p. 50	Holiday Inn Airport Conference Center	THREE DIAMOND		55
29 p. 50	Holiday Inn Express Airport	THREE DIAMOND		55
30 p. 50	Holiday Inn Express Hotel & Suites	THREE DIAMOND		55

LITTLE ROCK (cont'd)

Map Page	Hotels (cont'd)	Designation	Member Savings	Page
31 p. 50	Days Inn-Little Rock South	◈ APPROVED		54
32 p. 50	Tru by Hilton Little Rock West	◈ APPROVED	✔	55
33 p. 50	Super 8 Otter Creek Little Rock (47773)	◈ APPROVED		55

Map Page	Restaurants	Designation	Cuisine	Price Range	Page
1 p. 50	The Purple Cow	◈ APPROVED	American	$5-$10	56
2 p. 50	Trio's	◈ APPROVED	American	$8-$32	57
3 p. 50	Graffiti's	◈ APPROVED	Italian	$10-$32	56
4 p. 50	Zaza Fine Salad & Wood-Oven Pizza	◈ APPROVED	Pizza	$11-$16	57
5 p. 50	Baja Grill	◈ APPROVED	Mexican	$4-$12	55
6 p. 50	The Pantry	◈ APPROVED	European	$8-$25	56
7 p. 50	Fantastic China	◈ APPROVED	Chinese	$6-$15	56
8 p. 50	Sauced Bar and Oven	◈◈ THREE DIAMOND	American	$10-$20	56
9 p. 50	Petit & Keet	◈◈ THREE DIAMOND	American	$9-$35	56
10 p. 50	The Faded Rose	◈ APPROVED	Creole	$6-$28	56
11 p. 50	Maddie's Place	◈ APPROVED	American	$8-$22	56
12 p. 50	Loca Luna	◈◈ THREE DIAMOND	Southern	$7-$30	56
13 p. 50	The Fold: Botanas & Bar	◈ APPROVED	Mexican	$3-$35	56
14 p. 50	Red Door Restaurant	◈ APPROVED	American	$8-$34	56
15 p. 50	Table 28	◈◈ THREE DIAMOND	American	$12-$60	57
16 p. 50	Senor Tequila	◈ APPROVED	Mexican	$6-$15	57
17 p. 50	Brave New Restaurant	◈◈ THREE DIAMOND	New American	$11-$34	56
18 p. 50	Whole Hog Cafe	◈ APPROVED	Barbecue	$5-$13	57
19 p. 50	Kemuri	◈◈ THREE DIAMOND	Japanese Sushi	$6-$32	56
20 p. 50	Ciao Baci	◈◈ THREE DIAMOND	Mediterranean	$8-$45	56
21 p. 50	Star of India	◈ APPROVED	Indian	$7-$15	57
22 p. 50	Fu Lin	◈ APPROVED	Chinese	$8-$22	56
23 p. 50	Lazy Pete's	◈ APPROVED	Seafood	$8-$16	56
24 p. 50	Big Orange	◈ APPROVED	Burgers	$6-$13	56
25 p. 50	Shotgun Dan's Pizza	◈ APPROVED	Pizza	$5-$15	57
26 p. 50	David's Burgers	◈ APPROVED	Burgers	$3-$10	56
27 p. 50	Wasabi Sushi Bar Grill	◈ APPROVED	Japanese Sushi	$3-$28	57
28 p. 50	One Eleven at the Capital	◈◈ FOUR DIAMOND	American	$13-$39	56
29 p. 50	Capital Bar & Grill	◈◈ THREE DIAMOND	American	$10-$24	56
30 p. 50	Iriana's Pizza	◈ APPROVED	Pizza	$6-$19	56
31 p. 50	Sonny Williams' Steak Room	◈◈ THREE DIAMOND	Steak	$28-$57	57
32 p. 50	Forty Two	◈◈ THREE DIAMOND	Southern	$8-$13	56
33 p. 50	Dizzy's Gypsy Bistro	◈ APPROVED	American	$7-$30	56
34 p. 50	Samantha's Tap Room & Wood Grill	◈ APPROVED	American	$12-$34	56
35 p. 50	The Purple Cow	◈ APPROVED	American	$5-$10	56
36 p. 50	The Butcher Shop Steakhouse	◈ APPROVED	Steak	$16-$38	56
37 p. 50	Alley Oops	◈ APPROVED	Comfort Food	$6-$15	55
38 p. 50	South on Main	◈◈ THREE DIAMOND	American	$6-$25	57
39 p. 50	Raduno Brick Oven & Barroom	◈ APPROVED	Pizza	$9-$20	56
40 p. 50	Samurai Japanese Steakhouse & Sushi Bar	◈ APPROVED	Japanese	$9-$37	56
41 p. 50	Tacos 4 Life	◈ APPROVED	Mexican	$3-$10	57
42 p. 50	Sim's Bar-B-Que	◈ APPROVED	Barbecue	$6-$16	57

Map Page	Restaurants (cont'd)	Designation	Cuisine	Price Range	Page
㊸ p. 50	Homer's Restaurant	◆ APPROVED	American	$6-$9	56
㊹ p. 50	David's Burger	◆ APPROVED	Burgers	$3-$10	56

NORTH LITTLE ROCK

Map Page	Hotels	Designation	Member Savings	Page
㊱ p. 50	Courtyard by Marriott-Little Rock North	THREE DIAMOND	✔	60
㊲ p. 50	La Quinta Inn & Suites North Little Rock-McCain Mall	APPROVED		60
㊳ p. 50	Hampton Inn by Hilton North Little Rock McCain	THREE DIAMOND	✔	60
㊴ p. 50	Hilton Garden Inn North Little Rock	THREE DIAMOND	✔	60
㊵ p. 50	Holiday Inn Express Hotel & Suites	THREE DIAMOND		60
㊶ p. 50	Fairfield by Marriott	THREE DIAMOND	✔	60
㊷ p. 50	Residence Inn by Marriott-North	THREE DIAMOND	✔	60
㊸ p. 50	Red Roof Inn-North Little Rock	APPROVED		60
㊹ p. 50	Baymont Inn & Suites	THREE DIAMOND		60
㊺ p. 50	**Best Western Plus JFK Inn & Suites**	THREE DIAMOND	✔	60
㊻ p. 50	Wyndham Hotel and Resort Riverfront Little Rock	THREE DIAMOND		60
㊼ p. 50	Comfort Inn & Suites North Little Rock	THREE DIAMOND		60

Map Page	Restaurants	Designation	Cuisine	Price Range	Page
㊼ p. 50	Whole Hog Cafe North Little Rock	APPROVED	Barbecue	$5-$13	60
㊽ p. 50	David's Burger	APPROVED	Burgers	$3-$10	60
㊾ p. 50	Las Palmas	APPROVED	Mexican	$6-$11	60
㊿ p. 50	Ristorante Capeo	THREE DIAMOND	Italian	$8-$42	60

SHERWOOD

Map Page	Hotel	Designation	Member Savings	Page
㊾ p. 50	**Best Western Sherwood Inn & Suites**	THREE DIAMOND	✔	65

THE BURGUNDY HOTEL, TAPESTRY COLLECTION BY HILTON   501/224-8051 ❶

◆ **THREE DIAMOND**
Boutique Hotel

TAPESTRY COLLECTION BY HILTON

AAA Benefit: Members save up to 15%!

Address: 1501 Merrill Dr 72211 **Location:** I-430 exit 8, 0.5 mi w, then just s. **Facility:** The atrium lobby is brightened by skylights and colorful local artwork. Rooms are spacious and upscale, with custom furnishings that include a sectional sleeper sofa. 49 units. 3 stories, interior corridors. **Amenities:** safes. **Dining:** Table 28, see separate listing. **Pool:** outdoor. **Guest Services:** valet laundry.

THE CAPITAL HOTEL   501/374-7474 ❻

◆ **FOUR DIAMOND**
Historic Hotel

Address: 111 W Markham St 72201 **Location:** I-30 exit 141A, 0.6 mi w on 2nd St, just n on Main St, then just w; downtown. **Facility:** Striking historic details and personalized service make staying here a special experience. As you walk into the lobby, light gleams off white marble columns decorated with carved wood ornamentations. 94 units. 4 stories, interior corridors. **Parking:** valet only. **Amenities:** safes. **Dining:** 2 restaurants, also, Capital Bar & Grill, One Eleven at the Capital, see separate listings, entertainment. **Guest Services:** valet laundry, area transportation.

COMFORT INN & SUITES LITTLE ROCK AIRPORT   501/376-2466 ㉕

◆ **APPROVED**
Hotel

Address: 4301 E Roosevelt Rd 72206 **Location:** I-440 exit 3, just n. **Facility:** 107 units. 5 stories, interior corridors. **Activities:** exercise room. **Guest Services:** valet laundry. **Featured Amenity:** full hot breakfast.

COMFORT INN & SUITES PRESIDENTIAL   501/687-7700 ⑯
◆ **THREE DIAMOND** Hotel. **Address:** 707 I-30 72202

COMFORT SUITES   501/954-9300 ㉖
◆ **THREE DIAMOND** Hotel. **Address:** 11 Crossings Ct 72205

COURTYARD BY MARRIOTT DOWNTOWN LITTLE ROCK   501/975-9800 ❼

◆ **THREE DIAMOND**
Hotel

COURTYARD

AAA Benefit: Members save 5% or more!

Address: 521 President Clinton Ave 72201 **Location:** I-30 exit 141A, just w; downtown. **Facility:** 120 units. 6 stories, interior corridors. **Parking:** on-site (fee). **Pool:** heated indoor. **Activities:** exercise room. **Guest Services:** valet and coin laundry, boarding pass kiosk.

(See map & index p. 50.)

COURTYARD BY MARRIOTT-LITTLE ROCK WEST
501/227-6000 **14**

WWW THREE DIAMOND **COURTYARD** **AAA Benefit:** Members save 5% or more!

Hotel

Address: 10900 Financial Centre Pkwy 72211 **Location:** I-430 exit 5, 1 mi n on Shackleford Rd, then just w. **Facility:** 149 units. 3 stories, interior corridors. **Pool:** outdoor. **Activities:** exercise room. **Guest Services:** valet and coin laundry. *(See ad this page.)*

SAVE ECO TI+ Y CALL BIZ WiFi X

CROWNE PLAZA
501/223-3000 **4**

WWW THREE DIAMOND Hotel. **Address:** 201 S Shackleford Rd 72211

DAYS INN-LITTLE ROCK SOUTH
501/562-4448 **31**

WWW APPROVED Motel. **Address:** 8219 I-30 72209

DOUBLETREE BY HILTON HOTEL LITTLE ROCK
501/372-4371 **3**

WWW THREE DIAMOND **DOUBLETREE** **AAA Benefit:** Members save up to 15%!

Hotel

Address: 424 W Markham St 72201 **Location:** I-30 exit 141A, 0.6 mi w on 2nd St, then just n on Spring St; downtown. **Facility:** 288 units. 14 stories, interior corridors. **Parking:** on-site (fee). **Amenities:** safes. **Pool:** heated outdoor. **Activities:** exercise room. **Guest Services:** valet laundry, area transportation.

SAVE TI+ Y BIZ WiFi X / SOME UNITS

THE EMPRESS OF LITTLE ROCK
501/374-7966 **22**

WWW FOUR DIAMOND Historic Bed & Breakfast. **Address:** 2120 S Louisiana St 72206

FAIRFIELD INN & SUITES BY MARRIOTT LITTLE ROCK AIRPORT
501/210-0000 **27**

WWW THREE DIAMOND SAVE Hotel. **Address:** 4201 E Roosevelt Rd 72206 **AAA Benefit:** Members save 5% or more!

HAMPTON INN & SUITES BY HILTON/DOWNTOWN LITTLE ROCK AT THE RIVER MARKET
501/244-0600 **10**

WWW THREE DIAMOND **Hampton** **AAA Benefit:** Members save up to 15%!

Hotel

Address: 320 River Market Ave 72201 **Location:** I-30 exit 141A, just w on 2nd St, then just s; downtown. **Facility:** 119 units. 8 stories, interior corridors. **Parking:** on-site (fee). **Pool:** outdoor. **Activities:** exercise room. **Guest Services:** valet and coin laundry.

SAVE TI+ Y CALL WiFi HS X

HAMPTON INN & SUITES BY HILTON WEST LITTLE ROCK
501/537-3000 **20**

WWW THREE DIAMOND SAVE Hotel. **Address:** 1301 S Shackleford Rd 72211 **AAA Benefit:** Members save up to 15%!

HILTON GARDEN INN LITTLE ROCK DOWNTOWN
501/244-0044 **9**

WWW THREE DIAMOND SAVE Hotel. **Address:** 322 Rock St 72202 **AAA Benefit:** Members save up to 15%!

(See map & index p. 50.)

HILTON GARDEN INN WEST   501/227-4800 **18**
THREE DIAMOND SAVE Hotel. Ad-   **AAA Benefit:**
dress: 10914 Kanis Rd 72211   Members save up to
                                      15%!

HOLIDAY INN AIRPORT CONFERENCE CENTER
                                      501/490-1000 **28**
THREE DIAMOND Hotel. **Address:** 3201 Bankhead Dr 72206

HOLIDAY INN EXPRESS AIRPORT   501/490-4000 **29**
THREE DIAMOND Hotel. **Address:** 3121 Bankhead Dr 72206

HOLIDAY INN EXPRESS HOTEL & SUITES
                                      501/224-2600 **30**
THREE DIAMOND Hotel. **Address:** 4900 Talley Rd 72204

HOLIDAY INN-FINANCIAL CENTRE PARKWAY
                                      501/225-1075 **12**
THREE DIAMOND Hotel. **Address:** 10920 Financial Centre
Pkwy 72211

HOLIDAY INN PRESIDENTIAL   501/375-2100 **15**
THREE DIAMOND Hotel. **Address:** 600 I-30 72202

HOME2 SUITES BY HILTON   501/588-3000 **23**
THREE DIAMOND
                    HOME2   **AAA Benefit:**
Extended Stay   SUITES BY HILTON Members save up
   Hotel   to 15%!

Address: 2710 S Shackleford Rd 72205
Location: I-430 exit 5, 6 mi s. **Facility:**
93 units. 5 stories, interior corridors.
Pool: heated indoor. **Activities:** exercise room. **Guest Services:** complimentary and valet laundry.

SAVE CALL 🦽 🛏 ➕ BIZ HS
🛜 ✕ 🏠 📷 💻
/ SOME UNITS 🐾

HOMEWOOD SUITES BY HILTON LITTLE ROCK
                                      501/375-4663 **13**
THREE DIAMOND
                    HOMEWOOD   **AAA Benefit:**
Extended Stay   SUITES BY HILTON Members save up
   Hotel   to 15%!

Address: 400 River Market Ave 72201
Location: I-30 exit 141A, just w on 2nd
St, then just s; downtown. **Facility:** 116
kitchen units, some two bedrooms. 6
stories, interior corridors. **Parking:** on-
site (fee). **Terms:** check-in 4 pm. **Pool:**
heated outdoor. **Activities:** exercise
room. **Guest Services:** valet and coin
laundry.

SAVE CALL 🦽 🛏 ➕ BIZ HS
🛜 ✕ 🏠 📷 💻 / SOME UNITS 🐾

**HOTEL FREDERICA, AN ASCEND HOTEL COLLECTION
MEMBER**   501/379-8497 **11**
THREE DIAMOND Historic Boutique Hotel. **Address:** 625 W
Capitol Ave 72201

LITTLE ROCK MARRIOTT   501/906-4000 **5**
THREE DIAMOND SAVE Hotel. Ad-   **AAA Benefit:**
dress: 3 Statehouse Plaza Dr 72201   Members save 5%
                                      or more!

RAMADA   501/221-7666 **2**
APPROVED Hotel. **Address:** 8 Shackleford Dr 72211

RESIDENCE INN BY MARRIOTT   501/312-0200 **21**
THREE DIAMOND
                    Residence INN. **AAA Benefit:**
Extended Stay   Members save 5%
   Hotel   or more!

Address: 1401 S Shackleford Rd 72211
Location: I-430 exit 5, just n. **Facility:**
96 units, some two bedrooms, efficiencies and kitchens. 3-4 stories, interior
corridors. **Pool:** outdoor. **Activities:** exercise room. **Guest Services:** valet and
coin laundry. **Featured Amenity:** full
hot breakfast.

SAVE 🛏 ➕ ➕ 🛏 ➕ BIZ 🛜 ✕
🏠 📷 💻 / SOME UNITS 🐾

RESIDENCE INN BY MARRIOTT -DOWNTOWN
                                      501/376-7200 **8**
THREE DIAMOND
                    Residence INN. **AAA Benefit:**
Extended Stay   Members save 5%
   Hotel   or more!

Address: 219 River Market Ave 72201
Location: I-30 exit 141A, just w on 2nd
St, then just s; downtown. **Facility:** 107
units, some two bedrooms, efficiencies
and kitchens. 6 stories, interior corridors.
Parking: on-site (fee). **Terms:** check-in
4 pm. **Pool:** outdoor. **Activities:** exercise room. **Guest Services:** valet and
coin laundry, boarding pass kiosk.

SAVE 🛏 ➕ CALL 🦽 ➕ 🛏 ➕ BIZ
HS 🛜 ✕ 🏠 📷 💻 / SOME UNITS 🐾

STAYBRIDGE SUITES   501/406-6590 **17**
THREE DIAMOND Extended Stay Hotel. **Address:** 1020
South University 72204

SUPER 8 OTTER CREEK LITTLE ROCK (47773)
                                      501/455-2300 **33**
APPROVED Hotel. **Address:** 11701 I-30 72209

TOWNEPLACE SUITES BY MARRIOTT-LITTLE ROCK
                                      501/225-6700 **24**
THREE DIAMOND SAVE Extended   **AAA Benefit:**
Stay Hotel. **Address:** 12 Crossings Ct Members save 5%
72205   or more!

TRU BY HILTON LITTLE ROCK WEST   501/455-3300 **32**
APPROVED SAVE Hotel. Ad-
dress: 11320 Bass Pro Pkwy 72211   Members save up to
                                      15%!

WINGATE BY WYNDHAM   501/227-6800 **19**
THREE DIAMOND Hotel. **Address:** 1212 S Shackleford Rd
72211

WHERE TO EAT

ALLEY OOPS   501/221-9400 **37**
APPROVED Comfort Food. Casual Dining. **Address:**
11900 Kanis Rd 72211

BAJA GRILL   501/722-8920 **5**
APPROVED Mexican. Casual Dining. **Address:** 5923
Kavanaugh Blvd 72207

(See map & index p. 50.)

BIG ORANGE 501/379-8715 24
APPROVED Burgers. Casual Dining. **Address:** 207 N University Ave, Suite 100 72205

BIG ORANGE WEST 501/821-1515
APPROVED Burgers. Casual Dining. **Address:** 17809 Chenal Pkwy. Unit G-101 72223

BRAVE NEW RESTAURANT 501/663-2677 17
THREE DIAMOND New American. Casual Dining. **Address:** 2300 Cottondale Ln, Suite 105 72202

THE BUTCHER SHOP STEAKHOUSE 501/312-2748 36
APPROVED Steak. Casual Dining. **Address:** 10825 Hermitage Rd 72211

CANTINA CINCO DE MAYO 501/455-8500
APPROVED Mexican. Casual Dining. **Address:** 10401 Stagecoach Rd 72210

CANTINA LAREDO 501/280-0407
APPROVED Mexican. Casual Dining. **Address:** 207 N University Ave, Suite 130 72205

CAPERS RESTAURANT 501/868-7600
THREE DIAMOND American. Fine Dining. **Address:** 14502 Cantrell Rd 72202

CAPITAL BAR & GRILL 501/370-7013 29
THREE DIAMOND American. Casual Dining. **Address:** 111 W Markham St 72201

CIAO BACI 501/603-0238 20
THREE DIAMOND Mediterranean. Casual Dining. **Address:** 605 Beechwood St 72205

DAVID'S BURGER 501/455-6159 44
APPROVED Burgers. Casual Dining. **Address:** 6 Bass Pro Dr 72210

DAVID'S BURGERS 501/227-8333 26
APPROVED Burgers. Casual Dining. **Address:** 101 S Bowman Rd 72211

DIZZY'S GYPSY BISTRO 501/375-3500 33
APPROVED American. Casual Dining. **Address:** 200 River Market Ave 72201

EL CHICO 501/562-3762
APPROVED Tex-Mex. Casual Dining. **Address:** 8409 I-30 72209

THE FADED ROSE 501/663-9734 10
APPROVED Creole. Casual Dining. **Address:** 1619 Rebsamen Park Rd 72202

FANTASTIC CHINA 501/663-8999 7
APPROVED Chinese. Casual Dining. **Address:** 1900 N Grant St 72207

THE FOLD: BOTANAS & BAR 501/916-9706 13
APPROVED Mexican. Casual Dining. **Address:** 3501 Old Cantrell Rd 72202

FORTY TWO 501/537-0042 32
THREE DIAMOND Southern. Casual Dining. **Address:** 1200 President Clinton Ave 72201

FU LIN 501/225-8989 22
APPROVED Chinese. Casual Dining. **Address:** 200 N Bowman Rd, Suite 17 72211

GRAFFITI'S 501/224-9079 3
APPROVED Italian. Casual Dining. **Address:** 7811 Cantrell Rd 72227

HOMER'S RESTAURANT 501/374-1400 43
APPROVED American. Casual Dining. **Address:** 2001 E Roosevelt Rd 72206

IRIANA'S PIZZA 501/374-3656 30
APPROVED Pizza. Quick Serve. **Address:** 201 E Markham St 72201

KEMURI 501/860-4100 19
THREE DIAMOND Japanese Sushi. Casual Dining. **Address:** 2601 Kavanaugh Blvd 72205

LAZY PETE'S 501/907-6453 23
APPROVED Seafood. Casual Dining. **Address:** 200 N Bowman Rd. Suite 9 72211

LOCAL LIME 501/448-2226
APPROVED Mexican. Casual Dining. **Address:** 17815 Chenal Pwky, Unit F-105 72223

LOCA LUNA 501/663-4666 12
THREE DIAMOND Southern. Casual Dining. **Address:** 3519 Old Cantrell Rd 72202

MADDIE'S PLACE 501/660-4040 11
APPROVED American. Casual Dining. **Address:** 1615 Rebsamen Park Rd 72202

ONE ELEVEN AT THE CAPITAL 501/370-7011 28
FOUR DIAMOND American. Fine Dining. **Address:** 111 W Markham St 72201

THE PANTRY 501/353-1875 6
APPROVED European. Casual Dining. **Address:** 11401 Rodney Parham Rd 72212

PETIT & KEET 501/319-7675 9
THREE DIAMOND American. Casual Dining. **Address:** 1620 Market St 72211

THE PURPLE COW 501/221-3555 1
APPROVED American. Casual Dining. **Address:** 8026 Cantrell Rd 72207

THE PURPLE COW 501/224-4433 35
APPROVED American. Casual Dining. **Address:** 11602 Chenal Pkwy 72212

RADUNO BRICK OVEN & BARROOM 501/374-7476 39
APPROVED Pizza. Casual Dining. **Address:** 1318 Main St 72202

RED DOOR RESTAURANT 501/666-8482 14
APPROVED American. Casual Dining. **Address:** 3701 Old Cantrell Rd 72202

SAMANTHA'S TAP ROOM & WOOD GRILL 501/379-8019 34
APPROVED American. Casual Dining. **Address:** 322 Main St 72201

SAMURAI JAPANESE STEAKHOUSE & SUSHI BAR 501/224-5533 40
APPROVED Japanese. Casual Dining. **Address:** 2604 S Shackleford Rd, Suite A 72205

SAUCED BAR AND OVEN 501/353-1534 8
THREE DIAMOND American. Casual Dining. **Address:** 11121 N Rodney Parham Rd. Suite 9A 72212

(See map & index p. 50.)

SENOR TEQUILA   501/224-5505 (16)
APPROVED Mexican. Casual Dining. **Address:** 10300 N Rodney Parham Rd 72227

SHORTY SMALL'S   501/224-3344
APPROVED Barbecue. Casual Dining. **Address:** 11100 N Rodney Parham Rd 72212

SHOTGUN DAN'S PIZZA   501/224-9519 (25)
APPROVED Pizza. Casual Dining. **Address:** 10923 W Markham St 72211

SIM'S BAR-B-QUE   501/372-6868 (42)
APPROVED Barbecue. Casual Dining. **Address:** 2415 Broadway St 72206

SONNY WILLIAMS' STEAK ROOM   501/324-2999 (31)
THREE DIAMOND Steak. Fine Dining. **Address:** 500 President Clinton Ave 72201

SOUTH ON MAIN   501/244-9660 (38)
THREE DIAMOND American. Casual Dining. **Address:** 1304 Main St 72202

STAR OF INDIA   501/227-9900 (21)
APPROVED Indian. Casual Dining. **Address:** 301 N Shackleford Rd 72211

TABLE 28   501/224-2828 (15)
THREE DIAMOND American. Casual Dining. **Address:** 1501 Merrill Dr 72211

TACOS 4 LIFE   501/404-0144 (41)
APPROVED Mexican. Quick Serve. **Address:** 2630 S Shackleford Rd 72205

TRIO'S   501/221-3330 (2)
APPROVED American. Casual Dining. **Address:** 8201 Cantrell Rd, Suite 100 72227

WASABI SUSHI BAR GRILL   501/374-0777 (27)
APPROVED Japanese Sushi. Casual Dining. **Address:** 101 Main St 72201

WHOLE HOG CAFE   501/664-5025 (18)
APPROVED Barbecue. Quick Serve. **Address:** 2516 Cantrell Rd 72202

YAYA'S EURO BISTRO   501/821-1144
THREE DIAMOND American. Casual Dining. **Address:** 17711 Chenal Pkwy 72223

ZAZA FINE SALAD & WOOD-OVEN PIZZA   501/661-9292 (4)
APPROVED Pizza. Casual Dining. **Address:** 5600 Kavanaugh Blvd 72207

LONOKE pop. 4,245, elev. 242'

BEST WESTERN PLUS LONOKE HOTEL   501/676-8880
APPROVED
Hotel

Best Western PLUS

AAA Benefit: Members save up to 15% and earn bonus points!

Address: 102 Dee Dee Ln 72086 **Location:** I-40 exit 175, just n. **Facility:** 48 units. 2 stories, interior corridors. **Pool:** heated indoor. **Activities:** exercise room. **Guest Services:** coin laundry.

DAYS INN   501/676-5138
APPROVED Hotel. **Address:** 105 Dee Dee Ln 72086

HAMPTON INN & SUITES BY HILTON LONOKE   501/676-0602
THREE DIAMOND [SAVE] Hotel. **Address:** 240 Brownsville Loop 72086

AAA Benefit: Members save up to 15%!

HOLIDAY INN EXPRESS HOTEL & SUITES   501/676-7800
THREE DIAMOND Hotel. **Address:** 104 Dee Dee Ln 72086

MARION pop. 12,345

FAIRFIELD INN & SUITES MEMPHIS, MARION AR   870/739-8500
THREE DIAMOND
Hotel

Fairfield

AAA Benefit: Members save 5% or more!

Address: 101 Hannah Ln 72364 **Location:** I-55 exit 10, just e, then just s. **Facility:** 92 units. 4 stories, interior corridors. **Pool:** heated indoor. **Activities:** exercise room. **Guest Services:** valet and coin laundry. **Featured Amenity:** breakfast buffet.

HAMPTON INN BY HILTON   870/739-2800
THREE DIAMOND [SAVE] Hotel. **Address:** 310 Angelo's Grove Rd 72364

AAA Benefit: Members save up to 15%!

WHERE TO EAT

COLTON'S STEAKHOUSE & GRILL   870/739-1900
APPROVED Steak. Casual Dining. **Address:** 303 Angelo's Grove Rd 72364

SEAFOOD SHACK   870/559-5088
APPROVED Seafood. Casual Dining. **Address:** 308 Bancario Rd 72364

MAUMELLE pop. 17,163

HAMPTON INN BY HILTON MAUMELLE   501/851-6600
THREE DIAMOND **SAVE** Hotel. **Address:** 11920 Maumelle Blvd 72113

AAA Benefit: Members save up to 15%!

HOLIDAY INN EXPRESS & SUITES-MAUMELLE   501/851-4422
THREE DIAMOND Hotel. **Address:** 200 Holiday Dr 72113

WHERE TO EAT

CASA MEXICANA   501/812-2074
APPROVED Mexican. Casual Dining. **Address:** 13120 Crystal Hill Rd 72113

MONTICELLO pop. 9,467

DAYS INN   870/367-1881
APPROVED
Motel

Address: 317 Hwy 425 N 71655 **Location:** Jct US 278, just n. **Facility:** 55 units. 1-2 stories (no elevator), exterior corridors. **Pool:** outdoor. **Guest Services:** coin laundry. **Featured Amenity:** continental breakfast.

HAMPTON INN BY HILTON   870/367-6600
THREE DIAMOND
Hotel

AAA Benefit: Members save up to 15%!

Address: 480 Hwy 425 N 71655 **Location:** Jct US 278, 0.5 mi n. **Facility:** 64 units. 3 stories, interior corridors. **Pool:** heated indoor. **Activities:** hot tub, exercise room. **Guest Services:** valet and coin laundry. **Featured Amenity:** breakfast buffet.

MORRILTON (C-3) pop. 6,767, elev. 367'

Morrilton was built along the Little Rock & Fort Smith Railroad in the 1870s. The town's early trading business expanded after a highway bridge built over the Arkansas River increased Morrilton's accessibility. Local industries include plastics, food and automotive products.

Morrilton Area Chamber of Commerce: 115 E. Broadway St., P.O. Box 589, Morrilton, AR 72110. **Phone:** (501) 354-2393.

GEM **PETIT JEAN STATE PARK** is 9 mi. s. on SR 9, then 12 mi. w. on SR 154 to Petit Jean Mountain Rd. Perched on flat-topped Petit Jean Mountain, the park boasts an array of natural features including 95-foot Cedar Falls, Indian Cave, Bear Cave, Rock House Cave and two gravel scenic drives overlooking Cedar Creek Canyon, Red Bluff Drive and the Palisades. The Seven Hollows region contains the unusual Turtle Rocks, the Grotto and the Petit Jean Natural Bridge.

The mountain's name is taken from the legend of a French girl who disguised herself as a boy and accompanied her sailor sweetheart to America. Many points of interest are reached by foot trails. *See Recreation Areas Chart.*

Hours: Park open daily dawn-10 p.m. Visitor center open daily 8-8, Memorial Day weekend to mid-Aug.; Sun.-Thurs. 8-5, Fri.-Sat. 8-7, Apr. 1-day before Memorial Day weekend and mid-Aug. through Oct. 31; daily 8-5, rest of year; closed Christmas. **Cost:** Free. **Phone:** (501) 727-5441.

MOUNTAIN HOME pop. 12,448

QUALITY INN & SUITES   870/424-9000
APPROVED Hotel. **Address:** 1031 Highland Cir 72653

TEAL POINT RESORT   870/492-5145
THREE DIAMOND
Cabin

Address: 715 Teal Point Rd 72653 **Location:** Jct US 62 business route, 3.5 mi e on US 412/62, 0.6 mi n on CR 406. **Facility:** Units range from one-room cabins to four-bedroom houses, all with fully stocked kitchens, outdoor grills and most with lake views. Rental boats include pontoon, fishing, deck and ski boats. 24 cabins, some two bedrooms. 1 story, exterior corridors. **Terms:** check-in 4 pm, check-out 9 am. **Pool:** outdoor. **Activities:** motor boats, self-propelled boats, marina, fishing, playground, game room. **Guest Services:** coin laundry.

WHERE TO EAT

CHEN'S GARDEN   870/424-6899
APPROVED Chinese. Casual Dining. **Address:** 1310 Eastside Centre Ct, Suite 7 72654

COLTON'S STEAKHOUSE & GRILL   870/492-2663
APPROVED Steak. Casual Dining. **Address:** 2390 Hwy 62 E 72653

EL CHICO   870/492-4700
APPROVED Tex-Mex. Casual Dining. **Address:** 45 Charles Blackburn Dr 72653

FRED'S FISH HOUSE   870/492-5958
APPROVED American. Casual Dining. **Address:** 44 Hwy 101 Cutoff 72653

MOUNTAIN VIEW (B-4) pop. 2,748, elev. 770'

One of the Ozarks' most active crossroads is Mountain View, whose lively cultural heritage is evident in its community events. The annual Arkansas Folk Festival and the Dulcimer Jamboree and Southern Regional Dulcimer Competition are held in April; Mountains, Music and Motorcycles takes place in August; mid-September brings the Arkansas State Old-Time Fiddle Championship; and October brings BeanFest & Championship Outhouse Races.

Mountain View Chamber of Commerce: 107 N. Peabody Ave., Court Square, P.O. Box 133, Mountain View, AR 72560. **Phone:** (870) 269-8068 or (888) 679-2859.

BLANCHARD SPRINGS CAVERNS is 15 mi. n.w. on SR 14. Guided tours include three underground passageways. A visitor center has an exhibit hall and shows a 20-minute movie every half-hour.

The half-mile Dripstone Trail tour lasts 1 hour and covers a variety of cave formations in the upper level of the cave. The 1.2-mile Discovery Trail tour lasts 90 minutes and follows a cave stream and water-carved passages into the caverns' middle level. This trail has many steps and is not recommended for those with small children, limited mobility or respiratory problems. For the more adventurous, the strenuous 5-hour, 1-mile Wild Cave tour explores the undeveloped reaches of the underground system. Cave gear is provided. The caverns are 58 degrees Fahrenheit and damp; dress appropriately. Shoes with a low heel and non-slip sole are recommended. Boots are required for Wild Cave tour.

Hours: Dripstone Trail tour departs approximately every hour daily 9:30-6, Apr.-Oct.; Wed.-Sun. 9:30-6, rest of year. Last tour begins at 5. Discovery Trail tour departs approximately every hour daily 10:30-4:30, June-Aug. Last tour begins at 4:30. Wild Cave tour departs daily at 9:30, Apr.-Oct.; Wed.-Sun. at 9:30, rest of year. Visitors with reservations must arrive 30 minutes before departure. Visitor center open daily 9:30-6, Apr.-Oct.; Wed.-Sun. 9:30-6, rest of year.

Cost: Fee for trail tours $10.50; $5.50 (ages 6-15 and holders of National Forest Interagency Senior and Access passes); 50c (ages 0-5). Fee for Wild Cave tour $75.50; ages 10-12 must be with an adult and under 10 are not permitted. Reservations are suggested for the Dripstone Trail and Discovery Trail tours. Reservations are required for the Wild Cave tour. **Phone:** (870) 757-2211 for reservation information or to verify tour times or fees.

OZARK FOLK CENTER STATE PARK is 1.5 mi. n. via SRs 9/5/14, then 1 mi. w. on SR 382. The center focuses on the crafts, music, dance and oral history of an existing mountain folk culture. Local artisans demonstrate such skills as weaving, candle-making, broom-making and blacksmithing. Edible and medicinal herbs, and native plants are grown in the Heritage Herb Garden. Special events take place throughout the year.

Hours: Craft demonstrations are featured Tues.-Sat. 10-5, Apr.-Nov. Musical programs are presented in the auditorium Thurs.-Sat. at 7 p.m., Apr.-Nov. The center is open on a limited schedule rest of year for workshops, special events and holiday offerings. **Cost:** For craft area or for musical program $12; $7 (ages 6-12); $29.50 (family, two adults and children ages 0-17). Combination crafts and musical program $19.50; $10.25 (ages 6-12); $45 (family, two adults and children ages 0-17). Phone ahead to confirm schedule and rates. **Phone:** (870) 269-3851.

NORTH LITTLE ROCK (C-3)
elev. 280'
- Hotels p. 60 • Restaurants p. 60
- Hotels & Restaurants map & index

If one man could be said to have c... a city, William C. Faucette created North Little Rock. After he lost the 1903 mayoral election in Little Rock, Faucette and his lawyer friends introduced a bill in the Arkansas General Assembly making the section of Little Rock north of the Arkansas River a separate city. Faucette's bill was passed in 1917, making him a new mayor in a new city.

Spanning the Arkansas River, the Big Dam Bridge is the longest bridge built specifically for pedestrians and cyclists in the world. The 4,226-foot-long bridge rises 65 feet over the river. Also along the river is the North Shore Riverwalk, a promenade offering scenic views of the Arkansas River and the Little Rock skyline.

North Little Rock Convention and Visitors Bureau: 1 Eldor Johnson Dr. in Burns Park, P.O. Box 5511, North Little Rock, AR 72119. **Phone:** (501) 758-1424 or (800) 643-4690.

Shopping: McCain Mall, 3929 McCain Blvd. at US 67, counts Dillard's, JCPenney and Sears among its more than 80 stores. Specialty shops can be found along downtown Main Street and on John F. Kennedy Boulevard in the Park Hill Historic District.

THE OLD MILL AT T.R. PUGH MEMORIAL PARK is off Fairway Ave. at 3800 Lakeshore Dr. This picturesque replica of an 1830s gristmill appeared in the opening scene of "Gone With the Wind." It is believed to be the last surviving structure used in the film. Mexican sculptor Dionicio Rodríguez formed wet cement by hand to achieve the look of natural wood. Faux bois sculptures in the surrounding park include trees, benches, mushrooms and an ornate "timber" bridge, all crafted from concrete. **Hours:** Daily dawn-dusk. **Cost:** Free. **Phone:** (501) 758-1424 for the visitor center, or (800) 643-4690 out of Ark.

WILD RIVER COUNTRY is off I-40 exit 148, then .5 mi. w. to 6820 Crystal Hill Rd. This theme park offers water slides, a wave pool and other water-related amusements. A children's play area and facilities for volleyball also are provided. Lockers are available. **Hours:** Mon.-Tues. 10-6, Wed.-Sat. 10-7, Sun. noon-7, early June to mid-Aug.; Sat. 10-7, Sun. noon-6, Memorial Day weekend-early June; Sun. noon-7, mid-Aug. through Labor Day. Phone ahead to confirm schedule. **Cost:** $29.99; $24.99 (active military with ID); $20.99 (children under 48 inches tall); $10.99 (ages 61+ with ID); free (ages 0-2). After 3 p.m. $20.99. Phone ahead to confirm rates. **Phone:** (501) 753-8600.

For complete hotel, dining and attraction listings: AAA.com/travelguides

(… ee map & index p. 50.)

BAYMONT INN & SUITES   501/503-5537   **44**
THREE DIAMOND Hotel. **Address:** 110 E Pershing Blvd 72114

BEST WESTERN PLUS JFK INN & SUITES
    501/246-3300   **45**

THREE DIAMOND
Hotel

Best Western PLUS

AAA Benefit: Members save up to 15% and earn bonus points!

Address: 2500 Main St 72114 **Location:** I-40 exit 153A, just s on JFK Blvd. **Facility:** 64 units. 4 stories, interior corridors. **Pool:** heated indoor. **Activities:** hot tub, exercise room. **Guest Services:** valet and coin laundry.

[SAVE] [‡†→] CALL [♿] [≥] [🕯] [BIZ]
[HS] [📶] [✕] [🗐] [🖨] [💻]
/ SOME UNITS [🐾]

COMFORT INN & SUITES NORTH LITTLE ROCK
    501/801-1904   **47**
THREE DIAMOND Hotel. **Address:** 3915 McCain Park Dr 72116

COURTYARD BY MARRIOTT-LITTLE ROCK NORTH
    501/753-2000   **36**
THREE DIAMOND [SAVE] Hotel. **Address:** 4339 Warden Rd 72116

AAA Benefit: Members save 5% or more!

FAIRFIELD BY MARRIOTT   501/945-9777   **41**
THREE DIAMOND [SAVE] Hotel. **Address:** 4120 Healthcare Dr 72117

AAA Benefit: Members save 5% or more!

HAMPTON INN BY HILTON NORTH LITTLE ROCK MCCAIN
    501/537-7700   **38**
THREE DIAMOND [SAVE] Hotel. **Address:** 3629 McCain Blvd 72116

AAA Benefit: Members save up to 15%!

HILTON GARDEN INN NORTH LITTLE ROCK
    501/945-7444   **39**

THREE DIAMOND
Hotel

Hilton Garden Inn

AAA Benefit: Members save up to 15%!

Address: 4100 Glover Ln 72117 **Location:** US 67/167 exit 1 southbound; exit 1A northbound, 0.5 mi e on McCain Blvd, then just n. **Facility:** 119 units. 4 stories, interior corridors. **Pool:** heated indoor. **Activities:** hot tub, exercise room. **Guest Services:** valet and coin laundry.

[SAVE] [‡†] [≥] [Y] CALL [♿] [≥]
[🕯] [BIZ] [📶] [✕] [🗐] [🖨] [💻]

HOLIDAY INN EXPRESS HOTEL & SUITES
    501/945-4800   **40**
THREE DIAMOND Hotel. **Address:** 4306 E McCain Blvd 72117

LA QUINTA INN & SUITES NORTH LITTLE ROCK-MCCAIN MALL
    501/945-0808   **37**
APPROVED Hotel. **Address:** 4311 Warden Rd 72116

RED ROOF INN-NORTH LITTLE ROCK   501/945-0080   **43**
APPROVED Hotel. **Address:** 5711 Pritchard Dr 72117

RESIDENCE INN BY MARRIOTT-NORTH   501/945-7777   **42**
THREE DIAMOND [SAVE] Extended Stay Hotel. **Address:** 4110 Healthcare Dr 72117

AAA Benefit: Members save 5% or more!

WYNDHAM HOTEL AND RESORT RIVERFRONT LITTLE ROCK
    501/371-9000   **46**
THREE DIAMOND Hotel. **Address:** 2 Riverfront Pl 72114

WHERE TO EAT

DAVID'S BURGER   501/353-0387   **48**
APPROVED Burgers. Casual Dining. **Address:** 3510 Landers Rd 72116

LAS PALMAS   501/945-8010   **49**
APPROVED Mexican. Casual Dining. **Address:** 4154 E McCain Blvd 72117

RISTORANTE CAPEO   501/376-3463   **50**
THREE DIAMOND Italian. Casual Dining. **Address:** 425 Main St 72114

WHOLE HOG CAFE NORTH LITTLE ROCK
    501/753-9227   **47**
APPROVED Barbecue. Quick Serve. **Address:** 5107 Warden Rd 72116

OUACHITA NATIONAL FOREST (C-1)

Elevations in the forest range from 360 ft. on the Fourche-LaFave River to 2,681 ft. at Rich Tower. Refer to AAA maps for additional elevation information.

In west-central Arkansas and southeastern Oklahoma, the 1.8 million-acre Ouachita National Forest is known for its mountain scenery, recreational opportunities and varied wildlife. The Ouachita Mountains run east and west, rather than north and south as do most American ranges. The novaculite found in this area is highly valued for making Arkansas whetstones, used for sharpening blade tools.

Talimena Scenic Drive provides 54 miles of mountain views along SRs 88 and 1 from near Mena to near Talihina, Okla. The Ouachita National Recreation Trail is a 192-mile east-west route through the mountains from SR 9 near Little Rock to Talimena State Park in Oklahoma. A nature center and three hiking trails are available at Kerr Arboretum and Nature Center, 19 miles south of Heavener, Okla. The Jessieville Visitor Center is open Mon.-Fri. 8-4; closed federal holidays. The center is 18 miles north of Hot Springs in Jessieville and features the 1.5-mile Friendship Trail, a paved woodland loop.

Developed facilities are available at Lake Sylvia, south of Perryville off SR 9; Little Pines Recreation Area, 12 miles west of Waldron on SR 248; Shady Lake, 25 miles southeast of Mena; Cedar Lake, 10 miles south of Heavener, Okla., off US 270; and Charlton Recreation Area, 20 miles west of Hot Springs. Portions of Albert Pike Recreation Area, 6 miles north of Langley off SR 369 are open for day use only. Campers should phone ahead to verify accessibility to camping areas.

The forest contains six wilderness areas: Caney Creek, 14,460 acres 25 miles southeast of Mena; Black Fork Mountain, 13,579 acres shared with Oklahoma, 18 miles northwest of Mena; Poteau Mountain, 11,299 acres 35 miles south of Fort Smith; Flatside, 9,507 acres 16 miles southwest of Perryville; Dry Creek, 6,310 acres 12 miles southwest of Booneville; and Upper Kiamichi River, 10,819 acres 25 miles east of Talihina, Okla.

Forest admission is free. Information about additional recreation areas within the forest and about camping fees can be obtained from the Forest Supervisor's Office, Ouachita National Forest, 100 Reserve St., P.O. Box 1270, Hot Springs, AR 71902; phone (501) 321-5202. *See Recreation Areas Chart.*

OZARK NATIONAL FOREST (B-1)

Elevations in the forest range from 420 ft. near the town of New Blaine to 2,753 ft. at Mount Magazine. Refer to AAA maps for additional elevation information.

In the Ozark Highlands and Boston Mountains of northwestern Arkansas, the four principal divisions of the Ozark National Forest total more than a million acres. Recreational activities such as hiking, camping, canoeing, horseback riding, hunting, fishing, mountain bicycle riding, swimming and picnicking can be enjoyed in the rugged beauty of the forest.

Blanchard Springs Caverns Recreation Area, off SR 14 north of Mountain View, features a large spring that gushes 1,200 gallons of water per minute; nearby are Blanchard Springs Caverns *(see Mountain View p. 58)*.

Alum Cove Natural Bridge Recreation Area, north of Deer on FR 1206, preserves a 130-foot-long natural arch. Cove Lake, a 160-acre mountain lake southeast of Paris on SR 309 near Mount Magazine offers camping, picnicking, swimming, fishing and boating. The 150-mile-long Ozark Highland Trail affords opportunities for hiking and nature study. Campers should phone ahead to verify accessibility to camping areas. The Russellville visitor center is open Mon.-Fri. 8-4:30; closed federal holidays.

Information about the forest's many other recreation areas is available from the Forest Supervisor's Office, Ozark National Forest, 605 W. Main St., Russellville, AR 72801; phone (479) 964-7200. *See Recreation Areas Chart.*

PARAGOULD pop. 26,113

HAMPTON INN BY HILTON   870/565-1010
▼▼▼ THREE DIAMOND (SAVE) Hotel. Address: 3810 Linwood Dr 72450

AAA Benefit: Members save up to 15%!

WHERE TO EAT

KIMONO   870/240-8887
◆ APPROVED   Japanese. Casual Dining. **Address:** 2708 Linwood Dr 72450

PEA RIDGE NATIONAL MILITARY PARK (A-1)

On US 62 about 9 mi. n.e. of Rogers, in northwest Arkansas, the 4,300-acre park was the site of the Battle of Pea Ridge, also known to the Confederacy as the Battle of Elkhorn Tavern. A reconstruction of the tavern is on the original site. Largely as a result of this battle, fought March 7-8, 1862, Union forces succeeded in securing the state of Missouri. A 7-mile self-guiding driving tour through the park provides insight into the battle. A small portion of the "Trail of Tears" also is within the park.

Park and trails open daily 6 a.m.-sunset. Closed Jan. 1, Thanksgiving and Christmas. Phone ahead to confirm schedule. Admission $15 (per private vehicle); $10 (per motorcycle); $7 (individual); free (ages 0-15). Phone (479) 451-8122.

PEA RIDGE NATIONAL MILITARY PARK VISITOR CENTER is 10 mi. n.e. of Rogers via scenic US 62. Museum exhibits and a 28-minute movie, "Thunder in the Ozarks," provide background on the battle. A driving tour of the battlefield begins at the center and travels to 10 stops, including Elkhorn Tavern, with markers and descriptions of key points. An audio tour by cell phone is available. **Hours:** Center open daily 8:30-4:30. Phone ahead to confirm schedule. **Cost:** Included with park admission. **Phone:** (479) 451-8122.

PINE BLUFF (D-4) pop. 49,083, elev. 215'
• Hotels p. 62 • Restaurants p. 62

The second oldest city in the state, Pine Bluff was founded in 1819 as a trading post by Joseph Bonne, who dealt with the Quapaw Indians. Some of the properties in the city's historic district date from the Civil War period. A series of murals on downtown buildings depicts scenes from the city's history.

Tours of the restored 1887 childhood home of Pine Bluff native Martha Mitchell, 902 W. Fourth Ave., are offered by appointment; phone (870) 535-4973. Mitchell was a catalyst for national news during the Nixon administration and Watergate affair.

◆ Enchanted Land of Lights and Legends, a drive-through holiday festival featuring approximately 230 displays at some 165 locations, is held mid-Nov. through Dec. 31 at Pine Bluff/Jefferson County Regional Park, US 65B.

Pine Bluff Regional Chamber of Commerce: 510 S. Main St., P.O. Box 5069, Pine Bluff, AR 71611. **Phone:** (870) 535-0110.

Self-guiding tours: A brochure outlining a walking or driving tour of the murals in downtown Pine Bluff is available at the chamber of commerce.

GOVERNOR MIKE HUCKABEE DELTA RIVERS NATURE CENTER is at 1400 Black Dog Rd. Located within the Pine Bluff/Jefferson County Regional Park on 130 acres of woodlands, this center features exhibits that depict the natural history of Arkansas' Delta region. Nature trails provide viewing opportunities of the area's vegetation and wildlife. A 20,000-gallon freshwater outdoor aquarium contains native fish species, and other exhibits contain snakes, turtles, alligators and bald eagles. Interactive displays also are offered, including a weather exhibit and a taxidermy display. Videos offer a simulated boat ride and a crop-dusting airplane ride over the Arkansas Delta.

Hours: Trails open daily dawn-dusk. Nature center open Tues.-Sat. 8:30-4:30, Sun. 1-5. Fish feeding Tues.-Fri. at 11, Sat.-Sun. at 3. Eagle feeding and presentation Sat.-Sun. at 3:15. Alligator feeding Sat. after fish feeding, Memorial Day-Labor Day. Nature center closed Jan. 1, Easter, Thanksgiving, Christmas Eve and Christmas. **Cost:** Free. **Phone:** (870) 534-0011. 🎟

BEST WESTERN PRESIDENTIAL HOTEL & SUITES
870/535-6300

♦ **APPROVED**
Hotel

AAA Benefit: Members save up to 15% and earn bonus points!

Address: 3104 Market St 71601 **Location:** I-530 exit 46, just n on US 65 business route. **Facility:** 57 units. 3 stories, interior corridors. **Pool:** outdoor. **Activities:** exercise room. **Guest Services:** coin laundry. **Featured Amenity:** breakfast buffet.

COMFORT INN & SUITES
870/879-3800
THREE DIAMOND Hotel. **Address:** 3620 Camden Rd 71603

HAMPTON INN & SUITES BY HILTON PINE BLUFF
870/850-7488

THREE DIAMOND
Hotel

AAA Benefit: Members save up to 15%!

Address: 511 Mallard Loop 71603 **Location:** I-530 exit 43, just n. **Facility:** 80 units. 4 stories, interior corridors. **Pool:** heated indoor. **Activities:** hot tub, exercise room. **Guest Services:** coin laundry. **Featured Amenity:** full hot breakfast.

QUALITY INN & SUITES PINE BLUFF
870/535-5300
♦ **APPROVED** Hotel. **Address:** 2809 Pines Mall Dr 71601

WHERE TO EAT

BRIGG'S BBQ COOKING
870/718-9769
♦ **APPROVED** Barbecue. Quick Serve. **Address:** 2221 S Olive St 71601

COLONIAL STEAKHOUSE
870/536-3488
♦ **APPROVED** Steak. Casual Dining. **Address:** 111 W 8th Ave 71601

LYBRAND'S BAKERY & DELI
870/534-4607
♦ **APPROVED** American. Quick Serve. **Address:** 2900 Hazel St 71603

ROGERS (A-1) pop. 55,964, elev. 1,384'

The first train steamed into the settlement now known as Rogers in 1881, 22 years after the Butterfield Overland Mail established a way station in town. Spanish and French pioneers once walked this territory, as did Native Americans forced westward on the "Trail of Tears" and Civil War soldiers. Nearby recreation areas offer outdoor activities.

The historic War Eagle Mill, 11045 War Eagle Rd., is a reconstruction of an 1873 mill that burned down in 1924. This still working gristmill—the fourth mill built on this site along the War Eagle River, features an 18-foot undershot waterwheel made of cypress. The War Eagle Mill Arts and Crafts Fair is held here in October.

Rogers-Lowell Area Chamber of Commerce: 317 W. Walnut St., Rogers, AR 72756. **Phone:** (479) 636-5485 or (800) 364-1240.

WAR EAGLE CAVERN is 17 mi. e. on SR 12 to 21494 Cavern Dr. Set in the Ozark mountains on the shores of Beaver Lake, the cavern once sheltered Native Americans. Guided 1-hour tours reveal stalactites, stalagmites, fossils, Arkansas quartz crystal, an underground stream and a rimstone dam waterfall room; a nature trail is on the grounds. The cave also is home to 100,000 Arkansas brown and grey bats. Aboveground activities include gemstone panning and the "Lost in the Woods Maze."

Cave temperature is 58 degrees F year-around. Walkways are wide, level, and pet- and stroller-friendly. **Time:** Allow 1 hour minimum. **Hours:** Tours Mon.-Sat. 9:30-5, Sun. 11-5. Last tour begins at 4. **Cost:** $16.89; $10 (ages 4-12). **Phone:** (479) 789-2909. 🎟 🎟

ALOFT ROGERS-BENTONVILLE
479/268-6799

THREE DIAMOND
Hotel

aloft **AAA Benefit:** Members save 5% or more!

Address: 1103 S 52nd St 72758 **Location:** I-49 exit 83, just nw. **Facility:** 130 units. 6 stories, interior corridors. *Bath:* shower only. **Amenities:** safes. **Pool:** heated outdoor. **Activities:** exercise room. **Guest Services:** valet and coin laundry. **Featured Amenity:** continental breakfast.

CANDLEWOOD SUITES-ROGERS BENTONVILLE
479/636-2783
THREE DIAMOND Extended Stay Hotel. **Address:** 4601 W Rozell St 72757

COUNTRY INN & SUITES BY RADISSON   479/633-0055
THREE DIAMOND Hotel. **Address:** 4304 W Walnut St 72756

EMBASSY SUITES BY HILTON NORTHWEST ARKANSAS
479/254-8400
THREE DIAMOND SAVE Hotel. **Address:** 3303 Pinnacle Hills Pkwy 72758

AAA Benefit: Members save up to 15%!

FAIRFIELD INN & SUITES BY MARRIOTT   479/936-5900
THREE DIAMOND
Hotel

Fairfield
AAA Benefit: Members save 5% or more!

Address: 4611 W Rozell St 72756 **Location:** I-49 exit 85, 0.5 mi n on 46th St. **Facility:** 99 units. 3 stories, interior corridors. **Pool:** indoor. **Activities:** exercise room. **Guest Services:** valet and coin laundry.

HAMPTON INN BY HILTON-BENTONVILLE ROGERS
479/986-0500
THREE DIAMOND SAVE Hotel. **Address:** 4501 W Walnut St 72756

AAA Benefit: Members save up to 15%!

HOMEWOOD SUITES BY HILTON   479/636-5656
THREE DIAMOND SAVE Extended Stay Hotel. **Address:** 4302 W Walnut St 72756

AAA Benefit: Members save up to 15%!

HYATT PLACE ROGERS/BENTONVILLE   479/633-8555
THREE DIAMOND
Hotel

HYATT PLACE
AAA Benefit: Members save up to 10%!

Address: 4610 W Walnut St 72756 **Location:** I-49 exit 85, just e. **Facility:** 103 units. 5 stories, interior corridors. **Amenities:** video games. **Pool:** heated outdoor. **Activities:** exercise room. **Guest Services:** valet and coin laundry, area transportation. **Featured Amenity:** breakfast buffet.

MAINSTAY SUITES   479/636-3232
THREE DIAMOND Extended Stay Hotel. **Address:** 301 S 45th St 72758

MICROTEL INN & SUITES BY WYNDHAM ROGERS
479/636-5551
APPROVED Hotel. **Address:** 909 S 8th St 72756

RESIDENCE INN BY MARRIOTT   479/636-5900
THREE DIAMOND SAVE Extended Stay Hotel. **Address:** 4611 W Locust St 72756

AAA Benefit: Members save 5% or more!

STAYBRIDGE SUITES ROGERS-BENTONVILLE   479/845-5701
THREE DIAMOND Extended Stay Hotel. **Address:** 1801 S 52nd St 72758

WHERE TO EAT

COLTON'S STEAKHOUSE & GRILL   479/636-3336
APPROVED Steak. Casual Dining. **Address:** 4700 W Locust St 72756

CRABBY'S SEAFOOD BAR & GRILL   479/273-0222
THREE DIAMOND Seafood. Casual Dining. **Address:** 1800 S 52nd St 72758

JJ'S GRILL   479/372-4460
APPROVED American Casual Dining. **Address:** 4500 W Walnut St 72756

THE RAIL - A PIZZA COMPANY   479/633-8808
APPROVED Pizza. Casual Dining. **Address:** 218 S 1st St 72756

RUSSELLVILLE (C-2) pop. 27,920, elev. 348'
• Restaurants p. 64

About an hour northwest of Little Rock, Russellville borders Lake Dardanelle and the Arkansas River, and is located along the Arkansas Scenic 7 Byway. Lake Dardanelle State Park is a nationally known bass fishing tournament site, while across the river, Mount Nebo State Park offers views from above the city along with camping, swimming and hiking. Russellville is home to Arkansas State University as well as Arkansas Nuclear One, the state's only nuclear power plant.

BEST WESTERN INN   479/967-1000
APPROVED
Motel

Best Western.
AAA Benefit: Members save up to 15% and earn bonus points!

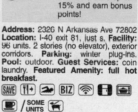

Address: 2326 N Arkansas Ave 72802 **Location:** I-40 exit 81, just s. **Facility:** 96 units. 2 stories (no elevator), exterior corridors. **Parking:** winter plug-ins. **Pool:** outdoor. **Guest Services:** coin laundry. **Featured Amenity:** full hot breakfast.

COURTYARD BY MARRIOTT RUSSELLVILLE
479/968-6000
THREE DIAMOND
Hotel

COURTYARD
AAA Benefit: Members save 5% or more!

Address: 154 E Aspen Ln 72802 **Location:** I-40 exit 81, just ne. **Facility:** 108 units. 4 stories, interior corridors. **Pool:** heated indoor. **Activities:** exercise room. **Guest Services:** complimentary and valet laundry, boarding pass kiosk.

🔗 **AAA.com/maps—Dream, plan, go with AAA travel planning tools**

DAYS INN & SUITES RUSSELLVILLE   479/280-1940
APPROVED   Hotel. **Address:** 109 E Harrell Dr 72802

FAIRFIELD INN & SUITES BY MARRIOTT   479/967-9030
THREE DIAMOND [SAVE] Hotel. **Address:** 120 E Harrell Dr 72802

| AAA Benefit: Members save 5% or more! |

HAMPTON INN BY HILTON RUSSELLVILLE
                                              479/858-7199
THREE DIAMOND
Hotel

| AAA Benefit: Members save up to 15%! |

Address: 2304 N Arkansas Ave 72802 **Location:** I-40 exit 81, just s. **Facility:** 83 units. 2 stories, interior corridors. **Pool:** heated indoor. **Activities:** hot tub, exercise room. **Guest Services:** valet and coin laundry. **Featured Amenity:** continental breakfast.

[SAVE] [T+] CALL [&] [≈] [⊞] [BIZ] [🛜] [✕] [🔒] [🖨] [🖥]

LA QUINTA INN & SUITES   479/967-2299
THREE DIAMOND Hotel. **Address:** 111 E Harrell Dr 72802

QUALITY INN   479/967-7500
APPROVED   Motel. **Address:** 3019 E Parkway Dr 72802

SUPER 8 RUSSELLVILLE   479/968-8898
APPROVED
Hotel

Address: 2404 N Arkansas Ave 72802 **Location:** I-40 exit 81, just s. **Facility:** 54 units. 3 stories (no elevator), interior corridors. **Guest Services:** valet laundry. **Featured Amenity:** full hot breakfast.

[SAVE] [⊟] [T+] [BIZ] [🛜] [🔒] [🖨] [🖥] / SOME UNITS [🐾]

WHERE TO EAT

COLTON'S STEAKHOUSE & GRILL   479/880-2333
APPROVED   Steak. Casual Dining. **Address:** 2320 N Arkansas Ave 72801

LA HUERTA MEXICAN RESTAURANT   479/880-9111
APPROVED   Mexican. Casual Dining. **Address:** 2005 N Arkansas Ave 72802

STOBY'S RESTAURANT   479/968-3816
APPROVED   American. Casual Dining. **Address:** 405 W Parkway Dr 72801

SUMO JAPANESE STEAKHOUSE   479/880-8855
APPROVED   Japanese. Casual Dining. **Address:** 2300 E Parkway Dr 72802

ST. CHARLES (D-5) pop. 230, elev. 200'

During the Civil War battle of June 17, 1862, a cannonball was shot through a porthole of the federal ironclad *Mound City* on the White River at St. Charles. Called by some historians the most destructive single shot of the war, it hit a steam pipe and killed nearly 100 soldiers.

ST. FRANCIS NATIONAL FOREST (D-6)

Elevations in the forest range from 150 ft. on the Mississippi River to 320 ft. at Crowley's Ridge. Refer to AAA maps for additional elevation information.

In east-central Arkansas, St. Francis National Forest covers 22,600 acres at the south end of a 200-mile-long ridge that rises above the surrounding flat farmlands. The forest offers picnicking, camping, fishing, boating, swimming and hiking.

Developed recreation areas are at 625-acre Bear Creek Lake, 8 miles south of Marianna on SR 44, and at 420-acre Storm Creek Lake, 6 miles north of West Helena on SR 44. The Mississippi River State Park visitor center is open daily 8-5; closed Jan. 1, Thanksgiving and Christmas. Christmas Eve hours are 8-noon. For additional information contact the Forest Supervisor, St. Francis National Forest, 2955 SR 44, Marianna, AR 72360; phone (870) 295-5278, or (870) 295-4040 for the visitor center. *See Recreation Areas Chart.*

SEARCY pop. 22,858

BEST WESTERN PLUS SEARCY INN   501/279-9191
THREE DIAMOND
Hotel

| AAA Benefit: Members save up to 15% and earn bonus points! |

Address: 501 Willow St 72143 **Location:** US 67/167 exit 46, just w, then just n. **Facility:** 71 units. 3 stories, interior corridors. **Pool:** heated indoor. **Activities:** exercise room. **Guest Services:** coin laundry. **Featured Amenity:** full hot breakfast.

[SAVE] [T+] [≈] [⊞] [BIZ] [HS] [🛜] [🔒] [🖨] [🖥] / SOME UNITS [🐾]

HOLIDAY INN EXPRESS & SUITES   501/279-9991
THREE DIAMOND Hotel. **Address:** 3660 Ferren Tr 72143

MICROTEL INN & SUITES BY WYNDHAM   501/268-1555
APPROVED   Hotel. **Address:** 3668 Ferren Tr 72143

SUPER 8 BY WYNDHAM - SEARCY   501/268-8988
APPROVED   Hotel. **Address:** 1200 Truman Baker Dr 72143

WHERE TO EAT

COLTON'S STEAKHOUSE & GRILL   501/268-5777
APPROVED   Steak. Casual Dining. **Address:** 3002 E Race Ave 72143

RIB CRIB BBQ AND GRILL   501/279-0440
APPROVED   Barbecue. Casual Dining. **Address:** 3204 E Race Ave 72143

ROCK HOUSE   501/268-3627
APPROVED   American. Casual Dining. **Address:** 1301 E Beebe Capps Expy 72143

SHERWOOD pop. 29,523
• Hotels & Restaurants map & index p. 50

BEST WESTERN SHERWOOD INN & SUITES
501/835-7556 (49)

WY THREE DIAMOND
Hotel

Best Western. **AAA Benefit:** Members save up to 15% and earn bonus points!

Address: 7533 Warden Rd 72120 **Location:** US 67/167 exit 5, 0.6 mi s on west service road. **Facility:** 60 units. 2 stories (no elevator), interior corridors. **Pool:** outdoor. **Activities:** exercise room. **Guest Services:** coin laundry.

[SAVE] [⊟] [Y!+] [➤] [♦] [BIZ] [HS]
[📶] [🔒] [▦] [▯]

SILOAM SPRINGS pop. 15,039

HAMPTON INN BY HILTON SILOAM SPRINGS   479/215-1000
WY THREE DIAMOND [SAVE] Hotel. **Address:** 2171 Ravenwood Plaza 72761

AAA Benefit: Members save up to 15%!

QUALITY INN   479/524-8080
WY APPROVED   Hotel. **Address:** 300 US Highway 412 W 72761

SUPER 8   479/524-8898
WY APPROVED   Motel. **Address:** 1800 Hwy 412 W 72761

SPRINGDALE (A-1) pop. 69,797, elev. 1,329'
• Restaurants p. 67

ARKANSAS AND MISSOURI RAILROAD departs from the depot at 306 E. Emma Ave. Travelers ride in comfort aboard restored late 19th- and early 20th-century passenger cars on an 8-hour, 134-mile round-trip train ride through the scenic Boston Mountains to Van Buren. The full-day ride includes a 2.5-hour stopover in Van Buren. Round-trips from Van Buren to Winslow and round-trips from Fort Smith to Winslow also are offered. Christmas-themed trips are available from Springdale in winter. *See also Van Buren p. 69.*

Hours: Springdale-to-Van Buren trips depart Wed. and Fri.-Sat. at 8, Apr.-Sept.; Fri.-Sat. at 8, Oct.-Nov. Van Buren-to-Winslow trips depart Wed. and Fri.-Sat. at 11, Apr.-Sept. and Oct.-Nov. Fort Smith-to-Winslow trips depart Sat. at 11, Jan.-Mar. All train rides are round trips. **Cost:** Springdale-to-Van Buren fare (Apr.-Sept.) $54-$95 and (Oct.-Nov.) $68-$110. Van Buren-to-Winslow fare (Apr.-Sept.) $39-$83 and (Oct.-Nov.) $49-$93. Fort Smith-to-Winslow fare (Jan.-Mar.) $44-$88. Phone to confirm schedules and fares. Reservations are recommended. **Phone:** (479) 725-4017 or (800) 687-8600.

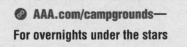

🅐 **AAA.com/campgrounds—**
For overnights under the stars

SHILOH MUSEUM OF OZARK HISTORY is at 118 W. Johnson Ave. This 3-acre regional history museum consists of various displays that focus on those who shaped Ozark history—the past residents of the area. Seven historic buildings, including a log cabin, outhouse, an oak barn and the Searcy House, also are on site. Free guided tours of the Searcy House are available. Changing exhibits are offered year-round. **Time:** Allow 30 minutes minimum. **Hours:** Mon.-Sat. 10-5. **Cost:** Donations. **Phone:** (479) 750-8165.

DOUBLETREE CLUB BY HILTON HOTEL SPRINGDALE
479/751-7200
WY THREE DIAMOND [SAVE] Hotel. **Address:** 4677 W Sunset Ave 72762

AAA Benefit: Members save up to 15%!

FAIRFIELD INN & SUITES BY MARRIOTT SPRINGDALE
479/419-5722
WY THREE DIAMOND [SAVE] Hotel. **Address:** 1043 Rieff St 72762

AAA Benefit: Members save 5% or more!

HAMPTON INN & SUITES   479/756-3500
WY THREE DIAMOND [SAVE] Hotel. **Address:** 1700 S 48th St 72762

AAA Benefit: Members save up to 15%!

HOLIDAY INN NORTHWEST AR HOTEL & CONVENTION CENTER   479/751-8300
WY THREE DIAMOND Hotel. **Address:** 1500 S 48th St 72762

INN AT THE MILL, AN ASCEND HOTEL COLLECTION MEMBER   479/443-1800
WY THREE DIAMOND Historic Hotel. **Address:** 3906 Johnson Mill Blvd 72762

LA QUINTA INN & SUITES SPRINGDALE   479/751-2626
WY APPROVED   Hotel. **Address:** 1300 S 48th St 72764

QUALITY SUITES   479/725-1777
WY THREE DIAMOND Hotel. **Address:** 1099 Rieff St 72762

RESIDENCE INN BY MARRIOTT   479/872-9100
WY THREE DIAMOND
Extended Stay Hotel

Residence INN. **AAA Benefit:** Members save 5% or more!

Address: 1740 S 48th St 72762 **Location:** I-49 exit 72, just e to 48th St, then just s. **Facility:** 72 units, some two bedrooms, efficiencies and kitchens. 3 stories, interior corridors. **Pool:** heated indoor. **Activities:** exercise room. **Guest Services:** valet and coin laundry.

[SAVE] [Y!+] [➤] [♦] [BIZ] [HS] [📶]

[✕] [⊟] [▦] [▯] / SOME UNITS [🐾]

THE EXPERIENCE YOU DESERVE

You can play all day and stay all night at Cherokee Casino & Hotel West Siloam Springs. We have 140 rooms, including seven suites, with all the amenities and accommodations you need to have a great time. As you enjoy your stay, check out the live entertainment at SEVEN Bar and the mouthwatering selections at Flint Creek Steakhouse or River Cane Buffet!

U.S. Hwy 412 & 59, West Siloam Springs, OK
800.754.4111 | CherokeeCasino.com

ONE★STAR

Cherokee
CASINO & HOTEL

WEST SILOAM SPRINGS

Know your limits. Gambling problem? Call 800.522.4700.

SLEEP INN & SUITES   479/756-5800
THREE DIAMOND Hotel. **Address:** 1056 Rieff St 72762

TOWNEPLACE SUITES BY MARRIOTT FAYETTEVILLE
NORTH/SPRINGDALE   479/966-4400
THREE DIAMOND SAVE Extended | **AAA Benefit:**
Stay Hotel. **Address:** 5437 S 48th St | Members save 5%
72762 | or more!

WHERE TO EAT

A Q CHICKEN HOUSE   479/751-4633
APPROVED Regional American. Casual Dining.
Address: 1207 N Thompson St 72765

BLUEFIN SUSHI BAR AND GRILL   479/717-2877
APPROVED Japanese. Casual Dining. **Address:** 4276
W Sunset Ave 72762

KRAKEN KILLER SEAFOOD   479/751-3649
APPROVED American. Casual Dining. **Address:** 2576
W Sunset Ave 72762

MARKETPLACE GRILL   479/750-5200
APPROVED American. Casual Dining. **Address:** 1636
S 48th St 72762

MJ PIZZERIA   479/717-6836
APPROVED American. Casual Dining. **Address:** 838
N 48th St 72762

TACOS 4 LIFE   479/225-9057
APPROVED Mexican. Quick Serve. **Address:** 1210
JTL Parkway 72762

WRIGHT'S BARBECUE   479/633-7229
APPROVED Barbecue. Casual Dining. **Address:** 2212
Main Dr 72762

STUTTGART (D-4) pop. 9,326, elev. 228'

Surrounding Stuttgart is the rice-producing section of the Grand Prairie region, also known as one of the finest fishing areas in the country. The rice fields and the many lakes and reservoirs in the area offer excellent feeding and resting places for waterfowl.

Stuttgart hosts the Wings Over the Prairie Festival, featuring the World Championship Duck Calling Contest, in November.

Stuttgart Chamber of Commerce: 507 S. Main St., P.O. Box 1500, Stuttgart, AR 72160. **Phone:** (870) 673-1602.

MUSEUM OF THE ARKANSAS GRAND PRAIRIE is just n. of the city park at 921 E. 4th St. The museum contains reproductions of an 1880 homestead and an 1890 village as well as a two-thirds scale model of an 1869 church, a 1914 schoolhouse and replicas of a fire station and a newspaper office. Included are exhibits about prairie farming, wildlife, duck hunting, toys and the Stuttgart Army Airfield.

Videos show local waterfowl and rice, soybean and fish farming; a mini-theater video traces the history of local crop dusting. A patch of rice is grown and harvested in summer. **Time:** Allow 1 hour minimum. **Hours:** Tues.-Fri. 8-4, Sat. 10-4. Closed major holidays. **Cost:** Donations. **Phone:** (870) 673-7001.

TRU BY HILTON STUTTGART   870/672-7505
APPROVED SAVE Hotel. **Ad-** | Members save up to
dress: 204 W 22nd St 72160 | 15%!

TEXARKANA (E-1) pop. 29,919
• Restaurants p. 68

The Arkansas-Texas state line runs approximately through the center of the dual municipality of Texarkana, which has a combined population of about 66,000.

For hundreds of years before European settlement in the area, the Great Southwest Trail, the major route between the Native American villages of the Mississippi Valley and the West and Southwest, crossed the area around what is now Texarkana. The Grand Caddoes, hospitable to explorers and settlers, farmed in the vicinity and maintained six villages along the banks of the Red River.

Shortly after 1840 a permanent settlement was established at Lost Prairie, 15 miles east of Texarkana. A number of mounds and other traces of former Native American civilizations remain within a 30-mile radius of the town.

During the 1850s the Cairo and Fulton Railroad served portions of Arkansas and by 1874 had crossed the Red River into Texas, establishing direct rail service to St. Louis. The Texas and Pacific Railroad had laid track to the Arkansas boundary, and the place where the two lines met became a town—Texarkana.

The state line runs through the middle of the Texarkana Post Office and Courthouse, said to be the only federal building situated in two states. Built in 1932 of pink granite from Texas and limestone from Arkansas, the post office has two separate zip codes. Residents on both sides of the border enjoy the Perot Theatre, 221 Main St., a restored 1924 facility that presents a variety of Broadway shows; phone (903) 792-4992.

BEST WESTERN PLUS TEXARKANA INN & SUITES
                                                        870/774-1534

THREE DIAMOND | Best Western PLUS | **AAA Benefit:** Members save up to
Hotel | | 15% and earn bonus points!

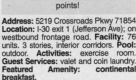

Address: 5219 Crossroads Pkwy 71854 **Location:** I-30 exit 1 (Jefferson Ave); on westbound frontage road. **Facility:** 76 units. 3 stories, interior corridors. **Pool:** outdoor. **Activities:** exercise room. **Guest Services:** valet and coin laundry. **Featured Amenity:** continental breakfast.

SAVE CALL ♿ 🏊 👪 BIZ HS
📶 ✕ ▯ ▭ ▭

HAMPTON INN   870/774-4267
THREE DIAMOND SAVE Hotel. **Ad-** | **AAA Benefit:**
dress: 5302 Crossroads Pkwy 71854 | Members save up to
                                                       | 15%!

HOLIDAY INN EXPRESS HOTEL & SUITES TEXARKANA EAST
870/216-0083
♦ **APPROVED**   Hotel. **Address:** 5210 Crossroads Pkwy 71854

HOLIDAY INN TEXARKANA   870/216-2000
♦ **THREE DIAMOND** Hotel. **Address:** 5200 Convention Plaza Dr 71854

WHERE TO EAT

CATTLEMANS STEAKHOUSE   870/774-4481
♦ **APPROVED**   Steak. Casual Dining. **Address:** 4018 State Line Ave 71854

EL CHICO   870/779-0300
♦ **APPROVED**   Tex-Mex. Casual Dining. **Address:** 420 Realtor Rd 71854

Nearby Texas

TEXARKANA pop. 36,411, elev. 290'

Texarkana Chamber of Commerce: 819 N. State Line Ave., Texarkana, TX 75501. **Phone:** (903) 792-7191 or (877) 275-5289.

ACE OF CLUBS HOUSE MUSEUM is at 420 Pine St. This 22-sided house was built in 1885 reputedly from the winnings of a poker game. The Italianate Victorian-style building has three octagonal wings and one rectangular wing and features original furniture. A 15-minute video presentation is followed by a 1-hour guided tour. High heels and photography are not permitted. **Time:** Allow 1 hour, 30 minutes minimum. **Hours:** Tours Tues.-Sat. at 10, 1 and 3:30, Sun. at 1 and 3:30. Closed major holidays. **Cost:** $5; $4 (ages 60+ and military with ID); free (ages 0-3). **Phone:** (903) 793-4831. GT

COURTYARD BY MARRIOTT   903/334-7400
♦ **THREE DIAMOND** SAVE Hotel. **Address:** 5001 N Cowhorn Creek Loop 75503

AAA Benefit: Members save 5% or more!

HAMPTON INN & SUITES   903/832-3499
♦ **THREE DIAMOND** SAVE Hotel. **Address:** 4601 Cowhorn Creek Rd 75503

AAA Benefit: Members save up to 15%!

HILTON GARDEN INN   903/792-1065
♦ **THREE DIAMOND** SAVE Hotel. **Address:** 2910 S Cowhorn Creek Loop 75503

AAA Benefit: Members save up to 15%!

🔗 **Save on travel, shopping and more: AAA.com/discounts**

HOLIDAY INN EXPRESS & SUITES CENTRAL MALL AREA   903/223-0008
♦ **THREE DIAMOND**   Hotel   **Address:** 4545 Cowhorn Creek Rd 75503 **Location:** I-30 exit 220B (Richmond Rd), 0.5 mi e on eastbound frontage road to Cowhorn Creek Loop, then just sw. **Facility:** 90 units. 3 stories, interior corridors. **Amenities:** safes. **Pool:** outdoor. **Activities:** exercise room. **Guest Services:** valet and coin laundry. **Featured Amenity: breakfast buffet.**

SAVE 🍴➕ 🏊 ♿ BIZ HS 📶 ✕ 🔒 📷 🖨

RESIDENCE INN BY MARRIOTT TEXARKANA   430/200-0742
♦ **THREE DIAMOND** SAVE Extended Stay Hotel. **Address:** 3900 St Michael Dr 75503

AAA Benefit: Members save 5% or more!

TOWNEPLACE SUITES BY MARRIOTT   903/334-8800
♦ **APPROVED** SAVE Extended Stay Hotel. **Address:** 5020 N Cowhorn Creek Loop 75503

AAA Benefit: Members save 5% or more!

WHERE TO EAT

GRANDY'S   903/832-5206
♦ **APPROVED**   Comfort Food. Quick Serve. **Address:** 1720 Richmond Rd 75503

IRONWOOD GRILL   903/223-4644
♦ **APPROVED**   American. Casual Dining. **Address:** 4312 Morris Ln 75503

PECAN POINT GASTROPUB & BREWERY   903/306-0661
♦ **APPROVED**   American. Gastropub. **Address:** 213 Main St 75501

This ends the Texarkana section and resumes the alphabetical city listings for Arkansas.

VAN BUREN (C-1) pop. 22,791, elev. 406'

Settled in 1818, Van Buren is one of the oldest settlements in western Arkansas. It was a steamboat landing, a stage stop for the Butterfield Line from St. Louis to California, a main artery for commerce and the border between the Cherokee and Choctaw tribes.

A six-block downtown area has been restored to its late 19th-century appearance, complete with old-fashioned lamps and period storefronts. Included in the restoration project are the Albert Pike Schoolhouse, Crawford County Courthouse, University of Arkansas - Fort Smith Drennen-Scott House, Fairview Cemetery, Mount Olive Church and the waterfront.

Van Buren Visitor Center: Old Frisco Depot at 813 Main St., P.O. Box 1518, Van Buren, AR 72957. **Phone:** (800) 332-5889.

Self-guiding tours: The Van Buren Walking Tour features 52 stops. A brochure featuring a map of the path and descriptions of the stops is available from the visitor center.

Shopping: Stroll around Van Buren's downtown historic district, centering around Main Street. Antique dealers, book stores, gift and specialty shops and bistros fill quaint Victorian-era red-brick buildings.

ARKANSAS AND MISSOURI RAILROAD departs from 813 Main in the Old Frisco Depot. A 70-mile round-trip train ride travels through the Boston Mountains. The 2.5-hour ride in restored late 19th- and early 20th-century passenger cars takes passengers over three trestles, through the Winslow tunnel and offers scenic views of the mountains. An 80-mile, 3-hour trip from Fort Smith to Winslow departs from the Fort Smith Trolley Museum at 100 S. 4th St. *See also Springdale p. 65.*

Hours: Round-trips to Winslow depart Wed. and Fri.-Sat. at 11, May-Nov.; Fri.-Sat. at 11, in Apr. Round-trips from Fort Smith to Winslow Sat. at 11, Jan.-Mar. **Cost:** Van Buren-to-Winslow fare (Apr.-Sept.) $41-$85. Van Buren-to-Winslow fare (Oct.-Nov.) $51-$95. Fort Smith-to-Winslow fare $44-$88. Phone to confirm schedules and fares. Reservations are recommended. **Phone:** (479) 725-4017 or (800) 687-8600.

BEST WESTERN VAN BUREN INN   479/474-8100

APPROVED

Hotel

Best Western

AAA Benefit: Members save up to 15% and earn bonus points!

Address: 1903 N 6th St 72956 **Location:** I-40 exit 5, just n, then just e. **Facility:** 58 units. 2 stories (no elevator), exterior corridors. **Pool:** outdoor. **Activities:** exercise room. **Guest Services:** valet laundry. **Featured Amenity:** full hot breakfast.

HAMPTON INN BY HILTON VAN BUREN   479/471-7447
THREE DIAMOND SAVE Hotel. **Address:** 1916 N 6th St 72956

AAA Benefit: Members save up to 16%!

WHERE TO EAT

EL LORITO   479/410-2463
APPROVED Mexican. Casual Dining. **Address:** 511 Broadway St 72956

WASHINGTON (E-2) pop. 180, elev. 375'

Founded in 1825, Washington was a crossroads for travelers in every direction during the 1800s. The Southwest Trail, the earliest road across Arkansas, ran from Missouri through Little Rock and Washington to Fulton, near the Texas border. From 1831 to 1833 more than 3,000 Choctaw Indians, forcibly evicted from Mississippi, passed through Washington on their way to Oklahoma.

Texas frontiersman Sam Houston planned the Texas Revolution of 1835-36 in a Washington tavern in 1834. During the Civil War the town became the Confederate state capital after Little Rock fell to Union forces. In 1875 and again in 1883 fires destroyed much of the business district, and Washington's glory began to fade. In 1938 Hope replaced Washington as Hempstead county seat.

WEST MEMPHIS pop. 26,245

DAYS INN WEST MEMPHIS   870/735-8600
APPROVED Hotel. **Address:** 1100 Ingram Blvd 72301

HOLIDAY INN EXPRESS & SUITES WEST MEMPHIS
                                     870/733-0570
THREE DIAMOND Hotel. **Address:** 1007 E Service Rd 72301

LA QUINTA INN & SUITES WEST MEMPHIS 870/551-4453
THREE DIAMOND Hotel. **Address:** 1550 North 6th St 72301

RAMADA WEST MEMPHIS   870/732-1102
APPROVED Hotel. **Address:** 2003 E Service Rd 72301

RODEWAY INN   870/735-7185
APPROVED Hotel. **Address:** 3401 Service Loop Rd 72301

Sunflower field

The Sunflower State. The Jayhawker State. The Wheat State. Midway, U.S.A.

All are fitting nicknames for Kansas, a state where the history is rich and the landscape surprisingly varied.

However, a strong argument could be made for The Pioneer State as an apropos moniker. Indeed, the state has seen its fair share of visionaries and has been the site of enough famous firsts.

Atchison native Amelia Earhart was the first woman to fly solo across the Atlantic. Frank E. Petersen of Topeka was the first African-American brigadier general in the Marine Corps. Argonian Susan Madora Salter was the first female mayor in the United States.

Kansas was the first state to ratify the amendment that allowed African-Americans the right to vote. A pair of brothers borrowed $600 to open the first Pizza Hut restaurant. And Independence was the hometown of Miss Able, the first monkey in space.

Wheat

Kansas

Kansas entrepreneurs invented the autopilot, the helicopter and the Oh Henry! candy bar. And native Walter P. Chrysler founded a cornerstone of the American automobile industry: the Chrysler Corporation.

Constant winds stir much more than fields of grain and flowers. They blow in ideas, visions and dreams.

More Than Just Flatlands

Fields of sunflowers stretch heavenward, their vivid yellow blooms jumping out of a subtle background of azure blue sky. Stalks of wheat bend to and fro as the wind blows fickle over the plains. Ruts of wagon wheels give evidence of a westward migration that rumbled across the Santa Fe Trail.

Explore sand dunes and irregular hills in the lowlands of the Arkansas River; rugged canyons and rocky bluffs around the lake at Historic Lake Scott State Park, north of Scott City; and salt mines and marshland near Wellington and McPherson.

Kansas boasts maple forests, the rolling Smoky Hills, Cimarron National Grasslands in its southwestern corner and scores of fence posts cut from rock due to a short supply of timber.

The posts aren't the only rock oddities. Many of the Mushroom Rocks, near Kanopolis Lake in Ellsworth County, resemble the giant fungus on which Alice found the contemplative, smoking caterpillar in "Alice in Wonderland." Elephant Rock, near Oberlin, suggests the hulking presence of a pachyderm.

Scenic wonders aren't all that make Kansas exceptional. The colorful characters who left behind volumes of legend and lore certainly set the state apart.

During its Wild West days, Kansas embraced a population in an epic struggle of good vs. evil. Peace officers James "Wild Bill" Hickok, Wyatt Earp and William "Bat" Masterson fought valiantly in towns such as Abilene, Dodge City and Wichita to curb the lawless elements—gunslingers, swindlers, brothel keepers and the like.

Meanwhile, outlaws set out to pillage and destroy. Of the three brothers in the notorious Dalton Gang, only Emmett survived a botched bank robbery in Coffeyville; Bob and Grat were shot dead. And Jesse James had a hand in a Lawrence raid that left more than 200 citizens dead and $1.5 million in damages.

Long documented in the annals of mystery is the fate of Atchison native Amelia Earhart, the intrepid aviator whose disappearance during an attempt to fly around the world endures as a puzzle unsolved.

The history and geography of Kansas can appeal to almost anyone. Even Dorothy, after her exotic adventures along the Yellow Brick Road and in the Emerald City, was eager to return to her aunt and uncle back home.

Recreation

In Kansas, ask not for whom the wind blows; it blows for thee. You might as well put the blustery gusts to good use.

When the air is moving, grab a sailboard and go windsurfing. Short, choppy waves give you a rough, but thrilling, ride on Cheney Lake, west of Wichita. If you like your rides smooth and speedy, head east out of Wichita to Eldorado Lake. Both lakes also are popular for sailing.

If the winds are blowing the same direction as the rivers are flowing, then it's a good day to go canoeing. A popular spot is the Fall River; rent a canoe in Eureka. Other waters that beckon to the paddler include the Kansas, Arkansas, Marais des Cygnes, Smoky Hill and Blue rivers.

Among the hottest spots for swimming, boating and water skiing are Shawnee Mission Park, northwest of Lenexa; John Redmond Reservoir, northwest of Burlington; and Lake Garnett, in Garnett.

Fishing is excellent in the basin below Webster Dam, where catches of trout (during the fall and winter), bass, catfish, crappie and bluegill are common. Drop a line in Keith Sebelius Reservoir, west of Norton,

where trophy wipers—hybrids of white and striped bass—put up a ferocious fight. Contact the Kansas Department of Wildlife, Parks and Tourism for information about fishing regulations and licensing; phone (620) 672-5911.

For a leisurely bicycle ride, try the Prairie Spirit Trail State Park, which runs between Ottawa and Welda. If you lean towards more grueling mountain biking adventures, head to Clinton Lake, southwest of Lawrence, where the 25-mile loop teems with protruding rocks, thick vegetation and soft soil.

To experience Kansas as the pioneers did, saddle up a horse and head to Horsethief Canyon in Kanopolis State Park. The park's 26 miles of multiuse trails are ideal for horseback riding. A 22-mile horseback trail follows the south side of Melvern Reservoir, south of Osage City.

Although it won't require much of an expenditure of sweat, an ascent up the state's highest point—4,039-foot Mount Sunflower, near the Colorado border in Wallace County- might provide some comic relief. At the less-than-daunting summit is a sunflower crafted of rail spikes, a rail fence and a mailbox that holds a log in which you can record your impressive feat.

Trout fishing

Historic Timeline

1804	Exploring the Louisiana Purchase territory, Meriwether Lewis and William Clark camp along the Missouri River.
1854	The Kansas-Nebraska Act is passed, and the Kansas Territory opens for settlement.
1862	The Homestead Act offers citizens federal land for a small fee and the promise to live on and improve the land for 5 years.
1899	In Medicine Lodge, prohibitionist Carry Nation begins her crusade against the consumption of liquor.
1917	The demands of World War I bring an agriculture boom to Kansas.
1953	Dwight D. Eisenhower, who grew up in Abilene, enters the White House.
1954	The Supreme Court decision in Brown vs. The Topeka Board of Education opens the door for school desegregation nationwide.
1978	Nancy Landon Kassebaum becomes the first Kansas woman elected to the U.S. Senate.
1993	Floods damage or destroy nearly one-fifth of the state's farmland.
1996	Native son Senator Bob Dole unsuccessfully runs for president.
2007	The town of Greensburg, ravaged by a tornado, begins an ongoing process to sustainably rebuild using only green techniques.

What To Pack

Temperature Averages Maximum/Minimum	JANUARY	FEBRUARY	MARCH	APRIL	MAY	JUNE	JULY	AUGUST	SEPTEMBER	OCTOBER	NOVEMBER	DECEMBER
Concordia	36 / 17	43 / 22	54 / 31	64 / 41	74 / 52	85 / 62	91 / 67	88 / 66	80 / 56	68 / 44	51 / 31	40 / 21
Dodge City	41 / 19	48 / 24	57 / 31	67 / 41	76 / 52	87 / 62	93 / 67	91 / 66	82 / 57	70 / 44	55 / 30	44 / 22
Goodland	39 / 16	45 / 20	53 / 26	63 / 35	72 / 46	84 / 56	89 / 61	87 / 60	78 / 50	66 / 38	50 / 25	41 / 18
Hays	39 / 15	46 / 20	55 / 29	66 / 40	75 / 51	86 / 61	92 / 66	90 / 64	81 / 54	70 / 41	53 / 27	43 / 18
Topeka	37 / 17	44 / 23	55 / 33	66 / 43	75 / 53	85 / 63	89 / 68	88 / 65	80 / 56	69 / 44	53 / 32	41 / 22
Wichita	40 / 20	47 / 25	57 / 34	67 / 44	76 / 54	87 / 64	93 / 69	92 / 68	82 / 59	70 / 47	55 / 34	43 / 24

From the records of The Weather Channel Interactive, Inc.

Good Facts To Know

ABOUT THE STATE

POPULATION: 2,688,418.

AREA: 82,278 square miles; ranks 15th.

CAPITAL: Topeka.

HIGHEST POINT: 4,039 ft., Mount Sunflower.

LOWEST POINT: 680 ft., Verdigris River.

TIME ZONE(S): Central/Mountain. DST.

REGULATIONS

TEEN DRIVING LAWS: Unless supervised, drivers under 16 are permitted to drive only to and from school or work and are not permitted to transport non-sibling passengers. Beginning at age 16, driving is not permitted 9 p.m.-5 a.m., and no more than one non-immediate family member under 18 may be a passenger. The minimum age for an unrestricted driver's license is 16 years, 6 months. For more information about Kansas driver's license regulations, phone (785) 296-3963.

SEAT BELT/CHILD RESTRAINT LAWS: Seat belts are required for driver and passengers 14 and older. Children ages 8-13, more than 80 pounds and taller than 57 inches are required to be in a child restraint or seat belt; child restraints are required for under age 8, less than 80 pounds and less than 57 inches. AAA recommends the use of seat belts and appropriate child restraints for the driver and all passengers.

CELLPHONE RESTRICTIONS: The use of a wireless communication device while driving is prohibited for instruction permit as well as restricted class C and M driver's license holders. Text messaging is prohibited for all drivers.

HELMETS FOR MOTORCYCLISTS: Required for riders under 18.

RADAR DETECTORS: Permitted. Prohibited for use by commercial vehicles.

MOVE OVER LAW: Driver is required to slow down and vacate the lane nearest stopped police, fire and rescue vehicles using audible or flashing signals. Law also requires driver to move over for tow truck drivers assisting motorists and municipal vehicles.

FIREARMS LAWS: Vary by state and/or county. Contact the Kansas Attorney General, Concealed Carry Licensing Unit, 120 S.W. 10th Ave., 2nd Floor, Topeka, KS 66612-1597; phone (785) 291-3765.

HOLIDAYS

HOLIDAYS: Jan. 1 ▪ Martin Luther King Jr. Day, Jan. (3rd Mon.) ▪ Washington's Birthday/President's Day, Feb. (3rd Mon.) ▪ Memorial Day, May (last Mon.) ▪ July 4 ▪ Labor Day, Sept. (1st Mon.) ▪ Columbus Day, Oct. (2nd Mon.) ▪ Veterans Day, Nov. 11 ▪ Thanksgiving, Nov. (last Thurs.) and following Fri. ▪ Christmas, Dec. 25.

MONEY

TAXES: The Kansas statewide sales tax is 6.5 percent (effective July 1, 2015), with local options for an additional increment up to 5 percent. Cities and counties also may levy a tax on lodgings; rates range from 1 to 5 percent.

VISITOR INFORMATION

INFORMATION CENTERS: State welcome centers are at Belle Plaine on I-35N as well as at I-70E Milepost 7 at Goodland. There are 14 community-owned welcome centers located throughout the state. Most information centers are open daily (except holidays) 8-6, May 15-Sept. 15 ▪ 9-5, rest of year.

FURTHER INFORMATION FOR VISITORS:
Kansas Department of Wildlife, Parks and Tourism
1020 S. Kansas Ave.
Suite 200
Topeka, KS 66612-1354
(785) 296-2009
(785) 296-3487 (TTY)

FISHING AND HUNTING REGULATIONS:
Kansas Department of Wildlife, Parks and Tourism
(Operations Office)
512 S.E. 25th Ave.
Pratt, KS 67124-8147
(620) 672-5911

RECREATION INFORMATION:
Kansas Department of Wildlife, Parks and Tourism
(Operations Office)
512 S.E. 25th Ave.
Pratt, KS 67124-8147
(620) 672-5911

ROAD AND WEATHER INFORMATION:
(800) 585-7623 (511 inside Kansas)

🔗 **For complete hotel, dining and attraction listings: AAA.com/travelguides**

Kansas Annual Events

Please call ahead to confirm event details.

Visit AAA.com/travelguides/events to find
AAA-listed events for every day of the year

WINTER

Dec. - Illuminations at Botanica, The Wichita Gardens / Wichita / 316-264-0448
- The Arc's Lights / Wichita 316-943-1191

Jan. - Starbird-Devlin Rod & Customs Charities Car Show / Wichita 316-734-2072
- Kaw Valley Eagles Day / Lawrence 785-843-3809

Feb. - Antiques and Collectible Show and Sale / Larned / 620-285-6916
- Kansas Silent Film Festival / Topeka 785-670-1100
- Kansas City Golf Show / Overland Park / 425-412-7070

SPRING

Mar. - KU Jazz Festival Concerts Lawrence / 785-864-3436
- St. Patrick's Day Parade and Celtic Street Fair / Topeka / 785-234-9336
- Mid America Farm Exposition / Salina 785-827-9301

Apr. - Wichita Jazz Festival / Wichita 316-978-6723
- Garmin Marathon in the Land of Oz Olathe / 913-764-1050

May - Fort Larned Memorial Day Weekend Larned / 620-285-6911

SUMMER

June - Smoky Hill River Festival / Salina 785-309-5770
- Riverfest / Wichita / 316-267-2817
- Country Stampede / Manhattan 785-539-2222

July - Wild West Festival / Hays 785-623-4476
- Amelia Earhart Festival / Atchison 913-367-2427
- Four State Farm Show / Pittsburg 800-356-8255

Aug. - Tumbleweed Festival / Garden City / 620-275-9141
- Dodge City Days / Dodge City / 620-227-3119

FALL

Sept. - Huff 'n Puff Hot Air Balloon Rally Topeka / 785-554-2003

Oct. - Bethel College Fall Festival / North Newton / 316-283-2500
- Neewollah Festival / Independence 877-633-9655

Nov. - Trail of Lights / Great Bend / 620-792-2750
- Miracle on Kansas Avenue Parade Topeka / 785-234-9336
- All Veterans Tribute Celebration Emporia / 620-342-1803

Sedgwick County Zoo, Wichita

The Old Mill Tasty Shop, Wichita

Kansas Cosmosphere and Space Center, Hutchinson

Union Station, Kansas City

Huff 'n Puff Hot Air Balloon Rally, Topeka

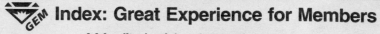

Index: Great Experience for Members

AAA editor's picks of exceptional note

Eisenhower
Presidential Library
and Museum

Rolling Hills Zoo

Cosmosphere

State Capitol

See Orientation map on p. 84 for corresponding grid coordinates, if applicable.
*Indicates the GEM is temporarily closed.

Abilene (C-6)
Eisenhower Presidential Library and Museum
(See p. 88.)

Hays (C-4)
Sternberg Museum of Natural History
(See p. 98.)

Hutchinson (D-5)
Cosmosphere *(See p. 99.)*

Lawrence (C-7)
Spencer Museum of Art *(See p. 103.)*
University of Kansas Natural History Museum
(See p. 104.)

Leavenworth (B-8)
Frontier Army Museum *(See p. 105.)*

Liberal (F-2)
Mid-America Air Museum *(See p. 106.)*

North Newton (D-5)
Kauffman Museum *(See p. 110.)*

Salina (C-5)
Rolling Hills Zoo *(See p. 115.)*

Topeka (C-7)
Kansas Historical Society *(See p. 118.)*
State Capitol *(See p. 118.)*

Wichita (E-5)
Exploration Place *(See p. 120.)*
Kansas Sports Hall of Fame *(See p. 121.)*
Museum of World Treasures *(See p. 121.)*
Sedgwick County Zoo *(See p. 121.)*

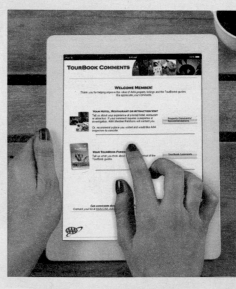

Save time and stay secure year-round

Continue receiving the benefits you love year after year. Renew your AAA membership or inquire about auto renewal. Leave your worries behind and enjoy everyday member savings, travel services, roadside assistance, and competitive financial and insurance services, and more!

Renew your membership today:
- Online at AAA.com/membership
- Visit your local club office
- Call 800-Join-AAA (564-6222)

Kansas

Atlas Section

ROADS/HIGHWAYS
- INTERSTATE
- CONTROLLED ACCESS
- CONTROLLED ACCESS TOLL
- TOLL ROAD
- PRIMARY DIVIDED
- PRIMARY UNDIVIDED
- SECONDARY DIVIDED
- SECONDARY UNDIVIDED
- LOCAL DIVIDED
- LOCAL UNDIVIDED
- UNPAVED ROAD
- UNDER CONSTRUCTION
- TUNNEL
- PEDESTRIAN ONLY
- AUTO FERRY
- PASSENGER FERRY
- SCENIC BYWAY
- **10** DISTANCE BETWEEN MARKERS
- EXIT NUMBER-FREE/TOLL
- INTERCHANGE FULL/PARTIAL
- WELCOME/INFORMATION CENTER
- REST AREA/ SERVICE CENTER

BOUNDARIES
- INTERNATIONAL
- STATE
- COUNTY
- TIME ZONE
- CONTINENTAL DIVIDE

ROAD SHIELDS
- **95 95** INTERSTATE/BUSINESS
- **22 22 22** U.S./STATE/COUNTY
- **127 127** FOREST/INDIAN
- TRANS- CANADA
- **1** PROVINCIAL AUTOROUTE/ KING'S HIGHWAY
- **1** MEXICO
- **66** HISTORIC ROUTE 66
- **VT 41** REFERENCE PAGE INDICATOR

AREAS OF INTEREST
- INDIAN
- MILITARY
- PARK
- FOREST
- GRASSLANDS
- HISTORIC
- INT'L/REGIONAL AIRPORT
- INCORPORATED CITY

POINTS OF INTEREST
- ○ TOWN
- NATIONAL CAPITAL
- STATE/PROVINCIAL CAPITAL
- AAA/CAA CLUB LOCATION
- FEATURE OF INTEREST
- COLLEGE/UNIVERSITY
- CUSTOMS STATION
- HISTORIC
- LIGHTHOUSE
- MONUMENT/MEMORIAL
- STATE/PROVINCIAL PARK
- NATIONAL WILDLIFE REFUGE
- SKI AREA
- SPORTS COMPLEX
- DAM

CITIES/TOWNS are color-coded by size, showing where to find AAA Inspected and Approved lodgings or restaurants listed in the AAA TourBook guides and on AAA.com:

- ● Red - major destinations and capitals; many listings
- ● Black - destinations; some listings
- ● Grey - no listings

AAA ROAD Atlas 2020
UNITED STATES · CANADA · MEXICO

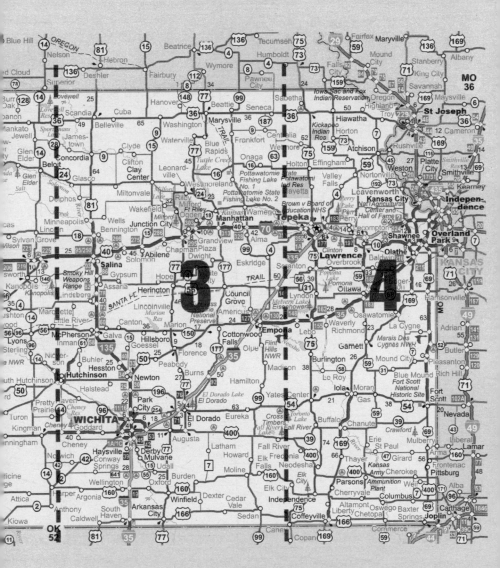

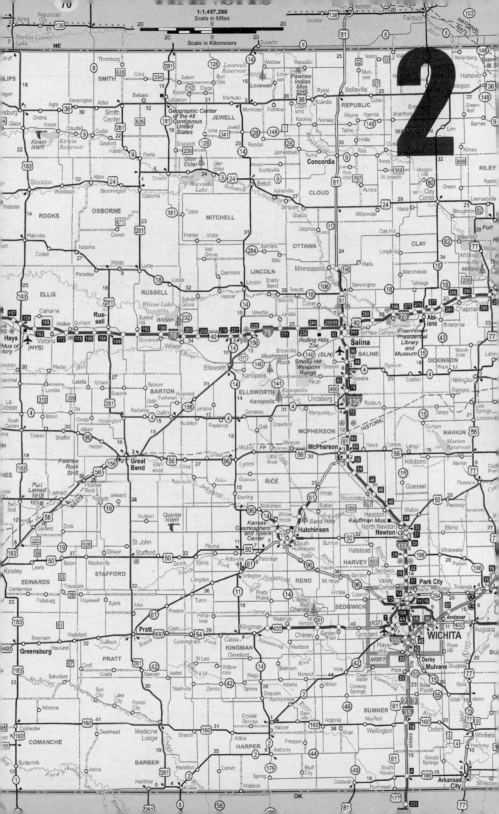

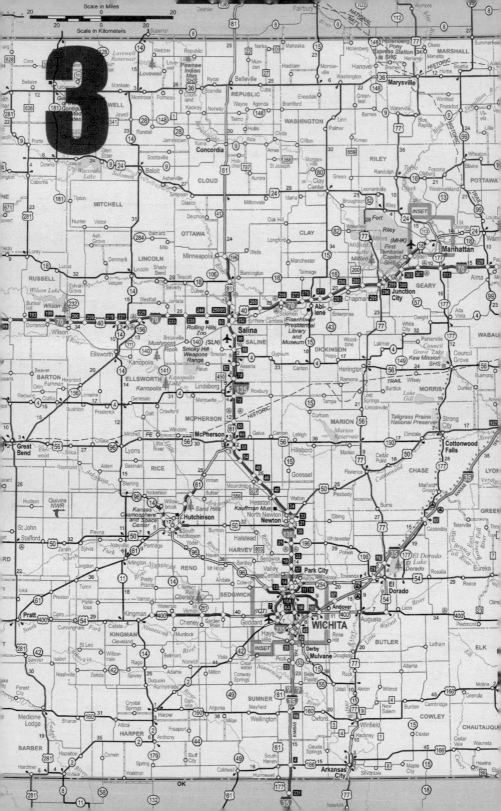

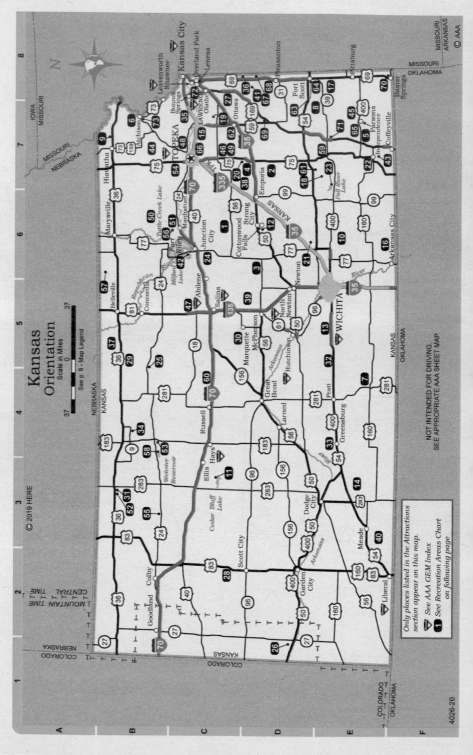

Kansas Orientation

Scale in Miles

See p. 6 - Map Legend

Only places listed in the Attractions section appear on this map.

See AAA GEM Index

See Recreation Areas Chart on following page

NOT INTENDED FOR DRIVING.
SEE APPROPRIATE AAA SHEET MAP.

© 2019 HERE

4026-20

© AAA

Recreation Areas Chart

The map location numerals in column 2 show an area's location on the preceding map.

Find thousands of places to camp at AAA.com/campgrounds

	MAP LOCATION	CAMPING	PICNICKING	HIKING TRAILS	BOATING	BOAT RAMP	BOAT RENTAL	FISHING	SWIMMING	PET FRIENDLY	BICYCLE TRAILS	WINTER SPORTS	VISITOR CENTER	LODGE/CABINS	FOOD SERVICE
ARMY CORPS OF ENGINEERS															
Council Grove Reservoir (C-6) 3,310 acres in Council Grove. ATV area, beach.	1	•	•	•	•	•		•	•	•	•		•		
John Redmond Reservoir (D-7) 9,400 acres 2 mi. n., then 1 mi. w. of Burlington off US 75. Horseback riding, hunting, water skiing; all-terrain vehicle trails.	2	•	•	•	•	•		•		•	•		•		
Marion Reservoir (D-6) 6,200 acres 3 mi. n.w. of Marion on the Cottonwood River off US 56. Hunting; beach, nature trail.	3	•	•	•	•	•		•	•	•	•				
Melvern Lake (D-7) 18,000 acres 30 mi. e. of Emporia off SR 276. Hunting; beach.	4	•	•	•	•	•	•	•	•	•	•		•	•	
Pearson-Skubitz Big Hill Lake (E-7) 1,200 acres 4.5 mi. e. of Cherryvale off county roads. Bird watching, disc golf, horseback riding.	5	•	•	•	•	•		•	•	•					
STATE															
Atchison State Fishing Lake (B-7) 66 acres 3.5 mi. n. and 2 mi. w. of Atchison off SR 7 at 318th St. Hunting.	6	•	•		•	•		•		•				•	
Barber State Fishing Lake (E-4) 190 acres .2 mi. n. of Medicine Lodge off US 281. Nature trail.	7	•	•	•	•	•		•		•					
Bourbon State Fishing Lake (D-7) 380 acres 4 mi. e. of Elsmore off US 59. Hunting.	8	•	•		•	•		•		•					
Brown State Fishing Lake (B-7) 148 acres 8 mi. s.e. of Hiawatha off US 36. Hunting.	9	•	•		•	•		•		•					
Butler State Fishing Lake (E-6) 320 acres 3 mi. n.w. of Latham off a county road. Hunting.	10	•	•		•	•		•		•					
Cedar Bluff (C-3) 900 acres 36 mi. s.w. of Hays off SR 147. Hunting; beach, playground.	11	•	•		•	•		•	•	•	•		•	•	•
Chase State Fishing Lake (D-6) 492 acres 2 mi. e. of Elmdale in Flint Hills. Bird watching, hunting.	12	•	•		•	•		•	•	•					
Cheney (E-5) 1,913 acres 20 mi. w. of Wichita via US 54 and SR 251 at 16000 N.E. 50th St. Hunting.	13	•	•	•	•	•		•	•	•	•		•	•	•
Clark State Fishing Lake (E-3) 1,243 acres 11 mi. s.w. of Kingsdown on SR 94. Hunting.	14	•	•		•	•		•		•			•		
Clinton (C-7) 1,500 acres 9 mi. s.w. of Lawrence off SR 10 at 798 N. 1415 Rd. Hunting; archery range, bicycle course, cross-country ski trail, fish cleaning station.	15	•	•	•	•	•	•	•	•	•	•	•	•	•	•
Cowley State Fishing Lake (E-6) 197 acres 13 mi. e. of Arkansas City off US 166. Hunting.	16	•	•		•	•		•		•					
Crawford (E-8) 589 acres 19 mi. s.w. of Fort Scott off SR 7 at 1 Lake Rd. Scuba diving, water skiing; playground.	17	•	•		•	•		•	•	•				•	•
Cross Timbers (D-7) 1,075 acres 12 mi. w. of Yates Center off US 54. Playground.	18	•	•	•	•	•		•	•	•			•	•	
Douglas State Fishing Lake (C-7) 718 acres n.e. of Baldwin City on US 56. Hunting.	19	•			•	•		•		•					
Eisenhower (C-7) 1,785 acres 4 mi. w. of Lawrence off US 40. Disc golf (18 holes), horseback riding, hunting; beach, playground, shooting range.	20	•	•	•	•	•		•	•	•	•		•		
El Dorado (D-6) 4,000 acres 3 mi. e., then 2 mi. n. of El Dorado on US 77 off US 54. Horseback riding, hunting; nature trail.	21	•	•	•	•	•		•	•	•	•		•		
Elk City (E-7) 857 acres 7 mi. n.w. of Independence off US 75. Playground.	22	•	•		•	•		•	•	•			•		
Fall River (E-7) 1,107 acres n.w. of Fall River next to Fall River Reservoir. Canoeing; playground.	23	•	•		•	•		•	•	•	•		•		
Geary State Fishing Lake (C-6) 179 acres 9 mi. s. of Junction City off US 77. Hunting.	24	•	•		•	•		•		•					
Glen Elder (B-5) 1,391 acres 12 mi. w. of Beloit on US 24. Marina, nature trails.	25	•	•	•	•	•	•	•	•	•			•	•	

Recreation Areas Chart

The map location numerals in column 2 show an area's location on the preceding map.

Find thousands of places to camp at AAA.com/campgrounds

	MAP LOCATION	CAMPING	PICNICKING	HIKING TRAILS	BOATING	BOAT RAMP	BOAT RENTAL	FISHING	SWIMMING	PET FRIENDLY	BICYCLE TRAILS	WINTER SPORTS	VISITOR CENTER	LODGE/CABINS	FOOD SERVICE
Hamilton State Fishing Lake (D-1) 620 acres 3 mi. w., then 2 mi. n. of Syracuse off US 50. Bird watching, hunting.	26	•		•	•	•		•		•					
Hillsdale (C-8) 2,830 acres 9 mi. n.w. of Paola off US 169. Horseback riding, hunting; model airplane field, shooting range.	27	•	•	•	•	•		•	•				•		
Historic Lake Scott (C-2) 1,020 acres 13 mi. n. of Scott City via US 83 and SR 95. Historic. Scenic. Canoeing, horseback riding, paddleboating, wildlife viewing; beach, equestrian and nature trails, historic buildings, playground, pueblo ruins.	28	•	•	•	•	•	•	•	•	•	•			•	
Jewell State Fishing Lake (B-5) 165 acres 10 mi. s.w. of Mankato on a county road. Hunting.	29	•	•		•	•		•	•						
Kanopolis (C-5) 1,585 acres 12 mi. s.e. of Kanopolis off SR 141. Horseback riding; beach, marina.	30	•	•	•				•	•	•	•		•	•	•
Keith Sebelius Reservoir (B-3) 700 acres 3 mi. w. of Norton off US 36. Also known as Norton Wildlife Area. Hunting.	31	•		•	•	•		•	•						
Kingman State Fishing Lake (E-5) 4,685 acres 8 mi. w. of Kingman on US 54. Bird watching, hunting; archery range.	32	•	•		•	•		•				•	•		
Kiowa State Fishing Lake (E-4) 43 acres just n.w. of Greensburg on Bay St.	33	•	•		•			•							
Kirwin Reservoir (B-4) 5,000 acres 15 mi. s.e. of Phillipsburg on SR 9. Hunting.	34			•	•	•	•	•		•	•				
Leavenworth State Fishing Lake (C-7) 341 acres 3 mi. w. and 1 mi. n. of Tonganoxie on SR 16. Hunting.	35	•	•		•	•		•	•						
Louisburg-Middle Creek State Fishing Lake (D-8) 281 acres 7 mi. s. of Louisburg on Metcalf Rd. Camping (primitive), hunting.	36	•			•	•		•							
Lovewell (B-5) 1,160 acres 15 mi. n.e. of Mankato off SR 14. Disc golf; beach, playground.	37	•	•	•	•	•	•	•	•	•	•		•	•	•
Lyon State Fishing Lake (D-7) 581 acres 11 mi. n.e. of Emporia on SR 170. Hunting; nature trail.	38	•	•	•	•	•		•	•						
McPherson State Fishing Lake (D-5) 2,245 acres 8 mi. n. of Canton off SR 86. Nature trail.	39	•	•	•	•	•		•						•	
Meade (E-3) 440 acres 12 mi. s.w. of Meade off SR 23. Kayaking, paddleboarding; beach.	40	•	•	•	•	•		•	•			•			
Miami State Fishing Lake (D-8) 267 acres 8 mi. e., then 5 mi. s. of Osawatomie off county roads. Hunting.	41	•		•	•	•		•							
Milford (C-6) 16,000 acres 4 mi. n.w. of Junction City on SR 57. Horseback riding; beach, marina, nature trails.	42	•	•	•	•	•	•	•	•	•			•	•	
Montgomery State Fishing Lake (E-7) 408 acres 4 mi. s. of Independence via county road.	43	•	•	•	•	•		•							
Nebo State Fishing Lake (B-7) 65 acres 7 mi. e., then 1 mi. s. of Holton on SR 116. Hunting.	44	•	•		•	•		•	•						
Neosho State Fishing Lake (E-7) 216 acres 7 mi. n.e. of Parsons off US 59.	45	•	•	•	•	•		•	•						
Osage State Fishing Lake (C-7) 506 acres 3 mi. s. of Carbondale off US 75. Hunting.	46	•	•	•	•	•		•	•						
Ottawa State Fishing Lake (C-5) 711 acres 8 mi. e. of Minneapolis on SR 106. Hunting.	47	•	•		•	•		•	•					•	
Perry (C-7) 1,597 acres 16 mi. n.e. of Topeka off US 24. Equestrian camping, horseback riding; ATV area.	48	•	•	•	•	•	•	•	•	•	•		•	•	•
Pomona (C-7) 490 acres 2 mi. n.e. of Vassar on SR 268. Disc golf (9 holes); playground.	49	•	•	•	•	•	•	•	•	•					
Pottawatomie State Fishing Lake No. 1 (B-6) 190 acres 5 mi. n. of Westmoreland on SR 99.	50	•	•		•	•		•							
Pottawatomie State Fishing Lake No. 2 (C-6) 247 acres 4 mi. n. of Manhattan off US 24.	51	•	•		•	•		•	•						
Prairie Dog (B-3) 1,150 acres 4 mi. w. of Norton on US 36. Historic. Beach.	52	•	•		•	•		•	•	•			•	•	

Recreation Areas Chart

The map location numerals in column 2 show an area's location on the preceding map.

🔗 **Find thousands of places to camp at AAA.com/campgrounds**

	MAP LOCATION	CAMPING	PICNICKING	HIKING TRAILS	BOATING	BOAT RAMP	BOAT RENTAL	FISHING	SWIMMING	PET FRIENDLY	BICYCLE TRAILS	WINTER SPORTS	VISITOR CENTER	LODGE/CABINS	FOOD SERVICE
Rooks State Fishing Lake (B-4) 313 acres 5 mi. s.w. of Stockton off US 183.	53	•	•		•	•		•		•					
Shawnee State Fishing Lake (C-7) 400 acres 3 mi. n.e. of Silver Lake off US 24. Hunting.	54	•	•		•	•		•		•					
Sheridan State Fishing Lake (B-3) 248 acres 3 mi. w. of Studley off US 24.	55	•	•		•	•		•		•					
Tuttle Creek (B-6) 13,350 acres 5 mi. n. of Manhattan on SR 177. Equestrian camping, horseback riding, hunting; beach.	56	•	•	•	•	•	•	•	•	•	•			•	•
Washington State Fishing Lake (B-5) 417 acres 12 mi. n.w. of Washington off county roads. Hunting.	57	•	•		•	•		•		•					
Webster (B-4) 880 acres 8 mi. w. of Stockton off US 24. Scenic. Bird-watching; beach.	58	•	•	•	•	•	•	•		•				•	•
Wilson State Fishing Lake (E-7) 291 acres 1.5 mi. s.e. of Buffalo on US 75.	59	•	•		•	•		•		•					
Wilson (C-4) 927 acres 10 mi. n. of Wilson via SR 232. Water skiing; beach, marina.	60	•	•	•	•	•	•	•	•	•	•			•	•
Woodson State Fishing Lake (D-7) 2,885 acres 10 mi. s.w. of Yates Center off US 54. Bird watching, hunting.	61	•	•		•	•		•		•					
OTHER															
Forest Park (C-7) 50 acres off Tecumseh and N. Locust sts. at Ottawa on the Marais des Cygnes River. Tennis (lighted); playground, swimming pool.	62		•							•	•				
Gunn Park (D-7) 155 acres on the w. side of Fort Scott. Disc golf (18 holes).	63	•	•		•		•	•		•					
Lake Fort Scott (D-8) 360 acres 4 mi. s.w. of Fort Scott on Lake Rd. Water skiing.	64	•	•		•	•		•	•	•					
Lake Parsons (E-7) 2,200 acres 3 mi. n. of Parsons on US 59, then 3 mi. w. on 20th Road. Beach.	65	•	•		•	•		•	•	•					
Lake Shawnee (C-7) 410 acres s.e. of Topeka just outside city limits on E. 29th St. Canoes, disc golf, golf (18 holes), tennis; beach, paddleboats.	66	•	•	•	•	•	•	•	•	•	•				
Linn County Park (D-8) 2,600 acres 5 mi. e. of La Cygne off US 69 at La Cygnes Lake. Horseback riding, hunting; marina.	67	•	•		•	•		•		•					•
Marais Des Cygnes Waterfowl Refuge (D-8) 7,600 acres 7 mi. n. of Pleasanton off US 69. Hunting.	68	•	•	•				•		•					
North Lake Park (D-7) 55 acres in downtown Garnett at Lake Garnett. Golf (18 holes), tennis, water skiing; fishing dock, race track, swimming pool.	69	•	•		•	•		•	•	•	•	•	•		
Riverside Park (E-8) In downtown Baxter Springs off US 166 at Spring River. Playground.	70	•	•		•	•		•		•					
Santa Fe Park (E-7) 249 acres 2 mi. s. of Chanute on Santa Fe Ave.	71	•	•		•	•		•	•	•					
Shawnee Mission Park (C-8) 1,236 acres 5 mi. n.w. of Lenexa off I-435 exit 5 at 7900 Renner Rd. Disc golf (18 holes), horseback riding, windsurfing; archery range, beach, dog park, marina, theater.	72		•	•	•	•	•	•	•	•	•	•	•	•	
Warnock Lake (B-7) 39 acres 2 mi. s.w. of Atchison at 17862 274th Rd. Fishing pier, playground.	73	•	•		•	•		•		•					

🔗 **For complete hotel, dining and attraction listings: AAA.com/travelguides**

ABILENE (C-6) pop. 6,844, elev. 1,155'

Though its name is of biblical origin, Abilene once was one of the unholiest and wildest towns in the West. Its reputation grew along with the city as hundreds of cowboys came to the town along the historic Chisholm Trail during the late 1800s. Nearly 3 million Texas longhorns passed through Abilene 1867-72 to be shipped east by rail. James "Wild Bill" Hickok, whose deadly accuracy with two pistols was as legendary as his icy willingness to use them, was marshal of the town in 1871.

Still, fame was not quite through with the City on the Plains; Dwight David Eisenhower, first the Supreme Allied Commander during World War II and then the 34th president of the United States, spent his boyhood years in Abilene. As president, he signed a truce to end the Korean War and passed the Federal Aid Highway Act in 1956, which created the present-day interstate highway system.

Eisenhower Park, a 57-acre tract near W. Third and Poplar sts., includes Bill Gravette Sports Complex; a swimming pool; basketball, tennis and sand volleyball courts; a skate park; picnic grounds; and landscaped gardens. The park also is the site of a fair and rodeo each year in late July-early August. Phone (785) 263-7266.

Great Plains Theatre, a live professional theater, presents Broadway plays June through December; phone (785) 263-4574. The city also is a major center for greyhound enthusiasts.

Abilene Convention & Visitors Bureau: 201 N.W. Second St., Abilene, KS 67410. **Phone:** (785) 263-2231 or (800) 569-5915.

Self-guiding tours: A free brochure detailing a tour past the historic houses of Abilene and Dickinson County is available from the visitors bureau and from Dickinson County Heritage Center and Museum.

EISENHOWER PRESIDENTIAL LIBRARY AND MUSEUM, 2 mi. s. of I-70 on SR 15 at 200 S.E. Fourth St., covers 22 acres of landscaped grounds and consists of five buildings, including the visitor center, in which a 23-minute orientation film is shown; the boyhood home of President Eisenhower; the presidential library; a museum detailing the president's life; and the final resting place of Dwight D. and Mamie Doud Eisenhower. **Time:** Allow 3 hours minimum. **Hours:** Grounds daily dawn-dusk. Museums and library daily 8-5:45, June-July; 9-4:45, rest of year. **Cost:** Grounds and visitor center free. Museums and library $12; $9 (ages 62+); $3 (ages 6-15); free (ages 0-5 and active military with ID). **Phone:** (785) 263-6700 or (877) 746-4453.

Eisenhower Home, on the grounds of Eisenhower Presidential Library and Museum, 200 S.E. Fourth St., was the boyhood home of President Dwight David Eisenhower. Representative of family houses in Kansas during the late 19th century, the frame house is kept as it was in 1946. **Hours:** Daily 8-5:45, June-July; 9-4:45, rest of year. **Cost:** (Includes

Eisenhower Museum and Eisenhower Presidential Library) $12; $9 (ages 62+); $3 (ages 6-15); free (ages 0-5 and active military with ID). **Phone:** (785) 263-6700 or (877) 746-4453.

Eisenhower Museum is on the grounds of Eisenhower Presidential Library and Museum, 200 S.E. Fourth St. The museum is constructed of Kansas limestone and features multiple galleries with items relating to President Dwight David Eisenhower's life and experiences from boyhood to the post-presidential years. Murals in the lobby depict events from Eisenhower's life and career.

Hours: Daily 8-5:45, June-July; 9-4:45, rest of year. **Cost:** (Includes Eisenhower Home and Eisenhower Presidential Library) $12; $9 (ages 62+); $3 (ages 6-15); free (ages 0-5 and active military with ID). **Phone:** (785) 263-6700 or (877) 746-4453.

Eisenhower Presidential Library, on the grounds of Eisenhower Presidential Library and Museum, 200 S.E. Fourth St., houses the papers, books and historical materials accumulated by Eisenhower during his military career and his term of office. While the archives are available to researchers only, a gallery of changing exhibits is open to all visitors. Anyone may apply as a researcher.

The extensive use of imported marble in the building's interior is offset by the Kansas limestone of the exterior. **Hours:** Daily 8-5:45, June-July; 9-4:45, rest of year. **Cost:** (Includes Eisenhower Home and Eisenhower Museum) $12; $9 (ages 62+); $3 (ages 6-15); free (ages 0-5 and active military with ID). **Phone:** (785) 263-6700 or (877) 746-4453.

Place of Meditation, on the grounds of Eisenhower Presidential Library and Museum, 200 S.E. Fourth St., is the final resting place of Dwight D. and Mamie Doud Eisenhower and their firstborn son, Doud Dwight Eisenhower. **Hours:** Daily dawn-dusk. **Cost:** Free. **Phone:** (785) 263-6700 or (877) 746-4453.

MUSEUM OF INDEPENDENT TELEPHONY is at 412 S. Campbell St., in the same building as Dickinson County Heritage Center and Museum. The museum relates the history of the telephone and its early independent proprietors since the original patent was issued to Alexander Graham Bell in 1876. Included are interactive exhibits of antique phones, insulators and switchboards. An outdoor exhibit includes an antique carousel, a blacksmith display and a log cabin.

Hours: Mon.-Fri. 9-4, Sat. 10-8, Sun. 1-5, Memorial Day-Labor Day; Mon.-Fri. 9-3, Sat. 10-5, Sun. 1-5, rest of year. Closed Jan. 1, Thanksgiving, Sun. after Thanksgiving and Dec. 21-31. **Cost:** Includes Dickinson County Heritage Center and Museum $6; $5 (ages 62+); $2 (ages 2-14; includes ride on carousel). Carousel $2. **Phone:** (785) 263-2681.

HOLIDAY INN EXPRESS HOTEL & SUITES 785/263-4049
▼▼▼ **APPROVED** Hotel. **Address:** 110 E Lafayette Ave 67410

WHERE TO EAT

BROOKVILLE HOTEL 785/263-2244
▼▼▼ **APPROVED** American. Casual Dining. **Address:** 105 E Lafayette Ave 67410

MR K'S FARMHOUSE RESTAURANT 785/263-7995
▼▼▼ APPROVED American. Casual Dining. Address: 407 S Van Buren St 67410

ANDOVER pop. 11,791

DAYS INN ANDOVER 316/733-0001
▼▼▼ **APPROVED**
Motel
Address: 222 W US Hwy 54 67002 **Location:** 2.2 mi e of jct SR 96. **Facility:** 38 units. 2 stories (no elevator), exterior corridors. **Pool:** outdoor. **Guest Services:** coin laundry.

[SAVE] [⊺↟⊹] [🚲] [BIZ] [🛜] [🔲] [🖨] / SOME UNITS [🐾]

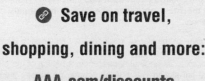

HOLIDAY INN EXPRESS & SUITES 316/733-8833
▼▼▼ THREE DIAMOND Hotel. **Address:** 600 S Allen St 67002

ARKANSAS CITY (F-6) pop. 12,415, elev. 1,075'

Arkansas (ar-KAN-sas) City's position, 4 miles north of the present Oklahoma border, made it a logical mustering point for one of the largest land rushes in the history of westward expansion. By the tens of thousands they lined up—eager boomers and homesteaders afoot, on horseback and with every horse-drawn conveyance possible—awaiting the gunshot that would signal the opening of the Cherokee Strip in 1893.

As the West lost its wildness, Arkansas City became what its Arkansas River site promised—a marketing and transportation center. The discovery of oil in the vicinity in the early 20th century added the refineries and other petroleum-related industries that dominated the economy through the middle part of the century.

Arkansas City Area Chamber of Commerce and Convention and Visitors Bureau: 106 S. Summit, Arkansas City, KS 67005. **Phone:** (620) 442-0230 or (620) 442-0236.

🔗 **Save on travel,**

shopping, dining and more:

AAA.com/discounts

BEST WESTERN PLUS PATTERSON PARK INN
620/307-6767
▼▼▼ THREE DIAMOND
Hotel

AAA Benefit: Members save up to 15% and earn bonus points!

Address: 6100 Patterson Pkwy 67005 **Location:** Just w of jct US 77. **Facility:** 69 units, some efficiencies. 3 stories, interior corridors. **Pool:** heated indoor. **Activities:** exercise room. **Guest Services:** coin laundry. **Featured Amenity:** full hot breakfast.

[SAVE] CALL [♿] [🚲] [👪] [BIZ] [HS] [🛜] [✕] [🔲] [🖨] [🖨] / SOME UNITS [🐾]

ATCHISON (B-7) pop. 11,021, elev. 798'

Independence Park, on the Atchison riverfront, marks where the Meriwether Lewis and William Clark expedition arrived on July 4, 1804. Five miles to the north lies Independence Creek, so named by Clark to commemorate the first Independence Day celebrated west of the Mississippi River.

Among the city's founders years after Lewis and Clark's travels were Benedictine monks, who established an abbey on the north bluffs, and the Benedictine Sisters, who started a convent. Atchison is known for the Atchison, Topeka & Santa Fe Railway, but before the railroad a steady stream of wagon and river traffic fed the infant town.

A marker at the Atchison courthouse commemorates a speech that Abraham Lincoln gave in 1859 and later delivered in the Cooper Union in New York City. The address brought Lincoln the recognition that resulted in his presidential nomination.

Atchison is the birthplace of Amelia Earhart, and monuments to the aviator can be seen at the downtown pedestrian mall, the International Forest of Friendship and Amelia Earhart Memorial Airport, 3 miles west. The Amelia Earhart Birthplace *(see attraction listing)* overlooks the Missouri River. In July the city hosts the 🎗 Amelia Earhart Festival, which features aerobatic performances, food, arts and crafts, games and a fireworks show.

The International Forest of Friendship honors aviation and aerospace pioneers. It features trees representing the 50 states, U.S. territories and 40 foreign countries. A "moon tree" grown from a sycamore seed taken to the moon on *Apollo 14* marks a memorial dedicated to the ill-fated Apollo and Challenger crews; a monument near the tree honors the Columbia crew. Memory Lane winds through the forest and offers tributes to Earhart, Charles Lindbergh, the Wright Brothers and others; phone (913) 367-1419.

The campus of Benedictine College, on the bluffs of the Missouri River, offers excellent views. Of interest near the campus are St. Benedict's Abbey, which is modeled after Benedictine monasteries of the Middle Ages, and the Abbey Chapel, which has 28 minor altars in its crypt.

Nearby Warnock Lake *(see Recreation Areas Chart)* features swimming, fishing, camping and picnic facilities. Just 3.5 miles north and 2 miles west of town on SR 7 to 318th Street is Atchison State Fishing Lake *(see Recreation Areas Chart)*, which also offers camping.

Atchison Area Chamber of Commerce: 200 S. 10th St., P.O. Box 126, Atchison, KS 66002. **Phone:** (913) 367-2427 or (800) 234-1854.

AMELIA EARHART BIRTHPLACE MUSEUM, overlooking the Missouri River at Santa Fe and N. Terrace sts., is the house where Amelia Earhart was born in 1897 and lived in until she was 12. The 1859 Victorian cottage on the bluffs of the Missouri River was owned by Earhart's grandparents. The house contains photographs, newspaper clippings and some of Earhart's belongings. **Time:** Allow 30 minutes minimum. **Hours:** Mon.-Fri. 9-4, Sat. 10-4, Sun. 1-4, mid-Feb. to mid-Dec.; Tues.-Sat. 10-4, Sun. 1-4, rest of year. **Cost:** $6; $1 (ages 0-12). **Phone:** (913) 367-4217.

THE MUCHNIC GALLERY is at 704 N. 4th St. A small art gallery resides in a three-story 1885 Queen Anne mansion built by a lumber merchant. The mansion is appointed with intricate parquet floors in various patterns, ornate carved woodwork, stained glass windows and a spiral staircase, as well as such antiques as Sevres porcelain, French furniture, oil paintings and mirrors. **Time:** Allow 30 minutes minimum. **Hours:** Sat.-Sun. and Wed. 1-5. **Cost:** Donations. **Phone:** (913) 367-4278.

BAXTER SPRINGS (F-8) pop. 4,238, elev. 843'

BAXTER SPRINGS HERITAGE CENTER AND MUSEUM is at 740 East Ave. The two-story facility's interpretive exhibits relate local history from the late 19th century and World Wars I and II as well as Native American history. Dioramas showcase books, clothing, letters, posters and other artifacts. An 1870s street display offers a blacksmith shop, and another interprets life in the 1930s and features a barber shop and beauty salon as well as dentist and optometrist offices.

Other displays interpret the significance of Route 66 and local mining history; many crystals, rocks and stones discovered in nearby mines are displayed in the Tri-State Mining Gallery. **Time:** Allow 2 hours minimum. **Hours:** Tues.-Sat. 10-4:30, Sun. 1-4. Closed major holidays. **Cost:** Donations. **Phone:** (620) 856-2385. GT

BELLEVILLE (B-5) pop. 1,991, elev. 1,550'

Located in north central Kansas, Belleville was founded in 1869 and named for early resident Anabelle Tutton. A Depression-era building boom, fueled by federal Works Project Administration (WPA) funding, resulted in many fine examples of Art Deco architecture, including the Republic County Courthouse.

A pond that formerly supplied water for Rock Island Railroad steam engines now provides year-round recreation. Rocky Pond Park offers picnicking, fishing, boating (electric motors only) and RV camping.

Belleville Chamber & Main Street: 1205 18th St., P.O. Box 261, Belleville, KS 66935. **Phone:** (785) 527-5524 or (866) 527-2355.

HIGH BANKS HALL OF FAME AND NATIONAL MIDGET AUTO RACING MUSEUM is 1.2 mi. n. of jct. US 36 and US 81 at 1204 H St. The museum preserves racing history and features vintage race cars, uniforms, flags, photographs and other memorabilia relating to all forms of auto racing. **Time:** Allow 30 minutes minimum. **Hours:** Tues.-Sun. 10-5, May 1-Apr. 30; 11-4, rest of year. Phone ahead to confirm schedule. **Cost:** Donations. **Phone:** (785) 527-2526.

BONNER SPRINGS (C-8) pop. 7,314, elev. 795'
• Part of Kansas City area — see map p. 199

Most of the year Bonner Springs, just west of the Kansas City metropolitan area, concentrates on light industry and the marketing of agricultural products. On weekends from early September to mid-October, however, the town exhibits a touch of 16th-century Europe when the popular 🚩 Kansas City Renaissance Festival is held. From May through September Providence Medical Center Amphitheater offers outdoor concerts featuring major rock, hip-hop and country artists; phone (913) 825-3400 or (800) 745-3000 for ticket information.

Bonner Springs/Edwardsville Area Chamber of Commerce: 129 N. Nettleton, Bonner Springs, KS 66012. **Phone:** (913) 422-5044.

COFFEYVILLE (F-7) pop. 10,295, elev. 736'

Though carefully planned, the simultaneous robbery of Coffeyville's two banks in October 1892 was not executed successfully. Because Eighth Street was being torn up where Bob, Grat and Emmett Dalton and their two confederates intended to tie their horses, they had to leave them in a parallel alley—too far for a safe getaway even under ideal circumstances.

Then, a warning of what was about to happen and a delaying ruse on the part of a bank employee gave townspeople time to arm. The running gun battle that followed left four citizens and all but one of the outlaws dead. Such was the Dalton Raid, one of the most notorious chapters in the annals of Kansas.

One of the banks involved, the Old Condon Bank (Perkins Building) at 811 Walnut St., has been restored to its original appearance. A replica of the old city jail sits in Death Alley, where the horses were left. The graves of Bob and Grat Dalton can be seen in Elmwood Cemetery, 2 blocks west of US 169.

Coffeyville once was the home of baseball pitcher Walter Johnson and of 1940 presidential candidate Wendell Willkie, who taught school in the town. A memorial to Johnson is in Walter Johnson Park.

The growth of the town is depicted in 13 murals on downtown walls, sidewalks and stores.

Coffeyville Area Chamber of Commerce: 807 Walnut St., Coffeyville, KS 67337. **Phone:** (620) 251-2550 or (800) 626-3357.

SLEEP INN & SUITES   620/688-6400
WW THREE DIAMOND Hotel. **Address:** 202 W 11th St 67337

SURESTAY PLUS HOTEL BY BEST WESTERN, COFFEYVILLE
                                                 620/251-3700
WW THREE DIAMOND Hotel. **Address:** 605 Northeast St 67337

COLBY (B-2) pop. 5,387, elev. 3,138'

Colby is a trading and service center for the surrounding wheat- and corn-producing area.

Colby Visitors Center: 2015 S. Range Ave., Colby, KS 67701. **Phone:** (785) 460-0076.

Shopping: Southwind Plaza, I-70 exit 53 at 2280 Southwind Ave., features artwork, Kansas products and Western memorabilia. Shops also line N. Franklin Avenue downtown.

COMFORT INN   785/462-3833
WW APPROVED Hotel. **Address:** 2225 S Range Ave 67701

HAMPTON INN BY HILTON   785/460-2333
WW THREE DIAMOND SAVE Hotel. **Ad-**   **AAA Benefit:**
dress: 1000 E Willow Dr 67701   Members save up to
                                             15%!

HOLIDAY INN EXPRESS HOTEL & SUITES   785/462-8787
WW THREE DIAMOND Hotel. **Address:** 645 W Willow St 67701

SLEEP INN & SUITES   785/460-0310
WW THREE DIAMOND Hotel. **Address:** 2075 Sewell Ave 67701

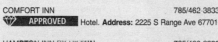

CITY LIMITS BAR & GRILL   785/462-6565
WW APPROVED American. Casual Dining. **Address:** 2227 S Range Ave 67701

CONCORDIA (B-5) pop. 5,395, elev. 1,363'

Concordia appeals to outdoor enthusiasts. Pheasants and quails are hunted, while the Republican River and area lakes provide good fishing. Concordia maintains five park and playground areas; camping by donation at Airport Park is popular with tourists traveling in recreational vehicles; phone (785) 243-2670.

Concordia Area Chamber of Commerce: 606 Washington St., Concordia, KS 66901. **Phone:** (785) 243-4290.

NATIONAL ORPHAN TRAIN COMPLEX is at 300 Washington St. The museum and research center tell the story of the 1854-1929 Orphan Train Movement during which more than 250,000 abandoned children were transported out of overpopulated eastern cities. The relocation, which laid the foundation for the present-day foster care system, is documented through exhibits. **Time:** Allow 45 minutes minimum. **Hours:** Tues.-Fri. 10-noon and 1-4, Sat. 10-4. **Cost:** $6; $3 (ages 4-12). **Phone:** (785) 243-4471.

EL PUERTO   785/243-6165
WW APPROVED Mexican. Casual Dining. **Address:** 217 W 6th St 66901

COTTONWOOD FALLS (D-6) pop. 903, elev. 1,191'

Cottonwood Falls was founded as a busy agricultural and livestock center in the late 1850s. It is home to the French Renaissance-style Chase County Courthouse, built in 1873. Constructed of locally mined limestone, the courthouse features a mansard roof, dormer windows and a cupola. Still in use, it was designed by John G. Haskell, who also designed the Kansas capitol building in Topeka. Guided tours of the courthouse are available; phone the chamber at (620) 273-8469.

Roniger Memorial Museum displays an extensive collection of Native American arrowheads and other artifacts discovered during archeological excavations; phone (620) 273-6310.

Chase County Chamber of Commerce: 318 Broadway Ave., Cottonwood Falls, KS 66845. **Phone:** (620) 273-8469.

GRAND CENTRAL HOTEL   620/273-6763
WW THREE DIAMOND **Address:** 215 Broadway 66845 **Loca-**
Historic   **tion:** US 177, just w on Main St, then
Country Inn just s; center of downtown. **Facility:** The
 hotel, built in 1884 and renovated in 1995, features rich Western flair with oversize guest rooms and large, spa-style showers. This sleepy little town provides a very peaceful escape destination. 10 units. 2 stories (no elevator), interior corridors. Bath: shower only. **Dining:** Grand Central Grill, see separate listing. **Guest Services:** valet laundry. **Featured Amenity:** continental breakfast.

SAVE [YI] [🛎] [Y] [HS] [🛜] [✕] [🖥] / SOME UNITS [🐾]

WHERE TO EAT

GRAND CENTRAL GRILL   620/273-6763
WW APPROVED American. Casual Dining. **Address:** 215 Broadway 66845

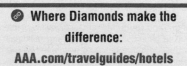

DERBY pop. 22,158

HAMPTON INN BY HILTON DERBY   316/425-7900
THREE DIAMOND [SAVE] Hotel. **Address:** 1701 Cambridge St 67037

AAA Benefit:
Members save up to 15%!

WHERE TO EAT

RIB CRIB BBQ AND GRILL   316/788-9902
APPROVED Barbecue. Casual Dining. **Address:** 1440 N Rock Rd 67037

DODGE CITY (E-3) pop. 27,340, elev. 2,496'

Fittingly called the "Wickedest Little City in America," Dodge City was a wide-open town during the late 1800s. Its infamous Front Street was one of the wildest on the frontier, with one well-stocked saloon for every 20 citizens. Cattlemen, buffalo hunters, soldiers, settlers, gunfighters, railroad men and mule skinners thronged the streets, to the delight and profit of the card sharks, brothel keepers and morticians.

Boot Hill Cemetery is named as such because many of its dead were buried with their boots on. Wyatt Earp and Bat Masterson were among the few able to control the city's lawless elements.

Dodge City began as a stopover on the Santa Fe Trail; wagon wheel ruts still are visible in the sod 9 miles west via US 50. By late 1872 the town was a station on the railroad. Buffalo hunting was intense in the area and the trading of hides, meat and ultimately bones brought considerable wealth to the town. By the time the buffaloes had nearly become extinct, bellowing herds of Texas cattle had become the primary source of income, and Dodge City became one of the largest cattle markets in the country.

While Dodge City's character has changed, its purpose has not. It remains a major cattle-shipping point and serves as a supply and trade center for a large wheat-growing region.

A look at the city's early days is provided by the mural that adorns the facade of the National Beef Packing Plant, southeast of town on SR 400. It is the work of muralist Stan Herd; another of his depictions can be seen at the Bank of America at 619 N. Second Ave.

Dodge City Days is a 10-day summertime celebration featuring more than 50 events, including art shows, street dances, rodeos and helicopter rides.

Dodge City Convention and Visitors Bureau: 400 W. Wyatt Earp Blvd., Dodge City, KS 67801. **Phone:** (620) 225-8186 or (800) 653-9378.

Self-guiding tours: More than 20 points of interest, including churches, monuments and buildings, are described in a free brochure distributed by the convention and visitors bureau. A recorded narrative to accompany the brochure can be rented for $2 (requires $8 refundable deposit) or purchased for $10. A driving tour features Fort Dodge.

BOOT HILL MUSEUM AND FRONT STREET is at 500 W. Wyatt Earp Blvd. On the original site of Boot Hill Cemetery, the museum contains exhibits featuring thousands of original historic items depicting life in 1876 Dodge City. Visitors can see an Old West gun collection and Native American artifacts along with buffalo, cattle and clothing items. Included in the complex are Boot Hill Cemetery, Ft. Dodge Jail, a one-room schoolhouse and an 1878 Victorian home once owned by cattle ranchers. A working general store and a saloon are along Front Street.

Food, gunfights and shows are available in summer. **Hours:** Daily 8-8, Memorial Day weekend-Labor Day; Mon.-Sat. 9-5, Sun. 1-5, rest of year. Gunfights start at noon and 7 p.m., Memorial Day weekend-Labor Day. **Cost:** $10; $8 (ages 5-10); $35 (family, 2 adults and 2 or more children ages 5-17). **Phone:** (620) 227-8188. [⑪]

BEST WESTERN NORTH EDGE INN   620/371-6441
THREE DIAMOND
Extended Stay Hotel

[BW] Best Western.

AAA Benefit:
Members save up to 15% and earn bonus points!

Address: 404 W Frontview 67801 **Location:** Jct US 50 and Central Ave, just n, just w. **Facility:** 61 efficiencies. 3 stories, interior corridors. **Pool:** heated outdoor. **Activities:** exercise room. **Guest Services:** valet and coin laundry, area transportation. **Featured Amenity:** full hot breakfast.

[SAVE] [⊁] [Y] CALL [&] [🚗] [👪]
[BIZ] [HS] [🛜] [✕] [🔌] [🍴] [💻] /SOME UNITS [🐾]

BEST WESTERN PLUS COUNTRY INN & SUITES
620/225-7378
THREE DIAMOND
Hotel

[BW] Best Western PLUS.

AAA Benefit:
Members save up to 15% and earn bonus points!

Address: 506 N 14th Ave 67801 **Location:** Just n of jct US 50 business route. **Facility:** 66 units. 3 stories, interior/exterior corridors. **Parking:** winter plug-ins. **Amenities:** safes. **Pool:** heated indoor. **Activities:** hot tub, exercise room. **Guest Services:** valet and coin laundry, area transportation. **Featured Amenity:** full hot breakfast.

[SAVE] [⑪] [Y] CALL [&] [🚗] [👪]
[BIZ] [HS] [🛜] [✕] [🔌] [🍴] [💻] /SOME UNITS [🐾]

COMFORT SUITES   620/801-4500
THREE DIAMOND Hotel. **Address:** 2700 W Wyatt Earp Blvd 67801

TOWNEPLACE SUITES BY MARRIOTT DODGE CITY
620/371-7171
THREE DIAMOND [SAVE] Extended Stay Hotel. **Address:** 2800 W Wyatt Earp Blvd 67801

AAA Benefit:
Members save 5% or more!

EL CHARRO RESTAURANT   620/225-0371
💎 **APPROVED**   Traditional Mexican. Casual Dining.
Address: 1209 W Wyatt Earp Blvd 67801

EL DORADO pop. 13,021, elev. 1,285'

HOLIDAY INN EXPRESS & SUITES   316/322-7275
💎**THREE DIAMOND** Hotel. **Address:** 3100 W El Dorado Ave 67042

FIESTA MEXICANA CANTINA MEXICA RESTAURANT
                                        316/320-1700
💎 **APPROVED**   Mexican. Casual Dining. **Address:** 127 Main St 67042

ELLIS (C-3) pop. 2,062, elev. 2,117'

ELLIS RAILROAD MUSEUM, 911 Washington St., tracks the history of the railroad in the area. Included are photographs, memorabilia, a re-created depot, cars, period clothing and some 1,600 dolls. Train rides aboard a one-third scale streamliner take passengers on a 2-mile track around the museum. **Time:** Allow 1 hour minimum. **Hours:** Tues.-Sat. 9-3, Apr.-Oct. **Cost:** Museum $4; $3 (ages 65+); $2 (ages 6-11). Train ride $4; $3 (ages 6-11). **Phone:** (785) 726-4493.

WALTER P. CHRYSLER BOYHOOD HOME AND MUSEUM is at 102 W. 10th St. The founder of Chrysler Corp. lived in this 1889 house until the age of 22. Early training as a machinist in local railroad yards helped shape his future course. Furnished in period, the house also contains Chrysler memorabilia, including the industrialist's corporate desk, which was donated to the museum after his death in 1940.

Hours: Tues.-Sat. 9-4, Sun. 1-4, Mar.-Oct.; Tues.-Sat. 10-3, Sun. 1-4, rest of year. Closed major holidays. **Cost:** $4; $3 (ages 65+); $2 (ages 6-11). **Phone:** (785) 726-3636.

DAYS INN   785/726-2511
💎 **APPROVED**   Hotel. **Address:** 205 N Washington St 67637

ARTHUR'S PIZZA & MEXICAN FOODS   785/726-4683
💎 **APPROVED**   Pizza. Casual Dining. **Address:** 103 W 9th St 67637

EMPORIA (D-6) pop. 24,916, elev. 1,135'
• Restaurants p. 94

Few cities are associated more widely with Kansas' journalistic tradition than Emporia, the home of William Allen White. As the outspoken editor and publisher of the *Emporia Gazette* 1895-1944, his incisive writing influenced national affairs. An essay on free speech, "To an Anxious Friend," won White a Pulitzer Prize in 1922.

Reminders of the "Sage of Emporia" are numerous. They include the William Allen White Library at the 6,000-student Emporia State University, William Allen White Memorial Drive and a commemorative statue in Peter Pan Park. Not the least of these memorials is the *Emporia Gazette* itself, still published by his family.

In 1953 the city became the first in the nation to observe Veterans Day thanks to the forward thinking of another patriotic citizen. Because Armistice Day honored only World War I veterans, Alvin J. King proposed renaming the holiday in order to include World War II and Korean War veterans. With the endorsement of a fellow Kansan, President Dwight D. Eisenhower, Congress officially changed the name to Veterans Day one year later, and in 2003, Congress declared Emporia its founding city.

The Howe House & Welsh Farmstead, 315 E. Logan Ave., is an 1867 limestone dwelling that reflects period style. Tours may be arranged; phone (620) 340-6310. Recreational facilities are available at several sites, including Peter Pan Park, Randolph and Rural streets, and at Soden's Grove Park, which features the David Traylor Zoo of Emporia. White Memorial Park, at Sixth and Merchant streets, contains park benches and street lamps in the style of the 1920s. A bust of White's son, William Lindsey White, is the main feature of the park.

Several nearby reservoirs offer fishing, boating and swimming: Lyon, Melvern, Council Grove, Pomona and John Redmond lakes *(see Recreation Areas Chart)* all are within a 45-minute drive.

Emporia Convention & Visitors Bureau: Trusler Business Center, 719 Commercial St., Emporia, KS 66801. **Phone:** (620) 342-1600 or (800) 279-3730.

Self-guiding tours: Brochures outlining walking, biking and driving tours of Emporia are available from the visitors bureau.

CANDLEWOOD SUITES   620/343-7756
💎 **APPROVED**   Extended Stay Hotel. **Address:** 2602 Candlewood Dr 66801

HAMPTON INN BY HILTON   620/412-9040
💎**THREE DIAMOND** 💾 Hotel. **Address:** 2900 Eaglecrest Dr 66801   **AAA Benefit:** Members save up to 15%!

SUPER 8   620/342-7567
💎 **APPROVED**   Hotel. **Address:** 2913 W US Hwy 50 66801

AMANDA'S BAKERY & CAFE   620/340-0620
W★ APPROVED   Sandwiches. Quick Serve. **Address:** 702
Commercial St, Suite 1F/G 66801

BOBBY D'S MERCHANT ST. BAR-B-QUE   620/342-1990
W★ APPROVED   Barbecue. Casual Dining. **Address:** 607
Merchant St 66801

HOUSE OF MA   620/342-3433
W★ APPROVED   Chinese. Casual Dining. **Address:** 1404
Industrial Rd 66801

FORT RILEY (C-6) elev. 1,063'

Reached from exit 301 off I-70, Fort Riley is the home of the 1st Infantry Division. The fort was built in 1853 to protect travelers along the Santa Fe Trail. Originally established as Camp Center, the fort later was named for Gen. Bennett Riley, who led the first military escort down the Santa Fe Trail in 1829. By 1855 the fort was a cavalry post, its soldiers credited with helping open the frontier for settlement.

The 101,000-acre, 11,600-personnel military reservation includes camps Forsyth, Funston and Whitside, Marshall Army Air Field and the Custer Hill area. A large historical district offers some 270 stone buildings. The Commanding General's Mounted Color Guard stables are open Monday through Friday. Tours are available; phone ahead to confirm schedule. A valid driver's license or photo ID, along with vehicle registration and proof of insurance are required for entry; phone (785) 239-0967 or (785) 239-2255.

1ST INFANTRY DIVISION MUSEUM, jct. Henry and Custer aves. in Bldg. 207, covers the four major campaigns — World War I to present operations — in which the First Infantry Division fought. The Vietnam section offers a reconstructed jungle trail, and the World War II area features an interactive trench. **Note:** Photo ID is required. **Time:** Allow 45 minutes minimum. **Hours:** Mon.-Sat. 10-4:30, Sun. noon-4:30. **Cost:** Donations. **Phone:** (785) 239-2737.

CUSTER HOUSE is on Sheridan Ave., Quarters 24A. Built in 1855 of native limestone, the house realistically depicts military life on the western frontier. Though Lt. Col. George A. Custer did not live in the house, it was named to honor him. A 30-minute guided tour explains about furnishings and other items. **Note:** Photo ID is required. **Hours:** Mon.-Sat. 9-4:30, Sun. noon-4:30, Memorial Day-Labor Day. Last tour begins 20 minutes before closing. **Cost:** Donations. **Phone:** (785) 239-2737. **GT**

FIRST TERRITORIAL CAPITOL STATE HISTORIC SITE is 3 mi. from I-70 exit 301, following signs. On the site of Pawnee, a struggling town at the edge of the Fort Riley cavalry post, the 1855 building hosted what became known as the "Bogus Legislature." Antislavery arguments here led to the conflict known as the "Bleeding Kansas" period of civil unrest. Restored in 1928, the capitol is now a museum furnished with period items. A self-guiding, .5-mile nature trail features native flora and fauna.

Note: Photo ID, vehicle registration and proof of insurance are required to enter the site. **Time:** Allow 1 hour minimum. **Hours:** Grounds and nature trail daily dawn-dusk. Museum Sat. 10-5, Sun. noon-5, Apr.-Oct. Closed major holidays. **Cost:** Donations. **Phone:** (785) 784-5535.

OLD TROOPER STATUE, on the cavalry parade ground across from the Custer House on Sheridan Ave., is a memorial to the U.S. Cavalry. The statue depicts a horse nicknamed Old Bill and its soldier rider, and is based upon Frederic Remington's pen and ink sketch "Old Bill." Chief, the last cavalry horse, died in 1968 and was buried in front of the memorial. **Note:** Photo ID is required. **Hours:** Daily dawn-dusk. **Cost:** Free. **Phone:** (785) 239-2737.

UNITED STATES CAVALRY MUSEUM is at the jct. of Henry and Custer aves. in Bldg. 205. The building, which dates from 1855, originally was a hospital. The museum tells the history of the mounted horse soldier of the U.S. Cavalry 1775-1950. **Note:** Photo ID is required. **Time:** Allow 1 hour minimum. **Hours:** Mon.-Sat. 9-4:30, Sun. noon-4:30. **Cost:** Donations. **Phone:** (785) 239-2737.

FORT SCOTT (D-8) pop. 8,087, elev. 801'

Formed around a military outpost established in 1842 to keep peace along the American frontier, the town of Fort Scott survived after the fort itself was abandoned and sold in 1855. During this time, proslavery versus Free State conflicts were common, and Fort Scott's location 6 miles from the Missouri border made it a frequent scene of violence during the turbulent period known as "Bleeding Kansas."

During the Civil War Fort Scott was divided, with "pro-slavers" living on the east side of town and "free-staters" living on the west side. After the war, the town became a leading city of eastern Kansas and challenged Kansas City's standing as the largest rail center west of the Mississippi River.

The town's many handsome commercial buildings and elegant Victorian residences were built from the 1850s to the 1920s. Narrated shuttle tours of historic Fort Scott depart hourly on Friday from 11-2 and Saturday 10-3 from March to October. Tours also are available on Friday and Saturday in November; call the information center for tour times.

Fort Scott was the boyhood home and is the final resting place of Gordon Parks, director of the popular 1970s film "Shaft."

Fort Scott Chamber & Tourism Center: 231 E. Wall St., Fort Scott, KS 66701. **Phone:** (620) 223-3566 or (800) 245-3678.

Self-guiding tours: A free brochure detailing a historic walking tour of downtown is available from the tourism center.

THE COURTLAND HOTEL & SPA   620/223-0098
APPROVED   Hotel. **Address:** 121 E 1st St 66701

LYONS' TWIN MANSIONS B & B HOTEL   620/224-6053
THREE DIAMOND Country Inn. **Address:** 742 S National Ave 66701

SLEEP INN & SUITES   620/223-2555
APPROVED   Hotel. **Address:** 302 E Wall St 66701

WHERE TO EAT

EL CHARRO   620/223-9944
APPROVED   Mexican. Casual Dining. **Address:** 2503 S Main St 66701

NATE'S PLACE RESTAURANT AND LOUNGE   620/224-6053
APPROVED   American. Casual Dining. **Address:** 750 S National Ave 66701

GARDEN CITY (D-2) pop. 26,658, elev. 2,830'

Founded in 1879 along the Arkansas River and the Santa Fe Trail, Garden City's early growth was followed by years of drought and declining population. This cycle continued until dependable irrigation systems were established at the turn of the 20th century.

The Arkansas River makes Garden City one of the state's most extensively irrigated regions; bumper crops of wheat, alfalfa and corn are produced. It also is a major cattle raising and shipping site. South of the city off US 83 a large herd of bison inhabits the nearly 4,000-acre, state-operated Sandsage Bison Range and Wildlife Area. Tours are available by reservation; phone (620) 276-8886 or (620) 276-9400 for tour information.

Finney County Convention and Visitors Bureau: 1513 E. Fulton Terr., Garden City, KS 67846-6165. **Phone:** (620) 276-0607 or (800) 879-9803.

BEST WESTERN PLUS EMERALD INN & SUITES
                                         620/277-7100
THREE DIAMOND
Hotel

Best Western PLUS. **AAA Benefit:** Members save up to 15% and earn bonus points!

Address: 2412 E Kansas Ave 67846 **Location:** Jct US 50, 83 and SR 156. **Facility:** 60 units. 3 stories, interior corridors. **Parking:** winter plug-ins. **Pool:** heated indoor. **Activities:** hot tub, exercise room. **Guest Services:** valet and coin laundry. **Featured Amenity:** full hot breakfast.

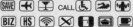

CLARION INN & CONFERENCE CENTER   620/275-7471
THREE DIAMOND Hotel. **Address:** 1911 E Kansas Ave 67846

COMFORT INN   620/275-5800
APPROVED   Hotel. **Address:** 2608 E Kansas Ave 67846

HAMPTON INN BY HILTON   620/272-0454
THREE DIAMOND **SAVE** Hotel. **Address:** 2505 E Crestway Dr 67846

AAA Benefit: Members save up to 15%!

THE HERITAGE INN & SUITES, AN ASCEND HOTEL COLLECTION MEMBER   620/277-7477
THREE DIAMOND Hotel. **Address:** 1212 Stone Creek Dr 67846

HOLIDAY INN EXPRESS HOTEL & SUITES   620/275-5900
THREE DIAMOND Hotel. **Address:** 2502 E Kansas Ave 67846

SLEEP INN & SUITES - CONFERENCE CENTER
                                         620/805-6535
APPROVED   Hotel. **Address:** 1931 E Kansas Plaza 67846

TOWNEPLACE SUITES BY MARRIOTT GARDEN CITY
                                         620/805-6717
THREE DIAMOND **SAVE** Extended Stay Hotel. **Address:** 3510 E Kansas Ave 67846

AAA Benefit: Members save 5% or more!

WHERE TO EAT

PHO HOA ONE   620/276-3393
APPROVED   Vietnamese. Casual Dining. **Address:** 713 E Fulton St, Suite 3 67846

SAMY'S SPIRITS & STEAKHOUSE   620/275-7471
APPROVED   American. Casual Dining. **Address:** 1911 E Kansas Ave 67846

GARDNER pop. 19,123
• Part of Kansas City area — see map p. 199

HAMPTON INN GARDNER CONFERENCE CENTER
                                         913/856-2100
THREE DIAMOND **SAVE** Hotel. **Address:** 151 S Cedar Niles Rd 66030

AAA Benefit: Members save up to 15%!

GOODLAND (B-2) pop. 4,489, elev. 3,687'
• Hotels p. 96 • Restaurants p. 96

Chosen as the county seat in 1887, the town became known in the 1880s for its rainmaking companies. The idea came from a man who claimed to produce rain by pouring sulfuric acid on zinc to release hydrogen, which would unite with the surrounding oxygen to form water. There was no immediate reaction after Melbourne's experiment, but within a day heavy rains reportedly fell.

Earlier the town had proved equally inventive: In its war with several nearby communities for the county seat, residents employed a combination of armed force, false arrest, staged trial and theft to obtain county records. Goodland also can claim that it is the home of America's first patented helicopter.

The brick surface that remains on Main Street and some side streets was laid in 1921 by Jim

Brown, a Native American whose skill was such that he reputedly could lay up to 150 bricks a minute—as fast as five men could supply him—so accurately that no later adjustment to the bricks was necessary.

Twenty miles northeast of Goodland, a historical marker indicates where Lt. Col. George Custer discovered the bodies of the Native American scout, Lt. Lyman Kidder and the 10 cavalrymen felled in the Kidder Massacre of 1867. A map to the site is available at the Sherman County Convention and Visitors Bureau.

Today, the city serves as major retail trade center for northwest Kansas. It also is known as one of the top sunflower producers in the nation; seeds are processed here for confectionery use and for oil. Because of this distinction, Goodland was chosen as one of seven sites worldwide to display giant outdoor reproductions of Vincent van Gogh's sunflower paintings. Visible from I-70, the 80-foot-tall easel and picture is the only one of its kind in the United States.

Sherman County Convention and Visitors Bureau: 925 Main St., P.O. Box 927, Goodland, KS 67735. **Phone:** (785) 890-3515 or (888) 824-4222.

Self-guiding tours: The convention and visitors bureau offers maps for walking and driving tours that highlight historic areas.

HOLIDAY INN EXPRESS HOTEL & SUITES
785/890-9060

THREE DIAMOND
Hotel

Address: 2631 Enterprise Rd 67735 **Location:** I-70 exit 17 (SR 27), just s. **Facility:** 73 units. 3 stories, interior corridors. **Parking:** winter plug-ins. **Pool:** heated indoor. **Activities:** hot tub, exercise room. **Guest Services:** coin laundry. **Featured Amenity:** full hot breakfast.

(SAVE) (CE) CALL (🔔) (➡) (🛏) (BIZ)
(HS) (📶) (✕) (🔒) (🖥) (🖨)

SUPER 8 BY WYNDHAM   785/890-7566
APPROVED   Hotel. **Address:** 2520 Commerce Rd 67735

WHERE TO EAT

TEQUILAS MEXICAN GRILL   785/899-2400
APPROVED   Mexican. Casual Dining. **Address:** 118 E 17th St 67735

GREAT BEND   (D-4) pop. 15,995, elev. 1,843'

While oil is pumped from underground reserves, wheat is harvested from the overlying fields in Great Bend, situated at the apex of the Arkansas River's sweeping arc through central Kansas.

Named for the big bend in the Arkansas River, Great Bend was established in 1872 along the Santa Fe Trail and around the shell of Fort Zarah, which guarded the trail until 1869 when diminished trail traffic and lessened Native American threats made the fort unnecessary. In 1872 the railroad arrived, bringing with it the cattle trade and all the

gambling, gunplay and other amusements typical of a cattle railhead. To establish order, state law decreed that the Texas herds could move no closer than a point 30 miles west of town.

Located in Lafayette Park on the historic Santa Fe Trail is the Kansas Quilt Walk. Seven patterns of quilts reflecting the early settlement of the area are etched in the surrounding sidewalks. Also noteworthy in town is the Great Bend Mural Project, a collection of outdoor murals painted on area buildings by local artists. Several are located in the Main Street business area.

Today, Great Bend is a destination for nature enthusiasts of all levels, with opportunities for hikers, bikers, paddlers, photographers and birders. In a vast natural sink, 6 miles northeast of town via US 281 or US 156, lies Cheyenne Bottoms Wildlife Area. As one of the nation's largest inland marshes, it is designated as a wetland of international importance. The 19,857-acre wildlife area attracts great numbers of birds, including the threatened bald eagle and endangered whooping crane. Forty-five percent of North America's shorebirds stop here on their migratory flight in the spring; phone (620) 793-7730 or (877) 243-9268.

Fort Zarah Park, 3 miles east of town on US 56, occupies 9 acres. Thirteen miles southwest on US 56, Pawnee Rock looms above the prairie.

From late November through New Year's Eve, three local parks are decorated with Christmas lights for the annual 🟢 Trail of Lights celebration. A Santa exhibit and an iceless skating rink add to the fun.

Great Bend Convention and Visitors Bureau: 3007 10th St., Great Bend, KS 67530. **Phone:** (620) 792-2750 or (877) 427-9299.

KANSAS WETLANDS EDUCATION CENTER is at 592 N.E. SR 156. The facility overlooks the 19,857-acre Cheyenne Bottoms Wildlife Area and the 7,694-acre Cheyenne Bottoms Preserve. Exhibits describe the history and development of the Cheyenne Bottoms wetlands, including its formation and its flora and fauna. The wetlands are home to about 340 species of migratory waterfowl and shorebirds, and birdwatching is a popular activity; cranes, herons, pelicans and sandpipers have been seen here. Spot wood rat nests, orioles and animal tracks on the 0.5-mile nature trail next to the center. Take a self-guiding driving tour, or a 30-minute or 1.5-hour guided van tour, of the area.

Hours: Mon.-Sat. 9-5, Sun. 1-5, Apr.-Oct.; Tues.-Sat. 9-5, Sun. 1-5, rest of year. Closed major holidays. **Cost:** Education center free. 1.5-hour van tour $5; $3 (ages 4-11). 30-minute van tour $3; $1.50 (ages 4-11). Reservations are required. **Phone:** (620) 566-1456 or (877) 243-9268. (GT)

SHAFER MEMORIAL ART GALLERY is 3 mi. n. on US 281, then 2 mi. e. to 245 N.E. 30th Rd. This gallery, on the Barton County Community College campus, features more than 800 watercolors, oil paintings, photographs and sculptures. Special emphasis is placed on Kansas artists, particularly the work of bronze sculptor L.E. "Gus" Shafer and painter Charles B. Rogers. The collection also contains works by John James Audubon, Marc Chagall, Pablo Picasso and Birger Sandzén. Educational displays and interactive activities are available for children. A digital gallery tour also is available.

Time: Allow 30 minutes minimum. **Hours:** Mon.-Sat. 10-5. Closed major holidays. Phone ahead to confirm schedule. **Cost:** Free. **Phone:** (620) 792-9342.

BEST WESTERN ANGUS INN   620/792-3541

♦ **APPROVED**

Hotel

Best Western. **AAA Benefit:** Members save up to 15% and earn bonus points!

Address: 2920 10th St 67530 **Location:** 0.8 mi w on US 56 and SR 96/156. **Facility:** 90 units. 2 stories, interior/exterior corridors. **Parking:** winter plug-ins. **Dining:** The Page-An American Bistro, see separate listing. **Pool:** heated indoor. **Activities:** hot tub, game room, exercise room. **Guest Services:** valet and coin laundry.

〔SAVE〕 〔✈〕 〔¶¶〕 〔🍽〕 CALL 〔♿〕 〔🏊〕

〔📶〕 〔BIZ〕 〔HS〕 〔📶〕 〔✕〕 〔🖥〕 〔🖨〕 〔🖥〕 / SOME UNITS 〔🐾〕

HOLIDAY INN EXPRESS & SUITES   620/603-6565
♦ **THREE DIAMOND** Hotel. **Address:** 3821 10th St 67530

SUPER 8 BY WYNDHAM GREAT BEND   620/793-9000
♦ **THREE DIAMOND** Hotel. **Address:** 911 Grant St 67530

WHERE TO EAT

THE PAGE-AN AMERICAN BISTRO   620/792-8700
♦ **APPROVED** American. Casual Dining. **Address:** 2920 10th St 67530

GREENSBURG (E-4) pop. 777, elev. 2,235'

The speed and dependability with which he drove the stagecoach between Wichita and Dodge City during the 1880s earned D.R. Green his nickname, "Cannonball." Legend has it that while riding as passenger, temperance reformer Carry Nation reached out of the coach, snatched Cannonball's cigar and hurled it onto the road. He drew rein, silently lifted the astounded lady to the roadway and left her to trudge the many remaining miles to town.

Despite Green's prowess, the day came when the Rock Island Railroad won the race against the Santa Fe Railroad, becoming the first rail line through present-day Greensburg and eliminating the need for stagecoach travel.

After a tornado leveled most of downtown Greensburg on May 4, 2007, the community made a decision to rebuild and reinvent the town as a national model for sustainable living, utilizing only

green building techniques and materials. A cell-phone audio tour highlights the town's history and reconstruction; phone (620) 805-3219.

The 5.4.7 Arts Center, 204 Wisconsin Ave., became the first building in Kansas to earn Leadership in Energy and Environmental Design (LEED) Platinum status. The center presents exhibits and educational programs; phone (620) 723-2600.

Kiowa County Chamber of Commerce: 101 S. Main St., Suite 103, Greensburg, KS 67054. **Phone:** (620) 723-3188.

BEST WESTERN PLUS NIGHT WATCHMAN INN & SUITES   620/723-2244

♦ **THREE DIAMOND**

Hotel

Best Western PLUS. **AAA Benefit:** Members save up to 15% and earn bonus points!

Address: 515 W Kansas Ave 67054 **Location:** Just e of jct US 54 and 183. **Facility:** 42 units. 2 stories, interior corridors. **Parking:** winter plug-ins. **Pool:** heated indoor. **Activities:** hot tub, exercise room. **Guest Services:** coin laundry.

〔SAVE〕 〔¶+〕 〔🏊〕 〔♿〕 〔BIZ〕 〔HS〕 〔📶〕 〔✕〕 〔🖥〕 〔🖨〕 〔🖥〕 / SOME UNITS 〔🐾〕

HAYS (C-4) pop. 20,510, elev. 1,997'
• Hotels p. 98 • Restaurants p. 98

By the early 1860s a rising tide of travelers, settlers and railroad builders was inching across the Kansas plains. Native Americans, whose lands were being usurped and whose food staple, the buffalo, was being slaughtered by the intruders, responded with increasing hostility.

For protection, Fort Fletcher was established on the banks of Big Creek on the Smoky Hill Trail. Renamed Fort Hays a year later, it became one of the era's prominent military posts. Unlike other typical frontier military outposts, however, Fort Hays had no stockade. All buildings and quarters were grouped around a parade ground.

At one time William "Buffalo Bill" Cody supplied the fort with buffalo meat. Lt. Col. George Custer's ill-fated 7th Cavalry also was encamped near the fort. By the time Fort Hays was abandoned in 1889, the town had become a thriving railroad and agricultural center.

Deeded to the state, the old military post became the site of 11,200-student Fort Hays State University and a 3,700-acre dryland agricultural research center and park, one of the largest in the world. The university also is home to the Sternberg Museum of Natural History (see attraction listing) which houses a world-class dinosaur and fossil collection. A small buffalo herd can be seen at Frontier Park across from Fort Hays State Historic Site.

In summer the Hays Aquatic Park, at 4th and Main streets, provides opportunities for swimming, diving or tubing down a lazy river; phone (785) 623-2653. The Kansas Merci Boxcar Museum, 13th and Canterbury streets, features one of 49 boxcars that arrived in the United States in 1949. Filled with French food and other goods, the gifts expressed the French people's gratitude for American assistance during World War II; phone (785) 625-9681 for tour reservations.

Hays Convention and Visitors Bureau: 2700 Vine St., Hays, KS 67601. **Phone:** (785) 628-8202 or (800) 569-4505.

Self-guiding tours: A series of 25 markers, beginning downtown at 12th and Fort streets, designates a self-guiding walking tour. Brochures are available at the convention and visitors bureau.

STERNBERG MUSEUM OF NATURAL HISTORY, off I-70 exit 159, 1 mi. s. on US 183, then following signs, re-creates the late Cretaceous period with dioramas of animated, life-size dinosaurs. The museum, part of Fort Hays State University, also contains one of the world's best collections of fossilized prehistoric flying reptiles and creatures from the Cretaceous sea. One particularly unusual specimen is a fish within a fish.

For children, the Discovery Room contains a giant spider model, computer workstations, live animals and hands-on activities. Changing exhibits are featured throughout the year. Guided tours are available by appointment. **Time:** Allow 2 hours minimum. **Hours:** Mon.-Sat. 9-6, Sun. 1-6, Apr.-Sept.; Tues.-Sat. 9-6, Sun. 1-6, rest of year. Closed Jan. 1, Thanksgiving, Christmas Eve, Christmas and Dec. 31. **Cost:** $9; $8 (ages 60+); $6 (ages 4-12). **Phone:** (785) 628-4286 or (877) 332-1165. (GT)

BEST WESTERN PLUS BUTTERFIELD INN
785/621-4337

THREE DIAMOND
Hotel

Best Western PLUS **AAA Benefit:** Members save up to 15% and earn bonus points!

Address: 1010 E 41st St 67601 **Location:** I-70 exit 159 (US 183), just n, then just e. **Facility:** 75 units. 3 stories, interior corridors. **Amenities:** safes. **Pool:** heated indoor. **Activities:** hot tub, exercise room. **Guest Services:** valet and coin laundry.

SAVE / CALL / BIZ / HS / SOME UNITS

COMFORT INN & SUITES NORTH 785/625-9322
APPROVED Hotel. **Address:** 1001 E 41st St 67601

FAIRFIELD BY MARRIOTT HAYS 785/625-3344
THREE DIAMOND SAVE Hotel. **Address:** 377 Mopar Dr 67601

AAA Benefit: Members save 5% or more!

HAMPTON INN BY HILTON 785/621-4444
APPROVED SAVE Hotel. **Address:** 4002 General Hays Rd 67601

AAA Benefit: Members save up to 15%!

HOLIDAY INN EXPRESS & SUITES 785/625-8000
THREE DIAMOND
Hotel
Address: 4650 Roth Ave 67601 **Location:** I-70 exit 159 (US 183), 0.5 mi n. **Facility:** 91 units. 3 stories, interior corridors. **Pool:** heated indoor. **Activities:** exercise room. **Guest Services:** valet and coin laundry. **Featured Amenity:** breakfast buffet.

SAVE CALL BIZ HS

SLEEP INN & SUITES 785/625-2700
APPROVED Hotel. **Address:** 1011 E 41st St 67601

TOWNEPLACE SUITES BY MARRIOTT HAYS 785/261-9630
THREE DIAMOND SAVE Extended Stay Contemporary Hotel. **Address:** 4001 General Hays Rd 67601

AAA Benefit: Members save 5% or more!

WHERE TO EAT

GELLA'S DINER & LB. BREWING CO. 785/621-2739
APPROVED Continental. Casual Dining. **Address:** 117 E 11th St 67601

GUTIERREZ COCINA MEXICANA 785/625-4402
APPROVED Traditional Mexican. Casual Dining. **Address:** 1106 E 27th St 67601

TRIO TAPHOUSE 785/621-2221
APPROVED American. Gastropub. **Address:** 1106 E 27th St 67601

HIAWATHA (B-7) pop. 3,172, elev. 1,085'

More than 100 varieties of maple trees, planted and cultivated by local citizens, line the streets of Hiawatha. Several city parks offer picnicking and fishing. A town clock dating from 1891 is at Seventh and Oregon streets.

Hiawatha Chamber of Commerce: 701 Oregon St., Hiawatha, KS 66434. **Phone:** (785) 742-7136.

Self-guiding tours: A brochure outlining a driving tour of late 19th-century houses is available from the chamber of commerce.

BEST WESTERN PLUS HIAWATHA HOTEL
785/740-7000

THREE DIAMOND

Hotel

Best Western PLUS
AAA Benefit: Members save up to 15% and earn bonus points!

Address: 119 E Lodge Rd 66434 **Location:** Jct US 73 and 36, just ne. **Facility:** 57 units. 3 stories, interior corridors. **Pool:** heated indoor. **Activities:** hot tub, exercise room. **Guest Services:** coin laundry.

SAVE CALL 🚪 🏊 🚼 BIZ 📶 ✕ 🛗 🖥 🖨 / SOME UNITS 🐾

HUGOTON pop. 3,904, elev. 3,110'

BEST WESTERN PLUS STEVENS COUNTY INN
620/544-7766

THREE DIAMOND

Hotel

Best Western PLUS
AAA Benefit: Members save up to 15% and earn bonus points!

Address: 1004 E 11th St 67951 **Location:** 1 mi e of center. **Facility:** 56 units. 3 stories, interior corridors. **Pool:** heated indoor. **Activities:** hot tub, exercise room. **Guest Services:** coin laundry.

SAVE CALL 🚪 🏊 🚼 BIZ HS 📶 ✕ 🛗 🖥 🖨

HUTCHINSON (D-5) pop. 42,080, elev. 1,529'
• Hotels p. 100 • Restaurants p. 100

"Salt of the Earth" has a special meaning in Hutchinson, where the mining and processing of salt has been a major industry since 1888. A bed of salt and salt/shale between 300 and 350 feet thick and some 600 feet below the surrounding wheat fields was discovered in 1887, to the consternation of drillers looking for natural gas.

Even exhausted mines are valuable; they are used by businesses, hospitals and film companies throughout the world for maximum-security storage of their records. Had the gas seekers persevered, they might have found some of the oil that now enriches the city's economy. However, it is the wheat fields themselves rather than the substances extracted from beneath them that support Hutchinson's leading industry. Other economic mainstays include agribusiness, aerospace equipment, health care, specialty vehicle manufacturing, grocery distribution and food processing.

The Fox Theatre, 18 E. First Ave., has been restored to its 1931 Art Deco splendor and is open for guided tours, films and live performances; phone (620) 663-5861. Nearly 550 acres of parks provide ample recreational opportunities. In early September the state's agricultural bounty is celebrated when Hutchinson hosts the Kansas State Fair.

Greater Hutchinson Convention/Visitors Bureau: 117 N. Walnut St., P.O. Box 519, Hutchinson, KS 67504-0519. **Phone:** (620) 662-3391.

COSMOSPHERE is at 1100 N. Plum St. The facility features the Hall of Space Museum, Carey Digital Dome Theater, Justice Planetarium, Dr. Goddard's Lab and changing exhibitions. Highlights include the Apollo 13 command module, an outstanding exhibit of space suits and one of the largest collections of Russian space artifacts outside Moscow.

Early space exploration is detailed through exhibits about Germany's V-1 and V-2 rockets and Russia's Sputnik programs. U.S. space artifacts include *Gemini X* and a full-scale replica of the space shuttle.

Various films are shown on a 44-foot dome screen; the planetarium presents programs about stars and space. Live shows at Dr. Goddard's Lab demonstrate the principles of rocket science.

Time: Allow 3 hours minimum. **Hours:** Mon.-Sat. 9-7, Sun. noon-7, Memorial Day-Labor Day; Mon.-Thurs. 9-5, Fri.-Sat. 9-7, Sun. noon-6, rest of year. Films, planetarium and Dr. Goddard's Lab demonstrations are presented daily. **Cost:** $26; $23 (ages 60+ and active military with ID); $17 (ages 4-12). Museum only $13.50; $11.50 (ages 60+ and active military with ID); $10 (ages 4-12). Single venue (Carey Digital Dome Theater, Justice Planetarium or Dr. Goddard's Lab) $6-$8; $6-$7 (ages 60+ and active military with ID); $6-$6.50 (ages 4-12). **Phone:** (620) 662-2305 or (800) 397-0330.

DILLON NATURE CENTER is at 3002 E. 30th Ave. The 10,000-square-foot visitor center houses a nature gallery featuring a diorama explaining the area's plants and animals. Other exhibits include an underground theater, aquariums and interactive displays. Three miles of mostly unpaved nature trails afford visitors an opportunity to enjoy the outdoors. **Time:** Allow 30 minutes minimum. **Hours:** Trails and grounds open Mon.-Fri. 8-8, Sat.-Sun. 9-8, Apr.-Sept.; Mon.-Fri. 8-6, Sat.-Sun. 9-6, rest of year. Trails and grounds closed Christmas. Visitor center open Mon.-Fri. 8-7, Sat. 10-5, Sun. and holidays 1-5, Apr.-Sept.; Mon.-Fri. 8-5, Sat. 10-5, Sun. and holidays 1-5, rest of year. Visitor center closed Thanksgiving and Christmas. **Cost:** Free. Admission is charged for programs and events. **Phone:** (620) 663-7411.

STRATACA—KANSAS UNDERGROUND SALT MUSEUM is at 3650 E. Ave. G. This tour starts with a safety video. A double-decked elevator then lowers visitors 650 feet underground into a working salt mine. A 30-minute guided tram tour and 15-minute ride on a miniature train into the salt caverns is available. Visitors learn about the mining process, geology and history in the museum's gallery of exhibits and displays. Safari Shuttle is a 1-hour underground tram tour beyond the museum boundaries. Only 12 participants are allowed and riders must be at least 10 years.

Note: For safety, children ages 0-3 are not permitted underground. Museum access is determined by elevator capacity. **Time:** Allow 1 hour, 30 minutes minimum. **Hours:** Tues.-Sat. 9-6, Sun. 1-6, Memorial Day-Labor Day; Tues.-Sat. 9-5, Sun. 1-5, rest of year. Last tour departs 2 hours before closing. Phone ahead to confirm schedule. **Cost:** $14; $12 (ages 60+ and active military with ID); $7.50 (ages 4-12). Tram tour or train fare $4. Safari Shuttle $12.50. Combination ticket (includes gallery, tram tour and train ride) $19; $17 (ages 60+ and active military with ID); $12.50 (ages 4-12). Reservations are recommended. **Phone:** (620) 662-1425 or (866) 755-3450. GT

COMFORT INN & SUITES — 620/669-5200
THREE DIAMOND Hotel. **Address:** 1601 Super Plaza 67501

HAMPTON INN BY HILTON — 620/665-9800
APPROVED SAVE Hotel. **Address:** 1401 1/2 E 11th St 67501

AAA Benefit: Members save up to 15%!

HOLIDAY INN EXPRESS HUTCHISON — 620/259-8656
THREE DIAMOND Hotel. **Address:** 911 Porter St 67501

WHERE TO EAT

AIRPORT STEAK HOUSE — 620/662-4281
APPROVED Steak. Casual Dining. **Address:** 1100 Airport Rd 67501

ANCHOR INN — 620/669-0311
APPROVED Mexican. Casual Dining. **Address:** 128 S Main St 67501

JILLIAN'S ITALIAN GRILL — 620/663-8466
APPROVED Italian. Casual Dining. **Address:** 216 N Main St 67501

ROY'S HICKORY PIT BBQ — 620/663-7421
APPROVED Barbecue. Quick Serve. **Address:** 1018 W 5th Ave 67501

INDEPENDENCE (E-7) pop. 9,483, elev. 798'

Formerly the site of the Osage Indian Reservation, the Independence area was opened to settlement in 1870 when the Osage agreed to move to the Indian Territory in what is now Oklahoma. In 1881 natural gas was discovered and Independence grew quickly, as it did again in 1903 with the discovery of oil. Today, with its gas and oil deposits depleted, the city relies on diversified manufacturing and agriculture.

Independence was the boyhood home of Pulitzer Prize winning playwright William Inge whose Midwestern upbringing shaped such dramas as "Splendor in the Grass" and "Come Back, Little Sheba." The William Inge Collection, housed at Independence Community College, contains original manuscripts, documents and memorabilia; phone (620) 332-5468. Nearby Elk City Reservoir and State Park offers water sports and other recreation *(see Recreation Areas Chart)*.

Independence Area Chamber of Commerce: 616 N. Penn Ave., P.O. Box 386, Independence, KS 67301. **Phone:** (620) 331-1890 or (800) 882-3606.

LITTLE HOUSE ON THE PRAIRIE MUSEUM, 13 mi. s.w. on US 75, following signs, is a log cabin reconstructed on the site where Laura Ingalls Wilder lived 1869-71. Of interest is the family's hand-dug well. A 19th-century post office, a one-room schoolhouse and a hiking trail also are on the grounds. **Hours:** Daily 10-5, Apr.-July; Thurs.-Sun. 10-5, Aug.-Sept.; Fri.-Sun. 10-5, in Oct. Phone ahead to confirm schedule. **Cost:** $3; $1 (ages 0-18). **Phone:** (620) 289-4238.

EL PUEBLITO — 620/331-5860
APPROVED Mexican. Casual Dining. **Address:** 1721 N Penn Ave 67301

JUNCTION CITY (C-6) pop. 23,353, elev. 1,080'

Trade has been a major occupation in Junction City since its founding in 1857 at the confluence of the Smoky Hill and Republican rivers. Early commerce was conducted with travelers on the Smoky Hill Trail and with the Kansa Indians, who often came into town to buy and sell. One notable day in 1867 the wares offered by a Cheyenne war party included some newly acquired scalps.

Although feathers and war paint have since disappeared—Junction City is now a commercial center—many of the military uniforms reminiscent of the hostile 1800s endure at historic Fort Riley *(see place listing p. 94),* which is just north.

Marking the history of Junction City and surrounding counties is Geary County Historical Society Museum, Sixth and Adams streets. Through the display of artifacts and photographs, the museum traces the progression of inhabitants since the area was settled; phone (785) 238-1666. The Spring Valley Historic Site, SR 18 and Spring Valley Road, contains a restored 1870s schoolhouse, a settler's log cabin, a barn and Wetzel's Log Cabin Church (the first Lutheran parish in the state).

Heritage Park, Sixth and Washington streets, contains the Kansas Vietnam Veterans Memorial, the 1st Infantry Division Monument, a Desert Storm Memorial and a limestone arch that commemorates participants from both sides of the Civil War. The 9-foot-tall bronze Buffalo Soldier Memorial, 18th Street and Buffalo Soldier Drive, commemorates the African-American soldiers who served in the 9th and 10th horse cavalry regiments during the Civil War.

Popular recreation sites are Milford Lake, Geary State Fishing Lake and Milford State Park. Milford Lake is the largest lake in the state. *See Recreation Areas Chart.*

Geary County Convention and Visitors Bureau: 222 W. 6th St., Junction City, KS 66441-6846. **Phone:** (785) 238-2885 or (800) 528-2489.

BEST WESTERN J C INN   785/210-1212

APPROVED

Hotel

Best Western. **AAA Benefit:** Members save up to 15% and earn bonus points!

Address: 604 E Chestnut St 66441 **Location:** I-70 exit 298, just w. **Facility:** 45 units. 2 stories (no elevator), interior corridors. **Parking:** winter plug-ins. **Pool:** heated indoor. **Activities:** exercise room. **Guest Services:** valet and coin laundry. **Featured Amenity:** full hot breakfast.

[SAVE] [TI+] [≈] [⊷] [BIZ] [HS] [≈]
[⊟] [▣] [▦] / SOME UNITS [⊷]

CANDLEWOOD SUITES JUNCTION CITY   785/238-1454

APPROVED   Extended Stay Hotel. **Address:** 100 S Hammons Dr 66441

COMFORT INN & SUITES   785/762-4200

APPROVED   Hotel. **Address:** 120 N East St 66441

COURTYARD BY MARRIOTT JUNCTION CITY   785/210-1500

THREE DIAMOND [SAVE] Hotel. **Address:** 310 Hammons Dr 66441

AAA Benefit: Members save 5% or more!

HAMPTON INN BY HILTON JUNCTION CITY   785/579-6950

THREE DIAMOND [SAVE] Hotel. **Address:** 1039 S Washington St 66441

AAA Benefit: Members save up to 15%!

KANSAS CITY (C-8) pop. 145,786, elev. 763'

The town of Wyandotte, established in 1850, was located in what is now the downtown area of present-day Kansas City. By the 1870s, railroads and stockyards were contributing to robust growth. Four municipalities—Armourdale, Armstrong, Kansas City and Wyandotte—consolidated in 1880 to form what today is the Kansas portion of the greater Kansas City metropolitan area.

Among those who migrated to Kansas looking for a better life in the latter part of the 19th century were African-Americans known as Exodusters. Free blacks who could read, were economically able to buy property and whose self-esteem had been bolstered by military service in the Civil War, pursued dreams of owning land and escaping the oppressive segregationist policies of Southern states, a legacy that remained despite the civil rights gains introduced by Reconstruction.

Their de facto leader was Benjamin "Pap" Singleton, who was born a slave in Tennessee, escaped to freedom in Detroit and returned to his native state after emancipation. An admirer of abolitionist John Brown's crusade against slavery in Kansas, he chose the state as a destination for the creation of organized African-American "colonies."

Singleton recruited impoverished blacks from throughout the South. Under his leadership, several

Exoduster communities took shape in Wyandotte County beginning in the early 1870s, including Hoggstown, Mississippi Town, Quindaro and Rattlebone Hollow, all later incorporated into Kansas City. Quindaro—today a neighborhood on the city's northern edge—was founded by freed African-Americans and abolitionists; it was a stop on the Underground Railroad and remained a thriving town until the early 20th century.

Although the organized movement to Kansas later became an unplanned rush (so much so that in 1880 Singleton was called before a U.S. Senate committee to explain the "alarming exodus" of blacks from the South), many who remained were indeed able to better their lives. But Singleton, dismayed with the racial prejudice he continued to encounter, eventually abandoned his efforts to establish African-American colonies in the United States.

These days you can find an exodus of racing fans heading to Kansas City. Grand National, Factory Stock and Modified events rev up the crowds at Lakeside Speedway, 1 mile west of I-435 exit 18 at 5615 Wolcott Dr., on Friday nights from April through September; phone (913) 299-9206.

The fall air is filled with the aroma of smoking hardwood, grilling meat, and tangy herbs and spices. One of the largest barbecue contests in the world, the ≫ American Royal World Series of Barbecue draws more than 600 barbecue circuit teams and renowned pitmasters for invitational and open contests. Held in late October at the Kansas Speedway, this barbecue competition season finale includes food, music, dancing, family activities and fireworks.

KANSAS SPEEDWAY is off I-70 exit 410 (110th St.) at jct. I-435/I-70. The 1,200-acre complex plays host to NASCAR races twice a year on its tri-oval track. The DC Solar FanWalk, accessed by separate admission on Friday and Saturday of event weekends, is an interactive area in the infield. Guests can view a working garage as well as access Autograph Alley, where fans can ask drivers for autographs, watch the presentation of the pole award and have their photo taken in Victory Lane before the race. The Pre-Race Pass (separate admission for each Monster Energy Cup Series races only) gives access to activities including the pre-race concert, driver introductions, DC Solar FanWalk and walking beside pit road to view the cars. General Parking is free and upgraded parking options are available, all with plenty of space for tailgating. Plus, make sure to visit the interactive Midway Display area before each race for the latest merchandise and to inquire about renting a scanner to hear the drivers discuss strategy with their crew chief and spotters during the race.

Hours: NASCAR Gander Outdoors Truck Series and NASCAR Monster Energy Cup Series night races in May and the NASCAR XFINITY Series and Monster Energy NASCAR Cup Series playoff races in Oct. Phone ahead to confirm race schedules.

(See map & index p. 218.)

Cost: Race ticket prices vary based on event. Fan-Walk $15; Pre-Race Pass $75 for select races only; Upgraded fan hospitality options available. **Phone:** (913) 328-3300 for tour information, or (866) 460-7223 for race information and tickets. GT

BEST WESTERN PREMIER KC SPEEDWAY INN & SUITES   913/334-4440   34
▼THREE DIAMOND
Hotel

AAA Benefit: Members save up to 15% and earn bonus points!

Address: 10401 France Family Dr 66111 **Location:** I-435 exit 13B (State Ave), just w. Adjacent to Sporting Park. **Facility:** 82 units. 3 stories, interior corridors. **Amenities:** safes. **Pool:** heated indoor. **Activities:** hot tub, exercise room. **Guest Services:** valet and coin laundry.

CANDLEWOOD SUITES KANSAS CITY SPEEDWAY   913/788-9929   31
APPROVED   Extended Stay Hotel. **Address:** 10920 Parallel Pkwy 66109

CHATEAU AVALON HOTEL   913/596-6000   36
▼THREE DIAMOND   Hotel. **Address:** 701 Village West Pkwy 66111

COMFORT SUITES SPEEDWAY   913/299-4466   29
▼THREE DIAMOND   Hotel. **Address:** 3000 N 103rd Terr 66109

COUNTRY INN & SUITES BY RADISSON, KC VILLAGE WEST   913/299-4700   33
▼THREE DIAMOND   Hotel. **Address:** 1805 N 110th St 66111

HAMPTON INN BY HILTON VILLAGE WEST   913/328-1400   35
▼THREE DIAMOND SAVE Hotel. **Address:** 1400 Village West Pkwy 66111

AAA Benefit: Members save up to 15%!

HOME2 SUITES BY HILTON KU MEDICAL CENTER   913/335-9950   37
▼THREE DIAMOND SAVE Extended Stay Hotel. **Address:** 3440 Rainbow Blvd 66103

AAA Benefit: Members save up to 15%!

HOMEWOOD SUITES BY HILTON KANSAS CITY SPEEDWAY   913/288-9999   30
▼THREE DIAMOND SAVE Extended Stay Hotel. **Address:** 10922 Parallel Pkwy 66109

AAA Benefit: Members save up to 15%!

RESIDENCE INN BY MARRIOTT KANSAS CITY AT THE LEGENDS   913/788-5650   32
▼THREE DIAMOND SAVE Extended Stay Hotel. **Address:** 1875 Village West Pkwy 66111

AAA Benefit: Members save 5% or more!

WHERE TO EAT

CHIUSANO'S BRICK OVEN PIZZERIA   913/299-8787   33
APPROVED   Pizza. Casual Dining. **Address:** 1713 Village West Pkwy 66111

EL TORO LOCO MEXICAN BAR & GRILL   913/400-3050   34
APPROVED   Tex-Mex. Casual Dining. **Address:** 1706 Village West Pkwy 66111

JAZZ A LOUISIANA KITCHEN   913/328-0003   30
APPROVED   Cajun. Casual Dining. **Address:** 1859 Village West Pkwy 66111

JOE'S KANSAS CITY BAR-B-QUE   913/722-3366   36
APPROVED   Barbecue. Quick Serve. **Address:** 3002 W 47th Ave 66103

JOSE PEPPER'S   913/328-0770   32
APPROVED   Southwestern. Casual Dining. **Address:** 1851 Village West Pkwy 66111

STIX   913/299-3788   31
APPROVED   Asian Sushi. Casual Dining. **Address:** 1847 Village West Pkwy 66111

YUKON BASE CAMP GRILL AT CABELA'S   913/328-3173   35
APPROVED   Wild Game Deli. Quick Serve. **Address:** 10300 Cabela Dr 66111

LARNED (D-4) pop. 4,054, elev. 2,002'

Midway along the Santa Fe Trail where Pawnee Creek joins the Arkansas River, the settlement of Larned emerged as the construction of the Santa Fe Railway neared Fort Larned. As the military usefulness of the fort declined, the attractiveness of the fertile agricultural lands became apparent, allowing Larned to develop into the prosperous trading center and county seat it is today.

Central States Scout Museum, 815 Broadway, displays Boy and Girl Scout memorabilia, including uniforms, awards and handbooks; phone (620) 285-6427.

Larned Area Chamber of Commerce: 502 Broadway, Larned, KS 67550. **Phone:** (620) 285-6916 or (800) 747-6919.

FORT LARNED NATIONAL HISTORIC SITE is 6 mi. w. via SR 156. Established in 1859 to protect mail coaches and commercial wagon trains traveling the Santa Fe Trail, the fort was an important post on the frontier until its deactivation in 1878. The site includes nine original sandstone buildings and a section of wagon-wheel rutted prairie. A visitor center has exhibits and a slide program; living-history programs are held in summer and on major holidays.

Guided tours are available by appointment. **Hours:** Daily 8:30-4:30. **Cost:** Free. **Phone:** (620) 285-6911. GT

SANTA FE TRAIL CENTER MUSEUM AND LIBRARY, 2 mi. w. on SR 156, depicts the history of one of America's most important frontier pathways as well as the lifestyles of early Kansas pioneers. Permanent displays include a Wichita Indian hunting lodge, mounted buffalo, a freight wagon, period rooms, a sod house, a limestone cooling house, a one-room schoolhouse, an early African-American church and a dugout house. Changing exhibits also are presented.

Time: Allow 1 hour minimum. **Hours:** Tues.-Sat. 9-5. **Cost:** $6; $3 (ages 12-18); $2 (ages 6-11). **Phone:** (620) 285-2054.

LAWRENCE (C-7) pop. 87,643, elev. 822'
• Hotels p. 104 • Restaurants p. 104

Founded as an abolitionist settlement in 1854 by the New England Emigrant Aid Society, Lawrence was at the center of the controversy concerning slavery that embroiled the state prior to the Civil War. Although the anti-slavery faction won, the other side ultimately had the last word. In 1863 Confederate guerrilla William Quantrill and 400 bushwhackers swept into Lawrence and attacked the ill-prepared home guard, leaving more than 200 dead and causing $1.5 million worth of damage, thus fueling animosities and retaliations between Kansans and Missourians.

Modern day Lawrence is a vibrant smaller city with many big-city amenities. Education, transportation, agriculture and light industry provide the basis for a diverse economy. The University of Kansas and Haskell Indian Nations University, the country's only intertribal Native American college, are focal points for education, arts and culture. Lectures, plays, films, performing arts and concerts are presented year-round at The Lied Center of Kansas; phone the box office at (785) 864-2787. The Lawrence Arts Center, 940 New Hampshire St., hosts visual art, theater and dance events; phone (785) 843-2787.

For recreational pursuits, the city has some 50 parks that offer opportunities for swimming, skateboarding, hiking, tennis, golf, camping and picnicking. Additional information and a map indicating bicycle routes and parks can be obtained at the Parks and Recreation Department, 1141 Massachusetts St., and at the Lawrence Visitor Information Center, 402 N. Second St.; phone (785) 856-3040. Clinton Lake State Park (see Recreation Areas Chart) is 4 miles west of town.

Downtown Lawrence has a number of historic buildings. The Old West Lawrence Historic District, bounded by Sixth, Eighth, Tennessee and Indiana streets, contains more than 40 Victorian- and Italianate-style residences. The 1912 Liberty Hall, 642 Massachusetts St., was the first motion picture theater west of the Mississippi River.

Lawrence Visitor Information Center: 402 N. 2nd St., Lawrence, KS 66044. **Phone:** (785) 856-3040.

Self-guiding tours: Maps for touring the city, its historic district and the University of Kansas campus are available from the visitor center at 402 N. 2nd St.

Shopping: The downtown district, running along Massachusetts Street between Sixth and 11th streets, has an eclectic mixture of locally owned shops, cafes and restaurants as well as large national chain stores.

UNIVERSITY OF KANSAS, s. of I-70 exit 202 via US 59, is on a 1,000-acre campus atop Mount Oread, which is bisected by the Oregon Trail and overlooks the valleys of the Kansas and Wakarusa rivers. A visitor center, at the corner of 15th and Iowa streets, offers maps as well as a brochure of a walking tour covering historic buildings on campus, including the Spencer Museum of Art, Natural History Museum, the World War II memorial campanile, Pharmacy Museum, Dole Institute of Politics and the Booth Hall of Athletics museum adjacent to the Allen Fieldhouse.

Hours: Visitor center Mon.-Fri. 8-5. Closed university holidays and semester breaks. **Cost:** Free. **Phone:** (785) 864-3911 for tour and general campus information or (785) 864-3506.

Kenneth Spencer Research Library is at 1450 Poplar Ln., on the University of Kansas campus. The library contains an extensive collection of rare books, manuscripts, old maps and early photographs. Among the specialties are European books printed in the 15th through 17th centuries; books relating to Ireland and 18th-century England; the history of such sciences as botany, ornithology and zoology; and broad collections of Italian, French and English manuscripts of the 11th through 20th centuries.

Items in the Kansas Collection range from the territorial period to the present. The University Archives contain information on the history of The University of Kansas.

Hours: Mon.-Fri. 9-5 (also Sat. 9-1 during spring and fall semesters). Closed major and university holidays. **Cost:** Free. **Phone:** (785) 864-4334.

Robert J. Dole Institute of Politics is off I-70 exit 202, 1.7 mi. s. on Iowa St. (US 59), then w. into University of Kansas via 19th St. to 2350 Petefish Dr. The bipartisan institute contains research and archival materials related to the careers Bob and Elizabeth Dole. A museum includes interactive exhibits about Kansas native Bob Dole's early life, military service and political accomplishments.

Memorials to the World Trade Center victims and the state's World War II veterans are included. **Time:** Allow 1 hour minimum. **Hours:** Mon.-Sat. 9-5, Sun. noon-5. **Cost:** Free. **Phone:** (785) 864-4900.

Spencer Museum of Art is at 1301 Mississippi St., on the University of Kansas campus; parking is available next to the university union. The museum, which contains more than 45,000 objects in its permanent collection, ranks among the finest university art museums in the country. Strengths are in Renaissance and baroque painting; American paintings and sculpture; the decorative arts of Europe,

America and Asia; and graphic arts, including photographs and Japanese prints.

Permanent and changing exhibits are displayed. **Time:** Allow 1 hour minimum. **Hours:** Tues.-Sat. 10-4 (also Wed.-Thurs. 4-8), Sun. noon-4. Closed major holidays. **Cost:** Donations. **Phone:** (785) 864-4710.

University of Kansas Natural History Museum is in Dyche Hall at 1345 Jayhawk Blvd., on the University of Kansas campus. The museum features native snakes and insects; a working beehive; fossils of animals from the Cretaceous period; and exhibits about microbes, parasites and global ecology. The museum also is home to mounted animals, including Comanche, a 7th Cavalry horse that survived the 1876 Battle of Little Bighorn.

Time: Allow 2 hours minimum. **Hours:** Tues.-Sat. 9-5, Sun. noon-4. Guided tours by appointment. Closed major holidays. **Cost:** Donations. **Phone:** (785) 864-4450. GT

BEST WESTERN PLUS WEST LAWRENCE
785/330-8009

▼▼ THREE DIAMOND		
Hotel	Best Western PLUS	**AAA Benefit:** Members save up to 15% and earn bonus points!

Address: 6101 Rock Chalk Dr 66049 **Location:** I-70 exit 197, 2 mi s, then 1.2 mi e. Adjacent to Rock Chalk Park. **Facility:** 112 units, some efficiencies. 4 stories, interior corridors. **Pool:** heated indoor. **Activities:** exercise room. **Guest Services:** coin laundry.

CIRCLE S RANCH & COUNTRY INN   785/843-4124
▼▼ THREE DIAMOND Ranch. **Address:** 3325 Circle S Ln 66044

COUNTRY INN & SUITES BY RADISSON LAWRENCE
785/749-6010
▼▼ THREE DIAMOND Hotel. **Address:** 2176 E 23rd St 66046

DOUBLETREE BY HILTON LAWRENCE   785/841-7077

▼▼ THREE DIAMOND 〔SAVE〕 Hotel. **Address:** 200 McDonald Dr 66044	**AAA Benefit:** Members save up to 15%!

ELDRIDGE HOTEL   785/749-5011
▼▼ THREE DIAMOND Historic Hotel. **Address:** 701 Massachusetts St 66044

HAMPTON INN BY HILTON   785/841-4994

▼▼ THREE DIAMOND 〔SAVE〕 Hotel. **Address:** 2300 W 6th St 66049	**AAA Benefit:** Members save up to 15%!

HOLIDAY INN EXPRESS HOTEL & SUITES   785/749-7555
▼▼ THREE DIAMOND Hotel. **Address:** 3411 Iowa St 66046

THE OREAD   785/843-1200
▼▼ THREE DIAMOND Hotel. **Address:** 1200 Oread Ave 66044

SPRINGHILL SUITES BY MARRIOTT LAWRENCE
785/841-2700

▼▼ THREE DIAMOND 〔SAVE〕 Hotel. **Address:** 1 Riverfront Plaza, Suite 300 66044	**AAA Benefit:** Members save 5% or more!

TOWNEPLACE SUITES BY MARRIOTT LAWRENCE DOWNTOWN   785/842-8800

▼▼ THREE DIAMOND 〔SAVE〕 Extended Stay Hotel. **Address:** 900 New Hampshire St 66044	**AAA Benefit:** Members save 5% or more!

TRU BY HILTON LAWRENCE   785/727-4244

▼▼ APPROVED 〔SAVE〕 Hotel. **Address:** 510 Wakarusa Dr 66049	Members save up to 15%!

WHERE TO EAT

23RD STREET BREWERY   785/856-2337
▼▼ APPROVED American. Casual Dining. **Address:** 3512 Clinton Pkwy 66047

EL POTRO MEXICAN CAFE   785/331-2500
▼▼ APPROVED Mexican. Casual Dining. **Address:** 3333 Iowa St 66046

FREE STATE BREWING COMPANY   785/843-4555
▼▼ APPROVED American. Casual Dining. **Address:** 636 Massachusetts St 66044

ZEN ZERO   785/832-0001
▼▼ APPROVED Asian. Casual Dining. **Address:** 811 Massachusetts St 66044

LEAVENWORTH (B-8) pop. 35,251, elev. 774'

Incorporated in 1854, Leavenworth is the oldest city in Kansas. In 1857 the firm of Russell, Majors & Waddell made the rapidly growing community the headquarters of their vast overland transportation system. In April 1860 the company's other venture, the Pony Express, used lightweight riders on fleet ponies to speed the mail from St. Joseph, Mo., to Sacramento, Calif., in as little as 9 days. Completion of the transcontinental telegraph in October 1861 rendered the service obsolete.

Leavenworth Landing Park, on the Missouri River at 100 Cherokee St., commemorates the city's role as "Gateway to the West." It features sculptures of a locomotive and a covered wagon as well as depictions of a railroad roundhouse and paddlewheel steamship. Interactive displays depict historical images along the 4-mile walking trail; phone (913) 651-2203.

Leavenworth Convention & Visitors Bureau: 100 N. 5th St., Leavenworth, KS 66048. **Phone:** (913) 682-4113.

Self-guiding tours: Maps featuring area driving and walking tours are available from the convention and visitors bureau.

C.W. PARKER CAROUSEL MUSEUM is .5 mi. e. on Springdale St./Spruce St. (SR 92), .4 mi. n. on S. 4th

St., .2 mi. e. on Choctaw St., then just n. to 320 S. Esplanade St. across from the riverfront. The museum offers artifacts and photographs depicting the work of carnival pioneer and carousel builder C.W. Parker. Guided tours explore the museum and a workshop area at which existing antique horses and carousel figures are repaired and refinished. Tours conclude with a ride on a 1913 Parker wooden carousel, one of three refurbished full-size carousels displayed.

Time. Allow 30 minutes minimum. **Hours:** Thur.-Sat. 11-5, Sun. 1-5, Feb.-Dec. Phone ahead to confirm schedule. **Cost:** Museum free. Guided tour $6; $3 (ages 0-12, includes ride on carousel). Carousel ride $1.50. **Phone:** (913) 682-1331 or (913) 897-2521. GT

FORT LEAVENWORTH is at Seventh St. and US 73. Established in 1827 to guard the Santa Fe and Oregon trails, the fort is the oldest active Army post west of the Mississippi River. It also was an important Army headquarters during the Mexican War 1846-48.

The Santa Fe and Oregon Trail markers, the Fort Leavenworth National Cemetery and the Buffalo Soldier Monument are of interest. Maps are available for self-guiding tours in the museum. All visitors should report to the visitor center. Photo ID is required for all visitors ages 17+ entering the base. **Hours:** Daily dawn-dusk. **Cost:** Free. **Phone:** (913) 684-3191.

Frontier Army Museum is at 100 Reynolds Ave., at Fort Leavenworth. Exhibits provide insight into the founding and development of Fort Leavenworth, the history of the frontier army and the Civil, Mexican and Indian wars. The museum includes the carriage in which Abraham Lincoln rode while visiting Leavenworth, army carriages and a full-size JN4 "Jenny" biplane.

Also displayed are examples of U.S. military dress and equipment up to World War I as well as several rare Mexican War items. Videos about the history of the fort are shown. Cellphone tours are available. All visitors should report to the visitor center. Photo ID is required for all visitors ages 17+ entering the base. **Hours:** Tues.-Fri. 9-4, Sat. 10-4. Closed major holidays. **Cost:** Free. **Phone:** (913) 684-3191.

RICHARD ALLEN CULTURAL CENTER AND MUSEUM is at 412 Kiowa St. The museum highlights the roles African-Americans have played in the history of Kansas and the West with exhibits about the Buffalo Soldiers, a nickname originally applied to members of the all-black Army regiments created after the Civil War. A restored Buffalo Soldiers home features furnishings and 1920s décor.

Other exhibits include an 1860 tallow light belonging to a runaway slave, a collection of historic photos and memorabilia belonging to former Secretary of State Colin Powell. An Underground Railroad guided tour also is offered. **Time:** Allow 1 hour minimum. **Hours:** Mon.-Thurs. 11-6, Fri. 11-4, Sat. by appointment. Closed major holidays. **Cost:** Museum

$5; $3 (ages 0-12). Underground Railroad tour $12.50; $5 (ages 0-12). Combination museum and Underground Railroad tour $15; $5 (ages 0-12). **Phone:** (913) 682-8772. GT

HAMPTON INN BY HILTON LEAVENWORTH KANSAS
913/680-1500

THREE DIAMOND SAVE Hotel. **Address:** 405 Choctaw St 66048

AAA Benefit: Members save up to 15%!

LEAWOOD pop. 31,867

- **Hotels & Restaurants map & index p. 218**
- **Part of Kansas City area — see map p. 199**

ALOFT LEAWOOD-OVERLAND PARK
913/345-9430 109

THREE DIAMOND
Hotel

aloft

AAA Benefit: Members save 5% or more!

Address: 11620 Ash St 66211 **Location:** I-435 exit 77B (Nall Ave), 1.1 mi s, then just e. Located in Town Center shopping area. **Facility:** 156 units. 6 stories, interior corridors. **Amenities:** safes. **Pool:** heated indoor. **Activities:** exercise room. **Guest Services:** coin laundry, area transportation.

SAVE ⑪◆ 🍴 CALL 🚹 🏊 👣 BIZ HS 🛜 ✉ 🖥 🖨 /SOME UNITS 🐾

WHERE TO EAT

THE BRISTOL SEAFOOD GRILL   913/663-5777   98
THREE DIAMOND Seafood. Fine Dining. **Address:** 5400 W 119th St 66209

HEREFORD HOUSE   913/327-0800   97
APPROVED Steak. Fine Dining. **Address:** 5001 Town Center Dr 66211

LA BODEGA   913/428-8272   99
THREE DIAMOND Spanish Small Plates. Casual Dining. **Address:** 4311 W 119th St 66209

PIG & FINCH   913/322-7444   96
THREE DIAMOND American. Gastropub. **Address:** 11570 Ash St 66211

RYE KC   913/642-5800   95
THREE DIAMOND New American. Gastropub. **Address:** 10551 Mission Rd 66206

LENEXA (C-8) pop. 48,190, elev. 1,052'

- **Hotels & Restaurants map & index p. 218**
- **Part of Kansas City area — see map p. 199**

Na-Nex-Se, the wife of a Shawnee Indian chief, lent her name to the Kansas City suburb of Lenexa in 1869. The community attracted German, Swiss and Belgian farmers by the early 1900s, and in the 1930s was known for its prolific spinach crops.

Shawnee Mission Park, 7900 Renner Rd., has one of the largest lakes in the area and offers archery, fishing, hiking trails, horseback riding trails, and canoes, swimming, and windsurfing. The outdoor Theatre in the Park presents plays and musicals; phone (913) 888-4713. *See Recreation Areas Chart.*

Lenexa Chamber of Commerce: 11180 Lackman Rd., Lenexa, KS 66219. **Phone:** (913) 888-1414 or (800) 950-7867.

CANDLEWOOD SUITES LENEXA - OVERLAND PARK AREA
913/888-3300 **80**
APPROVED Extended Stay Hotel. **Address:** 9630 Rosehill Rd 66215

HOLIDAY INN EXPRESS & SUITES - LENEXA - OVERLAND PARK AREA
913/492-4516 **79**
THREE DIAMOND Hotel. **Address:** 9620 Rosehill Rd 66215

HYATT PLACE KANSAS CITY/LENEXA CITY CENTER
913/742-7777 **78**

THREE DIAMOND
Hotel

HYATT PLACE **AAA Benefit:** Members save up to 10%!

Address: 8741 Ryckert St 66219 **Location:** I-435 exit 3, just w, then just s. **Facility:** 127 units. 6 stories, interior corridors. **Pool:** heated indoor. **Activities:** exercise room. **Guest Services:** valet and coin laundry. **Featured Amenity:** breakfast buffet.

SAVE ꠸꠸ CALL ꠸ ꠸ ꠸ BIZ
꠸ ꠸ ꠸ ꠸
/SOME UNITS ꠸ HS

SPRINGHILL SUITES BY MARRIOTT KANSAS CITY LENEXA/ CITY CENTER
913/225-9955 **77**
THREE DIAMOND SAVE Hotel. **Address:** 17190 W 87th St 66219

AAA Benefit: Members save 5% or more!

WHERE TO EAT

BO LING'S
913/888-6618
APPROVED Chinese. Casual Dining. **Address:** 9576 Quivira Rd 66215

SHOGUN SUSHI & STEAK RESTAURANT   913/438-3888 **75**
APPROVED Japanese Sushi Steak. Casual Dining. **Address:** 12028 W 95th St 66215

LIBERAL (F-2) pop. 20,525, elev. 2,839'

Now used by the Cotton Belt Railroad, the Rock Island Railroad Bridge across the Cimarron River is one of the largest of its kind. Called "Mighty Sampson," it is 1,268 feet long and 100 feet above the riverbed. Support pylons were driven to a depth of 165 feet to resist the shifting quicksand of the river.

Liberal Convention and Visitors Bureau: 1 Yellow Brick Rd., Liberal, KS 67901. **Phone:** (620) 626-0170 or (800) 542-3725.

DOROTHY'S HOUSE / LAND OF OZ / CORONADO MUSEUM is at 567 Yellow Brick Rd. Dorothy's House is a replica of the fictional Kansas farmhouse depicted in the 1939 motion picture "The Wizard of Oz." A re-creation of the Yellow Brick Road leads to the Land of Oz Museum, which features exhibits about the film as well as related memorabilia. The Coronado Museum contains pictures, documents and historical items pertaining to Seward County and early Kansas.

Time: Allow 1 hour minimum. **Hours:** Guided tours are offered Mon.-Sat. 9-6, Sun. 1-5, Memorial Day-Labor Day; Tues.-Sat. 9-5, Sun. 1-5, rest of year. Last tour departs 30 minutes before closing. **Cost:** Dorothy's House and Land of Oz $7; $5.50 (ages 65+); $4.50 (ages 6-18). Coronado Museum by donation. **Phone:** (620) 624-7624. **GT**

MID-AMERICA AIR MUSEUM, 2000 W. Second St., is Kansas' largest aviation museum. Collections consist of military and civilian aircraft as well as aerospace aviation exhibits. Visitors can see World War II fighters and bombers, experimental and golden age aircraft and planes used in the Korean and Vietnam wars.

Features include the Liberal Army Airfield, Korean War exhibits, the Col. Tom A. Thomas Jr. Historic Aircraft Collection and a NASA exhibit. More than 100 aircraft are displayed, including such rare planes as the Grumman TBM Avenger, North American B-25, Rutan aircraft, Vought F4U-5N Crusader and the Douglas A-4 Skyhawk. Wind tunnel and hot air balloon exhibits are part of the Aviation Hall of Science.

Time: Allow 1 hour minimum. **Hours:** Mon.-Fri. 8-5, Sat. 10-5, Sun. 1-5. Last admission 1 hour before closing. **Cost:** $7; $5 (ages 62+); $3 (ages 6-18). **Phone:** (620) 624-5263.

AMERICAS BEST VALUE INN   620/624-6203

APPROVED   Motel. **Address:** 564 E Pancake Blvd
67901

BEST WESTERN PLUS LIBERAL HOTEL & SUITES
620/624-9700

THREE DIAMOND
Hotel

Best Western PLUS
AAA Benefit: Members save up to 15% and earn bonus points!

Address: 1550 N Lincoln Ave 67901 **Location:** 1.5 mi n on US 83 business route. **Facility:** 67 units. 3 stories, interior corridors. **Pool:** heated indoor. **Activities:** exercise room. **Guest Services:** coin laundry. **Featured Amenity:** breakfast buffet.

HAMPTON INN & SUITES BY HILTON LIBERAL
620/604-0699

THREE DIAMOND
Hotel

Hampton
AAA Benefit: Members save up to 15%!

Address: 508 Hotel Dr 67901 **Location:** 1.2 mi w of jct US 54 and 83. **Facility:** 77 units. 4 stories, interior corridors. **Pool:** heated indoor. **Activities:** hot tub, exercise room. **Guest Services:** coin laundry. **Featured Amenity:** breakfast buffet.

MANHATTAN (C-6) pop. 52,281, elev. 1,019'
• Restaurants p. 108

Most of its residents having come from northern states, Manhattan maintained a decidedly free-state stance during the "Bleeding Kansas" era. As New England continued to send emigrants to Kansas to cement the abolitionist sympathies, organizations in the East often donated money to the settlers.

The city is nestled in the Flint Hills, so named for their bands of limestone and flint. The region, which remains largely untouched by the plow, includes the Konza Prairie. The Flint Hills are the largest remnants of tallgrass prairie on the continent; uncut or ungrazed, the native bluestem grasses can grow 8 feet high. A self-guiding hiking trail is open daily dawn to dusk and offers views of the tallgrass and limestone geology; a $2 trail fee is charged. No bikes or pets are allowed on the trail.

Kansas State Agricultural College, now Kansas State University, opened its doors in 1863; it was one of the first land-grant colleges in the nation. Tours of the more than 24,000-student campus are offered; phone (785) 532-6011.

Forty-five-acre City Park, on Poyntz Avenue between 11th and 14th streets, includes a pioneer log cabin, swimming pool, rose garden and a 30-foot statue of Johnny Kaw, a mythical Kansas wheat farmer. Tuttle Creek State Park (see Recreation

Areas Chart) offers 13,350 acres for sports, hunting and recreation, while Pottawatomie State Fishing Lake No. 2 (see Recreation Areas Chart) offers 247 acres.

In late June, country music fans flock to Tuttle Creek State Park for the Country Stampede, a 4-day music festival featuring big-name country-music stars as well as food, shopping opportunities and exhibits.

Manhattan Convention and Visitors Bureau: 501 Poyntz Ave., Manhattan, KS 66502. **Phone:** (785) 776-8829 or (800) 759-0134.

Shopping: Manhattan Town Center, at Third and Poyntz avenues, features Dillard's and JCPenney. Aggieville, near the Kansas State campus, is a mix of bars, restaurants and shops located within a six-square-block area that is the state's first dedicated shopping district.

KANSAS STATE UNIVERSITY INSECT ZOO is .7 mi. e. on Claflin Rd., then .1 mi. n. to 1500 Denison Ave. on the university's campus. Among the zoo's exhibits are freshwater and Amazonian rain forest displays, a honeybee observatory and a leaf-cutter ant colony spread throughout the building, viewable via glass panes and tubing. Terraria house a variety of arthropods including millipedes, scorpions, tarantulas and walking sticks; visitors may interact with selected insects during guided tours.

Time: Allow 45 minutes minimum. **Hours:** Zoo open Tues.-Fri. 1-6, Sat. noon-6. Guided tours are offered Mon. 9-6 and Tues.-Fri. 9-noon. Reservations for guided tours must be made at least 1 week in advance. **Cost:** $3; $2 (active military with ID); free (ages 0-2); Guided tour $4. **Phone:** (785) 532-2847, or (785) 532-5891 for guided tour reservations. GT

BEST WESTERN MANHATTAN INN
785/537-8300

APPROVED
Hotel

Best Western
AAA Benefit: Members save up to 15% and earn bonus points!

Address: 601 E Poyntz Ave 66502 **Location:** SR 177, 0.5 mi e on US 24 (Frontage Rd). **Facility:** 45 units. 2 stories (no elevator), interior corridors. **Parking:** winter plug-ins. **Pool:** heated indoor. **Activities:** exercise room. **Guest Services:** coin laundry.

CANDLEWOOD SUITES
785/320-7995

THREE DIAMOND Extended Stay Hotel. **Address:** 210 Blue Earth Pl 66502

FAIRFIELD BY MARRIOTT
785/539-2400

THREE DIAMOND SAVE Hotel. **Address:** 300 Colorado St 66502

AAA Benefit: Members save 5% or more!

HAMPTON INN BY HILTON   785/539-5000
THREE DIAMOND SAVE Hotel. **Address:** 501 E Poyntz Ave 66502

AAA Benefit: Members save up to 15%!

HILTON GARDEN INN & MANHATTAN CONFERENCE CENTER
785/532-9116
THREE DIAMOND SAVE Hotel. **Address:** 410 S 3rd St 66502

AAA Benefit: Members save up to 15%!

HOLIDAY INN AT THE CAMPUS   785/539-7531
THREE DIAMOND Hotel. **Address:** 1641 Anderson Ave 66502

HOLIDAY INN EXPRESS & SUITES   785/320-7454
THREE DIAMOND Hotel. **Address:** 115 Blue Earth Pl 66502

WHERE TO EAT

AJ'S NY PIZZERIA   785/587-0700
APPROVED Pizza. Casual Dining. **Address:** 301 Poyntz Ave 66502

BLUE MOOSE BAR & GRILL   785/370-3010
APPROVED American. Casual Dining. **Address:** 100 Manhattan Town Center 66502

BOURBON AND BAKER   785/320-4959
APPROVED Small Plates Soul Food. Casual Dining. **Address:** 312 Poyntz Ave 66502

THE CHEF A BREAKFAST CAFE   785/537-6843
APPROVED Breakfast. Casual Dining. **Address:** 111 S 4th St 66502

COCO BOLOS WOOD-FIRED GRILL & CANTINA
785/537-4700
APPROVED Mexican. Casual Dining. **Address:** 1227 Bluemont Ave 66502

DANCING GANESHA   785/323-7465
APPROVED Indian. Casual Dining. **Address:** 712 N Manhattan Ave 66502

HARRY'S   785/537-1300
THREE DIAMOND Continental. Fine Dining. **Address:** 418 Poyntz Ave 66502

LITTLE APPLE BREWING COMPANY   785/539-5500
APPROVED American. Casual Dining. **Address:** 1110 Westloop Shopping Center 66502

ROCK-A-BELLY BAR & DELI   785/539-8033
APPROVED Deli. Casual Dining. **Address:** 718 N Manhattan Ave 66502

SO LONG SALOON   785/537-9292
APPROVED American. Casual Dining. **Address:** 1130 Moro St 66502

TACO LUCHA   785/320-5255
APPROVED Mexican. Casual Dining. **Address:** 1130 Moro St 66502

MARQUETTE (D-5) pop. 641, elev. 1,388'

KANSAS MOTORCYCLE MUSEUM is at 120 N. Washington St. More than 100 motorcycles of various ages, makes and models fill this museum's two buildings. During his 6-decade-long racing career, the museum's owner won more than 600 trophies, which are on display. Visitors also will see an array of motorcycle memorabilia. **Time:** Allow 1 hour minimum. **Hours:** Mon.-Sat. 10-5, Sun. 11-5. Phone ahead to confirm holiday schedule. **Cost:** Donations. **Phone:** (785) 546-2449. GT

MARYSVILLE (B-6) pop. 3,294, elev. 1,154'

Marysville, known as the "Black Squirrel City," is one of few known spots in the country in which the black squirrel lives in the wild. The squirrels first came to the city in 1912 as part of a carnival's sideshow to entertain a group of Civil War veterans. Some local youngsters released the squirrels, which scampered from their cages to freedom in the city park, where their descendants still frolic.

Marysville was settled mainly by travelers along the Oregon Trail, seven emigrant trails and the Otoe Indian and Pony Express trails. The town was named for the wife of merchant Frank Marshall, who operated a ferry across the Big Blue River. Several emigrant parties camped near the ferry crossing 1840-60.

The state's first civilian post office was established in Marysville on Nov. 11, 1854. The town also was the home of the first state bank in Kansas. Marysville and surrounding Marshall County have several national historic landmarks, including old schools, houses and churches dating from the mid-1800s (some of these buildings are not open to the public).

A Union Pacific steam locomotive, schoolhouse, sod house and an 1870 railroad depot sit in Marysville's City Park. Three "Lifetile" murals created by artist Rufus Seder are displayed at the Pony Express Plaza at jct. N. 7th and Center sts.

Marysville Chamber of Commerce: 101 N. 10th St., P.O. Box 16, Marysville, KS 66508. **Phone:** (785) 562-3101 or (800) 752-3965.

Self-guiding tours: Maps detailing a walking tour of Marysville are available from the chamber of commerce.

ORIGINAL PONY EXPRESS HOME STATION NO. 1 MUSEUM, 106 S. Eighth St., served as an 1859 headquarters for the postal riders before the introduction of the telegraph to the Western territories. The museum displays post office boxes from the state's first civilian post office, established in Marysville in 1854. **Hours:** Mon.-Sat. 9-4, Sun. noon-4, mid-Apr. through the last weekend in Oct.; by appointment rest of year, depending on staffing. **Cost:** $4; $2 (ages 6-12). **Phone:** (785) 562-3825, or (785) 562-3101 (Marysville Chamber of Commerce).

HERITAGE INN EXPRESS   785/562-5588
APPROVED Hotel. **Address:** 1155 Pony Express Hwy 66508

WHERE TO EAT

WAGON WHEEL CAFE   785/562-3784
APPROVED American. Casual Dining. **Address:** 703 Broadway 66508

MCPHERSON (D-5) pop. 13,155, elev. 1,490'

McPherson bears the name of Union Civil War general James Birdseye McPherson, who was killed in the Battle of Atlanta in 1864. Although Gen. McPherson never visited the Kansas city named after him, his bronze likeness has watched over the city from its perch in Memorial Park since 1917. At 100 N. Maple St. is the historically maintained 1893 McPherson County Courthouse and its 105-foot-high clock tower. The Richardsonian-Romanesque building was designed by John G. Haskell, a prominent architect at the time. The Santa Fe Trail, which crosses just south of McPherson, is a present-day reminder of the area's pioneer heritage.

McPherson Convention and Visitors Bureau: 1111 E. Kansas Ave., McPherson, KS 67460. **Phone:** (620) 241-3340 or (800) 324-8022.

Self-guiding tours: Information detailing walking and driving tours is available from the convention and visitors bureau.

FAIRFIELD INN & SUITES BY MARRIOTT MCPHERSON
620/504-5353
THREE DIAMOND (SAVE) Hotel. **Address:** 2270 E Kansas Ave 67460
AAA Benefit: Members save 5% or more!

HAMPTON INN BY HILTON MCPHERSON   620/480 2900
THREE DIAMOND (SAVE) Hotel. **Address:** 200 N Centennial Dr 67460
AAA Benefit: Members save up to 15%!

MEADE (E-3) pop. 1,721, elev. 2,500'

Deep artesian wells contribute to the verdancy of Meade's tree-lined streets as well as to that of surrounding farms and ranches. Meade State Park is 12 miles southwest off SR 23 *(see Recreation Areas Chart)*.

Meade County Economic Development: P.O. Box 238, Meade, KS 67864-0238. **Phone:** (620) 873-8795.

MEADE COUNTY HISTORICAL SOCIETY MUSEUM, 200 E. Carthage, offers a maze of exhibits depicting the area's history. A one-room schoolhouse, church, sod house, general store and blacksmith shop are presented. Also featured is a livery barn with a horse-drawn wicker carriage, a sheepherder's wagon and saddles. **Time:** Allow 1 hour minimum. **Hours:** Tues.-Sat. 10-5, Sun. 1-5. **Cost:** Free. **Phone:** (620) 873-2359.

MERRIAM pop. 11,003
- **Hotels & Restaurants map & index p. 218**
- **Part of Kansas City area — see map p. 199**

DRURY INN-MERRIAM/SHAWNEE MISSION
913/236-9200 **68**
APPROVED Hotel. **Address:** 9009 Shawnee Mission Pkwy 66202

HAMPTON INN & SUITES BY HILTON   913/722-0800 **69**
THREE DIAMOND (SAVE) Hotel. **Address:** 7400 W Frontage Rd 66203
AAA Benefit: Members save up to 15%!

MULVANE pop. 6,111

HAMPTON INN & SUITES BY HILTON   316/524-3777
THREE DIAMOND (SAVE) Hotel. **Address:** 785 Kansas Star Dr 67110
AAA Benefit: Members save up to 15%!

NEWTON (D-5) pop. 19,132, elev. 1,445'

Newton's history began in 1870 when the site was chosen as a location for a new Atchison, Topeka & Santa Fe Railway terminal. Its position on the Chisholm Trail made the site a logical location. When the railroad pushed on to Dodge City and Wichita, so did Newton's wild and wicked cow town image.

As pressures against their beliefs mounted, Russian Mennonites looked to the North American prairies for a new home. Bernhard Warkentin visited central Kansas in 1872, his favorable reports elicited a wave of immigration. As a result, Newton and the surrounding area constitute the largest Mennonite settlement in the United States.

Mennonite farmers brought with them Turkey Red winter wheat seeds, which had flourished on the central European steppes. Warkentin built a gristmill at nearby Halstead and began promoting the use of this hardy new grain, which was well-suited to conditions in Kansas. His efforts at establishing hard winter wheat helped make Kansas known as the "wheat capital of the world." Warkentin's residence still stands at 211 E. First St.

Newton Convention and Visitors Bureau: 201 E. Sixth St., Newton, KS 67114. **Phone:** (316) 284-6015 or (316) 283-7633.

COMFORT INN & SUITES   316/804-4866
APPROVED Hotel. **Address:** 1205 E 1st St 67114

WHERE TO EAT

GENOVA ITALIAN RESTAURANT   316/587-8099
APPROVED Italian. Casual Dining. **Address:** 1021 Washington Rd 67114

NORTH NEWTON (D-5) pop. 1,759, elev. 1,440'

KAUFFMAN MUSEUM is .7 mi. s. of I-135 exit 34 at 2801 N. Main St., across from Bethel College. The museum is on a 5-acre site that consists of woods and a re-created prairie with native grasses and wildflowers. Indoor exhibits focus on Native Americans, the natural history of the Plains, and the culture and heritage of European Mennonites who immigrated to the Central Plains in the 1870s.

Permanent exhibits include Mennonite Immigrant Furniture, Mirror of the Martyrs and Of Land and People. Temporary exhibits often are available. Historical buildings include a late 19th-century homesteader's log cabin and a Kansas farmstead with an 1875 house and 1886 barn.

Time: Allow 1 hour minimum. **Hours:** Tues.-Fri. 9:30-4:30, Sat.-Sun. 1:30-4:30. Closed major holidays. **Cost:** $4; $2 (ages 6-16). **Phone:** (316) 283-1612.

OLATHE (C-8) pop. 125,872, elev. 1,023'
- Hotels & Restaurants map & index p. 218
- Part of Kansas City area — see map p. 199

In 1856 Dr. John T. Barton, appointed physician to the Shawnee Indians, staked a claim to land to which the Shawnees were giving up tribal title and named the land after the Shawnee word for beautiful, *Olathe.* Shortly after Olathe was established, it replaced the settlement of Shawnee as the county seat.

After Kansas was admitted to the Union as a free state in 1861, the town became an easy target for Confederate guerilla commander William Quantrill and his raiders, who invaded and destroyed much of the settlement. Once the Civil War ended, however, Olathe began to rebuild. The rich farmland and a railroad brought new settlers to the area.

Olathe Area Chamber of Commerce: 18001 W. 106th St., Suite 160, Olathe, KS 66061. **Phone:** (913) 764-1050.

BEST WESTERN PLUS OLATHE HOTEL   913/440-9762

THREE DIAMOND
Hotel

AAA Benefit: Members save up to 15% and earn bonus points!

Address: 1580 S Hamilton Cir 66061 **Location:** I-35 exit 215 (151st St), just nw. **Facility:** 67 units. 3 stories, interior corridors. **Pool:** heated indoor. **Activities:** hot tub, exercise room. **Guest Services:** valet and coin laundry.

FAIRFIELD INN & SUITES BY MARRIOTT
913/768-7000   106

THREE DIAMOND SAVE Hotel. **Address:** 12245 S Strang Line Rd 66062

AAA Benefit: Members save 5% or more!

HAMPTON INN BY HILTON   913/393-1111   104

THREE DIAMOND SAVE Hotel. **Address:** 12081 S Strang Line Rd 66062

AAA Benefit: Members save up to 15%!

HILTON GARDEN INN OLATHE   913/815-2345   103

THREE DIAMOND SAVE Hotel. **Address:** 12080 S Strang Line Rd 66062

AAA Benefit: Members save up to 15%!

HOLIDAY INN EXPRESS & SUITES OLATHE NORTH
913/397-0100   102

THREE DIAMOND Hotel. **Address:** 12070 S Strang Line Rd 66062

HOLIDAY INN EXPRESS & SUITES OLATHE SOUTH
913/948-9000

THREE DIAMOND Hotel. **Address:** 15475 S Rogers Rd 66061

RESIDENCE INN BY MARRIOTT   913/829-6700   105

THREE DIAMOND SAVE Extended Stay Hotel. **Address:** 12215 S Strang Line Rd 66062

AAA Benefit: Members save 5% or more!

WHERE TO EAT

JOE'S KANSAS CITY BARBEQUE   913/782-6858   91

APPROVED Barbecue. Quick Serve. **Address:** 11950 S Strang Line Rd 66062

KMACHO'S MEXICAN GRILL & CANTINA   913/768-7777   92

APPROVED Tex-Mex. Casual Dining. **Address:** 1229 E Santa Fe St 66061

OTTAWA (C-7) pop. 12,649, elev. 910'

OLD DEPOT MUSEUM, s.w. of jct. SR 68 and US 59 at 135 W. Tecumseh St., is in a two-story 1888 limestone building that originally was a passenger depot on the Santa Fe Railroad. A model train layout depicts local railroading in 1950. Displays focus on area history, including John Brown's Pottawatomie Massacre; changing exhibits are presented. **Hours:** Tues.-Sat. 10-4, Sun. 1-4. **Cost:** $3; $1 (students with ID); free (active military with ID and immediate family, Memorial Day-Labor Day). **Phone:** (785) 242-1250.

OVERLAND PARK (C-8) pop. 173,372, elev. 951'
- Restaurants p. 112
- Hotels & Restaurants map & index p. 218
- Part of Kansas City area — see map p. 199

One of the largest cities in the state, Overland Park is the leading business and commercial center for the Johnson County portion of the Kansas City metropolitan area.

(See map & index p. 218.)

Visit Overland Park: 9001 W. 110th St., Suite 100, Overland Park, KS 66210. **Phone:** (913) 491-0123 or (800) 262-7275.

Shopping: The historic Santa Fe Trail passes through downtown Overland Park where you can walk in any direction from 79th Street and Santa Fe Drive to find an eclectic variety of dining, entertainment and shopping venues. Some 300 locally owned, small businesses include restaurants and shops offering arts, gifts and hobby items.

The Overland Park Farmers Market is held Saturdays 8-1 at Matt Ross Community Center, 7950 Marty St., from April through November and features more than 70 vendors. The seasonal selection of fruits and vegetables is outstanding. Browse from a variety of baked goods, dairy and meat products, flowers, herbs and spices. Enjoy events including cooking demonstrations, healthy lifestyle fairs and live music.

Take a leisurely stroll past Tuscan-inspired architecture through tree-lined courtyards and enjoy the tranquil sounds of fountains and waterfalls at Corbin Park, 6503 W. 135th St., an open-air retail village. The sprawling mall is anchored by JCPenney, Scheels and Von Maur, and has more than 20 stores and 12 restaurants, from casual to fine dining.

Anchored by department store favorites Dillard's, JCPenney, Macy's and Nordstrom, the two-story Oak Park Mall, 11149 W. 95th St., has more than 185 boutiques, eateries and specialty stores.

JOHNSON COUNTY MUSEUM OF HISTORY is at 8788 Metcalf Ave. The Seeking the Good Life exhibit has more than 500 artifacts and explores three time periods in Johnson County. These eras are 1820-1880: Settling the Land; 1880-1945: Building the Suburbs; and 1945-present: Developing an Edge City. Interactive displays also highlight the county's history. KidScape offers hands-on exhibits for children that include a bookstore, park, city hall, hospital, fashion boutique and theater.

A research library also is available. **Time:** Allow 30 minutes minimum. **Hours:** Mon.-Sat. 10-4:30. Closed major holidays. Phone ahead to confirm schedule. **Cost:** Donations. **Phone:** (913) 715-2550.

OVERLAND PARK ARBORETUM AND BOTANICAL GARDENS is .5 mi. w. of US 69 at jct. 179th St. and Antioch Rd. Multiple gardens and ecosystems cover 300 acres. The Erikson Water Garden features bird and butterfly plants and ornamental grasses. Marder Woodland Garden has regional flora, wood and stone arbors, and a koi pond. The willow trees and annuals in the Monet Garden are similar to their namesake gardens in France.

A children's garden as well as an environmental education and visitor center are available. **Time:** Allow 1 hour minimum. **Hours:** Daily 8-7:30, Apr. 10 to Sept. 30; 8-5, rest of year. **Cost:** $3; $1 (ages 6-12); free (ages 0-5 and to all Tues.). **Phone:** (913) 685-3604.

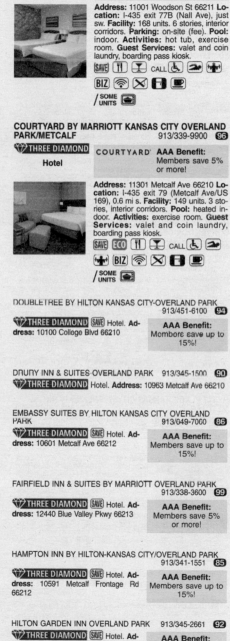

COURTYARD BY MARRIOTT KANSAS CITY/OVERLAND PARK CONVENTION CENTER 913/317-8500 **91**

THREE DIAMOND

Hotel

COURTYARD **AAA Benefit:** Members save 5% or more!

Address: 11001 Woodson St 66211 **Location:** I-435 exit 77B (Nall Ave), just sw. **Facility:** 168 units. 6 stories, interior corridors. **Parking:** on-site (fee). **Pool:** indoor. **Activities:** hot tub, exercise room. **Guest Services:** valet and coin laundry, boarding pass kiosk.

COURTYARD BY MARRIOTT KANSAS CITY OVERLAND PARK/METCALF 913/339-9900 **96**

THREE DIAMOND

Hotel

COURTYARD **AAA Benefit:** Members save 5% or more!

Address: 11301 Metcalf Ave 66210 **Location:** I-435 exit 79 (Metcalf Ave/US 169), 0.6 mi s. **Facility:** 149 units. 3 stories, interior corridors. **Pool:** heated indoor. **Activities:** exercise room. **Guest Services:** valet and coin laundry, boarding pass kiosk.

DOUBLETREE BY HILTON KANSAS CITY-OVERLAND PARK 913/451-6100 **94**

THREE DIAMOND SAVE Hotel. **Address:** 10100 College Blvd 66210

AAA Benefit: Members save up to 15%!

DRURY INN & SUITES-OVERLAND PARK 913/345-1500 **90**

THREE DIAMOND Hotel. **Address:** 10963 Metcalf Ave 66210

EMBASSY SUITES BY HILTON KANSAS CITY OVERLAND PARK 913/649-7000 **86**

THREE DIAMOND SAVE Hotel. **Address:** 10601 Metcalf Ave 66212

AAA Benefit: Members save up to 15%!

FAIRFIELD INN & SUITES BY MARRIOTT OVERLAND PARK 913/338-3600 **99**

THREE DIAMOND SAVE Hotel. **Address:** 12440 Blue Valley Pkwy 66213

AAA Benefit: Members save 5% or more!

HAMPTON INN BY HILTON-KANSAS CITY/OVERLAND PARK 913/341-1551 **85**

THREE DIAMOND SAVE Hotel. **Address:** 10591 Metcalf Frontage Rd 66212

AAA Benefit: Members save up to 15%!

HILTON GARDEN INN OVERLAND PARK 913/345-2661 **92**

THREE DIAMOND SAVE Hotel. **Address:** 5800 College Blvd 66211

AAA Benefit: Members save up to 15%!

(See map & index p. 218.)

HOLIDAY INN & SUITES CONVENTION CENTER OVERLAND PARK 913/312-0900 **88**
▼ THREE DIAMOND Hotel. **Address:** 10920 Nall Ave 66211

HOLIDAY INN & SUITES OVERLAND PARK-WEST 913/888-8440 **83**
▼ THREE DIAMOND Hotel. **Address:** 8787 Reeder Rd 66214

HOMEWOOD SUITES BY HILTON 913/341-5576 **84**
▼ THREE DIAMOND
Extended Stay Hotel

AAA Benefit: Members save up to 15%!
Address: 10556 Marty Ave 66212 **Location:** I-435 exit 79 (Metcalf Ave/US 169), just nw. **Facility:** 92 efficiencies, some two bedrooms. 4 stories, interior corridors. **Pool:** heated outdoor. **Activities:** hot tub, exercise room. **Guest Services:** valet and coin laundry, area transportation. **Featured Amenity:** breakfast buffet.
SAVE | CALL | 🚐 | ⚕ | BIZ
📶 ✕ 🖥 🍽 💻

HYATT PLACE KANSAS CITY/OVERLAND PARK/ CONVENTION CENTER 913/491-9002 **87**
▼ THREE DIAMOND
Contemporary Hotel
HYATT PLACE**AAA Benefit:** Members save up to 10%!
Address: 5001 W 110th St 66211 **Location:** I-435 exit 77B (Nall Ave), just se. **Facility:** 134 units. 6 stories, interior corridors. **Amenities:** safes. **Pool:** heated outdoor. **Activities:** exercise room. **Guest Services:** valet laundry. **Featured Amenity:** breakfast buffet.
SAVE CALL 🚐 ⚕ BIZ 📶
✕ 🎥 🖥 💻
/ SOME UNITS 🐾 HS

HYATT PLACE KANSAS CITY/OVERLAND PARK/ METCALF 913/451-2553 **95**
▼ THREE DIAMOND
Contemporary Hotel
HYATT PLACE**AAA Benefit:** Members save up to 10%!
Address: 6801 W 112th St 66211 **Location:** I-435 exit 79 (Metcalf Ave/US 169), 0.6 mi s. **Facility:** 124 units. 6 stories, interior corridors. **Amenities:** Some: safes. **Pool:** heated outdoor. **Activities:** exercise room. **Guest Services:** valet and coin laundry. **Featured Amenity:** breakfast buffet.
SAVE 🍽 CALL 🚐 ⚕ BIZ
📶 ✕ 🎥 🖥 💻
/ SOME UNITS 🐾

MARRIOTT KANSAS CITY OVERLAND PARK 913/451-8000 **89**
▼ THREE DIAMOND SAVE Hotel. **Address:** 10800 Metcalf Ave 66210
AAA Benefit: Members save 5% or more!

RESIDENCE INN BY MARRIOTT 913/491-4444 **97**
▼ THREE DIAMOND SAVE Extended Stay Hotel. **Address:** 12010 Blue Valley Pkwy 66213
AAA Benefit: Members save 5% or more!

SHERATON OVERLAND PARK HOTEL AT THE CONVENTION CENTER 913/234-2100 **93**
▼ THREE DIAMOND
Hotel
 SHERATON
AAA Benefit: Members save 5% or more!
Address: 6100 College Blvd 66211 **Location:** I-435 exit 79 (Metcalf Ave/US 169), just s to College Blvd, then 0.6 mi e. **Facility:** 412 units. 20 stories, interior corridors. **Parking:** on-site and valet. **Amenities:** safes. **Pool:** heated indoor. **Activities:** hot tub, exercise room. **Guest Services:** valet laundry, boarding pass kiosk.
SAVE ECO 🍽 🛗 🍽 CALL ♿
🚐 ⚕ BIZ SHS 📶 ✕ 🎥 🖥 💻
/ SOME UNITS 🐾

SPRINGHILL SUITES BY MARRIOTT 913/491-0010 **98**
▼ APPROVED SAVE Hotel. **Address:** 12000 Blue Valley Pkwy 66213
AAA Benefit: Members save 5% or more!

WHERE TO EAT

BARLEY'S KITCHEN + TAP 913/663-4099 **88**
▼ APPROVED American. Casual Dining. **Address:** 11924 W 119th St 66213

THE BURG & BARREL 913/444-0494 **78**
▼ APPROVED Burgers. Casual Dining. **Address:** 7042 W 76th St 66204

BURNT END BBQ 913/451-8888 **87**
▼ APPROVED Barbecue. Quick Serve. **Address:** 11831 Metcalf Ave 66210

FIORELLA'S JACK STACK BARBECUE - OVERLAND PARK 913/385-7427 **82**
▼ APPROVED Barbecue. Casual Dining. **Address:** 9520 Metcalf Ave 66212

GAROZZO'S OVERLAND PARK 913/491-8300 **85**
▼ APPROVED Italian. Casual Dining. **Address:** 9950 College Blvd 66210

INDIA PALACE 913/381-1680 **80**
▼ APPROVED Indian. Casual Dining. **Address:** 9918 W 87th St 66212

J. ALEXANDER'S RESTAURANT 913/469-1995 **86**
▼ THREE DIAMOND American. Casual Dining. **Address:** 11471 Metcalf Ave 66212

JOHNNY CASCONE'S ITALIAN RESTAURANT 913/381-6837 **81**
▼ APPROVED Italian. Casual Dining. **Address:** 6863 W 91st St 66212

JOSE PEPPER'S 913/341-5673 **83**
▼ APPROVED Southwestern. Casual Dining. **Address:** 10316 Metcalf Ave 66212

(See map & index p. 218.)

MR. GYROS GREEK FOOD AND PASTRY 913/381-4218 (79)
 APPROVED Greek. Quick Serve. **Address:** 8234
Metcalf Ave 66204

Q39 SOUTH 913/951-4500 (84)
APPROVED Barbecue. Casual Dining. **Address:**
11051 Antioch Rd 66210

PARK CITY pop. 7,297
• Hotels & Restaurants map & index p. 123

BEST WESTERN WICHITA NORTH HOTEL & SUITES
316/832-9387 (35)

APPROVED
Hotel

Best Western | **AAA Benefit:** Members save up to 15% and earn bonus points!

Address: 915 E 53rd St N 67219 **Location:** I-135 exit 13, just w. **Facility:** 149 units, some efficiencies. 2 stories, interior/exterior corridors. **Pool:** heated indoor. **Activities:** hot tub, game room, exercise room. **Guest Services:** valet and coin laundry, area transportation. **Featured Amenity:** breakfast buffet.

QUALITY INN & SUITES 316/927-3900 (34)
APPROVED Hotel. **Address:** 792 E Beaumont St 67219

SUPER 8-WICHITA NORTH/PARK CITY 316/744-2071 (33)
APPROVED Motel. **Address:** 6075 N Air Cap Dr 67219

PARSONS (E-7) pop. 10,500, elev. 902'

Parsons' history is closely intertwined with that of the Missouri-Kansas-Texas Railroad, also known as the KATY or MKT. It was home of the diesel shops for the line until it was sold to the Union Pacific in the 1980s.

Buildings of architectural note include the 1920s Carnegie Arts Center, formerly the town's library, and the Parsons Municipal Auditorium, which hosts concerts, theater productions and civic gatherings. The First Presbyterian Church's turrets and stained-glass windows make it a much-photographed structure. Hundreds of Civil War veterans are buried at Oakwood Cemetery, known for its wartime monuments and memorials.

The Parsons Arboretum, S. 21st Street and Briggs Avenue adjacent to Glenwood Park, includes a visitor center, wetlands area, observation deck and an 18-hole disc golf course; phone (620) 421-7088. Nearby, both Pearson-Skubitz Big Hill Lake and Neosho State Fishing Lake *(see Recreation Areas Chart)* offer camping and fishing facilities.

Parsons Chamber of Commerce and Labette County Tourism: 506 E. Main St., Parsons, KS 67357. **Phone:** (620) 421-6500 or (800) 280-6401.

BEST WESTERN PARSONS INN 620/423-0303
APPROVED
Hotel

Best Western | **AAA Benefit:** Members save up to 15% and earn bonus points!

Address: 101 E Main St 67357 **Location:** 1.5 mi e; center. **Facility:** 41 units. 2 stories (no elevator), interior corridors. **Pool:** heated indoor. **Activities:** exercise room. **Guest Services:** coin laundry.

QUALITY INN 620/421-6129
APPROVED
Hotel

Address: 1807 Harding Dr 67357 **Location:** Just sw of jct US 59 and 400. **Facility:** 50 units. 2 stories, interior corridors. **Pool:** heated indoor. **Activities:** hot tub, exercise room. **Guest Services:** coin laundry. **Featured Amenity:** full hot breakfast.

PITTSBURG (E-8) pop. 20,233, elev. 922'

Adopting and adapting the name of the Pennsylvania metropolis, Pittsburg was founded in 1876 as a mining camp. Over the years some 200 million tons of coal were excavated here. Pittsburg State University, with an enrollment of more than 7,000, offers educational and cultural opportunities. Nearby, several reclaimed strip pits provide swimming, fishing and other recreation.

Little Balkano Days, a festival held downtown on Labor Day weekend, celebrates the community's coal-mining origins. Highlights include sports tournaments, train rides, concerts, crafts and a quilt show.

Crawford County Convention and Visitors Bureau: 117 W. Fourth St., P.O. Box 1115, Pittsburg, KS 66762. **Phone:** (620) 231-1212.

COMFORT INN & SUITES 620/231-8800
APPROVED Hotel. **Address:** 4009 Parkway Dr 66762

HAMPTON INN & SUITES BY HILTON PITTSBURG AT KANSAS CROSSING 620/231-3100
THREE DIAMOND Hotel. **Address:** 1285 S US 69 66762

AAA Benefit: Members save up to 15%!

HOLIDAY INN EXPRESS & SUITES 620/231-1177
THREE DIAMOND Hotel. **Address:** 4011 Parkview Dr 66762

WHERE TO EAT

CHICKEN ANNIE'S ORIGINAL 620/231-9460
APPROVED Chicken. Casual Dining. **Address:** 1143 E 600th Ave 66762

CHICKEN MARY'S   620/231-9510
APPROVED   Chicken. Casual Dining. **Address:** 1133
E 600th Ave 66762

EL CHARRO   620/232-5763
APPROVED   Mexican. Casual Dining. **Address:** 3102
N Broadway Ave 66762

JIM'S STEAKHOUSE & LOUNGE   620/231-5770
APPROVED   American. Casual Dining. **Address:** 1912
N Broadway Ave 66762

PLEASANTON (D-8) pop. 1,216, elev. 862'

On Oct. 25, 1864, one of the last significant Civil War battles fought west of the Mississippi River occurred along this segment of Mine Creek. Retreating southward before a pursuing Union force, about 7,000 Confederate troops established a defense on the north side of the creek.

When the vanguard of the Union force topped the rise, they faced the muzzles of thousands of pistols and rifles and eight cannons—and charged. A half-hour later the numerically superior Confederates were routed, defeated by the Union's better weapons, position and cavalry. By forcing the Confederates out of Kansas and saving Fort Scott from attack, the Battle of Mine Creek extinguished the South's hope of success in the West.

Pleasanton City Hall: 1608 Laurel St., Pleasanton, KS 66075. **Phone:** (913) 352-8257.

MINE CREEK CIVIL WAR BATTLEFIELD STATE HISTORIC SITE is 2 mi. s. on US 69, then .5 mi. w. on SR 52. One of the last significant Civil War battles fought west of the Mississippi River occurred here in 1864. Walking trails, marked with interpretive signs, traverse the 600-acre battlefield site. A visitor center features Civil War exhibits and firsthand accounts of the battle. **Time:** Allow 1 hour minimum. **Hours:** Grounds daily dawn-dusk. Visitor Center Wed.-Sat. 10-5, May-Oct. Closed major holidays. Phone ahead to confirm schedule. **Cost:** Apr.-Oct. $5; $1 (students with ID); free (ages 0-5). Rest of year free. **Phone:** (913) 352-8890.

PRATT (E-4) pop. 6,835, elev. 1,896'

The bounty of the surrounding wheat and cattle ranches and the activity from being a shipping point on the Cotton Belt (Union Pacific) Railroad sustain Pratt.

Named for Civil War veteran Caleb Pratt, the community was established in 1884 as the railroad pushed westward. Until 1886 the community warred with neighboring Saratoga over the status of county seat. Years after Pratt's victory Saratoga citizens insisted that the Native American scare that had sent them fleeing had been fabricated so that Pratt could win a hastily called election.

During World War II the city served as a training base for crews who flew B-29 bombers. At the regional airport, the B-29 All Veterans Memorial, 30353 Morris Ave., honors these veterans and their contribution to history.

Pratt Area Chamber of Commerce: 114 N. Main St., Pratt, KS 67124. **Phone:** (620) 672-5501 or (888) 886-1164.

BEST WESTERN PLUS PRATT   620/508-6466
THREE DIAMOND
Hotel

Best Western PLUS   **AAA Benefit:** Members save up to 15% and earn bonus points!

Address: 112 NE SR Hwy 61 67124 **Location:** Just n of jct US 54 and SR 61. **Facility:** 70 units. 3 stories, interior corridors. **Pool:** heated indoor. **Activities:** hot tub, exercise room. **Guest Services:** coin laundry.

SAVE CALL 🛗 🛎 💻 BIZ HS 📶 ✉ 🔌 📷 📺 / SOME UNITS 🐾

COMFORT SUITES   620/672-9999
THREE DIAMOND Hotel. **Address:** 704 Allison Ln 67124

EVERGREEN INN - MOTEL & RV PARK   620/672-6431
APPROVED   Motel. **Address:** 20001 W US Hwy 54 67124

HAMPTON INN BY HILTON PRATT   620/508-6499
THREE DIAMOND SAVE Hotel. **Address:** 1705 Maple St 67124   **AAA Benefit:** Members save up to 15%!

HOLIDAY INN EXPRESS & SUITES   620/508-6350
THREE DIAMOND Hotel. **Address:** 1903 Pauline Pl 67124

RUSSELL (C-4) pop. 4,506, elev. 1,826'

Railroad station agents, section hands and military garrisons were the only inhabitants of Fossil Station until 1871, when a colony of some 60 families settled and later changed the name to Russell.

Today Russell is widely associated with former U.S. senator and 1996 presidential nominee Robert Dole, who was born here in 1923.

Architectural highlights from the city's past include the 1872 Gernon House, 808 Kansas St., and the 1879 Heym-Oliver House, 503 Kansas St. Both limestone dwellings are restored and furnished in period. Guided tours are offered by appointment; phone (785) 483-4796 or the Fossil Station Museum at (785) 483-3637.

Nearby Wilson Lake offers numerous outdoor activities. *See Recreation Areas Chart.*

Russell County Economic Development & Convention & Visitors Bureau: 331 E. Wichita Ave., Russell, KS 67665. **Phone:** (785) 483-4000 or (877) 830-3737.

MERIDY'S RESTAURANT & LOUNGE   785/483-4300
APPROVED   American. Casual Dining. **Address:** 1220
S Fossil St 67665

SALINA (C-5) pop. 47,707, elev. 1,222'

At the junction of I-70 and I-135, Salina is a major trade and distribution center for one of the greatest hard wheat belts in the world. Other agriculture as well as more than 100 diversified manufacturing firms complete the economic portrait of this city on the eastward bend of the Smoky Hill River.

Salina balances industrial growth with educational and cultural expansion. Kansas Wesleyan University and a branch of Kansas State University are important assets. The prize-winning Salina Bicentennial Center in Kenwood Park is the scene of expositions, trade shows, concerts and sporting events; phone (888) 826-7469.

For 4 days in June, the 🐟 Smoky Hill River Festival, held in Oakdale Park, offers a juried fine arts show, entertainment, food, music, children's activities and arts and crafts.

Visit Salina: 120 W. Ash St., P.O. Box 586, Salina, KS 67401. **Phone:** (785) 827-9301 or (877) 725-4625.

ROLLING HILLS ZOO is off I-70 exit 244, then 2 mi. s. to 625 N. Hedville Rd. Situated on 95 acres of Kansas prairie, the zoo features more than 100 species of rare or endangered animals and a wildlife museum. Sheltered observation areas permit up-close viewing of animals in natural outdoor settings.

The zoo's collection includes such endangered species as a greater one-horned and white rhinoceros, tigers, orangutans and Amur leopards. An indoor reptile house features a variety of reptiles and amphibians. A children's area allows hands-on interaction with domestic animals. Narrated tram rides operate seasonally.

Time: Allow 2 hours minimum. **Hours:** Daily 8-5, Memorial Day weekend-Labor Day weekend; Daily 9-5, early Mar.-late May and early Sept.-early Nov.; Daily 9-4, early Nov.-early Mar. **Cost:** Museum and zoo $13.95; $12.95 (ages 65+); $7 (ages 3-12). Seasonal tram rides, and giraffe, camel or ostrich feeding $3. **Phone:** (785) 827-9488. 🍴 🏕

Rolling Hills Wildlife Museum is at Rolling Hills Zoo, 625 N. Hedville Rd. The museum leads visitors through elaborate dioramas representing seven distinct environments. Realistic robots, representing peoples from around the world, carry on a dialogue with visitors and each other about the delicate balance between man and nature. The museum also features a 360-degree, domed movie theater, an interactive children's gallery filled with hands-on displays and an area for traveling exhibits.

Time: Allow 1 hour minimum. **Hours:** Daily 8-5, Memorial Day weekend-Labor Day; 9-5, mid-Mar. through day before Memorial Day weekend and day after Labor Day-Thanksgiving weekend; 9-4, rest of year. **Cost:** Museum and zoo $12.50; $11.50 (ages 65+); $6 (ages 3-12). Movie $2. **Phone:** (785) 827-9488.

BEST WESTERN PLUS MIDWEST INN & SUITES
785/493-9800

APPROVED
Hotel

Best Western PLUS.

AAA Benefit: Members save up to 15% and earn bonus points!

Address: 745 W Schilling Rd 67401 **Location:** I-135 exit 89 (Schilling Rd), just w. **Facility:** 51 units. 2 stories, interior corridors. **Pool:** heated indoor. **Activities:** exercise room. **Guest Services:** valet and coin laundry.

SAVE CALL ⬚ ⬚ ⬚ BIZ HS ⬚ ⬚ ⬚ ⬚ / SOME UNITS ⬚

CANDLEWOOD SUITES
785/823-6939
APPROVED   Extended Stay Hotel. **Address:** 2650 Planet Ave 67401

COMFORT SUITES
785/404-6944
THREE DIAMOND Hotel. **Address:** 715 W Schilling Rd 67401

COUNTRY INN & SUITES BY RADISSON-SALINA
785/827-1271
APPROVED   Hotel. **Address:** 2760 S 9th St 67401

COURTYARD BY MARRIOTT
785/309-1300
THREE DIAMOND SAVE Hotel. **Address:** 3020 Riffel Dr 67401

AAA Benefit: Members save 5% or more!

HOLIDAY INN EXPRESS & SUITES
785/404-3300
THREE DIAMOND Hotel. **Address:** 755 W Diamond Dr 67401

HOLIDAY INN SALINA
785/404-6767
THREE DIAMOND Hotel. **Address:** 3145 S 9th St 67401

QUALITY INN & SUITES
785/825-0709
APPROVED   Hotel. **Address:** 2110 W Crawford St 67401

SUPER 8 I-70
785/823-8808
APPROVED   Hotel. **Address:** 120 E Diamond Dr 67401

WHERE TO EAT

THE COZY INN
785/825-2699
APPROVED   Burgers. Quick Serve. **Address:** 108 N 7th St 67401

DAIMARU STEAK HOUSE
785/820-5500
APPROVED   Japanese Steak Sushi. Casual Dining. **Address:** 1601 W Crawford St 67401

HICKORY HUT BBQ
785/825-1588
APPROVED   Barbecue. Quick Serve. **Address:** 1617 W Crawford St 67401

HONG KONG BUFFET
785/820-8683
APPROVED   Chinese. Casual Dining. **Address:** 2515 S Market Pl 67401

MARTINELLI'S LITTLE ITALY
785/826-9190
APPROVED   Italian. Casual Dining. **Address:** 158 S Santa Fe Ave 67401

RUSSELL'S RESTAURANT　785/825-5733

◇ **APPROVED**　American. Casual Dining. **Address:** 649 Westport Blvd 67401

TUCSON'S STEAKHOUSE AND SALOON　785/820-9595

◇ **APPROVED**

Steak
Casual Dining
$9-$25

AAA Inspector Notes: A popular spot with the locals, this eatery features well-cooked steaks and appealing home-style sides. Most menu items are Southwest inspired, examples include Southwest egg rolls and Cajun pastas. The steaks are the stars here, and you can't go wrong with their delicious fillet or NY Strip. Homemade bread is served with all entrées for a fantastic addition. A light and fun atmosphere welcomes all patrons. **Features:** full bar, happy hour. **Address:** 2750 S 9th St 67401 **Location:** I-135 exit 89 (Schilling Rd), just e, then 0.3 mi n. ⓓ

SCOTT CITY (D-2) pop. 3,816, elev. 2,971'

Nearby, Historic Lake Scott State Park is an oasis of natural springs, deep wooded canyons and craggy bluffs. Recreation includes boating, camping, fishing, hiking, hunting, swimming and wildlife observation Historic sites within the park include the Steele Home Museum and the El Cuartelejo Indian Pueblo ruins. About one mile south of the park on SR 95 is Punished Woman's Fork, site of the last battle in Kansas between Native Americans and the U.S. Calvary. A monument overlooks a cave, canyon and the bluffs where the Northern Cheyenne hid waiting to ambush the U. S. Cavalry.

The El Quartelejo Museum and the Jerry Thomas Gallery & Collection offer free admission and guided tours of the area, including buffalo tours.

Scott City Chamber of Commerce: 113 E. Fifth St., Scott City, KS 67871. **Phone:** (620) 872-3525.

BEST WESTERN EL-QUARTELEJO INN & SUITES
620/872-7373

◇ **APPROVED**
Hotel

🅱️ **Best Western.**

AAA Benefit: Members save up to 15% and earn bonus points!

Address: 1610 S Main St 67871 **Location:** 1 mi s of jct US 83 and 96. **Facility:** 50 units. 2 stories, interior corridors. **Pool:** heated indoor. **Activities:** hot tub, exercise room. **Guest Services:** coin laundry. **Featured Amenity:** full hot breakfast.

SAVE 🔁 ➕ BIZ HS 🛜 ✕
🗄️ 📺 🛋️

SHAWNEE (C-8) pop. 62,209, elev. 1,066'
• **Hotels & Restaurants map & index p. 218**
• **Part of Kansas City area — see map p. 199**

Behind its modern-day suburban facade—the city is on the southwest edge of the Kansas City metropolitan area—Shawnee is part of a recorded history that dates back to 1724.

In subsequent years the settlement, first called Gum Springs, saw the opening of the Santa Fe Trail, the arrival of the Shawnee Indians from the East, the establishment of the Shawnee Mission and finally a raid by Civil War guerrilla William Quantrill.

Shawnee was the largest town in the territory until it lost the title of county seat to Olathe in 1858.

Visit Shawnee: 15100 W. 67th St., Suite 202, Shawnee, KS 66217-9344. **Phone:** (913) 631-6545.

WONDERSCOPE CHILDREN'S MUSEUM is off I-35 exit 229 (Johnson Dr.), then w. 1.4 mi. to 5700 King St. Hands-on activities encourage learning about art, health, science and space. Farm to Market, LEGO Ocean Adventure and H2Oh! exhibits teach children about farming, the ocean and its undersea life and the properties of water. **Time:** Allow 1 hour minimum. **Hours:** Tues.-Fri. 9-4:30, Sat. 9-5, Sun. noon-5. Closed major holidays. **Cost:** $7; $6 (ages 64+); free (ages 0-2). **Phone:** (913) 287-8888.

COURTYARD BY MARRIOTT　913/631-8800 72
◇◇◇ **THREE DIAMOND** SAVE Hotel. **Address:** 17250 Midland Dr 66217

AAA Benefit: Members save 5% or more!

HAMPTON INN BY HILTON-SHAWNEE　913/248-1900 74
◇◇◇ **THREE DIAMOND** SAVE Hotel. **Address:** 16555 Midland Dr 66217

AAA Benefit: Members save up to 15%!

HOLIDAY INN EXPRESS & SUITES　913/400-2509 73
◇◇◇ **THREE DIAMOND** Hotel. **Address:** 17346 Midland Dr 66217

WHERE TO EAT

BARLEY'S KITCHEN + TAP　913/268-5160 72
◇ **APPROVED**　American. Casual Dining. **Address:** 16649 Midland Dr 66217

PAULO AND BILL　913/962-9900 71
◇◇◇ **THREE DIAMOND** Italian. Casual Dining. **Address:** 16501 Midland Dr 66217

STRONG CITY (D-6) pop. 485, elev. 1,182'

At one time prairie grass blanketed a 400,000-square-mile swath of North America, stretching from the Rocky Mountains to east of the Mississippi River, and from Texas north to Saskatchewan. An 11,000-acre portion of this original grassland survives at the Tallgrass Prairie National Preserve *(see attraction listing).* Limestone just beneath the sod helped build Strong City's economy as well as countless public and private buildings throughout the west.

The annual Flint Hills Rodeo, held in early June in Strong City, is the state's oldest consecutively run professional rodeo; phone (620) 273-6480.

TALLGRASS PRAIRIE NATIONAL PRESERVE is .75 mi. w. on US 50, then 2 mi. n. on SR 177/Flint Hills National Scenic Byway. This 10,894-acre site protects a remnant of the continent's once vast tallgrass prairie. The visitor center offers exhibits, an orientation film and information. Self-guiding cell-phone tours of the 1881 Spring Hill Ranch include the restored Second Empire ranch house, a massive three-story limestone barn and a one-room schoolhouse. Via bus, rangers conduct 90-minute prairie tours, which focus on natural history, the ranching legacy and ecology. A bison herd roams Windmill Pasture.

Nature trails are available, and living-history programs are offered during summer. **Note:** Pets on leash are allowed in designated areas. **Hours:** Grounds daily 24 hours. Visitor center and ranch buildings open daily 8:30-4:30, May-Oct.; 9-4:30, rest of year. Buildings closed most major holidays. House tours are offered based on staff availability. Bus tours depart Sat.-Sun. at 11 a.m. and 1 p.m., and Mon.-Fri. at 11 a.m., late Apr.-late Oct. Closed major holidays. **Cost:** Free. **Phone:** (620) 273-8494, or (620) 805-3185 for cellphone tour. GT ⊠ 🐾

TOPEKA (C-7) pop. 127,473, elev. 940'
• Hotels p. 118 • Restaurants p. 119

Topeka was founded in 1854 when nine anti-slavery settlers met on the banks of the Kansas River, near the spot where Oregon Trail travelers made their first major river crossing on their journey to the West. The city was incorporated in 1857, and Cyrus K. Holliday, the founder of the Atchison, Topeka & Santa Fe Railway, was among the city's leaders.

When the railway began to extend its tracks westward 1854-69, Topeka defeated Tecumseh for county seat, became the state capital in 1861, survived the mayhem of the "Bleeding Kansas" era, suffered drought and withstood the fringes of the Civil War. In fact, Topeka flourished.

Almost 100 years after Topeka saw clashes between abolitionists and pro-slavery factions, it was the setting for the landmark 1954 Supreme Court ruling *Brown vs. The Topeka Board of Education*, the case that opened the door for school desegregation across the country.

Topeka hosts several annual events featuring entertainment and fun for visitors including Fiesta Mexicana Week, the Inter-tribal Pow Wow and the Huff-n-Puff Hot Air Balloon Rally. For the racing enthusiast, Heartland Park Topeka, 4 miles south on US 75, offers drag racing, road course racing, and dirt track and cycling events from March through October, and also is host to national motor sports events May through October; phone (785) 862-4781 or (800) 437-2237.

Lake Shawnee, 3137 E. 29th St., and Perry State Park, 16 miles northeast at 5441 Westlake Rd. in Ozawkie, offer water sports and other outdoor recreation *(see Recreation Areas Chart)*.

Visit Topeka Inc.: 618 S. Kansas Ave., Topeka, KS 66603. **Phone:** (785) 234-1030 or (800) 235-1030.

Shopping: West Ridge Mall, 1 mile south of I-70 on Wanamaker Road between 17th and 21st streets, features Burlington Coat Factory, Dillard's and JCPenney.

BROWN V. BOARD OF EDUCATION NATIONAL HISTORIC SITE is at 1515 S.E. Monroe St. The site commemorates the May 17, 1954, Supreme Court ruling that stated "separate educational facilities are inherently unequal," forcing desegregation of public schools in 21 states. The site consists of the Monroe Elementary School, one of the four segregated elementary schools for African-American children in Topeka, and its grounds. A visitor center contains interpretive exhibits. **Time:** Allow 1 hour minimum. **Hours:** Daily 9-5. Closed major holidays. **Cost:** Free. **Phone:** (785) 354-4273.

COMBAT AIR MUSEUM is at 7016 S.E. Forbes Ave., hangar 602, along the flight line of Topeka Regional Airport Forbes Field. This museum exhibits examples of aeronautical technology from all U.S. military conflicts from the early 1900s to the present, including aircraft and memorabilia. Among the more than 42 aircraft on display are an EC-121 Super Constellation, a Blue Angels F-11F Tiger, a Beech RU-8D and Meyers OTW, an F-14 Tomcat, a JN4 "Jenny" biplane and a flight simulator. Another exhibit re-creates a German prisoner of war barracks.

Time: Allow 1 hour, 30 minutes minimum. **Hours:** Mon.-Sat. 9-4:30, Sun. noon-4:30, Mar.-Dec.; daily noon-4:30, rest of year. Last admission 1 hour before closing. **Cost:** $7; $6 (ages 5-17 and active military with ID). **Phone:** (785) 862-3303.

THE GREAT OVERLAND STATION AND ALL VETERANS MEMORIAL is at 701 N. Kansas Ave. In 2004, a local preservation group completed restoration of North Topeka's neglected Union Pacific passenger depot, returning it to its 1927 splendor. The station's grand waiting room features 34-foot-high ornamented ceilings, large windows and impressive 12-foot-wide, 120-bulb chandeliers. A former pantry houses the Fink Gallery, which has exhibits about Topeka's history and railroad heritage as well as pop culture.

Outside the station, flags of the 50 states flank a flame-shaped sculpture, the centerpiece of the All Veterans Memorial. **Time:** Allow 45 minutes minimum. **Hours:** Tues.-Sat. 10-4. Last admission 45 minutes before closing. Closed major holidays. **Cost:** $5; $4 (ages 62+ and active military with ID); $2 (ages 3-12). **Phone:** (785) 232-5533. GT

HOLLEY MUSEUM OF MILITARY HISTORY is inside the Ramada Topeka Downtown Hotel and Convention Center at 420 S.E. 6th Ave. The museum's five galleries display approximately 30 dioramas depicting poignant scenes in U.S. military history, including D-Day and the Battle of the Bulge, as well as military artifacts from around the world. Exhibits and model aircraft explore the evolution of military aviation and the history of such groups as the Naval Air Forces and the Tuskegee Airmen as well as their contributions. **Time:** Allow 30 minutes minimum. **Hours:** Daily 10-8. Phone ahead to confirm schedule. **Cost:** Free. **Phone:** (785) 633-1166.

KANSAS HISTORICAL SOCIETY is at 6425 S.W. Sixth Ave. Set on 80 acres of woodlands and prairies, the complex is home to the Kansas Museum of History *(see attraction listing)*. The museum features exhibits relevant to Kansas history and the West such as an 1880s steam locomotive, a full-size Southern Cheyenne teepee, a stagecoach and a Civil War section. The State Archives *(see attraction listing)* contains genealogical information as well as a collection of historic documents, photographs and manuscripts relating Kansas history.

The Nature Trail winds 2.5 miles through native grassland, along creek banks and into a wooded area. Accessible to physically impaired visitors, the East Trail portion is a .25-mile loop with interpretive signs that describe the area's natural and cultural histories. While exploring the North Trail section, visitors might see red-tailed hawks, white-tailed deer and wild turkeys.

Time: Allow 1 hour, 30 minutes minimum. **Hours:** Nature trail open daily dawn-dusk. Museum open Tues.-Sat. 9-5, Sun. 1-5. State Archives open Wed.-Sat. 9-4:30 (also Tues. 9-4:30, Mar.-Oct.). Closed major holidays. **Cost:** Museum $10; $7 (ages 65+ and active military with ID); $6 (students with ID); free (ages 0-5). Archives free. **Phone:** (785) 272-8681. 🅰️

Kansas Museum of History is in the Kansas Historical Society complex, 6425 S.W. Sixth Ave. Exhibits at the complex detail state history from its earliest days to the present and include displays about Native American history, forts and trails, Civil War settlement, frontier life, the arrival of the railroad, fast food, African-American history and Kansas families. In the Discovery Place children experience history firsthand by dressing in frontier costumes and visiting a Plains Indian teepee. Of interest is a full-size Southern Cheyenne tipi and an 1880s steam locomotive.

Time: Allow 1 hour minimum. **Hours:** Tues.-Sat. 9-5, Sun. 1-5. Discovery Place Tues.-Sat. 1-5. Closed major holidays. **Cost:** $8; $7 (ages 65+ and active military with ID); $6 (students with ID); free (ages 0-5 with adult). **Phone:** (785) 272-8681, ext. 414.

State Archives is in the Kansas Historical Society complex, 6425 S.W. Sixth Ave. Headquarters of the Kansas Historical Society, the center offers extensive resources for genealogists and researchers of Kansas history and the West. **Time:** Allow 1 hour minimum. **Hours:** Wed.-Sat. 9-4:30 (also Tues. 9-4:30, Mar.-Oct.). Closed major holidays. **Cost:** Free. **Phone:** (785) 272-8681, ext. 117. 🅰️

STATE CAPITOL, on Capitol Sq. between Jackson and Harrison sts. facing 8th Ave., contains murals by Kansas native John Steuart Curry as well as artists David H. Overmyer, Lumen Martin Winter and Michael Young. Interesting outdoor sculptures include the "Pioneer Mother" and a bronze of Abraham Lincoln by Robert Merrill Gage.

The capitol, built with native limestone and classically inspired, dates from 1866. Atop the dome is the 22-foot-high statue of Ad Astra, a Kansa Indian warrior, after whose tribe the state was named. During the 50-minute guided historical tour, visitors see the Representative Hall, Senate chamber, former Supreme Court chamber and governor's ceremonial office. The 40-minute dome tour affords panoramic views and an up-close look at the dome's architectural features; visitors must climb 296 steps.

Hours: Mon.-Fri. 8-5, Sat. 10-4. Guided historical tour departs daily at 9, 11 and 3 (also at 10 and 2, Jan.-May). Sat. at 10, 11, 1, 2, and 3. Dome tour departs every hour Mon.-Fri. 9:15-3:15, Sat. 10:15-3:15. **Cost:** Free. Tour reservations are recommended Mar.-May. **Phone:** (785) 296-3966. 🅶🆃

TOPEKA FIRST PRESBYTERIAN CHURCH is off I-70 exit 362B, .4 mi. n.w. on 8th St., then just s. to 817 S.W. Harrison St. The church is illuminated by ten Favrile glass windows designed in 1911 by artist Louis Comfort Tiffany, whose use of cobalt, copper and gold additives gives the glass its remarkably deep colors. The sanctuary houses a 1935 Möller pipe organ. Guided tours are available by appointment. **Hours:** Mon.-Fri. 8:30-4. **Cost:** Donations. **Phone:** (785) 233-9601. 🅶🆃

BEST WESTERN TOPEKA INN & SUITES   785/228-2223

▼ **APPROVED**
Hotel

🅱️🆆 **Best Western.**

AAA Benefit: Members save up to 15% and earn bonus points!

Address: 700 SW Fairlawn Rd 66606 **Location:** I-70 exit 357A, just ne. **Facility:** 45 units. 2 stories (no elevator), interior corridors. **Pool:** heated indoor. **Activities:** hot tub, exercise room.

🆂🅰🆅🅴 🔜 🅗➕ 🅱🅸🆉 🅷🆂 📶 ❌ 🔲 🔳 🖥 /SOME UNITS 🐾

CLUBHOUSE INN & SUITES   785/273-8888
▼ **APPROVED**   Hotel. **Address:** 924 SW Henderson Rd 66615

COMFORT SUITES   785/246-6777
▼ **THREE DIAMOND** Hotel. **Address:** 6213 SW 10th Ave 66615

FAIRFIELD BY MARRIOTT   785/273-6800
▼ **APPROVED** 🆂🅰🆅🅴 Hotel. **Address:** 1530 SW Westport Dr 66604

AAA Benefit: Members save 5% or more!

HAMPTON INN BY HILTON TOPEKA   785/228-0111
▼ **THREE DIAMOND** 🆂🅰🆅🅴 Hotel. **Address:** 1515 SW Arrowhead Rd 66604

AAA Benefit: Members save up to 15%!

HOLIDAY INN EXPRESS HOTEL & SUITES   785/228-9500
▼ **THREE DIAMOND** Hotel. **Address:** 901 SW Robinson Ave 66606

HOMEWOOD SUITES BY HILTON TOPEKA   785/861-7840

THREE DIAMOND **SAVE** Extended Stay Hotel. **Address:** 1519 SW Arrowhead Rd 66604

| AAA Benefit: Members save up to 15%! |

HYATT PLACE TOPEKA   785/273-0066

THREE DIAMOND
Contemporary Hotel

HYATT PLACE
AAA Benefit: Members save up to 10%!

Address: 6021 SW 6th Ave 66615 **Location:** I-70 exit 356 (Wanamaker Rd), just n. **Facility:** 126 units. 6 stories, interior corridors. **Amenities:** safes. **Pool:** heated outdoor. **Activities:** exercise room. **Guest Services:** valet and coin laundry. **Featured Amenity: breakfast buffet.**

SAVE 🍴 🍸 CALL ♿ 🏊 👶
BIZ 📶 ✕ 🎥 🔌 📺 / SOME UNITS 🐾

WHERE TO EAT

ANNIE'S PLACE   705/273-0048
APPROVED American. Casual Dining. **Address:** 4014 Gage Center Dr 66604

BLIND TIGER BREWERY & RESTAURANT   785/267-2739
APPROVED American. Casual Dining. **Address:** 417 SW 37th St 66611

BLUE MOOSE BAR & GRILL   785/272-6800
APPROVED American. Casual Dining. **Address:** 3030 SW Wanamaker Dr 66614

PAISANO'S ITALIAN RISTORANTE   785/273-0100
APPROVED Italian. Casual Dining. **Address:** 4043 SW 10th Ave 66604

WAKEENEY pop. 1,862

BEST WESTERN PLUS WAKEENEY INN & SUITES
785/743-2700

APPROVED
Hotel

BW Best Western PLUS
AAA Benefit: Members save up to 15% and earn bonus points!

Address: 525 S 1st St 67672 **Location:** I-70 exit 127, just n. **Facility:** 50 units, some efficiencies. 3 stories, interior corridors. **Pool:** heated indoor. **Activities:** hot tub, exercise room. **Guest Services:** coin laundry.

SAVE 🍴 CALL ♿ 🏊 👶 BIZ
📶 ✕ 🔌 📺 📺 / SOME UNITS 🐾 HS

WHERE TO EAT

THE BRAZEN BULL   785/743-2653
APPROVED American. Casual Dining. **Address:** 717 S 2nd St 67672

🔗 **Get an expert view from AAA inspectors:**
AAA.com/travelguides/hotels

WICHITA (E-5) pop. 382,368, elev. 1,397'
• Hotels p. 126 • Restaurants p. 128
• Hotels & Restaurants map & index p. 123

For 11,000 years Wichita served as a trading center and meeting place for nomadic people, but it wasn't until 1863 that the first permanent settlement of Wichita Indians was recorded. Shortly after, J.R. Mead became the first white settler when he opened a trading post and established the area as a base for the Chisholm Trail.

By 1870 Wichita, now incorporated as a city, had become a destination for cattle drives from Texas, hence the city's nickname, "Cowtown." When the cattle trade moved west to take advantage of new rail lines, Wichita fell on hard times. The city bounced back in the 1890s as commerce centered on grain began to surpass the wealth once generated by cattle.

The population of Wichita nearly doubled in 1918 after a great oil reserve was discovered nearby. In turn, the oil money allowed local entrepreneurs Lloyd Stearman, Walter Beech and Clyde Cessna to further develop Wichita's fledgling airplane industry. During World War II Wichita was the major manufacturing center for airplanes needed in the war effort, and today Wichita produces more than 40 percent of the world's general aviation aircraft.

Lake Afton Public Observatory is southwest of downtown Wichita in Goddard at 25000 W. 39th St. S. Telescopes are available and astronomy exhibits are displayed in a museum; phone (316) 883-4329.

A lively cultural life centers on the city's symphony orchestra, Music Theatre of Wichita, Wichita Grand Opera and three institutions of higher learning: Friends University, with 2,800 students; Newman University, with 3,000 students; and Wichita State University, with an enrollment of 14,500.

Recreation is as much a part of the city's life as industry and culture. Several municipal parks offer golf, swimming and other pastimes. Information can be obtained from the Park Board; phone (316) 268-4638.

From late May to early June, crowds gather downtown for 🚩 Riverfest, a celebration featuring parades, concerts, sporting events, fireworks, food and more.

Go Wichita Convention and Visitors Bureau: 515 S. Main St., Suite 115, Wichita, KS 67202. **Phone:** (316) 265-2800 or (800) 288-9424.

Shopping: Towne East Square, US 54/400 at Rock Road, features Dillard's, JCPenney, Sears and Von Maur. Towne West Square, on US 54/400 at Tracy Street, features Dillard's, JCPenney and Sears. Sheplers, 6501 W. Kellogg St., specializes in western wear.

The Coleman Factory Outlet Store, 235 N. St. Francis, offers outdoor gear and displays of vintage Coleman products. Bradley Fair, 2000 N. Rock Rd., includes Banana Republic, Chico's, Eddie Bauer and Talbots.

Wichita
Attractions
Scale in Miles
1.8   0   1.8
See p. 6 - Map Legend

© 2019 HERE   © AAA

2037-20

(See map & index p. 123.)

In the heart of downtown, renovated 19th-century warehouses are the setting for Old Town, which features some 100 trendy urban shops, galleries, nightclubs and restaurants.

BOTANICA, THE WICHITA GARDENS, 701 Amidon St., presents a diversity of native and exotic plants in 28 themed gardens on a 17-acre site. Gardens include the Downing Children's Garden; the Jayne Milburn Aquatic Collection; the Xeriscape Demonstration Garden; the Chinese Garden of Friendship; the Project Beauty Shakespearean Garden; and rose, butterfly, woodland bird, wildflower and sensory gardens. In the Butterfly House hundreds of free-flight butterflies put on a colorful show June through September.

Time: Allow 1 hour minimum. **Hours:** Mon.-Sat. 9-5 (also Tues. and Thurs. 5-8, Apr.-Sept.; Sun. 1-5, Apr.-Oct.). Closed most major holidays. **Cost:** $7; $6 (ages 62+ and active military with ID); $5 (ages 3-12). **Phone:** (316) 264-0448.

EXPLORATION PLACE, at 300 N. McLean Blvd., has hands-on exhibits exploring such topics as flight, medieval life, health and Kansas. Changing exhibits also are featured. In Design Build Fly, a completely renovated 5,100 square-foot aviation exhibit gallery, encounter dozens of hands-on activities that reveal what happens behind-the-scenes in Wichita's aircraft plants. Featuring a three-story stone castle, the Where Kids Rule area gives children the opportunity to launch a catapult or build a bridge across a moat. In the Kansas Kids Connect, children can plant a garden, fix a tractor, climb through the Earth's layers and nestle inside a giant meadowlark nest.

In the newly updated Digital Dome Theater and Planetarium digitally produced shows are presented on a 60-foot, 360-degree screen. A playground and recreation paths are offered at the outdoor Exploration Park during summer.

Time: Allow 1 hour, 30 minutes minimum. **Hours:** Tues.-Sat. 10-5 (also Mon. 10-5, mid-Mar. through Labor Day), Sun. noon-5. **Cost:** $10.50; $9 (ages 65+); $7 (ages 3-11). Theater show $5; $4 (ages

(See map & index p. 123.)

65+); $3 (ages 3-11). Combination tickets are available. 🅰️

▼ **KANSAS SPORTS HALL OF FAME** is at 515 S. Wichita St. A historic boathouse contains profiles of the 228 hall of fame inductees. Galleries are dedicated to basketball, football, baseball, track and field and Olympic sports at the professional, college and high school levels. Exhibits include uniforms, photographs, equipment and a virtual sports game. Information about such famous sports personalities as Barry Sanders and Wilt Chamberlain also are featured. **Hours:** Mon.-Fri. 10-4. **Cost:** Donations. **Phone:** (316) 262-2038.

MARK ARTS 1307 N. Rock Rd., is a 40,000-square-foot building on 17 landscaped acres. The modern, prairie-style art center includes a premier gallery space, nine studios for art education and an events center that can host up to 600 people. **Time:** Allow 30 minutes minimum. **Hours:** Mon.-Sat. 10-5. Closed major holidays. **Cost:** Free.

THE MID-AMERICA ALL-INDIAN CENTER, 650 N. Seneca St., depicts past and present Native American heritage, traditions and cultures. "Keeper of the Plains," a 44-foot-high sculpture by Blackbear Bosin, stands near the grounds. The Gallery of Nations displays tribal flags. **Time:** Allow 1 hour minimum. **Hours:** Tues.-Sat. 10-4. Closed major holidays. **Cost:** $7; $5 (ages 55+, and military and students with ID); $3 (ages 6-12). **Phone:** (316) 350-3340.

▼ **MUSEUM OF WORLD TREASURES** is at 835 E. 1st St. in Old Town. Within the museum's impressive collection of artifacts and fossils is Ivan, reputedly one of the most complete T. rex skeletons on display in the world. The Egyptian area showcases genuine Egyptian mummies and coffins, and the Hall of Royalty depicts the grandeur of European monarchs.

Form & Function explores life after the extinction of the dinosaurs and survival during the Ice Age. Founding of America explores the birth and growth of our country and features a signature from every United States President. Other exhibits contain memorabilia related to the frontier era, music and composers, wars, sports and American pop culture.

Time: Allow 2 hours minimum. **Hours:** Mon.-Sat. 10-5, Sun. noon-5. **Cost:** $9.95; $8.95 (ages 65+); $7.95 (ages 4-12). **Phone:** (316) 263-1311 or (888) 700-1311.

OLD COWTOWN MUSEUM, 1865 W. Museum Blvd., consists of restorations and reproductions of more than 40 buildings dating 1865-80. Among them is the Darius Munger House, Wichita's first residential structure; the city's first jail; a general store; a newspaper shop; a carpenter shop; a drugstore; a school; a saloon; and a railroad depot. Many buildings are furnished in period.

A 5-acre working farm depicts agricultural history. A blacksmith demonstrates his craft, and costumed interpreters perform living-history demonstrations. The Dickens Christmas Splendor is featured during the first three weekends in December. **Time:** Allow 1 hour minimum. **Hours:** Tues.-Sat. 10-5, Sun. noon-5, mid-Apr. to late Oct.; Tues.-Sat. 10-5, rest of year. **Cost:** $7.75; $6.50 (ages 62+); $6 (ages 12-17); $5.50 (ages 4-11); free (active military with ID and their family, Memorial Day-Labor Day). **Phone:** (316) 219-1871. 🄶🅃 🍴

▼ **SEDGWICK COUNTY ZOO,** near I-235 exit 10, at 5555 Zoo Blvd., contains 247 acres with more than 3,000 animals representing 400 species. Exhibit areas include the Children's Farms; the Amphibian & Reptile Building; the Tropics, presenting tropical sights, sounds and animals; recreated habitats of Africa with giraffes and lions; and one of the largest outdoor, walk-through aviaries representing the wild regions of Australia and South America.

A close-up look at primates is offered at the Koch Orangutan and Chimpanzee Habitat. A bridge takes visitors out of the village atmosphere of Nganda Island and into the Downing Gorilla Forest of Africa. An elevated boardwalk traverses the 12-acre exhibit of North America, which features native plants, bears, bison, eagles, otters and wolves. The Cessna Penguin Cove, featuring Humboldt penguins and Inca terns, reflects the coasts of Chile and Peru. The Slawson Family Tiger Trek houses Burmese brow-antlered deer, red pandas and Amur tigers. The Reed Family Elephants of the Zambezi River Valley is designed to give the elephants choices to ensure their well-being, all while immersing guests into the habitat with nearly 360-degree views of the area.

Time: Allow 3 hours minimum. **Hours:** Daily 8:30-5, Mar.-Oct.; 10-5, rest of year. **Cost:** $15.95; $11.95 (ages 62+); $9.95 (ages 3-11). **Phone:** (316) 660-9453.

ULRICH MUSEUM OF ART is e. on 17th St. to 1845 Fairmount St., on the Wichita State University campus. The museum showcases contemporary art by such artists as Andy Warhol, Alexander Calder, Louise Nevelson, Gordon Parks and W. Eugene Smith. The outdoor collection includes more than 70 modern sculptures displayed throughout the campus, featuring works by Andy Goldsworthy, Tom Otterness, Henry Moore and Robert Indiana. **Time:** Allow 1 hour minimum. **Hours:** Tues.-Fri. 11-5, Sat.-Sun. 1-5. Closed major holidays. **Cost:** Free. **Phone:** (316) 978-3664.

WICHITA ART MUSEUM is at 1400 W. Museum Blvd. An extensive exhibit of American art includes works by Mary Cassatt, Winslow Homer, Edward Hopper, Charles M. Russell and others. Art glass installations by Dale Chihuly also are featured. Changing exhibits are presented. The Art Garden surrounds the museum with paved walking paths and features a 13-piece sculpture collection, with works by Henry Moore and Tom Otterness. **Time:** Allow 1 hour minimum. **Hours:** Tues.-Sat. 10-5, Sun. noon-5. The Art Garden is open daily 24 hours.

(See map & index p. 123.)

Closed major holidays. **Cost:** $7; $5 (ages 60+); $3 (ages 5-17 and college students with ID); free (to all on Sat.). Art Garden free. **Phone:** (316) 268-4921. 🍴

WICHITA STATE UNIVERSITY is between 17th and 21st sts. Highlights of the 330-acre campus include the Corbin Education Center, designed by Frank Lloyd Wright, and a collection of more than 70 outdoor sculptures from the university's Ulrich Museum of Art *(see attraction listing)*. The student body consists of about 14,500 undergraduates and 3,500 graduate students. Approximately 350 fine arts performances are held on campus each year.

Free maps detailing the sculptures' sites are available at the museum. Campus tours are offered. **Phone:** (316) 978-3085. GT

Wichita State University Libraries, Special Collections and University Archives, 1845 Fairmount St. on the Wichita State University campus, contain the university's archives, rare books and manuscripts. Collections highlight aviation, abolition, and state and local history. The library contains numerous historic Kansas photographs and maps as well as more than 400 digitized maps pertaining to the state. Changing exhibits are presented. **Hours:** Mon.-Thurs. 8-4:45. Closed major holidays. **Cost:** Free. **Phone:** (316) 978-3590.

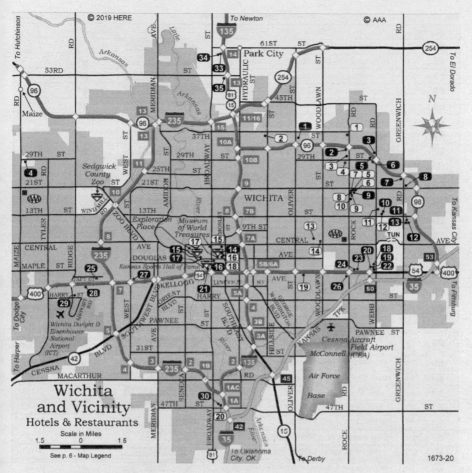

Wichita
and Vicinity
Hotels & Restaurants

Scale in Miles
1.5   0   1.5

See p. 6 - Map Legend

1673-20

✈ Airport Hotels

Map Page	WICHITA MID-CONTINENT (Maximum driving distance from airport: 2.7 mi)	Designation	Member Savings	Page
25 this page	Candlewood Suites, 2.7 mi	◈ APPROVED		127
29 this page	Hampton Inn & Suites by Hilton Wichita Airport, 1.3 mi	◈ THREE DIAMOND	✔	127
28 this page	SpringHill Suites by Marriott Wichita Airport, 1.9 mi	◈ THREE DIAMOND	✔	128

Wichita and Vicinity

This index helps you "spot" where hotels and restaurants are located on the corresponding detailed maps. Restaurant price range is a combination of lunch and/or dinner. Turn to the listing page for more information and consult display ads for special promotions.

🔗   **For more details, rates and reservations: AAA.com/travelguides/hotels**

WICHITA

Map Page	Hotels	Designation	Member Savings	Page
1 this page	**Aloft Wichita Northeast** *(See ad p. 126.)*	◈ THREE DIAMOND	✔	126
2 this page	**Best Western Wichita Northeast**	◈ APPROVED	✔	127

WICHITA (cont'd)

Map Page	Hotels (cont'd)	Designation	Member Savings	Page
3 p. 123	Candlewood Suites-Wichita Northeast	APPROVED		127
4 p. 123	Hampton Inn by Hilton Wichita Northwest	THREE DIAMOND	✔	127
5 p. 123	TownePlace Suites by Marriott	APPROVED	✔	128
6 p. 123	Courtyard by Marriott	THREE DIAMOND	✔	127
7 p. 123	Hampton Inn & Suites Wichita/Northeast	THREE DIAMOND	✔	127
8 p. 123	Staybridge Suites	THREE DIAMOND		128
9 p. 123	Hilton Garden Inn-Wichita	THREE DIAMOND	✔	127
10 p. 123	Homewood Suites by Hilton at The Waterfront	THREE DIAMOND	✔	127
11 p. 123	Tru by Hilton Wichita Northeast	APPROVED	✔	128
12 p. 123	SpringHill Suites by Marriott Wichita East at Plazzio	THREE DIAMOND	✔	128
13 p. 123	Residence Inn by Marriott at Plazzio	THREE DIAMOND	✔	128
14 p. 123	Hotel At Old Town	THREE DIAMOND		127
15 p. 123	Drury Plaza Hotel Broadview-Wichita	THREE DIAMOND		127
16 p. 123	**Ambassador Hotel Wichita, Autograph Collection**	FOUR DIAMOND	✔	126
17 p. 123	**Hyatt Regency Wichita**	THREE DIAMOND	✔	127
18 p. 123	Country Inn & Suites by Radisson, Wichita East	fyi		127
19 p. 123	Comfort Inn by Choice Hotels	APPROVED		127
20 p. 123	Hampton Inn by Hilton	THREE DIAMOND	✔	127
21 p. 123	Fairfield Inn & Suites by Marriott Wichita Downtown	THREE DIAMOND	✔	127
22 p. 123	Fairfield Inn & Suites by Marriott Wichita East	THREE DIAMOND	✔	127
23 p. 123	**Best Western Plus Eastgate Inn & Suites**	APPROVED	✔	126
24 p. 123	Super 8 Wichita East	APPROVED		128
25 p. 123	Candlewood Suites	APPROVED		127
26 p. 123	Holiday Inn Wichita East I-35	THREE DIAMOND		127
27 p. 123	**Best Western Plus Wichita West Airport Inn**	THREE DIAMOND	✔	127
28 p. 123	SpringHill Suites by Marriott Wichita Airport	THREE DIAMOND	✔	128
29 p. 123	Hampton Inn & Suites by Hilton Wichita Airport	THREE DIAMOND	✔	127
30 p. 123	**Best Western Governors Inn & Suites**	APPROVED	✔	126

Map Page	Restaurants	Designation	Cuisine	Price Range	Page
1 p. 123	Hot Stone Korean Grill	APPROVED	Korean	$6-$14	128
2 p. 123	Stroud's Restaurant Bar & Grill	APPROVED	American	$9-$20	128
3 p. 123	Jimmie's Diner	APPROVED	American	$4-$9	128
4 p. 123	Two Olives	APPROVED	Middle Eastern	$7-$14	128
5 p. 123	Ya Ya's Euro Bistro	THREE DIAMOND	European	$8-$29	128
6 p. 123	The Good Egg	APPROVED	Breakfast	$7-$10	128
7 p. 123	Bella Luna Cafe	APPROVED	Mediterranean	$8-$26	128
8 p. 123	Il Vicino Wood Oven Pizza	APPROVED	Italian Pizza	$6-$11	128
9 p. 123	Newport Grill	THREE DIAMOND	Seafood	$19-$38	128
10 p. 123	Red Rock Canyon Grill	APPROVED	American	$9-$27	128
11 p. 123	Chester's Chophouse & Wine Bar	THREE DIAMOND	Steak	$6-$38	128
12 p. 123	Doc Green's Gourmet Salads & Grill	APPROVED	Sandwiches	$8-$11	128
13 p. 123	Thai Tradition	APPROVED	Thai	$7-$18	128
14 p. 123	Wichita Brewing Co	APPROVED	American	$9-$33	128
15 p. 123	Sabor Latin Bar & Grille	APPROVED	Latin American	$8-$29	128
16 p. 123	River City Brewery Co	APPROVED	American	$8-$16	128

Map Page	Restaurants (cont'd)	Designation	Cuisine	Price Range	Page
⑰ p. 123	Old Mill Tasty Shop	◆ APPROVED	Sandwiches	$6-$8	128
⑱ p. 123	Larkspur Bistro & Bar	◆ APPROVED	American	$9-$36	128
⑲ p. 123	Scotch & Sirloin	◆ THREE DIAMOND	Steak	$7-$37	128
⑳ p. 123	Hog Wild Pit Bar-B-Q	◆ APPROVED	Barbecue	$4-$10	128

PARK CITY

Map Page	Hotels	Designation	Member Savings	Page
㉝ p. 123	Super 8-Wichita North/Park City	◆ APPROVED		113
㉞ p. 123	Quality Inn & Suites	◆ APPROVED		113
㉟ p. 123	**Best Western Wichita North Hotel & Suites**	◆ APPROVED	✔	113

iStockphoto.com_LeoPatrizi

Make a good trip great with insight from AAA's travel experts. Use their recommended picks and itineraries to find best places to go, stay, dine and play.

Photo source iStockphoto.com

 Get AAA travel information at club offices and on AAA.com for experiences you'll remember for a lifetime.

(See map & index p. 123.)

ALOFT WICHITA NORTHEAST   316/744-1100 **1**

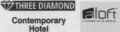 **THREE DIAMOND**

Contemporary Hotel

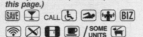 **AAA Benefit:** Members save 5% or more!

Address: 3642 N Oliver Ave 67220 **Location:** Just n of jct SR 96. **Facility:** 126 units. 5 stories, interior corridors. *Bath:* shower only. **Amenities:** safes. **Pool:** heated outdoor. **Activities:** exercise room. **Guest Services:** valet and coin laundry, area transportation. *(See ad this page.)*

SAVE ⬛ CALL ♿ 🚐 📶 BIZ
📶 ✖ 🛎 🖥 / SOME UNITS 🐾

AMBASSADOR HOTEL WICHITA, AUTOGRAPH COLLECTION   316/239-7100 **16**

FOUR DIAMOND

Historic Boutique Hotel

AUTOGRAPH COLLECTION HOTELS **AAA Benefit:** Members save 5% or more!

Address: 104 S Broadway 67202 **Location:** Jct Douglas Ave; downtown. **Facility:** This refined hotel is situated in a former bank building. Premium bedding packages are a welcome luxury after a long day of business or sight-seeing. 117 units. 14 stories, interior corridors. **Parking:** on-site (fee) and valet. **Amenities:** safes. **Activities:** exercise room. **Guest Services:** valet laundry, area transportation.

SAVE ➕ 🍽 🐾 ⬛ CALL ♿ 📶 BIZ HS 📶
✖ 🛎 🖥 / SOME UNITS 🐾

BEST WESTERN GOVERNORS INN & SUITES   316/522-0775 **30**

APPROVED

Hotel

Best Western. **AAA Benefit:** Members save up to 15% and earn bonus points!

Address: 4742 S Emporia St 67216 **Location:** I-135 exit 1A/B (47th St S), just sw. **Facility:** 58 units. 3 stories, interior corridors. **Pool:** outdoor. **Activities:** exercise room. **Guest Services:** coin laundry.

SAVE 🛏 CALL ♿ 🚐 📶 BIZ
📶 ✖ 🛎 🖥 🖥
/ SOME UNITS 🐾

BEST WESTERN PLUS EASTGATE INN & SUITES   316/682-3000 **23**

APPROVED

Hotel

Best Western PLUS. **AAA Benefit:** Members save up to 15% and earn bonus points!

Address: 8300 E Kellogg Dr 67207 **Location:** I-35 exit 50, 0.4 mi w via frontage road. **Facility:** 65 units. 3 stories, interior corridors. **Pool:** heated indoor. **Activities:** hot tub, exercise room. **Guest Services:** coin laundry. **Featured Amenity: full hot breakfast.**

SAVE CALL ♿ 🚐 📶 BIZ HS
📶 ✖ 🛎 🖥 🖥

🔗 **Book and save at AAA.com/hertz**

(See map & index p. 123.)

BEST WESTERN PLUS WICHITA WEST AIRPORT INN
316/945-4100 **27**

THREE DIAMOND
Hotel

Best Western **PLUS**

AAA Benefit: Members save up to 15% and earn bonus points!

Address: 3800 W Kellogg Dr 67213 **Location:** US 54 exit West St, just e on north service road. **Facility:** 121 units. 4 stories, interior corridors. **Amenities:** safes. **Pool:** heated outdoor. **Activities:** exercise room. **Guest Services:** valet laundry, area transportation.

BEST WESTERN WICHITA NORTHEAST
316/634-3900 **2**

APPROVED
Hotel

Best Western

AAA Benefit: Members save up to 15% and earn bonus points!

Address: 7824 E 32nd St N 67226 **Location:** SR 96 E exit Rock Rd, just sw. **Facility:** 67 units. 3 stories, interior corridors. **Pool:** heated indoor. **Activities:** exercise room. **Guest Services:** coin laundry.

CANDLEWOOD SUITES
316/942-0400 **25**
APPROVED Extended Stay Hotel. **Address:** 570 S Julia St 67209

CANDLEWOOD SUITES-WICHITA NORTHEAST
316/634-6070 **3**
APPROVED Extended Stay Hotel. **Address:** 3141 N Webb Rd 67226

COMFORT INN BY CHOICE HOTELS
316/686-2844 **19**
APPROVED Hotel. **Address:** 9525 E Corporate Hills Dr 67207

COUNTRY INN & SUITES BY RADISSON, WICHITA EAST
316/685-0333 **18**
fyi Hotel. Under major renovation, call for details. **Last Designation:** Three Diamond. **Address:** 333 S Webb Rd 67207

COURTYARD BY MARRIOTT
316/636-4600 **6**
THREE DIAMOND **SAVE** Hotel. **Address:** 2975 N Webb Rd 67726

AAA Benefit: Members save 5% or more!

DRURY PLAZA HOTEL BROADVIEW-WICHITA
316/262-5000 **15**
THREE DIAMOND Hotel. **Address:** 400 W Douglas Ave 67202

FAIRFIELD INN & SUITES BY MARRIOTT WICHITA DOWNTOWN
316/201-1400 **21**
THREE DIAMOND **SAVE** Hotel. **Address:** 525 S Main St 67202

AAA Benefit: Members save 5% or more!

FAIRFIELD INN & SUITES BY MARRIOTT WICHITA EAST
316/685-3777 **22**
THREE DIAMOND **SAVE** Hotel. **Address:** 417 S Webb Rd 67207

AAA Benefit: Members save 5% or more!

HAMPTON INN & SUITES BY HILTON WICHITA AIRPORT
316/942-2000 **29**
THREE DIAMOND **SAVE** Hotel. **Address:** 7230 W Harry St 67209

AAA Benefit: Members save up to 15%!

HAMPTON INN & SUITES WICHITA/NORTHEAST
316/636-5594 **7**
THREE DIAMOND **SAVE** Hotel. **Address:** 2433 N Greenwich Rd 67226

AAA Benefit: Members save up to 15%!

HAMPTON INN BY HILTON
316/686-3576 **20**
THREE DIAMOND **SAVE** Hotel. **Address:** 9449 E Corporate Hills Dr 67207

AAA Benefit: Members save up to 15%!

HAMPTON INN BY HILTON WICHITA NORTHWEST
316/925-6600 **4**
THREE DIAMOND **SAVE** Hotel. **Address:** 10047 W 29th St N 67205

AAA Benefit: Members save up to 15%!

HILTON GARDEN INN-WICHITA
316/219-4444 **9**
THREE DIAMOND **SAVE** Hotel. **Address:** 2041 N Bradley Fair Pkwy 67206

AAA Benefit: Members save up to 15%!

HOLIDAY INN WICHITA EAST I-35
316/686-7131 **26**
THREE DIAMOND Hotel. **Address:** 549 S Rock Rd 67207

HOMEWOOD SUITES BY HILTON AT THE WATERFRONT
316/260-8844 **10**
THREE DIAMOND **SAVE** Extended Stay Hotel. **Address:** 1550 N Waterfront Pkwy 67206

AAA Benefit: Members save up to 15%!

HOTEL AT OLD TOWN
316/267-4800 **14**
THREE DIAMOND Extended Stay Hotel. **Address:** 830 E First St 67202

HYATT REGENCY WICHITA
316/293-1234 **17**
THREE DIAMOND
Hotel

HYATT REGENCY

AAA Benefit: Members save up to 10%!

Address: 400 W Waterman St 67202 **Location:** Just w of jct Main and Waterman sts; downtown. **Facility:** 303 units. 18 stories, interior corridors. **Parking:** on-site (fee) and valet. **Amenities:** safes. **Pool:** heated indoor. **Activities:** hot tub, exercise room. **Guest Services:** valet laundry, boarding pass kiosk, area transportation.

(See map & index p. 123.)

RESIDENCE INN BY MARRIOTT AT PLAZZIO
316/682-7300 **13**
THREE DIAMOND **SAVE** Extended
Stay Hotel. **Address:** 1212 N Greenwich Rd 67206

AAA Benefit:
Members save 5%
or more!

SPRINGHILL SUITES BY MARRIOTT WICHITA AIRPORT
316/260-4404 **28**
THREE DIAMOND   **SAVE**
Contemporary Hotel. **Address:** 6633 W
Kellogg Dr 67209

AAA Benefit:
Members save 5%
or more!

**SPRINGHILL SUITES BY MARRIOTT WICHITA EAST AT
PLAZZIO**   316/681-1800 **12**
THREE DIAMOND **SAVE** Hotel. **Ad-
dress:** 1220 N Greenwich Rd 67206

AAA Benefit:
Members save 5%
or more!

STAYBRIDGE SUITES   316/927-3888 **8**
THREE DIAMOND Extended Stay Hotel. **Address:** 2250 N
Greenwich Rd 67226

SUPER 8 WICHITA EAST   316/685-8291 **24**
APPROVED Hotel. **Address:** 8220 E Kellogg Dr 67207

TOWNEPLACE SUITES BY MARRIOTT   316/631-3773 **5**
APPROVED **SAVE** Extended
Stay Hotel. **Address:** 9444 E 29th St N
67226

AAA Benefit:
Members save 5%
or more!

TRU BY HILTON WICHITA NORTHEAST   316/925-5100 **11**
APPROVED **SAVE** Hotel. **Ad-
dress:** 1236 N Greenwich Rd 67206

Members save up to
15%!

WHERE TO EAT

BELLA LUNA CAFE   316/634-0008 **7**
APPROVED Mediterranean. Casual Dining. **Address:**
2132 N Rock Rd, Suite 107 67206

CHESTER'S CHOPHOUSE & WINE BAR   316/201-1300 **11**
THREE DIAMOND Steak. Fine Dining. **Address:** 1550 N
Webb Rd 67206

DOC GREEN'S GOURMET SALADS & GRILL
316/636-8997 **12**
APPROVED Sandwiches. Quick Serve. **Address:**
10096 E 13th St, Suite 102 67206

THE GOOD EGG   316/315-0110 **6**
APPROVED Breakfast. Casual Dining. **Address:** 2141
N Bradley Fair Pkwy 67206

HOG WILD PIT BAR-B-Q   316/522-7636 **20**
APPROVED Barbecue. Quick Serve. **Address:** 662 E
47th St 67216

HOT STONE KOREAN GRILL   316/425-7082 **1**
APPROVED Korean. Casual Dining. **Address:** 3743 N
Rock Rd 67226

IL VICINO WOOD OVEN PIZZA   316/636-2121 **8**
APPROVED Italian Pizza. Quick Serve. **Address:**
2132 N Rock Rd 67226

JIMMIE'S DINER   316/636-1818 **3**
APPROVED American. Casual Dining. **Address:** 3111
N Rock Rd 67226

KANAI   316/719-2929
THREE DIAMOND Japanese. Casual Dining. **Address:**
12111 W Maple St, Suite 131 67235

LARKSPUR BISTRO & BAR   316/262-5275 **18**
APPROVED American. Casual Dining. **Address:** 904
E Douglas Ave 67202

NEWPORT GRILL   316/636-9555 **9**
THREE DIAMOND Seafood. Casual Dining. **Address:** 1900
N Rock Rd 67226

OLD MILL TASTY SHOP   316/264-6500 **17**
APPROVED Sandwiches. Casual Dining. **Address:**
604 E Douglas Ave 67202

RED ROCK CANYON GRILL   316/636-1844 **10**
APPROVED American. Casual Dining. **Address:** 1844
N Rock Rd 67226

RIVER CITY BREWERY CO   316/263-2739 **16**
APPROVED American. Casual Dining. **Address:** 150
N Mosley St 67202

SABOR LATIN BAR & GRILLE   316/201-4880 **15**
APPROVED Latin American. Casual Dining. **Address:**
309 N Mead St 67202

SCOTCH & SIRLOIN   316/685-8701 **19**
THREE DIAMOND Steak. Casual Dining. **Address:** 5325 E
Kellogg St 67218

STROUD'S RESTAURANT BAR & GRILL   316/838-2454 **2**
APPROVED American. Casual Dining. **Address:** 3661
N Hillside St 67219

THAI TRADITION   316/687-1500 **13**
APPROVED Thai. Casual Dining. **Address:** 650 N
Carriage Pkwy, Suite 120 67208

TWO OLIVES   316/681-1100 **4**
APPROVED Middle Eastern. Casual Dining. **Address:**
2949 N Rock Rd 67226

WICHITA BREWING CO   316/440-4885 **14**
APPROVED American. Brewpub. **Address:** 535 N
Woodlawn St 67208

YA YA'S EURO BISTRO   316/634-1000 **5**
THREE DIAMOND European. Fine Dining. **Address:** 8115 E
21st St N 67226

Turn dreams into plans using
AAA travel planning tools: AAA.com/maps

Kansas City

Missouri

Missouri has always provided an open door to adventure, from the footpaths blazed by Lewis and Clark to historic Route 66. Travel one of Missouri's legendary trails to discover the state's delightful mix of frontier heritage and scenic treasures.

Wander the cobblestone streets of Laclede's Landing in cosmopolitan St. Louis. Explore the converted warehouses along the Mississippi riverfront, now filled with restaurants and clubs. A brief stroll south is rewarded with a nighttime view of The Gateway Arch.

Then, like the pioneers before you, head westward. Running beside the Missouri River is the Katy Trail, a monumental rails-to-trails conversion. The whistles of the trains and the rumble along the tracks have been replaced by the crunch of gravel beneath your feet or your bicycle's wheels.

After you pass the striking capitol building in Jefferson City, leave the trail and follow

The Gateway Arch, St. Louis

the river's path to Independence and Kansas City. Once trailheads for the Santa Fe and Oregon trails, these cities have maintained their rich history and Western sensibilities.

And don't forget a side trip to Branson. Immerse yourself in the entertainment flowing from the town's theater's before heading to the peaceful wooded hills of the Ozarks.

Gateway to the West

When Meriwether Lewis and William Clark returned to St. Louis with tales of their discoveries in the West, they sparked a wave of national expansion. The burgeoning towns of Independence and Kansas City became trailheads for the long and arduous journey into the unknown.

Today's explorers can retrace the Santa Fe, Oregon and California trails, following in the footsteps of people who dared to go in search of a better life. They reveal many stories, from the sad steps of the Cherokees along the Trail of Tears near Cape Girardeau to the hoof beats of the Pony Express, once headquartered in St. Joseph.

The Gateway Arch, rising majestically above St. Louis' modern skyline, remains a symbol of Missouri's early role as a gateway to a new frontier. Bicycle paths wind through Forest Park, originally the site of the 1904 St. Louis World's Fair and now home to the city's art, history and science museums.

While known for its jazz and barbecue, Kansas City has much more to offer. The city harbors some pretty big surprises, from the 322-foot-wide waterfall beyond the right field fence of Kauffman Stadium to the 18-foot shuttlecocks on the lawn of The Nelson-Atkins Museum of Art.

In the minds of many (including those who have never been there), Branson equals music theaters. But while the sheer number and variety of live entertainment offerings are indeed noteworthy, this southwestern Missouri town also lies in the heart of Ozarks country, where deep blue springs flow through lushly forested hills and valleys.

Dreamers and Doers

The state's pioneering spirit does not just apply to those who ventured west. Missouri has been more than a gateway out; it has been a stepping stone up. Mark Twain based the adventures of Tom Sawyer and Huckleberry Finn on his own childhood in Hannibal, while Walt Disney modeled the "Main Street USA" portion of Disneyland after Marceline, his hometown.

A former slave, George Washington Carver took the knowledge that sprouted in his garden in Diamond and used it to revolutionize agriculture in the southern United States. And Independence resident and former Kansas City Automobile Club employee Harry S. Truman steered our country out of World War II, paving the way for prosperity.

Ragtime composer Scott Joplin, rock 'n' roller Chuck Berry, and jazz greats Duke Ellington and Miles Davis are just a few of the musical pioneers who started out in the saloons of St. Louis and Kansas City.

Recreation

South-central Missouri is a water lover's paradise. Surrounded by spectacular rolling hills, Lake of the Ozarks' 54,000 acres of water beckon boaters, water skiers, and those who want to enjoy the area's tranquil beauty. Farther south, the crystal clear waters of Table Rock Lake offer scuba divers unparalleled views of an underwater forest.

Canoeing on the Meramec River in eastern Missouri is a tranquil retreat. Meramec State Park near Sullivan features miles of picturesque riverbank scenery, bubbling springs and more than 40 caves. Paddle your way past open glades dotted with Indian paintbrush and fern-covered ravines.

Fishing is the classic pastime in Missouri. The cold water of Lake Taneycomo near Branson is a trout haven year-round. Other lakes throughout the state are teeming with smallmouth and largemouth bass, eye, walleye, channel cat and blu

The oak and hickory forests and grass that surround all this water myriad hunting opportunities. Migrating ducks and geese rest at Swan Lake and Mingo national wildlife refuges, near Brookfield and Poplar Bluff, respectively. Quails, wild turkeys, squirrels, rabbits, raccoons and deer are plentiful throughout the state.

In 1986 the Missouri-Kansas-Texas Railroad (the "Katy") stopped running between Sedalia and St. Charles, opening the door for one of the largest rails-to-trails conversions in history. The trail starts at the restored M-K-T Depot in St. Charles and runs west between towering bluffs and the curvaceous Missouri River. Trailheads with facilities are spaced about every 10 miles. Favorite pit stops along the 240-mile trek include the Stone Hill Winery in Hermann and the charming bistros and cafés of Rocheport.

Another popular hiking route across the state is the still-evolving Ozark Trail, a series of trails that will one day form a continuous route from St. Louis to northern Arkansas. The Taum Sauk section, generally regarded as the trail's most rugged and scenic stretch, winds over sculpted ridges and mossy glades, ascends the summit of Taum Sauk Mountain (the highest in the state) and takes in Mina Sauk Falls.

Hiking in the Ozarks

Historic Timeline

1764	A French trading post is established at present-day St. Louis.
1804	The Lewis and Clark expedition departs from St. Charles.
1811	The New Madrid earthquakes rock the Mississippi Valley.
1820	A compromise admits Missouri to the Union as a slave state while prohibiting slavery in the remaining Louisiana Territory.
1835	Samuel Langhorne Clemens, better known as Mark Twain, is born in the town of Florida.
1860	The Pony Express begins its run from St. Joseph to Sacramento.
1945	Missouri native and former AAA sales representative Harry S. Truman becomes the 33rd U.S. president.
1993	Flooding on the Missouri and Mississippi rivers causes billions of dollars in damage across the state.
2011	A deadly tornado cuts a 13-mile path through Joplin.
2014	The death of Michael Brown in the St. Louis suburb of Ferguson sparks a nationwide debate.
2015	The Gateway Arch celebrates its 50th anniversary in October as part of the national park's expansion project.

What To Pack

Temperature Averages Maximum/Minimum	JANUARY	FEBRUARY	MARCH	APRIL	MAY	JUNE	JULY	AUGUST	SEPTEMBER	OCTOBER	NOVEMBER	DECEMBER
Branson	44 / 21	50 / 25	59 / 33	69 / 41	77 / 50	85 / 59	90 / 64	89 / 62	82 / 55	72 / 43	58 / 34	47 / 25
Columbia	37 / 18	44 / 24	55 / 33	66 / 43	75 / 53	84 / 62	89 / 66	87 / 64	79 / 55	68 / 44	53 / 33	41 / 22
Kansas City	38 / 21	44 / 26	56 / 36	67 / 46	76 / 57	86 / 67	90 / 72	89 / 70	80 / 61	69 / 49	53 / 36	42 / 25
New Madrid	41 / 25	48 / 29	58 / 38	69 / 48	78 / 57	87 / 66	91 / 70	89 / 67	83 / 59	72 / 47	57 / 38	46 / 29
St. Joseph	37 / 16	43 / 22	55 / 32	66 / 42	76 / 54	86 / 63	90 / 67	88 / 64	81 / 55	70 / 43	53 / 32	40 / 21
St. Louis	38 / 21	45 / 26	55 / 36	66 / 47	77 / 57	86 / 66	91 / 71	88 / 69	81 / 61	69 / 49	54 / 38	42 / 27

From the records of The Weather Channel Interactive, Inc.

Good Facts To Know

ABOUT THE STATE

POPULATION: 5,988,927.

AREA: 69,707 square miles; ranks 21st.

CAPITAL: Jefferson City.

HIGHEST POINT: 1,772 ft., Taum Sauk Mountain.

LOWEST POINT: 230 ft., St. Francis River.

TIME ZONE(S): Central. DST.

GAMBLING

MINIMUM AGE FOR GAMBLING: 21.

REGULATIONS

TEEN DRIVING LAWS: Driving is not permitted 1 a.m.-5 a.m. One unrelated passenger (family members exempt) under age 19 is permitted for the first six months; afterwards, no more than three passengers under age 19 are permitted. The minimum age for an unrestricted driver's license is 18. Phone (573) 751-4600 for more information about Missouri's driver's license regulations.

SEAT BELT/CHILD RESTRAINT LAWS: Seat belts are required for driver and front-seat passengers age 16 and over. Children ages 8-16 and at least 57 inches or 80 lbs. are required to be in a child restraint or seat belt; child restraints or booster seats are required for children who are under age 8, weigh less than 80 pounds and are less than 57 inches tall. AAA recommends the use of seat belts and appropriate child restraints for the driver and all passengers.

CELLPHONE RESTRICTIONS: Persons age 21 and under are prohibited from driving while sending, reading or writing a text message.

HELMETS FOR MOTORCYCLISTS: Required for all riders.

RADAR DETECTORS: Permitted. Prohibited for use by commercial vehicles.

MOVE OVER LAW: State law requires drivers approaching a stationary emergency vehicle displaying flashing lights, including towing and recovery vehicles, traveling in the same direction, to vacate the lane closest if safe and possible to do so. Or slow to a speed safe for road conditions.

FIREARMS LAWS: Vary by state and/or county. Contact the Missouri State Highway Patrol, Attn.: Public Information and Education Division, 1510 East Elm St., Jefferson City, MO 65101; phone (573) 526-6115.

HOLIDAYS

HOLIDAYS: Jan. 1 ■ Martin Luther King Jr. Day, Jan. (3rd Mon.) ■ Lincoln's Birthday, Feb. 12 ■ Washington's Birthday/Presidents Day, Feb. (3rd Mon.); Truman Day, May 8 ■ Memorial Day, May (last Mon.) ■ July 4 ■ Labor Day, Sept. (1st Mon.) ■ Columbus Day, Oct. (2nd Mon.) ■ Veterans Day, Nov. 11 ■ Thanksgiving ■ Christmas, Dec. 25.

MONEY

TAXES: Missouri's statewide sales tax is 4.225 percent. Cities and counties may also impose additional increments to the sales tax. Cities may levy taxes on lodging, food and beverages.

VISITOR INFORMATION

INFORMATION CENTERS: State welcome centers are 2 miles east of the Missouri-Oklahoma state line on I-44 near Joplin ■ in north St. Louis on Dunn Road off I-270 (Riverview exit 34) ■ west of I-29, a half-mile south of the junction with US 136 near Rock Port ■ in Hannibal, US 61S, 2 miles south of junction with US 36 ■ in Kansas City, on the grounds of the Truman Sports Complex off I-70 exit 9 at the Blue Ridge Cut-Off ■ and in Eagleville, I-35S, 2 miles south of the Iowa state line and I-35, at mile marker 112.

The centers are open daily 8-5, Mar.-Nov., Mon.-Sat. 8-5, rest of year. The Missouri Division of Tourism office in the Truman State Office Building, 301 W. High St., second floor, Jefferson City, provides travel information Mon.-Fri. 8-5.

FURTHER INFORMATION FOR VISITORS:
Missouri Division of Tourism
301 W. High St. #290
Jefferson City, MO 65101
(573) 751-4133

NATIONAL FOREST INFORMATION:
Mark Twain National Forest
401 Fairgrounds Rd.
Rolla, MO 65401
(573) 364-4621
(877) 444-6777 (reservations)

FISHING AND HUNTING REGULATIONS:
Missouri Department of Conservation
2901 W. Truman Blvd.
Jefferson City, MO 65109
(573) 751-4115

RECREATION INFORMATION:
Missouri Department of Natural Resources
Division of State Parks
1101 Riverside Dr.
Jefferson City, MO 65102
(573) 751-3443
(800) 334-6946

Missouri Annual Events

Please call ahead to confirm event details.

Visit **AAA.com/travelguides/events** to find
AAA-listed events for every day of the year

WINTER

Dec. - Garden Glow Light Exhibit / St.
Louis / 314-577-5100
- Christmas Candlelight / Defiance
636-798-2005

Jan. - Saint Louis Auto Show / St.
Louis / 314-822-0333
- Ag Expo / Poplar
Bluff / 573-686-8064
- Soulard 12th Night / St.
Louis / 314-771-5110

Feb. - St. Louis Boat & Sportshow / St.
Louis / 314-567-0020
- Missouri Botanical Garden Orchid
Show / St. Louis / 314-577-5100
- Ozarks Super Plunge & Polar Bear
Strut / Osage Beach / 573-635-1660

SPRING

Mar. - Heart of America Chili Challenge / St.
Joseph / 816-364-3836
- Greater Kansas City Home Show
Kansas City / 816-942-8800

Apr. - Show Me Gourd Festival / Springfield
417-754-2558
- Ozark Mountain Spring / Branson
800-619-5708
- Dogwood Festival / Camdenton
573-346-2227

May - Twain on Main Festival / Hannibal
573-470-3492
- Art Fair at Laumeier / St.
Louis / 314-821-1209

SUMMER

June - Shakespeare Festival St. Louis in the
Park / St. Louis / 314-531-9800, ext.
101
- Scott Joplin Ragtime Festival
Sedalia / 660-826-2271

July - Riverfest / St.
Charles / 636-946-7776
- Fair St. Louis / St.
Louis / 314-434-3434
- National Tom Sawyer Days
Hannibal / 573-795-6233

Aug. - Festival of Nations / St.
Louis / 314-773-9090
- Festival of the Little Hills / St.
Charles / 636-940-0095
- Missouri State Fair / Sedalia
660-530-5600

FALL

Sept. - Roots N Blues N BBQ Festival
Columbia / 573-442-5862
- Great Forest Park Balloon Race / St.
Louis / 314-993-2468
- Greek Food Fest / Kansas
City / 816-942-9100

Oct. - Autumn Historic Folklife Festival
Hannibal / 573-221-6545
- Heritage Days / Warsaw
660-438-5922

Nov. - KCP&L Plaza Lighting Ceremony
Kansas City / 816-753-0100
- Veterans Homecoming Week
Branson / 417-337-8387

STAY CONNECTED

GET THE APP

AAA.com/mobile
CAA.ca/mobile

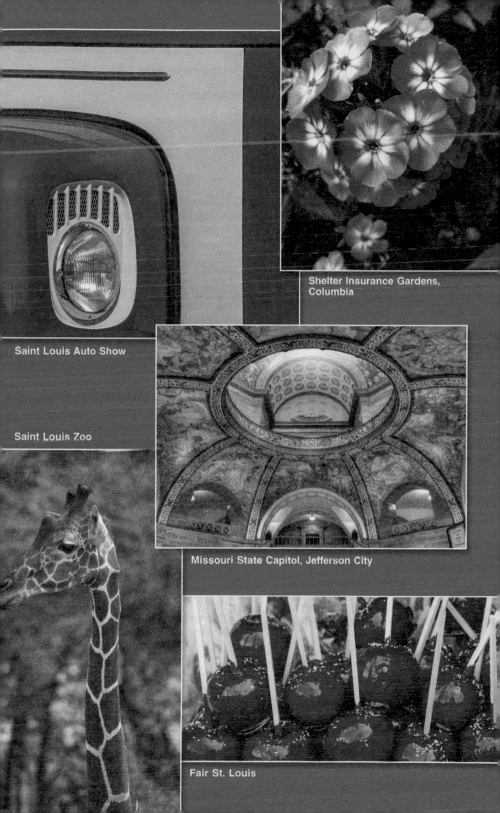

Shelter Insurance Gardens, Columbia

Saint Louis Auto Show

Saint Louis Zoo

Missouri State Capitol, Jefferson City

Fair St. Louis

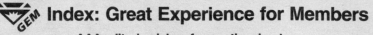

Index: Great Experience for Members

AAA editor's picks of exceptional note

Onondaga Cave
State Park

Saint Louis Zoo

Missouri State Capitol

Missouri Botanical
Garden

See Orientation map on p. 144 for corresponding grid coordinates, if applicable.
*Indicates the GEM is temporarily closed.

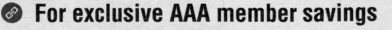

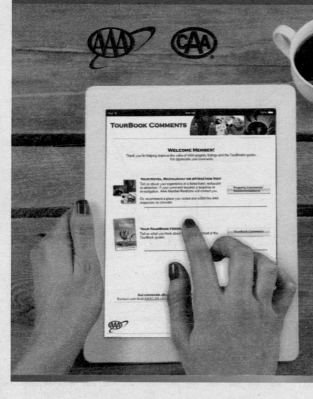

Let Your Voice Be Heard

We Want To Hear From You

- If a AAA listed establishment doesn't meet your expectations, send us the details so we can look into it.
- Or, if you've got a favorite hotel, restaurant or attraction you'd like us to consider for AAA inspection, send us your recommendation.

Visit us at **AAA.com/MemberFeedback**

Missouri
Atlas Section

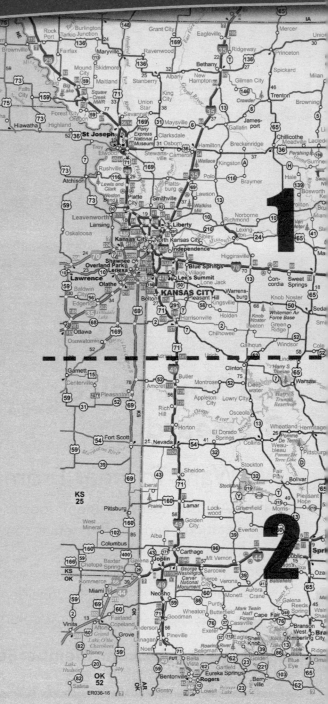

MISSOURI

3

4

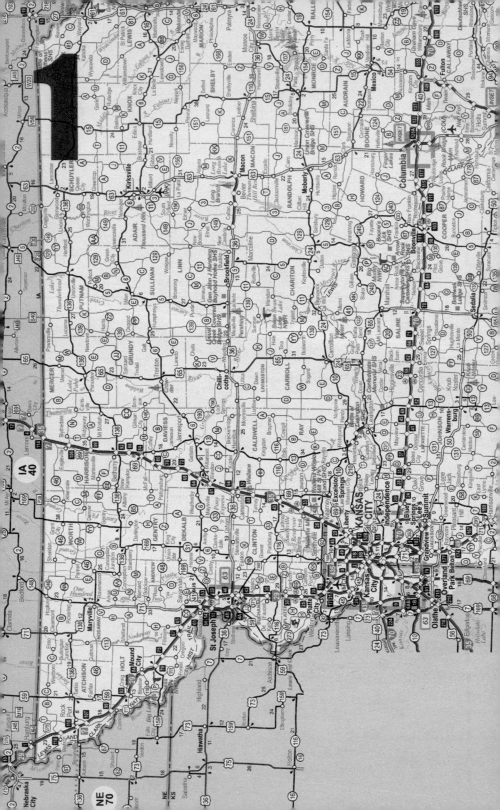

MISSOURI

1:1,552,320
Scale in Miles

Scale in Kilometers

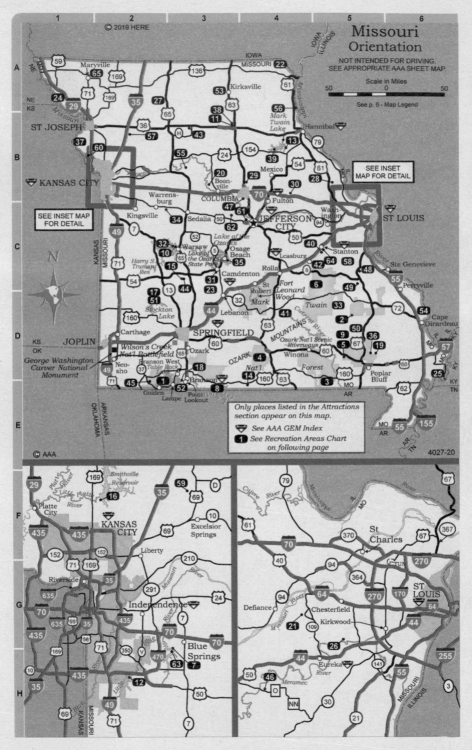

© 2019 HERE

Missouri
Orientation

NOT INTENDED FOR DRIVING.
SEE APPROPRIATE AAA SHEET MAP

Scale in Miles
50   0   50

See p. 6 - Map Legend

IOWA
MISSOURI

NE
MO

NE
KS

ST JOSEPH

KANSAS CITY

Maryville

Kirksville

Hannibal

Mark Twain Lake

SEE INSET MAP FOR DETAIL

ST LOUIS

SEE INSET MAP FOR DETAIL

Warrensburg

Kingsville

COLUMBIA

Boonville

Mexico

Fulton

JEFFERSON CITY

Washington

KANSAS
MISSOURI

Sedalia

Lake of the Ozarks

Osage Beach

Leasburg

Stanton

Ste Genevieve

Harry S Truman Res

Lake of the Ozarks State Park

Camdenton

Rolla

St Robert

Fort Leonard Wood

Perryville

Stockton Lake

Lebanon

Mark Twain

National Forest

Cape Girardeau

JOPLIN

Carthage

SPRINGFIELD

Ozark Nat'l Scenic Riverways

KS
OK

Wilson's Creek Nat'l Battlefield

George Washington Carver National Monument

Neosho

Ozark

Winona

Ozark Nat'l

Poplar Bluff

Branson West

Branson

Golden

Lampe

Point Lookout

Ozark

MO
AR

AR
TN

MO
KY

KY
TN

OKLAHOMA

ARKANSAS

MISSOURI

Only places listed in the Attractions section appear on this map.

⬥ See AAA GEM Index

1 See Recreation Areas Chart on following page

© AAA

4027-20

Smithville Reservoir

Platte City

KANSAS CITY

Excelsior Springs

Liberty

Riverside

Independence

Blue Springs

Cuivre River

Mississippi River

St Charles

ST LOUIS

Defiance

Chesterfield

Kirkwood

Eureka

Meramec River

MISSOURI
ILLINOIS

KANSAS
MISSOURI

Recreation Areas Chart

The map location numerals in column 2 show an area's location on the preceding map.

Find thousands of places to camp at AAA.com/campgrounds

	MAP LOCATION	CAMPING	PICNICKING	HIKING TRAILS	BOATING	BOAT RAMP	BOAT RENTAL	FISHING	SWIMMING	PET FRIENDLY	BICYCLE TRAILS	WINTER SPORTS	VISITOR CENTER	LODGE/CABINS	FOOD SERVICE
NATIONAL FORESTS *(See place listings.)*															
Mark Twain (D-4) 1,500,000 acres. Southern Missouri.			•	•	•	•	•	•	•	•	•				
Big Bay (E-2) 680 acres 1 mi. s.e. of Shell Knob on SR 39, then 3 mi. s.e. on CR YY.	1		•					•	•	•					
Crane Lake (D-5) 100 acres 12 mi. s. of Ironton off SR 49 and CR E. Electric boat motors only. Hunting; horse trails.	2		•	•	•	•		•	•	•					
Fourche Lake (E-5) 40 acres 18 mi. w. of Doniphan on US 160.	3		•	•	•	•		•		•					
Noblett Lake (D-4) 8 acres 8 mi. w. of Willow Springs on SR 76, then 1.4 mi. s. on SR 181, 3 mi. s.e. on CR AP and 1 mi. s.w. on CR 857. Electric boat motors only. Bird-watching, canoeing; horse trails.	4	•	•	•	•	•		•		•	•				
Pinewoods Lake (D-5) 32 acres 2 mi. w. of Ellsinore on SR 60. Electric boat motors only. Note: Swimming is permitted but not recommended; this is a managed fishery lake.	5		•	•	•	•		•	•	•		•			
Red Bluff (C-5) 133 acres 1 mi. e. of Davisville on CR V, then 1 mi. n. on FR 2011.	6	•	•					•	•	•					
NATIONAL SCENIC RIVERWAYS *(See place listings.)*															
Ozark (D-4) 134 miles. Southeastern Missouri. Hunting; horse trails.			•	•	•	•	•	•	•	•	•		•	•	•
ARMY CORPS OF ENGINEERS															
Blue Springs Lake (H-3) 720 acres .5 mi. e. of I-470 off Bowlin Rd. in Blue Springs. Marina.	7	•	•	•	•	•	•	•	•	•					
Bull Shoals Lake (E-3) 60,000 acres s.e. of Branson on the Missouri-Arkansas state line.	8	•	•	•	•	•	•	•	•	•			•	•	•
Clearwater Lake (D-5) 1,630 acres 7 mi. w. of Piedmont. Tennis; exercise trail, marina, playground.	9	•	•	•	•	•	•	•	•	•			•	•	•
Harry S. Truman Lake (C-2) 55,600 acres 1.5 mi. n.w. of Warsaw on the Osage River. Horse trails, marina.	10	•	•	•	•	•	•	•	•	•					
Long Branch Lake (B-3) 2,430 acres 2 mi. w. of Macon on US 36. Hunting; marina, playground, shooting range.	11	•	•	•	•	•	•	•	•	•					
Longview Lake (H-2) 930 acres 1 mi. s. of I-470 off Raytown Rd. in Kansas City. Golf; marina.	12	•	•	•	•	•	•	•	•	•	•				
Mark Twain Lake (B-4) 18,600 acres 9 mi. n. of Perry on CR J. Golf (nine holes), hunting; horse trails, marina, playground, shooting range.	13	•	•	•	•	•	•	•	•	•			•	•	•
Norfork Lake (D-4) 22,000 acres at Tecumseh off US 160. Marinas, playground.	14	•	•	•	•	•	•	•	•	•					•
Pomme De Terre Lake (C-3) 7,800 acres 3 mi. s. of Hermitage off SR 64. Marina, playground.	15	•	•	•	•	•	•	•	•	•			•	•	•
Smithville Lake (F-2) 7,190 acres 15 mi. n. of Kansas City on US 169, then 2 mi. e. on SR DD. Golf (36 holes); horse trails, marina, playground.	16	•	•	•	•	•	•	•	•	•				•	•
Stockton Lake (D-2) 24,900 acres 1 mi. s. of Stockton on SR 32. Horse trails, marina, playground.	17	•	•	•	•	•	•	•	•	•			•	•	•
Table Rock Lake (D-3) 52,300 acres 5 mi. w. of Branson via SRs 76 and 165. Marina.	18	•	•	•	•	•	•	•	•	•			•	•	•
Wappapello Lake (D-5) 8,900 acres 16 mi. n.e. of Poplar Bluff via US 60 and CR T. Canoeing, kayaking; horse trails.	19	•	•	•	•	•	•	•	•	•			•		
STATE															
Arrow Rock (B-3) 167 acres 3 blks. n. of SR 41.	20	•	•	•				•		•			•		•
Babler Memorial (G-4) 2,441 acres 20 mi. w. of St. Louis on SR 109. Tennis; horse rental, nature center, playground.	21	•	•	•					•	•	•		•		
Battle of Athens (A-4) 408 acres 8 mi. n. of Revere off SR 81. Historic. Playground.	22	•	•	•	•	•		•							
Bennett Spring (C-3) 3,216 acres 12 mi. w. of Lebanon on SR 64.	23	•	•	•	•	•	•	•	•	•			•	•	•

Recreation Areas Chart

The map location numerals in column 2 show an area's location on the preceding map.

Find thousands of places to camp at AAA.com/campgrounds

	MAP LOCATION	CAMPING	PICNICKING	HIKING TRAILS	BOATING	BOAT RAMP	BOAT RENTAL	FISHING	SWIMMING	PET FRIENDLY	BICYCLE TRAILS	WINTER SPORTS	VISITOR CENTER	LODGE/CABINS	FOOD SERVICE
Big Lake (A-1) 407 acres 11 mi. s.w. of Mound City off SR 118 on SR 111. Playground.	24	•	•		•	•		•	•	•				•	•
Big Oak Tree (D-6) 1,028 acres 2 mi. e. of East Prairie on SR 80, then 12.5 mi. s. on SR 102. Bird-watching, boating (electric motors only); boardwalk trail, interpretive programs, playground.	25		•	•	•	•		•		•			•		
Castlewood (G-5) 1,818 acres 6 mi. e. of Ballwin on Kiefer Creek Rd. off SR 100. Canoeing; horse trails, playground.	26		•	•				•		•					
Crowder (A-2) 1,912 acres 4 mi. w. of Trenton on SR 146. Canoeing, tennis; horse trails, playground. Electric boat motors only.	27	•	•	•	•	•		•	•	•					
Cuivre River (B-5) 6,393 acres 3 mi. e. of Troy off SR 47. Boating (electric motors only), orienteering; horse trails.	28	•	•	•	•	•		•	•	•				•	
Finger Lakes (B-4) 1,128 acres 10 mi. n. of Columbia on US 63. Boating (electric motors only); ATV and motorcycle trails.	29	•	•	•	•	•		•	•	•					
Graham Cave (B-4) 386 acres 2 mi. w. of I-70 on SR TT. Interpretive trails, playground.	30	•	•	•	•	•		•		•					
Ha Ha Tonka (C-3) 3,709 acres 5 mi. s.w. of Camdenton off US 54 on CR D. Scenic. Historic ruins, playground. Boat docks are only available outside park boundaries at the Big Niangua arm of the Lake of the Ozarks.	31		•	•	•			•	•	•					
Harry S. Truman (C-2) 1,440 acres 5 mi. w. of Warsaw off SR 7 on CR UU. Kayaking; marina, playground.	32	•	•	•	•	•	•	•	•	•			•		•
Johnson's Shut-Ins (D-5) 8,550 acres 8 mi. n. of Lesterville on CR N. Scenic. Pets are not permitted on Shut-Ins Trail. Rock climbing; horse trails, playground.	33	•	•	•				•	•	•			•		
Knob Noster (C-3) 3,934 acres 2 mi. s. of Knob Noster off US 50 on SR 23. Kayaking; horse trails, playground. Electric boat motors only.	34	•	•	•	•			•		•	•		•		
Lake of the Ozarks (C-3) 17,626 acres. Caverns, horse rental, marina.	35	•	•	•	•	•	•	•	•	•			•	•	•
Lake Wappapello (D-5) 1,854 acres 16 mi. n. of Poplar Bluff on US 67 and 9 mi. e. on SR 172. Canoeing, kayaking; bicycle and horse trails, marina.	36	•	•	•	•	•	•	•	•	•				•	
Lewis and Clark (B-1) 189 acres 20 mi. s.w. of St. Joseph via US 59 and SR 45 on SR 138. Bird-watching; playground.	37	•	•					•	•	•					
Long Branch (A-3) 1,828 acres 2 mi. w. of Macon on US 36. Kayaking; marina.	38	•	•	•	•	•		•	•	•					•
Mark Twain (B-4) 2,775 acres .5 mi. s. of Florida on SR 107. Historic. Playground.	39	•	•	•	•	•		•	•	•					
Meramec (C-4) 6,896 acres 4 mi. e. via SR 185. Scenic. Canoeing, rafting; cavern tours, playground.	40	•	•	•	•	•		•	•	•			•	•	•
Montauk (D-4) 1,396 acres 21 mi. s.w. of Salem via SR 119. Historic. Playground.	41	•	•	•				•		•			•	•	•
Onondaga Cave (C-5) 1,317 acres 5 mi. s. on SR H. Scenic. Cavern tours; playground.	42	•	•	•				•		•			•		•
Pershing (B-3) 3,565 acres 2 mi. w. of Laclede off US 36 on SR 130. Interpretive trail, playground. Electric boat motors only.	43	•	•	•				•	•	•					
Pomme De Terre (C-3) 734 acres 5 mi. s. of Hermitage via SR 64. Canoeing, kayaking; marina, playground.	44	•	•	•	•	•	•	•		•				•	•
Roaring River (E-2) 4,093 acres 7 mi. s. of Cassville on SR 112. Interpretive trail, playground.	45	•	•	•				•	•	•			•	•	•
Robertsville (H-4) 1,224 acres 15 mi. s.w. of Eureka off I-44. Canoeing, kayaking; playground.	46	•	•	•				•		•					
Rock Bridge Memorial (C-3) 2,273 acres 5 mi. s. of Columbia on SR 163. Cross-country skiing, orienteering; horse trails, playground.	47		•	•				•		•	•	•			
Saint Francois (C-5) 2,735 acres 4 mi. n. of Bonne Terre on US 67. Boating (motors not recommended); horse trails, playground.	48	•	•	•	•			•	•	•					

Recreation Areas Chart

The map location numerals in column 2 show an area's location on the preceding map.

Find thousands of places to camp at AAA.com/campgrounds

	MAP LOCATION	CAMPING	PICNICKING	HIKING TRAILS	BOATING	BOAT RAMP	BOAT RENTAL	FISHING	SWIMMING	PET FRIENDLY	BICYCLE TRAILS	WINTER SPORTS	VISITOR CENTER	LODGE/CABINS	FOOD SERVICE
Saint Joe (C-5) 8,243 acres 3 mi. s. of Flat River off CR B via SR 32. Canoeing, kayaking; ATV trails, horse trails. Electric boat motors only.	49	•	•	•	•	•	•	•	•	•	•	•	•		
Sam A. Baker (D-5) 5,324 acres 6 mi. n. of Patterson via SRs 34 and 143. Horse trails, nature center, playground.	50	•	•	•	•	•	•	•	•	•	•		•	•	•
Stockton (D-2) 2,176 acres 8 mi. s.e. of Stockton on SR 215. Canoeing, kayaking; marina.	51	•	•	•	•	•	•	•	•	•				•	•
Table Rock (E-3) 356 acres 5 mi. w. of Branson on SR 165. Scuba diving; marina, playground. Food service in summer only.	52	•	•	•	•	•	•	•	•						•
Thousand Hills (A-3) 3,080 acres 2 mi. w. of Kirksville off SR 6 on SR 157. Historic. Marina, playground.	53	•	•	•	•	•	•	•	•	•				•	•
Trail of Tears (D-6) 3,415 acres 10 mi. n. on SR 177. Boating (electric motors only); horse trails, playground.	54	•	•	•	•			•	•	•			•		
Van Meter (B-3) 1,105 acres on SR 122 via SR 41 in Miami. Nature trails, playground. Electric boat motors only.	55	•	•	•	•			•		•			•		
Wakonda (A-4) 1,054 acres 3 mi. s. of La Grange off US 61. Kayaking; playground.	56	•	•	•	•	•		•	•	•					
Wallace (B-2) 502 acres 6 mi. s. of Cameron on SR 121. Boating (electric motors only); amphitheater, playground.	57	•	•	•	•			•	•	•					
Washington (C-5) 2,148 acres 9 mi. s.w. of De Soto off SR 21. Historic. Boating (no motors); nature center, playground.	58	•	•	•	•			•	•	•				•	•
Watkins Woolen Mill (F-3) 1,500 acres 6 mi. n. of Excelsior Springs off SR 92 on CR RA. Historic mill tours; horse trails, interpretive trails.	59	•	•	•	•	•		•	•	•			•		
Weston Bend (B-2) 1,133 acres 1 mi. s. of Weston on SR 45. Playground.	60	•	•	•				•		•	•				
OTHER															
Binder (C-4) 650 acres off US 50W in Jefferson City. Playground, sand volleyball court, softball field.	61	•	•	•	•			•		•					•
Cole County (C-3) 80 acres off Country Club Dr. in Jefferson City	62		•	•				•	•						
Fleming Park (H-3) 7,809 acres e. of Kansas City on US 40 and Woods Chapel Rd.	63	•	•	•	•	•	•	•	•			•	•		•
Meramec Caverns (C-5) 110 acres 3 mi. s. of Stanton off I-44. Canoeing, gold panning; cavern tours, riverboat rides, ziplines. Note: Swimming is permitted but not recommended due to dangerous undertows.	64	•	•		•	•	•	•	•				•	•
Mozingo Lake (A-2) 3,000 acres 4 mi. e. of Maryville on US 136. Golf, hunting; horse trails.	65	•	•	•	•			•	•					•	•

BELTON pop. 23,116

HAMPTON INN BY HILTON   816/416-8006
THREE DIAMOND **SAVE** Hotel. **Address:** 16410 Cornerstone Dr 64012

AAA Benefit: Members save up to 15%!

BERKELEY pop. 8,978
- **Hotels & Restaurants map & index p. 274**
- **Part of St. Louis area — see map p. 248**

HILTON GARDEN INN ST. LOUIS AIRPORT
314/521-6444   **23**

THREE DIAMOND
Hotel

Hilton Garden Inn

AAA Benefit: Members save up to 15%!

Address: 4450 Evans Place Dr 63134 **Location:** I-70 exit 239, just n on Hanley Rd, just w on Evans Ave, then just s. **Facility:** 136 units. 3 stories, interior corridors. **Terms:** check-in 4 pm. **Pool:** heated indoor. **Activities:** hot tub, exercise room. **Guest Services:** valet and coin laundry, area transportation.

SAVE ✈ 🍴 🍽 CALL ♿ 🏊
➕ **BIZ** **HS** 📶 ✖ 🔌 ▤
▣

RENAISSANCE ST. LOUIS AIRPORT HOTEL
314/429-1100   **22**

THREE DIAMOND **SAVE** Hotel. **Address:** 9801 Natural Bridge Rd 63134

AAA Benefit: Members save 5% or more!

BLUE SPRINGS (G-3) pop. 52,575, elev. 962'
- **Part of Kansas City area — see map p. 199**

Drawn to the cool, deep springs of the Little Blue River, settlers heading westward in the 1800s made Blue Springs one of their final stopping points before leaving civilized territory. Today it's a center of outdoor activity revolving around lakes, parks and golf courses. Blue Springs made an appearance on pop culture radar in 2008, when resident David Cook won the seventh season of the reality show singing competition "American Idol."

More than a dozen city parks feature sports courts and fields, jogging trails, picnic facilities and playgrounds. You can sled down the town's largest hill after the snow begins to fall at Keystone Park, 2214 S.W. Keystone Dr. Let canine family members run loose at Dog Park, 1049 N.E. 20th St., a 2.7-acre off-leash area for dogs of all sizes at Gregory O. Grounds Park. Skateboarders will find thrills at the skate park at 14-acre Burrus Old Mill Park, 112 N.W. Woods Chapel Rd., which is also the original site of Blue Springs.

There may not be water, water *everywhere* in Blue Springs, but there's more than enough to go around at Lake Jacomo and Blue Springs Lake, both in Fleming Park, 22807 Woods Chapel Rd. Boaters and windsurfers on 970-acre Lake Jacomo enjoy smooth sailing, in part because horsepower is limited to no more than 40 hp for pontoon boats and sailboats, and no more than 25 hp for other types of boats. There are no horsepower limits at 720-acre Blue Springs Lake, where visitors engage in water skiing, tubing and jet skiing. There's also good fishing to be had at both lakes. Phone (816) 228-0137 for more park information.

Blue Springs Chamber of Commerce: 1000 W. Main St., Blue Springs, MO 64015. **Phone:** (816) 229-8558.

COURTYARD BY MARRIOTT KANSAS CITY EAST/BLUE SPRINGS   816/228-8100
THREE DIAMOND **SAVE** Hotel. **Address:** 1500 NE Coronado 64014

AAA Benefit: Members save 5% or more!

HAMPTON INN BY HILTON BLUE SPRINGS   816/220-3844
THREE DIAMOND **SAVE** Hotel. **Address:** 900 NW South Outer Rd 64015

AAA Benefit: Members save up to 15%!

WHERE TO EAT

LEGEND OF ASIA   816/220-9833
APPROVED Chinese. Buffet Style. **Address:** 1853 SW 7 Hwy 64014

RANCHO GRANDE CANTINA   816/228-5550
APPROVED Mexican. Casual Dining. **Address:** 501 NW Jefferson St 64014

ZARDA BAR-B-Q   816/229-9999
APPROVED Barbecue. Quick Serve. **Address:** 214 N 7 Hwy 64014

BOLIVAR pop. 10,325

BEST WESTERN PLUS BOLIVAR HOTEL AND SUITES
417/326-0188

THREE DIAMOND
Hotel

Best Western PLUS

AAA Benefit: Members save up to 15% and earn bonus points!

Address: 777 San Martin St 65613 **Location:** On US 83. **Facility:** 61 units, some kitchens. 4 stories, interior corridors. **Parking:** winter plug-ins. **Pool:** heated indoor. **Activities:** exercise room. **Guest Services:** coin laundry.

SAVE ➤ ➕ **BIZ** 📶 ✖ 🔌
▤ ▣ / **SOME UNITS** 🐾

COMFORT INN BOLIVAR   417/326-6169
APPROVED Hotel. **Address:** 2451 Tower Dr 65613

BOONVILLE (B-3) pop. 8,319, elev. 579'

Boonville, on the Missouri River, was an early distribution center from which wagon trains with provisions started over the old Santa Fe Trail to the Southwest. The first battle of the Civil War in Missouri was fought in Boonville on June 17, 1861, when Union troops under Gen. Nathaniel Lyon defeated state troops led by Gov. Claiborne Jackson.

Boonville has seven historic districts; venerable buildings include the 1836 Hain House and the renovated 1848 Old Cooper County Jail. The Katy Depot Caboose Museum, on First Street, is in a restored caboose that also houses the chamber of commerce.

Thespian Hall, built in 1855, is one of the oldest surviving theater buildings west of the Alleghenies. Its exterior is restored to its 1857 appearance and the interior recalls 1901. The hall is open for tours by appointment and is the site of spring and fall concerts; phone (660) 882-7977.

Boonville Area Chamber of Commerce: 320 First St., Suite A, Boonville, MO 65233. **Phone:** (660) 882-2721.

COMFORT INN BOONVILLE-COLUMBIA   660/882-5317

APPROVED
Hotel

Address: 2427 Mid America Industrial Dr 65233 **Location:** I-70 exit 101, just sw. **Facility:** 51 units. 2 stories, interior corridors. **Pool:** heated indoor. **Activities:** hot tub. **Guest Services:** coin laundry. **Featured Amenity: full hot breakfast.**

HOLIDAY INN EXPRESS   660/882-6882

APPROVED
Hotel

Address: 2419 Mid America Industrial Dr 65233 **Location:** I-70 exit 101, just nw. **Facility:** 56 units. 3 stories, interior corridors. **Pool:** heated indoor. **Activities:** hot tub, exercise room. **Guest Services:** coin laundry. **Featured Amenity: full hot breakfast.**

Branson

Then & Now

Monster cinnamon buns. A half-scale replica of the *Titanic*. Heartfelt displays of patriotic pride. Dale Evans, Lawrence Welk and Andy Williams. Sausage gravy and biscuits. Theme parks and showboats. Branson unashamedly revels in maximum Americana. It's the kind of place where a total stranger will greet you with a smile, a handshake and a heartfelt "Welcome to the heart of the Ozarks!" Anywhere else it would sound scripted or ring false, but friendliness Branson style feels neither forced nor fabricated.

Little more than 25 years after it was proclaimed "the live country music capital of the universe" in a feature profile on "60 Minutes," this town's enormous popularity is still something of a shocker. A small southwestern Missouri burg with a population of more than 11,000 being visited by millions of people a year is unlikely enough. The fact that it's tucked deep into the hills and hollows of the Ozarks, relatively isolated from big cities and major interstates, makes this an even more impressive success story.

Country is no longer the only game in town. Not when you've got popular headliner Shoji Tabuchi—a Japanese-born, classically trained musician who learned how to play the violin at age 7 and performs fleet-fingered versions of standards like "Orange Blossom Special" on fiddle in a glitzy, gaudy theater that's straight outa Vegas.

AAA.com/travelguides— more ways to look, book and save

Titanic—World's Largest Museum Attraction

Branson's Famous Baldknobbers show has been packin' 'em in for more than half a century, back when brothers Bill, Jim, Lyle and Bob Mabe set up folding chairs in Branson's City Hall and played banjo, dobro and washtub bass. It's still a show where grown men dressed in suspenders, loud shirts and funny hats engage in bawdy comedy routines guaranteed to make you laugh. Oh, and there's plenty of music, too.

A key catalyst in Branson's beginnings was the 1907 publication of Harold Bell Wright's second novel "The Shepherd of the Hills." Said to be the first American novel to sell a million copies, it told the inspirational story of an itinerant former pastor who chose to stay and live his life with the citizens of rural Mutton Hollow, offering a spiritual message based on simple values. The story's Ozark Mountains setting was what sparked an initial interest in Branson as a place to visit.

Tourism began on a small scale, with humble attractions like summer lakeside

(Continued on p. 152.)

Destination Branson

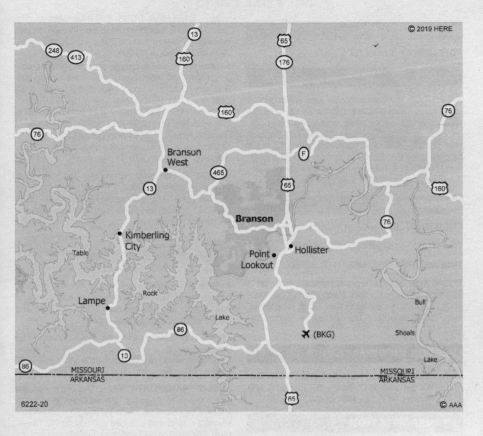

This map shows cities in the Branson vicinity where you will find attractions, hotels and restaurants. Cities are listed alphabetically in this book on the following pages.

Fast Facts

ABOUT THE CITY

POP: 10, 520 ▪ **ELEV:** 722 ft.

MONEY

SALES TAX: The Branson/Lakes area levies general retail sales, tourism sales and food and beverage sales taxes based on three different jurisdictions: Branson Landing/downtown, citywide and Branson Hills. General retail sales taxes range from 8.6 to 9.6 percent; sales that include a tourism sales tax range from 11.6 to 12.6 percent; food and beverage sales taxes range from 8.975 to 9.975 percent.

WHOM TO CALL

EMERGENCY: 911

POLICE (non-emergency): (417) 334-3300

TIME AND TEMPERATURE: (417) 336-5000

HOSPITALS: Skaggs Regional Medical Center, (417) 335-7000 ▪ CoxHealth Cox North (Springfield, Mo.), (417) 269-3000 ▪ CoxHealth Cox South (Springfield, Mo.), (417) 269-6000 ▪ Mercy Hospital (Springfield, Mo.), (417) 820-2000.

VISITOR INFORMATION

Branson/Lakes Area Convention and Visitors Bureau: 269 SR 248, P.O. Box 1897, Branson, MO 65615. **Phone:** (417) 334-4084 or (800) 214-3661.

TRANSPORTATION

AIR TRAVEL: Branson Airport (BKG), 1 mile south of the Hollister exit off US 65, east on Branson Creek Boulevard, then following signs to 4000 Branson Airport Blvd., is served by Buzz Airways and Frontier and handles commercial and general aviation; phone (417) 334-7813. Springfield-Branson National Airport (SGF), 5000 W. Kearney St. in Springfield, is about 45 miles

north of Branson via US 65. The drive takes 45 minutes to an hour, depending on traffic. Domestic airlines serving the airport include Allegiant Air, American, Delta and United; (417) 868-0500.

Several shuttle and limousine services transport passengers to and from Branson and the Springfield-Branson National Airport, including Branson Gray Line, (417) 335-4466 or (800) 542-6768; Fisk Transportation, (417) 862-2900; and Branson Coach/Tri-Lakes Shuttle, (417) 339-4888 or (800) 841-2313. At Branson Airport, only Branson Gray Line transports passengers from the airport; the other companies may only drop off passengers.

RENTAL CARS: Hertz, which only operates out of Springfield-Branson National Airport, offers discounts to AAA members; phone (417) 597-5313, (800) 654-3131 or (800) 654-3080. Rental cars are available at Branson Airport.

 Book and save at AAA.com/hertz

BUSES: Gray Line Branson, (800) 542-6768, provides chartered motor coach service to Branson and one-way transfers to and from Branson Airport and Springfield-Branson National Airport.

TAXIS: Cab companies include Jerry's Shuttle, (417) 348-1419 ▪ and Checker Cab, City Cabs and Yellow Cab, all of which can be reached at (417) 332-2227 (Branson Cab Service).

PUBLIC TRANSPORTATION: Unless you're part of a motor coach tour, getting around Branson is much easier if you have your own vehicle. One convenient alternative to driving is a free ride aboard the Downtown Trolley. The red-and-gold, hop-on and hop-off trolley makes 12 stops in the historic downtown area, including two stops at Branson Landing. It operates daily 9-6, Mar.-Dec.; closed Thanksgiving and Christmas. Trolley maps are available at downtown retail locations and at the Downtown Branson Betterment Association, 112 W. College St.; phone (417) 334-1548 or (866) 523-1190.

(Continued from p. 150.)

cottages on man-made Lake Taneycomo, an underground cave tour and lavish Christmastime lighting ceremonies. In 1959 the play "The Shepherd of the Hills" was first presented in the Old Mill Theater on the Shepherd of the Hills Farm, perched high on a ridge just west of Dewey Bald. The farm became a

tourist attraction, as did Silver Dollar City, a replica of an Ozark frontier town that has morphed into a major theme park complete with thrill rides, but at the same time maintains a dedicated commitment to the preservation of Ozarks artistic heritage. The loyal Branson fans keep coming back for these wholesome, family-friendly pleasures and the natural beauty of the area.

Must Do: AAA Editor's Picks

- Spend the day at  Silver Dollar City (399 Silver Dollar City Pkwy.). This 1880s village-themed park preserves Ozarks heritage with its working crafters and a bevy of festivals devoted to holidays, music and folk culture. It also has some pretty awesome thrill rides and downright tasty theme park eats.

- With so much live entertainment on the Branson Strip, what (or who) should you see? Put Branson's Famous Baldknobbers at the **Branson Famous Theatre** (645 SR 165) and the **Presleys' Country Jubilee** (2920 SR 76W) near the top of your list—both of these down-home music and comedy shows are pure family fun.

- See how small a third-class cabin actually was, feel the icy ocean water and clamber into a lifeboat at  **Titanic—World's Largest Museum Attraction** (3235 SR 76W). It's not only a total immersion experience; you'll relive James Cameron's 1997 movie blockbuster all over again.

- Handpicked by Louise Harrison (George's big sister), the Liverpool Legends are the ultimate Beatles experience. They perform songs from the time of the band's first U.S. appearance on the Ed Sullivan show to the music of the Sgt. Pepper's album at the **Andy Williams Performing Arts Center & Theatre** (2500 W. 76 Country Blvd.).

- Have breakfast at the **Farmhouse Restaurant** (119 W. Main St.) and then amble the downtown streets, which still conjure up small-town charm in an age of iPhone apps. **Dick's 5 & 10** (103 W. Main St.) has everything from coconut incense to Lucy and Ethel lunch boxes; it's certain to stir up some nostalgia.

- "See you at the Landing!" The 2006 opening of **Branson Landing** (100 Branson Landing) was the biggest thing to hit town since the early days of music theaters. This village-style shopping and entertainment complex spreads out along the shore of winding Lake Taneycomo. Non-shoppers won't want to miss the daily dancing fountain water show combining water fountains, fire cannons and lights choreographed to music.

- Branson shopping isn't all about T-shirts and souvenirs. Explore **Branson Mill Craft Village** (3300 Gretna Rd.), where local artists sell a wide array of high-quality crafts.

- Watch contortionists, acrobats and jugglers perform astounding (and in a few cases, death-defying) feats at the **Grand Shanghai Theatre** (3455 SR 76W). This mesmerizing show by the Amazing Acrobats of Shanghai is a dazzling display of bravura skill.

- With its Ozark Mountains setting, Harold Bell Wright's 1907 novel "The Shepherd of the Hills" sparked initial interest in Branson as a place to visit. The  **Shepherd of the Hills Homestead** (5586 SR 76W) re-creates the farm at the center of Wright's inspirational story, which also is dramatized at **The Shepherd of the Hills Outdoor Theatre**.

- Once upon a time Branson was a speck of a town in the middle of the Ozarks, and you can still appreciate the region's natural beauty on a relaxing cruise around Table Rock Lake aboard the **Showboat Branson Belle** (4800 SR 165). The scenic cruise on board a late 1800s-style paddle wheeler includes a three-course meal and a sensational show with talented performers and live music.

- Indulge yourself at the Spa Chateau. This luxurious retreat at the **Chateau on the Lake Resort & Spa** (415 N. SR 265) offers deep massages, salt scrubs, mud baths, facials and other treatments, with pampering touches like chamomile-infused towels added for good measure.

Silver Dollar City

Branson 1-day Itinerary

AAA editors suggest these activities for a great short vacation experience. Those staying in the area for a longer visit can access a 3-day itinerary at AAA.com/TravelGuides.

Morning

- Stroll downtown Branson, a compact area just a couple of blocks square (park in one of the downtown lots or the Branson Landing garage). Have breakfast at the **Farmhouse Restaurant** (119 W. Main St.). Don't expect upscale décor or fancy preparation; what you'll get is a basic lineup of eggs, bacon, pancakes, home fries and such, plus a friendly "hon" when your coffee cup is refilled.

- Browse the shops, where more than a touch of 1960s Mayberry lives on. The time warp really kicks in at **Dick's 5 & 10** (103 W. Main St.). It's a must-see: narrow aisles packed to the rafters with everything from clothing to wooden back scratchers to horehound candy. There are loads of ceramic figurines and knickknacks, model airplanes and trains, toys, Christmas ornaments—you name it.

- Head to the Branson Strip for an immersion experience at ≋ *Titanic*-World's Largest Museum Attraction (3235 SR 76W). From the moment you enter this half-scale reproduction of the ill-fated ocean liner you'll be taken to another time and place as the doomed maiden voyage of the RMS *Titanic* unfolds. The exhibits are interesting (those third-class rooms were indeed tiny), and the layout approximates the feeling of being an actual passenger. Pay your pop culture respects at the gallery saluting the Unsinkable Molly Brown.

Afternoon

- **Branson Landing** (100 Branson Landing) is an open-air mall with a backdrop of wooded slopes and serpentine Lake Taneycomo. Have lunch here and hang around for the fountain show, which takes place on the hour beginning at noon. Water fountains shoot 120-foot geysers accompanied by fire, fancy lights and rousing music, a spectacle you can watch from the terraced "town square" or while ambling along the lakeshore boardwalk.

- The **Bass Pro Shops** outlet at the Landing's south end is worth wandering through even if you're not an outdoor person. It has an A-to-Z assemblage of everything related to hunting, fishing, camping and other recreational activities, and an attention to detail that extends to wildlife tracks etched into the concrete floor. Check out the freshwater aquarium stocked with some of the game species—brown and rainbow trout, large and small-mouth bass, blue gill—that contribute to this region's considerable sport-fishing reputation.

- If you're not a shopper, you might want to catch a 3 o'clock matinee at one of the areas many theaters with offerings from acrobatics to vocal

Chateau on the Lake Resort & Spa

feats. For sheer entertainment it's hard to beat the Amazing Acrobats of Shanghai show at the **Grand Shanghai Theatre** (3455 SR 76W). These gifted young athletes exhibit breathtaking agility, strength and flexibility as they spin plates, balance by one hand atop precariously stacked chairs and bend their bodies into human pretzels, all without seeming to break a sweat. It's a nonstop parade of flamboyant costumes and acrobatic thrills. The Branson's Famous Baldknobbers show at the **Branson Famous Theatre** (645 SR 165) offers a mix of comedy, classic country music, gospel numbers and a patriotic finale. The Mabe family has been putting the show on for nearly 6 decades.

Evening

- Forgo the all-you-can-eat buffets and dine in style at the **Chateau Grille at Chateau on the Lake** (in the **Chateau on the Lake Resort & Spa** at 415 N. SR 265). The wine list is extensive and well chosen, and in season the veranda offers a prime view of Table Rock Lake.

- One of the flashier extravaganzas in town takes place at the **Shoji Tabuchi Theatre,** on Shepherd of the Hills Expressway near Branson's IMAX complex. Tabuchi and his troupe serve up a musical menu that includes country fiddling as well as Broadway hits. Lavish is the word, from costumes to special effects to the plusher-than-usual theater seats. The ladies' powder room and gentlemen's lounge are ornate with a capital "O": onyx and marble, crystal chandeliers, fresh orchids, billiards table and black leather chairs.

Top Picks for Kids

Under 13

- The indoor-outdoor water park **Splash Country** (1945 SR 76W) offers something for both thrill seekers and those just wanting to chill out. The complex at the Grand Country Resort offers 40,000 square feet of waterslides, several play areas (including one that dumps 1,000 gallons of water on kids at a time), lazy rivers, an infant splash zone and hot tubs—one is reserved especially for adults.

- For a mildly educational but completely colorful experience, seek out the round white building at the end of the main drag. **The Butterfly Palace & Rainforest Adventure** (4106 SR 76W) features flowers AND animals in a climate controlled room—and, of course, 1,000 butterflies at any given time. Check the schedule so you can watch the butterfly releases.

- No matter what you choose, you'll be hungry at the end of the day. Solve that with a spread for foragers of all sizes at the **Grand Country Buffet** in the **Grand Country Inn** (1945 W. 76 Country Blvd.). It specializes in serving picky eaters with many kinds of meats and sides in its "scatter bars." If all else fails, there's a pizza buffet and a self-serve ice cream station.

Teens

- When the main exhibit room is called the "odditorium," it's no surprise that what's waiting inside **Ripley's Believe it or Not!** (3326 SR 76W) is a vampire killing kit. The museum features some of the 25,000 strange and interesting items collected by anthropologist (and hoarder?) Robert Leroy Ripley.

- Looking for other larger-than-life experiences? **Branson's IMAX Entertainment Complex** (3562 Shepherd of the Hills Expwy.) offers standing adventure features such as "Tornado Alley 3D" and "Ozarks Legacy & Legend." New films shot in this large-format, immersive film technology are also played here.

- More adventurous and outdoors-driven teens will be lured by ☞ **Marvel Cave** (399 Silver Dollar City Pkwy.). No, it's not a place where superheroes retire for the night, but after exploring the 3 miles of passageways and climbing more than 600 stairs, you'll feel like one for keeping up. This strenuous 1-hour tour is worth the work as you get to see the underground cathedral room. And good news: there's a cable railway car to take you back.

- There are many quality, family-friendly shows that are a major draw of this Ozark town. But what sets **Dolly Parton's Dixie Stampede Dinner Attraction** (1525 SR 76W) apart is simple: those other shows don't have ostrich racing, stunt riding or a buffalo stampede. (Did we mention ostrich racing?)

All Ages

- If ever there was a more unlikely theme for a theme park than an 1880s-era Ozark pioneer village, we can't think of it. But ☞ **Silver Dollar City** (399 Silver Dollar City Pkwy.) manages to blend all of the charm of the heritage of the past with the rides of the future. And there's an event for EVERY season. ☞ **Bluegrass & BBQ**, the **Southern Gospel Picnic**, the **Harvest Festival** and **An Old Time Christmas** all feature food, activities and music appropriate for each occasion.

- It would be a shame to be in the area and not take advantage of the many outdoor recreation opportunities in southwestern Missouri. You can boat, fish, camp, picnic or bike through the oak and hickory trees at **Table Rock State Park** (5272 SR 165).

- You can't come back from vacation without a couple of souvenirs, and the shopping village of **Branson Landing** (100 Branson Landing) offers plenty at both local specialty stores like Branson Quilts and Cardinals Clubhouse Shops, and nationally known stores like Bass Pro Shops, Chico's and Tervis. There are also plenty of local restaurants when you're ready to grab a bite to eat.

Grand Country Buffet

Arriving
By Car

Branson receives an estimated 8 million visitors annually, and more than 90 percent of them drive. This can present a challenge to the existing road network, which was never meant to accommodate the number of vehicles that arrive throughout the year. However, more than $200 million spent on new highway construction has helped lessen the bottleneck conditions that can occur in summer, the busiest season.

I-44 funnels traffic to Springfield from St. Louis and points east, and from Tulsa, Oklahoma City and points west. South from Springfield or north from Little Rock and Harrison, Ark., the main approach is via US 65, which is four lanes from Springfield south to Branson, facilitating access into town. US 65 has been widened to four lanes from Hollister, just across Lake Taneycomo from Branson, south to the Arkansas border.

More locally, the Ozark Mountain Highroad (SR 465) runs east-west for 8 miles between US 65 and SR 76 just west of the Shepherd of the Hills Homestead, offering a relaxed and less-traveled route to Table Rock Lake, the Silver Dollar City theme park and other attractions on the west side of town. North-south SR 13, which branches off SR 76, and east-west SR 86, which branches off US 65 south of Hollister, are other easy ways to get to Table Rock Lake. For a delightfully scenic day trip from Branson to popular Eureka Springs, Ark., take US 65 south to US 62, then US 62 west.

Parking in Branson is plentiful

Getting Around
Street System

Historic downtown Branson, just east of US 65 via US 65 Business Route/Veterans Boulevard, forms a small, compact grid of streets running about six blocks north-south and east-west. East-west Main Street, the eastward extension of SR 76, and north-south Commercial Street are the main thoroughfares. Main Street runs into Branson Landing Boulevard, which fronts Branson Landing and beyond, Lake Taneycomo.

Branson's main drag is, of course, SR 76W, sometimes known as Country Music Boulevard and widely named simply "the Strip." The 5-mile stretch within the city limits, a two-lane highway with a center turning lane, is the heart of many Branson activities, winding past a seemingly endless procession of music theaters, attractions, shopping centers, hotels, motels and restaurants.

The other major roads are SR 248/Shepherd of the Hills Expressway, Gretna Road and Green Mountain Drive. SR 248 branches west off US 65, providing a northerly route that eventually intersects with SR 265 west of SR 76 via Shepherd of the Hills Expressway. Several popular theaters and attractions are along this stretch. Gretna Road, between SR 248 and SR 76, is lined with shopping complexes. Green Mountain Drive runs south of and parallel to SR 76.

Traffic is frequently congested along much of SR 76, particularly so before and after evening performances at the theaters, and major intersections—for example, SR 76 and Gretna Road—can become gridlocked at times. But fortunately, driving the Strip is a choice and not a necessity, thanks to three east-west color-coded "relief routes" that can be time-saving options.

Two routes are north of SR 76, and one is south. The Red Route is SR 248 from US 65 west to Shepherd of the Hills Expressway and Shepherd of the Hills Expressway west to SR 265. The Blue Route is Roark Valley Road from SR 76 to Gretna Road and Gretna Road back to SR 76. The Yellow Route is Fall Creek Road to Wildwood Drive, Wildwood Drive to Green Mountain Drive and Green Mountain Drive to SR 76.

Red, blue and yellow route signs are posted regularly along the respective roads. The Yellow Route is the most crowded of the three, so consider using the Blue or Red routes instead. Once you become familiar with these routes, however, getting around Branson is pretty much a snap. You can pick up a Time-Saver road map (created by the Branson/Lakes Area Convention and Visitors Bureau) showing these routes as well as the location of many theaters and attractions from just about any local hotel or restaurant.

Parking

Finding a place to park in Branson is rarely a problem. Almost all of the theaters have their own large lots, and parking for most shopping centers and restaurants is plentiful. Although you may have to hunt for a space downtown on weekends, there are two parking garages and four lots serving the historic downtown and Branson Landing areas.

Shopping

Loads of people come to Branson to shop, and it's easy to see why: with a historic downtown that could almost double for Mayberry, a new waterfront shopping and dining complex at downtown's doorstep and specialty stores and centers practically everywhere you turn, the opportunities are legion.

Branson Landing, a shopping "village" with lovely Lake Taneycomo as a backdrop, is divided into six different districts, each with its own style of architecture. Branson Landing's blue-and-silver shuttle runs up and down the promenade back and forth to the parking lots. Anchors Belk Department Store and Bass Pro Shops are augmented by more than 100 additional stores and shops, including national retailers like Brookstone, Chico's, Jos. A. Bank and White House/Black Market. Eateries include both fast-food outlets and popular franchises like Famous Dave's Bar-B-Q, Joe's Crab Shack and gourmet Mexican at Cantina Laredo.

Branson's **Bass Pro Shops** outlet isn't as large as the flagship store in Springfield but the atmosphere is similar, right down to the beautifully done nature dioramas and freshwater trout aquarium. Be sure to look up as you wander around; some of the most interesting things are above eye level. There's also a floating restaurant and a marina where boats and fishing equipment can be tested.

The town square at the center of the Landing is an open space with terraces that slope down to a waterfront boardwalk where free concerts take place throughout the year. The square also is the site of hourly shows incorporating 186 water jet fountains and 15 cannons blasting fireballs, choreographed to special lighting and a variety of music. The dancing water display is most impressive in the evening, especially when seen from the vantage point of the boardwalk. And since Branson is famous for live performances, the Landing also features street entertainment in the form of jugglers, dancers, clowns, musicians, and singers from country and bluegrass to jazz and gospel.

Branson Landing is a stone's throw from historic downtown Branson, which offers a much more down-home experience. Streets are lined with brick sidewalks and adorned with Victorian-style lampposts, all maintained by the **Downtown Branson Betterment Association.** Strolling the streets does seem like taking a step back in time.

Browsers will love **Dick's 5 & 10,** at 103 W. Main St. The narrow aisles of this classic "dime store" are crammed with thousands of nostalgic items. You'll see more miniature figurines and key chains than you ever thought possible, but Dick's also carries practical items like kitchen dish towels and jars of homemade jam. **Plum Bazaar,** 123 E. Main St., is located in what is reputedly downtown's oldest building. For elegant girls' and women's clothing as

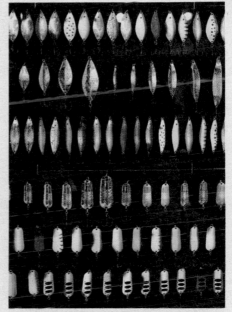

Bass Pro Shops

well as home accessories and Victorian-style furnishings, wander through **Victorian House,** 101 W. Main St.

All sorts of specialty shopping complexes are along SR 76. If you love Christmas, by all means visit **The Grand Village Shops,** 2800 SH 76W, which offers a collection of clothing, craft and specialty stores. A must-browse here is Kringles Christmas Store, where you can search for angels, collectibles, ornaments, stockings, nutcrackers, candleholders, fiber-optic Christmas trees and a host of other seasonal decorations. There also are shops specializing in art, woodcrafts and hand-blown glass, all in an open-air setting of winding cobblestone paths accented with fountains and flowers.

Victorian Village, on Shepherd of the Hills Expressway next to the Hamners' Variety Theater, offers a variety of collectibles, including candles, gifts, jewelry, quilts and dolls, along with circus memorabilia and reproductions of paintings by inspirational artist Thomas Kinkade. About a mile west are the shops in **Branson's IMAX Entertainment Complex** *(see attraction listing p. 164),* where you can grab a bite to eat at the food court while hunting for toys, jewelry, collectibles and souvenirs.

The **Branson Mill Craft Village** on North Gretna Road is a combination specialty retail shopping center and working craft village where luthiers, silversmiths, wood carvers, scrimshaw crafters, stained- and etched-glass makers and other artisans demonstrate their skills. You'll find everything from wind chimes, pottery, gift baskets and custom picture frames to pewter items, carved walking sticks and hand-painted gourds.

[SAVE] Tanger Outlets Branson, off SR 76 in the middle of the Strip, offers discounted bargains on men's, women's and children's clothing from retailers like Polo Ralph Lauren, Tommy Hilfiger and Gap, plus shoes, housewares and fashion accessories. **The Shoppes at Branson Meadows,** 4562 Gretna Rd. near the Branson Mill Craft Village, has a Victorian-style look and discount retailers like Consignment Clothing Exchange, Hush Puppies and V.F. Factory Outlet. There are other stores here as well, and a movie multiplex will keep restless kids happy.

If you don't like crowds, shop the outlet malls in January and February. The weekend following Thanksgiving, when holiday specials go on sale, is the year's busiest.

Last but certainly not least are the ubiquitous gift shops at the music theaters. Every theater has one, and some are ostentatious indeed. The **Shoji Tabuchi Theatre** has several separate shops in an ornate lobby filled with potted palms and Art Deco furniture, while the gift shop at the **Andy Williams Performing Arts Center & Theatre** is notable because it is so discreet (more like a boutique).

Show DVDs, performer CDs and cast posters are all big sellers, but you also can purchase such keepsakes as a Baldknobbers ball cap. The most personal, of course, is an autograph, so if you happen to own an old Lennon Sisters, Righteous Brothers or Mickey Gilley album, bring it along for a personal signature—Branson's stars are very obliging of their fans.

Play billiards at Outback Pub

Nightlife

There's no shortage of live entertainment in Branson, but when the footlights turn dark in the big theaters there's still fun to be had. **Ernie Biggs Dueling Piano Bar**, 505 Branson Landing Blvd., offers daily drink specials along with a menu of appetizers, sandwiches and pizza. Phone (417) 239-3670.

At **Big Whiskey's American Restaurant & Bar**, 301 Branson Landing Blvd., you can watch your favorite sport on more than 25 HDTVs inside or on the outdoor patio. Quench your thirst with more than 100 whiskeys and whiskey flights as well as cocktails highlighting the flavors of the season. On Sunday Funday, some 20 draft beers on tap perfectly compliment the wing specials. Happy hour is popular with the locals; Steak Night features a savings on steak Thursday evenings. A variety of chicken, pasta, seafood, hand-cut steaks, and street tacos and quesadillas make ordering your meal as difficult as choosing your beverage. Phone (417) 334-4478.

The **Outback Pub**, 1922 SR 76W, offers a two-fer nighttime experience with a pub party deck upstairs and a "Down Under" section that offers billiards and the popular NTN trivia. Monday is open mic night; Thursdays feature karaoke. Happy hour is daily 4-7 p.m., with a choice of more than 100 beers and beverages. Phone (417) 334-7003.

Entertainment

For many visitors, the No. 1 reason to visit Branson is to sample the incredible variety of live entertainment. The city has long outgrown its tag "the country music capital of the universe" that was bestowed by "60 Minutes" back in the early 1990s: Today you can choose from more than 100 different shows at 50 venues. And while country is still king, it is by no means the only game in town.

There's still plenty of traditional country music, of course, and tribute bands at the Little Opry, as well as shows starring generation-spanning families (Branson's Famous Baldknobbers, Presleys' Country Jubilee, the Duttons).

But you also can choose from shows devoted to the 1950s ("New Jersey Nights"), baby boomer favorites like Bill Medley, tributes ("Legends in Concert") and flashy glitz ("Puttin' On the Ritz"). The Legend of Kung Fu: Return of the Dragon, a world-class extravaganza, and the religious-themed shows at Sight & Sound Theatres *(see attraction listing p. 165)* add some welcome diversity.

Performances take place year-round, with the majority occurring March through December. Top-name artists who headline their own shows appear in Branson at least part of the year. Show schedules are subject to change; new theaters open, old theaters close and existing theaters occasionally change names. Many brochures and free newspapers publish current show schedules. If you want to see a certain show at a particular time, call ahead.

Most evening shows start at 8 p.m. Matinees usually begin at 3 p.m. There are also a couple of morning shows that usually begin at 10 a.m., including the Bretts Show and "A Tribute to John Denver" at the Little Opry Theatre.

Adult ticket prices range from about $20-$60; children's ticket prices range from free to about $30. Tickets can be purchased at the theater box office or through various ticket agencies in the area. Free show guide brochures and coupon sheets, available for the taking at most area hotels, restaurants, theaters and attractions, offer a bewildering assortment of special offers; diligently collecting and sorting through these deals can end up saving you quite a bit of money. AAA members can purchase discounted theater tickets at any AAA Missouri branch office.

Branson is a conservative town, and traditional values are emphasized. Flag-waving patriotism and pro-military sentiments are often expressed in production numbers, and evangelical Christian themes are presented at some shows. Most shows also include a merchandising spiel during intermission, encouraging customers to buy CDs, DVDs, autographed posters and sundry other memorabilia. Many of the performers generously share their time with the audience, coming out during intermission to meet fans and signing autographs in the lobby after the show.

It would take weeks to see every performance in town, and few visitors have that luxury of time. The following theater rundown emphasizes proven longevity and popularity and includes current big-name stars as well as newer acts.

Note: In some theater parking lots the rear slopes sharply; visitors with limited mobility or special needs should be dropped off at the main entrance.

The **Caravelle Theatre** presents such shows as the Beatles tribute "Liverpool Legends."

Yakov's Theatre, just off US 65 on SR 248 used to be the home of Russian-born comic Yakov Smirnoff. Now it's where you'll find The Acrobats of China. The performers—all in their teens and 20s—juggle, leap, contort and cavort across the stage. This is the kind of show where poised young women balance a dizzying number of spinning plates atop sticks simultaneously—and that's the easy part. It's all fast-paced, colorful and thrilling.

A similar razzle-dazzle show, the Amazing Acrobats of Shanghai, is presented at the **Grand Shanghai Theatre** (at 3455 SR 76W). This eye-popping spectacle will have you cheering as these gifted athletes display jaw-dropping strength, outrageous flexibility and amazing balance while performing one amazing feat after another.

The stars are out in force at **Dick Clark's American Bandstand Theater,** on SR 76 across from Dolly Parton's Dixie Stampede Dinner Attraction, where the "Legends in Concert" celebrity impersonator tribute show plays. In Branson you'll naturally see country icons like Garth Brooks and Shania Twain, plus the likes of Ray Charles, Judy Garland, Justin Timberlake and, of course, Elvis. Video screens flanking both sides of the stage

Watch an evening theater show

project footage of the real-life legend, which can invite comparisons both favorable and unfavorable. The good news: no lip syncing. There's also a crack house band.

The **Welk Resort Theatre** on SR 165 (3 miles south of the SR 76/Gretna Road intersection) is home to the "Million Dollar Quartet" musical and occasionally presents such stars as Charley Pride, Herman's Hermit and Pam Tillis.

One of the flashiest shows in town is at the **Shoji Tabuchi Theatre** on Shepherd of the Hills Expressway (near the Branson's IMAX theater complex). Tabuchi, his wife, daughter, a troupe of dancers and a band of superbly talented professional musicians put on a show that encompasses practically every style of popular music, from swing and big band to gospel, Dixieland jazz and Broadway show tunes, as well as Japanese Taiko drums, a nod toward Shoji's country of birth.

Tabuchi plays everything from "Flight of the Bumblebee" to "Over the Rainbow" on his fiddle, and the production numbers feature top-notch choreography and cool laser special effects. If nothing else, you must see this show just to experience the ladies' powder room or gentlemen's lounge; the rich wood paneling, potted palms, chandeliers, beveled-glass wall tiles, onyx sinks, fresh orchids and hand-carved mahogany billiard table are all the last word in lavish.

The ancient art of kung fu gets a theatrical makeover in a show closer to Cirque de Soleil in "The Legend of Kung Fu: Return of the Dragon," at the **White House Theatre.** The troupe has a permanent home in Branson after being the opening act at the 2008 Beijing Olympics and traveling the world.

The Mabe family is still going strong at the **Branson Famous Theatre,** on SR 165. They carry on a show-business tradition that began in 1959. The show, Branson's Famous Baldknobbers (formerly The Baldknobbers Jamboree Show), has a little bit of everything—crowd-pleasing comedy routines, classic country, hot new country hits, roof-raising gospel music and a rousing patriotic finale.

The Presley family stars in another longtime Branson favorite at the **Presleys' Country Jubilee** theater, on SR 76. Three generations of this talented family appear on stage. It's a fast-paced show, with one musical number after another. There's impassioned Southern gospel singing, classic country tunes and even a bit of "new country" (i.e., current hits). Herkimer and Cecil provide the requisite comic relief.

King's Castle Theatre, on SR 76 across from the Andy Williams Performing Arts Center & Theatre, presents a varied entertainment menu. Shows include Puttin' on the Ritz, Broadway's Greatest Hits, Christmas Wonderland, New Jersey Nights and Dublin's Irish Tenors & Celtic Ladies, who offer perfect harmonies and Irish charm.

The five talented Hughes brothers take the stage at the **Hughes Brothers Theatre,** on SR 76, along with their wives and children: 45 talented family members in all, plus a five-piece band. The brothers' bond shines both vocally and during moments of good-natured banter, which recalls the brothers Smothers. Their schedule includes a poplar Christmas show.

Another family, the Duttons, display their multiple talents at the **Dutton Family Theater** on SR 76

Bluegrass & BBQ

(next to the Caravelle). With a repertoire that manages to include both Pachelbel's "Canon in D major" and the revved-up surf instrumental "Wipeout," the Duttons obviously have music in their genes.

The Oak Ridge Boys appear throughout the year at the **Mansion Theatre.** Venerable stars like Clint Black, Charlie Daniels, Johnny Mathis and Kenny Rogers also appear here. Longtime Branson entertainer Clay Cooper headlines his own show at the **Clay Cooper Theatre,** on SR 76 across from Titanic—World's Largest Museum Attraction. The Haygoods, #1 Hits of the '60s, and Hot Rods & High Heels (yet another '50s tribute) also appear at Clay Cooper's.

The **Starlite Theatre,** on SR 76 across from the Hollywood Wax Museum, presents The Texas Tenors; AYO; Voices of Glory; Raiding the Country Vault; Raiding the Rock Vault; Larry's Country Diner; and the comedy percussion show Buckets N Boards. **Hamners' Variety Theater** on Shepherd of the Hills Expressway (across from the **Pierce Arrow Theater**) offers several different shows, including the Hamners' Unbelievable Variety Show, co-starring comedian and ventriloquist Jim Barber and the Hamner family's exotic illusions, which incorporate a bevy of colorful macaws and cockatoos. Other performances include the Magnificent 7 Variety Show and a Conway Twitty tribute.

Sight & Sound Theatres, 1001 Shepherd of the Hills Expwy., presents elaborate live theatrical and musical performances based on Bible stories. The current show, "Samson," is packed full of dazzling sets, special effects and music.

Many theaters also present their own special Christmas shows during November and December, and many people come to Branson during these two months to celebrate an old-fashioned holiday season. Contact the individual theaters for details.

For a list of current theaters, see Branson Theaters on p. 163.

Big Events

For many years, Branson was traditionally a summer destination, and tourist activities pretty much shut down during the winter. But these days, the "season" is all year. The **Hot Winter Fun Big Show** at Dick Clark's American Bandstand Theater, in late January or early February, brings a slew of Branson performers together on one stage.

Ozark Mountain Spring runs from March through May and features more than 40 special events and festivals, including collector car auctions and sporting events. **Kewpiesta** in April is one of the planned events; it honors Ozarks artist Rose O'Neill, creator of the Kewpie doll.

Spring also brings 🔹**Bluegrass & BBQ.** Hundreds of bluegrass performances feature both up-and-coming artists and big-name headliners. The singing and fiddling is complemented by a lip-smackin' lineup of barbecue—pit-cooking demonstrations highlight everything from Texas smoked beef brisket to St. Louis-style ribs and Memphis dry-rubbed meats, which can be doused with all kinds of different barbecue sauces.

The rousing **Southern Gospel Picnic** brings together the rich harmonies of top-name gospel vocal groups along with another Southern tradition—an old-fashioned picnic spread featuring chicken and all the fixings plus a tempting array of desserts. This family-style music celebration runs from late August to early September.

During the **Harvest Festival** from mid-September to late October, more than 150 artisans and craftspeople present their work. A lumberjack show, an art show, sand sculpting, a barn dance, musical performances and harvest foods also are offered. Silver Dollar City's final event of the year is **An Old Time Christmas** in November and December.

In September, the 3-day **Autumn Daze Arts, Crafts & Music Festival** takes place in downtown Branson.

From Nov. 5-11 Branson hosts the **Veterans Homecoming Week** celebration, which draws tens of thousands of veterans, their friends and families. The week features a variety of events, including special appearances by high-ranking military personnel, tribute shows and military reunions. It concludes with a downtown Veterans Day parade.

Branson pulls out the stops for the holidays. Throughout November and December, more than 5 million twinkling lights adorn the streets during the **Branson's Gift of Lights.** The **Branson Adoration Parade** rolls through the downtown area in early December. This nighttime parade is a joyful expression of small-town pride and a faith-based celebration of Christmas, with lighted floats, high school marching bands, musicians and singers all ringing in the season.

The parade starts with the lighting of the enormous **Adoration Nativity Scene** on Mount Branson, a tradition that goes back almost 70 years. Incorporating figures nearly 28 feet tall, it remains lit through Dec. 31. Branson's music theaters also get into the spirit, presenting literally dozens of special holiday-themed productions in November and December during the **Ozark Mountain Christmas Lights & Village** celebration.

Sports & Rec

You could quite easily spend a week in Branson doing nothing but seeing shows, visiting attractions and going shopping. You would, however, be missing out on one of the area's most delightful assets: the great outdoors. The recreational opportunities that attracted Branson's first vacationers still abound.

Branson's location in the midst of **Table Rock Lake, Bull Shoals Lake** and **Lake Taneycomo** makes what is known as the Tri-Lakes area a terrific place for **boating, fishing** and **camping.** All kinds of activities can be enjoyed at **Table Rock Lake and Dam,** which was created by the U.S. Army Corps of

Autumn Daze Arts, Crafts & Music Festival

Engineers to control floods and generate hydroelectric power. The deep-blue lake teems with bass, bluegill, crappie and catfish, making it rewarding for both novice and serious anglers. With nearly 800 miles of shoreline to explore, Table Rock *(see Recreation Areas Chart)* also is a good location for **swimming** and **scuba diving.**

Table Rock State Park, 5272 SR 165 at the south end of Table Rock Dam, has a public marina offering easy lake access and a full range of boat rentals, including WaveRunners and fishing, pontoon and Jet Ski boats. Two camping areas shaded by oak and hickory trees are located along the winding shoreline, and picnic sites are scattered throughout the park. For more information phone (417) 334-4704. *See Recreation Areas Chart.*

Just to the south is **State Park Marina,** 380 State Park Marina Rd., offering boat rentals including WaveRunners. There's also parasailing, shopping, a restaurant and shaved ice. Feeling adventurous? Stop into the dive shop and explore the underwater world of Table Rock Lake. Phone (417) 334-2628.

The **Dewey Short Visitor Center** has natural history exhibits and shows a fascinating 20-minute film that details the construction of Table Rock Dam. Be sure to walk the **Table Rock Lakeshore Trail,** which begins at the visitor center and runs south 2.2 miles to the park marina. The scenic views of the lake are heightened in the spring by flowering dogwood and redbud trees and in the fall by a display of colorful foliage. The trail is open daily dawn-dusk. The visitor center is open daily 10-5, March-December; Tuesday-Saturday, rest of year; phone (501) 340-1943.

Indian Point Park, at the south end of Indian Point Road near the entrance to Silver Dollar City, has campgrounds, a marina and a variety of lakeside resorts. The port of Kimberling City, on SR 13 south of Branson West, proclaims itself "The Bass Fishing Capital of the Ozarks." It offers boat rentals, fishing and camping.

Due to their proximity to Branson, Indian Point and the area around Table Rock Dam have the region's greatest concentration of recreation facilities. But the lake spreads out far beyond the dam in a meandering series of arms and inlets, and some nature lovers prefer its western end, which has equally good fishing along with a more remote, primitive atmosphere. **Cape Fair Park,** in a lovely wooded setting on Table Rock's James River Arm, is a favorite with both campers and fishermen. There are prime angling spots below Virgin Bluff and across the channel from the park's boat launch ramp. For information phone (417) 538-2220.

Also administered by the U.S. Army Corps of Engineers is Bull Shoals Lake. Although it extends into southern Missouri, most of its area is in northern Arkansas. Less developed than Table Rock Lake, Bull Shoals offers many of the same activities. The 1,050-mile shoreline is indented with coves ideal for boating, fishing, swimming and water sports. This is a deep, clean lake and the water is very clear—which makes it just about unbeatable for landing crappie, bluegill, walleye and largemouth, smallmouth, white and striped bass; phone (870) 425-2700. *See Recreation Areas Chart.*

In between these two lakes stretches 22-mile-long Lake Taneycomo. Created by the impounding

Spend an afternoon at a golf course

of the White River, Taneycomo was a warm-water lake from 1913 until the completion of Table Rock Dam in 1958. Virtually overnight it was turned into a cold-water fishery due to the temperature of the water flowing through the dam's power generators. The Missouri Department of Conservation took advantage of this change, constructing the Shepherd of the Hills Fish Hatchery at the foot of the dam.

When Table Rock Dam is generating power the water temperature drops, and for all practical purposes Taneycomo becomes a deep, cold, fast-running river. The bracing water makes it one of the best brown and rainbow trout-fishing spots in the Midwest. The lake's headwaters at the foot of Table Rock Dam offer excellent wading and fly rod fishing when power is not being generated. Only flies and hard artificial baits are permitted in this "trophy trout" area, which covers approximately 3 miles from the dam north to the mouth of Fall Creek.

Although officially a lake, serpentine Taneycomo, with its lush green banks, certainly looks more like a river. The Branson Landing Boardwalk offers a pleasant waterside stroll, and you also can walk along the shoreline via N. Lake Drive to **North Beach Park,** where there is a lakeside trail.

Dogwood Canyon Nature Park *(see attraction listing p. 234)* has a 6.5-mile round-trip paved path that is popular for **hiking** and **bicycling.** The gently sloping trail traverses wooded terrain along the canyon floor, passing waterfalls, burbling streams and stone bridges created by local stonemasons from native dolomite rock. Points of interest along the way include the Glory Hole, a 16-foot-deep, blue-green pool of water inhabited by rainbow and brown trout, and a huge sycamore tree estimated to be more than 250 years old.

Although fishing and boating still rule in the Tri-Lakes area, Branson also is gaining a reputation for **golf.** The backdrop of Ozark Mountains scenery is certainly a big part of what makes golf so appealing in Branson, in addition to the mild weather that allows practically year-round play.

Area courses include the **Buffalo Ridge Golf Course,** off US 65 about 4 miles south of SR 76; the **Holiday Hills Resort and Golf Club,** about 3 miles east of downtown Branson via SR 76E; the **LedgeStone Golf Course,** 1600 LedgeStone Way in west Branson; the **Branson Hills Golf Club,** just north of Branson Hills Parkway between SR 248 and US 65; the **Pointe Royale Golf Course,** on SR 165 3 miles south of SR 76W; the **Thousand Hills Golf Resort,** on Wildwood Drive just south of SR 76W; and the nine-hole, par-3 **Top of the Rock Golf Course,** off US 65 just north of the junction with SR 86.

The high-tech scavenger hunt known as **geocaching** is a popular family and group activity; hundreds of caches, or treasure locations, are scattered throughout the Branson/Tri-Lakes area. For additional information contact the Branson/Lakes Area Convention and Visitors Bureau; phone (417) 334-4084 or (800) 214-3661.

If you feel like catching a **baseball** game, head up to Springfield and cheer on the **Springfield Cardinals** AA minor league team. And if you need some exercise, the Branson RecPlex, half a mile east of SR 248 on Branson Hills Parkway, has a fitness center, track and basketball courts, and an outdoor aquatic park. Guest memberships are available; phone (417) 335-2368.

INSIDER INFO:
Branson Theaters

- **ANDY WILLIAMS PERFORMING ARTS CENTER & THEATRE**
  (417) 334-4500 or (800) 666-6094
- **BRANSON FAMOUS THEATRE**
  (417) 334-4528 or (800) 998-8908
- **BRANSON HOT HITS THEATRE**
  (417) 337-7426 or (800) 691-2207
- **CARAVELLE THEATRE**
  (417) 334-5100
- **CLAY COOPER THEATRE**
  (417) 332-2529 or (877) 317-2604
- **DICK CLARK'S AMERICAN BANDSTAND THEATER**
  (417) 339-3003 or (800) 374-7469
- **DOLLY PARTON'S DIXIE STAMPEDE DINNER ATTRACTION**
  (417) 336-3000 or (800) 520-5544
- **DUTTON FAMILY THEATER**
  (417) 332-2772 or (888) 388-8661
- **GRAND COUNTRY MUSIC HALL**
  (417) 335-2485 or (888) 506-6278
- **GRAND SHANGHAI THEATRE**
  (417) 336-0888
- **HAMNERS' VARIETY THEATER**
  (417) 334-4363 or (888) 335-2080
- **HISTORIC OWEN THEATRE & BRANSON'S HOUSE OF COMEDY**
  (417) 464-8497

- **HUGHES BROTHERS THEATRE**
  (417) 334-0076 or (800) 422-0076
- **JERRY PRESLEY'S GOD AND COUNTRY THEATRES**
  (417) 334-6806
- **KING'S CASTLE THEATRE**
  (417) 334-2500 or (888) 462-7267
- **LITTLE OPRY THEATRE**
  (417) 335-3533 or (800) 419-4832
- **THE MANSION THEATRE**
  (417) 239-1333 or (866) 707-4100
- **PIERCE ARROW THEATER**
  (417) 336-8742 or (877) 687-4241
- **PRESLEYS' COUNTRY JUBILEE**
  (417) 334-4874 or (800) 335-4874
- **THE SHEPHERD OF THE HILLS OUTDOOR THEATRE**
  (417) 334-4191 or (800) 653-6288
- **SHOJI TABUCHI THEATRE**
  (417) 334-7469
- **SHOWBOAT BRANSON BELLE**
  (417) 336-7171 or (800) 775-2628
- **SIGHT & SOUND THEATRES**
  (800) 377-1277
- **SILVER DOLLAR CITY**
  (800) 475-9370
- **STARLITE THEATRE**
  (417) 337-9333
- **WELK RESORT THEATRE**
  (417) 337-7469 or (800) 505-9355
- **WHITE HOUSE THEATRE**
  (417) 335-2396
- **YAKOV'S THEATRE**
  (417) 339-2568 or (417) 336-8888

ATTRACTIONS

For a complete list of attractions,
visit AAA.com/travelguides/attractions

BRANSON AUTO AND FARM MUSEUM, 1335 SR 76W, houses a collection of antique and collectible cars. Some of the vehicles are for sale while some, like Evel Knievel's Cadillac and motorcycle, are for display only. There also is a large collection of antique toys and farm equipment. The Sculpture World gallery contains bronze sculptures, fountains and home furnishings (some are for sale).

Time: Allow 1 hour minimum. **Hours:** Daily 9-8. Phone ahead to confirm schedule. **Cost:** $19.95; $17.95 (ages 55+ and military with ID); $15.95 (ages 6-13). **Phone:** (417) 335-2600.

BRANSON'S IMAX ENTERTAINMENT COMPLEX is just e. of SR 76 at 3562 Shepherd of the Hills Expwy. This family-oriented entertainment center features several different larger-than-life IMAX adventures (including "National Parks Adventure" and "Ozarks Legacy & Legend") shown on a screen six stories tall and 83 feet wide. The center also has a three-screen movie theater and gift shops. The Little Opry Theatre presents live musical shows with an emphasis on traditional country and bluegrass.

Time: Allow 2 hours minimum. **Hours:** IMAX box office opens daily at 8:30 a.m.; film screenings daily 10-7. Little Opry Theatre live performance times vary. Good News Gospel Hour Sun. at 9 a.m. **Cost:**

The Butterfly Palace & Rainforest Adventure

IMAX VIP Reserved $12-$15. IMAX General Admission $8-$12.75. Live show tickets $30.50-$33.75; free (ages 0-12). Good News Gospel Hour free. **Phone:** (417) 335-4832 or (800) 419-4832.

THE BUTTERFLY PALACE & RAINFOREST ADVENTURE is at 4106 SR 76W. This state-of-the-art complex has a climate-controlled room where various tropical butterfly species flit among flowering plants. Other six-legged critters, plus a few four-legged tree frogs, reside in the Living Rainforest Science Center. Visitors also can watch a 15-minute 3-D film about the life cycle of a butterfly and navigate their way through the Emerald Forest Mirror Maze.

Time: Allow 2 hours minimum. **Hours:** Daily 9-5. Last ticket is sold 30 minutes before closing. **Cost:** $18.95; $16.95 (ages 55+); $9.95 (ages 4-12). **Phone:** (417) 332-2231.

COLLEGE OF THE OZARKS—see Point Lookout p. 240.

DOGWOOD CANYON NATURE PARK—see Lampe p. 234.

DOLLY PARTON'S DIXIE STAMPEDE DINNER ATTRACTION is at 1525 SR 76W (Country Blvd.). Trick horseback riding, a lumberjack relay, buffaloes and other live animals, singing, dancing and audience participation are all part of the entertainment at this dinner theater. **Time:** Allow 2 hours minimum. **Hours:** Shows daily at 5:30p.m., with matinees at 3 and evening shows at 8 p.m. added on select days throughout the year. Phone ahead to confirm dates and show times. **Cost:** $49.99-$59.99; $29.99-$39.99 (ages 4-11); free (ages 0-3 on lap). Ticket prices vary depending on show time and preferred seating location. **Phone:** (800) 520-5544.

HOLLYWOOD WAX MUSEUM is at 3030 SR 76W in the Hollywood Wax Museum Entertainment Center. Visitors can take photos with lifelike wax celebrities and learn about the charities they support, their pets, pet peeves and accomplishments. Celebrities featured include classic to current stars: Judy Garland to George Clooney; Bob Hope to Robert Downey, Jr.; and Willie Nelson to Will Smith. One exhibit pays tribute to Hollywood awards, with a red carpet scene where guests can pose with favorites such as Angelina Jolie, Harrison Ford, Vin Diesel and Samuel L. Jackson. Sets and figures change regularly.

Time: Allow 1 hour minimum. **Hours:** Daily 8 a.m.-midnight, late Feb-early Oct.; Sun.-Thurs. 8 a.m.-11 p.m., Fri.-Sat. 8 a.m.-midnight, early Oct.-early Jan.; 8-8, rest of year. Phone ahead to confirm schedule. **Cost:** Wax museum $22.99; $12.99 (ages 4-11). Castle of Chaos $15.99; $10.99 (ages 4-11). Mirror Maze $12.99; $9.99 (ages 4-11). All Access Pass (includes all three) $29.99; $19.99 (ages 4-11). **Phone:** (417) 337-8277.

MARVEL CAVE—see Silver Dollar City p. 168.

RALPH FOSTER MUSEUM—see Point Lookout p. 240.

RIPLEY'S BELIEVE IT OR NOT! is at 3326 SR 76W. More than 400 odd and unusual exhibits from around the world are featured inside creatively themed galleries. Visitors can learn about the world's tallest man, see such pranks of nature as a two-headed cow and witness optical illusions. Interactive displays explore entrepreneur and anthropologist Robert Leroy Ripley's obsession with the strange and unusual.

Time: Allow 1 hour minimum. **Hours:** Daily 9:30 a.m.-11 p.m., mid-Mar. to mid-Oct.; 9:30-8, mid-Oct. through Dec. 31; 9:30-6, rest of year. Last ticket sold 1 hour before closing. Phone ahead to confirm schedule. **Cost:** $19.99; $18.99 (ages 55+); $10.99 (ages 4-12). **Phone:** (417) 337-5300.

SHEPHERD OF THE HILLS HOMESTEAD is 2 mi. w. at 5586 W. 76 Country Blvd. This working homestead evokes the farm featured in Harold Bell Wright's novel "The Shepherd of the Hills." Jeep-driven guided tours take visitors past Old Matt's Cabin, home of the leading characters, which contains most of its original furnishings. Also on the site are a gristmill, sawmill and a reconstructed church similar to those in which Wright preached during his years in the Ozarks.

Stone statues of the book's characters stand on Inspiration Point, where the author lived. Inspiration Tower, standing 230 feet high, affords panoramic views of the hills and valleys surrounding the homestead. ATV and horseback tours also are available. During the Trail of Lights celebration, which takes place nightly in November and December, the homestead is decorated with more than 80 festively illuminated drive-through displays.

Hours: Homestead open daily 10-5, May-Oct. Guided tours depart on the hour beginning at 10. Last tour begins 30 minutes before closing. Tower open daily at 9 a.m. Closing time varies from 5 to 8 p.m. (midnight when the tower is lighted for the holidays). Trail of Lights daily dusk-midnight, Nov.-Dec. Phone ahead to confirm schedule. **Cost:** Homestead tour $15; $8 (ages 4-16). Inspiration Tower $8.75; $4.28 (ages 4-16). Trail of Lights drive $12; $6 (ages 4-16); $35 (carload). Family packages are available; phone for details. **Phone:** (417) 334-4191 or (800) 653-6288.

The Shepherd of the Hills Outdoor Theatre is at 5586 SR 76W at Shepherd of the Hills Homestead. The story of "The Shepherd of the Hills" is dramatized in this outdoor amphitheater. Kids can participate in bullfrog races Memorial Day-Labor Day. **Hours:** Evening performances Mon., Wed. and Sat. at 8:30 p.m. (pre-show begins at 7:30), May-Aug.; at 7:30 p.m. (pre-show begins at 6:45), Sept.-Oct.

Cost: $37; $18 (ages 4-16). **Phone:** (417) 334-4191 or (800) 653-6288.

SIGHT & SOUND THEATRES is at 1001 Shepherd of the Hills Expwy. The 2,080-seat theater presents original musical shows based on biblical stories. Performed on one of the largest stages in the country, these epic productions utilize stunning sets, elaborate costumes, live animals and the latest theatrical technology to bring the Bible to life.

Time: Allow 2 hours, 30 minutes minimum. **Hours:** Shows are offered Tues.-Sat. Show times vary by show and season; phone ahead for schedules. Behind-the-scenes tours are offered some show days and begin at 1; phone ahead for schedule. **Cost:** $45; $19 (ages 3-12). Behind-the-scenes tour $5. Reservations are recommended. **Phone:** (800) 377-1277 Mon.-Sat. 8:30-6 for reservations. [T]

SILVER DOLLAR CITY is 5 mi. w. on SR 76W to Indian Point Rd., then about .4 mi. s. on Silver Dollar City Pkwy. to the entrance. This theme park combines the atmosphere of an 1880s Ozark pioneer village with 21st-century rides and thrills, and plays host to festivals throughout the year. Rides include the Outlaw Run roller coaster, which boasts the world's first triple inversions and double-barrel roll on a wooden coaster. Time Traveler, a spinning roller coaster with a 10-story vertical drop is expected to open in 2018. Other attractions include the PowderKeg roller coaster, which goes from 0 to 53 mph in 2.8 seconds; the multi-looping WildFire; Thunderation, a runaway mine train; and the Giant Barn Swing, which launches riders more than seven stories and nearly upside down. Fireman's Landing features rides and attractions with a volunteer firefighter recruitment fair theme.

The Grand Exposition, modeled after the renowned World's Fairs and expositions held since the mid-19th century, features family-themed rides. Performances are given daily on various stages throughout the park, including music and comedy shows in the 4,000-seat Echo Hollow Amphitheater. Artisans demonstrate woodcarving, blacksmithing, leatherwork, pottery making, furniture making and glassblowing; many of their beautiful creations are for sale.

Silver Dollar City also has a well-deserved reputation for serving up some of the country's tastiest theme park food. The Culinary & Craft School presents courses on food preparation, including breads, cookies, pies and soups. Attendees can partake in hands-on demonstrations, taste samples and take home recipes compiled by the school's culinary artisans and guest chefs.

Allow a full day. **Hours:** Park generally opens daily at 9:30 a.m., late May-early Aug., with closing times extended to 10 p.m. or later from mid-July to early Aug. Park generally opens Sun.-Fri. at 10 a.m., Sat. at 9:30 a.m. (closing times vary), early Aug. through Oct. 31. Park generally opens Thurs.-Sun.

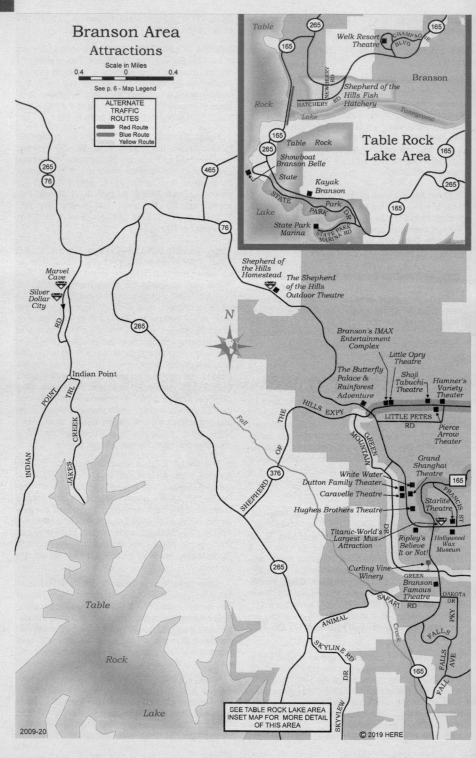

Branson Area
Attractions

Scale in Miles
0.4   0   0.4

See p. 6 - Map Legend

ALTERNATE
TRAFFIC
ROUTES
Red Route
Blue Route
Yellow Route

Table Rock Lake Area

Welk Resort Theatre

CHAMPAGNE BLVD

Branson

Shepherd of the Hills Fish Hatchery

HATCHERY

NEWBERRY RD

Taneycomo

Table Rock Lake

Showboat Branson Belle

State

Kayak Branson

State Park Marina

STATE PARK DR

STATE PARK MARINA RD

Lake

Marvel Cave

Silver Dollar City

SDC RD

Indian Point

INDIAN POINT

JAKES CREEK

INDIAN POINT TRL

Shepherd of the Hills Homestead

The Shepherd of the Hills Outdoor Theatre

N

Fall

Branson's IMAX Entertainment Complex

Little Opry Theatre

The Butterfly Palace & Rainforest Adventure

Shoji Tabuchi Theatre

Hamner's Variety Theater

HILLS EXPY

SHEPHERD OF THE

GREEN MOUNTAIN

LITTLE PETES RD

Pierce Arrow Theater

Grand Shanghai Theatre

White Water

Dutton Family Theater

Caravelle Theatre

Hughes Brothers Theatre

Titanic-World's Largest Mus Attraction

Starlite Theatre

FRANCIS ST

Hollywood Wax Museum

Ripley's Believe It or Not!

Curling Vine Winery

GREEN

Branson Famous Theatre

SAFARI RD

ANIMAL

Creek

DAKOTA DR

SKYLINE RD

SKYVIEW DR

FALLS PKY

FALLS AVE

FALL

Table

Rock

Lake

SEE TABLE ROCK LAKE AREA
INSET MAP FOR MORE DETAIL
OF THIS AREA

2009-20

© 2019 HERE

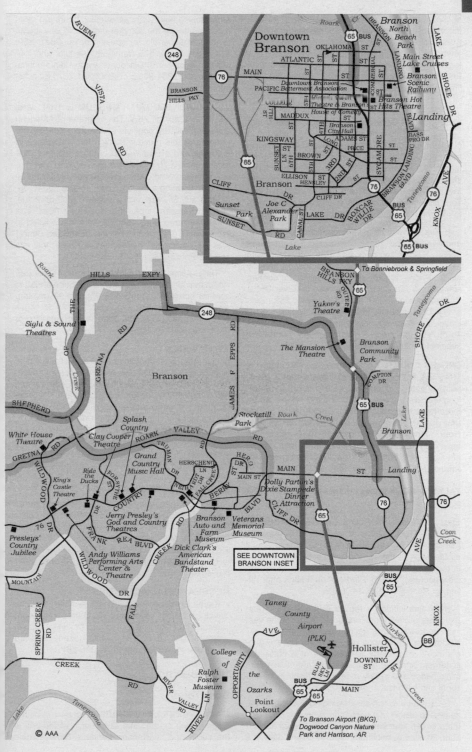

Downtown Branson

Branson North Beach Park

Main Street Lake Cruises
Branson Scenic Railway

Downtown Branson Betterment Association

Branson Hot Hits Theatre

House of Comedy

Branson City Hall

Sunset Park

Joe C Alexander Park

To Bonniebrook & Springfield

Sight & Sound Theatres

Yukon's Theatre

The Mansion Theatre

Branson Community Park

Branson

Stockstill Park

Branson

White House Theatre

Splash Country

Clay Cooper Theatre

Ride the Ducks

Grand Country Music Hall

King's Castle Theatre

Jerry Presley's God and Country Theatres

Dolly Parton's Dixie Stampede Dinner Attraction

Landing

SEE DOWNTOWN BRANSON INSET

Presleys' Country Jubilee

Andy Williams Performing Arts Center & Theatre

Branson Auto and Farm Museum

Veterans Memorial Museum

Dick Clark's American Bandstand Theater

Coon Creek

Taney County Airport (PLK)

Hollister

College of the Ozarks

Ralph Foster Museum

Point Lookout

To Branson Airport (BKG), Dogwood Canyon Nature Park and Harrison, AR

© AAA

at 1 p.m. (closing times vary), Nov. 1-Dec. 30, with extended hours during the Thanksgiving holiday week. Schedule varies mid-Mar. to late May; phone ahead to confirm. **Cost:** $62; $60 (ages 62+); $51 (ages 4-11). Culinary & Craft School classes $15. Prices are subject to change; phone ahead to confirm. **Phone:** (417) 336-7100 or (800) 831-4386. ⑪

Marvel Cave lies 500 ft. below Silver Dollar City. This wet limestone cave includes 3 miles of explored passageways and a cathedral room 400 feet long and 20 stories high. The 1-hour tour includes more than 600 stairs and is considered strenuous. A cable railway train returns visitors to the surface. Each night a 1.5-hour Lantern Light Tour (maximum 20 guests) is offered; guides lead tours by lantern and share the history of the cave.

Hours: Cave tours depart approximately every 30 minutes, weather permitting. Lantern Light Tours begin 1.5 hours before closing. Park hours vary with extended hours during the Thanksgiving holiday week. Phone ahead or check online to confirm schedule. **Cost:** Cave tour included in Silver Dollar City admission of $68; $66 (ages 62+); $58 (ages 4-11). Lantern Light Tour fee an additional $14. Under age 8 are not permitted on the Lantern Light Tour; reservations are recommended. Rates are subject to change. **Phone:** (800) 831-4386.

SPLASH COUNTRY is at Grand Country Square at 1945 SR 76W. This 40,000-square-foot indoor-outdoor water park features waterslides, a 250-foot-long lazy river, a pool with basketball hoops, and a three-level tree house with a 1,000-gallon bucket that dumps cascades of water every 8 minutes. **Hours:** Indoor park open daily 10-10. Outdoor park open daily 10-9. Hours vary in fall and winter; phone ahead to verify schedule. **Cost:** $15; free (under 2). **Phone:** (417) 335-3535 or (888) 514-1088. ⑪

TALKING ROCKS CAVERN—see Branson West p. 180.

TITANIC—WORLD'S LARGEST MUSEUM ATTRACTION is at jct. SRs 76W and 165 (Gretna Rd.). Built at half-scale to the original vessel as far back as the second smokestack, this walk-through experience focuses on the passengers and crew aboard the RMS *Titanic* when it sank after hitting an iceberg on April 14, 1912.

Highlights include a replica of the ship's Grand Staircase and a 26-foot-long scale model of the vessel's underwater bow section as seen in the 1997 blockbuster film. Among other exhibits are a regenerating "live" iceberg, re-creations of a first-class stateroom and third-class cabin, an interactive captain's bridge and gallery rooms with displays of personal and historical artifacts.

Each visitor receives a boarding pass with the name and history of a passenger who was on the ill-fated ocean liner's maiden voyage. **Time:** Allow 1 hour, 30 minutes minimum. **Hours:** Opens daily at 9

a.m. Closing hours vary seasonally; hours are often extended during the summer months. Phone ahead to confirm schedule for specific days. **Cost:** $30; $14 (ages 5-12); $95 (family, two adults and four children ages 5-18). Discounts are available online. **Phone:** (417) 334-9500, or (800) 381-7670 for ticket information.

VETERANS MEMORIAL MUSEUM is 1 mi. w. of US 65 at 1250 SR 76W. The veterans of American wars and military conflicts of the 20th century are honored at this museum, which has collections of uniforms and art as well as artifact exhibits. The focal point is a 70-foot-long bronze sculpture by museum founder and owner Fred Hoppe, depicting 50 soldiers storming a beach. Each life-size figure represents a U.S. state and is modeled after an actual combat veteran, including Hoppe's father. The names of more than 400,000 Americans killed in World War II are listed on the museum walls. Similar rolls are dedicated to casualties in Korea, Vietnam and the Persian Gulf.

Time: Allow 1 hour minimum. **Hours:** Daily 9-5. Hours may be extended in summer. Phone ahead to confirm schedule. **Cost:** $16.95; $13.99 (military and veterans with ID); $10 (ages 13-17); $5 (ages 6-12). **Phone:** (417) 336-2300 for information, or (877) 554-8387 for tickets.

WHITE WATER is 3.7 mi. w. on SR 76W. The water park's rides and attractions include Aloha River at Hula Hula Bay, an 800-plus-foot tropical river adventure for floating, with fountains, misters, geysers and more; the 500,000-gallon Surf's Up Wave Pool; waterslides, including Ohana Falls, Raging River Rapids and Pipeline Plunge; the Coconut Cove children's play area; and Splashaway Cay Island Adventure. Kalani Towers is a seven-and-a-half-story contraption with six different slides. White Water's biggest ride is KaPau Plummet, featuring a drop-floor launch from atop a four-story tower with a near-vertical plunge through two 240-foot dueling slides.

Hours: Open daily at 10 a.m. (closing times vary), late May to mid-Aug.; Sat.-Sun. and Labor Day, mid- to late May and mid-Aug. through Labor Day. Phone ahead to confirm schedule. **Cost:** $42; $32 (ages 62+); $20 (ages 4-11). Rates are subject to change; phone ahead to confirm. **Phone:** (800) 831-4386.

RECREATIONAL ACTIVITIES
• **Kayak Branson,** 5403 SR 165, provides tours as well as canoe, kayak and stand-up paddleboard rentals for Lake Taneycomo and Table Rock Lake. **Hours:** Daily 8-4:30, Mar.-Nov. Reservations are recommended. **Phone:** (417) 336-2811.

Sightseeing

Boat Tours

MAIN STREET LAKE CRUISES depart from the Gage Marina on the Lake Taneycomo waterfront, at the south end of Branson Landing. Ninety-minute sightseeing cruises (some with meals served) as well as dinner and cocktail cruises are offered on two 100-foot-long ships. The *Landing Princess* yacht offers three open-air decks, while the *Lake Queen* is a riverboat replica with a climate-controlled lower deck and an outdoor upper deck. During the cruise passengers might spot bald eagles, coyotes, foxes, herons and other wildlife.

Hours: Sightseeing cruises depart daily at 11:45 (with optional lunch) and 1:45. Dinner cruises depart at 6:45. **Cost:** Sightseeing cruise $38; $18 (ages 4-12). Sightseeing cruise with lunch (available on the 11:45 cruise only) $48; $28 (ages 4-12). Dinner cruise $52.95; $39.95 (ages 4-12). Reservations are required. **Phone:** (417) 239-3980 or (877) 382-6287.

SHOWBOAT *BRANSON BELLE* departs from White River Landing on SR 165, 6 mi. s. of jct. SR 76W and .5 mi. s. of Table Rock Dam. This turn-of-the-20th-century-style paddle wheeler is 278 feet long and holds 700 passengers. A scenic cruise on Table Rock Lake, which lasts approximately 2.25 hours, includes a three-course lunch or dinner and a show starring a troupe of talented entertainers and a live band.

Hours: Cruises depart most days at noon, 4 and 8, early Mar.-Dec. 31. Boarding begins 1 hour before departure. Phone ahead to confirm schedule. **Cost:** $53-$73; $27-$37 (ages 4-11). Fares are subject to change; phone ahead to confirm. Reservations are recommended. **Phone:** (417) 336-7171 or (800) 775-2628.

Bus Tours

Gray Line Branson/Springfield offers sightseeing tours of the Tri-Lakes area as well as nearby Eureka Springs, Ark.; phone (800) 542-6768.

Rail Tours

BRANSON SCENIC RAILWAY departs from the 1906 depot at 206 E. Main St. Passengers enjoy a narration of the history of the area and the railroad as the 1940s and '50s rolling stock embarks on a 40-mile round trip of the scenic Ozark foothills, crossing bridges and passing through two tunnels. A dinner train also is offered (not recommended for ages 12 and under).

Time: Allow 2 hours minimum. **Hours:** Departures Mon.-Fri. at 9, 11:30, 2 and 4:30, June-July and 2 weeks in mid-Oct.; Mon.-Fri. at 9, 11:30 and 2, in May and on select days from Aug. through Nov.; Mon.-Fri. at 11:30 and 2, Mar.-Apr. and on select days in Aug.-Sept. and Nov.; otherwise varies. Dinner train departs Sat. at 5, Apr.-Oct. Polar Express train runs on select days in Nov.-Dec. Phone ahead for schedule details on specific days. **Cost:** $27.50; $17 (ages 3-12). Dinner train fare $62. **Phone:** (417) 334-6110 or (800) 287-2462. 🍽

▼ *See AAA listing p. 11* ▼

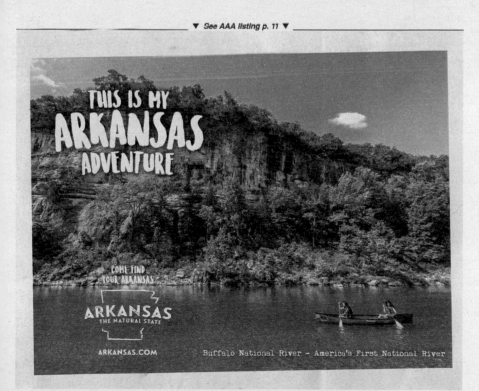

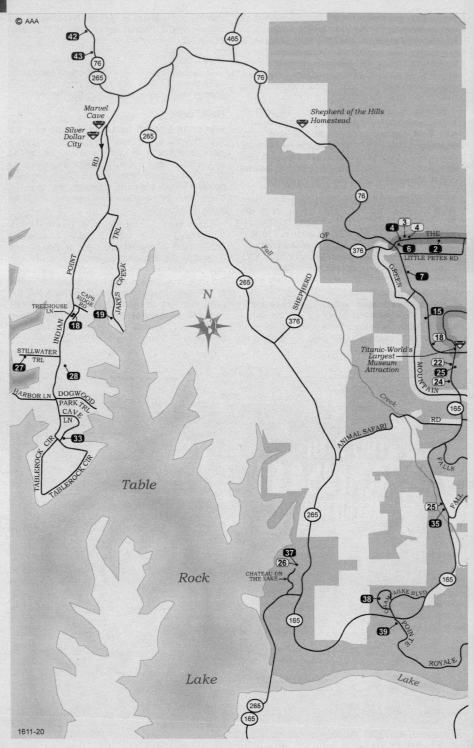

© AAA

42
43
76
265

Marvel Cave
Silver Dollar City
RD

POINT

TRL

JAKES CREEK

465

76

76

265

265

Fall

SHEPHERD

265

376

376

OF

GREEN

Shepherd of the Hills Homestead

76

4   3
4   THE

6   2
LITTLE PETES RD

7

15

18

Titanic-World's Largest Museum Attraction

MOUNTAIN

22
25
24

165

N

CAPS RIDGE RD

TREEHOUSE LN

INDIAN

19

18

STILLWATER TRL

27

28

HARBOR LN

DOGWOOD PARK TRL

CAVE LN

TABLEROCK CIR

TABLEROCK CIR

33

Table

Rock

Lake

Creek

RD

ANIMAL SAFARI

FALLS

Fall

25
35

265

37
26

CHATEAU ON THE LAKE

165

165

CHAMPAGNE BLVD

38

39

POINT

ROYALE

Lake

165

265
165

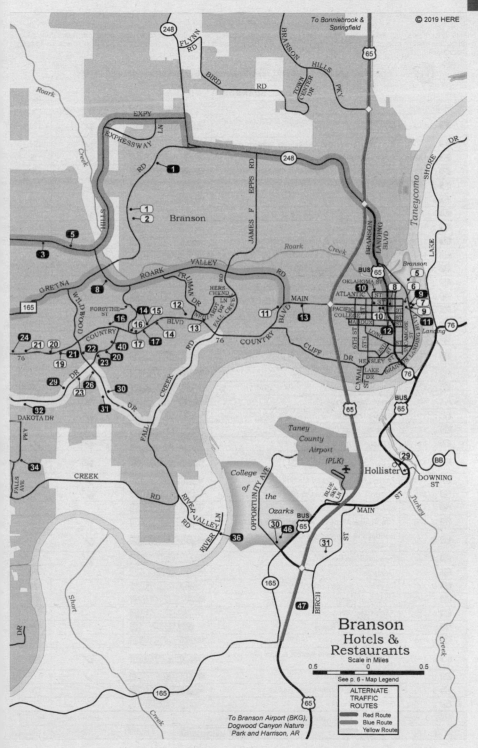

Branson
Hotels &
Restaurants
Scale in Miles
0.5   0   0.5
See p. 6 - Map Legend

ALTERNATE
TRAFFIC
ROUTES
Red Route
Blue Route
Yellow Route

© 2019 HERE

Branson

This index helps you "spot" where hotels and restaurants are located on the corresponding detailed maps. Restaurant price range is a combination of lunch and/or dinner. Turn to the listing page for more information and consult display ads for special promotions.

For more details, rates and reservations: AAA.com/travelguides/hotels

BRANSON

Map Page	Hotels	Designation	Member Savings	Page
1 p. 170	**Comfort Inn & Suites-Branson Meadows** *(See ad p. 174.)*	APPROVED	✔	176
2 p. 170	**Best Western Music Capital Inn** *(See ad p. 174.)*	APPROVED	✔	174
3 p. 170	Ozark Valley Inn	APPROVED		178
4 p. 170	Honeysuckle Inn & Conference Center	APPROVED		177
5 p. 170	Scenic Hills Inn	APPROVED		178
6 p. 170	Quality Inn West *(See ad p. 174.)*	APPROVED		178
7 p. 170	Hampton Inn by Hilton-On the Strip	THREE DIAMOND	✔	177
8 p. 170	Rosebud Inn	APPROVED		178
9 p. 170	Hilton Promenade at Branson Landing	THREE DIAMOND	✔	177
10 p. 170	**Best Western Plus Landing View Inn & Suites**	THREE DIAMOND	✔	175
11 p. 170	**Hilton Branson Convention Center Hotel**	THREE DIAMOND	✔	177
12 p. 170	The Branson Hotel	THREE DIAMOND		175
13 p. 170	**Baymont Inn & Suites**	APPROVED	✔	174
14 p. 170	**Grand Country Inn**	APPROVED	✔	177
15 p. 170	The Dutton Inn	APPROVED		176
16 p. 170	**Hotel Grand Victorian** *(See ad p. 178.)*	APPROVED	✔	178
17 p. 170	**Holiday Inn Express Hotel & Suites Branson 76 Central**	THREE DIAMOND	✔	177
18 p. 170	Treehouse Condo Rentals Inc	APPROVED		178
19 p. 170	Calm Waters Resort	APPROVED		176
20 p. 170	Green Gables Inn	APPROVED		177
21 p. 170	**Clarion Hotel**	APPROVED	✔	176
22 p. 170	Radisson Hotel Branson	THREE DIAMOND		178
23 p. 170	**Branson Super 8** *(See ad p. 175.)*	APPROVED	✔	175
24 p. 170	**Best Western Center Pointe Inn** *(See ad p. 174.)*	APPROVED	✔	174
25 p. 170	Fairfield Inn & Suites by Marriott	THREE DIAMOND	✔	177
26 p. 170	**Comfort Inn at Thousand Hills** *(See ad p. 174.)*	APPROVED	✔	176
27 p. 170	Still Waters Condominium Resort	THREE DIAMOND		178
28 p. 170	**The Village At Indian Point** *(See ad p. 179.)*	THREE DIAMOND	✔	179
29 p. 170	**Holiday Inn Express Green Mtn Drive** *(See ad p. 174.)*	THREE DIAMOND	✔	177
30 p. 170	Residence Inn by Marriott	THREE DIAMOND	✔	178
31 p. 170	Thousand Hills Golf Resort	THREE DIAMOND		178
32 p. 170	Days Inn & Suites Branson	APPROVED		176
33 p. 170	Tribesman Resort	APPROVED		178
34 p. 170	Ramada by Wyndham Branson	APPROVED		178
35 p. 170	Fall Creek Inn & Suites	APPROVED		177
36 p. 170	Lazy Valley Resort	APPROVED		178
37 p. 170	**Chateau on the Lake Resort & Spa** *(See ad p. 176.)*	FOUR DIAMOND	✔	176
38 p. 170	**Welk Resort Branson**	THREE DIAMOND	✔	179
39 p. 170	Pointe Royale Condominium Resort	APPROVED		178
40 p. 170	Grand Oaks Hotel	THREE DIAMOND		177

Map Page	Restaurants	Designation	Cuisine	Price Range	Page
1 p. 170	Tequila's 2	APPROVED	Mexican	$8-$25	180

Map Page	Restaurants (cont'd)	Designation	Cuisine	Price Range	Page
② p. 170	Vasken's Deli	APPROVED	Greek Deli Pizza	$6-$12	180
③ p. 170	Little Hacienda	APPROVED	Mexican	$9-$23	180
④ p. 170	McFarlain's Family Restaurant	APPROVED	American	$6-$18	180
⑤ p. 170	Black Oak Grill	APPROVED	American	$8-$18	179
⑥ p. 170	Momo Sushi & Grill	APPROVED	Japanese	$8-$22	180
⑦ p. 170	Big Whiskey's	APPROVED	American	$8-$24	179
⑧ p. 170	Farmhouse Restaurant	APPROVED	American	$6-$15	180
⑨ p. 170	Waxy O'Shea's	APPROVED	Irish	$9-$15	180
⑩ p. 170	Ruby Lena's Tea Room & Antiques	APPROVED	American	$6-$8	180
⑪ p. 170	Casa Fuentes Mexican Grill	APPROVED	Mexican	$7-$14	179
⑫ p. 170	Mitsu Neko Fusion Cuisine and Sushi Bar	APPROVED	Asian	$13-$30	180
⑬ p. 170	Thai Thai Cuisine	APPROVED	Thai	$6-$17	180
⑭ p. 170	Outback Steak & Oyster Bar	APPROVED	Steak	$8-$30	180
⑮ p. 170	Grand Country Buffet	APPROVED	American	$9-$13	180
⑯ p. 170	WaKyoto Japanese Restaurant & Sushi	APPROVED	Japanese	$6-$20	180
⑰ p. 170	Indian Clay Oven	APPROVED	Northern Indian	$13-$26	180
⑱ p. 170	Pizza World	APPROVED	Pizza	$6-$22	180
⑲ p. 170	**Buckingham's Prime Rib & Steakhouse**	THREE DIAMOND	Steak	$12-$40	179
⑳ p. 170	Gettin' Basted	APPROVED	Barbecue	$9-$23	180
㉑ p. 170	Charlie's Steak Ribs & Ale	APPROVED	American	$5-$23	179
㉒ p. 170	Uptown Cafe	APPROVED	American	$7-$14	180
㉓ p. 170	Florentina's Ristorante Italiano	APPROVED	Italian	$7-$35	180
㉔ p. 170	St. James Winery & Restaurant	APPROVED	American	$12-$19	180
㉕ p. 170	Danna's Bar B Que and Burger Shop	APPROVED	Barbecue	$5-$10	180
㉖ p. 170	**Chateau Grille at Chateau on the Lake**	THREE DIAMOND	American	$7-$70	180

BRANSON WEST

Map Page	Hotels	Designation	Member Savings	Page
㊷ p. 170	Shady Acre Motel	APPROVED		181
㊸ p. 170	**Best Western Branson Inn & Conference Center** *(See ad p. 175.)*	APPROVED	✔	180

HOLLISTER

Map Page	Hotels	Designation	Member Savings	Page
㊻ p. 170	Mabee Lodge of the Keeter Center at College of the Ozarks	THREE DIAMOND		194
㊼ p. 170	**La Quinta Inn & Suites**	THREE DIAMOND	✔	194

Map Page	Restaurants	Designation	Cuisine	Price Range	Page
㉙ p. 170	Downing Street Pour House	APPROVED	American	$8-$22	194
㉚ p. 170	The Keeter Center at College of the Ozarks	THREE DIAMOND	American	$9-$25	194
㉛ p. 170	Pizza by the Chef	APPROVED	Pizza	$7-$20	194

🔗 Get the scoop from AAA inspectors:

AAA.com/travelguides/restaurants

BRANSON
- Restaurants p. 179
- Hotels & Restaurants map & index p. 170

BAYMONT INN & SUITES   417/334-1985   13

APPROVED

Hotel

Address: 1000 W Main St 65616 **Location:** Just sw of jct US 65 and SR 76 (Country Blvd). **Facility:** 87 units. 5 stories, interior corridors. **Amenities:** safes. **Pool:** heated indoor. **Activities:** hot tub, exercise room. **Guest Services:** coin laundry. **Featured Amenity: full hot breakfast.**

BEST WESTERN CENTER POINTE INN
417/334-1894   24

APPROVED

Best Western

Hotel

AAA Benefit: Members save up to 15% and earn bonus points!

Address: 3215 W Hwy 76 (Country Blvd) 65616 **Location:** Just e of jct SR 165. **Facility:** 162 units. 2-4 stories, interior/exterior corridors. **Terms:** check-in 4 pm. **Pool:** outdoor, heated indoor. **Activities:** hot tub, game room, exercise room. **Guest Services:** coin laundry. *(See ad this page.)*

BEST WESTERN MUSIC CAPITAL INN
417/334-8378   2

APPROVED

Best Western

Hotel

AAA Benefit: Members save up to 15% and earn bonus points!

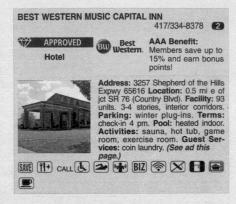

Address: 3257 Shepherd of the Hills Expwy 65616 **Location:** 0.5 mi e of jct SR 76 (Country Blvd). **Facility:** 93 units. 3-4 stories, interior corridors. **Parking:** winter plug-ins. **Terms:** check-in 4 pm. **Pool:** heated indoor. **Activities:** sauna, hot tub, game room, exercise room. **Guest Services:** coin laundry. *(See ad this page.)*

Let Your Voice Be Heard

If your visit to a listed property doesn't meet your expectations, tell us about it.

AAA.com/MemberFeedback

(See map & index p. 170.)

BEST WESTERN PLUS LANDING VIEW INN & SUITES
417/334-6464 **10**

THREE DIAMOND

Hotel

Best Western PLUS

AAA Benefit: Members save up to 15% and earn bonus points!

Address: 403 W Main (Hwy 76) 65616 **Location:** 0.3 mi e of jct SR 76 (Country Blvd) and US 65. **Facility:** 109 units. 3 stories (no elevator), exterior corridors. **Pool:** heated indoor. **Activities:** exercise room. **Guest Services:** complimentary and valet laundry, area transportation. **Featured Amenity:** breakfast buffet.

[SAVE] [≡] [¶↑] CALL [⚑] [≈] [♿]

[BIZ] [HS] [🛜] [✕] [🔌] [🍽] [🖥] /SOME UNITS [🐾]

THE BRANSON HOTEL
417/544-9814 **12**

THREE DIAMOND Historic Boutique Hotel. **Address:** 214 W Main St 65616

BRANSON SUPER 8
417/334-8880 **23**

APPROVED

Hotel

Address: 2490 Green Mountain Dr 65616 **Location:** Just s of jct SR 76 (Country Blvd). **Facility:** 70 units. 2-3 stories (no elevator), interior corridors. **Pool:** outdoor. **Guest Services:** coin laundry. **Featured Amenity:** full hot breakfast. *(See ad this page.)*

[SAVE] [¶↑] [≈] [BIZ] [🛜] [✕] [🔌]

[🖥] /SOME UNITS [🍽]

▼ See AAA listing p. 180 ▼

▼ See AAA listing this page ▼

(See map & index p. 170.)

CALM WATERS RESORT   417/338-8963   **19**
♦ **APPROVED**   Cabin. **Address:** 1043 Jakes Creek Tr 65616

CHATEAU ON THE LAKE RESORT & SPA
417/334-1161   **37**

♦ **FOUR DIAMOND**
Resort Hotel

Address: 415 N State Hwy 265 65616 **Location:** Waterfront. Just n of jct SR 165. **Facility:** This exceptional property offers elegance and many unique features, including a mixture of Ozark hospitality and sophisticated service. Rooms feature stunning views of Table Rock Lake. 301 units. 10 stories, interior corridors. **Parking:** on-site and valet. **Terms:** check-in 4 pm. **Amenities:** safes. **Dining:** 3 restaurants, also, Chateau Grille at Chateau on the Lake, see separate listing. **Pool:** heated outdoor, heated indoor. **Activities:** hot tub, marina, fishing, scuba diving, tennis, recreation programs in season, kids club, playground, game room, trails, exercise room, spa. **Guest Services:** complimentary and valet laundry. (See ad this page.)

[icons] SAVE ⊶ ⤋ ☗ CALL ⑤ ⤱ ⚐ BIZ 🛜 ✕ 🖥 / SOME UNITS ⊞ 🗄 🖳

CLARION HOTEL
417/334-7666   **21**

♦ **APPROVED**
Hotel

Address: 2820 W Hwy 76 65616 **Location:** 2.5 mi w of jct US 65. **Facility:** 166 units, some two bedrooms and kitchens. 5-7 stories, interior/exterior corridors. **Amenities:** safes. **Dining:** Buckingham's Prime Rib & Steakhouse, see separate listing. **Pool:** heated outdoor, heated indoor. **Activities:** sauna, hot tub, exercise room, massage. **Guest Services:** coin laundry. **Featured Amenity:** full hot breakfast.

[icons] SAVE ⊶ ⊶ CALL ⑤ ⤱ ⚐ BIZ 🛜 ✕ 🖥 🗄 🖳

COMFORT INN & SUITES-BRANSON MEADOWS   **1**
417/335-4731

♦ **APPROVED**
Hotel

Address: 5150 N Gretna Rd 65616 **Location:** 2.9 mi n of jct SR 76 (Country Blvd). **Facility:** 102 units, some cottages. 4 stories, interior corridors. **Terms:** check-in 4 pm. **Amenities:** safes. **Pool:** heated indoor. **Activities:** sauna, hot tub, game room, trails, exercise room. **Guest Services:** valet and coin laundry. **Featured Amenity:** full hot breakfast. (See ad p. 174.)

[icons] SAVE ECO CALL ⑤ ⤱ ⚐ BIZ HS 🛜 ✕ 🖥 🗄 🖳

COMFORT INN AT THOUSAND HILLS
417/335-4727   **26**

♦ **APPROVED**
Hotel

Address: 203 S Wildwood Dr 65616 **Location:** Just s of jct SR 76 (Country Blvd). **Facility:** 108 units, some two bedrooms. 4 stories, interior corridors. **Terms:** check-in 4 pm. **Pool:** heated indoor. **Activities:** sauna, hot tub, game room, exercise room. **Guest Services:** coin laundry. **Featured Amenity:** full hot breakfast. (See ad p. 174.)

[icons] SAVE ECO ⊶ CALL ⑤ ⤱ ⚐ BIZ 🛜 ✕ 🖥 🗄 🖳

DAYS INN & SUITES BRANSON   417/336-2200   **32**
♦ **APPROVED**   Hotel. **Address:** 3010 Green Mountain Dr 65616

THE DUTTON INN   417/334-8873   **15**
♦ **APPROVED**   Motel. **Address:** 3454 W 76 Country Blvd 65616

▼ See AAA listing this page ▼

(See map & index p. 170.)

FAIRFIELD INN & SUITES BY MARRIOTT 417/336-5665 **25**
▼▼ THREE DIAMOND SAVE Hotel. Address: 220 Hwy 165 S 65616

AAA Benefit: Members save 5% or more!

FALL CREEK INN & SUITES 417/348-1683 **35**
▼▼ APPROVED Hotel. Address: 995 Hwy 165 65616

GRAND COUNTRY INN 417/335-3535 **14**
▼▼ APPROVED Hotel
Address: 1945 W 76 Country Blvd 65616 Location: Jct US 65, 1.9 mi w. Adjacent to the mall; 76 Music Hall Theater on premises. Facility: 319 units. 2-3 stories, exterior corridors. Dining: 2 restaurants, also, Grand Country Buffet, see separate listing, entertainment. Pool: outdoor, heated indoor. Activities: hot tub, miniature golf, game room. Guest Services: coin laundry.

GRAND OAKS HOTEL 417/336-6423 **40**
▼▼ THREE DIAMOND Hotel. Address: 2315 Green Mountain Dr 65616

GREEN GABLES INN 417/336-3400 **20**
▼▼ APPROVED Hotel. Address: 2400 Green Mountain Dr 65616

HAMPTON INN BY HILTON-BRANSON HILLS 417/243-7800
▼▼ THREE DIAMOND SAVE Hotel. Address: 200 Payne Stewart Dr 65616

AAA Benefit: Members save up to 15%!

HAMPTON INN BY HILTON-ON THE STRIP
417/337-5762 **7**
▼▼ THREE DIAMOND SAVE Hotel. Address: 3695 W Hwy 76 (Country Blvd) 65616

AAA Benefit: Members save up to 15%!

HILTON BRANSON CONVENTION CENTER HOTEL
417/336-5400 **11**
▼▼ THREE DIAMOND Hotel

Hilton HOTELS & RESORTS

AAA Benefit: Members save up to 15%!

Address: 200 E Main St 65616 Location: Center. Facility: 294 units, some two bedrooms and condominiums. 12 stories, interior corridors. Parking: on-site (fee) and valet. Terms: check-in 4 pm. Amenities: safes. Pool: heated outdoor, heated indoor. Activities: hot tub, exercise room. Guest Services: valet laundry.

HILTON PROMENADE AT BRANSON LANDING
417/336-5500 **9**
▼▼ THREE DIAMOND SAVE Hotel. Address: 3 Branson Landing 65616

AAA Benefit: Members save up to 15%!

HOLIDAY INN EXPRESS GREEN MTN DRIVE
417/336-2100 **29**
▼▼ THREE DIAMOND Hotel
Address: 2801 Green Mountain Dr 65616 Location: Just s of jct Wildwood Dr. Facility: 120 units. 5 stories, interior corridors. Amenities: Some: safes. Pool: heated indoor. Activities: sauna, hot tub, game room, exercise room. Guest Services: coin laundry. Featured Amenity: full hot breakfast. (See ad p. 174.)

HOLIDAY INN EXPRESS HOTEL & SUITES BRANSON 76 CENTRAL 417/336-1100 **17**
▼▼ THREE DIAMOND Hotel
Address: 1970 W Hwy 76 (Country Blvd) 65616 Location: 1.8 mi w of jct US 65. Facility: 141 units, some two bedrooms. 5 stories, interior corridors. Pool: heated outdoor. Activities: hot tub, exercise room. Guest Services: coin laundry. Featured Amenity: full hot breakfast.

HONEYSUCKLE INN & CONFERENCE CENTER
417/335-2030 **4**
▼▼ APPROVED Hotel. Address: 3598 Shepherd of the Hills Expwy 65616

Expert Travel Insight

Get AAA travel information at club offices and on AAA.com for experiences you'll remember for a lifetime.

(See map & index p. 170.)

HOTEL GRAND VICTORIAN
417/336-2935 **16**

APPROVED

Hotel

Address: 2325 W Hwy 76 (Country Blvd) 65616 **Location:** 2.3 mi w of jct US 65. **Facility:** 151 units. 5 stories, interior corridors. **Terms:** check-in 4 pm. **Pool:** heated outdoor, heated indoor. **Activities:** hot tub, game room, exercise room. **Guest Services:** coin laundry. **Featured Amenity: breakfast buffet.** *(See ad this page.)*

SAVE ⏹ ⏹ ⏹ BIZ 📶 ⏹
⏹ ⏹ ⏹ /SOME UNITS ⏹

LAZY VALLEY RESORT
417/334-2397 **36**

APPROVED   Motel. **Address:** 285 River Ln 65616

OZARK VALLEY INN
417/336-4666 **3**

APPROVED   Motel. **Address:** 2693 Shepherd of the Hills Expwy 65616

POINTE ROYALE CONDOMINIUM RESORT
417/334-5614 **39**

APPROVED   Vacation Rental Condominium. **Address:** 158 Pointe Royale Dr, Suite 100 65616

QUALITY INN WEST
417/334-8694 **6**

APPROVED   Hotel. **Address:** 3601 Shepherd of the Hills Expwy 65616 *(See ad p. 174.)*

RADISSON HOTEL BRANSON
417/335-5767 **22**

THREE DIAMOND Hotel. **Address:** 120 S Wildwood Dr 65616

RAMADA BY WYNDHAM BRANSON
417/334-1717 **34**

APPROVED   Hotel. **Address:** 3140 Falls Pkwy 65616

RESIDENCE INN BY MARRIOTT
417/336-4077 **30**

THREE DIAMOND SAVE Extended Stay Hotel. **Address:** 280 Wildwood Dr S 65616

AAA Benefit: Members save 5% or more!

ROSEBUD INN
417/336-4000 **8**

APPROVED   Hotel. **Address:** 1415 Roark Valley Rd 65616

SCENIC HILLS INN
417/336-8855 **5**

APPROVED   Hotel. **Address:** 2422 Shepherd of the Hills Expwy 65616

STILL WATERS CONDOMINIUM RESORT
417/338-2323 **27**

THREE DIAMOND Resort Condominium. **Address:** 21 Stillwater Tr 65616

THOUSAND HILLS GOLF RESORT
417/336-5873 **31**

THREE DIAMOND Resort Condominium. **Address:** 245 S Wildwood Dr 65616

TREEHOUSE CONDO RENTALS INC
417/338-5199 **18**

APPROVED   Condominium. **Address:** 129 Treehouse Ln 65616

TRIBESMAN RESORT
417/338-2616 **33**

APPROVED   Resort Cottage. **Address:** 416 Cave Ln 65616

▼ *See AAA listing this page* ▼

🔗 **Turn dreams into plans using**

AAA travel planning tools: AAA.com/maps

(See map & index p. 170.)

THE VILLAGE AT INDIAN POINT   417/338-8800 ㉘

THREE DIAMOND

Resort Condominium

Address: 24 Village Tr 65616 **Location:** Waterfront. 2.5 mi s of jct SR 76 (Country Blvd) on Indian Point Rd. **Facility:** Nestled on lush wooded acreage, this resort offers fully equipped, handsomely furnished cabin-like units, all with a stone wood-burning fireplace. 67 condominiums. 3 stories (no elevator), exterior corridors. **Terms:** check-in 4 pm. **Pool:** outdoor, heated indoor. **Activities:** sauna, hot tub, boat dock, fishing, playground, game room, exercise room. **Guest Services:** complimentary laundry. *(See ad this page.)*

[SAVE] [icons] / SOME UNITS [icons]

WELK RESORT BRANSON   417/336-3575 ㊳

THREE DIAMOND

Hotel

Address: 1984 State Hwy 165 65616 **Location:** 2.9 mi s of jct SR 76 (Country Blvd). **Facility:** 159 units. 4 stories, interior corridors. **Terms:** check-in 4 pm. **Amenities:** safes. **Pool:** heated outdoor, heated indoor. **Activities:** hot tub, miniature golf, recreation programs, playground, game room, exercise room. **Guest Services:** coin laundry.

[SAVE] [icons] CALL [icons]

BIG WHISKEY'S   417/334-4478 ⑦

APPROVED American. Casual Dining. **Address:** 301 Branson Landing Blvd 65616

BLACK OAK GRILL   417/239-0063 ⑤

APPROVED American. Casual Dining. **Address:** 601 Branson Landing 65616

BUCKINGHAM'S PRIME RIB & STEAKHOUSE   417/337-7777 ⑲

THREE DIAMOND

Steak
Casual Dining
$12-$40

AAA Inspector Notes: Beef, wild-game meats, seafood and pasta are served in a dining room that has an unusual African-safari theme. **Features:** full bar. **Reservations:** suggested. **Address:** 2820 W Hwy 76 65616 **Location:** 2.5 mi w of jct US 65; in Clarion Hotel. [D] CALL [icon]

CANTINA LAREDO   417/334-6062

APPROVED Mexican. Casual Dining. **Address:** 1001 Branson Landing 65616

CASA FUENTES MEXICAN GRILL   417/339-3888 ⑪

APPROVED Mexican. Casual Dining. **Address:** 1107 W Hwy 76 65616

CHARLIE'S STEAK RIBS & ALE   417/334-6090 ㉑

APPROVED American. Casual Dining. **Address:** 3009 W Hwy 76 65616

(See map & index p. 170.)

CHATEAU GRILLE AT CHATEAU ON THE LAKE
417/243-1777 26

THREE DIAMOND **AAA Inspector Notes:** Patrons enjoy a
view of Table Rock Lake while waiting
American   for their meal. Locally caught fish is a
Fine Dining   menu highlight alongside aged steaks.
$7-$70   The staff is polished, knowledgeable and
able to help you pair a good wine from
an extensive collection to your menu choice. **Features:** full bar,
patio dining, Sunday brunch. **Reservations:** suggested. **Address:** 415 N State Hwy 265 65616 **Location:** Just n of jct SR
165; in Chateau on the Lake Resort & Spa. **Parking:** on-site and
valet. D

DANNA'S BAR B QUE AND BURGER SHOP
417/337-5527 25
APPROVED Barbecue. Casual Dining. **Address:** 963
Hwy 165 65615

FARMHOUSE RESTAURANT
417/334-9701 8
APPROVED American. Casual Dining. **Address:** 119
W Main St 65616

FLORENTINA'S RISTORANTE ITALIANO
417/337-9882 23
APPROVED Italian. Casual Dining. **Address:** 2690
Green Mountain Dr 65616

GETTIN' BASTED
417/320-6357 20
APPROVED Barbecue. Casual Dining. **Address:** 2845
W Hwy 76 65616

GRAND COUNTRY BUFFET
417/335-2434 15
APPROVED American. Casual Dining. **Address:** 1945
W 76 Country Blvd 65616

INDIAN CLAY OVEN
417/973-0044 17
APPROVED Northern Indian. Casual Dining. **Address:**
2005 W 76 Country Blvd 65616

LITTLE HACIENDA
417/335-2008 3
APPROVED Mexican. Casual Dining. **Address:** 9
Treasure Lake Dr 65616

MCFARLAIN'S FAMILY RESTAURANT
417/336-4680 4
APPROVED American. Casual Dining. **Address:** 3562
Shepherd of the Hills Expwy 65616

MITSU NEKO FUSION CUISINE AND SUSHI BAR
417/336-1819 12
APPROVED Asian. Casual Dining. **Address:** 1819 W
76 Country Blvd, Unit D 65616

MOMO SUSHI & GRILL
417/320-6125 6
APPROVED Japanese. Casual Dining. **Address:** 120
N Sycamore St 65616

OUTBACK STEAK & OYSTER BAR
417/334-6306 14
APPROVED Steak. Casual Dining. **Address:** 1914 W
Hwy 76 65616

PIZZA WORLD
417/337-7778 18
APPROVED Pizza. Quick Serve. **Address:** 3405 W 76
Country Blvd 65616

RIB CRIB BBQ AND GRILL
417/337-7427
APPROVED Barbecue. Casual Dining. **Address:** 1855
W Hwy 76 65616

RUBY LENA'S TEA ROOM & ANTIQUES
417/239-2919 10
APPROVED American. Casual Dining. **Address:** 224
W Main St 65616

ST. JAMES WINERY & RESTAURANT
417/544-8283 24
APPROVED American. Casual Dining. **Address:** 405
Highway 165 65616

SHORTY SMALL'S
417/337-9716
APPROVED Barbecue. Casual Dining. **Address:** 2600
SR 76 W (Country Blvd) 65616

TEQUILA'S 2
417/239-0099 1
APPROVED Mexican. Casual Dining. **Address:** 3300
N Gretna Rd 65616

THAI THAI CUISINE
417/334-9070 13
APPROVED Thai. Casual Dining. **Address:** 1615 W
Hwy 76 65616

UPTOWN CAFE
417/336-3535 22
APPROVED American. Casual Dining. **Address:** 285
SR 165 65616

VASKEN'S DELI
417/334-9182 2
APPROVED Greek Deli Pizza. Quick Serve. **Address:**
3200 Gretna Rd 65616

WAKYOTO JAPANESE RESTAURANT & SUSHI
417/336-1177 16
APPROVED Japanese. Casual Dining. **Address:** 2005
W Hwy 76, Unit 201 65616

WAXY O'SHEA'S
417/348-1759 9
APPROVED Irish. Casual Dining. **Address:** 235
Branson Landing 65616

BRANSON WEST (D-3) pop. 478, elev. 1,368'
• **Hotels & Restaurants map & index p. 170**
• **Part of Branson area — see map p. 151**

TALKING ROCKS CAVERN is on SR 13 at 423
Fairy Cave Ln. Drapery helictites, stalactites and a
100-foot-tall formation called the Cathedral can be
seen in the cave, which has approximately 140
steps to climb; electric lighting, concrete walks and
railings are provided. A 5-minute sound and light
presentation and a 400-acre nature area with
walking trails also are featured.

   Time: Allow 1 hour minimum. **Hours:** Daily 9-6,
June-Aug.; 9:30-5, Feb.-May and Sept.-Dec.;
noon-5, rest of year. **Cost:** $17.95; $9.95 (ages
4-12). **Phone:** (417) 272-3366 or (800) 600-2283.

(See map & index p. 170.)

SHADY ACRE MOTEL   417/338-2316   **42**
🔷 **APPROVED** Motel. **Address:** 8722 State Hwy 76 65737

WHERE TO EAT

DANNA'S BAR-B-QUE & BURGER SHOP   417/272-1945
🔷 **APPROVED** Barbecue. Quick Serve. **Address:** 15 Hope Way (SR 13 business route) 65737

BRENTWOOD pop. 8,055
- **Hotels & Restaurants map & index p. 274**
- **Part of St. Louis area — see map p. 248**

DRURY INN & SUITES BRENTWOOD   314/968-3704   **78**
🔷 **THREE DIAMOND** Hotel. **Address:** 8700 Eager Rd 63144

SPRINGHILL SUITES BY MARRIOTT BRENTWOOD
                                                    314/647-8400   **79**
🔷 **THREE DIAMOND** 〔SAVE〕 Hotel. **Address:** 1231 Strassner Dr 63144

| AAA Benefit: |
| Members save 5% |
| or more! |

WHERE TO EAT

BONEFISH GRILL   314/918-1649   **97**
🔷 **THREE DIAMOND** Seafood. Fine Dining. **Address:** 8780 Eager Rd 63144

FRANK PAPA'S RISTORANTE   314/961-3344   **99**
🔷 **APPROVED** Italian. Casual Dining. **Address:** 2241 S Brentwood Blvd 63144

HOULIHAN'S   314/863-9116   **98**
🔷 **THREE DIAMOND** American. Casual Dining. **Address:** 1221 Strassner Dr 63144

MAI LEE RESTAURANT   314/645-2835   **96**
🔷 **APPROVED** Asian. Casual Dining. **Address:** 8396 Musick Memorial Dr 63144

BRIDGETON pop. 11,550
- **Hotels & Restaurants map & index p. 274**
- **Part of St. Louis area — see map p. 248**

COURTYARD BY MARRIOTT-AIRPORT/EARTH CITY
                                                    314/209-1000   **26**
🔷 **THREE DIAMOND** 〔SAVE〕 Hotel. **Address:** 3101 Rider Tr S 63044

| AAA Benefit: |
| Members save 5% |
| or more! |

CROWNE PLAZA ST. LOUIS AIRPORT
                                                    314/291-6700   **31**
🔷 **THREE DIAMOND**
Hotel

Address: 11228 Lone Eagle Dr 63044 **Location:** I-70 exit 235A (Lindbergh Blvd/US 67), just s, then just w. **Facility:** 350 units. 8 stories, interior corridors. **Parking:** on-site (fee). **Pool:** heated indoor. **Activities:** exercise room. **Guest Services:** valet laundry, area transportation.

〔SAVE〕 〔🏋〕 〔🍴〕 〔🛎〕 〔🍸〕 CALL 〔🔔〕
〔🛁〕 〔♿〕 〔BIZ〕 〔HS〕 〔📶〕 〔✕〕 〔🖥〕
/SOME UNITS 〔🔒〕 〔📷〕

EMBASSY SUITES BY HILTON ST. LOUIS AIRPORT
                                                    314/739-8929   **28**
🔷 **THREE DIAMOND** 〔SAVE〕 Hotel. **Address:** 11237 Lone Eagle Dr 63044

| AAA Benefit: |
| Members save up to |
| 15%! |

MAINSTAY SUITES   314/528-5550   **30**
🔷 **THREE DIAMOND** Extended Stay Hotel. **Address:** 11225 Lone Eagle Dr 63044

SLEEP INN   314/344-1954   **29**
🔷 **THREE DIAMOND** Hotel. **Address:** 11225 Lone Eagle Dr 63044

SPRINGHILL SUITES BY MARRIOTT-ST. LOUIS AIRPORT/
EARTH CITY   314/739-9991   **27**
🔷 **THREE DIAMOND** 〔SAVE〕 Hotel. **Address:** 3099 Rider Tr S 63044

| AAA Benefit: |
| Members save 5% |
| or more! |

WHERE TO EAT

MASSA'S   314/739-3894   **46**
🔷 **APPROVED** Italian. Casual Dining. **Address:** 4210 N Lindbergh Blvd 63044

BROOKFIELD pop. 4,542

BEST WESTERN BROOKFIELD   660/258-4900
🔷 **APPROVED**
Hotel

| Best Western. | AAA Benefit: Members save up to 15% and earn bonus points! |

Address: 28622 Hwy 11 64628 **Location:** US 36 exit Business Rt 36, just se. **Facility:** 31 units. 2 stories, interior corridors. **Parking:** winter plug-ins. **Pool:** outdoor. **Featured Amenity: full hot breakfast.**

〔SAVE〕 CALL 〔♿〕 〔🛁〕 〔BIZ〕 〔📶〕 〔✕〕
〔🔒〕 〔📷〕 〔🖥〕 /SOME UNITS 〔🐾〕 〔HS〕

CAMDENTON (C-3) pop. 3,718, elev. 1,000'
- **Hotels p. 182**

Camdenton, the seat of Camden County, is in south-central Missouri. Osage and Delaware Indians inhabited this area prior to the onset of white settlement in the 1820s. The 1,150-mile shoreline of the nearby Lake of the Ozarks can be explored by boat.

Camdenton Area Chamber of Commerce: 739 W. US 54, P.O. Box 1375, Camdenton, MO 65020. **Phone:** (573) 346-2227 or (800) 769-1004.

BRIDAL CAVE is 2 mi. n. on SR 5, then 1.5 mi. w. on Lake Rd. 5-88. Guided 1-hour tours depart every few minutes and follow concrete walks through the cave, which maintains a constant temperature of 60 F and is known for its massive onyx formations and colorful mineral deposits. The stalactite-adorned Bridal Chapel is a popular site for weddings, with more than 3,600 ceremonies performed. On the grounds are a visitor center, mining sluice, rock shop, observation tower and a boat dock. Visitors may spot such wildlife as the bald eagle, deer, turkeys and red foxes along a half-mile outdoor walking trail offering sweeping views of Thunder Mountain's rock bluffs. Lantern Tours are offered on Saturday nights Memorial Day through Labor Day; reservations are required.

Hours: Daily 9-6, mid-June to mid-Aug.; 9-5, mid-Mar. to mid-June and mid-Aug. to mid-Oct.; 9-4, rest of year. Lantern tour Sat. at 7, Memorial Day-Labor Day; reservations are required. **Cost:** $20; $10 (ages 5-12). Lantern tour $25. **Phone:** (573) 346-2676. 🎂

_____ ▼ See AAA listing this page ▼ _____

A rich history and thriving culture collide *here*

Baseball, vineyards, hiking trails, art galleries, award-winning cafés... Find *your* escape along the Mississippi.

visit**cape**
CAPE GIRARDEAU

VisitCape.com | 📘📷📹
#GetHere

MISS🌻URI
enjoy the show

THE LODGE AT OLD KINDERHOOK   573/317-4314
💎 **THREE DIAMOND** Hotel. **Address:** 678 Old Kinderhook Dr 65020

SLEEP INN & SUITES   573/346-4501
💎 **THREE DIAMOND** Hotel. **Address:** 1390 E Hwy 54 65020

CAPE GIRARDEAU (D-6) pop. 37,941, elev. 350'

Named after Jean Baptiste Girardot, who established a trading post here in 1733, Cape Girardeau, on the banks of the Mississippi River, was settled by Spanish immigrants drawn to the area by Spain's offer of inexpensive, tax-exempt land. Flourishing river trade characterized the town before the Civil War. Cape Girardeau experienced an industrial resurgence in the 1880s with the establishment of new railroad lines.

A look at area heritage and culture is available at the Cape River Heritage Museum, 538 Independence St.; phone (573) 334-0405. The city contains many scenic parks. Ivers Square overlooks the Mississippi, while Capaha Park boasts a notable rose garden. A scenic portion of I-55 runs 57 miles north from Cape Girardeau to St. Mary.

Cape Girardeau Convention and Visitors Bureau: 220 N. Fountain St., Cape Girardeau, MO 63701. **Phone:** (573) 335-1631 or (800) 777-0068. *(See ad this page.)*

Self-guiding tours: A pamphlet outlining a walking tour of historic downtown Cape Girardeau is available from the convention and visitors bureau.

CRISP MUSEUM is at 518 S. Fountain St. in the Holland School of Visual and Performing Arts on the River Campus of Southeast Missouri State University. The collections represent regional archeology, fine art and history. Of special interest is the museum's extensive collection of prehistoric Native American artifacts, including ceramic conch shell effigies, stone tools, and cups and bowls. The museum also contains an interactive Lewis and Clark exhibit, a life-size diorama of a Native American hut, exhibits about native wildlife and regional history, a river board display and a small art museum with changing exhibits.

Time: Allow 1 hour minimum. **Hours:** Tues.-Fri. 10-5, Sat.-Sun. 1-4, mid-Aug. to mid-May; Tues.-Fri. 10-4, Sat.-Sun. 1-4, rest of year. Also open first Fri. of the month 4-8, with extended hours on performance evenings. Closed major holidays. **Cost:** Free. **Phone:** (573) 651-2260.

AUBURN PLACE HOTEL & SUITES   573/651-4486
💎 **APPROVED** Hotel. **Address:** 3265 William St 63701

CANDLEWOOD SUITES   573/334-6868
💎 **THREE DIAMOND** Extended Stay Hotel. **Address:** 485 S Mount Auburn Rd 63703

DRURY PLAZA HOTEL CAPE GIRARDEAU CONFERENCE CENTER   573/334-7151
💎 **THREE DIAMOND** Hotel. **Address:** 3351 Percy Dr 63701

DRURY SUITES-CAPE GIRARDEAU   573/339-9500
THREE DIAMOND Hotel. **Address:** 3303 Campster Dr 63701

HOLIDAY INN EXPRESS HOTEL & SUITES   573/334-4491
THREE DIAMOND Hotel. **Address:** 3253 William St 63701

PEAR TREE INN BY DRURY CAPE GIRARDEAU WEST
                                     573/651-3000
APPROVED Hotel. **Address:** 103 Cape W Pkwy 63701

PEAR TREE INN CAPE GIRARDEAU MEDICAL CENTER
                                     573/334-3000
APPROVED Hotel. **Address:** 3248 William St 63701

WHERE TO EAT

BELLA ITALIA   573/332-7800
APPROVED Italian. Casual Dining. **Address:** 20 N
Spanish St 63701

BG'S OLDE TYME DELI & SALOON   573/335-8860
APPROVED American. Casual Dining. **Address:** 205
S Plaza Way 63703

CARTHAGE (D-2) pop. 14,378, elev. 1,008'

Virtually destroyed during the Civil War, Carthage was subsequently rebuilt largely with marble quarried from the surrounding area. The city's historic square contains several Victorian houses built with the local stone, which also was used in the construction of the Missouri State Capitol in Jefferson City.

Another marble building is the castle-like Jasper County Courthouse, 302 S. Main St., which bristles with turrets and a tall clock spire. Inside, the mural "Forged in Fire" by Lowell Davis depicts the history of Carthage from the time of its first settlers, the Osage Indians, through the Civil War to the present.

Myra Belle Shirley—later to become Belle Starr, infamous Confederate spy and outlaw—was in her teens when the war forced her family to move from the area. Other residents were Annie Baxter, the first woman in the United States to hold elected office; ragtime musician and composer James Scott; and zoologist and lecturer Marlin Perkins, who is honored with a bronze statue in Central Park.

During the Civil War the Battle of Carthage was fought July 5, 1861. Different stages of the battle are shown by markers that begin on Civil War Road, at the baseline 8 miles north of town, and extend to Carter Park on River Street in Carthage. The Battle of Carthage State Historic Site on Chestnut Street provides an interpretive shelter that depicts the history of the battle. For further information about the battle markers contact the convention and visitors bureau.

The Powers Museum at 1617 W. Oak St. recounts the history of Carthage and the surrounding region during the late 19th and early 20th centuries; phone (417) 237-0456. ArtCentral at 1110 E. 13th St. displays the works of local artists; phone (417) 358-4404.

Carthage Convention and Visitors Bureau: 402 S. Garrison Ave., Carthage, MO 64836. **Phone:** (417) 359-8181 or (866) 357-8687.

Self-guiding tours: A historical drive about 4 miles long is defined by green street markers posted throughout the business and residential districts, both of which are distinguished by Victorian architecture.

PRECIOUS MOMENTS CHAPEL AND GARDENS is at 4321 S. Chapel Rd. The chapel was conceived and designed by artist Samuel J. Butcher, who in the 1970s began drawing teardrop-eyed children called "Precious Moments" to convey messages to family and friends. He further developed his signature style by depicting biblical events, which are reflected in 30 stained-glass windows and 84 murals covering the chapel's walls and ceiling. The east gallery displays a large collection of porcelain figurines and some of Butcher's early artistic work. The grounds are adorned with flower gardens, fountains and statues of inspirational figures.

Time: Allow 1 hour minimum. **Hours:** Chapel open daily 9-5, visitor center daily 9-5:30, early Mar. through Dec. 31; chapel and visitor center daily 10-4, rest of year. **Cost:** Free. **Phone:** (800) 543-7975.

DAYS INN CARTHAGE   417/358-3900
APPROVED Hotel. **Address:** 1441 W Central Ave 64836

WHERE TO EAT

SIRLOIN STOCKADE   417/358-1765
APPROVED Steak. Quick Serve. **Address:** 1027 W Central Ave 64836

CHESTERFIELD (G-5) pop. 47,484, elev. 472'
- **Hotels p. 184 • Restaurants p. 185**
- **Hotels & Restaurants map & index p. 271**
- **Part of St. Louis area — see map p. 248**

FAUST COUNTY PARK is off I-64 exit 19B, then 1.1 mi. n.e. on Clarkson Rd./Olive Blvd. (Olive Street Rd.) to 15185 Olive Blvd. A popular spot for picnicking, the nearly 200-acre public park features a playground, loop trail, a landscaped pond, gardens and the preserved home of Missouri's second governor as well as Faust Historical Village, a re-created 19th-century town. The 1920s-era St. Louis Carousel, with some 60 hand-carved animals, is open to the public.

Hours: Park open daily dawn-30 minutes after dusk. Carousel Tues.-Sun. 10-4 (last ride at 3:50), Feb.-Dec. **Cost:** Free. Carousel $2 (single ride); $5 (three tickets); free (ages 0-1 with paid adult). Ages 0-4 must ride the carousel with an adult. **Phone:** (314) 615-8328, or (314) 615-8345 for the carousel.

Sophia M. Sachs Butterfly House is off I-64 exit 19B, then 1.3 mi. n.e. on Clarkson Rd./Olive Blvd.

(See map & index p. 271.)

(Olive Street Rd.) to 15193 Olive Blvd., within Faust County Park. Hundreds of tropical butterflies representing more than 60 species fly freely within this 8,000-square-foot glass conservatory. A chrysalis exhibit showcases the amazing process of metamorphosis. The exhibit hall features dozens of other living insect and arachnid displays.

Special events are held throughout the year, including Winter Jewels in December and Morpho Mardi Gras in February and March, when thousands of bright blue morpho butterflies, raised in Costa Rica, can be seen flying throughout the tropical conservatory and information about their native environment is shared. Step into the BOOTerfly House in October. **Time:** Allow 1 hour minimum. **Hours:** Tues.-Sun. 10-4, Feb.-Dec. Phone for schedule in Jan. Last ticket is sold 30 minutes before closing. **Cost:** $8; $6 (ages 3-12); $5 (ages 65+). **Phone:** (636) 530-0076.

COURTYARD BY MARRIOTT ST. LOUIS-CHESTERFIELD
636/778-3230 **25**
THREE DIAMOND SAVE Hotel. **Address:** 17369 Chesterfield Airport Rd 63005
AAA Benefit: Members save 5% or more!

DOUBLETREE BY HILTON HOTEL ST. LOUIS - CHESTERFIELD
636/532-5000 **29**
THREE DIAMOND
Hotel
DOUBLETREE BY HILTON
AAA Benefit: Members save up to 15%!

Address: 16625 Swingley Ridge Rd 63017 **Location:** I-64/US 40 exit 19A (Chesterfield Pkwy), just n, then just w. **Facility:** 224 units. 12 stories, interior corridors. **Amenities:** safes. **Pool:** outdoor, heated indoor. **Activities:** sauna, hot tub, tennis, health club, massage. **Guest Services:** valet laundry, area transportation.

DRURY PLAZA HOTEL-CHESTERFIELD 636/532-3300 **34**
THREE DIAMOND Hotel. **Address:** 355 Chesterfield Center E 63017

HAMPTON INN & SUITES BY HILTON-CHESTERFIELD
636/530-0770 **27**
THREE DIAMOND SAVE Hotel. **Address:** 5 McBride and Son Center Dr 63005
AAA Benefit: Members save up to 15%!

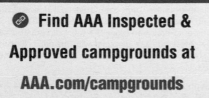
Find AAA Inspected & Approved campgrounds at AAA.com/campgrounds

HAMPTON INN BY HILTON ST. LOUIS/CHESTERFIELD
636/537-2500 **31**
THREE DIAMOND SAVE Hotel. **Address:** 16201 Swingley Ridge Rd 63017
AAA Benefit: Members save up to 15%!

HILTON GARDEN INN ST. LOUIS/CHESTERFIELD
636/532-9400 **28**
THREE DIAMOND
Hotel
Hilton Garden Inn
AAA Benefit: Members save up to 15%!

Address: 16631 Chesterfield Grove Rd 63005 **Location:** I-64/US 40 exit 17, just s on Boone's Crossing St, 1.2 mi e on Chesterfield Airport Rd, just s on Baxter Rd, then just e. **Facility:** 100 units. 4 stories, interior corridors. **Pool:** heated indoor. **Activities:** hot tub, exercise room. **Guest Services:** valet and coin laundry, area transportation.

HOLIDAY INN EXPRESS & SUITES ST. LOUIS-CHESTERFIELD
636/590-6240 **26**
THREE DIAMOND Hotel. **Address:** 11 Arnage Dr 63005

HOMEWOOD SUITES BY HILTON ST. LOUIS - CHESTERFIELD
636/530-0305 **30**
THREE DIAMOND SAVE Extended Stay Hotel. **Address:** 840 Chesterfield Pkwy W 63017
AAA Benefit: Members save up to 15%!

HYATT PLACE ST. LOUIS/CHESTERFIELD
636/536-6262 **35**
THREE DIAMOND
Hotel
HYATT PLACE
AAA Benefit: Members save up to 10%!

Address: 333 Chesterfield Center E 63017 **Location:** I-64/US 40 exit 19B (Clarkson Rd/Olive Blvd), just s on Clarkson Rd, then just w. **Facility:** 145 units. 8 stories, interior corridors. **Pool:** heated indoor. **Activities:** exercise room. **Guest Services:** valet laundry, area transportation. **Featured Amenity:** breakfast buffet.

SONESTA ES SUITES ST. LOUIS - CHESTERFIELD
636/537-1444 **33**
THREE DIAMOND Extended Stay Hotel. **Address:** 15431 Conway Rd 63017

SPRINGHILL SUITES BY MARRIOTT ST. LOUIS/CHESTERFIELD
636/519-7500 **32**
THREE DIAMOND SAVE Hotel. **Address:** 1065 Chesterfield Pkwy E 63017
AAA Benefit: Members save 5% or more!

TOWNEPLACE SUITES ST. LOUIS CHESTERFIELD
636/778-5100 **24**
THREE DIAMOND SAVE Extended Stay Hotel. **Address:** 748 Premium Way 63005
AAA Benefit: Members save 5% or more!

(See map & index p. 271.)

WHERE TO EAT

ANNIE GUNN'S   636/532-7684   26
THREE DIAMOND Regional American. Casual Dining. **Address:** 16806 Chesterfield Airport Rd 63005

CHARLIE GITTOS FROM THE HILL   636/536-2199   30
THREE DIAMOND Italian. Fine Dining. **Address:** 15525 Olive Blvd 63017

THE CHEESECAKE FACTORY   636/536-9662   33
THREE DIAMOND International. Casual Dining. **Address:** 2028 Chesterfield Mall 63017

EAST COAST PIZZA   636/536-7888   27
APPROVED Pizza. Quick Serve. **Address:** 17304 Chesterfield Airport Rd 63005

EDGEWILD RESTAURANT & WINERY   636/532-0550   32
APPROVED American. Casual Dining. **Address:** 550 Chesterfield Center 63017

EL MAGUEY   314/878-5988
APPROVED Mexican. Casual Dining. **Address:** 13377 Olive Blvd 63017

GIANFABIO'S ITALIAN CAFE   636/532-6686   29
APPROVED Italian. Casual Dining. **Address:** 127 Hilltown Village Center 63017

P.F. CHANG'S CHINA BISTRO   636/532-0215   34
THREE DIAMOND Chinese. Fine Dining. **Address:** 1295 Chesterfield Pkwy E 63017

TAJ PALACE   636/728-1000   28
APPROVED Indian. Casual Dining. **Address:** 92 THF Blvd 63005

YAYA'S EURO BISTRO   636/537-9991   31
THREE DIAMOND European. Casual Dining. **Address:** 15601 Olive Blvd 63017

CHILLICOTHE pop. 9,515

COMFORT INN & SUITES CHILLICOTHE   660/646-9900
THREE DIAMOND Hotel. **Address:** 250 Business Hwy 36 64601

FAIRFIELD BY MARRIOTT CHILLICOTHE   660/646-3100
THREE DIAMOND SAVE Hotel. **Address:** 220 W Business 36 64601

> **AAA Benefit:**
> Members save 5% or more!

WHERE TO EAT

WABASH BBQ   660/646-6777
APPROVED Barbecue. Casual Dining. **Address:** 1 Elm St 64601

CLAYTON pop. 15,939
- **Hotels & Restaurants map & index p. 274**
- **Part of St. Louis area — see map p. 248**

CLAYTON PLAZA HOTEL   314/726-5400   66
THREE DIAMOND Hotel. **Address:** 7750 Carondelet Ave 63105

HAMPTON INN & SUITES CLAYTON/BRENTWOOD-GALLERIA AREA   314/727-0700   63
THREE DIAMOND SAVE Hotel. **Address:** 216 N Meramec Ave 63105

> **AAA Benefit:**
> Members save up to 15%!

THE RITZ-CARLTON, ST. LOUIS   314/863-6300   65
FOUR DIAMOND SAVE Hotel. **Address:** 100 Carondelet Plaza 63105

> **AAA Benefit:**
> Unequaled service at special member savings!

SEVEN GABLES INN   314/863-8400   64
THREE DIAMOND Historic Boutique Hotel. **Address:** 26 N Meramec Ave 63105

SHERATON CLAYTON PLAZA HOTEL
314/863-0400   67

fyi
Hotel

SHERATON

> **AAA Benefit:**
> Members save 5% or more!

Under major renovation, call for details. **Last Designation:** Three Diamond. **Address:** 7730 Bonhomme Ave 63105 **Location:** I-64/US 40 exit 31B (Brentwood/Hanley Rd), 1.2 mi n on Hanley Rd, then just w. **Facility:** 259 units, some two bedrooms. 16 stories, interior corridors. **Parking:** on-site (fee) and valet. **Pool:** heated indoor. **Activities:** exercise room. **Guest Services:** valet and coin laundry, area transportation.

WHERE TO EAT

BARCELONA TAPAS RESTAURANT   314/863-9909   73
APPROVED Spanish Small Plates. Casual Dining. **Address:** 34 N Central Ave 63105

CAFÉ NAPOLI   314/863-5731   77
APPROVED Italian. Casual Dining. **Address:** 7754 Forsyth Blvd 63105

THE CROSSING   314/721-7375   75
THREE DIAMOND New American. Fine Dining. **Address:** 7823 Forsyth Blvd 63105

DOMINIC'S TRATTORIA   314/863-4567   80
THREE DIAMOND Italian. Casual Dining. **Address:** 200 S Brentwood Blvd 63105

THE GRILL   314/863-6300   79
FOUR DIAMOND American. Fine Dining. **Address:** 100 Carondelet Plaza 63105

MORTON'S THE STEAKHOUSE   314/725-4008   81
THREE DIAMOND Steak. Fine Dining. **Address:** 7822 Bonhomme Ave 63105

PASTARIA   314/862-6603   76
APPROVED New Italian Pizza. Casual Dining. **Address:** 7734 Forsyth Blvd 63105

RUTH'S CHRIS STEAK HOUSE   314/783-9900   74
THREE DIAMOND Steak. Fine Dining. **Address:** 1 N Brentwood Blvd, Suite 150 63105

SARDELLA   314/773-7755   78
THREE DIAMOND New Italian. Casual Dining. **Address:** 7734 Forsyth Blvd 63105

CLINTON pop. 9,008

HAMPTON INN BY HILTON   660/885-4488
THREE DIAMOND SAVE Hotel. **Ad-dress:** 900 Kansas Ave 64735

AAA Benefit: Members save up to 15%!

PARKFIELD INN   660/890-6188
APPROVED Hotel. **Address:** 506 Kansas Ave 64735

WHERE TO EAT

EL CAMINO REAL   660/885-9992
APPROVED Mexican. Casual Dining. **Address:** 417 Kansas Ave 64735

COLUMBIA (B-4) pop. 108,500, elev. 738'
• Restaurants p. 188

Columbia began in 1819 as Smithton; it was renamed and made the seat of Boone County in 1821. After Boone's Lick Trail was rerouted south through Columbia, the town became a prosperous outfitting station for westbound emigrants, some of whom chose to remain.

Columbia's residents responded to the competition to secure the appointment for a state university with the fervor of a political campaign. As a result of door-to-door canvassing and torchlight parades, a subscription of $117,000 was raised by 900 patrons, some of whom sold their houses and farms to meet their pledges. The University of Missouri, the first public university west of the Mississippi River, opened its doors in 1839.

MU is Missouri's national flagship university, with more than 280 degree programs and the largest library collection in the state. Its school of journalism, founded in 1908, is distinguished as the world's first. As one of only six universities in the country with medicine, veterinary medicine and law on one campus, MU also plays a significant role in professional education.

"Mizzou" is a member of the Southeastern Conference and features the state's only Division 1-A athletic program for football. For sports event schedules and ticket information phone (800) 228-7297.

Columbia College and Stephens College confirm Columbia's identity as a college town, though the insurance industry and medical services reinforce its economic base. The Davis Art Gallery at Stephens College mounts exhibits throughout the year; phone (573) 876-7233.

Columbia's downtown area, known as The District, offers a vibrant mix of shopping, dining and gallery-hopping, while the North Village Arts District is an enclave of artists, artisans, musicians and media types, with nightlife venues and a great market. Columbia also hosts a number of annual festivals, including the popular True/False Film Festival.

The 8.9-mile M-K-T Trail connects downtown Columbia to the 240-mile Katy Trail, a rails-to-trails conversion that crosses the state. At the Stadium Boulevard trailhead is the Martin Luther King Jr. Memorial Garden. Trail maps are available from the convention and visitors bureau.

Columbia Convention & Visitors Bureau: 300 S. Providence Rd., Columbia, MO 65203. **Phone:** (573) 875-1231.

Self-guiding tours: Brochures outlining a driving tour of publicly accessible art are offered by the convention and visitors bureau.

MASONIC MUSEUM AND LIBRARY is off US 63 exit Prathersville Rd. (4 mi. n. from jct. I-70 and US 63), then .3 mi. n. to 6033 Masonic Dr. and approximately 100 yards beyond the first Masonic complex parking lot. The museum's five themed galleries—Pathmakers and Patriots, Living Well, Generosity, Leadership and Everyman, the latter a space for rotating exhibits—present the memorabilia of and impart the significant contributions made by such famous Masons as explorers William Clark and Meriwether Lewis; President Harry S. Truman, who once served as Grand Master of Missouri Masons; and Laura Ingalls Wilder, a member of the Order of the Eastern Star, an organization for relatives of Masons.

Displayed are a medallion from Truman's Masonic collared apron, his gavel and pieces donated by local Masons. Exhibits outline the history of Eastern Star and Masonic chapters across the country. **Time:** Allow 30 minutes minimum. **Hours:** Mon.-Fri. 8:30-5. Closed major holidays. **Cost:** Free. **Phone:** (573) 814-4663 or (800) 434-9804.

SHELTER INSURANCE GARDENS is off I-70 exit 124, s. on Stadium Blvd., then e. to 1817 W. Broadway St., behind the insurance company's headquarters. Tucked behind stone and wrought-iron gates at the home office complex of Shelter Insurance Companies are 5 acres planted with more than 300 varieties of native trees and shrubs, along with more than 15,000 annuals and perennials. Rose, shade, rock, conifer and desert gardens as well as a garden for the blind are all tagged for identification.

The site is also graced by a gazebo, a waterfall, sundial, pools and a memorial to Vietnam veterans. A free summer concert series is presented Sunday evenings, June through July. **Time:** Allow 30 minutes minimum. **Hours:** Daily 8 a.m.-dusk. **Cost:** Free. **Phone:** (573) 445-8441.

UNIVERSITY OF MISSOURI-COLUMBIA is on Eighth St., 3 blks. s. of Broadway St. "Mizzou," the oldest state university west of the Mississippi, has 30,000 students and 1,700 faculty and staff members. The 1,358-acre campus features a number of historic buildings. Six Ionic columns on Francis Quadrangle are all that remains of Academic Hall, destroyed by fire in 1892. Thomas Jefferson's original tombstone is on the quadrangle. With more than 5,000 trees and 650 varieties of plants, the MU grounds have been officially designated as a botanic garden.

In the lobby of the Electrical Engineering Building on Sixth Street is Thomas Edison's restored dynamo, used on the campus for the first demonstration of incandescent lighting west of the Mississippi.

The Geology Building has more than 100,000 fossil and rock specimens, many displayed in its ground and first-floor corridors. A collection of mounted waterfowl is exhibited in the corridors of Lefevre Hall on University Avenue.

Hours: Campus walking tours are given Mon.-Fri. during the school year and are arranged on an individual basis. Two weeks' advance notice is recommended. **Cost:** Free. **Phone:** (573) 882-2456 for Jesse Hall, or (800) 856-2181 for the Office of Visitor Relations.

George Caleb Bingham Gallery is on the University of Missouri–Columbia campus in room A125 of the Fine Arts Building at Hitt St. and University Ave. Changing exhibits of artwork by faculty and students as well as artists of national and international stature are mounted. **Hours:** Mon.-Fri. 7:30-4, mid-May to mid-Aug.; Mon.-Thurs. 8-5, Fri. 8-4, rest of year. Closed campus holidays and between semesters. **Cost:** Free. **Phone:** (573) 882-3555.

Museum of Art and Archaeology is on the University of Missouri–Columbia campus in the Mizzou North building. The museum contains a collection of ancient Egyptian, Greek and Roman art; American artworks; and European paintings, drawings, prints and sculpture from the 15th century to the present. Other exhibits feature Asian, African and pre-Columbian art. The Cast Gallery displays plaster casts of Greek and Roman sculptures. **Hours:** Tues.-Fri. 9-4, Sat.-Sun. noon-4. Closed university holidays. **Cost:** Free. **Phone:** (573) 882-3591.

State Historical Society of Missouri is on the University of Missouri–Columbia campus on the ground floor of Ellis Library at Hitt St. and Lowry Mall. Missouri newspapers, books and publications about state history and genealogy are part of an extensive collection that includes editorial cartoons and artworks by John J. Audubon, Thomas Hart Benton, George Caleb Bingham, Karl Bodmer and other Missouri artists. Tours are given by appointment. **Hours:** Tues.-Fri. 8-4:45, Sat. 8-3:30. Closed major holidays. **Cost:** Free. **Phone:** (573) 882-7083 Mon.-Fri., or (573) 882-1187 on Sat.

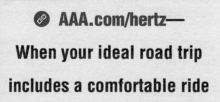

BEST WESTERN PLUS - COLUMBIA INN   573/397-6471

🔷 APPROVED

Hotel

Best Western PLUS.

AAA Benefit: Members save up to 15% and earn bonus points!

Address: 2904 Clark Ln 65202 **Location:** I-70 exit 128A, just nw. **Facility:** 78 units. 3 stories, interior corridors. **Pool:** heated indoor. **Activities:** hot tub, exercise room. **Guest Services:** complimentary and valet laundry.

THE BROADWAY COLUMBIA - A DOUBLETREE BY HILTON HOTEL   573/875-7000
🔷 THREE DIAMOND SAVE Hotel. **Address:** 1111 E Broadway 65201   **AAA Benefit:** Members save up to 15%!

CANDLEWOOD SUITES HWY 63 & I-70   573/256-0200
🔷 THREE DIAMOND Extended Stay Hotel. **Address:** 1400 Creekwood Pkwy 65202

COUNTRY INN & SUITES BY RADISSON   573/445-8585
🔷 THREE DIAMOND Hotel. **Address:** 817 N Keene St 65201

COURTYARD BY MARRIOTT-COLUMBIA   573/443-8000
🔷 THREE DIAMOND SAVE Hotel. **Address:** 3301 Lemone Industrial Blvd 65201   **AAA Benefit:** Members save 5% or more!

DRURY INN & SUITES COLUMBIA STADIUM BOULEVARD   573/445-1800
🔷 THREE DIAMOND Hotel. **Address:** 1000 Knipp St 65203

DRURY PLAZA HOTEL COLUMBIA EAST   573/441-0090
🔷 THREE DIAMOND Hotel. **Address:** 3100 I-70 Dr SE 65201

HAMPTON INN & SUITES BY HILTON COLUMBIA AT THE UNIVERSITY OF MISSOURI   573/214-2222
🔷 THREE DIAMOND SAVE Hotel. **Address:** 1225 Fellows Pl 65201   **AAA Benefit:** Members save up to 15%!

HAMPTON INN BY HILTON   573/886-9392
🔷 THREE DIAMOND SAVE Hotel. **Address:** 3410 Clark Ln 65202   **AAA Benefit:** Members save up to 15%!

HOLIDAY INN COLUMBIA-EAST   573/474-4444
🔷 THREE DIAMOND Hotel. **Address:** 915 Port Way 65201

RAMADA   573/443-4141
🔷 APPROVED Hotel. **Address:** 901 Conley Rd 65201

RESIDENCE INN BY MARRIOTT   573/442-5601
🔷 THREE DIAMOND SAVE Extended Stay Hotel. **Address:** 1100 Woodland Springs Ct 65202   **AAA Benefit:** Members save 5% or more!

SPRINGHILL SUITES BY MARRIOTT COLUMBIA
573/554-9024

THREE DIAMOND SAVE Extended Stay Contemporary Hotel. **Address:** 3415 Clark Ln 65202

AAA Benefit: Members save 5% or more!

STONEY CREEK HOTEL & CONFERENCE CENTER
573/442-6400

APPROVED Hotel. **Address:** 2601 S Providence Rd 65203

THE TIGER HOTEL 573/875-8888

THREE DIAMOND

Historic Boutique Hotel

Address: 23 S 8th St 65201 **Location:** Jct Cherry St. **Facility:** Luxurious modern day styling plays with hints of 1930s history at this wonderfully redone hotel. Take in the original flooring and gilded columns in the lobby on your way up to the sleek modern rooms. 62 units. 9 stories, interior corridors. **Parking:** valet and street only. **Amenities:** safes. **Dining:** Glenn's Cafe, see separate listing, nightclub, entertainment. **Activities:** exercise room. **Guest Services:** valet laundry.

SAVE [icons] BIZ

HS [icons]

TOWNEPLACE SUITES BY MARRIOTT 573/817-0012

THREE DIAMOND

TOWNEPLACE —SUITES— MARRIOTT

Extended Stay Hotel

AAA Benefit: Members save 5% or more!

Address: 4400 Nocona Pkwy 65201 **Location:** US 63 exit Discovery Pkwy, 0.4 mi sw, then 0.4 mi n. **Facility:** 96 units, some efficiencies and kitchens. 4 stories, interior corridors. **Pool:** heated outdoor. **Activities:** exercise room. **Guest Services:** valet and coin laundry, area transportation.

SAVE [icons] CALL [icons] / SOME UNITS [icons] HS

WINGATE BY WYNDHAM COLUMBIA 573/817-0500
THREE DIAMOND Hotel. **Address:** 3101 Wingate Ct 65201

WHERE TO EAT

44 STONE PUBLIC HOUSE 573/443-2726
APPROVED Continental. Gastropub. **Address:** 3910 Peachtree Dr 65203

ADDISON'S 573/256-1995
APPROVED American. Casual Dining. **Address:** 709 Cherry St 65201

BARRED OWL BUTCHER & TABLE 573/442-9323
THREE DIAMOND New American. Casual Dining. **Address:** 47 E Broadway 65203

FLAT BRANCH PUB & BREWING 573/499-0400
APPROVED American. Casual Dining. **Address:** 115 S Fifth St 65201

🔗 **What's for dinner?**

AAA.com/travelguides/restaurants

FLYOVER 573/825-6036
THREE DIAMOND American. Casual Dining. **Address:** 212 E Green Meadows 65205

GLENN'S CAFE 573/447-7100
APPROVED Southern Creole. Casual Dining. **Address:** 29 S 8th St 65201

GRAND CRU 573/443-2600
APPROVED American. Casual Dining. **Address:** 2600 S Providence Rd 65203

JAZZ A LOUISIANA KITCHEN 573/443-5299
APPROVED Cajun. Casual Dining. **Address:** 217 N Stadium Blvd, Suite 100 65203

LE BAO ASIAN EATERY 573/443-2867
APPROVED Asian. Quick Serve. **Address:** 1009 Park Ave 65201

MURRY'S 573/442-4969
APPROVED American. Casual Dining. **Address:** 3107 Green Meadows Way 65203

THE PASTA FACTORY 573/449-3948
APPROVED Italian. Casual Dining. **Address:** 3103 W Broadway, Suite 109 65201

SOPHIA'S 573/874-8009
THREE DIAMOND Mediterranean. Casual Dining. **Address:** 3915 S Providence Rd 65203

TELLERS GALLERY AND BAR 573/441-8355
APPROVED American. Casual Dining. **Address:** 820 E Broadway St 65201

CREVE COEUR pop. 17,833

- **Hotels & Restaurants map & index p. 274**
- **Part of St. Louis area — see map p. 248**

COURTYARD BY MARRIOTT-CREVE COEUR
314/993-0515 **59**

THREE DIAMOND SAVE Hotel. **Address:** 828 N New Ballas Rd 63146

AAA Benefit: Members save 5% or more!

DRURY INN & SUITES-CREVE COEUR 314/989-1100 **60**
THREE DIAMOND Hotel. **Address:** 11980 Olive Blvd 63141

WHERE TO EAT

BRISTOL BAR & SEAFOOD GRILL 314/567-0272 **70**
THREE DIAMOND Seafood. Casual Dining. **Address:** 11801 Olive Blvd 63141

HOULIHAN'S 314/469-1167 **66**
THREE DIAMOND American. Casual Dining. **Address:** 1085 N Mason Rd 63141

IL BEL LAGO 314/994-1080 **69**
THREE DIAMOND Italian. Fine Dining. **Address:** 11631 Olive Blvd 63141

LA BONNE BOUCHÉE 314/576-6606 **68**
APPROVED French. Casual Dining. **Address:** 12344 Olive Blvd 63141

NUDO HOUSE STL 314/274-8046 **67**
APPROVED Asian Noodles. Quick Serve. **Address:** 11423 Olive Blvd 63141

DEFIANCE (G-4) pop. 155, elev. 469'
• Part of St. Louis area — see map p. 248

Daniel Boone, 69 years old and heavily in debt, settled here in 1799 with his wife and some of their children. Defective titles had caused the loss of his land in Kentucky; good reports from one of his sons as well as promises of land grants and honors from the Spanish brought him to Defiance.

Boone received a grant of 845 acres and served 1800-04 as the *syndic* (judge) of the Femme Osage District, a position that gave him control of all civil and military matters. The great explorer died in Defiance a number of years after being forced to sell his land to satisfy his creditors in Kentucky.

Defiance serves as an access point to the Katy Trail, known for its scenery and historic legacy. The trail, which runs almost parallel to the Missouri River, is enjoyed by hikers and bicyclists alike.

THE HISTORIC DANIEL BOONE HOME AT LINDENWOOD PARK is 5 mi. w. on SR F. The frontiersman supervised construction of this four-story, Georgian-style structure, which took 7 years to build, and lived in it until his death in 1820. The house contains many Boone family belongings. More than a dozen 19th-century structures on the grounds, including a gristmill, chapel and schoolhouse, were relocated to create Boonesville Village and restored to represent life in Boone's day. Several of them can be visited. Special events include living history days and Candlelight Christmas Tours, which are offered the first two Friday and Saturday nights in December.

Hours: Property open Mon.-Sat. 8:30-5, Sun. 11:30-5. From March through mid-Dec. guided tours of the Boone home and historic buildings are given Mon.-Sat. on the hour beginning at 9, Sun. beginning at noon. Tours of the village grounds begin Mon.-Sat. at 9, 11, 1 and 3, Sun. at 1 and 3. Tours offered Sat.-Sun. only, rest of year. Last home tour begins 1 hour before closing. Phone ahead to confirm schedule. **Cost:** Grounds free. Guided home and village tour $8; $6 (ages 60+); $5 (ages 5-12); free (ages 0-4 and active duty and retired military with ID). Rates may vary on special event days. **Phone:** (636) 798-2005.

EARTH CITY
• Hotels & Restaurants map & index p. 274
• Part of St. Louis area — see map p. 248

CANDLEWOOD SUITES ST. LOUIS   314/770-2744 (15)
APPROVED   Extended Stay Hotel. **Address:** 3250 Rider Tr S 63045

RESIDENCE INN BY MARRIOTT ST. LOUIS AIRPORT/EARTH CITY   314/209-0995 (14)
THREE DIAMOND SAVE Extended Stay Hotel. **Address:** 3290 Rider Tr S 63045

| AAA Benefit: |
| Members save 5% or more! |

EDMUNDSON pop. 834
• Hotels & Restaurants map & index p. 274
• Part of St. Louis area — see map p. 248

DRURY INN & SUITES ST. LOUIS AIRPORT   314/423-7700 (19)
THREE DIAMOND Hotel. **Address:** 10490 Natural Bridge Rd 63134

MARRIOTT-ST. LOUIS AIRPORT   314/423-9700 (18)
THREE DIAMOND
Hotel

AAA Benefit: Members save 5% or more!

Address: 10700 Pear Tree Ln 63134 **Location:** I-70 exit 236 (Lambert Airport), just s. **Facility:** 600 units. 8-9 stories, interior corridors. **Parking:** on site (fee). **Amenities:** *Some:* safes. **Pool:** outdoor, heated outdoor, heated indoor. **Activities:** hot tub, exercise room. **Guest Services:** valet and coin laundry, boarding pass kiosk.

WHERE TO EAT

LOMBARDO'S RESTAURANT   314/429-5151 (43)
THREE DIAMOND Italian. Casual Dining. **Address:** 10488 Natural Bridge Rd 63134

EMINENCE pop. 600

ECHO BLUFF STATE PARK   573/858-3059
THREE DIAMOND Hotel. **Address:** 34489 Echo Bluff Dr 65466

EUREKA (H-5) pop. 10,189, elev. 465'
• Hotels p. 190 • Restaurants p. 190
• Hotels & Restaurants map & index p. 271
• Part of St. Louis area — see map p. 248

Eureka began as a railroad construction camp in 1853. The triumphant name was chosen by a surveyor upon discovering a route through the valley that would eliminate the difficult cutting and grading required by the original route. After the railroad was finished, a town was laid out, and the name remained.

Eureka Chamber of Commerce: 22 Dreyer Ave., Eureka, MO 63025. **Phone:** (636) 938-6062.

GEM SAVE **SIX FLAGS ST. LOUIS,** off I-44 at 4900 Six Flags Rd., has more than 100 rides, shows and attractions. The park's lineup of roller coasters includes American Thunder, an eight-story-tall wooden coaster; Boomerang; The Boss; Mr. Freeze: Reverse Blast; Batman: The Ride; Screamin' Eagle; Ninja; Pandemonium; and the River King Mine Train. Other thrill rides include the Superman: Tower of Power free-fall ride and Skyscreamer, a 236-foot-tall swing ride. In 2019, Six Flags St. Louis debuted SUPERGIRL. Drawing on Supergirl's powers of stamina and strength, thrill seekers spin and tilt, all while suspended from the whirling wheel of justice. Riders are raised up by a giant arm, feet dangling, and then launched into a high-speed spin.

(See map & index p. 271.)

Just for kids, Bugs Bunny National Park offers eight rides, a tree house play structure and an interactive fountain. Visitors also can experience Thunder River, a white-water raft ride; Colossus, an 18-story Ferris wheel; Xcalibur's spinning wheel and the family-friendly Tsunami Soaker ride, featuring nine spinning boats equipped with huge water guns.

Hurricane Harbor, a 12-acre tropical-themed water park that is free with park admission, has a wave pool, a lazy river, a five-story tree house, speed and tube slides, the funnel-shaped Tornado ride and the Bonzai Pipeline body slide, which features Skybox launching capsules.

Holiday in the Park features rides, treats and holiday season entertainment for the whole family. On select days November through December, enjoy a winter wonderland as the park is illuminated by thousands of festive lights. Carolers sing yuletide favorites, and park guests delight in a meet-and-greet with Santa Claus and *Looney Tunes* characters.

Hours: Park open late Mar. through Dec.; days and hours vary. Hurricane Harbor open Memorial Day weekend-Labor Day; days and hours vary. Phone ahead to confirm schedule. **Cost:** (Includes Hurricane Harbor) $71.99; $54.99 (children under 48 inches tall); free (ages 0-2). Prices may vary; phone ahead. AAA members save on select services. See guest relations for details. **Parking:** $25. **Phone:** (636) 938-5300.

HOLIDAY INN AT SIX FLAGS 636/938-6661 ㊷
THREE DIAMOND Hotel. **Address:** 4901 Six Flags Rd 63025

WHERE TO EAT

POOR RICHARD'S 636/938-4666 ㊸
APPROVED American. Casual Dining. **Address:** 108A Hilltop Village Center 63025

EXCELSIOR SPRINGS (F-3) pop. 11,084, elev. 939'

• Part of Kansas City area — see map p. 199

The presence of saline, soda, calcium and iron manganese mineral waters made Excelsior Springs a well-known spa. A visitor center is in The Hall of Waters building, 201 E. Broadway St.

Excelsior Springs Area Chamber of Commerce: 461 S. Thompson Ave., P.O. Box 632, Excelsior Springs, MO 64024. **Phone:** (816) 630-6161.

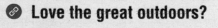

THE ELMS HOTEL & SPA 816/630-5500
THREE DIAMOND
Historic Hotel

DESTINATION HOTELS
AAA Benefit: Members save up to 10%!

Address: 401 Regent St 64024 **Location:** Off SR 10; at Elms Blvd. **Facility:** On the National Register of Historic Places, this beautiful hotel features a world-class spa, elaborate grounds and a piano-shaped pool. Rooms are embellished with soft colors and quality materials. 153 units. 5 stories, interior corridors. **Parking:** on-site and valet. **Terms:** check-in 4 pm. **Amenities:** safes. **Pool:** heated outdoor, heated indoor. **Activities:** sauna, hot tub, steamroom, bicycles, lawn sports, exercise room, spa. **Guest Services:** area transportation.

SAVE BIZ / SOME UNITS

WHERE TO EAT

WILLOW SPRING MERCANTILE 816/630-7467
APPROVED Sandwiches. Casual Dining. **Address:** 249 E Broadway St 64024

FARMINGTON pop. 16,240, elev. 915'

CROWN POINTE LODGE, BW SIGNATURE COLLECTION 573/701-9747
APPROVED SAVE Hotel. **Address:** 4245 Hunt Rd 63640

AAA Benefit: Members save up to 15% and earn bonus points!

WHERE TO EAT

SPOKES PUB & GRILL 573/756-6220
APPROVED American. Casual Dining. **Address:** 1627 W Columbia St 63640

FENTON pop. 4,022

• **Hotels & Restaurants map & index p. 274**
• **Part of St. Louis area — see map p. 248**

DRURY INN & SUITES-FENTON 636/343-7822 (85)
THREE DIAMOND Hotel. **Address:** 1088 S Highway Dr 63026

HOLIDAY INN EXPRESS HOTEL & SUITES 636/349-4444 (88)
APPROVED Hotel. **Address:** 1848 Bowles Ave 63026

PEAR TREE INN BY DRURY-FENTON 636/343-8820 (86)
APPROVED Hotel. **Address:** 1100 S Highway Dr 63026

TOWNEPLACE SUITES BY MARRIOTT 636/305-7000 (87)
APPROVED SAVE Extended Stay Hotel. **Address:** 1662 Fenton Business Park Ct 63026

AAA Benefit: Members save 5% or more!

WHERE TO EAT

BANDANA'S BAR-B-Q 636/305-8855
APPROVED Barbecue. Casual Dining. **Address:** 1160 S Highway Dr 63026

(See map & index p. 274.)

POOR RICHARD'S   636/349-3438 106
▼▼ APPROVED Wings Burgers. Casual Dining. **Address:**
960 Brookwood Center 63026

FESTUS pop. 11,602

COMFORT INN FESTUS   636/937-2888
▼▼ APPROVED Hotel. **Address:** 1303 Veterans Blvd
63028

HOLIDAY INN EXPRESS & SUITES-FESTUS   636/937-7100
▼▼ THREE DIAMOND Hotel. **Address:** 1802 Gamel Cemetery Rd
63028

LA QUINTA INN & SUITES   636/638-1800
▼▼ THREE DIAMOND Hotel. **Address:** 1001 Veterans Blvd
63028

QUALITY INN   636/933-1999
▼▼ THREE DIAMOND Hotel. **Address:** 1200 W Gannon Dr
63028

WHERE TO EAT

MAIN & MILL BREWING COMPANY   636/543-3031
▼▼ APPROVED American. Casual Dining. **Address:** 240
E Main St 63028

FORT LEONARD WOOD (D-4)

Fort Leonard Wood, in the Ozark foothills 2 miles
south of I-44 from the Fort Leonard Wood exit, is a
major U.S. Army training center and headquarters of
the Army Engineer, Military Police and Chemical
Corp. schools. Established in 1940, the fort is
named for the general who helped organize the 1st
U.S. Cavalry, The Rough Riders.

JOHN B. MAHAFFEY MUSEUM COMPLEX is at
495 South Dakota Ave. The complex contains four
museums: The U.S. Army Chemical Corps Museum,
the U.S. Army Engineer Museum, the U.S. Army
Military Police Corps Museum and the Fort Leonard
Wood Museum. Walk-through dioramas and artifacts from each corps are featured. The Fort
Leonard Wood Museum is a group of World War
II-era buildings with items portraying daily military
life at the fort. **Time:** Allow 1 hour minimum. **Hours:**
Mon.-Fri. 8-4, Sat. 10-4. Closed federal holidays.
Fort Leonard Wood may be closed due to bad
weather. **Cost:** Free. **Phone:** (573) 596-0604.

FRONTENAC pop. 3,482
• Hotels & Restaurants map & index p. 274
• Part of St. Louis area — see map p. 248

HILTON ST. LOUIS FRONTENAC   314/993-1100 70
▼▼ THREE DIAMOND (SAVE) Hotel. Ad-   **AAA Benefit:**
dress: 1335 S Lindbergh Blvd 63131   Members save up to
                                      15%!

WHERE TO EAT

BRIO TUSCAN GRILLE   314/432-4410 85
▼▼ THREE DIAMOND Italian. Fine Dining. **Address:** 1601 S
Lindbergh Blvd 63131

CANYON CAFE   314/872-3443 86
▼▼ APPROVED Southwestern. Casual Dining. **Address:**
1707 S Lindbergh Blvd, Suite 2 63131

FLEMING'S PRIME STEAKHOUSE & WINE BAR
                                      314/567-7610 87
▼▼ THREE DIAMOND Steak. Fine Dining. **Address:** 1855 S
Lindbergh Blvd 63131

KREIS' STEAKHOUSE & BAR   314/993-0735 84
▼▼ THREE DIAMOND **AAA Inspector Notes:** Classic. A time-
                    less dining institution in the St. Louis
   Steak   area since the 1930s, this restaurant ex-
   Fine Dining udes a traditional English hunt-club at-
   $13-$68   mosphere with a lively business crowd
                    on weeknights. Known for its prime rib,
steak and fresh seafood, this place also prepares a few German
dishes. **Features:** full bar. **Reservations:** suggested. **Address:**
535 S Lindbergh Blvd 63131 **Location:** I-64/US 40 exit 28B (N
Lindbergh Blvd), 0.8 mi n. D

FULTON (B-4) pop. 12,790, elev. 813'
• Hotels p. 192 • Restaurants p. 192

Fulton, named for steamboat inventor Robert
Fulton, also was the birthplace of musician, poet,
novelist and reviewer Henry Bellamann, who published three books of poetry and seven novels over
more than 2 decades. Bellamann's best-known
novel was "Kings Row"; the 1942 film adaptation of
life in a small Midwestern town at the turn of the
20th century starred Ann Sheridan and Ronald
Reagan. It was filmed on location, and downtown
Fulton's brick-paved streets and historic architecture
have been carefully preserved in the years since.

**Callaway Chamber of Commerce & Visitor's
Center:** 510 Market St., Fulton, MO 65251. **Phone:**
(573) 642-3055.

AUTO WORLD MUSEUM is just off US 54 (exit SR
HH) to 200 Peacock Dr., following signs. Approximately 80 vehicles are displayed, arranged against
backdrops of building facades and enlarged
photos—such as a drive-in movie theater showing a
John Wayne film—to provide historical context.
Background information includes production details
and history on each vehicle. Among the rare cars
are a 1909 Ford Model T Touring vehicle and examples from the 1920s and '30s (including a
Marmon 16), along with more recognizable icons (a
'57 T-Bird, a '66 Mustang, a VW bug and a 1982 De-
Lorean). The collection also includes vintage fire
trucks.

Time: Allow 1 hour minimum. **Hours:** Daily 9-5,
Apr.-Dec.; other times by appointment. **Cost:** $8; $7
(ages 50+ and military with ID); $4 (ages 5-11).
Phone: (573) 642-2080.

▼▼ GEM **NATIONAL CHURCHILL MUSEUM** is at jct.
Westminster Ave. and W. 7th St. The Westminster College Gymnasium was the site of Churchill's prophetic "Iron Curtain" speech on March 5,

1946. To commemorate that visit, the college acquired London's historic Church of St. Mary the Virgin, Aldermanbury and reassembled it on the campus as a memorial to his speech and life.

The church destroyed by the Great Fire in 1666 was rebuilt by Sir Christopher Wren. Damaged again in the London Blitz of 1940, the ruins were shipped to Fulton and restored to their original glory. Beneath this magnificent building sits the Churchill Museum, recognized by Congress as America's "National Churchill Museum," replete with interactive displays, artifacts, films and exhibits that bring Churchill and his times to life.

Additionally, eight pieces of the Berlin Wall have been relocated and erected on the grounds, and in 2011 the evocative "Iron Curtain" sculpture by Don Wiegand was installed in front of the museum.

Time: Allow 1 hour minimum. **Hours:** Daily 10-4:30. Closed Jan. 1, Thanksgiving and Christmas. **Cost:** $10; $9 (ages 65+ and active duty military with ID); $6.50 (ages 12-18 and college students with ID); free (ages 0-11). **Phone:** (573) 592-5369.

BAYMONT INN & SUITES   573/642-2600
APPROVED   Hotel. **Address:** 2205 Cardinal Dr 65251

LOGANBERRY INN BED & BREAKFAST   573/642-9229
THREE DIAMOND   Bed & Breakfast. **Address:** 310 W 7th St 65251

WHERE TO EAT

BEKS   573/592-7117
APPROVED   American. Casual Dining. **Address:** 511 Court St 65251

GEORGE WASHINGTON CARVER NATIONAL MONUMENT (D-1)

George Washington Carver National Monument is southeast of Joplin and 2.5 miles southwest of Diamond on SR V. The 240-acre park preserves the birthplace of the noted scientist. Carver developed more than 300 byproducts from the peanut and more than 100 from the sweet potato, as well as new uses for cotton, soybeans, cowpeas and other crops.

Museum exhibits and a 28-minute film in the visitor center pertain to Carver's life and work in the field of botany and his career as a teacher of scientific agriculture. The Discovery Center gives visitors the chance to try hands-on experiments and learn more about Carver's endeavors and achievements.

A self-guiding .7-mile trail winds through woods and fields Carver walked as a boy. Sites along the trail include the birthplace site, the "Boy Carver" statue by Robert Amendola and the Carver family cemetery. Ranger-led tours are offered daily at 10 and 2. Allow 1 hour minimum. Daily 9-5; closed Jan. 1, Thanksgiving and Christmas. Free. Phone (417) 325-4151.

GOLDEN (E-2) pop. 280, elev. 1,155'

GOLDEN PIONEER MUSEUM is at SR 86 and SR J at the northern edge of town. Don't let the faded yellow metal exterior fool you; this museum contains an extensive and impressive collection of artifacts. Neatly displayed in glass cases are pre-Columbian, Aztec and Oaxacan black pottery, razor-sharp obsidian knives, axes, arrowheads, miniature clay figures and beautiful pieces of quartz (including a cluster that weighs more than 1,250 lbs.).

Other objects are giant mastodon teeth and bones, pocket watches in mint condition, antique Kewpie dolls and a coin collection featuring the first U.S. silver dollar and some 3-cent nickels. One highlight is a beautiful turquoise carving, said to be the world's largest.

Historical exhibits pay tribute to the Native Americans who died during the 1837 Trail of Tears forced westward migration. The museum also has plenty of 20th-century Americana—Elvis displays, a huge collection of 1960s lunch boxes, baseball cards, and hundreds of antique glass plates and pitchers in vivid colors. **Time:** Allow 2 hours minimum. **Hours:** Tues.-Sat. 10:30-4:30, mid-Apr. through Oct. 31. **Cost:** Free. **Phone:** (417) 271-3300.

GRANDVIEW pop. 24,475, elev. 1,070'
• **Hotels & Restaurants map & index p. 218**
• **Part of Kansas City area — see map p. 199**

HOLIDAY INN EXPRESS HOTEL & SUITES
                       816/268-5858 (65)

THREE DIAMOND
Hotel

Address: 12801 S Hwy 71 64030 **Location:** I-49 exit 179, on Outer Rd, east side. **Facility:** 72 units. 4 stories, interior corridors. **Pool:** heated indoor. **Activities:** hot tub, exercise room. **Guest Services:** coin laundry. **Featured Amenity:** breakfast buffet.

SAVE CALL ⬅ ➡ ✦ BIZ HS
🛜 ✕ 🔌 📺 📱

HANNIBAL (B-4) pop. 17,916, elev. 470'
• **Restaurants p. 194**

Samuel Clemens (Mark Twain) lived in Hannibal as a boy and later used the town as the setting for incidents in "The Adventures of Huckleberry Finn" and "The Adventures of Tom Sawyer." Another Hannibal resident was Margaret Tobin, who, after being encouraged by Clemens to tap the wealth in the Rocky Mountains, went West and became adored by Denver society. She married and later was dubbed the Unsinkable Molly Brown after rowing passengers to safety from the sinking *Titanic*.

Already imbued with a distinctly American character through its association with Mark Twain, Hannibal also is the southern migration destination for bald eagles that live on the high Mississippi River bluffs. Many of the majestic birds can be seen at the dam at Saverton, about 9 miles south of Hannibal on SR 79.

Hannibal is at the northern end of the scenic portion of SR 79 that runs 86 miles south to St. Peters, following the Mississippi River much of the way. Tom Sawyer look-alikes, aged 10 to 13, descend upon Hannibal yearly to compete in the fence-painting contest during National Tom Sawyer Days, held the week of July 4.

Hannibal Convention & Visitors Bureau: 505 N. 3rd St., Hannibal, MO 63401. **Phone:** (573) 221-2477.

◆ MARK TWAIN BOYHOOD HOME & MUSEUM, a National Historic Landmark, is at 206 Hill St. The complex consists of six historic buildings and two interactive museums related to Hannibal's most famous resident. The home where Samuel Clemens lived between the ages of 9 and 17 was built by his father, John Marshall Clemens, in 1843. The restored two-story frame house is decorated with period furnishings, and the museum properties contain interpretive displays, including photographs, first editions of Twain's books, original manuscripts and the desk where he wrote "The Adventures of Tom Sawyer." A 10-minute video presentation about his life is shown in the annex behind the home and museum.

The Becky Thatcher House is the home of Laura Hawkins, a childhood friend of Twain's who was the inspiration for his Thatcher character. The Huckleberry Finn House is a reconstruction of Tom Blankenship's house, Twain's inspiration for Huck Finn. Pilaster House (closed for renovations), an old drugstore, was the home of Dr. Orville Grant, a close Clemens family friend. The family moved into Dr. Grant's house after losing their own home. There also is an interpretive center with a Clemens family timeline, and you can visit the John M. Clemens Justice of the Peace Office on Hill Street (originally located on Bird Street).

The Mark Twain Museum gallery, 2 blocks south at 120 N. Main St., features 15 original Norman Rockwell oil paintings that were used as illustrations in special editions of "The Adventures of Tom Sawyer" and "The Adventures of Huckleberry Finn"; sketches for the paintings were done by Rockwell in Hannibal 1935-36. Interactive exhibits depict scenes from five of Twain's famous books, and live performances take place May through October.

Note: Pilaster House (also referred to as Grant's Drugstore) is scheduled to re-open in 2020 after a major restoration. **Time:** Allow 1 hour minimum. **Hours:** Daily 9-5, Apr.-Dec; 10-4, rest of year. Closed Jan. 1, Easter, Thanksgiving and Christmas. **Cost:** (includes all museum buildings) $12; $10 (ages 60+); $6 (ages 6-17); Free (retired military with ID and spouse). **Phone:** (573) 221-9010.

MARK TWAIN CAVE is 2 mi. s.e. on SR 79 to 300 Cave Hollow Rd. Samuel Clemens immortalized this underground labyrinth in "The Adventures of Tom Sawyer" as the cave in which Tom and Becky Thatcher were lost. The cave's dry, lighted passageways have a constant temperature of 52 F. The Mark Twain Live show is a 1-hour, one-man presentation about the author.

Hours: Guided 1-hour tours depart based on the number of visitors daily 9-8, Memorial Day weekend-late Aug (also Labor Day weekend); 9-6, Apr. 1-day before Memorial Day weekend and late Aug.-Oct. 31, 10-4, rest of year. Mark Twain Live presented Wed.-Sun. at 2, Memorial Day-Oct. 31. **Cost:** $18.95; $9.95 (ages 6-12); $4 (ages 2-5). Combination ticket with Cameron Cave $34.90; $18.95 (ages 6-12); $9 (ages 2-5). Live Show $14.95; $7.50 (ages 8-12). **Phone:** (573) 221-1656.

Cameron Cave is 2 mi. s.e. on SR 79, at Mark Twain Cave. Visitors carry lanterns during the 90-minute tour of this cave, which is in an almost entirely natural state. **Hours:** Tours depart from the Mark Twain Cave visitor center daily at 10, noon, 1:30, 3 and 4:30, Memorial Day to mid-Aug.; Mon.-Fri. at 2:30, Sat. at 10, noon, 1:30, 3 and 4:30, mid-Aug. through Labor Day. Phone ahead to confirm schedule. **Cost:** $20.95; $12.95 (ages 6-12); $5 (ages 2-5). Combination ticket with Mark Twain Cave $34.90; $18.95 (ages 6-12); $9 (ages 2-5). **Phone:** (573) 221-1656.

MARK TWAIN RIVERBOAT docks at the foot of Center St. This triple-deck riverboat offers narrated sightseeing cruises on the Mississippi River. A 2-hour dinner cruise with live entertainment also is available. **Hours:** One-hour sightseeing trips depart daily at 11, 1:30 and 4, Apr.-Oct. (times vary early and late in the season). Dinner cruises depart daily at 6:30 p.m. Phone ahead to confirm schedule. **Cost:** $18; $11 (ages 5-12). Dinner cruise $40.95; $21.95 (ages 5-12); $5 (ages 2-4). Phone ahead to confirm rates. **Phone:** (573) 221-3222.

SLEEP INN & SUITES 573/221-1500

▼▼ THREE DIAMOND

Hotel

Address: 105 Lakeside Dr 63401 **Location:** 2 mi w on US 36 exit Shinn Ln to south service road, then 0.6 mi e. **Facility:** 67 units. 3 stories, interior corridors. **Pool:** heated indoor. **Activities:** exercise room. **Guest Services:** coin laundry. **Featured Amenity:** breakfast buffet.

⟨SAVE⟩ ⟨†¶⟩ CALL ⟨⟪⟫⟩ ⟨⟫⟩ ⟨⟪⟫⟩ ⟨BIZ⟩
⟨HS⟩ ⟨⟫⟩ ⟨⟫⟩ ⟨⟫⟩ ⟨⟫⟩ ⟨⟫⟩
/ SOME UNITS ⟨🐾⟩

WHERE TO EAT

FIDDLESTIKS FOOD & SPIRITS CO 573/406-0493

▼▼ APPROVED American. Casual Dining. **Address:** 8945 Hwy 36 63401

LOGUE'S RESTAURANT 573/248-1854

▼▼ APPROVED American. Casual Dining. **Address:** 121 Huckleberry Heights Dr 63401

HOLLISTER pop. 4,426

• Hotels & Restaurants map & index p. 170
• Part of Branson area — see map p. 151

LA QUINTA INN & SUITES 417/239-0066 ⟨47⟩

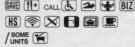

▼▼ THREE DIAMOND

Hotel

Address: 291 Financial Dr 65672 **Location:** Just e of jct US 65. **Facility:** 93 units. 4 stories, interior corridors. **Pool:** heated indoor. **Activities:** hot tub, exercise room. **Guest Services:** coin laundry. **Featured Amenity:** full hot breakfast.

⟨SAVE⟩ CALL ⟨⟪⟫⟩ ⟨⟫⟩ ⟨⟪⟫⟩ ⟨BIZ⟩ ⟨HS⟩
⟨⟫⟩ ⟨⟫⟩ ⟨⟫⟩ ⟨⟫⟩ ⟨⟫⟩
/ SOME UNITS ⟨🐾⟩

MABEE LODGE OF THE KEETER CENTER AT COLLEGE OF THE OZARKS 417/239-1900 ⟨46⟩

▼▼ THREE DIAMOND Hotel. **Address:** 1 Opportunity Way 65726

WESTGATE BRANSON LAKES RESORT 417/334-4944

▼▼ THREE DIAMOND

Resort Condominium

Address: 750 Emerald Pointe Dr 65672 **Location:** Waterfront. Jct US 65 and SR 265, 1 mi w to Hill Haven Rd, then 2 mi s. **Facility:** Located on the shores of Table Rock Lake and a short distance from Branson's attractions, the one- and two-bedroom units offer luxury and comfort with great guest amenities. 158 kitchen condominium units. 4 stories, exterior corridors. **Terms:** check-in 4 pm. **Pool:** outdoor, heated indoor. **Activities:** hot tub, marina, fishing, miniature golf, recreation programs, game room, lawn sports, picnic facilities, exercise room. **Guest Services:** complimentary laundry.

⟨SAVE⟩ CALL ⟨⟪⟫⟩ ⟨⟫⟩ ⟨⟪⟫⟩ ⟨⟫⟩ ⟨⟫⟩ ⟨⟫⟩ ⟨⟫⟩
/ SOME UNITS ⟨🐾⟩

WHERE TO EAT

DOWNING STREET POUR HOUSE 417/320-6106 ⟨29⟩

▼▼ APPROVED American. Gastropub. **Address:** 24 Downing St 65672

THE KEETER CENTER AT COLLEGE OF THE OZARKS 417/239-1900 ⟨30⟩

▼▼ THREE DIAMOND American. Fine Dining. **Address:** 1 Opportunity Way 65726

PIZZA BY THE CHEF 417/239-1415 ⟨31⟩

▼▼ APPROVED Pizza. Casual Dining. **Address:** 180 Mall Rd, Suite D 65672

INDEPENDENCE (G-2) pop. 116,830, elev. 1,012'

• Hotels & Restaurants map & index p. 218
• Part of Kansas City area — see map p. 199

Upon his return following the end of his presidency, Harry S. Truman called Independence "the greatest town in the United States" and "the center of things for me." Truman thought the world of his hometown, and a day spent in the town's center, Independence Square, will help newcomers understand why.

Independence Square is where you'll find Clinton's Soda Fountain, 100 W. Maple Ave., where young Harry had his first job as a store clerk, doing everything from sweeping the floors to dispensing flavored phosphates. Sit at the fountain's 100-year-old marble counter and slurp a cherry phosphate or feast on an ice cream sundae in Harry's honor.

Take a leisurely stroll through Independence Square, much like Harry did every day during his retirement, and you'll happen upon delightful one-of-a-kind clothing boutiques, family-owned restaurants and specialty shops selling home interiors, gifts and antiques. In the Englewood Station Arts District, galleries stay open late and offer demonstrations, children's activities and meet-the-artist events on the third Friday of every month. A covered wagon historical tour, offered April through October by Pioneer Trails Adventures, panders to aching feet and pioneer spirits, with fun 45-minute ghost tours, led by paranormal experts, on October Friday evenings; phone (816) 254-2466 for reservations. With the past in mind, a large number of visitors come to check out their ancestry at the Midwest Genealogy Center, reputedly the nation's largest; phone (816) 252-7228 for information.

During the holiday season, Independence Square turns into a winter wonderland. On the third Saturday in November, townspeople gather for the annual tree lighting ceremony. Festivities include live music and dancing, children's activities, visits with Santa and sleigh rides. Other major events include Truman Days in May, the Vaile Mansion Strawberry Festival in June and the 4-day ▼▼ Santa-Cali-Gon Days Festival in late August and early September.

While Independence is well-known for its Truman-related historic sites, it was a major "jumping off" point for the Santa Fe, Oregon and California trails, earning the city the nickname "Queen City of the Trails." The moniker still holds true today. The Little Blue Trace Trail runs north for 11 scenic miles along

(See map & index p. 218.)

the Blue River and is accessible from the Hartman Heritage Center, I-70 and Little Blue River Road.

Independence Department of Tourism: 112 W. Lexington Ave., Independence, MO 64050. **Phone:** (816) 325-7890 or (800) 748-7323.

Self-guiding tours: The Missouri Mormon Walking Trail, which begins at Walnut and River streets across from the Community of Christ Auditorium, is a 1-mile trail with 14 plaques commemorating early Mormon sites. The Truman Walking Trail, beginning at the Harry S Truman National Historic Site ticket office at Main Street and Truman Road, meanders 2.7 miles through the Truman neighborhood, with 44 plaques embedded in sidewalks along the way.

HARRY S. TRUMAN PRESIDENTIAL LIBRARY & MUSEUM is on the n.e. edge of US 24 at Delaware St. The focal point of the museum, an exhibit about the Missouri native's presidential years, features a film presentation in the State of Missouri Auditorium that traces Truman's life from childhood to his swearing in as the 33rd president of the United States. In addition, a 45-minute documentary and audiovisual presentations dealing with difficult decisions Truman was faced with during his presidency are shown in two theaters. Exhibits and objects of artistic and historic interest examine such topics as the challenges faced in the post-World War II years, the beginning of the Cold War and the status of the nation as Truman left office in 1952.

Other permanent exhibits include Harry S. Truman: His Life and Times, which covers the periods before and after his White House years; a replica of Truman's Oval Office, with the original "The Buck Stops Here" sign; and the office in the Truman Library that he used every day until his health failed. The grave sites of President and Mrs. Truman, their daughter Margaret and son-in-law E. Clifton Daniel are in the courtyard.

Note: The museum is undergoing major renovations and plans to re-open late summer 2020. The Research Room will remain open during the closure of the museum. **Time:** Allow 2 hours minimum. **Hours:** Research room open Mon.-Fri. 8:45-4:45. Check website for Research Room Regulations. Closed federal holidays. **Cost:** $8; $7 (ages 65+); $3 (ages 6-15). **Phone:** (816) 268-8200 or (800) 833-1225.

HARRY S TRUMAN NATIONAL HISTORIC SITE is on Delaware St. off Truman Rd.; a visitor center is at 223 N. Main St. This is the house in which President and Mrs. Truman, when not in Washington, D.C., lived from their marriage in 1919 until their deaths. The Victorian home is crowded with their furnishings and other possessions. The visitor center offers a short audiovisual program and exhibits.

Note: The visitor center distributes tickets on a first-come, first-served basis beginning at 8:30 a.m. for each day's tours. Tours may sell out. Parking in front of the Truman Home on Delaware Street is limited.

Hours: Visitor center open daily 8:30-5. Guided house tours are given every 15-30 minutes daily 9-4:30, Memorial Day-Oct. 31; Tues.-Sun. 9-4:30, rest of year. Each tour is limited to eight people. Closed major holidays. Phone ahead to confirm schedule. **Cost:** $5; free (ages 0-15). **Phone:** (816) 254-9929 or (816) 254-2720.

DRURY INN & SUITES KANSAS CITY-INDEPENDENCE
816/795-9393 **57**
THREE DIAMOND Hotel. **Address:** 20300 E 42nd St S 64015

HILTON GARDEN INN INDEPENDENCE   816/350-3000 **54**
THREE DIAMOND SAVE Hotel. **Address:** 19677 E Jackson Dr 64057

> **AAA Benefit:** Members save up to 15%!

HOLIDAY INN EXPRESS & SUITES-INDEPENDENCE/KANSAS CITY   816/795-8889 **56**
THREE DIAMOND Hotel. **Address:** 19901 E Valley View Pkwy 64057

MY PLACE HOTEL   816/491-2598 **58**
APPROVED Extended Stay Hotel. **Address:** 20105 E Valley View Pkwy 64057

STONEY CREEK HOTEL & CONFERENCE CENTER
816/908-9600 **55**
THREE DIAMOND Hotel. **Address:** 18011 Bass Pro Dr 64055

SUPER 8 INDEPENDENCE   816/833-1888 **53**
APPROVED Hotel. **Address:** 4032 S Lynn Court Dr 64055

TRUMAN INN   816/254-0100 **52**
APPROVED Hotel. **Address:** 4048 S Lynn Court Dr 64055

WHERE TO EAT

CORNER CAFE   816/350-7000 **62**
APPROVED Comfort Food. Casual Dining. **Address:** 4215 S Little Blue Pkwy 64057

HEREFORD HOUSE   816/795-9200 **59**
THREE DIAMOND Steak. Casual Dining. **Address:** 19721 E Jackson Dr 64057

JAZZ A LOUISIANA KITCHEN   816/912-1096 **60**
APPROVED Cajun. Casual Dining. **Address:** 19700 E Valley View Pkwy 64057

OPHELIA'S RESTAURANT & INN   816/461-4525 **56**
THREE DIAMOND American. Casual Dining. **Address:** 201 N Main St 64050

THE RHEINLAND RESTAURANT   816/461-5383 **55**
APPROVED German. Casual Dining. **Address:** 208 N Main St 64050

SALVATORE'S ITALIAN RESTAURANT   816/737-2400 **61**
APPROVED Italian. Casual Dining. **Address:** 12801 E 40 Hwy S 64055

(See map & index p. 218.)

SMOKEHOUSE BAR-B-QUE   816/795-5555   58
▼ APPROVED   Barbecue. Casual Dining. **Address:** 19000 E 39th St 64057

V'S ITALIANO RISTORANTE   816/353-1241   57
▼ APPROVED   Italian. Casual Dining. **Address:** 10819 E Hwy 40 64055

JACKSON   pop. 13,758, elev. 463'

DRURY INN & SUITES-JACKSON, MO   573/243-9200
▼▼ THREE DIAMOND   Hotel. **Address:** 225 Drury Ln 63755

JEFFERSON CITY   (C-4) pop. 43,079, elev. 630'

The first building denoting Missouri's capital city, completed in 1826, was destroyed by fire in 1837; a new one begun the same year burned after it was struck by lightning in 1911. The present structure was built in 1918. The Governor's Mansion was built in 1871 on the site of the original Capitol. Guided tours of the residence are given Tues.-Thurs. 9-11:30, May-July and Sept.-Nov. To arrange a tour contact the governor's office; phone (573) 751-7929.

Jefferson Landing State Historic Site, on the river at the end of Jefferson Street, preserves three buildings that were the center of Jefferson City's 19th-century river trade: The 1839 Lohman Building, the 1854 Christopher Maus House and the 1855 Union Hotel. A visitor center in the Lohman Building offers a small museum and an audiovisual presentation about the history of the landing and Jefferson City.

Also of interest is the Safety Education Center and Law Enforcement Museum at the Missouri State Highway Patrol, 1510 E. Elm St. Exhibits include law enforcement antiques and five completely equipped patrol cars dating from 1931 to the present. Phone (573) 526-6149 Mon.-Fri. 8-5.

Stretching more than 200 miles from St. Charles to beyond Sedalia, Katy Trail State Park follows the former route of the Missouri-Kansas-Texas Railroad. Running parallel to the Missouri River, the trail takes hikers and bicyclists through open fields, forests and wetlands and past towering bluffs, and winds through such historic towns as Augusta, Boonville, Columbia, Defiance, Franklin and Marthasville as well as St. Charles and Jefferson City. For further information contact the Department of Natural Resources, P.O. Box 176, Jefferson City, MO 65102-0176; phone (800) 361-4827 or (573) 751-3443.

Jefferson City Convention & Visitors Bureau : 700 E. Capitol Ave., Jefferson City, MO 65101. **Phone:** (573) 632-2820 or (800) 769-4183.

Self-guiding tours: Visitor guides and maps describing Jefferson City's historic attractions are available at the Jefferson City Convention & Visitors Bureau Mon.-Fri. 8-5.

MISSOURI STATE CAPITOL is at 201 W. Capitol Ave. Built of Carthage stone and completed in 1917, the building contains paintings by Thomas Hart Benton, Frank Brangwyn, N.C. Wyeth and other artists who have captured the state's legends, history and landscapes. The State Museum has a large collection of exhibits interpreting Missouri's natural and cultural heritage on display in the History and Resources halls, including a Missouri Veterans Gallery. **Hours:** Daily 8-5. Tours are given Mon.-Fri. on the hour 9-11 and 1-4, Sat.-Sun. at 11 and 2. Closed Jan. 1, Thanksgiving and Christmas. **Cost:** Free. **Phone:** (573) 751-2854.

BEST WESTERN PLUS CAPITAL INN   573/635-4175
▼▼ THREE DIAMOND   Hotel   Best Western PLUS.   **AAA Benefit:** Members save up to 15% and earn bonus points!

Address: 1937 Christy Dr 65101 **Location:** US 54 exit Ellis Blvd, just se. **Facility:** 75 units. 3 stories, interior corridors. **Parking:** winter plug-ins. **Pool:** heated indoor. **Activities:** hot tub, exercise room. **Guest Services:** valet and coin laundry. **Featured Amenity:** full hot breakfast.

SAVE ▮▮+ CALL ⬇ ⬆ ✚ BIZ
HS 🛜 ⊠ ▮ ▭ ▭

CAPITOL PLAZA HOTEL & CONVENTION CENTER   573/635-1234
▼▼ APPROVED   Hotel. **Address:** 415 W McCarty St 65101

TRAVELODGE BY WYNDHAM JEFFERSON CITY   573/636-5456
▼▼ APPROVED   Hotel. **Address:** 1710 Jefferson St 65110

WHERE TO EAT

DAS STEIN HAUS   573/634-3869
▼▼ APPROVED   German. Casual Dining. **Address:** 1436 Southridge Dr 65109

MADISON'S CAFE   573/634-2988
▼▼ APPROVED   Italian. Casual Dining. **Address:** 216 Madison St 65101

MEL'S COUNTRY CAFE   573/893-9115
▼▼ APPROVED   American. Casual Dining. **Address:** 2421 Industrial Dr 65109

JOPLIN   (D-2) pop. 50,150, elev. 1,002'

Following the Civil War, mining companies that had established smelters along the Joplin Creek Valley engaged in fierce rivalry, splitting the town into two factions controlled by competing companies. The valley endured a reign of terror until the state general assembly came to the rescue in 1873 and reincorporated the two towns as the city of Joplin.

Once peace was established in Joplin, the railroad arrived and stimulated development of the zinc industry. Small plots produced great fortunes in zinc, which soon overtook lead production. Joplin's boom stabilized as smelters moved to new deposits outside town, and the more sedate industry of buying and selling ore developed. A railroad center by 1900, the city consequently attracted a number of industrial and wholesale companies.

Joplin is the home of Missouri Southern State University, which offers tours of its 310-acre campus.

The Post Art Library, inside the Joplin Public Library at 1901 E. 20th St., houses a 2,500-piece collection of art reference material, focused on English architecture and furniture of the 16th and 17th centuries. Phone (417) 623-7953.

In May 2011 a deadly EF-5 tornado ripped through the city, destroying entire neighborhoods and causing more deaths than any single tornado since 1950. Almost immediately after the devastation a coordinated rebuilding effort, Rebuild Joplin, was put into place. In May 2016 the fifth anniversary of the tornado was commemorated with a memorial for those who passed away as well as a celebration of the city's successful reconstruction.

Joplin Convention & Visitors Bureau : 602 S. Main St., Joplin, MO 64801. **Phone:** (417) 625-4789 or (800) 657-2534.

BEST WESTERN OASIS INN & SUITES   417/781-6776

APPROVED

Hotel

Best Western.

AAA Benefit: Members save up to 15% and earn bonus points!

Address: 3508 S Range Line Rd 64804 **Location:** I-44 exit 8, just nw. **Facility:** 97 units. 2 stories (no elevator), exterior corridors. **Pool:** outdoor. **Activities:** exercise room.

CANDLEWOOD SUITES   417/623-9595
APPROVED   Extended Stay Hotel. **Address:** 3512 S Range Line Rd 64804

COMFORT INN & SUITES   417/627-0400
APPROVED   Hotel. **Address:** 3400 S Range Line Rd 64804

DRURY INN & SUITES-JOPLIN   417/781-8000
THREE DIAMOND Hotel. **Address:** 3601 S Range Line Rd 64804

HAMPTON INN BY HILTON-JOPLIN   417/659-9900
THREE DIAMOND SAVE Hotel. **Address:** 3107 E 36th St 64804

AAA Benefit: Members save up to 15%!

HILTON GARDEN INN   417/206-6700
THREE DIAMOND SAVE Hotel. **Address:** 2644 E 32nd St 64804

AAA Benefit: Members save up to 15%!

HOLIDAY INN JOPLIN   417/624-9000
THREE DIAMOND Hotel. **Address:** 3402 Arizona Ave 64804

HOMEWOOD SUITES BY HILTON   417/623-1900
THREE DIAMOND SAVE Extended Stay Hotel. **Address:** 2642 E 32nd St 64804

AAA Benefit: Members save up to 15%!

RESIDENCE INN BY MARRIOTT-JOPLIN   417/782-0908
THREE DIAMOND SAVE Extended Stay Hotel. **Address:** 3128 E Hammons Blvd 64804

AAA Benefit: Members save 5% or more!

SLEEP INN   417/782-1212
APPROVED   Hotel. **Address:** 4100 Hwy 43 S 64803

TOWNEPLACE SUITES BY MARRIOTT JOPLIN
417/659-8111

THREE DIAMOND

Extended Stay Hotel

TOWNEPLACE SUITES MARRIOTT

AAA Benefit: Members save 5% or more!

Address: 4026 S Arizona Ave 64804 **Location:** I-44 exit 8, just sw. **Facility:** 74 efficiencies. 4 stories, interior corridors. **Pool:** heated indoor. **Activities:** exercise room. **Guest Services:** valet and coin laundry. **Featured Amenity:** full hot breakfast.

WHERE TO EAT

CRABBY'S SEAFOOD BAR & GRILL   417/206-3474
APPROVED   Seafood. Casual Dining. **Address:** 815 W 7th St 64801

DEL RIO BORDERTOWN CAFE   417/206-0423
APPROVED   Tex-Mex. Casual Dining. **Address:** 1801 Range Line Rd 64801

GUSANO'S CHICAGO STYLE PIZZERIA   417/623-9090
APPROVED   Pizza. Casual Dining. **Address:** 3929 E 7th St, Suite E 64801

RED ONION CAFE   417/623-1004
APPROVED   American. Casual Dining. **Address:** 203 E 4th St 64801

RIB CRIB BBQ AND GRILL   417/206-7427
APPROVED   Barbecue. Casual Dining. **Address:** 2915 E 24th St 64804

WILDER'S STEAKHOUSE   417/623-7230
APPROVED   Steak. Casual Dining. **Address:** 1216 Main St 64801

Kansas City

Then & Now

"I'm goin' to Kansas City, Kansas City here I come." So goes the 1950s hit with the catchy melody. Ditto for Kansas City—once you've sniffed its barbecue-scented air, felt a fountain's cool spray and tapped your feet to its home-grown jazz, you'll never forget the experience, and you'll find yourself singing the city's praises.

From "Possumtrot" to "The Paris of the Plains," Kansas City has known many names. In 1821, fur trader François Chouteau established a trading post near the Missouri River and called it "Chouteau's Town." Kansas City's prime location at the confluence of the Missouri and Kansas rivers as well as at the starting point of the Santa Fe and Oregon trails was instrumental to the area's growth.

Nicknames "Kawsmouth," "Possumtrot," and "Westport Landing" were used during the 1800s when Kansas City was the last stop for travelers to pick up provisions during the great westward migration, including those heading to California during the Gold Rush.

During the heyday of jazz in the 1920s and '30s, Kansas City was heralded as "The Paris of the Plains" because of its numerous jazz clubs

AAA.com/travelguides—
more ways to look, book and save

and gambling halls and local government's bold disregard of Prohibition. Today, names like "The City of Fountains" and "Barbecue Capital of the World" describe this Midwestern city.

A $4.5 billion revitalization transformed downtown into a flourishing metropolis offering plenty of things to

J.C. Nichols Memorial Fountain

do. The Power & Light District is an entertainment complex spanning 8 city blocks brimming with hip local restaurants, live music venues, dance clubs, and free rock and country music concerts in the summer.

Just footsteps away from the Power & Light District is the Sprint Center, a sparkling wedding-band shaped entertainment and sports venue. Glance at its mirror-like glass façade and you'll see a reflection of Kansas City's past and present in turn-of-the-20th-century red-brick buildings juxtaposing gleaming stick-straight skyscrapers.

Today's popular music scene jumps, jives and wails, but in the 1920s and '30s, blues-influenced Kansas City jazz was *really* hot. Back then, jazz aficionados had the pleasure of seeing musicians such as Count Basie and Charlie "Bird" Parker perform live. Known as one of the cradles of jazz due to its heavily influential style, Kansas City also is where the jam session was born. After performances, musicians couldn't put their instruments down and jammed into

(Continued on p. 200.)

Destination Kansas City

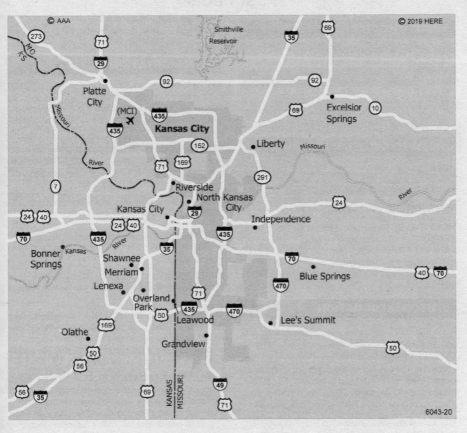

This map shows cities in the Kansas City vicinity where you will find attractions, hotels and restaurants. Cities are listed alphabetically in this book on the following pages.

Fast Facts

ABOUT THE CITY

POP: 459,787 ▪ ELEV: 1,005 ft.

MONEY

SALES TAX: The sales tax rate in the city of Kansas City is 7.99 percent. The city's lodging tax is 11.98 percent and there is a rental car tax of $4 per day.

WHOM TO CALL

EMERGENCY: 911

POLICE (non-emergency): (816) 234-5111

TEMPERATURE: (816) 540-6021

HOSPITALS: Research Medical Center, (816) 276-4000 ▪ St. Joseph Medical Center, (816) 942-4400 ▪ Saint Luke's Hospital, (816) 932-2000 ▪ Saint Luke's North Hospital, (816) 891-6000 ▪ Truman Medical Center Hospital Hill, (816) 404-1000.

VISITOR INFORMATION

Visit KC: 1321 Baltimore Ave., Kansas City, MO 64105. Phone: (816) 221-5242, (816) 691-3800, or (800) 767-7700 Mon.-Fri. 9-5, Sat. 10-3.

Located in The City Center Square Building, the association distributes free brochures Mon.-Fri. 8:30-5; closed Jan. 1, Memorial Day, July 4, Labor Day, Thanksgiving, day after Thanksgiving and Dec. 25.

Missouri Welcome Center: 4010 Blue Ridge Cut-Off, Kansas City, MO 64133. Phone: (816) 889-3330.

The center is off I-70 exit 9 and Blue Ridge Cut-Off at the Harry S. Truman Sports Complex. It is open daily 8-5, Apr.-Oct.; Mon.-Sat. 8-5, rest of year.

TRANSPORTATION

AIR TRAVEL: Kansas City International Airport (MCI) is 17 miles northwest of downtown and is served by several major airlines. Taxi fare into the city is about $50. Many larger hotels offer airport shuttle and limousine service.

RENTAL CARS: Hertz, at the airport, offers discounts to AAA members; phone (816) 243-5765 or (800) 654-3080.

 Book and save at AAA.com/hertz

RAIL SERVICE: The Amtrak station, (816) 421-3622 or (800) 872-7245, is at W. Pershing Road and Main Street.

BUSES: Greyhound Lines Inc., (800) 231-2222, is at 1101 Troost Ave. Jefferson Lines also serves Kansas City.

TAXIS: Yellow Cab, (816) 471-5000, is the city's major taxi service. Cabs are deregulated, so fares vary widely. Rates are posted on each cab, and you are not required to take the first cab in a line. Up to five people can share a ride for a single fare.

PUBLIC TRANSPORTATION: Ride KC, the metro bus system, serves all of Greater Kansas City except Johnson County. The exact-change fare minimum is $1.50 ($3 for an all-day pass) and varies by distance. For more details and for route information regarding construction, phone (816) 221-0660.

(Continued from p. 198.)

the wee hours. Kansas City's fluid, spontaneous style of jazz eventually gave birth to an improvisational style called bebop; city native and saxophonist Parker was instrumental in this transition.

Besides its legendary contributions to jazz, Kansas City's cultural scene comprises a mix of art and history museums, theater, ballet, opera and an annual Shakespeare festival. Culture vultures will feel right at home in the city's high-caliber museums.

Fountain lovers are in the right place too. Kansas City has more than 200 fountains, earning it another nickname: "The City of Fountains." There are more fountains here than almost anywhere; only Rome is said to have more. Used in the late 1800s as water troughs for the horses that provided transportation, the fountains are now appreciated for their beauty. Near Country Club Plaza in Mill Creek Park is the J.C. Nichols Memorial Fountain. This dramatic 80-foot-round fountain features four 10-foot-high rearing horses, dolphins, cherubs and nine arching streams of water.

Other landmark fountains in Kansas City include the Henry Wollman Bloch Fountain outside Union Station and the splashing columns of water synchronized to music at nearby Crown Center Square. On the south end of Penn Valley Park stands the impressive Firefighter Fountain and Memorial, which pays tribute to fallen firefighters. Even Kauffman Stadium has a 322-foot-wide fountain with a waterfall that provides a show before games. Of course, after the Royals' 2015 World Series win, the baseball is the main attraction.

But man cannot live by water alone. Roll down your car window as you drive around town, and inhale the mouthwatering fragrance of barbecue sauce. Follow your nose to any of the many local restaurants; residents brag that Kansas City has more barbecue places to eat per capita than any city in the country. You'll see why so many call Kansas City the "Barbecue Capital of the World."

Must Do: AAA Editor's Picks

- When in Kansas City, try the **barbecue**, a time-honored KC tradition. You'll have a tough time deciding where to dine because there are so many local restaurants to choose from, so ask around. Kansas City natives are proud of their favorites, including **Gates Bar-B-Q** (3205 Main St.) or **Smokebox BBQ** (10020 N. Ambassador Dr.).

- If you're looking for fun things to with friends, catch a **jazz** band or two. Warm up at **The Blue Room** at the **American Jazz Museum** (1616 E. 18th St.) or at **The Phoenix** (302 W. 8th St.), then head over to the **Mutual Musicians Foundation** (1823 Highland Ave.), where things start heating up at midnight and go on until the break of dawn.

- Wander around **Country Club Plaza** (4750 Broadway St.), a Midwestern mecca for outdoor mall maniacs. The plaza's exquisite Spanish and Moorish architecture, highlighted by European sculptures and fountains, surrounds upscale shops, the usual mall standards (Banana Republic and the like) and popular local restaurants. If you're there during the holidays, don't miss the ▽ **KCP&L Plaza Lighting Ceremony** on Thanksgiving night. When the switch is thrown, more than 80 miles of twinkling lights illuminate the plaza for the season.

- Drive to nearby **Independence**, where our 33rd president Harry S. Truman was born and raised. Visit the ▽ **Harry S. Truman Presidential Library & Museum** (500 US 24W) and **Harry S Truman National Historic Site** (219 N. Delaware St.) and stroll along the 2.7-mile-long Truman Walking Trail, Harry's favorite path, now marked with plaques featuring facts about Harry.

- Check out the spectacular collection at ▽ **The Nelson-Atkins Museum of Art** (4525 Oak St.) and then relax on its lawn, which also happens to be the Kansas City Sculpture Park. Recline next to 18-foot-tall shuttlecocks made by artists Claes Oldenburg and Coosje van Bruggen or any of the park's 30 other sculptures.

- After sunset, get into the groove at **Kansas City Power & Light District**, bordered by Baltimore Avenue, Grand Boulevard, 12th Street and I-670. Encompassing eight blocks of nightclubs and restaurants, the entertainment district revitalized downtown KC when it opened in 2008.

- The **Crossroads Arts District**, just south of the downtown loop and north of Union Station, offers up art galleries galore and modern cafés, both of which double as entertainment venues depending on the night. You'll also find one-of-a-kind shops such as **Retro Inferno** (1500 Grand Blvd.) for midcentury-modern furniture (think "The Jetsons" or "Bewitched"); **Christopher Elbow Chocolates** (1819 McGee St.), nirvana for lovers of artfully designed chocolate; and **Webster House** (1644 Wyandotte St.), an antique store and restaurant.

- Drop into **Union Station** (30 W. Pershing Rd.), an eye-catching Kansas City landmark built in 1914 for use as a train station. The resplendent interior of the 850,000-square-foot Beaux Arts building boasts a 6-foot-wide clock, three 3,500-pound chandeliers suspended from a 95-foot-high ceiling, marble floors and plaster ceilings. Today there's a small collection of shops and local restaurants as well as **Science City** (a family-oriented science museum with fun things to do with kids) and exhibits about railroad history.

- Both children and adults will ooh and aah at the toys that fill 38 rooms at the ▽ **National Museum of Toys and Miniatures** (5235 Oak St.). The treasures date back to the Victorian era and include a 9-foot-tall Victorian dollhouse complete with running water, tiny glassware and ceramic pieces, cast iron cars and trains, teddy bears, dolls and toy soldiers.

- For a tasty, one-of-a-kind, elegant evening out, visit **Bluestem Restaurant** (900 Westport Rd.). Every visit will be different, as the menu changes daily and seasonally. The presentation is as delightful as the taste because the chefs use fresh, local ingredients.

Union Station

Kansas City 1-day Itinerary

AAA editors suggest these activities for a great short vacation experience. Those staying in the area for a longer visit can access a 3-day itinerary at AAA.com/TravelGuides.

Morning

- See how many fountains you can count during your day trip; according to the latest total, KC had about 200. One of the most beautiful is the J.C. Nichols Memorial Fountain near Country Club Plaza; it's 80 feet in diameter with horses, dolphins and cherubs. Find more fountains in Country Club Plaza, including fountains of Bacchus and Neptune, and the humorous Boy and Frog fountain.

- Sports aficionados will want to check out a Kansas City Royals baseball game April through late fall at Kaufmann Stadium (One Royal Way), though you can visit the ⟐ **Royals Hall of Fame** there any time of the year. Step out of the sidelines at ⟐ **The College Basketball Experience** (1401 Grand Blvd.), where you can work on your lay-ups and 3-pointers while you walk or run in the shoes of your favorite college hoop-shooter.

- Explore some of Kansas City's fascinating museums. Don't miss ⟐ **The Nelson-Atkins Museum of Art** (4525 Oak St.), housed in the 1933 Beaux Art Nelson-Atkins Building and the modern 2007 Bloch Building. The lawn is marked by gigantic shuttlecocks, statuary and large pools. The museum's collections survey art from across the globe, including Japan, Europe, South and Southeast Asia, Africa, China and the United States. Highlights include the indoor Noguchi Sculpture Court; Bauhaus, Cubist, Expressionist and Surrealist works; a comprehensive collection of bronzes by sculptor Henry Moore; ancient Egyptian, Greek and Roman art; and Claude Monet's Water Lilies.

Afternoon

- Take a ride to the top of the 217-foot-tall Liberty Memorial Tower at the ⟐ **National World War I Museum and Memorial** (2 Memorial Dr.) for breathtaking views of downtown Kansas City. The limestone tower is flanked by a sphinx and a museum building. Inside the museum, you'll find soldiers' uniforms from past wars, photographs, letters, weapons, battle plans and other artifacts describing the war in great detail.

- Kill two birds with one stone at **The Museums at 18th & Vine** (1616 E. 18th St.), home to the **American Jazz Museum** and the **Negro Leagues Baseball Museum,** a true score if you love both sports *and* music. The American Jazz Museum pays tribute to the originators of jazz with memorabilia, listening stations, film clips and neon lights that once glowed outside nightclubs. Check out **The Blue Room,** a part of the museum that is transformed into a live jazz club when night falls. The Negro Leagues

National World War I Museum and Memorial

Baseball Museum presents the history of the leagues from the 1800s through 1960.

- Shopaholics will find it difficult to tear themselves away from **Country Club Plaza** (4750 Broadway St.), Kansas City's prestigious shopping venue. Spanish and Moorish buildings with terra-cotta roofs, colorful tile murals, fountains, statues and lush greenery everywhere you look distinguish this shopping mecca. Grab lunch at one of the hip local restaurants, such as **Kona Grill** (444 Ward Pkwy.) for Pacific Rim cuisine.

- Get a warm-and-fuzzy feeling at the **Hallmark Visitors Center** (2450 Grand Blvd.), where displays of greeting cards and holiday ornaments from the early 1900s to the present are bound to bring back sweet memories. Fun things to do include learning how cards are made and making your own bow to take home.

Evening

- Kansas City is famous for a few things, not the least of which is barbecue. When dinner time rolls around, chow down at such tried-and-true restaurants as **Fiorella's Jack Stack Barbecue - Freight House** (101 W. 22nd St.) and **Gates Bar-B-Q** (3205 Main St.).

- Jazz: It's another of Kansas City's claims to fame. Have a hot time in the old town with a return trip to the 18th & Vine Jazz District. Live musicians play **The KC Blues & Jazz Juke House** (1700 E. 18th St.) and the **Gem Theater** (1615 E. 18th St.), a renovated venue with a colorful marquee. There's good rockin' after midnight on weekends at the **Mutual Musicians Foundation** (1823 Highland Ave.), where the jamming goes on until dawn.

Top Picks for Kids

Under 13

- Kids in the 5-7 age range will love the  LEGOLAND Discovery Center Kansas City (2475 Grand Blvd.). It has a couple of small-scale rides, short films to watch, a kiddie play area and—most importantly—the opportunity to build something awesome with those beloved plastic bricks. Adults will appreciate the ingenious LEGO re-creations of Kansas City landmarks at MiniLand.

- The Cabela's store (10300 Cabela Dr.) is filled to the rafters with outdoor clothing and gear. Kids will enjoy the wildlife taxidermy throughout the store including more than 80 deer in lifelike scenery in the Mule Deer Country Museum, the Aquarium with giant tanks full of locally found fish, and the fudge and nut shop.

- Kids can scamper through room after room of vintage toys, collectibles, puppets and teddy bears at the National Museum of Toys and Miniatures (5235 Oak St.). Little girls in particular will be entranced by the old-fashioned dollhouses in all shapes and sizes, including one 9-foot-tall mansion complete with running water.

Teens

- Hip-hop and pop divas may rule the charts today, but encourage musically inclined teens to explore musical roots at the American Jazz Museum (1616 E. 18th St.), part of the 18th & Vine Jazz District. Kansas City was a prime breeding ground for musicians creating "America's Classical Music" in the 1920s and '30s, and exhibits focusing on greats like Ella Fitzgerald, Duke Ellington and Charlie Parker will be an eye-opening musical education lesson.

- Unleash the tribe for the day at Worlds of Fun (4545 Worlds of Fun Ave.), where fearless teens can ride hair-raising roller coasters like Prowler, Mamba, Boomerang and Timber Wolf, then experience the gut-clutching thrill of Zulu, a circular ride that spins riders upside down.

All Ages

- Beautifully restored Union Station (30 W. Pershing Rd.) offers a fun family outing and is one of Kansas City's most popular things to see. Of course, there are hands-on railroad exhibits—the Missouri Pacific Railroad, known as MoPac by train aficionados, reached KC in 1865. But there's also a planetarium, 3D films on the Regnier "Extreme Screen" and Science City, which is loaded with Interactive features.

- Shooters, cobbles, jumbos, toebreakers—they're all marbles, and you'll find 'em at the Moon Marble Company store (600 E. Front St. in Bonner Springs). In addition to marbles that look like baseballs and eyeballs and handmade, legitimate works of art (check out Dichroic Swirl, a clear marble with swirls of translucent green), marble-making demonstrations are given on Tuesdays, Fridays and Saturdays (and sometimes on other days too).

- Watching the Kansas City Royals play ball at Kauffman Stadium is a summertime tradition, and the team's World Series win in 2015 fired up their loyal fans more than ever. If you can't make a home game, visit the Royals Hall of Fame (One Royal Way) and learn more about Bret Saberhagen, Frank White, George Brett and other hall of famers who have worn the iconic blue uniform.

- On a blazing hot summer—or frigid winter—day, while away some time at the Lakeside Nature Center (4701 E. Gregory Blvd.) in Swope Park. It not only exhibits native wildlife but is one of the state's largest wildlife rehabilitation facilities.

- Kansas City barbecue is world famous, and there are plenty of joints where you can sample it. Gates Bar-B-Q (3205 Main St.) regularly wins awards for the best 'cue in town, and the not-so-secret secret behind their success is the sauce (original, sweet or extra hot). Regardless of your preference, it's best slathered on ribs, and you should know the lingo—slab, short end, center cut or long end—before you place your order at the noisy counter.

- Who doesn't love munching on a giant turkey leg while wandering around looking at people dressed up in all sorts of costumes? At the Kansas City Renaissance Festival you can watch jousting knights, get a psychic reading or shop for cool crafts. It's open on weekends from early September until mid-October.

Moon Marble Company store

Arriving
By Car

From the north, Kansas City is approached by two major controlled-access highways, I-35 and I-29, which merge into I-29/35, or US 71, and cross the Missouri River before leading into the downtown area via 13th Street. Running into Kansas City, Kan., from the south, I-35 provides direct controlled access to downtown via Washington Avenue and 12th Street.

On the Missouri side the fastest southern approach is via US 71, which connects with the I-435 bypass. The bypass circles the city and can be taken north to I-70. Beginning in St. Louis, I-70 bisects the state and enters Kansas City via the 13th Street exit. I-70 also is the controlled-access route from the west to downtown.

Getting Around
Street System

The Greater Kansas City area follows a basic grid pattern, slightly complicated by the Kansas and Missouri rivers. North Kansas City and Kansas City, Mo., are separated by the Missouri River, from which cross streets are numbered in ascending order well into the suburbs. The reference point for the east-west block designation in downtown Kansas City, Mo., is Main Street. Conversely, numbered streets in Kansas City, Kan., run on a north-south axis, paralleling the abrupt S-curve of the Missouri River.

State Line Road separates the Missouri and Kansas sides of the city. The street systems of both are peculiar to their own states, although several

KCP&L Plaza Lighting Ceremony

streets continue across the border unchanged. The main east-west artery over the Kansas River connecting the twin cities is I-70, which leads into US 24/40, the main route through downtown Kansas City, Kan.

I-70 also intersects other major thoroughfares that travel through and around town. The Southwest Trafficway provides rapid access into the central part of Kansas City, Mo.

Generally downtown speed limits are 25 mph or as posted. Right turns on red are permitted unless otherwise posted. Avoid rush hours, from about 6:30 to 8:30 a.m. and 3:30 to 6 p.m.

Parking

On-street parking is controlled by meters, but finding an empty space in the right spot can be difficult. Numerous commercial lots and garages are concentrated around Central and Grand avenues, between 9th and 14th streets, and at the southern edge of town. Rates average $1 per half-hour, with a maximum of $7.

Parking also is available for $10-$20 around the Truman Sports Complex, home to Arrowhead and Kauffman stadiums. Several major downtown hotels are connected to the Kansas City Convention Center by an underground concourse.

Shopping

The original model for the "outdoor shopping village" concept, **Country Club Plaza** (47th Street and J.C. Nichols Parkway) is the jewel in the crown of Kansas City shopping experiences. Built by J.C. Nichols, a wealthy developer with vision, the plaza opened in 1923 and was the nation's first suburban shopping complex designed expressly for consumers who owned an automobile. Doubting townspeople dubbed the plaza "Nichols' Folly" because it was built in a swampy area used for pig farming, but the plaza was a success from the start.

In addition to chain restaurants, local bistros and the Cinemark Palace at the Plaza Theater, the plaza's collection of some 150 retailers includes designer names like Coach and Tiffany & Co., trendsetters like Anthropologie and J.Crew, and traditional clothiers like Burberry and Talbots.

Spanish and Moorish influences are evident in the 12 towers looming over the terra-cotta rooftops; the most notable is a 130-foot-tall reproduction of Spain's Giralda Tower. More than 40 fountains and statues imported from Europe fill the plaza; intricate mosaic murals made of Spanish tile adorn storefronts; and terra-cotta planters, window boxes and street medians overflow with colorful plants. You can take a horse-drawn carriage ride throughout the year; gondola rides are available on adjacent Brush Creek from April through November.

Special events are held year-round. During a free concert series from May through September, reggae, rock, R&B and bluegrass music fills the air Thursday through Sunday evenings. The ⏚ **KCP&L Plaza Lighting Ceremony** celebrates the holiday season. Held every Thanksgiving night since 1925, the event draws thousands who wait for the moment when a switch is thrown and 80 miles of sparkling lights outline shops and restaurants in a kaleidoscope of colors—definitely one of most wonderful things to see at this time of year.

In contrast to Country Club Plaza's European ambience, **Crown Center** (2450 Grand Blvd., in the heart of downtown adjacent to Hallmark Cards headquarters) is contemporary in design. About 30 shops on three levels sell jewelry, toys, gifts, clothing and housewares; local restaurants run the gamut from fast food to fine dining.

The fashion-forward youngster will love the child-size versions of Kate Spade, Lacoste and Ugg in the Kid Oh! department at Halls Kansas City. There are Crayola products galore at the Crayola Store, while the LEGO Discovery Center features every imaginable LEGO creation as well as an interactive play area and a LEGO model of Kansas City.

The turn-of-the-20th-century redbrick buildings in the **Westport** district house shops, cafés, pubs and entertainment venues that attract a young, hip crowd. Enter **Pryde's Kitchen & Necessities** (115 Westport Rd.) and within minutes you'll be handed a mug of coffee or tea to sip while you shop. This divine emporium overflows with charm as well as everything you need for your kitchen, from Fiestaware, gourmet foods, knife blocks and teapots to bakeware, potato peelers and nutmeg graters. On Thursday, Friday and Saturday scrumptious, made-from-scratch fruit or cream pies can be purchased at the store's bakery, Ashleigh's Bake Shop. **Vulcan's Forge** (3936 Broadway) sells distinctive jewelry created by on-site designers and jewelers.

Pryde's Kitchen & Necessities

For a true Main Street-style shopping experience, explore the **Brookside** shopping district (on 63rd Street between Wornall and Main streets). Cafés and shops beneath blue and red-striped awnings include **Brookside Barkery & Bath** (118 W. 63rd St.), purveyor of pet-pampering products; **The (New) Dime Store** (314 W. 63rd St.), an old-fashioned five-and-dime complete with creaky wood floors; **Stuff** (316 W. 63rd St.), an artsy bazaar offering affordable art in the forms of jewelry, home goods and other stuff; **World's Window** (332 W. 63rd St.), packed with eco-friendly and fair-trade art, crafts, clothing, accessories and home décor from around the world; and **ShopGirls** (6245 Brookside Plaza), a funky fashion boutique.

Scenesters flock to the **Crossroads Art District,** centered around 20th Street and Baltimore Avenue downtown. Here you'll find **Retro Inferno** (1500 Grand Blvd.), a wonderland of fabulous mid-century furnishings and collectibles housed in a groovy 1960s-era building; **Bob Jones Shoes** (1914 Grand Blvd.), a local footwear institution; and **Christopher Elbow Chocolates** (1819 McGee St.), offering a tempting array of unusual and artistic treats.

On the prowl for antiques? The **45th & State Line Antique, Art & Design Center** is a quaint enclave of more than 20 shops clustered along the 1700 and 1800 blocks of 45th Street, just steps away from the Kansas/Missouri state line. The merchants here deal in American, Asian and European fine art, furnishings and architectural salvage.

Thirteen miles north of downtown, **Zona Rosa** (8640 N. Dixson Ave.) is a little out of the way but worth the trip if you like the old-fashioned feel of Main Street shopping combined with nationally known mall stores. Fountains and park benches enhance the relaxing experience. Retailers include American Eagle Outfitters, Chico's, Dick's Sporting Goods, Gap and Sephora, plus more than a dozen local restaurants.

Other regional shopping malls include **Independence Center,** I-70 and SR 291 in Independence; **Legends Outlets Kansas City,** 1843 Village West Pkwy. in Kansas City, Kan.; **Oak Park Mall,** 11149 W. 95th St. in Overland Park, Kan.; **Town Center Plaza & Crossing,** 5000 W. 119th St. in Leawood, Kan.; and **Ward Parkway Center,** 8600 Ward Pkwy.

Nightlife

Kansas City is well-known for its jazz scene—that's a given. But there's also some good rockin' to be found, and not just at midnight. One of the city's premier entertainment districts is downtown's **Kansas City Power & Light District** (bordered by Grand Boulevard, Baltimore Street, 12th Street and Truman Road). The "P & L," as it's locally known, is an eight-block area of bars, nightclubs, shops and places to eat. The focal point is **KC Live Block,** where crowds gather in a covered outdoor courtyard for free summer shows by national rock and country acts.

More than a dozen nightclubs surround the Live Block, which has an open liquor permit and heaters for cooler nights. The Power & Light District is also a great place to hang out for some wining and dining before or after shows at the nearby Sprint Center arena.

P & L perennials include the **Shark Bar** (1340 Grand Blvd.) and the **Mosaic Ultra Lounge** (1331 Walnut St.); both draw a crowd of mostly twenty-somethings with thumping DJ music. Mosaic has a swanky lounge vibe with comfy seating and a balcony view of downtown's glimmering lights, while Shark Bar's beachy décor and surf music is summed up by the motto "retro surf...retro dance...r-etro cool." Phone (816) 442-8140 for the Shark Bar or (816) 679-5454 for the Mosaic Ultra Lounge.

Things often get a little rowdy at **Angels Rock Bar** (1323 Walnut St.), where you can order a beer, a mixed drink or a glass of fine champagne at the 130-foot-long bar and get your groove on to live or DJ music, depending on the night; phone (816) 379-9813. Or sashay into **PBR Big Sky** (111 E. 13th St.), where country and western reigns and there's a mechanical bull by the name of Norman; phone (816) 442-8145.

P & L pubs have that traditional warm walnut wood décor as well as a wide selection of international brews (there's also whiskey or wine if you want it). Keep your thirst at bay at the **Flying Saucer Draught Emporium** (101 E. 13th St.) and **McFadden's Sports Saloon** (1330 Grand Blvd.). Boisterous barkeeps and patrons hoisting frosty mugs contribute to the homey neighborhood bar atmosphere. Phone (816) 221-1900 or (816) 471-1330, respectively.

The **Westport District**, centered around the intersection of Westport Road and Pennsylvania Avenue, has a diverse assortment of local restaurants and bars ensconced in 100-year-old brick buildings. It attracts locals as well as out-of-towners in search of a friendly neighborhood joint. **Kellys Westport Inn** (500 Westport Rd.) has walls festooned with sports memorabilia and neon beer signs. U2 singer Bono once stopped in for a pint and gave the place his seal of approval. Throw your extra quarters in the jukebox, toss back a few and stay awhile. Phone (816) 561-5800.

Revisit the 1970s at **The Foundry** (424 Westport Rd.). Paneled walls, bean bag chairs and even the font on the sign outside will remind you of your aunt's basement circa 1975, except your aunt probably didn't have 140 varieties of beer to choose from (including McCoy's own hand-crafted beers, ranging from lager to pale ales). The drink menu also includes wine and classic cocktails. Phone (816) 960-0866.

Harry's Bar & Tables (501 Westport Rd.) is a chic martini bar that also serves up delicious steak and seafood; the kitchen stays open until 2 a.m. so you can satisfy those midnight munchies. More than 50 brands of scotch are also on the menu. Phone (816) 561-3950.

Local bands and the occasional touring act play at **recordBar** (1520 Grand Blvd.). The venue moved to a downtown location in early 2016 and is currently open only on the days shows take place; tickets can be purchased online or in person on show nights. Phone (816) 753-5207 for the latest updates on an expanded opening schedule.

The beat goes on at the **18th & Vine Jazz District,** which is home to some smokin' nightclubs. If you love *le jazz hot*, this is your territory. Rated among the top jazz venues on the planet by Downbeat magazine, by day **The Blue Room** (1616 E. 18th St.), with memorabilia tucked under glass-topped tables, is a part of the American Jazz Museum, but at night the jazz is so hot it burns. Phone (816) 474-6262.

After midnight, swing by the **Mutual Musicians Foundation** (1823 Highland Ave.), where jazz and blues players burn the midnight oil during intense all-night jam sessions. Alcoholic beverages are served until 6 a.m. Elsewhere in town, **The Phoenix** (302 W. 8th St.) has live performances Tuesday through Sunday; the cozy brick-walled club attracts a crowd of sophisticated ladies and gentlemen. Phone (816) 471-5212 for the Mutual Musicians Foundation or (816) 221-5299 for The Phoenix.

It's almost a requirement for big cities to have a monthly art walk, and Kansas City is no exception. First Friday happens at the **Crossroads Art District** (20th Street and Baltimore Avenue), about a mile south of the Power & Light District and one of KC's fun places to go. Kick off your evening with a stroll through art galleries and boutiques from 7-9 p.m., then grab a meal or a glass of wine at one of the district's casually elegant bistros and lounges. Street performers and live music add to the fun atmosphere.

recordBar

Big Events

Things heat up in Kansas City beginning in late March with the **Greater Kansas City Home Show** at Bartle Hall, presented by the Home Builders Association of Greater Kansas City. Also in March is the **St. Patrick's Day Parade,** which threads through downtown and is followed by festivities that continue throughout the city well into the night. The **NAIA Division 1 Men's Basketball Championship,** which features smaller colleges and universities, takes place in mid-March.

Say Ciao L'Italia! to **Festa Italiana,** a 3-day weekend festival in late May and/or early June that's guaranteed to bring out your inner Italian.

The Crown Center sponsors free outdoor Summer on the Square activities, including concerts and children's entertainment, the **Hospital Hill Run** in June and the **Kansas City Irish Fest** in early September.

Over the July 4th weekend **KC Riverfest,** at Berkley Park on the Missouri River, salutes the nation's birthday with entertainment, games, crafts, food and a spectacular fireworks display.

The third full weekend of August brings the **Ethnic Enrichment Festival** to Swope Park, where the world's cultures are celebrated with live music and dance performances, craft exhibitions and a tempting lineup of food booths. Among the fun things to do with friends: watch Scottish Highland games and the colorful pageantry of the Parade of Nations.

In early September, the 3-day **Greek Food Fest** will have you shouting "Opa!" as you load up on souvlaki, baklava, gyros (pronounce it like "hero" if you want to sound authentic) with tzatziki sauce and other goodies. It takes place at the Annunciation Greek Orthodox Church, 120th Street and Wornall Road. **Fiesta Kansas City** is held in early September in the Kansas City Power & Light District. The event celebrates Hispanic culture with a day of Latin-American food, drink, art, crafts and entertainment.

Thanksgiving evening marks the  **KCP&L Plaza Lighting Ceremony,** which illuminates Country Club Plaza's fanciful towers with miles of tiny, colored light bulbs. The display lasts until mid-January. The day after Thanksgiving, a nearly 100-foot-tall Christmas tree is illuminated during the **Mayor's Christmas Tree Lighting Ceremony** at Crown Center Square. Decorated with more than 900 red and gold ornaments and white lights, the tree stands as the symbol of a citywide charity drive to help people in need during the holidays.

Festa Italiana

Sports & Rec

Major league all the way, Kansas City offers a wide range of professional sports. Following their teams with a passionate involvement, fans pile into the 118,000-seat **Harry S. Truman Sports Complex,** with its outstanding stadiums for **baseball** and **football.**

On any given year the **Kansas City Royals** draw a loyal baseball following from April through September to **Kauffman Stadium.** The team thrilled fans in 2015, besting the New York Mets in just five games and winning the World Series for the first time since 1985. Kauffman claims to have Major League Baseball's largest replay system; phone (800) 676-9257.

Football is a passion for the die-hard fans of the National Football League's **Kansas City Chiefs,** who play to capacity crowds in **Arrowhead Stadium**; phone (816) 920-9300.

College **basketball** is popular during the winter months. Major league **soccer's Sporting KC** place their spell over fans at **Children's Mercy Park** April through October; phone (913) 387-3400 or (888) 452-4625 for schedule and ticket information.

Kansas City's 302 public parks provide opportunities for a variety of fun things to do outdoors, including **boating, hiking** and **picnicking.** Three parks in particular are known for their natural beauty and developed facilities: **Jacob L. Loose Park,** 51st Street and Wornall Road; **Swope Park,** Meyer Boulevard and Swope Parkway; and **Fleming Park,** at US 40 and Woods Chapel Road in Lee's Summit and Blue Springs, in eastern Jackson County.

Swope Park has two of the oldest **golf** courses in the city. The **Minor Park Golf Course,** 11215 Holmes Rd., offers a challenging 18 holes. **River Oaks** is at 14204 St. Andrews Dr. in Grandview, just south of the Kansas City limits.

Courses outside Kansas City, Mo., include **Shamrock Hills,** 3161 S. SR 291 in Lee's Summit.

Courses outside Kansas City, Kan., include the **Sykes/Lady Overland Park Golf Club,** 12501 Quivira Rd. in Overland Park; the **St. Andrews Golf Club,** 11099 W. 135th St. in Overland Park; and **Tomahawk Hills,** 17501 Midland Dr. in Shawnee.

More than 200 public **tennis** courts are within the Kansas City metropolitan area. Most are free and available on a first-come, first-served basis. Phone the Parks and Recreation Department, (816) 513-7500, for locations. In **Swope Park** there are courts at the picnic area north of the Starlight Theatre.

The following parks have at least four courts: **The Concourse Park,** at Benton Boulevard and St. John Avenue; **Martin Luther King, Jr. Square Park,** at Swope Parkway and Woodland Avenue; **Loose Park,** at 5200 Wornall Rd.; and **Central Park** at 31st Street and Indiana Avenue.

Bicycling is popular on the trails in Swope Park.

In the winter Kansas City's parks draw visitors for **cross-country skiing.** Ice Terrace, an outdoor rink at Crown Center, 2450 Grand Ave., is open November to mid-March for **ice skating.**

Kansas Speedway, at I-70 and I-435, draws **motorsports** fans for NASCAR Monster Energy Cup Series, XFINITY Series and additional racing events; phone (866) 460-7223.

Performing Arts

Kansas City's opera and ballet companies as well as its symphony orchestra perform at the stunning **Kauffman Center for the Performing Arts** (1601 Broadway). **Lyric Opera of Kansas City** performs in the center's **Muriel Kauffman Theatre;** for information or tickets to its two fall and two spring presentations phone (816) 471-7344 or (877) 673-7252. The **Kansas City Ballet** mounts four productions a year, also in the Muriel Kauffman Theatre, including "The Nutcracker" in December;

Kansas City Ballet

phone (816) 931-2232 for schedule information. The **Kansas City Symphony** presents its October through May concert season in the center's Helzberg Hall; phone (816) 471-0400 for information and tickets.

If you're looking for things for couples to do, local and national acts in a variety of genres take the stage at the 3,000-seat **Arvest Bank Theatre at The Midland** (1228 Main St.). Thirsty concertgoers can grab a cold one at the Midland's in-house bar The Indie on Main before and after shows; those in the bar before a show are allowed to enter the venue first. Phone (816) 283-9900 for general information, or (816) 283-9921 for tickets.

A tremendous reconstruction effort turned the once-dilapidated **Gem Theater,** 1615 E. 18th St. in the 18th & Vine Historic District, into a center for multicultural arts, entertainment and education programming. Phone (816) 474-6262 (Gem Theater) or (816) 474-8463 (American Jazz Museum, part of the district) for information about upcoming performances and exhibitions.

The University of Missouri-Kansas City's **Conservatory of Music and Dance,** 4949 Cherry St., draws patrons from within as well as outside the university. Concert series also are sponsored by William Jewell College's Department of Music.

The university-based equity company of the **Kansas City Repertory Theater** stages classic and modern productions in the on-campus **Spencer Theater,** 4949 Cherry St., September through June; phone (816) 235-2700. Musical comedy productions, light opera and concerts of all types are on the bill at Swope Park's **Starlight Theatre,** the nation's second-largest outdoor amphitheater. Top stars perform during the mid-June through September season; phone (816) 363-7827 for the box office.

From mid-June to mid-July, works by the Bard of Avon are presented in Southmoreland Park during the **Heart of America Shakespeare Festival;** phone (816) 531-7728. The Theatre League brings the national touring companies of Broadway musicals to the **Music Hall,** 301 W. 13th St.; phone (816) 513-5000.

The **Folly Theater,** W. 12th and Central streets, is a restored turn-of-the-20th-century burlesque house that presents a variety of entertainment, from children's theater to jazz concerts; phone (816) 842-5500. The **New Theatre Restaurant,** 9229 Foster St. in Overland Park, offers evening performances Tuesday through Sunday as well as Sunday matinees; phone (913) 649-7469.

Other area theaters include the **Providence Medical Center Amphitheater,** 633 N. 130th St. in Bonner Springs, Kan., (913) 825-3400; **Comedy City** at 3600 Broadway, (816) 842-2744; **Coterie Theatre** (on the Crown Center's first level), (816) 474-6552; the **Quality Hill Playhouse** at 303 W. 10th St., (816) 421-1700; **Theatre for Young America** at 30 W. Pershing Rd., (816) 460-2083; the **Unicorn Theatre** at 3828 Main St., (816)

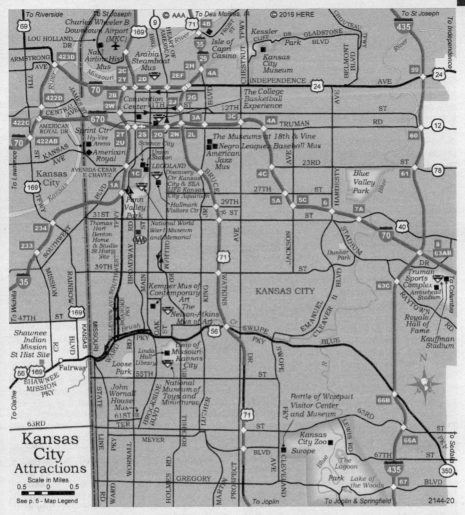

Kansas City Attractions

Scale in Miles
0.5   0   0.5

See p. 6 - Map Legend

2144-20

531-7529; and the **Just Off Broadway Theatre** at 3051 Central in Penn Valley Park, (816) 784-5020.

The events section of the *Kansas City Star* has current information about the city's performing arts offerings and is a great resource when looking for fun things to do with friends.

ATTRACTIONS

For a complete list of attractions, visit AAA.com/travelguides/attractions

AMERICAN ROYAL is 1 mi. w. from jct. 12th St. and Broadway, then .5 mi. s. on Genesee St. to 1701 American Royal Ct., following signs for Kemper Arena. American Royal began in 1899 at the Kansas City Stockyards as the nation's first purebred cattle show. From September through November, such events as

livestock and horse shows, rodeos, barbecue contests and parades are held. A museum offers interactive displays relating to the agriculture and livestock industries, livestock judging and western lifestyle. Show clothing and memorabilia as well as a film detailing Kansas City history may be seen.

Note: The barbecue contest moved to Kansas in 2017. The museum and events are scheduled to relocate to Kansas in late 2018; phone ahead for updates. Food is available during events. **Time:** Allow 1 hour minimum. **Hours:** Mon.-Fri. 8:30-5, Sat.-Sun. by appointment. Phone ahead for event schedule. Closed major holidays. **Cost:** Museum free. Event tickets $15-$70. **Phone:** (816) 221-9800.

ARABIA **STEAMBOAT MUSEUM** is at 400 Grand Blvd. in the River Market area. The *Arabia* sank in the Missouri River in 1856 with a 200-ton cargo. This museum displays a vast collection of frontier supplies and personal belongings recovered from the steamboat in 1989, including clothing and shoes, medicines, guns, bottled fruits and vegetables, jewelry and perfume. The 6-ton stern and a paddle-wheel are preserved with a full-size reproduction of the main deck. Guided tours include a theater presentation describing the excavation effort, and visitors may view a working preservation lab.

Time: Allow 1 hour, 30 minutes minimum. **Hours:** Mon.-Sat. 10-5, Sun. noon-5. Last admission is at 3:30. Tours depart every 30 minutes. Closed Jan. 1, Easter, Thanksgiving, Christmas Eve and Christmas. Phone ahead to confirm schedule. **Cost:** $14.50; $13.50 (ages 60+); $5.50 (ages 4-14). **Phone:** (816) 471-1856 or (816) 471-4030. ⒪

THE COLLEGE BASKETBALL EXPERIENCE is connected to the Sprint Center at 1401 Grand Blvd. Ever dream of making a game-winning jump shot or announcing the scores of your favorite basketball teams from behind a news desk? This interactive facility allows you to do that and more. Whether you're a hard-core college basketball fanatic or a casual spectator, the museum will lure you out on to the court to experience the excitement of being a top college athlete.

Exhibits highlight various aspects of the game. You can rebound a ball for a lay-up at Clean the Glass, practice 3-point shots at Shoot From Downtown or slam dunk at a hoop that's just your height at the Throw It Down exhibit. Compare your shoe and hand sizes to those of college players at the Measure Up display and make as many free throws before the buzzer goes off in Step Up to the Line.

Complete your visit with a walk through the National Collegiate Basketball Hall of Fame. Here the greats—players, coaches and contributors—are enshrined in a slick, high-tech room filled with interactive floor displays and colorful graphics. Nearby, the Honor Theater presents an immersive film about the sport. **Note:** Only shoes with soft soles are allowed on the basketball courts. **Time:** Allow 1 hour, 30 minutes minimum. **Hours:** Mon.-Sat. 10-6, Sun. 11-6, Memorial Day through mid-Aug.; Wed.-Sat. 10-6, Sun. 11-6. Last admission 1 hour before closing. Closed major holidays. **Cost:** $15; $12 (ages 4-17); $11 (65+ and active military with ID). **Phone:** (816) 949-7500.

KANSAS CITY MUSEUM is at 3218 Gladstone Blvd., adjacent to Cliff Drive Scenic Byway and Kessler Park. The museum is housed in Corinthian Hall, a 50-room mansion built in 1910 by industrialist Robert A. Long and named for the six Corinthian columns at its entrance. The 50-seat StoryTarium theater, in what was formerly the museum's planetarium, presents documentaries, films, lectures and other history programming. The Long Family and Corinthian Hall outdoor exhibit offers vibrantly colored panels detailing the history of the Long family and the 3-acre estate and also presents a collection of vintage Kansas City postcards.

Note: The museum was closed for ongoing restoration at press time; phone for updates. Special events are held on the lawn. **Phone:** (816) 513-0720.

KANSAS CITY ZOO—see Swope Park p. 212.

KEMPER MUSEUM OF CONTEMPORARY ART is just e. of 45th and Main sts. at 4420 Warwick Blvd. Georgia O'Keeffe, Robert Mapplethorpe and William Wegman are among the artists represented in a permanent collection of diverse, modern works. **Time:** Allow 1 hour minimum. **Hours:** Tues.-Fri. 10-4 (also Thurs.-Fri. 4-9), Sat.-Sun. 10-4. Closed major holidays. **Cost:** Free. **Phone:** (816) 753-5784. ⒪

LEGOLAND DISCOVERY CENTER KANSAS CITY is at 2475 Grand Blvd., at the south end of Crown Center Square. Kids are introduced to an exhibit of a LEGO factory showing how the classic bricks are made, then ushered onto a ride where they get to shoot dragons and monsters with a laser gun from the moving car. Also featured is a 15-minute 4-D movie.

An impressive display of Kansas City's landmarks make up MiniLand, which consists of 1.5 million individual LEGO bricks and several interactive features; over the course of 6 minutes the room changes from day to night, and includes a LED fireworks display. Several stations are set up inside the Discovery Center, ranging from a LEGO racer build and test workshop to a girls' karaoke shop.

LEGO Master Builder Academy classes are offered every half-hour, during which participants create a unique piece that can be purchased and taken home. There is a large soft play area with slides, rope walls and huge blocks, including a giant wrecking ball that inspires more thoughts of demolition than creation. You must accompany a child under the age of 16 to visit the attraction. Adult only night is 6 p.m.-8 p.m. on the second Thursday of the month. Children must wear socks to enter the soft play area. **Time:** Allow 2 hours minimum. **Hours:** Mon.-Thurs. 10-6, Fri. and Sun. 10-7, Sat. 10-8. Center opens at 9 a.m. Labor Day weekend, Thanksgiving weekend and Dec. 26-31. Last admission is 2 hours before closing. **Cost:** $27.95; free (ages 0-2). Combination ticket with Sea Life Kansas City Aquarium $39.95; free (ages 0-2). **Phone:** (816) 471-4386. ⒪

THE MUSEUMS AT 18TH & VINE are .3 mi. s. off I-70 Paseo exit, then e. to 1616 E. 18th St. This complex, in the heart of one of the country's most celebrated jazz and blues districts, encompasses the American Jazz Museum and the Negro Leagues Baseball Museum. The Horace M. Peterson III Visitor Center offers a brief video celebrating the African-American community that thrived at 18th and Vine for more than 40 years.

Hours: Museums and visitor center open Tues.-Sat. 9-6, Sun. noon-6. Closed major holidays. **Cost:** Visitor center free. Each museum $10; $9 (ages 65+); $6 (ages 5-12). Combination ticket for both museums $15; $13 (ages 65+); $8 (ages 5-12). **Phone:** (816) 474-8463.

American Jazz Museum, 1616 E. 18th St., is part of The Museums at 18th & Vine complex and recalls jazz greats Louis Armstrong, Duke Ellington, Ella Fitzgerald, Charlie Parker and others through listening stations, photographs, videos and memorabilia. **Time:** Allow 1 hour minimum. **Hours:** Tues.-Sat. 9-6, Sun. noon-6. Closed Jan. 1, July 4, Veterans Day, Thanksgiving and Christmas. **Cost:** $10; $9 (ages 65+); $6 (ages 5-12). Combination ticket with the Negro Leagues Baseball Museum $15; $13 (ages 65+); $8 (ages 5-12). **Phone:** (816) 474-8463.

Negro Leagues Baseball Museum, 1616 E. 18th St., is part of The Museums at 18th & Vine complex and recounts the formation and history of the Negro Baseball League prior to 1945, the year Jackie Robinson was signed by the Brooklyn Dodgers. Displays include pennants, autographed baseballs, photographs, biographies and an 8-minute video about the league narrated by former CNN anchorman Bernard Shaw.

Time: Allow 30 minutes minimum. **Hours:** Tues.-Sat. 9-6, Sun. noon-6. Closed Jan. 1, July 4, Veterans Day, Thanksgiving and Christmas. **Cost:** $10; $9 (ages 65+); $6 (ages 5-12). Combination ticket with the American Jazz Museum $15; $13 (ages 65+); $8 (ages 5-12). **Phone:** (816) 221-1920 or (888) 221-6526.

NATIONAL MUSEUM OF TOYS AND MINIATURES is at 5235 Oak St. exhibits the world's largest collection of fine-scale miniatures and one of the nation's largest collections of historic toys on view Highlights from the toy collection include the 9-foot tall Coleman dollhouse circa 1864, a Baby Moss doll by doll artist Leo Moss circa 1895 and a floor-to-ceiling kinetic marble sculpture.

The fine-scale miniature collection features contemporary artworks that are created in exquisite detail, right down to the dovetailed drawers and often function like their full-scale counterparts. Notable architectural works include a replica of the Palace of Versailles, Twin Manors (a Colonial Georgian mansion) and the Studiolo Gubbio from the Gubbio Palace in Italy.

Such special events as storytelling, scavenger hunts, family days, holiday events, craft workshops and temporary toy exhibits take place throughout the year. **Time:** Allow 1 hour minimum. **Hours:** Wed.-Mon. 10-4. Closed major holidays. **Cost:** $8; $7 (ages 65+); $5 (ages 6-17 and college students with ID); free (ages 0-5, UMKC faculty, staff and students, and active and retired military with ID). **Phone:** (816) 235-8000.

NATIONAL WORLD WAR I MUSEUM AND MEMORIAL, 2 Memorial Dr., is dedicated to remembering, interpreting and understanding World War I and its enduring impact on the global community. The museum and memorial hold one of the

National Museum of Toys and Miniatures

most comprehensive collections of World War I objects and documents in the world. Visitors take an epic journey through personal stories of courage, honor, patriotism and sacrifice that make the experiences of the war era meaningful and relevant for present and future generations

The 217-foot-tall Liberty Memorial Tower takes visitors to an open-air observation deck at the top for panoramic views of downtown Kansas City. Several fountains grace the landscaped grounds.

Time: Allow 2 hours minimum. **Hours:** Sun.-Fri. 10-5, Sat. 9-5, Memorial Day-Labor Day; Tues.-Sun. 10-5, rest of year. Closed Jan. 1, Thanksgiving, Christmas Eve, Christmas and Dec. 31. **Cost:** $18; $14 (ages 65+ and military with ID); $10 (ages 6-18); Combination ticket with tower $20; $16 (ages 65+ and military with ID); $12 (ages 6-18). Tower only $5. **Phone:** (816) 888-8100.

THE NELSON-ATKINS MUSEUM OF ART is 4.5 mi. s. on US 56 at 45th and Oak sts. The museum's permanent collection of more than 41,000 art objects is one of the country's finest. Highlights include Asian, American and European paintings; modern sculpture; ancient Egyptian, Etruscan, Greek and Roman pieces; and an extensive collection of English ceramics. Works by modern artists are featured in the 22-acre Kansas City Sculpture Park, notably a large collection of monumental bronzes by English sculptor Henry Moore.

The Bloch Building contains the museum's collection of African and contemporary art, a reference library and a sculpture court. The impressive Hallmark Photography Collection features works from the origins of photography to the present; practically every key American photographer is represented. An Egyptian gallery features tomb discoveries, including the inner coffin of a 2,300-year-old noblewoman. A reflecting pool highlights the building's north entrance.

Hours: Mon. and Wed.-Sun. 10-5 (also Thurs.-Fri. 5-9). Collection Highlights tours depart Mon. and Wed.-Fri. at 1:30, Thurs.-Fri. at 6:15 and 7:30, Sat.-Sun. at 1:15 and 2:30. Other tours are offered; phone for details. Closed Jan. 1, July 4, Thanksgiving, Christmas Eve and Christmas. **Cost:** Free. A fee is charged for ticketed exhibitions. **Parking:** Garage $10. **Phone:** (816) 751-1278. ⑪

OCEANS OF FUN—see Worlds of Fun p. 213.

ROYALS HALL OF FAME is at Kaufmann Stadium, at the jct. of I-70 and the Blue Ridge Cutoff. A short movie shown in the Dugout Theater highlights the history of the Royals, the stadium and individual players going back to the beginning of baseball in Kansas City. Interactive exhibits include one that lets you design your own ballpark and another that lets you call plays in an announcer's booth.

The hall of fame gallery displays photos and biographies of 25 Royals Hall of Fame members. Legendary players George Brett and Frank White are highlighted in an interactive exhibit. The Royals' 1985 World Series trophy is on display in the Crowning Moments section, along with division titles and pennants won by the team through the years. Cooperstown Corner is dedicated to items on loan from the National Baseball Hall of Fame.

Time: Allow 2 hours minimum. **Hours:** Open non-game days Tues.-Sat. 10-2, day after Memorial Day through Aug. 30; Tues. and Fri.-Sat. 10-2, early Apr.-Memorial Day and Sept. 1 to mid-Sept. Open game days 10-2 (also 90 minutes before game opening until the top of the 8th inning). Open by appointment rest of year. Holiday hours vary. Phone ahead to confirm schedule. **Cost:** $10; $9 (ages 55+); $7 (ages 4-12); Free during games with paid admission. **Parking:** $15 (on game days); free (on non-game days in lot M). **Phone:** (816) 504-4222 for tour information or (816) 921-8000.

Kauffman Stadium Tours is at jct. I-70 and Blue Ridge Cutoff at One Royal Way. The tours provide a behind-the-scenes look at the Kansas City Royals' home facility. Packages include a 90-minute experience that visits the Royals Hall of Fame, dugout, press box and outfield, a tour that includes a visit to a diamond suite and souvenirs like signed caps, and an all-access pass on game day.

Note: The shortest tour requires walking 1.5 miles. Some of the stops along the tour routes may not be included due to limited availability. **Time:** Allow 1 hour, 15 minutes minimum. **Hours:** Schedule varies based on season game days; visit the website or phone ahead for details. **Cost:** Legends tour $17; $15 (ages 55+); $12 (ages 0-12). All-Star tour $30; $27 (ages 55+); $22 (ages 0-12).

Grand Slam tour $55; $50 (ages 55+); $40 (ages 0-12). Reservations are recommended. **Parking:** $15 (on game days); free (on non-game days in lot M). **Phone:** (816) 504-4222.

SEA LIFE KANSAS CITY AQUARIUM is at 2475 Grand Blvd., at the south end of Crown Center Square. Thousands of sea creatures are displayed, including a huge variety of fresh and saltwater fish species, sharks, rays, crabs and eels. Habitats with interactive features include a display about Missouri lakes.

Glass tunnels enhance the up-close feeling while observing the aquarium's inhabitants. The Touch Tank offers hands-on experiences like petting a star fish or tickling a sea urchin. Plenty of background information is provided, staff are on hand to answer questions, and quizzes help keep kids interested and involved. **Time:** Allow 2 hours minimum. **Hours:** Sun.-Thurs. 10-5, Fri.-Sat. 10-6. Last admission is 2 hours before closing. **Cost:** $21.95; $17.95 (ages 3-12). Combination ticket with LEGOLAND Discovery Center $39.95; $34.95 (ages 3-12). **Phone:** (816) 471-4386.

SWOPE PARK is s.e. of downtown at jct. Meyer Blvd. and Swope Pkwy. This 1,805-acre park contains golf courses, tennis courts, picnic grounds and a swimming pool. A lagoon offers fishing, boating and ice-skating. During the summer, musicals and popular entertainers are presented nightly in the outdoor Starlight Theatre.

The park's Lakeside Nature Center houses native Missouri wildlife, has educational displays and offers nature trails. The center's staff rehabilitates injured wildlife. **Hours:** Park open daily 5 a.m.-midnight. Lakeside Nature Center open Tues.-Sat. 9-4, Sun. 11-3. **Cost:** Free. **Phone:** (816) 513-7500, (816) 513-8960 for the nature center, or (816) 363-7827 for the Starlight Theatre.

Kansas City Zoo is in Swope Park at 6800 Zoo Dr. This 202-acre zoo exhibits animals in the Tropics; Australian Outback; Penguin Plaza; Asian Tiger Trail; Discovery Barn; a 3-acre chimp exhibit; and a 95-acre African Plains exhibit, overlooked by the African Sky Safari gondola ride. An endangered species carousel and train, tram and boat rides are offered seasonally for an additional fee.

Time: Allow a full day. **Hours:** Mon.-Fri. 8-4, Sat.-Sun. 8-5, Memorial Day-Labor Day; daily 9:30-4, Nov.-Feb.; Mon.-Fri. 9:30-4; Sat.-Sun. 9:30-5, rest of year. Phone ahead to confirm schedule. **Cost:** $14.50; $13.50 (ages 55+); $11.50 (ages 3-11). Admission for Jackson and Clay County residents with ID $7; $6.50 (ages 55+); $6 (ages 3-11). **Phone:** (816) 595-1234.

UNION STATION is at 30 W. Pershing Rd. More than 79,000 trains passed through this terminal at its peak in 1917, and half of all GIs deployed in World War II traveled under its great clock. Restored in 1999, the station is now home to Science City (see *attraction listing)* and hosts world-class touring exhibitions. It also includes hands-on exhibits highlighting American railroad history such as the Model Railroad Experience and KC Rail Experience. The Grand Hall features 95-foot ceilings with intricate plaster ornaments, along with two restaurants. The Theater District includes a five-story digital movie theater, live performances on City Stage and a state-of-the-art planetarium.

Hours: Union Station open daily 6 a.m.-midnight. Attractions open Tues.-Sat. 10-5 (also Mon. 10-5, June-Aug.), Sun. noon-5. Hours for Union Station shops and restaurants vary. Phone ahead to confirm attraction and performance schedules. **Cost:** Union Station building free. Science City (includes KC Rail Experience) $13.25; free (ages 0-2). Planetarium $7. Model Railroad Experience free with any ticket. Touring Exhibition prices vary. **Parking:** $3-$15. **Phone:** (816) 460-2020.

Science City is in Union Station at 30 W. Pershing Rd. Interactive exhibits include Science on a Sphere, a huge, dome-shaped room with a 7-foot sphere suspended in the center, that features global images, planetary data and earth science programs. A local school's "Battle of the Brains" contest resulted in the Unplugged energy exhibit. There's also an animal and nature center, a crime lab, a bicycle suspended 30 feet above ground and more than 50 hands-on interactive areas. DinoLab offers a behind-the-scenes look at a working lab where a paleontologist prepares dinosaur fossils for exhibition.

Hours: Tues.-Sat. 10-5 (also Mon. 10-5, June-Aug.), Sun. noon-5. Closed 1 week in Sept. for annual maintenance. Phone ahead to confirm schedule. **Cost:** Union Station free. Science City $13.25; free (ages 0-2). **Phone:** (816) 460-2020.

WORLDS OF FUN is off I-435 exit 54 (Parvin Rd.) at 4545 Worlds of Fun Ave. This 235-acre entertainment complex combines an amusement park and a tropical water park. Worlds of Fun offers 175 acres of rides, shows and attractions in five internationally themed areas. Featured are Mamba, one of the tallest, longest and fastest coasters in the world; Timber Wolf, a world-class wooden coaster; and The Prowler, a wooden coaster reaching 51 mph. Camp Snoopy is a 1-acre playland with Peanuts-themed rides and characters. Nordic Chaser, speedy mini ships that rotate along a circuit, is scheduled to open in 2018.

Hours: Park opens daily at 10, mid-May to late Aug. and Labor Day weekend; Sat.-Sun. at 10, early Apr. to mid-May and day after Labor Day weekend-late Oct. Closing times vary. **Cost:** (includes Oceans of Fun) $59.99; $39.99 (ages 62+ and under 48 inches tall); free (ages 0-2). After 4 p.m. $39.99 (Sat.); $36.99 (Sun.-Fri.). Phone ahead to confirm rates. **Parking:** $17; $20 (Sat.). **Phone:** (816) 454-4545.

Oceans of Fun is off I-435 exit 54 (Parvin Rd.) at 4545 Worlds of Fun Ave. This 60-acre tropical-themed water park features the Surf City Wave Pool, a million-gallon pool with 4-foot waves; Hurricane Falls, an eight-story-high family raft ride; and a variety of other waterslides. Special areas of the park are designed specifically for children and for adults.

Hours: Water park opens daily at 11, late May to mid-Aug.; opens Sat.-Sun. at 11, mid-Aug. to early Sept. Closing time varies. Phone ahead to confirm schedule. **Cost:** (includes Worlds of Fun) $59.99; $39.99 (ages 62+ and under 48 inches tall); free (ages 0-2). After 4 p.m. $39.99 (Sat.); $36.99 (Sun.-Fri.). Phone ahead to confirm rates. **Parking:** $17; $20 (Sat.). **Phone:** (816) 454-4545.

Sightseeing
Driving Tours
"Day Tours from Kansas City," a 40-page booklet detailing eight trips within a day's drive, is available to AAA/CAA members free at any AAA service office in Missouri. *See AAA Offices.*

Industrial Tours

HARLEY-DAVIDSON ASSEMBLY PLANT AND VISITORS CENTER is at 11401 N. Congress. This is one of two Harley-Davidson motorcycle final assembly plants in the United States. The free tour includes a video presentation and a chance to see the actual production line where the Dyna, Sportster and V-Rod models and the V-Rod's Revolution Powertrain motor are assembled. Audio headsets and safety glasses are provided. Two-hour behind-the-scenes Steel Toe Tours also are offered.

Note: Tour participants must wear completely enclosed low-heeled shoes. Cameras are permitted in the tour center but not on the plant tour. **Time:** Allow 1 hour, 30 minutes minimum. **Hours:** Center open Mon.-Fri. 9-3. General tours are given Mon.-Fri. 9-1:30. Closed during model change and year-end maintenance periods; production not always scheduled on Friday. Steel Toe Tours are offered Mon.-Thurs. at 9:15 and noon. Closed major holidays. Phone ahead to confirm schedule. **Cost:** Ages 0-11 are not permitted on tours; ages 12-17 must be accompanied by an adult. General Tours free. Steel Toe Tours $38. **Phone:** (816) 270-8488 or (877) 883-1450. GT

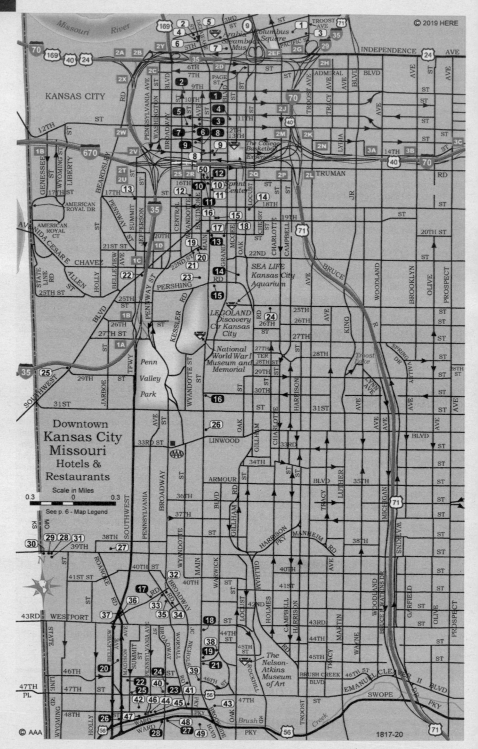

© 2019 HERE

KANSAS CITY

Downtown
Kansas City
Missouri
Hotels &
Restaurants

Scale in Miles

0.3   0   0.3

See p. 6 - Map Legend

© AAA

1817-20

Downtown Kansas City

This index helps you "spot" where hotels and restaurants are located on the corresponding detailed maps. Restaurant price range is a combination of lunch and/or dinner. Turn to the listing page for more information and consult display ads for special promotions.

 For more details, rates and reservations: AAA.com/travelguides/hotels

DOWNTOWN KANSAS CITY

Map Page	Hotels	Designation	Member Savings	Page
1 p. 214	Hampton Inn by Hilton Kansas City Financial District	THREE DIAMOND	✔	226
2 p. 214	**21c Museum Hotel Kansas City by MGallery**	FOUR DIAMOND	✔	225
3 p. 214	Hotel Indigo Kansas City Downtown	THREE DIAMOND		227
4 p. 214	The Ambassador Kansas City, Autograph Collection	FOUR DIAMOND	✔	225
5 p. 214	**Kansas City Marriott Downtown**	THREE DIAMOND	✔	227
6 p. 214	**Hotel Phillips Kansas City, Curio Collection by Hilton**	FOUR DIAMOND	✔	227
7 p. 214	**Aladdin Holiday Inn Downtown Kansas City**	THREE DIAMOND	✔	225
8 p. 214	**Crowne Plaza Kansas City Downtown**	THREE DIAMOND	✔	225
9 p. 214	**Hilton President Kansas City**	FOUR DIAMOND	✔	226
10 p. 214	Courtyard by Marriott Kansas City Downtown/ Convention Center	THREE DIAMOND	✔	225
11 p. 214	Residence Inn by Marriott Kansas City Downtown/ Convention Center	THREE DIAMOND	✔	227
12 p. 214	Hampton Inn & Suites Kansas City Downtown Crossroads	THREE DIAMOND	✔	226
13 p. 214	Home2 Suites Kansas City Downtown	THREE DIAMOND	✔	227
14 p. 214	**The Sheraton Kansas City Hotel at Crown Center**	THREE DIAMOND	✔	227
15 p. 214	**The Westin Kansas City at Crown Center**	THREE DIAMOND	✔	228
16 p. 214	Fairfield by Marriott Kansas City/Union Hill	THREE DIAMOND	✔	225
17 p. 214	**AC Hotels by Marriott Kansas City Westport**	THREE DIAMOND	✔	225
18 p. 214	**Best Western Plus Seville Plaza Hotel**	THREE DIAMOND	✔	225
19 p. 214	Kansas City Marriott Country Club Plaza	THREE DIAMOND	✔	227
20 p. 214	SpringHill Suites by Marriott	THREE DIAMOND	✔	228
21 p. 214	**Holiday Inn Country Club Plaza** (See ad p. 226.)	THREE DIAMOND	✔	226
22 p. 214	Hampton Inn & Suites By Hilton - Kansas City Country Club Plaza	APPROVED	✔	225
23 p. 214	Courtyard by Marriott-Country Club Plaza	THREE DIAMOND	✔	225
24 p. 214	Residence Inn by Marriott Kansas City Country Club Plaza	THREE DIAMOND	✔	227
25 p. 214	**Sheraton Suites Country Club Plaza** (See ad p. 228.)	THREE DIAMOND	✔	228
26 p. 214	**The Fontaine Country Club Plaza Kansas City**	THREE DIAMOND	✔	225
27 p. 214	**The Raphael Hotel, Autograph Collection**	FOUR DIAMOND	✔	227
28 p. 214	**The InterContinental Kansas City at the Plaza**	FOUR DIAMOND	✔	227

Map Page	Restaurants	Designation	Cuisine	Price Range	Page
① p. 214	Garozzo's Ristorante	APPROVED	Italian	$15-$32	229
② p. 214	The Farmhouse	THREE DIAMOND	Natural/Organic	$9-$26	229
③ p. 214	Happy Gillis	APPROVED	Natural/Organic	$6-$14	229
④ p. 214	Tribe Street Kitchen	APPROVED	Continental	$11-$14	230
⑤ p. 214	Brown & Loe	THREE DIAMOND	American	$11-$27	228
⑥ p. 214	Il Lazzarone Pizza	APPROVED	Pizza	$9-$15	229
⑦ p. 214	Harry's Country Club	APPROVED	American	$8-$22	229
⑧ p. 214	Drunken Fish	THREE DIAMOND	Japanese Sushi	$5-$27	229
⑨ p. 214	Bristol Seafood + Steak + Social	THREE DIAMOND	Seafood	$10-$39	228
⑩ p. 214	Anton's Taproom Restaurant	APPROVED	American	$12-$24	228
⑪ p. 214	Nara	APPROVED	Japanese Sushi	$12-$28	229

Map Page	Restaurants (cont'd)	Designation	Cuisine	Price Range	Page
⑫ p. 214	Webster House	THREE DIAMOND	American	$11-$32	230
⑬ p. 214	Blue Bird Bistro	APPROVED	Natural/Organic	$5-$32	228
⑭ p. 214	Mission Taco Joint	APPROVED	Mexican	$6-$22	229
⑮ p. 214	**Corvino Tasting Room**	FOUR DIAMOND	New American	$105-$200	229
⑯ p. 214	Corvino Supper Club	THREE DIAMOND	New American	$12-$28	229
⑰ p. 214	The Rieger Hotel Grill & Exchange	THREE DIAMOND	American	$10-$29	230
⑱ p. 214	The Rockhill Grille	THREE DIAMOND	New American	$12-$34	230
⑲ p. 214	Lidia's Kansas City	THREE DIAMOND	Northern Italian	$12-$35	229
⑳ p. 214	Grunauer	THREE DIAMOND	Austrian	$9-$30	229
㉑ p. 214	Fiorella's Jack Stack Barbecue - Freight House	APPROVED	Barbecue	$8-$32	229
㉒ p. 214	La Bodega	APPROVED	Spanish Small Plates	$5-$22	229
㉓ p. 214	Pierponts At Union Station	THREE DIAMOND	Steak Seafood	$10-$48	229
㉔ p. 214	The Antler Room	THREE DIAMOND	Mediterranean Small Plates	$8-$18	228
㉕ p. 214	Ponak's Mexican Kitchen & Bar	APPROVED	Mexican	$6-$17	229
㉖ p. 214	Gates Bar-B-Q	APPROVED	Barbecue	$8-$20	229
㉗ p. 214	Q39	APPROVED	Barbecue	$7-$30	230
㉘ p. 214	d'Bronx Authentic Deli and Pizzeria	APPROVED	Pizza Deli	$6-$26	229
㉙ p. 214	Blue Koi Noodles & Dumplings	APPROVED	Asian	$8-$17	228
㉚ p. 214	Jazz, A Louisiana Kitchen	APPROVED	Cajun	$8-$20	229
㉛ p. 214	Genghis Khan Mongolian Grill	APPROVED	Mongolian Barbecue	$7-$16	229
㉜ p. 214	Jerusalem Cafe	APPROVED	Middle Eastern	$7-$19	229
㉝ p. 214	Harry's Bar & Tables	APPROVED	American	$7-$17	229
㉞ p. 214	Port Fonda	APPROVED	Mexican	$5-$19	229
㉟ p. 214	Californos	APPROVED	American	$9-$27	228
㊱ p. 214	Bluestem Restaurant	FOUR DIAMOND	New American	$80-$115	228
㊲ p. 214	PotPie	APPROVED	American	$7-$23	229
㊳ p. 214	Cafe Sebastienne	THREE DIAMOND	American	$11-$27	228
㊴ p. 214	Cafe Trio	APPROVED	New American	$5-$29	228
㊵ p. 214	Cooper's Hawk Winery & Restaurant	THREE DIAMOND	American	$12-$34	229
㊶ p. 214	Fiorella's Jack Stack Barbecue	APPROVED	American	$7-$21	229
㊷ p. 214	The Capital Grille	THREE DIAMOND	Steak	$18-$55	228
㊸ p. 214	Grand Street Cafe	THREE DIAMOND	American	$9-$36	229
㊹ p. 214	Hogshead Kansas City	APPROVED	American	$13-$29	229
㊺ p. 214	Kona Grill	THREE DIAMOND	Pacific Rim Fusion	$9-$30	229
㊻ p. 214	Gram & Dun	THREE DIAMOND	New American	$11-$25	229
㊼ p. 214	Parkway Social Kitchen	THREE DIAMOND	New American	$12-$35	229
㊽ p. 214	Chaz on the Plaza	THREE DIAMOND	Continental	$8-$39	229
㊾ p. 214	Stock Hill	FOUR DIAMOND	New Steak	$22-$52	230
㊿ p. 214	Streetcar Grille & Tavern	APPROVED	American	$12-$26	230

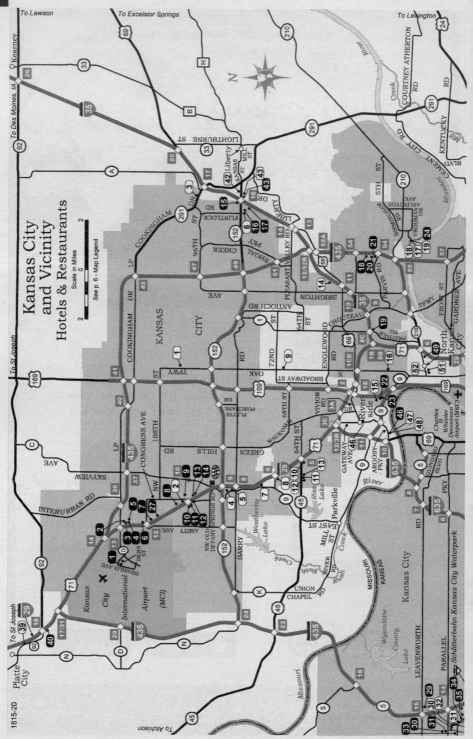

Kansas City and Vicinity
Hotels & Restaurants

See p. 6 – Map Legend

Scale in Miles

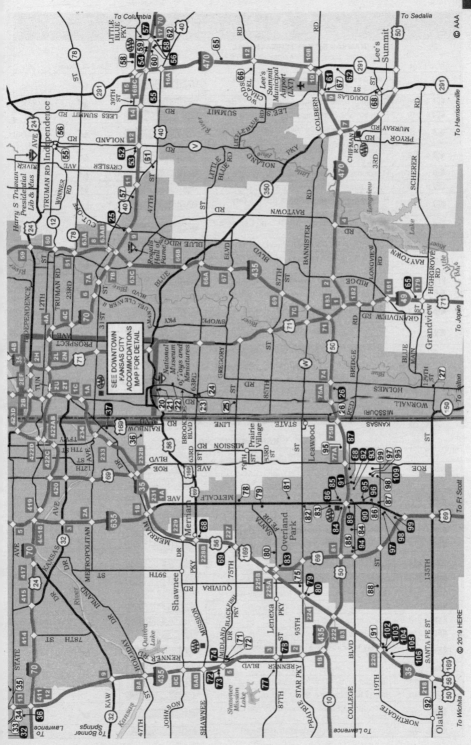

© AAA

© 2019 HERE

✈ Airport Hotels

Map Page	KANSAS CITY INTERNATIONAL (Maximum driving distance from airport: 5.6 mi)	Designation	Member Savings	Page
7 p. 218	**Best Western Plus Kansas City Airport-KCI East, 3.7 mi**	💎 THREE DIAMOND	✔	230
11 p. 218	Courtyard by Marriott-KCI, 5.1 mi	💎 THREE DIAMOND	✔	231
10 p. 218	Drury Inn & Suites-Kansas City Airport, 5.1 mi	💎 THREE DIAMOND		231
3 p. 218	Fairfield Inn & Suites by Marriott/Kansas City Airport, 2.8 mi	💎 THREE DIAMOND	✔	231
2 p. 218	Four Points by Sheraton Kansas City Airport, 2.7 mi	💎 THREE DIAMOND	✔	231
6 p. 218	Hampton Inn by Hilton Kansas City Airport, 3.5 mi	💎 THREE DIAMOND	✔	231
27 p. 218	Hilton Garden Inn Kansas City Airport, 4.0 mi	💎 THREE DIAMOND	✔	231
13 p. 218	**Holiday Inn Express & Suites Kansas City Airport, 5.5 mi**	💎 THREE DIAMOND	✔	231
5 p. 218	**Holiday Inn KCI Airport & KCI Expo Center, 2.9 mi**	💎 THREE DIAMOND	✔	231
14 p. 218	Home2 Suites by Hilton KCI Airport, 5.6 mi	💎 THREE DIAMOND	✔	231
9 p. 218	Homewood Suites by Hilton Kansas City Airport, 5.3 mi	💎 THREE DIAMOND	✔	231
12 p. 218	**Hyatt Place Kansas City/Airport, 5.3 mi**	💎 THREE DIAMOND	✔	231
1 p. 218	Marriott Kansas City Airport, on airport property	💎 THREE DIAMOND	✔	232
8 p. 218	Residence Inn by Marriott, Kansas City Airport, 4.9 mi	💎 THREE DIAMOND	✔	232
4 p. 218	TownePlace Suites by Marriott Kansas City Airport, 2.9 mi	💎 THREE DIAMOND	✔	232

Kansas City and Vicinity

This index helps you "spot" where hotels and restaurants are located on the corresponding detailed maps. Restaurant price range is a combination of lunch and/or dinner. Turn to the listing page for more information and consult display ads for special promotions.

 For more details, rates and reservations: AAA.com/travelguides/hotels

KANSAS CITY, MO

Map Page	Hotels	Designation	Member Savings	Page
1 p. 218	Marriott Kansas City Airport	💎 THREE DIAMOND	✔	232
2 p. 218	Four Points by Sheraton Kansas City Airport	💎 THREE DIAMOND	✔	231
3 p. 218	Fairfield Inn & Suites by Marriott/Kansas City Airport	💎 THREE DIAMOND	✔	231
4 p. 218	TownePlace Suites by Marriott Kansas City Airport	💎 THREE DIAMOND	✔	232
5 p. 218	**Holiday Inn KCI Airport & KCI Expo Center**	💎 THREE DIAMOND	✔	231
6 p. 218	Hampton Inn by Hilton Kansas City Airport	💎 THREE DIAMOND	✔	231
7 p. 218	**Best Western Plus Kansas City Airport-KCI East**	💎 THREE DIAMOND	✔	230
8 p. 218	Residence Inn by Marriott, Kansas City Airport	💎 THREE DIAMOND	✔	232
9 p. 218	Homewood Suites by Hilton Kansas City Airport	💎 THREE DIAMOND	✔	231
10 p. 218	Drury Inn & Suites-Kansas City Airport	💎 THREE DIAMOND		231
11 p. 218	Courtyard by Marriott-KCI	💎 THREE DIAMOND	✔	231
12 p. 218	**Hyatt Place Kansas City/Airport**	💎 THREE DIAMOND	✔	231
13 p. 218	**Holiday Inn Express & Suites Kansas City Airport**	💎 THREE DIAMOND	✔	231
14 p. 218	Home2 Suites by Hilton KCI Airport	💎 THREE DIAMOND	✔	231
15 p. 218	Hampton Inn by Hilton-Kansas City/Liberty	💎 THREE DIAMOND	✔	231
16 p. 218	Holiday Inn Express & Suites Kansas City/Liberty	💎 APPROVED		231
17 p. 218	Fairfield Inn & Suites by Marriott Kansas City Liberty	💎 THREE DIAMOND	✔	231
18 p. 218	Candlewood Suites Kansas City Northeast	💎 THREE DIAMOND		230

KANSAS CITY, MO (cont'd)

Map Page	Hotels (cont'd)	Designation	Member Savings	Page
19 p. 218	**Best Western Country Inn North**	APPROVED	✔	230
20 p. 218	Hampton Inn by Hilton Kansas City near Worlds of Fun	THREE DIAMOND	✔	231
21 p. 218	Comfort Inn & Suites near Worlds of Fun	APPROVED		231
22 p. 218	Courtyard by Marriott Kansas City at Briarcliff	THREE DIAMOND	✔	231
23 p. 218	TownePlace Suites by Marriott Kansas City at Briarcliff	THREE DIAMOND	✔	232
24 p. 218	Ameristar Casino Hotel Kansas City	THREE DIAMOND		230
25 p. 218	Drury Inn & Suites-Kansas City Stadium	APPROVED		231
26 p. 218	Courtyard by Marriott	THREE DIAMOND	✔	231
27 p. 218	Hilton Garden Inn Kansas City Airport	THREE DIAMOND	✔	231

Map Page	Restaurants	Designation	Cuisine	Price Range	Page
1 p. 218	White Horse Pub	APPROVED	English	$8-$17	233
2 p. 218	Smokebox BBQ	APPROVED	Barbecue	$6-$15	232
3 p. 218	Masabi Japanese Sushi Bar & Grill	APPROVED	Japanese Sushi	$4-$28	232
4 p. 218	Bo Lings	APPROVED	Chinese	$7-$20	232
5 p. 218	Smokehouse Bar-B-Que	APPROVED	Barbecue	$7-$24	232
6 p. 218	Corner Cafe	APPROVED	Comfort Food	$5-$15	232
7 p. 218	LC's Hamburgers Etc	APPROVED	Burgers	$4-$10	232
8 p. 218	Tasty Thai	APPROVED	Thai	$8-$20	232
9 p. 218	Summit Grill	APPROVED	American	$10-$26	232
10 p. 218	Saki Asian Restaurant	APPROVED	Asian Sushi	$10-$33	232
11 p. 218	Dominic's Casual Italian	APPROVED	Italian	$5-$12	232
12 p. 218	Bonefish Grill	THREE DIAMOND	Seafood	$7-$33	232
13 p. 218	Luna Azteca Mexican Grill	APPROVED	Mexican	$8-$17	232
14 p. 218	Stroud's Oak Ridge Manor	APPROVED	Chicken	$8-$25	232
15 p. 218	Trezo Mare Restaurant and Lounge	THREE DIAMOND	Italian	$7-$33	233
16 p. 218	Cascone's Italian Restaurant	APPROVED	Italian	$7-$23	232
17 p. 218	Horizon's Buffet	APPROVED	International	$12-$26	232
18 p. 218	DeliLux	APPROVED	Deli	$5-$8	232
19 p. 218	Great Plains Cattle Company	THREE DIAMOND	Steak	$18-$55	232
20 p. 218	Black Dirt	THREE DIAMOND	New American	$11-$24	232
21 p. 218	**Osteria Il Centro**	THREE DIAMOND	Northern Italian	$8-$19	232
22 p. 218	Aixois French Bistro	APPROVED	French	$12-$42	232
23 p. 218	Avenues Bistro	APPROVED	European	$12-$32	232
24 p. 218	Carmen's Cafe	APPROVED	Italian	$8-$26	232
25 p. 218	Summit Grill & Bar	THREE DIAMOND	American	$8-$34	232
26 p. 218	Jasper's Ristorante	THREE DIAMOND	Traditional Italian	$13-$27	232
27 p. 218	Fiorella's Jack Stack Barbecue - Martin City	APPROVED	Barbecue	$9-$32	232

KANSAS CITY, KS

Map Page	Hotels	Designation	Member Savings	Page
29 p. 218	Comfort Suites Speedway	THREE DIAMOND		102
30 p. 218	Homewood Suites by Hilton Kansas City Speedway	THREE DIAMOND	✔	102
31 p. 218	Candlewood Suites Kansas City Speedway	APPROVED		102
32 p. 218	Residence Inn by Marriott Kansas City at The Legends	THREE DIAMOND	✔	102
33 p. 218	Country Inn & Suites by Radisson, KC Village West	THREE DIAMOND		102
34 p. 218	**Best Western Premier KC Speedway Inn & Suites**	THREE DIAMOND	✔	102
35 p. 218	Hampton Inn by Hilton Village West	THREE DIAMOND	✔	102
36 p. 218	Chateau Avalon Hotel	THREE DIAMOND		102

KANSAS CITY, KS (cont'd)

Map Page	Hotels (cont'd)	Designation	Member Savings	Page
37 p. 218	Home2 Suites by Hilton KU Medical Center	THREE DIAMOND	✔	102

Map Page	Restaurants	Designation	Cuisine	Price Range	Page
30 p. 218	Jazz a Louisiana Kitchen	APPROVED	Cajun	$8-$20	102
31 p. 218	STIX	APPROVED	Asian Sushi	$6-$27	102
32 p. 218	Jose Pepper's	APPROVED	Southwestern	$6-$17	102
33 p. 218	Chiusano's Brick Oven Pizzeria	APPROVED	Pizza	$5-$20	102
34 p. 218	El Toro Loco Mexican Bar & Grill	APPROVED	Tex-Mex	$10-$22	102
35 p. 218	Yukon Base Camp Grill at Cabela's	APPROVED	Wild Game Deli	$5-$12	102
36 p. 218	Joe's Kansas City Bar-B-Que	APPROVED	Barbecue	$7-$16	102

PLATTE CITY

Map Page	Hotel	Designation	Member Savings	Page
40 p. 218	Ramada by Wyndham Platte City KCI Airport	APPROVED		240

Map Page	Restaurant	Designation	Cuisine	Price Range	Page
39 p. 218	Maria's Authentic Mexican Restaurant	APPROVED	Mexican	$7-$14	240

LIBERTY

Map Page	Hotel	Designation	Member Savings	Page
43 p. 218	TownePlace Suites by Marriott Kansas City/Liberty	THREE DIAMOND	✔	235

Map Page	Restaurants	Designation	Cuisine	Price Range	Page
42 p. 218	Tasty Thai - Liberty	APPROVED	Thai	$8-$20	235
43 p. 218	Margarita's	APPROVED	Mexican	$6-$16	235

RIVERSIDE

Map Page	Hotel	Designation	Member Savings	Page
45 p. 218	Argosy Casino Hotel & Spa *(See ad p. 230.)*	FOUR DIAMOND	✔	242

Map Page	Restaurants	Designation	Cuisine	Price Range	Page
46 p. 218	Corner Cafe	APPROVED	American	$7-$14	242
47 p. 218	The Journey	THREE DIAMOND	Steak	$20-$40	242
48 p. 218	Terrace Buffet	APPROVED	International	$14-$30	242

NORTH KANSAS CITY

Map Page	Hotel	Designation	Member Savings	Page
49 p. 218	Holiday Inn Express Hotel & Suites	THREE DIAMOND		239

Map Page	Restaurants	Designation	Cuisine	Price Range	Page
51 p. 218	Chappell's Restaurant & Sports Museum	APPROVED	American	$7-$21	239
52 p. 218	Paul & Jack's Tavern	APPROVED	American	$6-$20	239

INDEPENDENCE

Map Page	Hotels	Designation	Member Savings	Page
52 p. 218	Truman Inn	APPROVED		195
53 p. 218	Super 8 Independence	APPROVED		195
54 p. 218	Hilton Garden Inn Independence	THREE DIAMOND	✔	195
55 p. 218	Stoney Creek Hotel & Conference Center	THREE DIAMOND		195
56 p. 218	Holiday Inn Express & Suites-Independence/ Kansas City	THREE DIAMOND		195
57 p. 218	Drury Inn & Suites Kansas City-Independence	THREE DIAMOND		195
58 p. 218	My Place Hotel	APPROVED		195

Map Page	Restaurants	Designation	Cuisine	Price Range	Page
55 p. 218	The Rheinland Restaurant	APPROVED	German	$7-$23	195
56 p. 218	Ophelia's Restaurant & Inn	THREE DIAMOND	American	$8-$32	195
57 p. 218	V's Italiano Ristorante	APPROVED	Italian	$7-$26	196
58 p. 218	Smokehouse Bar-B-Que	APPROVED	Barbecue	$8-$22	196
59 p. 218	Hereford House	THREE DIAMOND	Steak	$7-$38	195
60 p. 218	Jazz A Louisiana Kitchen	APPROVED	Cajun	$11-$22	195

Map Page	Restaurants (cont'd)	Designation	Cuisine	Price Range	Page
61 p. 218	Salvatore's Italian Restaurant	APPROVED	Italian	$8-$26	195
62 p. 218	Corner Cafe	APPROVED	Comfort Food	$5-$14	195

LEE'S SUMMIT

Map Page	Hotels	Designation		Member Savings	Page
61 p. 218	Hampton Inn by Hilton	THREE DIAMOND		✔	235
62 p. 218	Fairfield Inn & Suites by Marriott Lee's Summit	APPROVED		✔	235

Map Page	Restaurants	Designation	Cuisine	Price Range	Page
65 p. 218	Summit Grill & Bar	THREE DIAMOND	American	$8-$34	235
66 p. 218	Tiff N' Jay's	APPROVED	American	$8-$22	235
67 p. 218	Jose Pepper's	APPROVED	Southwestern	$7-$16	235
68 p. 218	Smoke Brewing Co	APPROVED	American	$9-$16	235

GRANDVIEW

Map Page	Hotel	Designation	Member Savings	Page
65 p. 218	**Holiday Inn Express Hotel & Suites**	THREE DIAMOND	✔	192

MERRIAM, KS

Map Page	Hotels	Designation	Member Savings	Page
68 p. 218	Drury Inn-Merriam/Shawnee Mission	APPROVED		109
69 p. 218	Hampton Inn & Suites by Hilton	THREE DIAMOND	✔	109

SHAWNEE, KS

Map Page	Hotels	Designation	Member Savings	Page
72 p. 218	Courtyard by Marriott	THREE DIAMOND	✔	116
73 p. 218	Holiday Inn Express & Suites	THREE DIAMOND		116
74 p. 218	Hampton Inn by Hilton-Shawnee	THREE DIAMOND	✔	116

Map Page	Restaurants	Designation	Cuisine	Price Range	Page
71 p. 218	Paulo and Bill	THREE DIAMOND	Italian	$10-$31	116
72 p. 218	Barley's Kitchen + Tap	APPROVED	American	$7-$27	116

LENEXA, KS

Map Page	Hotels	Designation	Member Savings	Page
77 p. 218	SpringHill Suites by Marriott Kansas City Lenexa/City Center	THREE DIAMOND	✔	106
78 p. 218	**Hyatt Place Kansas City/Lenexa City Center**	THREE DIAMOND	✔	106
79 p. 218	Holiday Inn Express & Suites - Lenexa - Overland Park Area	THREE DIAMOND		106
80 p. 218	Candlewood Suites Lenexa - Overland Park Area	APPROVED		106

Map Page	Restaurant	Designation	Cuisine	Price Range	Page
75 p. 218	Shogun Sushi & Steak Restaurant	APPROVED	Japanese Sushi Steak	$7-$23	106

OVERLAND PARK, KS

Map Page	Hotels	Designation	Member Savings	Page
83 p. 218	Holiday Inn & Suites Overland Park-West	THREE DIAMOND		112
84 p. 218	**Homewood Suites by Hilton**	THREE DIAMOND	✔	112
85 p. 218	Hampton Inn by Hilton-Kansas City/Overland Park	THREE DIAMOND	✔	111
86 p. 218	Embassy Suites by Hilton Kansas City Overland Park	THREE DIAMOND	✔	111
87 p. 218	**Hyatt Place Kansas City/Overland Park/Convention Center**	THREE DIAMOND	✔	112
88 p. 218	Holiday Inn & Suites Convention Center Overland Park	THREE DIAMOND		112
89 p. 218	Marriott Kansas City Overland Park	THREE DIAMOND	✔	112
90 p. 218	Drury Inn & Suites-Overland Park	THREE DIAMOND		111
91 p. 218	**Courtyard by Marriott Kansas City/Overland Park Convention Center**	THREE DIAMOND	✔	111
92 p. 218	Hilton Garden Inn Overland Park	THREE DIAMOND	✔	111

OVERLAND PARK, KS (cont'd)

Map Page	Hotels (cont'd)	Designation	Member Savings	Page
93 p. 218	Sheraton Overland Park Hotel at the Convention Center	THREE DIAMOND	✔	112
94 p. 218	DoubleTree by Hilton Kansas City-Overland Park	THREE DIAMOND	✔	111
95 p. 218	Hyatt Place Kansas City/Overland Park/Metcalf	THREE DIAMOND	✔	112
96 p. 218	Courtyard by Marriott Kansas City Overland Park/Metcalf	THREE DIAMOND	✔	111
97 p. 218	Residence Inn by Marriott	THREE DIAMOND	✔	112
98 p. 218	SpringHill Suites by Marriott	APPROVED	✔	112
99 p. 218	Fairfield Inn & Suites by Marriott Overland Park	THREE DIAMOND	✔	111

Map Page	Restaurants	Designation	Cuisine	Price Range	Page
78 p. 218	The Burg & Barrel	APPROVED	Burgers	$10-$14	112
79 p. 218	Mr. Gyros Greek Food and Pastry	APPROVED	Greek	$6-$12	113
80 p. 218	India Palace	APPROVED	Indian	$6-$15	112
81 p. 218	Johnny Cascone's Italian Restaurant	APPROVED	Italian	$6-$24	112
82 p. 218	Fiorella's Jack Stack Barbecue - Overland Park	APPROVED	Barbecue	$7-$33	112
83 p. 218	Jose Pepper's	APPROVED	Southwestern	$6-$17	112
84 p. 218	Q39 South	APPROVED	Barbecue	$8-$25	113
85 p. 218	Garozzo's Overland Park	APPROVED	Italian	$14-$34	112
86 p. 218	J. Alexander's Restaurant	THREE DIAMOND	American	$8-$28	112
87 p. 218	Burnt End BBQ	APPROVED	Barbecue	$9-$16	112
88 p. 218	Barley's Kitchen + Tap	APPROVED	American	$8-$28	112

OLATHE, KS

Map Page	Hotels	Designation	Member Savings	Page
102 p. 218	Holiday Inn Express & Suites Olathe North	THREE DIAMOND		110
103 p. 218	Hilton Garden Inn Olathe	THREE DIAMOND	✔	110
104 p. 218	Hampton Inn by Hilton	THREE DIAMOND	✔	110
105 p. 218	Residence Inn by Marriott	THREE DIAMOND	✔	110
106 p. 218	Fairfield Inn & Suites by Marriott	THREE DIAMOND	✔	110

Map Page	Restaurants	Designation	Cuisine	Price Range	Page
91 p. 218	Joe's Kansas City Barbeque	APPROVED	Barbecue	$5-$14	110
92 p. 218	Kmacho's Mexican Grill & Cantina	APPROVED	Tex-Mex	$8-$18	110

LEAWOOD, KS

Map Page	Hotel	Designation	Member Savings	Page
109 p. 218	Aloft Leawood-Overland Park	THREE DIAMOND	✔	105

Map Page	Restaurants	Designation	Cuisine	Price Range	Page
95 p. 218	Rye KC	THREE DIAMOND	New American	$11-$50	105
96 p. 218	Pig & Finch	THREE DIAMOND	American	$13-$27	105
97 p. 218	Hereford House	APPROVED	Steak	$8-$25	105
98 p. 218	The Bristol Seafood Grill	THREE DIAMOND	Seafood	$8-$35	105
99 p. 218	La Bodega	THREE DIAMOND	Spanish Small Plates	$5-$22	105

AAA.com/maps—Dream, plan, go

with AAA travel planning tools

DOWNTOWN KANSAS CITY

- Restaurants p. 228
- Hotels & Restaurants map & index p. 214

21C MUSEUM HOTEL KANSAS CITY BY MGALLERY
816/443-4200 2

FOUR DIAMOND

Historic Boutique Hotel

Address: 219 W 9th St 64105 **Location:** Jct W 9th & Central sts; downtown. **Facility:** This unique hotel is perfect for guests with an appreciation for modern contemporary art, as the public areas are gallery spaces. Rooms are very large and feature sleek décor with upscale accents. 120 units. 7 stories, interior corridors. **Parking:** on-site (fee) and valet. **Terms:** check-in 4 pm. **Amenities:** safes. **Activities:** exercise room. **Guest Services:** valet laundry.

SAVE ⊤⊤ ⊹ ⊤ CALL ⌖ ⊹⊹
BIZ HS ⊚ ⊠ ⊟
/ SOME UNITS ⊞

AC HOTELS BY MARRIOTT KANSAS CITY WESTPORT
816/931-0001 17

THREE DIAMOND

Hotel

AAA Benefit: Members save 5% or more!

Address: 560 Westport Rd 64111 **Location:** Jct Main St, 0.4 mi w; in Westport Plaza area. **Facility:** 123 units. 4 stories, interior corridors. **Amenities:** safes. **Activities:** exercise room. **Guest Services:** valet and coin laundry, area transportation.

SAVE ECO ⊤⊤ ⊤ CALL ⌖ ⊹⊹
BIZ ⊚ ⊠ ⊡ ⊟ ⊟
/ SOME UNITS HS

ALADDIN HOLIDAY INN DOWNTOWN KANSAS CITY
010/421-8888 7

THREE DIAMOND

Boutique Hotel

Address: 1215 Wyandotte St 64105 **Location:** Jct 12th St, just se. **Facility:** In a historic building (circa 1920s) near the convention center, the property boasts its original marble floors and pillars in the atrium lobby. Rooms have splashy decor and a wide variety of styles. 193 units. 16 stories, interior corridors. **Parking:** valet only. **Terms:** check-in 4 pm. **Activities:** exercise room. **Guest Services:** valet and coin laundry.

SAVE ⊤⊤ ⊹ ⊤ ⊹⊹ BIZ HS
⊚ ⊠ ⊟ / SOME UNITS ⊟ ⊟

THE AMBASSADOR KANSAS CITY, AUTOGRAPH COLLECTION
816/298-7700 4

FOUR DIAMOND SAVE Historic Boutique Hotel. **Address:** 1111 Grand Blvd 64106

AAA Benefit: Members save 5% or more!

@ **AAA.com/campgrounds—**

For overnights under the stars

BEST WESTERN PLUS SEVILLE PLAZA HOTEL
816/561-9600 18

THREE DIAMOND

Hotel

Best Western PLUS

AAA Benefit: Members save up to 15% and earn bonus points!

Address: 4309 Main St 64111 **Location:** Jct 43rd St, just s. **Facility:** 76 units. 4 stories, interior corridors. **Activities:** exercise room.

SAVE ⊤⊤ CALL ⌖ ⊹⊹ BIZ ⊚
⊠ ⊟ ⊟ / SOME UNITS ⊟ ⊟

COURTYARD BY MARRIOTT-COUNTRY CLUB PLAZA
816/285-9755 23

THREE DIAMOND SAVE Historic Hotel. **Address:** 4600 J.C. Nichols Pkwy 64112

AAA Benefit: Members save 5% or more!

COURTYARD BY MARRIOTT KANSAS CITY DOWNTOWN/CONVENTION CENTER
816/221-7400 10

THREE DIAMOND SAVE Hotel. **Address:** 1535 Baltimore Ave 64108

AAA Benefit: Members save 5% or more!

CROWNE PLAZA KANSAS CITY DOWNTOWN
816/474-6664 8

THREE DIAMOND

Hotel

Address: 1301 Wyandotte St 64105 **Location:** Just s of I-70, US 24 and 40. **Facility:** 385 units. 28 stories, interior corridors. **Parking:** on-site (fee) and valet. **Pool:** heated outdoor. **Activities:** exercise room. **Guest Services:** valet laundry, area transportation.

SAVE ⊤⊤ ⊹ ⊤ ⊃⊃ ⊹⊹ BIZ
⊚ ⊠ ⊟ ⊟

FAIRFIELD BY MARRIOTT KANSAS CITY/UNION HILL
816/931-5700 16

THREE DIAMOND SAVE Hotel. **Address:** 3001 Main St 64108

AAA Benefit: Members save 5% or more!

THE FONTAINE COUNTRY CLUB PLAZA KANSAS CITY
816/753-8800 26

THREE DIAMOND

Boutique Hotel

Address: 901 W 48th Pl 64112 **Location:** Jct Madison Ave; in Country Club Plaza area. **Facility:** This polished and sophisticated hotel is conveniently located at Country Club Plaza. The views from many guest rooms and the on-site restaurant are unequaled by any other hotel in the city. 132 units. 7 stories, interior corridors. **Parking:** on-site (fee) and valet. **Amenities:** safes. **Pool:** heated outdoor. **Activities:** exercise room, massage. **Guest Services:** valet laundry, area transportation.

SAVE ⊤⊤ ⊹ ⊤ CALL ⌖ ⊃⊃ ⊹⊹ BIZ HS ⊚
⊠ ⊟ / SOME UNITS ⊟

HAMPTON INN & SUITES BY HILTON - KANSAS CITY COUNTRY CLUB PLAZA
816/448-4600 22

APPROVED SAVE Hotel. **Address:** 4600 Summit St 64112

AAA Benefit: Members save up to 15%!

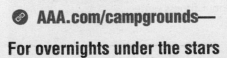

(See map & index p. 214.)

HAMPTON INN & SUITES KANSAS CITY DOWNTOWN CROSSROADS   816/255-3915 **12**

THREE DIAMOND **SAVE** Hotel. **Address:** 1571 Main St 64108

AAA Benefit: Members save up to 15%!

HAMPTON INN BY HILTON KANSAS CITY FINANCIAL DISTRICT   816/474-9200 **1**

THREE DIAMOND **SAVE** Historic Hotel. **Address:** 801 Walnut St 64105

AAA Benefit: Members save up to 15%!

HILTON PRESIDENT KANSAS CITY   816/221-9490 **9**

FOUR DIAMOND

Historic Hotel

Hilton HOTELS & RESORTS

AAA Benefit: Members save up to 15%!

Address: 1329 Baltimore Ave 64105 **Location:** Jct 14th St. **Facility:** Built in the 1920s and recently refurbished, this hotel is a cornerstone of the popular Power & Light District. Guest rooms are large and designed with a fashionable and stylish elegance. 213 units. 13 stories, interior corridors. **Parking:** on-site (fee) and valet. **Amenities:** safes. **Dining:** 2 restaurants. **Activities:** exercise room. **Guest Services:** valet laundry, area transportation.

HOLIDAY INN COUNTRY CLUB PLAZA
816/753-7400 **21**

THREE DIAMOND

Hotel

Address: 1 E 45th St 64111 **Location:** Jct Main St; in Country Club Plaza. **Facility:** 240 units. 2-5 stories, interior corridors. **Pool:** outdoor. **Activities:** exercise room. **Guest Services:** valet and coin laundry, area transportation. (See ad this page.)

(See map & index p. 214.)

HOME2 SUITES KANSAS CITY DOWNTOWN
816/987-7300 **13**

 THREE DIAMOND **SAVE** Extended Stay Hotel. **Address:** 2001 Main St 64108

AAA Benefit: Members save up to 15%!

HOTEL INDIGO KANSAS CITY DOWNTOWN
816/283-8000 **3**

THREE DIAMOND Historic Boutique Hotel. **Address:** 101 W 11th St 64105

HOTEL PHILLIPS KANSAS CITY, CURIO COLLECTION BY HILTON
816/221-7000 **6**

FOUR DIAMOND

Historic Boutique Hotel

AAA Benefit: Members save up to 15%!

Address: 106 W 12th St 64105 **Location:** Jct Wyandotte St, just e. **Facility:** Located in central downtown, this restored boutique property features a stunning 1930s Art Deco design. The on-trend and polished rooms boast lush accents. 216 units. 20 stories, interior corridors. **Parking:** valet only. **Activities:** exercise room. **Guest Services:** valet laundry, area transportation. **Featured Amenity:** full hot breakfast.

THE INTERCONTINENTAL KANSAS CITY AT THE PLAZA
816/756-1500 **28**

FOUR DIAMOND

Hotel

Address: 401 Ward Pkwy 64112 **Location:** Jct Wornall Rd; in Country Club Plaza. **Facility:** This fashionable hotel offers guests easy access to upscale shops and restaurants at nearby Country Club Plaza. The spacious guest rooms have lovely décor and offer a range of luxury amenities. 371 units. 6-12 stories, interior corridors. **Parking:** on-site (fee) and valet. **Terms:** check-in 4 pm. **Amenities:** safes. **Pool:** outdoor. **Activities:** sauna, steamroom, health club. **Guest Services:** valet laundry.

KANSAS CITY MARRIOTT COUNTRY CLUB PLAZA
816/531-3000 **19**

THREE DIAMOND **SAVE** Hotel. **Address:** 4445 Main St 64111

AAA Benefit: Members save 5% or more!

KANSAS CITY MARRIOTT DOWNTOWN
816/421-6800 **5**

THREE DIAMOND

Hotel

AAA Benefit: Members save 5% or more!

Address: 200 W 12th St 64105 **Location:** Jct Wyandotte St. **Facility:** 971 units. 18-22 stories, interior corridors. **Parking:** on-site (fee) and valet. **Amenities:** safes. **Pool:** heated indoor. **Activities:** health club. **Guest Services:** valet laundry, boarding pass kiosk, area transportation.

THE RAPHAEL HOTEL, AUTOGRAPH COLLECTION
816/756-3800 **27**

FOUR DIAMOND

Historic Boutique Hotel

 AUTOGRAPH COLLECTION HOTELS

AAA Benefit: Members save 5% or more!

Address: 325 Ward Pkwy 64112 **Location:** Corner of Wornall Rd; in Country Club Plaza. **Facility:** A large circular drive with a picturesque statue greets guests as they arrive at this quaint hotel. Rooms feature lush appointments and very nice bedding; some units have restricted bathroom space. 126 units. 9 stories, interior corridors. **Parking:** on-site (fee) and valet. **Terms:** check-in 4 pm. **Amenities:** safes. **Dining:** Chaz on the Plaza, see separate listing, entertainment. **Activities:** exercise room. **Guest Services:** valet laundry.

RESIDENCE INN BY MARRIOTT KANSAS CITY COUNTRY CLUB PLAZA
816/753-0033 **24**

THREE DIAMOND **SAVE** Extended Stay Hotel. **Address:** 4601 Broadway Blvd 64112

AAA Benefit: Members save 5% or more!

RESIDENCE INN BY MARRIOTT KANSAS CITY DOWNTOWN/CONVENTION CENTER
816/221-1400 **11**

THREE DIAMOND **SAVE** Extended Stay Hotel. **Address:** 1535 Baltimore Ave 64108

AAA Benefit: Members save 5% or more!

THE SHERATON KANSAS CITY HOTEL AT CROWN CENTER
816/841-1000 **14**

THREE DIAMOND

Hotel

 SHERATON

AAA Benefit: Members save 5% or more!

Address: 2345 McGee St 64108 **Location:** In Crown Center area. **Facility:** 720 units. 42 stories, interior corridors. **Parking:** on-site (fee) and valet. **Terms:** check-in 4 pm. **Amenities:** safes. **Pool:** heated outdoor. **Activities:** hot tub, exercise room. **Guest Services:** valet and coin laundry, area transportation.

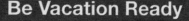

(See map & index p. 214.)

SHERATON SUITES COUNTRY CLUB PLAZA
816/931-4400 ㉕

THREE DIAMOND

Hotel

AAA Benefit: Members save 5% or more!

Address: 770 W 47th St 64112 **Location:** Jct Summit St; in Country Club Plaza. **Facility:** 257 units. 18 stories, interior corridors. **Parking:** on-site (fee) and valet. **Amenities:** safes. **Pool:** heated outdoor, heated indoor. **Activities:** exercise room. **Guest Services:** valet and coin laundry. *(See ad this page.)*

SPRINGHILL SUITES BY MARRIOTT
816/285-4900 ⑳

THREE DIAMOND SAVE Hotel. **Address:** 4500 Madison Ave 64111

AAA Benefit: Members save 5% or more!

THE WESTIN KANSAS CITY AT CROWN CENTER
816/474-4400 ⑮

THREE DIAMOND

Hotel

WESTIN HOTELS & RESORTS

AAA Benefit: Members save 5% or more!

Address: 1 E Pershing Rd 64108 **Location:** 0.5 mi s. **Facility:** 724 units. 18 stories, interior corridors. **Parking:** on-site (fee) and valet. **Terms:** check-in 4 pm. **Amenities:** safes. **Pool:** heated outdoor. **Activities:** sauna, hot tub, steamroom, tennis, health club, massage. **Guest Services:** valet laundry, boarding pass kiosk, area transportation.

▼ See AAA listing this page ▼

WHERE TO EAT

THE ANTLER ROOM 816/605-1967 ㉔
THREE DIAMOND Mediterranean Small Plates. Casual Dining. **Address:** 2506 Holmes St 64108

ANTON'S TAPROOM RESTAURANT 816/888-8800 ⑩
APPROVED American. Casual Dining. **Address:** 1610 Main St 64108

BLUE BIRD BISTRO 816/221-7559 ⑬
APPROVED Natural/Organic. Casual Dining. **Address:** 1700 Summit St 64108

BLUE KOI NOODLES & DUMPLINGS 816/561-5003 ㉙
APPROVED Asian. Casual Dining. **Address:** 1803 W 39th St 64111

BLUESTEM RESTAURANT 816/561-1101 ㊱
FOUR DIAMOND New American. Fine Dining. **Address:** 900 Westport Rd 64111

BRISTOL SEAFOOD + STEAK + SOCIAL 816/448-6007 ⑨
THREE DIAMOND Seafood. Casual Dining. **Address:** 51 E 14th St 64106

BROWN & LOE 816/472-0622 ⑤
THREE DIAMOND American. Gastropub. **Address:** 429 Walnut St 64106

CAFE SEBASTIENNE 816/561-7740 ㊳
THREE DIAMOND American. Casual Dining. **Address:** 4420 Warwick Blvd 64111

CAFE TRIO 816/756-3227 ㊴
APPROVED New American. Casual Dining. **Address:** 4558 Main St 64111

CALIFORNOS 816/531-7878 ㉟
APPROVED American. Casual Dining. **Address:** 4124 Pennsylvania Ave 64111

THE CAPITAL GRILLE 816/531-8345 ㊷
THREE DIAMOND Steak. Fine Dining. **Address:** 4740 Jefferson St 64112

(See map & index p. 214.)

CHAZ ON THE PLAZA 816/802-2152 (48)
THREE DIAMOND Continental. Fine Dining. **Address:** 325 Ward Pkwy 64112

COOPER'S HAWK WINERY & RESTAURANT 816/531-1500 (40)
THREE DIAMOND American. Casual Dining. **Address:** 4686 Broadway St 64112

CORVINO SUPPER CLUB 816/832-4564 (16)
THREE DIAMOND New American. Casual Dining. **Address:** 1830 Walnut St 64108

CORVINO TASTING ROOM 816/832-4564 (15)
FOUR DIAMOND **AAA Inspector Notes:** This chic Crossroads Arts District restaurant offers a
New American Fine Dining $105-$200
very unique and intimate experience. Enjoy the tasting menu prepared by the restaurant's namesake chef. Expect eight to 10 courses featuring wild and exotic ingredients masterfully prepared in front of you. The attentive servers display their knowledge and are impeccably precise. **Features:** full bar. **Reservations:** required, Deposit required. **Address:** 1830 Walnut St 64108 **Location:** Jct 18th and Walnut sts. **Parking:** street only.
D CALL

D'BRONX AUTHENTIC DELI AND PIZZERIA 816/531-0550 (28)
APPROVED Pizza Deli. Casual Dining. **Address:** 3904 Bell St 64111

DRUNKEN FISH 816/474-7177 (8)
THREE DIAMOND Japanese Sushi. Casual Dining. **Address:** 14 E 14th St 64106

THE FARMHOUSE 816/569-6032 (2)
THREE DIAMOND Natural/Organic. Casual Dining. **Address:** 300 Delaware St 64105

FIORELLA'S JACK STACK BARBECUE 816/531-7427 (41)
APPROVED American. Casual Dining. **Address:** 4747 Wyandotte St 64112

FIORELLA'S JACK STACK BARBECUE - FREIGHT HOUSE 816/472-7427 (21)
APPROVED Barbecue. Casual Dining. **Address:** 101 W 22nd St 64108

GAROZZO'S RISTORANTE 816/221-2455 (1)
APPROVED Italian. Casual Dining. **Address:** 526 Harrison St 64106

GATES BAR-B-Q 816/753-0828 (26)
APPROVED Barbecue. Quick Serve. **Address:** 3205 Main St 64111

GENGHIS KHAN MONGOLIAN GRILL 816/753-3600 (31)
APPROVED Mongolian Barbecue. Casual Dining. **Address:** 3906 Bell St 64111

GRAM & DUN 816/389-2900 (46)
THREE DIAMOND New American. Gastropub. **Address:** 600 Ward Pkwy 64112

GRAND STREET CAFE 816/561-8000 (43)
THREE DIAMOND American. Casual Dining. **Address:** 4740 Grand Ave 64112

GRUNAUER 816/283-3234 (20)
THREE DIAMOND Austrian. Casual Dining. **Address:** 101 W 22nd St 64108

HAPPY GILLIS 816/471-3663 (3)
APPROVED Natural/Organic. Casual Dining. **Address:** 549 Gillis St 64106

HARRY'S BAR & TABLES 816/561-3950 (33)
APPROVED American. Casual Dining. **Address:** 501 Westport Rd 64111

HARRY'S COUNTRY CLUB 816/421-3505 (7)
APPROVED American. Casual Dining. **Address:** 112 E Missouri Ave 64106

HOGSHEAD KANSAS CITY 816/321-2929 (44)
APPROVED American. Gastropub. **Address:** 4743 Pennsylvania Ave 64112

IL LAZZARONE PIZZA 816/541-3695 (6)
APPROVED Pizza. Casual Dining. **Address:** 412 Delaware St , Suite A 64105

JAZZ, A LOUISIANA KITCHEN 816/531-5556 (30)
APPROVED Cajun. Casual Dining. **Address:** 1823 W 39th St 64111

JERUSALEM CAFE 816/756-2770 (32)
APPROVED Middle Eastern. Casual Dining. **Address:** 431 Westport Rd 64111

KONA GRILL 816/931-5888 (45)
THREE DIAMOND Pacific Rim Fusion. Casual Dining. **Address:** 444 Ward Pkwy 64112

LA BODEGA 816/472-8272 (22)
APPROVED Spanish Small Plates. Casual Dining. **Address:** 703 Southwest Blvd 64108

LIDIA'S KANSAS CITY 816/221-3722 (19)
THREE DIAMOND Northern Italian. Fine Dining. **Address:** 101 W 22nd St 64108

MISSION TACO JOINT 816/844-3707 (14)
APPROVED Mexican. Casual Dining. **Address:** 409 E 18th St 64108

NARA 816/221-6272 (11)
APPROVED Japanese Sushi. Casual Dining. **Address:** 1617 Main St 64108

PARKWAY SOCIAL KITCHEN 816/214-5616 (47)
THREE DIAMOND New American. Casual Dining. **Address:** 616 Ward Pkwy 64112

PIERPONTS AT UNION STATION 816/221-5111 (23)
THREE DIAMOND Steak Seafood. Fine Dining. **Address:** 30 W Pershing Rd, Suite 900 64108

PONAK'S MEXICAN KITCHEN & BAR 816/753-0775 (25)
APPROVED Mexican. Casual Dining. **Address:** 2856 Southwest Blvd 64108

PORT FONDA 816/216-6462 (34)
APPROVED Mexican. Casual Dining. **Address:** 4141 Pennsylvania Ave 64111

POTPIE 816/561-2702 (37)
APPROVED American. Casual Dining. **Address:** 904 Westport Rd 64111

(See map & index p. 214.)

Q39 816/255-3753 27
 APPROVED Barbecue. Casual Dining. **Address:** 1000 W 39th St 64111

THE RIEGER HOTEL GRILL & EXCHANGE 816/471-2177 17
THREE DIAMOND American. Casual Dining. **Address:** 1924 Main St 64108

THE ROCKHILL GRILLE 816/389-5800 18
THREE DIAMOND New American. Gastropub. **Address:** 2000 Grand Blvd 64108

STOCK HILL 816/895-8400 49
FOUR DIAMOND New Steak. Fine Dining. **Address:** 4800 Main St 64112

STREETCAR GRILLE & TAVERN 816/216-6187 50
APPROVED American. Casual Dining. **Address:** 1580 Main St 64108

TRIBE STREET KITCHEN 816/214-6058 4
APPROVED Continental. Casual Dining. **Address:** 316 Delaware St 64105

WEBSTER HOUSE 816/221-4713 12
THREE DIAMOND American. Casual Dining. **Address:** 1644 Wyandotte St 64111

KANSAS CITY
- **Restaurants p. 232**
- **Hotels & Restaurants map & index p. 218**

AMERISTAR CASINO HOTEL KANSAS CITY 816/414-7000 24
THREE DIAMOND Hotel. **Address:** 3200 N Ameristar Dr 64161

BEST WESTERN COUNTRY INN NORTH 816/459-7222 19

APPROVED
Hotel

Best Western. **AAA Benefit:** Members save up to 15% and earn bonus points!

Address: 2633 NE 43rd St 64117 **Location:** I-35 exit 8C (Antioch Rd), just s on SR 1, then just e. **Facility:** 44 units. 2 stories (no elevator), exterior corridors. **Pool:** outdoor. **Guest Services:** coin laundry. **Featured Amenity:** full hot breakfast.

BEST WESTERN PLUS KANSAS CITY AIRPORT-KCI EAST 816/891-9111 7

THREE DIAMOND
Hotel

Best Western PLUS. **AAA Benefit:** Members save up to 15% and earn bonus points!

Address: 11130 NW Ambassador Dr 64153 **Location:** I-29 exit 12, just se. **Facility:** 79 units. 3 stories, interior corridors. **Pool:** heated indoor. **Activities:** exercise room. **Guest Services:** valet and coin laundry, area transportation.

CANDLEWOOD SUITES KANSAS CITY NORTHEAST 816/886-9311 18
THREE DIAMOND Extended Stay Hotel. **Address:** 4450 N Randolph Rd 64117

▼ See AAA listing p. 242 ▼

Save on travel, shopping, dining and more: AAA.com/discounts

(See map & index p. 218.)

COMFORT INN & SUITES NEAR WORLDS OF FUN
816/454-3500 **21**
APPROVED Hotel. **Address:** 7300 NE Parvin Rd 64117

COURTYARD BY MARRIOTT
816/941-3333 **26**
THREE DIAMOND [SAVE] Hotel. **Address:** 500 E 105th St 64131
AAA Benefit: Members save 5% or more!

COURTYARD BY MARRIOTT KANSAS CITY AT BRIARCLIFF
816/841-3300 **22**
THREE DIAMOND [SAVE] Hotel. **Address:** 4000 N Mulberry Dr 64116
AAA Benefit: Members save 5% or more!

COURTYARD BY MARRIOTT-KCI
816/891-7500 **11**
THREE DIAMOND [SAVE] Hotel. **Address:** 7901 NW Tiffany Springs Pkwy 64153
AAA Benefit: Members save 5% or more!

DRURY INN & SUITES-KANSAS CITY AIRPORT
816/880-9700 **10**
THREE DIAMOND Hotel. **Address:** 7900 NW Tiffany Springs Pkwy 64153

DRURY INN & SUITES-KANSAS CITY STADIUM
816/923-3000 **25**
APPROVED Hotel. **Address:** 3830 Blue Ridge Cutoff 64133

FAIRFIELD INN & SUITES BY MARRIOTT/KANSAS CITY AIRPORT
816/464-2424 **3**
THREE DIAMOND [SAVE] Hotel. **Address:** 11820 NW Plaza Cir 64153
AAA Benefit: Members save 5% or more!

FAIRFIELD INN & SUITES BY MARRIOTT KANSAS CITY LIBERTY
816/792-4000 **17**
THREE DIAMOND [SAVE] Hotel. **Address:** 8101 N Church Rd 64158
AAA Benefit: Members save 5% or more!

FOUR POINTS BY SHERATON KANSAS CITY AIRPORT
816/464-2345 **2**
THREE DIAMOND [SAVE] Hotel. **Address:** 11832 NW Plaza Cir 64153
AAA Benefit: Members save 5% or more!

HAMPTON INN BY HILTON KANSAS CITY AIRPORT
816/464-5454 **6**
THREE DIAMOND [SAVE] Hotel. **Address:** 11212 N Newark Cir 64153
AAA Benefit: Members save up to 15%!

HAMPTON INN BY HILTON-KANSAS CITY/LIBERTY
816/415-9600 **15**
THREE DIAMOND [SAVE] Hotel. **Address:** 8551 N Church Rd 64158
AAA Benefit: Members save up to 15%!

HAMPTON INN BY HILTON KANSAS CITY NEAR WORLDS OF FUN
816/452-1010 **20**
THREE DIAMOND [SAVE] Hotel. **Address:** 4233 N Corrington Ave 64117
AAA Benefit: Members save up to 15%!

HILTON GARDEN INN KANSAS CITY AIRPORT
816/321-1900 **27**
THREE DIAMOND [SAVE] Hotel. **Address:** 10920 N Ambassador Dr 64153
AAA Benefit: Members save up to 15%!

HOLIDAY INN EXPRESS & SUITES KANSAS CITY AIRPORT
816/923-4100 **13**
THREE DIAMOND Hotel
Address: 9550 NW Polo Dr 64153 **Location:** I-29 exit 10, just e. **Facility:** 109 units. 4 stories, interior corridors. **Terms:** check-in 4 pm. **Pool:** heated indoor. **Activities:** hot tub, exercise room. **Guest Services:** coin laundry, area transportation. **Featured Amenity: continental breakfast.**

HOLIDAY INN EXPRESS & SUITES KANSAS CITY/LIBERTY
816/781-5555 **16**
APPROVED Hotel. **Address:** 8230 N Church Rd 64158

HOLIDAY INN KCI AIRPORT & KCI EXPO CENTER
816/801-8400 **5**
THREE DIAMOND Hotel
Address: 11728 NW Ambassador Dr 64153 **Location:** I-29 exit 13, just e on CR D, then just s. Adjacent to KCI Airport and Expo Center. **Facility:** 141 units. 6 stories, interior corridors. **Pool:** heated indoor. **Activities:** exercise room. **Guest Services:** valet and coin laundry, area transportation. **Featured Amenity: breakfast buffet.**

HOME2 SUITES BY HILTON KCI AIRPORT
816/800-5500 **14**
THREE DIAMOND [SAVE] Extended Stay Contemporary Hotel. **Address:** 9500 NW Polo Dr 64153
AAA Benefit: Members save up to 15%!

HOMEWOOD SUITES BY HILTON KANSAS CITY AIRPORT
816/880-9880 **9**
THREE DIAMOND [SAVE] Extended Stay Hotel. **Address:** 7312 NW Polo Dr 64153
AAA Benefit: Members save up to 15%!

HYATT PLACE KANSAS CITY/AIRPORT
816/891-0871 **12**
THREE DIAMOND Hotel
HYATT PLACE
AAA Benefit: Members save up to 10%!
Address: 7600 NW 97th Terr 64153 **Location:** I-29 exit 10, just sw. **Facility:** 134 units. 6 stories, interior corridors. **Amenities:** safes. **Pool:** heated outdoor. **Activities:** exercise room. **Guest Services:** valet laundry, area transportation. **Featured Amenity: breakfast buffet.**

(See map & index p. 218.)

MARRIOTT KANSAS CITY AIRPORT   816/464-2200   **1**
▼▼ **THREE DIAMOND** [SAVE] Hotel. **Address:** 775 Brasilia Ave 64153

AAA Benefit: Members save 5% or more!

RESIDENCE INN BY MARRIOTT, KANSAS CITY AIRPORT   816/741-2300   **8**
▼▼ **THREE DIAMOND** [SAVE] Extended Stay Hotel. **Address:** 10300 N Ambassador Dr 64153

AAA Benefit: Members save 5% or more!

TOWNEPLACE SUITES BY MARRIOTT KANSAS CITY AIRPORT   816/464-0525   **4**
▼▼ **THREE DIAMOND** [SAVE] Extended Stay Hotel. **Address:** 11812 NW Plaza Cir 64153

AAA Benefit: Members save 5% or more!

TOWNEPLACE SUITES BY MARRIOTT KANSAS CITY AT BRIARCLIFF   816/587-4600   **23**
▼▼ **THREE DIAMOND** [SAVE] Extended Stay Hotel. **Address:** 3950 N Mulberry Dr 64116

AAA Benefit: Members save 5% or more!

WHERE TO EAT

AIXOIS FRENCH BISTRO   816/333-3305   **22**
▼▼ **APPROVED** French. Casual Dining. **Address:** 251 E 55th St 64113

AVENUES BISTRO   816/333-5700   **23**
▼▼ **APPROVED** European. Casual Dining. **Address:** 338 W 63rd St 64113

BLACK DIRT   816/214-5947   **20**
▼▼ **THREE DIAMOND** New American. Casual Dining. **Address:** 5070 Main St 64112

BO LINGS   816/587-7880   **4**
▼▼ **APPROVED** Chinese. Casual Dining. **Address:** 8670 NW Prairie View Rd 64153

BONEFISH GRILL   816/746-8179   **12**
▼▼ **THREE DIAMOND** Seafood. Fine Dining. **Address:** 6332 N Lucerne Ave 64151

CARMEN'S CAFE   816/333-4048   **24**
▼▼ **APPROVED** Italian. Casual Dining. **Address:** 6307 Brookside Plaza 64113

CASCONE'S ITALIAN RESTAURANT   816/454-7977   **16**
▼▼ **APPROVED** Italian. Casual Dining. **Address:** 3737 N Oak Trafficway 64116

CORNER CAFE   816/415-0050   **6**
▼▼ **APPROVED** Comfort Food. Casual Dining. **Address:** 8301 N Flintlock Rd 64157

DELILUX   816/414-7000   **18**
▼▼ **APPROVED** Deli. Quick Serve. **Address:** 3200 N Ameristar Dr 64161

DOMINIC'S CASUAL ITALIAN   816/437-7200   **11**
▼▼ **APPROVED** Italian. Quick Serve. **Address:** 6209 NW 63rd Terrace 64151

FIORELLA'S JACK STACK BARBECUE - MARTIN CITY   816/942-9141   **27**
▼▼ **APPROVED** Barbecue. Casual Dining. **Address:** 13441 Holmes St 64145

GREAT PLAINS CATTLE COMPANY   816/414-7420   **19**
▼▼ **THREE DIAMOND** Steak. Fine Dining. **Address:** 3200 N Ameristar Dr 64161

HORIZON'S BUFFET   816/414-7000   **17**
▼▼ **APPROVED** International. Casual Dining. **Address:** 3200 N Ameristar Dr 64161

JASPER'S RISTORANTE   816/941-6600   **26**
▼▼ **THREE DIAMOND** Traditional Italian. Fine Dining. **Address:** 1201 W 103rd St 64114

LC'S HAMBURGERS ETC   816/741-6027   **7**
▼▼ **APPROVED** Burgers. Quick Serve. **Address:** 7612 NW Prairie View Rd 64151

LUNA AZTECA MEXICAN GRILL   816/437-8038   **13**
▼▼ **APPROVED** Mexican. Casual Dining. **Address:** 5918 NW 63rd Terrace 64151

MASABI JAPANESE SUSHI BAR & GRILL   816/792-8881   **3**
▼▼ **APPROVED** Japanese Sushi. Casual Dining. **Address:** 9763 N Cedar Ave 64157

MINSKY'S PIZZA CAFE & BAR   816/741-2737   **15**
▼▼ **APPROVED** Pizza. Casual Dining. **Address:** 7007 NW Barry Rd 64153

OSTERIA IL CENTRO   816/561-2369   **21**
▼▼ **THREE DIAMOND**

Northern Italian
Casual Dining
$8-$19

AAA Inspector Notes: With its engaging music and colorful, creative décor, the trendy bistro exudes relaxed sophistication. Menu options are tempting, and a large wine list offers great pairing potential. The house made pastas are popular and full of flavor. Although the dress code is casual, dressy casual is the norm. **Features:** full bar, happy hour. **Address:** 5101 Main St 64112 **Location:** Jct 51st St; in Country Club Plaza area. **D**

SAKI ASIAN RESTAURANT   816/584-8888   **10**
▼▼ **APPROVED** Asian Sushi. Casual Dining. **Address:** 5225 NW 64th St 64151

SMOKEBOX BBQ   816/891-8011   **2**
▼▼ **APPROVED** Barbecue. Casual Dining. **Address:** 10020 N Ambassador Dr 64153

SMOKEHOUSE BAR-B-QUE   816/587-3337   **5**
▼▼ **APPROVED** Barbecue. Casual Dining. **Address:** 8451 NW Prairie View Rd 64152

STROUD'S OAK RIDGE MANOR   816/454-9600   **14**
▼▼ **APPROVED** Chicken. Casual Dining. **Address:** 5410 NE Oak Ridge Rd 64119

SUMMIT GRILL   816/768-6100   **9**
▼▼ **APPROVED** American. Casual Dining. **Address:** 501 NE 70th St 64118

SUMMIT GRILL & BAR   816/361-9788   **25**
▼▼ **THREE DIAMOND** American. Casual Dining. **Address:** 520 W 75th St 64114

TASTY THAI   816/584-8801   **8**
▼▼ **APPROVED** Thai. Casual Dining. **Address:** 7104 NW Prairie View Rd 64151

(See map & index p. 218.)

TREZO MARE RESTAURANT AND LOUNGE
816/505-3200 (15)
THREE DIAMOND Italian. Casual Dining. **Address:** 4105 N Mulberry Dr 64116

WHITE HORSE PUB   816/500-7472 (1)
APPROVED English. Casual Dining. **Address:** 10221 N Oak Trafficway 64155

KIMBERLING CITY pop. 2,400
• Part of Branson area — see map p. 151

PORT OF KIMBERLING MARINA & RESORT   417/739-3883
THREE DIAMOND Hotel. **Address:** 201 Marina Way 65686

KINGSVILLE (C-2) pop. 269, elev. 904'
POWELL GARDENS is at 1609 N.W. US 50, just e. of jct. SR W. Visitors may walk or take a trolley to the Perennial Garden, featuring more than 500 varieties of plants; the Fountain Garden; the Island Garden with a "living" wall; the Beals Woodland and Stream Garden; and the Marjorie Powell Allen Chapel. A 3.25-mile nature trail also traverses the 900-acre park. Horticultural displays are located in the Visitor Education Center. The 12-acre Heartland Harvest Garden is a vast edible landscape, featuring more than 2,000 types of food plants and the Fun Foods Farm youth garden.

Time: Allow 1 hour minimum. **Hours:** Daily 9-6, May-Sept.; 10-4, rest of year. **Cost:** Admission $10; $9 (ages 60+); $4 (ages 5-12). An additional fee may be charged during special events. **Phone:** (816) 697-2600. [T]

KIRKSVILLE (A-3) pop. 17,505, elev. 965'
Founded in 1841 as the seat of Adair County, Kirksville was named for Jesse Kirk, who exchanged a turkey dinner for the right to name the town after himself. Truman State University and the A.T. Still University have transformed this former farming community into an important educational center.

The area's rural character still can be enjoyed in such nearby areas as the Big Creek and Sugar Creek conservation areas and at the larger Thousand Hills State Park *(see Recreation Areas Chart)*. Thousand Hills offers petroglyphs with an interpretive shelter, and recreational facilities are offered at 573-acre Forest Lake.

Kirksville Area Chamber of Commerce: 304 S. Franklin, P.O. Box 251, Kirksville, MO 63501-3581. **Phone:** (660) 665-3766.

HAMPTON INN BY HILTON   660/956-4686
THREE DIAMOND [SAVE] Hotel. **Address:** 2604 N Baltimore St 63501

AAA Benefit:
Members save up to 15%!

HOLIDAY INN EXPRESS & SUITES - UNIVERSITY AREA
660/956-4682
THREE DIAMOND Hotel. **Address:** 2523 S Franklin St 63501

WHERE TO EAT

THOUSAND HILLS DINING LODGE   660/665-7119
APPROVED American. Casual Dining. **Address:** 20431 State Hwy 157 63501

KIRKWOOD (G-5) pop. 27,540, elev. 659'
• Hotels & Restaurants map & index p. 274
• Part of St. Louis area — see map p. 248

THE NATIONAL MUSEUM OF TRANSPORTATION is w. off the I-270 Dougherty Ferry Rd. exit at 2933 Barrett Station Rd. Trains, automobiles, buses, streetcars, horse-drawn vehicles, aircraft and boats represent 150 years of American history. In addition to more than 70 locomotives, the collection includes Bobby Darin's 1960 dream car, which cost more than $93,000 and took 7 years to build. Miniature train rides are offered mid-May through December.

Creation Station is a separate hands-on educational area where young children can explore different modes of transportation. The various play stations utilize puzzles, puppets, arts and crafts and other learning tools.

Time: Allow 1 hour, 30 minutes minimum. **Hours:** Mon.-Sat. 9-4, Sun. 11-4, Mar.-Oct.; Wed.-Sat. 9-4, Sun. 11-4, Nov.-Dec.; Thurs.-Sat. 9-4, Sun. 11-4, rest of year. Phone for Creation Station and miniature train schedule. Closed Jan. 1, Easter, Thanksgiving, Christmas Eve, Christmas and Dec. 31. Phone ahead to confirm schedule. **Cost:** Museum $8; $5 (ages 3-12). Creation Station additional $2. Ride wristband $5. **Phone:** (314) 965-6212.

BEST WESTERN KIRKWOOD INN   314/821-3950 (82)
APPROVED
Hotel

[BW] Best Western. **AAA Benefit:** Members save up to 15% and earn bonus points!

Address: 1200 S Kirkwood Rd 63122 **Location:** I-44 exit 277B (Lindbergh Blvd), just n. **Facility:** 112 units. 6 stories, interior corridors. **Amenities:** safes. **Pool:** heated outdoor. **Activities:** exercise room. **Guest Services:** coin laundry. **Featured Amenity:** full hot breakfast.

[SAVE] [≡] [¶] [▼] [Y] CALL [♿]
[⊇] [✚] [BIZ] [≈] [✕] [🖥] [🖵]

/ SOME UNITS [🐾] [HS]

WHERE TO EAT

CITIZEN KANE'S STEAK HOUSE   314/965-9005 (103)
APPROVED Steak. Fine Dining. **Address:** 133 W Clinton Pl 63122

SUNSET 44   314/965-6644 (102)
APPROVED American. Casual Dining. **Address:** 118 W Adams Ave 63122

LAKE OF THE OZARKS (C-3)

The Bagnell Dam was built on the Osage River in 1931 to form Lake of the Ozarks, Missouri's largest inland body of water and the largest man-made lake in the world at the time of its creation. Fishing, boating and swimming are popular pastimes on the 54,000-acre reservoir, which offers 1,150 miles of shoreline—more than the length of the California coast.

Osage Indians once hunted in the woods surrounding the lake, and it is said they left directions by bending and tying oak saplings. Hundreds of years later, examples of these strangely bent "thong trees" can still be seen.

The Community Bridge, completed in 1998, links the east and west sides of the lake. The toll bridge runs from Lake Ozark to Shawnee Bend.

The following towns on the Lake of the Ozarks are listed separately under their individual names: Camdenton, Linn Creek, Osage Beach and Warsaw (see place listings).

Lake of the Ozarks Convention & Visitor Bureau: 5815 Osage Beach Pkwy., P.O. Box 1498, Osage Beach, MO 65065. **Phone:** (573) 348-1599 or (800) 386-5253.

LAMPE (E-3) elev. 1,316'
• Part of Branson area — see map p. 151

DOGWOOD CANYON NATURE PARK is s. on SR 13 to jct. SR 86, then w. about 2 mi. on SR 86 following signs to the park turnoff. Dogwood Canyon is a private refuge encompassing some 2,200 acres of Ozark wilderness. The terrain of ridges, hollows and limestone bluffs is honeycombed with caves and provides a backdrop for waterfalls, meandering streams and woodlands dominated by oaks, pines and cedars.

Activities include walking, hiking or biking along a 6-mile round-trip paved trail, trout fishing and horseback riding. A 2-hour wildlife tram tour winds along the canyon floor before crossing the Arkansas border to encounter herds of Texas longhorn cattle, American bison and elk that live in the park.

Note: All recreational activities are subject to weather conditions and availability. **Time:** Allow 2 hours minimum. **Hours:** Park open daily 8:30-7, May 1-late Oct.; 8:30-5, late Oct-late Nov.; 8:30-4, late Nov. through Dec. 31 (weather permitting). Most activities offered May-Nov. (horseback riding not available Sun.-Mon.). **Cost:** Fees for individual activities vary. Wildlife tram tour $28-$35; $19-$26 (ages 3-11). One-day Adventure Pass combining

various activities $55; $30 (ages 3-11). **Phone:** (417) 779-5983 or (800) 225-6343. ⊓ ⊠

LAURIE pop. 945, elev. 965'

VAL'S   573/374-0922
▼▼ APPROVED   American. Casual Dining. **Address:** 601 N Hwy 5 65038

LEASBURG (C-4) pop. 338, elev. 1,019'

ONONDAGA CAVE STATE PARK is 5 mi. s. on SR H to 7556 SR H. One of the largest lighted caves in Missouri, Onondaga features formations ranging from lacy patterns to massive pieces of onyx. The temperature is always 57 F. Concrete walks wind through the interior. Park staff give weekend kerosene lantern tours of nearby Cathedral Cave, which features a large column of flowstone, wind-bent stalactites and fossilized beds of algae known as stromatolites. See Recreation Areas Chart. **Time:** Allow 1 hour minimum. **Hours:** Park open daily for camping and day use. Onondaga Cave tour daily 10-4, early Apr. to late Oct. Cathedral Cave tour mid-May to mid Oct. Phone ahead to confirm schedule. **Cost:** $15; $9 (ages 6-12). Combination ticket with Cathedral Cave tour $20; $12 (ages 6-12). **Phone:** (573) 245-6576 or (800) 334-6946. GT ⊼ ⊓ ⊠ 🐾 ⊞

LEBANON (D-3) pop. 14,474, elev. 1,265'

Originally named after the Wyota Indians, Lebanon was later renamed after Lebanon, Tenn. In the late 1800s residents discovered that the city's water contained magnetic properties. People flocked to the Gasconade Hotel to bathe in water that was said to contain healing qualities.

Bennett Spring State Park is located 12 miles west on SR 64. The 3,100-acre park offers nature programs and guided tours; phone (417) 532-4338, (800) 334-6946 or (417) 532-4307 for fishing licenses and lodging. See Recreation Areas Chart.

Lebanon Area Chamber of Commerce: 186 N. Adams, Lebanon, MO 65536. **Phone:** (417) 588-3256.

HAMPTON INN BY HILTON   417/533-3100
▼▼ THREE DIAMOND SAVE Hotel. **Ad-**   **AAA Benefit:**
dress: 930 Ivey Ln 65536   Members save up to 15%!

HOLIDAY INN EXPRESS   417/532-1111
▼▼ THREE DIAMOND Hotel. **Address:** 1955 W Elm St 65536

SUPER 8   417/588-2574
▼▼ APPROVED Hotel. **Address:** 1831 W Elm St 65536

LEE'S SUMMIT pop. 91,364, elev. 1,037'

- Hotels & Restaurants map & index p. 218
- Part of Kansas City area — see map p. 199

FAIRFIELD INN & SUITES BY MARRIOTT LEE'S SUMMIT
816/524-7572 **62**
▼▼ APPROVED [SAVE] Hotel. **Ad-dress:** 1301 NE Windsor Dr 64086

AAA Benefit:
Members save 5%
or more!

HAMPTON INN BY HILTON 816/347-8600 **61**
▼▼ THREE DIAMOND [SAVE] Hotel. **Ad-dress:** 1751 NE Douglas St 64086

AAA Benefit:
Members save up to
15%!

WHERE TO EAT

JOSE PEPPER'S 816/246-9555 **67**
▼▼ APPROVED Southwestern. Casual Dining. **Address:** 1667 NE Douglas Rd 64086

MINSKY'S PIZZA CAFE & BAR 816/524-3112
▼▼ APPROVED Pizza Sandwiches. Casual Dining. **Address:** 1251 NE Rice Rd 64086

SMOKE BREWING CO 816/525-2337 **68**
▼▼ APPROVED American. Brewpub. **Address:** 209 SE Main St 64063

SUMMIT GRILL & BAR 816/795-5553 **65**
▼▼ THREE DIAMOND American. Casual Dining. **Address:** 4835 NE Lakewood Way 64064

TIFF N' JAY'S 816/373-4300 **66**
▼▼ APPROVED American. Casual Dining. **Address:** 700 NE Woods Chapel Rd 64064

LIBERTY (F-2) pop. 29,149, elev. 852'

- Hotels & Restaurants map & index p. 218
- Part of Kansas City area — see map p. 199

Self-guiding tours: Numerous sites are highlighted in the "Tour, Taste, Play, Stay" brochure and map, available at local shops and restaurants. The tour covers the downtown business district; the Dougherty, Jewell and Lightburne historic residential districts; William Jewell College; the Clay County Historical Museum; and sites related to African American history, early resident Alexander Doniphan and outlaw Jesse James. A self-guiding tour can be accessed via the Historic Downtown Liberty, Inc. mobile app.

Shopping: Downtown streets are lined with book, clothing, home décor and jewelry stores. The Historic Downtown Liberty Farmers Market is held at Liberty Square—bordered by Kansas Avenue and Franklin, Main and Water streets—Sat. 7-noon from May through September; 8-noon in October.

JESSE JAMES BANK MUSEUM is at 103 N. Water St. on Liberty Square. The nation's first bank robbery carried out during daylight hours was at this site, committed by the James gang Feb. 13, 1866. The 1858 building houses Jesse James memorabilia, period furnishings and antebellum-era banking displays. **Time:** Allow 30 minutes minimum. **Hours:**

Mon.-Sat. 10-4. **Cost:** $6.50; $6 (ages 62+); $4 (ages 8-15). **Phone:** (816) 736-8510. [GT]

TOWNEPLACE SUITES BY MARRIOTT KANSAS CITY/LIBERTY 816/415-9200 **43**
▼▼ THREE DIAMOND [SAVE] Extended Stay Contemporary Hotel. **Address:** 130 S Stewart Rd 64068

AAA Benefit:
Members save 5%
or more!

WHERE TO EAT

MARGARITA'S 816/781-3031 **43**
▼▼ APPROVED Mexican. Casual Dining. **Address:** 1910 Victory Dr 64068

TASTY THAI - LIBERTY 816/781-7800 **42**
▼▼ APPROVED Thai. Casual Dining. **Address:** 1912 Star Dr 64068

MACON pop. 5,471

COMFORT INN 660/395-8000
▼▼ THREE DIAMOND Hotel. **Address:** 1821 N Missouri St 63552

SUPER 8 660/385-5788
▼▼ APPROVED Hotel. **Address:** 203 E Briggs Dr 63552

WHERE TO EAT

PEAR TREE KITCHEN & BAR 660/385-1500
▼▼ APPROVED American. Casual Dining. **Address:** 1407 N Missouri St 63552

MARK TWAIN NATIONAL FOREST (D-4)

Elevations in the forest range from 230 ft. at the boot-heel drainage ditches to 1,772 ft. on Taum Sauk Mountain.

In southern and central Missouri, Mark Twain National Forest encompasses 1.5 million acres in 29 counties. Scenic drives, hunting, camping, fishing, canoeing and hiking are among the many activities available in nine wilderness areas. Pinewoods Lake Recreation Area near Ellsinore features a 1.5-mile trail around the lake. A more challenging 5-mile national recreation trail skirts 99-acre Crane Lake, approximately 12 miles south of Ironton off SR 49 and SR E.

Big Bay Recreation Area, southeast of Shell Knob on SR 39, offers swimming, boating and fishing. Swimming in the Huzzah River is available at Red Bluff Recreation Area, east of Davisville on SR V. Activities at Noblett Lake Recreation Area, west of Willow Springs, include hiking, boating, camping and picnicking. Also within the forest is 49-acre Fourche Lake, about 18 miles west of Doniphan on SR 142, then 1 mile south on SR 160.

Skyline Scenic Drive, a 4-mile automobile loop, is 2 miles south of Van Buren on SR 103 and features views of the Ozark countryside. The 8-mile Sugar Camp Scenic Drive, off SR 112 near Cassville, also offers a drive through the Ozarks. Near I-70 is the 35-mile Cedar Creek Trail System. Glade Top Trail Scenic Drive, southeast of Springfield near SR 125, offers 23 miles through open glades.

Information about the forest's many national recreation areas can be obtained from the Forest Supervisor, 401 Fairgrounds Rd., Rolla, MO 65401; phone (573) 364-4621. *See Recreation Areas Chart.*

MARYLAND HEIGHTS pop. 27,472
- **Hotels & Restaurants map & index p. 274**
- **Part of St. Louis area — see map p. 248**

COMFORT INN ST. LOUIS - WESTPORT   314/878-1400 **49**
THREE DIAMOND   Hotel. **Address:** 12031 Lackland Rd 63146

COURTYARD BY MARRIOTT-WESTPORT   314/997-1200 **44**
THREE DIAMOND SAVE Hotel. **Address:** 11888 Westline Industrial Dr 63146
AAA Benefit: Members save 5% or more!

DOUBLETREE BY HILTON HOTEL ST. LOUIS-WESTPORT   314/434-0100 **50**
THREE DIAMOND
Hotel

AAA Benefit: Members save up to 15%!
Address: 1973 Craigshire Rd 63146 **Location:** I-270 exit 16A (Page Ave), just e, then 0.4 mi s on Concourse Dr, just w on Lackland Rd, then just w. **Facility:** 327 units. 11 stories, interior corridors. **Amenities:** safes. **Pool:** heated indoor. **Activities:** hot tub, exercise room. **Guest Services:** valet laundry, area transportation.

DRURY INN & SUITES-ST. LOUIS-WESTPORT   314/576-9966 **42**
THREE DIAMOND   Hotel. **Address:** 12220 Dorsett Rd 63043

FAIRFIELD INN & SUITES BY MARRIOTT ST. LOUIS WESTPORT   314/762-1630 **47**
THREE DIAMOND SAVE Hotel. **Address:** 11920 Westline Industrial Dr 63146
AAA Benefit: Members save 5% or more!

HAMPTON INN BY HILTON ST. LOUIS/WESTPORT   314/298-7878 **40**
THREE DIAMOND SAVE Hotel. **Address:** 2454 Old Dorsett Rd 63043
AAA Benefit: Members save up to 15%!

HAWTHORN SUITES BY WYNDHAM ST. LOUIS WESTPORT PLAZA   314/469-0060 **51**
THREE DIAMOND Extended Stay Hotel. **Address:** 1881 Craigshire Rd 63146

📎 **Use the free travel planning tools at AAA.com/maps**

HOLLYWOOD CASINO & HOTEL   314/770-8100 **38**
THREE DIAMOND Hotel. **Address:** 777 Casino Center Dr 63043

HOMEWOOD SUITES BY HILTON ST. LOUIS RIVERPORT - AIRPORT WEST   314/739-3900 **39**
THREE DIAMOND SAVE Extended Stay Hotel. **Address:** 13639 Riverport Dr 63043
AAA Benefit: Members save up to 15%!

HOMEWOOD SUITES BY HILTON ST. LOUIS WESTPORT   314/733-9800 **41**
THREE DIAMOND
Extended Stay Hotel

HOMEWOOD SUITES BY HILTON
AAA Benefit: Members save up to 15%!
Address: 2434 Old Dorsett Rd 63043 **Location:** I-270 exit 17 (Dorsett Rd), just e, then just n. **Facility:** 121 efficiencies. 4 stories, interior corridors. **Pool:** heated indoor. **Activities:** exercise room. **Guest Services:** complimentary and valet laundry, area transportation. **Featured Amenity:** full hot breakfast.

RESIDENCE INN BY MARRIOTT ST. LOUIS WESTPORT   314/762-1600 **46**
THREE DIAMOND SAVE Extended Stay Hotel. **Address:** 11918 Westline Industrial Dr 63146
AAA Benefit: Members save 5% or more!

SHERATON WESTPORT LAKESIDE CHALET   314/878-1500 **45**
THREE DIAMOND
Hotel
SHERATON
AAA Benefit: Members save 5% or more!
Address: 191 Westport Plaza Dr 63146 **Location:** I-270 exit 16A (Page Ave), just e, then s on Concourse Dr, just w on Lackland Rd, then 0.4 mi n. Located in Westport Plaza Shopping Center. **Facility:** 299 units. 4-6 stories, interior corridors. **Amenities:** safes. **Pool:** outdoor. **Activities:** trails, exercise room. **Guest Services:** valet laundry, area transportation.

SHERATON WESTPORT PLAZA TOWER   314/878-1500 **48**
THREE DIAMOND
Hotel
SHERATON
AAA Benefit: Members save 5% or more!

Address: 900 Westport Plaza 63146 **Location:** I-270 exit 16A (Page Ave), just e, just s on Concourse Dr, just w on Lackland Rd, then 0.4 mi n. Located in Westport Plaza Shopping Center. **Facility:** 210 units. 12 stories, interior corridors. **Pool:** heated indoor. **Activities:** sauna, exercise room. **Guest Services:** valet laundry, area transportation.

(See map & index p. 274.)

SONESTA ES SUITES ST. LOUIS WESTPORT
314/878-1555 52

THREE DIAMOND
Extended Stay Hotel
Address: 1855 Craigshire Rd 63146 **Location:** I-270 exit 16A (Page Ave), just e, just s on Concourse Dr, just s on Craig Rd, then just w. **Facility:** 106 kitchen units, some two bedrooms. 2 stories (no elevator), interior/exterior corridors. **Amenities:** safes. **Pool:** heated outdoor. **Activities:** exercise room. **Guest Services:** valet and coin laundry, area transportation. **Featured Amenity: breakfast buffet.**

/ SOME UNITS

STAYBRIDGE SUITES ST. LOUIS - WESTPORT
314/628-1155 43

THREE DIAMOND Extended Stay Hotel. **Address:** 25 Progress Pkwy 63146

WHERE TO EAT

BALDUCCI'S WINEFEST RESTAURANT & BAR
314/576-5024 60
APPROVED Italian. Casual Dining. **Address:** 12527 Bennington Pl 63146

BANDANA'S BAR-B-Q
314/439-1123
APPROVED Barbecue. Casual Dining. **Address:** 12222 Dorsett Rd 63043

CASA JUÁREZ
314/317-9404 53
APPROVED Mexican. Casual Dining. **Address:** 12710 Dorsett Rd 63043

CHARLIE GITTO'S AT HOLLYWOOD CASINO
314/770-7663 51
THREE DIAMOND Italian. Casual Dining. **Address:** 777 Casino Center Dr 63043

DD MAU VIETNAMESE EATERY
314/942-2300 52
APPROVED Vietnamese. Quick Serve. **Address:** 11982 Dorsett Rd 63043

THE DRUNKEN FISH SUSHI BAR AND LOUNGE
314/275-8300 56
APPROVED Japanese. Sushi. Casual Dining. **Address:** 639 Westport Plaza 63146

EAT UP! BUFFET
314/770-8100 50
APPROVED International. Casual Dining. **Address:** 777 Casino Center Dr 63043

THE FINAL CUT STEAKHOUSE
314/770-8248 49
THREE DIAMOND Steak. Fine Dining. **Address:** 777 Casino Center Dr 63043

IMO'S PIZZA
314/548-2848 55
APPROVED Pizza. Sandwiches. Quick Serve. **Address:** 318 Port Plaza Dr 63146

KEMOLL'S CHOPHOUSE
314/421-0555 54
THREE DIAMOND Italian Steak. Fine Dining. **Address:** 323 Westport Plaza 63146

KOBE STEAK HOUSE OF JAPAN
314/469-3900 57
APPROVED Japanese. Casual Dining. **Address:** 111 Westport Plaza, Suite 1200 63146

TRAINWRECK SALOON WESTPORT
314/434-7222 58
APPROVED American. Casual Dining. **Address:** 314 Westport Plaza 63146

WESTPORT SOCIAL
314/548-2876 59
APPROVED American. Sports Bar. **Address:** 910 W Port Plaza Dr 63146

MARYVILLE (A-1) pop. 11,972, elev. 1,034'

Maryville is named for Mary Graham, the first woman of European descent to settle in the village. She and her husband Amos built the first house in Maryville in 1844.

Mozingo Lake, 3 miles east on US 136, offers fishing, boating and hiking trails as well as camping and picnic areas. *See Recreation Areas Chart.*

Greater Maryville Chamber of Commerce: 408 N. Market St., Maryville, MO 64468. **Phone:** (660) 582-8643.

Self-guiding tours: The Nodaway County Historical Society publishes a driving tour brochure, available from the chamber of commerce, that covers historic buildings and houses in town.

HOLIDAY INN EXPRESS HOTEL & SUITES
660/562-9949
THREE DIAMOND Hotel. **Address:** 2929 S Main St 64468

MEHLVILLE pop. 28,380
• Hotels & Restaurants map & index p. 274
• Part of St. Louis area — see map p. 248

BEST WESTERN ST. LOUIS INN
314/416-7639 97
APPROVED
Hotel

 Best Western.
AAA Benefit: Members save up to 15% and earn bonus points!

Address: 6224 Heimos Industrial Park Dr 63129 **Location:** I-55 exit 193, just e on Meramec Bottom Rd, then just n. **Facility:** 85 units. 3 stories, interior corridors. **Amenities:** safes. **Pool:** heated indoor. **Activities:** exercise room. **Guest Services:** valet and coin laundry. **Featured Amenity: full hot breakfast.**

/ SOME UNITS

HAMPTON INN & SUITES BY HILTON, ST. LOUIS SOUTH I-55
314/894-1900 95
THREE DIAMOND Hotel. **Address:** 4200 MidAmerica Ln 63129
AAA Benefit: Members save up to 15%!

HOLIDAY INN EXPRESS & SUITES ST. LOUIS SOUTH-I-55
314/894-0700 96
THREE DIAMOND Hotel. **Address:** 4250 Midamerica Ln 63129

HOLIDAY INN SOUTH COUNTY CENTER 314/892-3600 94
THREE DIAMOND Hotel. **Address:** 6921 S Lindbergh Blvd 63125

MEXICO (B-4) pop. 11,543, elev. 818'

Many Mexico residents share a love of championship horses. Located near the Salt River in Missouri's upland prairie region and established in 1837, early Mexico was encircled by racetracks. These tracks were the scene of Saturday afternoon events well attended by the locals. The trotting and pacing races at Mexico's fair in 1908 were purportedly the first in the nation to offer purses of as much as $1,500.

In the early 20th century Mexico was the center of one of the world's most important fireclay manufacturing areas. The refractories and brick factories here once held a virtual monopoly on the production of many types of fireclay products.

Rated by the Department of the Army and the Department of Education as one of the nation's top military schools, the Missouri Military Academy is the home of the Fusiliers, a national champion drill team. The public is invited to watch the battalion march in review on select Sundays from September through May; phone for schedule. Campus tours are available daily year-round; phone (573) 581-1776 or (888) 564-6662.

Mexico Area Chamber of Commerce: 100 W. Jackson, Mexico, MO 65265. **Phone:** (573) 581-2765 or (800) 581-2765.

BEST WESTERN TEAL LAKE INN   573/582-0700

[V] APPROVED
Hotel

[BW] Best Western. **AAA Benefit:** Members save up to 15% and earn bonus points!

Address: 3602 S Clark St 65265 **Location:** Jct US 54 and 54 S business route, 1.4 mi n. **Facility:** 48 units. 2 stories (no elevator), interior corridors. **Pool:** heated indoor. **Activities:** exercise room. **Guest Services:** coin laundry.

[SAVE] [🏊] [📶] [BIZ] [🛜] [✕] [🔌] [📠] [💻]

MINER pop. 984

BEST WESTERN PLUS SIKESTON   573/481-9500

[V] APPROVED
Hotel

[BW] Best Western PLUS. **AAA Benefit:** Members save up to 15% and earn bonus points!

Address: 120 S Interstate Dr 63801 **Location:** I-55 exit 67, just e, 0.4 mi s on Interstate Dr (frontage road). **Facility:** 55 units. 2 stories, interior corridors. **Pool:** heated indoor. **Activities:** limited exercise equipment. **Guest Services:** valet and coin laundry.

[SAVE] [CALL] [♿] [🏊] [BIZ] [HS] [🛜]
[✕] [🔌] [📠] [💻] [/SOME UNITS] [🐾]

DRURY INN & SUITES-SIKESTON   573/472-2299
[V] THREE DIAMOND Hotel. **Address:** 2608 E Malone Ave 63801

PEAR TREE INN BY DRURY   573/471-4100
[V] APPROVED   Hotel. **Address:** 2602 E Malone Ave 63801

WHERE TO EAT

LAMBERT'S CAFE   573/471-4261
[V] APPROVED Comfort Food. Casual Dining. **Address:** 2305 E Malone Ave 63801

MOBERLY pop. 13,974

COMFORT INN & SUITES   660/269-9700

[V] APPROVED
Hotel

Address: 1801 W Outer Rd 65270 **Location:** Jct US 36 and 24, 0.4 mi e. **Facility:** 63 units. 3 stories, interior corridors. **Pool:** heated indoor. **Activities:** hot tub, exercise room. **Featured Amenity:** full hot breakfast.

[SAVE] [🏊] [📶] [BIZ] [HS] [🛜] [✕]
[🔌] [📠] [💻]

WHERE TO EAT

THE BRICK   660/263-1414
[V] APPROVED American. Casual Dining. **Address:** 107 N Williams St 65270

MOUND CITY pop. 1,159, elev. 877'

SUPER 8 MOUND CITY   660/442-4000
[V] APPROVED Hotel. **Address:** 109 W 8th St 64470

MOUNT VERNON pop. 4,575

BEST WESTERN MT VERNON INN   417/461-0230

[V] APPROVED
Hotel

[BW] Best Western. **AAA Benefit:** Members save up to 15% and earn bonus points!

Address: 1200 E Industrial Dr 65712 **Location:** I-44 exit 46, just n, then just se. **Facility:** 49 units. 2 stories, interior corridors. **Pool:** heated indoor. **Activities:** limited exercise equipment. **Guest Services:** coin laundry. **Featured Amenity:** full hot breakfast.

[SAVE] [CALL] [♿] [🏊] [BIZ] [🛜] [✕]
[🔌] [📠] [💻] [/SOME UNITS] [🐾]

NEOSHO (D-2) pop. 11,835, elev. 1,019'

Neosho was named for the Osage word describing the clear water of a large spring near the center of town. The community was the boyhood home of artist Thomas Hart Benton, whose bold caricature-like paintings and murals portrayed the nation's ideas of life west of the Mississippi River in the early 1800s.

Neosho Area Chamber of Commerce: 216 W. Spring St., P.O. Box 605, Neosho, MO 64850. **Phone:** (417) 451-1925.

BEST WESTERN BIG SPRING LODGE 417/455-2300

APPROVED

Hotel

AAA Benefit: Members save up to 15% and earn bonus points!

Address: 1810 Southern View Dr 64850 **Location:** I-49 exit 24, 0.9 mi e. **Facility:** 63 units. 3 stories, interior corridors. **Pool:** outdoor. **Activities:** exercise room. **Guest Services:** coin laundry.

NORTH KANSAS CITY pop. 4,208
- **Hotels & Restaurants map & index p. 218**
- **Part of Kansas City area — see map p. 199**

HOLIDAY INN EXPRESS HOTEL & SUITES
816/218-1100 49
THREE DIAMOND Hotel. **Address:** 1995 Macon St 64116

WHERE TO EAT

CHAPPELL'S RESTAURANT & SPORTS MUSEUM
816/421-0002 51
APPROVED American. Casual Dining. **Address:** 323 Armour Rd 64116

PAUL & JACK'S TAVERN 816/221-9866 52
APPROVED American. Casual Dining. **Address:** 1808 Clay St 64116

O'FALLON pop. 79,329
- **Hotels & Restaurants map & index p. 271**
- **Part of St. Louis area — see map p. 248**

SLEEP INN & SUITES 636/329-1000 20
THREE DIAMOND Hotel. **Address:** 1147 Technology Dr 63368

STAYBRIDGE SUITES O'FALLON 636/300-0999 21
THREE DIAMOND Extended Stay Hotel. **Address:** 1155 Technology Dr 63368

WHERE TO EAT

SUGARFIRE SMOKE HOUSE 636/265-1234 23
APPROVED Barbecue. Quick Serve. **Address:** 9955 Winghaven Blvd 63368

OSAGE BEACH (C-3) pop. 4,351, elev. 860'

Osage Beach's location on Lake of the Ozarks makes it a popular vacation site. Music and comedy shows take place at the Main Street Music Hall, on Main Street at Blair's Landing.

HOLIDAY INN EXPRESS OSAGE BEACH-LAKE OF THE OZARKS 573/302-0330
APPROVED Hotel. **Address:** 4533 Osage Beach Pkwy 65065

MARGARITAVILLE LAKE RESORT LAKE OF THE OZARKS
573/348-3131
THREE DIAMOND Resort Hotel. **Address:** 494 Tan Tar A Dr 65065

RED ROOF INN & SUITES 573/348-4773
APPROVED Hotel. **Address:** 5927 Osage Beach Pkwy 65065

SCOTTISH INNS 573/348-3123
APPROVED Motel. **Address:** 5404 Osage Beach Pkwy 65065

WHERE TO EAT

LIL RIZZO'S 573/302-1500
APPROVED Italian. Casual Dining. **Address:** 929 Premium Outlets Dr 65065

MICHAEL'S STEAK CHALET & SWISS VILLAGE 573/348-3611
APPROVED Steak. Casual Dining. **Address:** 1440 Swiss Village Rd 65065

ON THE RISE BAKERY & BISTRO 573/348-4224
THREE DIAMOND American. Casual Dining. **Address:** 5439 Hwy 54 65065

VISTA GRANDE MEXICAN RESTAURANT 573/348-1231
APPROVED Tex-Mex. Casual Dining. **Address:** 4579 Hwy 54 65065

OZARK (D-3) pop. 17,820, elev. 1,168'

SMALLIN CIVIL WAR CAVE is at 3575 N. Smallin Rd. A 1-hour guided walking cave tour that involves inclines and ramps covers half a mile. Background information about the cave's geology and history is provided. In addition rock formations and various carvings, such cave dwellers such as bats, crayfish and salamanders might be spotted. Other tours are offered; phone for details. **Time:** Allow 1 hour minimum. **Hours:** Mon.-Sat. 9:30-5, Sun. 1-5, Mar.-Dec.; phone for schedule rest of year. **Cost:** $17.95; $9.95 (ages 4-12). **Phone:** (417) 551-4545.

LAMBERT'S CAFE 417/501-7655
APPROVED Comfort Food. Casual Dining. **Address:** 1800 W State Hwy J 65721

PRIMAS CANTINA & GRILL 417/582-2776
APPROVED Mexican. Casual Dining. **Address:** 1769 W James River Rd 65721

RIB CRIB BBQ AND GRILL 417/581-5566
APPROVED Barbecue. Casual Dining. **Address:** 750 N 18th St 65721

OZARKS AND OZARK NATIONAL SCENIC RIVERWAYS (D-4)

Encompassing the northeastern corner of Oklahoma, most of northern Arkansas and the majority of southern Missouri, the Ozarks comprise one of the oldest mountain ranges in North America. The hardwood forests that blanket these mountains also conceal approximately 4,000 caves, giving Missouri its well-deserved reputation as the "cave state."

Immortalized for their exceptional beauty in Harold Bell Wright's novel "The Shepherd of the Hills," the Ozarks are rich in folklore and tradition. The mountains were settled before the Civil War by Scottish, Irish, French and German mountaineers and homesteaders from Kentucky, Virginia, the Carolinas and Tennessee.

The Ozark National Scenic Riverways embrace portions of the Current and Jacks Fork rivers. Land along both sides of the rivers is protected. Forests, with many varieties of trees, shrubs and wildflowers, cover three-fourths of the riverways. Wildlife is abundant; hunting is permitted in season.

The riverways area is noted for its many springs—more than 300 in all. Big Spring, south of Van Buren on US 60 and then 4 miles east on SR 103, is one of the nation's largest springs. Flowing from a collapsed cave, it emits an average of 286 million gallons of water a day. A three-story historic roller mill, 6 miles west of Eminence via SR 106, is preserved at Alley Spring, one of the riverways' largest springs.

Lantern tours of Round Spring Cavern near Round Spring are offered by park interpreters during the summer. Recreational facilities in the park include camping and picnic areas. Most visitors come to enjoy the float trips on the Current and Jacks Fork rivers and there are several outfitters catering to them; hiking the trails and horseback riding also are very popular.

For information about seasonal interpretive programs, craft demonstrations and other activities phone (573) 323-4236. *See Recreation Areas Chart.*

Towns in the Ozarks region listed in this book under their own descriptions are Branson, Hermann, Ironton, Jefferson City, Joplin, Osage Beach, Rolla, St. James, Springfield and Warsaw *(see place listings).*

PERRYVILLE (C-6) pop. 8,225, elev. 581'

The Kings Highway, which the Spanish extended from New Madrid to St. Louis in 1789, once ran through the present site of Perryville. The rolling barrens of Perry County were named for the geographically similar small plains areas of southwestern Kentucky.

Perryville Chamber of Commerce: 2 W. St. Maries St., Perryville, MO 63775. **Phone:** (573) 547-6062.

HOLIDAY INN EXPRESS & SUITES PERRYVILLE I-55
573/605-1385
▼▼ **THREE DIAMOND** Hotel. **Address:** 2020 Jefferson St 63775

SUPER 8 PERRYVILLE   573/517-7888
▼▼ **APPROVED** Hotel. **Address:** 1119 Vincent Dr 63775

🔗 **For complete hotel,**

dining and attraction listings:

AAA.com/travelguides

PLATTE CITY (F-1) pop. 4,691, elev. 850'
• **Hotels & Restaurants map & index p. 218**
• **Part of Kansas City area — see map p. 199**

When Missouri joined the Union in 1821, the northwestern corner of the state was still part of the Native American Territory. The Platte Purchase of 1836 negotiated the transfer of this area from the Iowa, Sac and Fox Indians.

Platte County Convention and Visitors Bureau: 11724 N.W. Plaza Cir., Suite 200, Kansas City, MO 64153. **Phone:** (816) 270-3979 or (888) 875-2883.

RAMADA BY WYNDHAM PLATTE CITY KCI AIRPORT
816/858-0200 **40**
▼▼ **APPROVED** Motel. **Address:** 2512 NW Prairie View Rd 64079

WHERE TO EAT

MARIA'S AUTHENTIC MEXICAN RESTAURANT
816/858-2600 **39**
▼▼ **APPROVED** Mexican. Casual Dining. **Address:** 1205 Branch St 64079

POINT LOOKOUT (E-3) elev. 928'
• **Part of Branson area — see map p. 151**

COLLEGE OF THE OZARKS is off US 65 Bus. Rte. exit. This liberal arts college is maintained largely by students as one way of defraying the cost of education. Highlights include The College of the Ozarks Greenhouses, containing a collection of more than 7,000 orchids; the neo-Gothic Williams Memorial Chapel, which has impressive stained-glass windows; and the Ralph Foster Museum. The water-powered Edwards Mill produces whole-grain meal; visitors can observe weaving and basket-making demonstrations.

Three memorials are on the grounds. The Missouri Vietnam Veterans Memorial honors the 1,410 Missouri men and women who gave the ultimate sacrifice in the Vietnam conflict. The 9-11 "Lest We Forget" Memorial features a World Trade Center column and honors the 2,996 lives lost on Sept. 11, 2001. The Missouri Gold Star Families Memorial honors those who have lost immediate family members in their service to the country, to preserve the memory of the fallen and stand as a stark reminder that freedom is not free. All memorials are open daily sunrise-10 p.m.

The Keeter Center, at the entrance to the campus, houses a lodge and Dobyns Dining Room. It features architectural details created almost entirely by students, who also prepare and serve the food. **Phone:** (417) 334-6411.

Ralph Foster Museum is at 100 Opportunity Ave. on the College of the Ozarks campus. Named after local radio pioneer and avid hunter, angler and conservationist Ralph Foster, the displays at this museum cover Ozarks history and life. Collections include coins, stamps, timepieces, dolls, musical instruments, Native American artifacts and an extensive display of weapons that features gold-plated handguns and flintlocks.

Other highlights include beautiful ornate saddles, Western gear, wildlife displays (polar bears, deer and waterfowl), antique cameos and the vintage vehicle that took the Clampett family to California in the popular 1960s TV series "The Beverly Hillbillies." The Discovery Room has interactive exhibits for kids. **Time:** Allow 2 hours minimum. **Hours:** Mon.-Sat. 9-5. Closed Thanksgiving, day after Thanksgiving and Christmas week. **Cost:** $6; $5 (ages 62+); $4 (retired military with ID); free (ages 0-18). **Phone:** (417) 690-3407.

POPLAR BLUFF (D-5) pop. 17,023, elev. 344'

Greater Poplar Bluff Area Chamber of Commerce: 1111 W. Pine St., Poplar Bluff, MO 63901. **Phone:** (573) 785-7761.

COMFORT INN   573/686-5200
THREE DIAMOND Hotel. **Address:** 2582 N Westwood Blvd 63901

DRURY INN-POPLAR BLUFF   573/686-2451
APPROVED Hotel. **Address:** 2220 N Westwood Blvd 63901

FAIRFIELD INN & SUITES BY MARRIOTT POPLAR BLUFF   573/250-7020
THREE DIAMOND SAVE Hotel. **Address:** 3109 Oak Grove Rd 63901

	AAA Benefit: Members save 5% or more!

HAMPTON INN BY HILTON POPLAR BLUFF   573/300-4550
THREE DIAMOND SAVE Hotel. **Address:** 2420 Crestwood Dr 63901

	AAA Benefit: Members save up to 15%!

MOTEL 6 POPLAR BLUFF   573/776-6400
APPROVED Motel. **Address:** 4101 N US 67 63901

WHERE TO EAT

COLTON'S STEAKHOUSE & GRILL   573/686-3880
APPROVED Steak. Casual Dining. **Address:** 2114 N Westwood Blvd 63901

EL ACAPULCO AUTHENTIC MEXICAN RESTAURANT   573/776-7000
APPROVED Mexican. Casual Dining. **Address:** 2260 N Westwood Blvd 63901

MAYA'S MEXICAN GRILL   573/785-7966
APPROVED Mexican. Casual Dining. **Address:** 940 S Westwood Blvd 63901

REPUBLIC pop. 14,751

AMERICINN LODGE & SUITES OF REPUBLIC   417/732-5335
APPROVED Hotel. **Address:** 950 N Austin Ln 65738

RICHMOND HEIGHTS pop. 8,603
• **Hotels & Restaurants map & index p. 274**
• **Part of St. Louis area — see map p. 248**

COURTYARD BY MARRIOTT ST. LOUIS BRENTWOOD   314/647-2998 **75**

THREE DIAMOND Hotel   COURTYARD **AAA Benefit:** Members save 5% or more!

Address: 8101 Dale Ave 63117 **Location:** I-64/US 40 exit 31B (Brentwood/Hanley Rd), 0.5 mi s on Hanley Rd, then just w. **Facility:** 141 units. 5 stories, interior corridors. **Activities:** exercise room. **Guest Services:** valet and coin laundry.

HOMEWOOD SUITES BY HILTON ST. LOUIS GALLERIA   314/863-7700 **73**
THREE DIAMOND SAVE Extended Stay Hotel. **Address:** 8040 Clayton Rd 63117

AAA Benefit: Members save up to 15%!

RESIDENCE INN BY MARRIOTT-ST. LOUIS GALLERIA   314/862-1900 **74**
THREE DIAMOND SAVE Extended Stay Hotel. **Address:** 8011 Galleria Pkwy 63117

AAA Benefit: Members save 5% or more!

WHERE TO EAT

BLUE SKY TOWER GRILL   314/726-2583 **90**
APPROVED American. Casual Dining. **Address:** 1034 S Brentwood Blvd 63117

THE CHEESECAKE FACTORY   314/721-0505 **91**
THREE DIAMOND International. Casual Dining. **Address:** 1062 St. Louis Galleria 63117

MAGGIANO'S LITTLE ITALY   314/824-2402 **92**
THREE DIAMOND Italian. Fine Dining. **Address:** 2 The Boulevard 63117

P.F. CHANG'S CHINA BISTRO   314/862-2624 **93**
THREE DIAMOND Chinese. Fine Dining. **Address:** 25 The Boulevard 63117

RIVERSIDE (G-1) pop. 2,937, elev. 440'
• Hotels & Restaurants map & index p. 218
• Part of Kansas City area — see map p. 199

GAMBLING ESTABLISHMENTS

• **Argosy Casino** is e. of jct. I-635 and US 69 at 777 N.W. Argosy Casino Pkwy., following signs. **Hours:** Daily 24 hrs. **Phone:** (816) 746-3100 or (800) 270-7711. *(See ad p. 230.)*

ARGOSY CASINO HOTEL & SPA   816/746-3700 46
🔷 **FOUR DIAMOND**   **Address:** 777 NW Argosy Pkwy 64150 **Location:** I-635 exit 9, just s, then 1 mi e. **Facility:** This hotel is a mini playground for adults with its on-site gaming, dining and spa. Rooms are nice and spacious, but the bathrooms really impress with rain shower heads and spa-style amenities. 258 units. 9 stories, interior corridors. **Parking:** on-site and valet. **Terms:** check-in 4 pm. **Amenities:** safes. **Dining:** 3 restaurants, also, The Journey, Terrace Buffet, see separate listings. **Activities:** exercise room, spa. **Guest Services:** valet laundry. *(See ad p. 230.)*

Hotel

SAVE 🚭 🍴 🕎 🍸 CALL 👥 🛜 BIZ 📶 📹 🔲 💻

WHERE TO EAT

CORNER CAFE   816/741-2570 46
🔷 **APPROVED**   American. Casual Dining. **Address:** 4541 NW Gateway Ave 64150

THE JOURNEY   816/746-3100 47
🔷 **THREE DIAMOND**   Steak. Casual Dining. **Address:** 777 NW Argosy Pkwy 64150

TERRACE BUFFET   816/746-3100 48
🔷 **APPROVED**   International. Casual Dining. **Address:** 777 NW Argosy Pkwy 64150

ROLLA (C-4) pop. 19,559, elev. 1,095'

Rolla was founded in 1855 when a group of railroad contractors built an office and a few warehouses near the farm of John Webber. The prospect of the railroad attracted 600 people within the following 6 months, and in 1857 a search for a town name began.

Webber, who had farmed in the area, wanted to call the town Hardscrabble. A railroad official wanted to call it Phelps Center. The suggestion of a nostalgic North Carolinian who wanted to call it Raleigh was finally approved, but the new name was spelled as the Southerner had pronounced it.

Rolla is the home of the Mid-Continent Mapping Center, National Mapping Division, US Geological Survey. The center, 1400 Independence Rd., offers tours; phone (573) 308-3500.

St. Patrick, the patron saint of engineers, is honored every March by students attending the Missouri University of Science and Technology at Rolla (MS&T), who are dubbed knights in the Order of St. Patrick. Other festivities include a parade, a beard competition and painting Main Street a shade of green.

On the UMR campus near US 63 and State Street is Missouri S&T Stonehenge, a partial replica of the ancient megaliths in England. The stone circle has apertures that allow the date to be told by the position of the sun's rays and permit the viewing of the North Star, features not present in the original construction. The replica is an official triangulation point in the National Geodetic Survey's North American Triangulation Network.

Rolla Area Chamber of Commerce: 1311 Kingshighway, Rolla, MO 65401. **Phone:** (573) 364-3577 or (888) 809-3817.

BEST WESTERN COACHLIGHT   573/341-2511
🔷 **APPROVED**   Best Western.
Motel

AAA Benefit: Members save up to 15% and earn bonus points!

Address: 1403 Martin Springs Dr 65401 **Location:** Jct I-44 and Business Rt 44 S exit 184. **Facility:** 76 units. 2 stories (no elevator), exterior corridors. **Amenities:** safes. **Pool:** outdoor. **Guest Services:** coin laundry. **Featured Amenity:** continental breakfast.

SAVE 🍴 🛜 BIZ 📶 🔲 💻 / SOME UNITS 🐾

COMFORT SUITES   573/368-4300
🔷 **THREE DIAMOND**   Hotel. **Address:** 1650 Old Wire Outer Rd 65401

HAMPTON INN BY HILTON   573/308-1060
🔷 **THREE DIAMOND** SAVE   Hotel. **Address:** 2201 N Bishop Ave 65401

AAA Benefit: Members save up to 15%!

HOLIDAY INN EXPRESS HOTEL & SUITES   573/426-2900
🔷 **THREE DIAMOND**   Hotel. **Address:** 1610 Old Wire Outer Rd 65401

PEAR TREE INN BY DRURY-ROLLA   573/364-4000
🔷 **APPROVED**   Hotel. **Address:** 2006 N Bishop Ave 65401

WHERE TO EAT

ALEX'S PIZZA PALACE   573/364-2669
🔷 **APPROVED**   Pizza. Casual Dining. **Address:** 122 W 8th St 65401

JUST DELICIOUS!   573/426-6463
🔷 **APPROVED**   Sandwiches. Quick Serve. **Address:** 1375 E 10th St 65401

MOTTOMO SUSHI   573/341-1200
🔷 **APPROVED**   Asian Sushi. Casual Dining. **Address:** 1011 Kingshighway St 65401

ST. ANN pop. 13,020
- **Hotels & Restaurants map & index p. 274**
- **Part of St. Louis area — see map p. 248**

HAMPTON INN BY HILTON - ST. LOUIS AIRPORT
314/429-2000 **34**

THREE DIAMOND **SAVE** Hotel. **Ad-dress:** 10820 Pear Tree Ln 63074

AAA Benefit:
Members save up to 15%!

PEAR TREE INN BY DRURY-ST. LOUIS AIRPORT
314/427-3400 **35**
APPROVED Hotel. **Address:** 10810 Pear Tree Ln 63074

WHERE TO EAT

BANDANA'S BAR-B-Q 314/426-9955
APPROVED Barbecue. Casual Dining. **Address:** 10800 Pear Tree Ln, Suite 2 63074

ST. CHARLES (F-5) pop. 65,794, elev. 467'
- **Hotels p. 244 • Restaurants p. 244**
- **Hotels & Restaurants map & index p. 271**
- **Part of St. Louis area — see map p. 248**

Founded by French Canadians in 1769, St. Charles was first known as *Les Petites Cotes*—"the little hills"—a reference to the low bluffs that form a picturesque backdrop along the Missouri River. Present-day Missouri was then part of a vast territory under Spanish rule, although many of those who came to the region to start a new life were French nationals. But also among the arrivals was an American pioneer and soon-to-be folk hero named Daniel Boone; he and much of his extended family settled in nearby Defiance.

In 1804 Upper Louisiana was formally transferred from France to the United States, and the district of San Carlos was renamed St. Charles. That same year Meriwether Lewis arrived from St. Louis to meet up with William Clark, and the two men, along with several boats and an expedition party, left the relative comforts of civilization to embark on a great journey of discovery that would lead them all the way to the Pacific Ocean.

Take a walk around the grounds of the Lewis & Clark Boat House and Nature Center and you'll spot a couple of pawpaw trees. This small tree, which flourishes in the lower Missouri River Valley, produces a large, yellowish-brown, edible fruit that bears a resemblance to another edible yellow fruit, hence the pawpaw's local name—Missouri banana. On the return trip the Lewis and Clark expedition party had depleted most of their rations and ended up subsisting largely on pawpaw fruit.

Missouri was admitted to the Union on Aug. 10, 1821, and St. Charles became the state's first capital. It also was an early center for education west of the Mississippi; the Academy of the Sacred Heart was established in 1818 by Rose Philippine Duchesne, who was canonized in 1988.

In mid-August the entire city celebrates Fête des Petites Côtes, or the Festival of the Little Hills. The 19th century is revisited at this major summertime event, which offers craft demonstrations, food and musical entertainment courtesy of the St. Charles Municipal Band and other acts like Catfish Willie and Borderline.

Pay tribute to yesteryear at the Lewis & Clark Statue in Frontier Park (off Riverside Drive at the foot of Perry Street). Dedicated in 2003, it depicts the intrepid explorers and their dog, Seaman. Also in the park is the Katy Depot; St. Charles is the starting point of the Katy Trail, the former railroad line turned scenic bike trail that stretches west to Clinton.

Switch gears from the past to the present and stop by the Foundry Art Centre, 520 N. Main St. This gallery has studios where you can chat with local artists about their work. The center also contains several rooms with rotating exhibits of high-quality art; phone (636) 255-0270.

St. Charles is home to the River City Raiders professional indoor football team and the St. Louis Ambush men's soccer team. Both play at the Family Arena, 2002 Arena Pkwy.; phone (636) 896-4200 for the box office.

Greater St. Charles Convention and Visitors Bureau: 230 S. Main St., St. Charles, MO 63301. **Phone:** (636) 946-7776 or (800) 366-2427.

Shopping: If you're a fan of gift and specialty shops—all quaint with a capital "Q" and conveniently located along one street for easy browsing—you're in luck: Main Street in St. Charles has perfected this particular shopping experience.

The street, part of the St. Charles Historic District, parallels the Missouri River. Shady, brick-paved sidewalks are lined with barrel planters and hanging flower baskets. Just when you're thinking about cooling your heels for a minute an inviting bench seems to appear; the gazebo near the convention and visitors bureau (where there also are public restrooms) is a particularly pretty spot.

Many of the shops are in handsomely restored old brick and wood-frame buildings. Even if you're on a mission to find that certain something, take time to check out The Enchanted Attic (304 S. Main St.) for funky jewelry, wind chimes, crystals and such, and Cobblestone Cottage (803 S. Main St.) for Colonial-style furniture, period lighting fixtures, historical prints and other Americana.

The boutique Ooh La La (703 S. Main St.) has women's clothing. Look for children's books and tomes about local history at Main Street Books (307 S. Main St.).

Have lunch in the cozy dining room at the Mother-in-Law House Restaurant (500 S. Main St.), or sit on the leafy patio if the weather's nice. Picasso's (101 N. Main St.) is a coffee house with a relaxed air and a good selection of coffee and espresso drinks.

Of course Main Street isn't the only shopping game in town. Outdoor enthusiasts not on the hunt for tea cozies and collectible dolls head to Bass Pro Shops Sportsman's Warehouse, 1365 S. 5th St. It's a sprawling place with every conceivable type of

(See map & index p. 271.)

recreational gear, plus wildlife exhibits, an indoor waterfall and a game fish aquarium.

FIRST MISSOURI STATE CAPITOL STATE HISTORIC SITE is at 200-216 S. Main St. on the riverfront. These adjoining Federal-style brick buildings were the seat of government 1821-26. The first state General Assembly met upstairs while the building's owners lived and operated a general store on the first floor. Gov. Alexander McNair's office and a committee room were off the legislative chambers. Several rooms in the 1820 complex have been restored and decorated with period furnishings. Behind the building, overlooking the riverfront, gardens are laid out in period style. An interpretive center offers exhibits and a slide show.

Time: Allow 1 hour minimum. **Hours:** Guided tours are given Mon.-Sat. on the hour 10-4, Sun. noon-4, Apr.-Oct.; Tues.-Sat. on the hour 10-4, Sun. noon-4, Nov.-Dec. and in Mar.; Tues.-Sat. on the hour 10-4, rest of year. Last tour begins 1 hour before closing. **Cost:** $4.50; $3 (ages 6-17). **Phone:** (636) 940-3322 or (800) 334-6946.

AMERISTAR ST. CHARLES CASINO RESORT & SPA
636/940-4300 **11**

FOUR DIAMOND Hotel

Address: One Ameristar Blvd 63301 **Location:** I-70 exit 229 and 229B, just n on 5th St, then just e. **Facility:** Spacious, upscale rooms will make you feel like a high roller; all feature plump bedding and a sunken living rooms with conversational seating. 397 units. 25 stories, interior corridors. **Parking:** on-site and valet. **Terms:** check-in 4 pm. **Amenities:** safes. **Dining:** 3 restaurants, also, Amerisports Bar & Grill, Bugatti's Steak & Pasta, The Falcon Diner, The Landmark Buffet, see separate listings. **Pool:** heated outdoor, heated indoor. **Activities:** hot tub, game room, exercise room, spa. **Guest Services:** valet laundry.

SAVE 🎰 🍴 🌭 🍸 CALL 🚹 🏊 ♿ BIZ 📶 🔌 💻

BEST WESTERN PLUS THE CHARLES HOTEL
636/946-6936 **8**

THREE DIAMOND Hotel

Best Western PLUS. **AAA Benefit:** Members save up to 15% and earn bonus points!

Address: 1425 S 5th St 63301 **Location:** I-70 exit 229B (5th St N), just n, then w. **Facility:** 133 units. 8 stories, interior corridors. **Amenities:** safes. **Pool:** heated indoor. **Activities:** exercise room. **Guest Services:** valet and coin laundry.

SAVE 🍴 CALL 🚹 🏊 ♿ BIZ 📶 ❌ 🔌 📺 💻 / SOME UNITS 🐾

COMFORT SUITES-ST. CHARLES 636/949-0694 **10**
THREE DIAMOND Hotel. **Address:** 1400 S 5th St 63301

COUNTRY INN & SUITES BY RADISSON 636/724-5555 **7**
THREE DIAMOND Hotel. **Address:** 1190 S Main St 63301

DRURY PLAZA ST. LOUIS ST. CHARLES 636/724-5772 **12**
THREE DIAMOND Hotel. **Address:** 380 Mulholland Dr 63303

EMBASSY SUITES BY HILTON ST. LOUIS-ST. CHARLES HOTEL 636/946-5544 **9**
THREE DIAMOND SAVE Hotel. **Address:** Two Convention Center Plaza 63303 — **AAA Benefit:** Members save up to 15%!

HAMPTON INN BY HILTON - ST. LOUIS/ST. CHARLES 636/947-6800 **5**
THREE DIAMOND SAVE Hotel. **Address:** 3720 W Clay St 63301 — **AAA Benefit:** Members save up to 15%!

TOWNEPLACE SUITES BY MARRIOTT 636/949-6800 **6**
THREE DIAMOND SAVE Extended Stay Hotel. **Address:** 1800 Zumbehl Rd 63303 — **AAA Benefit:** Members save 5% or more!

TRU BY HILTON ST. CHARLES ST. LOUIS 636/669-2500 **13**
APPROVED SAVE Hotel. **Address:** 333 Camelback Rd 63303 — Members save up to 15%!

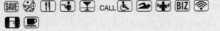

WHERE TO EAT

AMERISPORTS BAR & GRILL 636/940-4935 **13**
APPROVED American. Casual Dining. **Address:** One Ameristar Blvd 63301

BELLA VINO WINE BAR & TAPAS 636/724-3434 **8**
APPROVED Small Plates. Casual Dining. **Address:** 325 S Main St 63301

BRADDENS RESTAURANT 636/493-9303 **9**
APPROVED American. Casual Dining. **Address:** 515 S Main St 63301

BUGATTI'S STEAK & PASTA 636/940-4471 **15**
THREE DIAMOND Steak. Fine Dining. **Address:** One Ameristar Blvd 63301

THE FALCON DINER 636/940-4955 **14**
APPROVED American. Casual Dining. **Address:** One Ameristar Blvd 63301

FRATELLI'S RISTORANTE 636/949-9005 **6**
APPROVED Italian. Casual Dining. **Address:** 2061 Zumbehl Rd 63303

THE LANDMARK BUFFET 636/940-4470 **12**
APPROVED International. Buffet Style. **Address:** One Ameristar Blvd 63301

LEWIS AND CLARK'S AN AMERICAN RESTAURANT & PUBLIC HOUSE 636/947-3334 **7**
APPROVED American. Casual Dining. **Address:** 217 S Main St 63301

LLYWELYN'S PUB 636/724-8520 **5**
APPROVED Irish. Casual Dining. **Address:** 100 N Main St 63301

MAGPIE'S 636/947-3883 **10**
APPROVED American. Casual Dining. **Address:** 903 S Main St 63301

(See map & index p. 271.)

MISSION TACO JOINT   636/442-1620   (17)
◈ **APPROVED**   Mexican. Gastropub. **Address:** 1650
Beale St 63303

PRASINO   636/277-0202   (16)
◈**THREE DIAMOND** New American. Casual Dining. **Address:**
1520 S 5th St 63303

SUGARFIRE SMOKE HOUSE   636/724-7601   (4)
◈ **APPROVED**   Barbecue. Quick Serve. **Address:** 3150
Elm Point Industrial Dr 63301

TRAILHEAD BREWING COMPANY   636/946-2739   (11)
◈ **APPROVED**   American. Casual Dining. **Address:** 921
S Riverside Dr 63301

ST. JOSEPH (B-1) pop. 76,780, elev. 823'
• Hotels p. 246 • Restaurants p. 246

St. Joseph was founded in 1826 by Joseph Robidoux, who established a fur trading post in the Blacksnake Hills. The mass migrations following the discovery of gold in California in 1848 and Colorado in 1858 transformed the frontier town into a major wagon train staging area and supply depot. In 1859 Robidoux drove the last spike on the Hannibal and St. Joseph Railroad, which made St. Joseph the westernmost railroad terminal.

The Pony Express launched its famous mail service on Apr. 3, 1860, from St. Joseph to Sacramento, Calif. Riders traveled the 10-day route twice a week.

Notorious outlaw Jesse James lived quietly with his family in St. Joseph, where he was known as the mild-mannered, respected Mr. Howard. He was killed in 1882 by fellow gang member Bob Ford, whose brother Charles claimed the $10,000 reward.

The Buchanan County Courthouse, 411 Jules St., originally was constructed at Fifth and Felix streets in 1873. During the Centennial Exhibition of 1876, the classical Renaissance building was called one of the most outstanding buildings in the country. Its exterior is lighted at night; the interior houses county offices.

St. Joseph Convention & Visitors Bureau: 911 Frederick Ave., P.O. Box 445, St. Joseph, MO 64501. **Phone:** (816) 233-6688 or (800) 785-0360.

THE GLORE PSYCHIATRIC MUSEUM is at 3406 Frederick Ave. It surveys the portrayal and treatment of mental illness over the years, including exhibits of antique ward furniture and such primitive early equipment as lobotomy instruments, a hydrotherapy tub, a tranquilizing chair, a restraint cage and wet sheet packs. The museum also recounts the history of a facility once known as "State Lunatic Asylum No. 2."

Time: Allow 1 hour minimum. **Hours:** Mon.-Sat. 10-5, Sun. 1-5. Closed major holidays. **Cost:** (includes The Black Archives Museum, the Doll Museum and the St. Joseph Museum) $6; $5 (ages 62+); $4 (students with ID). **Phone:** (816) 232-8471 or (800) 530-8866.

The Black Archives Museum, 3406 Frederick Ave. on The Glore Psychiatric Museum grounds, has exhibits depicting the history and cultural heritage of the African-American community in St. Joseph. **Hours:** Mon.-Sat. 10-5, Sun. 1-5. Closed major holidays. **Cost:** (includes The Glore Psychiatric Museum, the Doll Museum and the St. Joseph Museum) $6; $5 (ages 62+); $4 (students with ID). **Phone:** (816) 232-8471 or (800) 530-8866.

St. Joseph Museum, 3406 Frederick Ave. on The Glore Psychiatric Museum grounds, contains extensive Native American exhibits including clothing, accessories, fans, pottery, pipes, weapons, jewelry and archeological artifacts from 10 different cultural regions. Occupying another wing is the Black Archives Museum, featuring area African-American history, and the Doll Museum, displaying life-size child dolls dating from the 1860s as well as dolls created from such materials as wood and corn husks.

Hours: Mon.-Sat. 10-5, Sun. 1-5. Closed major holidays. **Cost:** (includes The Glore Psychiatric Museum, the Doll Museum and The Black Archives Museum) $6; $5 (ages 62+); $4 (students with ID). **Phone:** (816) 232-8471 or (800) 530-8866.

PONY EXPRESS NATIONAL MUSEUM is at 914 Penn St. This was the original site of the business venture that developed from the War Department's demand for speedy communications with California. Riders routinely made the 1,966-mile trip between St. Joseph and Sacramento, Calif., in 10 days. Exhibits explore the creation, operation and demise of the Pony Express. **Hours:** Mon.-Sat. 9-5, Sun. 11-4, Mar.-Nov.; Mon.-Sat. 9-4, Sun. 11-4, rest of year. Closed Jan. 1, Thanksgiving, Christmas Eve, Christmas and Dec. 31. **Cost:** $6; $5 (ages 60+); $3 (ages 7-17); $1 (ages 4-6). **Phone:** (816) 279-5059.

REMINGTON NATURE CENTER OF ST. JOSEPH is at 1502 MacArthur Dr. Natural history displays include a life-size mammoth and her calf as well as exhibits of preserved animals including a bison, wolf and black bear. Also featured are more than a thousand Native American artifacts from the area and a 7,000-gallon aquarium filled with native Missouri River fish. A variety of interactive educational exhibits appeal to kids. Outside, an observation deck overlooks the Missouri River and a walkway provides views of the Loess Hills Bluffs. **Time:** Allow 1 hour minimum. **Hours:** Mon.-Sat. 10-5, Sun. 1-5. Closed major holidays. **Cost:** $3; $2 (ages 60+); $1 (ages 4-15). **Phone:** (816) 271-5499. (Ⅱ)

THE WYETH-TOOTLE MANSION is at 11th and Charles sts. Overlooking the Missouri River, this 1879 Gothic sandstone mansion was designed with a north side turret to create a resemblance to European castles. It is one of many turn-of-the-20th-century residences in the city and has ornate walnut woodwork and staircases and stained-glass windows. The first floor is furnished in period, with oil-on-canvas paintings on the ceilings, and displays photographs of the home taken in the early 1900s, while exhibits on the upper floors impart local history.

Time: Allow 30 minutes minimum. **Hours:** Fri.-Sat. 10-4, Apr.-Oct. Closed major holidays. **Cost:** $6; $5 (ages 62+); $4 (students with ID); free (ages 0-6). **Phone:** (816) 232-8471. GT

CANDLEWOOD SUITES   816/232-2600
▼▼ THREE DIAMOND Extended Stay Hotel. **Address:** 3505 N Village Dr 64506

DRURY INN & SUITES-ST. JOSEPH   816/364-4700
▼▼ THREE DIAMOND Hotel. **Address:** 4213 Frederick Blvd 64506

FAIRFIELD INN & SUITES BY MARRIOTT - ST. JOSEPH
816/232-2700
▼▼ THREE DIAMOND SAVE Hotel. **Address:** 4779 Tuscany Dr 64506

> **AAA Benefit:**
> Members save 5% or more!

HAMPTON INN BY HILTON   816/390-9300
▼▼ THREE DIAMOND SAVE Hotel. **Address:** 3928 Frederick Blvd 64506

> **AAA Benefit:**
> Members save up to 15%!

HOLIDAY INN EXPRESS & SUITES   816/232-2500
▼▼ THREE DIAMOND Hotel. **Address:** 3600 N Village Dr 64506

STONEY CREEK HOTEL & CONFERENCE CENTER
816/901-9600
▼▼ THREE DIAMOND Hotel. **Address:** 1201 N Woodbine Rd 64506

WHERE TO EAT

GYRO PARADISE-MEDITERRANEAN GRILL   816/279-2990
▼▼ APPROVED Mediterranean. Quick Serve. **Address:** 1209 N Belt Hwy 64506

IL LAZZARONE   816/273-0582
▼▼ APPROVED Italian Pizza. Casual Dining. **Address:** 1628 Frederick Ave 64501

RIB CRIB BBQ AND GRILL   816/279-7422
▼▼ APPROVED Barbecue. Casual Dining. **Address:** 3704 Faraon St 64506

St. Louis

Then & Now

What do Judy Garland, Nelly, Joe Garagiola, Pierre Laclede and Provel have in common? The movie star, the rapper, the baseball player, the French fur trader and the cheese all have a St. Louis connection.

Back in 1764, Laclede established a trading post on a bluff 18 miles south of the mouth of the Mississippi and Missouri rivers. With a surrounding area rich in natural resources and the river providing an easily navigable link to New Orleans, this new settlement seemed destined for success.

And prosper it did. After being governed by Spain and France the United States acquired the town in 1803 as part of the Louisiana Purchase. Lewis and Clark set off from nearby St. Charles on their 1804 trip to the Pacific. The arrival of the *Zebulon M. Pike* in 1817 inaugurated the steamboat era.

The 1904 World's Fair—held at Forest Park, the crown jewel of the city's parks—celebrated the Louisiana Purchase centennial and put the city in the world spotlight. (This is the Judy Garland connection; in the film "Meet Me in St. Louis" Garland plays a 17-year-old whose family is leaving St. Louis for New York and will miss the extravaganza.) The fair introduced and popularized food items that have achieved who-hasn't-had-one status, among them the hot dog and the waffle cone. And from this beginning comes the city's reputation for regional specialties.

AAA.com/travelguides—
more ways to look, book and save

Provel? This mild and creamy blend of Swiss, provolone and cheddar cheeses is the defining ingredient in St. Louis-style pizza, which has a thin, crackery crust, a sweet tomato sauce and finely chopped toppings, that is then cut into square or rectangular slices.

Another specialty is toasted ravioli, a Sicilian concoction of pasta squares encasing meat or cheese, given a twist by being breaded and deep fried. In St. Louis, "toasted rav" typically has a ground beef filling and a sprinkling of Parmesan cheese on top and is served with a side of marinara sauce.

All things Italian are found on the Hill, one of St. Louis' best-known neighborhoods. Even the fire hydrants are painted the colors of Italy's flag. In addition to primo Italian groceries, bakeries and restaurants, the Hill is noted for two baseball giants—Yogi Berra and Joe Garagiola—who grew up on Elizabeth Avenue.

Forest Park

(Continued on p. 249.)

Destination St. Louis

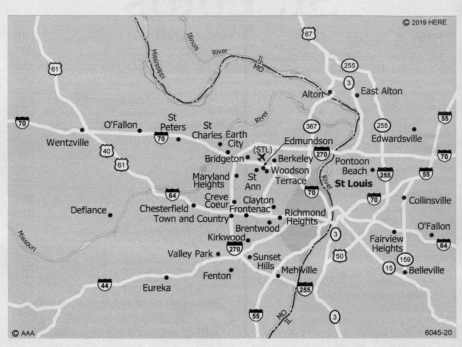

This map shows cities in the St. Louis vicinity where you will find attractions, hotels and restaurants. Cities are listed alphabetically in this book on the following pages.

Fast Facts

ABOUT THE CITY

POP: 319,294 ▪ **ELEV:** 585 ft.

MONEY

SALES TAX: The sales tax rate in the city of St. Louis is 8.49 percent. The city's lodging tax is 14.9 percent and there is a rental car tax of 7.82 percent.

WHOM TO CALL

EMERGENCY: 911

POLICE (non-emergency): (314) 231-1212

TIME AND TEMPERATURE: (314) 321-2222 or (636) 441-8467

HOSPITALS: Barnes-Jewish Hospital, (314) 747-3000 ▪ Missouri Baptist Medical Center (Town and Country, Mo.), (314) 996-5000 ▪ St. Alexius Hospital, (314) 865-7000 ▪ St. Anthony's Medical Center, (314) 525-1000 ▪ Saint Louis University Hospital, (314) 577-8000.

VISITOR INFORMATION

Missouri Welcome Center: I-270, exit 34 at Riverview Dr., St. Louis, MO 63138. **Phone:** (314) 869-7100 daily 8-5, Apr.-Oct.; Mon.-Sat. 8-5, rest of year.

St. Louis Convention and Visitors Commission (Explore St. Louis): 701 Convention Plaza, Suite 300, St. Louis, MO 63101. **Phone:** (314) 421-1023, or (800) 325-7962 for general information.

TRANSPORTATION

AIR TRAVEL: Lambert-St. Louis International Airport (STL) is on I-70 in the northwestern section of the metropolitan area. Taxi fare from the airport is usually about $40. The area's light-rail system, MetroLink, originates at the airport and culminates at Scott Air Force Base in Shiloh, Ill.

RENTAL CARS: Hertz offers discounts to AAA members; phone (314) 426-7555 or (800) 654-3080.

 Book and save at **AAA.com/hertz**

RAIL SERVICE: The Amtrak terminal, (800) 872-7245, is at 430 S. 15th St.

BUSES: The Greyhound Lines Inc. terminal, (800) 231-2222, is at 430 S. 15th St.

TAXIS: Cab companies include St. Louis County Cab & Yellow Cab, (314) 991-5300 or (314) 993-8294 ▪ and Laclede, (314) 652-3456 or (314) 403-7000 (to request a taxi via text message). All cabs in St. Louis are on the meter system. Base fare is approximately $2 to $3.50 for the first mile, with a rate of $2 to $2.50 per mile. The base fare goes up $1 for each additional passenger. A fuel surcharge of at least $1 also is added to the fare, and there is a $4 surcharge for airport pick-ups.

PUBLIC TRANSPORTATION: Metro, the public transportation system—which includes MetroBus, the MetroLink light-rail train and the Metro Call-A-Ride para-transit van service—transports passengers throughout the St. Louis metropolitan area. The base bus fare is $2; $1 (ages 5-12, ages 65+ and customers with disabilities). Exact cash fare is required. A MetroLink one-ride ticket is $2.50; $1.25 (ages 5-12, ages 65+ and customers with disabilities). A 2-hour system pass (with transfers) is $3; $1.50 (ages 5-12, ages 65+ and customers with disabilities), or $4 from Lambert Airport. Weekly and monthly passes also are available. For route information, current fares and hours of system operation contact MetroTransit Information Mon.-Fri. 7-7; phone (314) 231-2345, or (618) 271-2345 in Illinois.

(Continued from p. 247.)

The city claims some famous music exports, too. Besides Nelly, the St. Louis area produced such luminaries as Chuck Berry and Miles Davis. Their brass stars are embedded in the sidewalk on Delmar Boulevard with other cultural contributors, collectively making up the St. Louis Walk of Fame.

Then there's the city's architectural facets. Head over to Lindell Boulevard and prepare to be impressed by the turn-of-the-20th-century brick and stone mansions and the Cathedral Basilica of Saint Louis, a massive Romanesque building. At the foot of Ashley Street along the downtown riverfront is the Ashley Street Power House, a squat building standing in stark contrast to its most prominent neighbor, Lumière Place. This glitzy casino/hotel complex is the latest salvo in an ongoing effort to re-establish downtown as a place to live and play.

But perhaps the most well-known symbol of the city is the 630-foot-tall Gateway Arch, which is the symbolic starting point for the arduous trek across the American West undertaken by countless 19th-century pioneers. Taking the tram to the observation room at the top for views of the city is a necessary sightseeing pilgrimage.

Must Do: AAA Editor's Picks

- Stroll through **Soulard Farmers Market** (730 Carroll St.) and participate in a tradition with origins dating back to 1838. This is reputedly the oldest farmers market west of the Mississippi River, and with that little historical tidbit, you'll treasure your purchases even more. If you're there in February, you have several fabulous events to choose from, including the **Soulard Mardi Gras** and the 🎷 **Cruzan Rum Taste of Soulard.**

- Ride the tram to the top of 🎷 **The Gateway Arch** (at Memorial Drive and Market Street) for an extraordinary view of St. Louis and the Mississippi River.

- Spend some time inside the Catholic 🎷 **Cathedral Basilica of Saint Louis** (4431 Lindell Blvd.). You'll discover impressive religious imagery created with more than 41 million individual pieces of glass, marble and stone.

- Visit the 🎷 **Missouri History Museum** (5700 Lindell Blvd.), 🎷 **Saint Louis Art Museum** (One Fine Arts Dr.), 🎷 **Saint Louis Science Center** (5050 Oakland Ave.) or 🎷 **Saint Louis Zoo** (1 Government Dr.). These AAA GEM attractions are all in 🎷 **Forest Park** (5595 Grand Dr.), which is nestled in the center of the city. The 1904 World's Fair—immortalized in the 1944 film "Meet Me in St. Louis"—was held on the park grounds.

- Go to 🎷 **City Museum** (750 N. 16th St.) without any preconceived ideas, except to be wowed. Some of the exhibits are even on the roof. Just be sure to allot plenty of time for this crazy, one-of-a-kind adventure since you'll have to find your way around the mazelike structure, built by artisans using recycled and found materials, without a map.

- Explore **Laclede's Landing** (710 N. 2nd St.) to get a feel for old St. Louis. This nine-block historic district, complete with cobblestone streets, marks St. Louis founder Pierre Laclede's original settlement. You'll marvel at the wonderfully preserved mid-19th- to early 20th-century warehouses that now feature bars, nightclubs, restaurants and offices.

- Canvass **The Hill,** the city's Little Italy. The district is bounded by Manchester, Columbia and Hampton avenues and South Kingshighway Boulevard. Pick up some imported products to take home with you as you peruse the meat markets, bakeries and specialty markets. Be sure to schedule your visit around a meal; there are a variety of Italian restaurants worth patronizing.

- Tour the **Anheuser-Busch Brewery** (at 12th and Lynch streets) and see the famous Clydesdales. The company's origins date to the mid-19th century, so this is definitely a St. Louis institution.

- Check out the **St. Louis Walk of Fame** along Delmar Boulevard, in the Delmar Loop neighborhood. It's entertaining as well as educational, with brass stars and biographical bronze plaques embedded in the pavement paying tribute to St. Louis area notables both past and present.

- Join in some local team spirit at the **Cardinals Hall of Fame and Museum** (601 Clark St.) at the **Ballpark Village** near **Busch Stadium** (700 Clark Ave.). If you're there during the season, be sure to catch a game and see the team. Even if you don't love baseball, the village is a huge entertainment complex with food, drinks and fun.

- Relive the city's celebrated musical past with a trip to the **Scott Joplin House State Historic Site** (2658 Delmar Blvd.). The ragtime composer and his wife, Belle, had a second-floor flat in this beautiful brick structure, which is simply furnished to reflect their early years. A player piano belts out tunes from the ragtime era.

- Attend a performance by one of America's oldest symphony orchestras, the **St. Louis Symphony**. Powell Hall (718 N. Grand Blvd.), the former 1925 St. Louis Theatre, has been the symphony's home since 1968.

The Gateway Arch

St. Louis 1-day Itinerary

AAA editors suggest these activities for a great short vacation experience. Those staying in the area for a longer visit can access a 3-day itinerary at AAA.com/TravelGuides.

Morning

- Start off with an early visit to **Soulard Farmers Market** (730 Carroll St.), especially if it's a Saturday, the busiest day of the week and when most vendors are open. A trip to this historic site is as much for the atmosphere as it is for the shopping. In addition to produce, meat, dairy and bakery stalls, there are vendors selling flowers, soaps and a variety of gift items.

- Then it's off to see what ▽ **The Gateway Arch** (at Memorial Drive and Market Street) looks like up close. The arch, the nation's tallest monument, is on the grounds of the **Gateway Arch National Park** (on the riverfront at Market Street). Try to arrive soon after it opens. You'll receive a timed ticket for your ride to the top. While you're waiting for your turn, peruse the **Museum of Westward Expansion**, where exhibits and artifacts showcase Western history, including pioneer tales, Native American life and Lewis and Clark's trailblazing adventures. In order to get to the top, you'll have to take a 4-minute ride in a small five-seat pod. This will likely be an uncomfortable ride if you don't like tight quarters, but the viewing area at the top offers great sights if you're up for it.

Afternoon

- A plate of toasted ravioli—known locally as t-ravs and served with a side of marinara sauce—is a St. Louis culinary tradition. These breaded morsels show up on many local restaurants' menus, and a great place to try them is at **Charlie Gitto's Downtown** (207 N. 6th St.).

- After lunch, make a quick stop at the ▽ **Cathedral Basilica of Saint Louis** (4431 Lindell Blvd.). You've never seen mosaics like the ones that adorn the inside of this structure. More than 41 million individual pieces of glass, marble and stone have been meticulously arranged to create beautiful religious imagery as well as local historical scenes.

- Then head over to ▽ **Forest Park** (5595 Grand Dr.) and venture into the remarkable galleries at the ▽ **Saint Louis Art Museum** (One Fine Arts Dr.). Nearly every culture and time period is represented, including pieces of African, American, Asian, European, Islamic, Native American, Oceanic and Pre-Columbian art as well as art from ancient cultures like Egypt and Greece. The collection includes such well-known names as Albert Bierstadt, John Singleton Copley, Edgar Degas, Claude Monet, Georgia O'Keeffe, Pablo Picasso and Vincent van Gogh.

- An alternative, especially if you've got kids in tow, is to spend the afternoon at ▽ **City Museum** (750 N. 16th St.). But don't

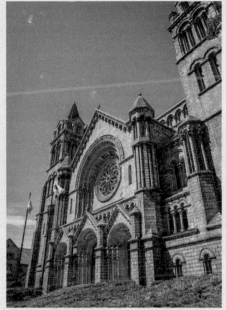
Cathedral Basilica of St. Louis

worry; this place is also fun for adults. It's definitely not your average children's museum—everything in the former International Shoe Co.'s building has been salvaged from around St. Louis. Things like bridges, chimneys, construction cranes, metal washers, tile and assembly line parts have been put to new structural use, and in many cases are works of art in themselves.

Evening

- If your wallet can accommodate a pricey meal and your suitcase contains something fairly dressy, make reservations for dinner at **Tony's** (410 Market St.). Many locals consider this sophisticated Italian restaurant one of the city's best.

- Whether you gamble or not, **Lumière Place Casino & Hotels** (999 N. 2nd St.) is a popular nightspot. It's a trendy spot to sip a cocktail while listening to live music. If you do hit the gaming floor, keep in mind that smoking is permitted; you'll definitely notice it.

- An alternative evening plan if you'll be in town between mid-June and mid-August is to attend a show at the Muny (1 Theatre Dr.), an outdoor amphitheater in Forest Park. Roughly 1,450 free seats at the top of the house are reserved for each performance, so if you're willing to wait in line (first-come, first-served) you might be able to get in for an unbeatable price. Afterward, have a late supper in the nearby Central West End district (just northeast of Forest Park). **Dressel's Public House** (419 N. Euclid Ave.), a popular destination for theatergoers, has walls adorned with pictures of authors and musicians.

Top Picks for Kids

Under 13

- **Myseum** (283 Lamp and Lantern Village) combines scientific learning and fun with exhibits such as the Dual Super Radar Slide, Magnetic Wall Ball and Vertical Wind Tubes. Kids can create faces with forensics software or pretend to be paleontologists in the Dino Dig exhibit. There's a place for fine arts, too: where kids learn about sound and music through some unconventional materials.

- The **Saint Louis Zoo** (1 Government Dr.) is home to more than 600 species of animals. Immerse yourself in the Rivers Edge exhibit to see hippos and black rhinos. Grizzlies and gorillas inhabit The Wild Zone, while lions and tigers prowl in Big Cat Country. See meerkats, tree kangaroos and insects in the Discovery Zone. Pet lovers can enjoy wagon rides and cuddle baby bunnies, chicks and piglets at **Purina Farms** (500 William Danforth Way in Gray Summit). Meet horses, cows, chickens and sheep and swing on a rope in the Animal Barn & Hayloft Play Area and watch rescued dogs demonstrate their athletic skills in the Incredible Dog Arena.

- Sip a frosty mug of root beer and savor American fare while watching sodas being bottled on a restored 1940s bottling line at **Fitz's** (6605 Delmar Blvd.). Try one of the seasonal flavors or specially labeled bottles if you're there in the fall (Pumpkin Pop), the summer (Happy 4th of July) or St. Patrick's Day.

Saint Louis Zoo

- **The Magic House, St. Louis Children's Museum** (516 S. Kirkwood Rd.) features hundreds of hands-on exhibits and fun things to do. Catch fish or fix a car in the Children's Village, become a detective or try out the Oval Office. Wee ones can ride a toddler-size boat or climb in the Peekaboo House in a special space for infants, toddlers and their grown-ups.

Teens

- Board an egg-shaped pod for a ride to the top of **The Gateway Arch** (at Memorial Drive and Market Street). The views stretch up to 30 miles away on clear days, taking in downtown St. Louis, Busch Stadium to the east and the Mississippi River to the west.

- "Bake" your own custom-designed shirt, shorts or other wearables in minutes at **Baked T's** (6368 Delmar Blvd.). The bakery-themed shop will package your finished design to look like cookies, doughnuts or cupcakes.

- The **Endangered Wolf Center** (6750 Tyson Valley Rd. in Eureka) offers the opportunity to learn about and interact with several species of wolves through tours, programs and events. Work alongside the animal trainers who care for wolves, swift foxes and African painted dogs, or practice your photography on a special tour of the wooded enclosures.

All Ages

- Baseball fans can tour **Busch Stadium** (700 Clark Ave.) any time of year for a close-up look at the home of the Cardinals. View the field from the radio broadcast booth or the Cardinals dugout, and see the World Series trophies in the Champions Club. After the tour, visit **Ted Drewes Custard** (4224 S. Grand Blvd. and 6726 Chippewa St.). Locals have lined up for Ted's rich and creamy frozen treats here since 1930.

- Kids from 8 to 80 can slide, crawl and climb through **City Museum** (750 N. 16th St.), an eclectic mixture of playground, fun house and architectural marvel constructed entirely from recycled and found materials.

- Join the 150,000 spectators who turn out every September to see 70 world-class balloon pilots take to the sky in the **Great Forest Park Balloon Race.** Festivities begin Friday with the Balloon Glow at Central Field in **Forest Park** (5595 Grand Dr.), followed by fireworks. Children's activities and live entertainment lead up to the impressive race launch on Saturday.

- With more than 100 rides, shows and attractions, **Six Flags St. Louis** (4900 Six Flags Rd. in Eureka) is packed with fun things to do for the entire family. Match wits against Lex Luthor in the 4-D Justice League: Battle for Metropolis or experience gut-wrenching 50-mph drops on American Thunder. Find fun for little ones in Bugs Bunny National Park, cool off in Hurricane Harbor or see a show.

Arriving
By Car

As befits the Gateway to the West, a network of major interstate highways flows into St. Louis, bringing goods and people from all points of the compass. From the east come I-55, I-64, I-70 and US 40; all these highways converge at the Poplar Street Bridge to pour into the downtown area and through the western suburbs as I-64/US 40 (the Daniel Boone Expressway).

I-55 approaches from the south and I-44 from the southwest; I-70 enters from the northwest to combine in the downtown area with I-55. A bypass route is formed by I-270, with connections to I-70, I-64, I-55, I-44 and I-170. I-270 becomes I-255 southeast of the city before connecting with I-64 and I-70 to the east in Illinois.

Getting Around
Street System

Streets in downtown St. Louis follow a basic grid pattern complicated by a system of one-way streets. Numbered streets run parallel to the Mississippi River; numbers begin at the river and run westward. The north-south dividing line is Market Street.

After a complete stop, a right turn on red is permitted unless otherwise posted. Driving during rush hours, generally from 7 to 9 a.m. and 4 to 6 p.m., should be avoided.

Parking

On-street parking is controlled by meter, but your chance of finding a space where and when you want one is slight. Many commercial lots and garages are in the downtown business core and around Memorial Plaza; several multilevel garages are in the vicinity of Busch Stadium as well. Rates average $2 per hour for the first 5 hours, $4 for 6 to 13 hours, and $8 for 14 to 24 hours. For stadium events, day or night, the charge is $5-$20.

Rates for parking near the Gateway Arch are $1-$2 for the first 20 minutes, then $1 per 20-30 minutes after that; $16-$20 maximum per day. Additional parking, which costs from $3 to $5 per day, can be found at private lots on the landing.

Shopping

Our No. 1 tip for a rewarding St. Louis shopping experience: zero in on the neighborhoods. This is a spread-out city of many separate communities, each with its own distinct character. Here's a quick rundown that can help you plan your shopping strategy.

The **Central West End,** just north and east of Forest Park, was created in the flush of expansion and prosperity that followed the 1904 World's Fair. Today it's one of the city's most pleasant shopping destinations, a neighborhood of stately turn-of-the-20th-century homes, ornate lampposts, streets lined with giant oaks and lots of sidewalk cafés for people-watching when the weather's nice.

Euclid Avenue is thick with specialty shops, pubs and restaurants. Peruse the selection at cozy **Left**

Vintage Vinyl

Bank Books (399 N. Euclid Ave.), then wander through the once-abandoned auto repair warehouse now occupied by **Bowood Farms** (4605 Olive St.), a combination garden center, greenhouse and café that's a lush respite from the concrete jungle.

Another trendy district is the **Delmar Loop.** The six or so blocks of Delmar Boulevard between Kingsland and Des Peres avenues form the heart of The Loop. It's a shopping, dining and nightlife destination with a lively street life courtesy of neighboring Washington University. The district's name comes from the streetcar turnaround, or loop, that runs through the area. The vintage electric trolley's 2.2-mile fixed-track links the Delmar Loop to Forest Park with 10 stops along the way. From University City Hall, the trolley travels along Delmar Boulevard turning at DeBaliviere Avenue to the Missouri History Museum. Trolley cars run daily every 20 minutes. A 2-hour pass is $2; $1 (ages 65+ and the physically impaired); free (ages 0-5 with adult supervision). An all-day pass is $5; $2.50 (ages 65+ and the physically impaired); free (ages 0-5 with adult supervision).

Eclectic is the keyword here. **Vintage Vinyl** (6610 Delmar Blvd.) has a discriminating collection of CDs, DVDs, LPs, T-shirts and posters. Next door is **Sunshine Daydream,** an all-purpose head shop (incense, candles, more T-shirts). Browse art galleries like the **Compônere Gallery** (6509 Delmar Blvd.) and the **Craft Alliance Center of Art + Design** (6640 Delmar Blvd.). For handcrafted jewelry, locally made art and Mexican Day of the Dead dolls, check out **Phoenix Rising** (6331 Delmar Blvd.).

The Hill, south of Manchester Avenue between Hampton Avenue and S. Kingshighway Boulevard, is an old, established residential neighborhood with a gaggle of great Italian restaurants and specialty food markets. The shelves at **J. Viviano & Sons** (5139 Shaw Ave.) are loaded with jars of black olive paste, cans of anchovy-stuffed olives, bags of lupine beans, almond confetti candy and blocks of Parmigiano-Reggiano ("the crown jewel of cheeses"). **Girasole Gifts & Imports** (2103 Marconi Ave.) sells ceramics, jewelry, handbags and gift items; a miniature replica of the Italian Immigrants statue (which stands across the street in front of St. Ambrose Catholic Church) is an appropriate Hill souvenir.

South Grand is one of the city's more ethnically diverse neighborhoods, and that's reflected in the shops and restaurants that line the eight-block stretch of S. Grand Boulevard between Crittenden Street and McDonald Avenue. **Bali Cargo Company,** (3203 S. Grand Blvd.) has genuine Balinese goods, including furniture, art and jewelry. Shop for Indian spices, Japanese eggplants and green tea ice cream at **Jay International Food Co.** (3172 S. Grand Blvd.) or contemplate a tattoo or piercing from one of the friendly folks at **TRX** (3207 S. Grand Blvd.).

South of downtown is **Cherokee Antique Row,** centered along Cherokee Street between Nebraska Avenue and DeMenil Place. In addition to antique stores and art galleries this city neighborhood has some interesting specialty shops. One of the best is **Retro 101/Cherry Bomb Vintage** (2303 Cherokee St.), a treasure trove of vintage stuff (think "mod" '60s furniture, funky costume jewelry, vintage clothing and kitschy bar accessories). There's more

Union Station

nostalgic browsing at **Bella** (1934 Cherokee St.), two buildings loaded with an eclectic range of antiques, collectibles, arts, crafts and housewares.

You can't miss **Union Station,** the hulking, red-roofed, turreted former train terminal that stands downtown on Market Street (between 18th and 20th streets). Stop by the [SAVE] **Hard Rock Cafe** for a look at memorabilia like a custom-built Peavey bass played by former Van Halen member Michael Anthony, then scope out their line of T-shirts, pins and gifts.

The city has a couple of worthy destination malls. Upscale **Plaza Frontenac,** just south of I-64/40 at the intersection of Clayton Road and Lindbergh Boulevard, caters to well-to-do St. Louisans with the only Saks Fifth Avenue and Neiman Marcus stores in town, along with trendy retailers like Tiffany & Co. and Louis Vuitton. The atmosphere here is elegant throughout; even the seating areas and restrooms are smartly stylish.

West County Center, at I-270 and Manchester Road in Des Peres, is a major mall anchored by JCPenney, Macy's and Nordstrom. Among the more than 150 other retailers are familiar names like Ann Taylor, Brooks Brothers and The North Face. Anchors at the **Saint Louis Galleria,** I-64 and S. Brentwood Boulevard, are Dillard's, Macy's and Nordstrom, plus some 165 additional stores and boutiques.

Westport Plaza, in a mixed-use office complex just off I-270 and Page Avenue in the western burbs, is more a place to relax after shopping since it has pick-me-ups like Starbucks and the St. Louis Bread Co., a variety of casual and higher-end restaurants, happy hour hangouts and pubs with live music.

Bargain hunters head for **St. Louis Outlet Mall,** SR 370 (exit 11) and St. Louis Mills Boulevard. With more than 100 outlets—everything from Old Navy and The Children's Place to Burlington and Bed, Bath and Beyond—there's something for everyone. Refuel with a Wetzel's pretzel.

Missouri farmers supply St. Louis farmers markets, and one of the best reasons to visit is for the cornucopia of locally grown fruits and veggies. The markets are also good places to pick up locally produced cheese, eggs, honey and baked goods. Shoppers in the know arrive early to snap up seasonal goodies like berries and heirloom tomatoes. And of course it's fun to just wander around soaking up the sights and smells.

The granddaddy of them all is the **Soulard Farmers Market** (south of downtown at the corner of 7th and Carroll streets), which has been in business in one form or another since 1779. If you're a first timer go on Saturday morning, when this big, bustling market is at its busiest and best. Shaped like a giant "H," it has stall after stall of produce—fat melons, baskets of grapes, just-picked zucchini—as well as butchers, bakers and vendors selling everything from balsamic black bean dip to aromatic soaps. It's open Wed.-Thurs. 8-5, Fri. 7-5, Sat.

7-5:30, year-round. Hint: Street parking is not plentiful and also metered, and regulations are strictly enforced; park in the free lot across 7th Street from the market.

Much smaller but equally appealing is the **Kirkwood Farmers Market** in downtown Kirkwood (150 E. Argonne Dr. at Taylor Avenue). Fresh, locally grown produce varies by season; in summer look for ripe peaches grown in Missouri's "boot heel," and ask about the recipe for turning them into a scrumptious peach pie. The Tropical Moose ("Tro Mo" to its loyal customers) snow cone stand sells the icy treats in more than 50 different flavors. The market is open from mid-April to late September (Mon.-Fri. 9-8, Sat. 8-5, Sun. varies by vendor), but Saturday mornings offer the best selection. In October it morphs into a pumpkin patch, stays open longer hours (daily 9-8) and has lots of activities for kids. From mid-November to December 24, the Christmas Market is open daily 9-9.

And if your sweet tooth demands satisfaction, do as many longtime residents do and head for **Lubeley's Bakery & Deli** (7815 Watson Rd. in South St. Louis). Family-owned Lubeley's has been in business for more than 75 years, turning out St. Louis specialties like the super-sweet gooey butter cake, German treats like stollen and custom-made, multi-tiered wedding cakes. A fresh-out-of-the-oven caramel pecan roll and coffee to go is as good a way as any to start your day.

Smaller-scale shopping with a healthy dollop of historic charm prevails in nearby St. Charles. If you're into antiques, crafts, gifts and collectibles, put **St. Charles' Main Street** at the top of your day-trip list. See place listing p. 243.

Lubeley's Bakery & Deli

Nightlife

Begin an evening on the town with drinks at the **Rooftop Terrace Bar,** eight stories above Delmar Boulevard at the top of the luxury boutique Moonrise Hotel (6177 Delmar Blvd. in The Loop). A hip crowd lounges on fancy white couches or mingles at the patio under what is reputedly the world's largest rotating man-made moon, snacking on marinated olives while nursing a glass of wine or a classic cocktail. A bonus is the view of the downtown skyline and the Arch in the distance, a nice backdrop for a sunset or later when the lights of the Delmar Loop twinkle below. Phone (314) 721-1111.

Another place to kick off an evening is **Cielo**, a restaurant and bar on the eighth floor of the Four Seasons Hotel St. Louis (999 N. 2nd St., adjacent to **Lumière Place Casino & Hotels**). The setting is swank—elegant flower arrangements, a roaring fire on freezing winter days, and an outdoor patio with canopy beds and a great view of the Arch that's perfect for people-watching on warm summer evenings. The atmosphere helps take the sting out of pricey drinks like the vodka pear mojito.

The casino offers plenty of flash for a night out. In addition to the usual table games and a poker room, some 2,000 slots feature the latest in video technology. Nonsmokers take note: The smell of smoke

hangs pretty heavily in the air. You also can hit Lumière Place for dinner. Enjoy an upscale meal at The Wok, scarf down a plate full at The Kitchen Buffet & Bistro or sip a beer and catch a game at Ozzie's Sports Bar & Grill. Phone (314) 881-7777 for the casino.

The vibe is similar at the **Hollywood Casino St. Louis** (777 Casino Center Dr. in Maryland Heights). There's a poker room with more than 20 tables, 31 Black Jack tables, six roulette tables, five craps tables and 2,100 slots, and there are nonsmoking areas. The casino's Boogie Nights club has dancing Friday and Saturday nights. Among the dining options here is Charlie Gitto's, a branch of the celebrated Italian restaurant. Phone (314) 770-8100 for the casino.

Laclede's Landing (710 N. 2nd St. on the banks of the Mississippi) is an area of eateries, bars and entertainment venues occupying former warehouse buildings.

For live music, **The Loop** is tops. Rock, pop and blues bands jam it up several nights a week at the **Duck Room**, inside the Blueberry Hill diner (6504 Delmar Blvd.). For schedule information phone (314) 727-4444. Pop, rock, acoustic and metal bands and comedians, including some big names, perform at **The Pageant** (6161 Delmar Blvd.). Patrons can chill out at the venue's Halo Bar before and/or after the main show. The Halo Bar also has live performances and DJ sets most nights, and there's no cover. For concert info phone (314) 726-6161.

Local scenesters congregate at **Pin-up Bowl** (6191 Delmar Blvd.), a lounge where the bartenders whip up killer martinis and specialty cocktails in outlandish colors. The kitschy décor includes display cases full of vintage bowling and pin-up paraphernalia. There are eight lanes here as well, but if you're serious about the game this is not the place to work on your delivery. Phone (314) 727-5555.

In the Grand Center arts district, **Jazz at the Bistro** (3536 Washington Ave.) is an intimate jazz club where you can have dinner and catch local talent as well as name acts. Reservations for music performances are recommended; for tickets phone the box office at (314) 571-6000.

Two downtown watering holes are especially popular for live music. **BB's Jazz, Blues and Soups** (700 S. Broadway) brings top jazz and blues musicians to town. Memorabilia adorns the walls of this old brick building. Within spitting distance of BB's is **The Beale on Broadway** (701 S. Broadway). Down-home blues is the music of choice here, with dashes of R&B, old-school soul and roots rock. Phone (314) 436-5222 for BB's or (314) 621-7880 for The Beale on Broadway.

Off Broadway (3509 Lemp Ave. in the Cherokee-Lemp Historic District) is basically a dive bar, but it's also one of the best spots in the city for live music. Acts run to folk, alt country, blues and rock, plus the occasional tribute show (Jerry Garcia, Gram Parsons and the like). This is also a good place to catch up-and-coming local bands. Another plus: The smoking area is outside. **The Focal Point** (2720 Sutton Blvd. in the suburb of Maplewood) provides a casual showcase for folk and acoustic performers, local singer-songwriters and bluegrass musicians.

Soulard Mardi Gras

The eclectic offerings extend to poetry slams and folk dancing. Phone (314) 328-4810.

The **Moolah Theatre & Lounge** (3821 Lindell Blvd. near the St. Louis University campus) is housed in a renovated, Moorish-style brick building that was once the Moolah Temple, a meeting place for the Shriners. The screen is huge, and the theater has a beautiful ceiling dome. A full bar and a retro eight-lane bowling alley downstairs encourage hanging out afterward, but arrive early to snag one of the comfy leather sofas that make up the front rows. Phone (314) 446-6868.

Is there a better way to spend a summer evening in St. Louis than attending a Cardinals game at **Busch Stadium**? A stone's throw from the Arch, the ballpark is invariably packed with die-hard Cards fans cheering on their team. So grab a dog and a couple of bags of peanuts and take a seat under the stars. Evening home games usually start at 6:15. Single game tickets can be purchased at the 8th Street ticket windows, located just north of Gate 3, Mon.-Fri. from 9 a.m. until 2 hours after game time; to charge by phone call (314) 345-9000.

Note: RFT (Riverfront Times), a free newsweekly available all over town, has arts and entertainment listings.

Big Events

From early January to mid-February, **Soulard Mardi Gras** shakes St. Louis out of its winter doldrums with colorful parades, a wiener dog derby, a Creole food fair and more. Soulard neighborhood restaurants and bars participate in the ▽ **Cruzan Rum Taste of Soulard,** another popular February event where you can sample signature culinary creations, many of the Cajun and Creole variety.

St. Louis warms up to spring with the **St. Louis Storytelling Festival** in early May, when both professionals and amateurs celebrate the art of tale spinning. Presentations of The Bard's plays are given during the **Shakespeare Festival St. Louis,** held at **Forest Park** from early May to late June. These free outdoor performances include dance, music and a plot synopsis.

May also celebrates another art form at the **Art Fair at Laumeier.** On Mother's Day weekend nearly 150 artists travel to **Laumeier Sculpture Park** to sell their works among the park's outdoor sculptures. You'll see a range of media, including clay, paper, wood, jewelry, glass and photography. Musical performances and art demonstrations enhance the festive atmosphere.

Fourth of July festivities send sparks flying during **Fair Saint Louis in Forest Park,** held over the July 4 weekend. The celebration attracts huge crowds of revelers with big-name entertainment, an air show, a parade and fireworks.

Festival of Nations at **Tower Grove Park** is an August favorite. For 2 days St. Louisans honor and celebrate the city's ethnic diversity as the park becomes a showcase for traditional music and dance performances, fashion, craft displays and cuisine representing dozens of ethnic cultures.

Several events close out the summer, beginning in late August or early September with the 3-day **Japanese Festival,** held at the **Missouri Botanical Garden.** This time of year also brings the 2-day **Big Muddy Blues Festival** at **Laclede's Landing.** The Mississippi river provides a backdrop for performances by blues bands and other artists. In the suburb of Clayton, the **Saint Louis Art Fair** attracts artsy types for 3 days of art and entertainment. The **Great Forest Park Balloon Race** takes place in mid-September.

Soulard Oktoberfest, held in mid-October, is a celebration of German heritage that includes hearty fare like bratwurst, schweinshaxe and strudel, live music on four stages, dancing and a beer tent. There are also crowd-pleasing contests for bratwurst eating, stein holding and the strongest barmaid.

The Christmas holiday season kicks off in late November with **Winter Wonderland** in **Tilles Park,** which features thousands of twinkling lights.

Sports & Rec

Major League Baseball's **St. Louis Cardinals** were founded in 1882 as an American Association team called the St. Louis Brown Stockings. The team has had an enviable record in recent years, winning multiple National League pennants since 2004 and the World Series in 2006 and 2011. The 2014 team also advanced to the National League Championship Series as Central Division champions.

Both World Series clinchers were played at home in **Busch Stadium** *(see attraction listing p. 260)* in front of more than 46,000 enthusiastic local fans. Other fun facts about this retro-style ballpark that opened in 2006: It hosted the 80th All-Star Game in 2009 and sells more than 540,000 hot dogs over the course of a season.

The design incorporates wide concourses, elevators and escalators between levels and excellent spectator sight lines, as well as dramatic views of downtown and the Gateway Arch. A statue of Cards slugger Stan "the Man" Musial stands at the arched 8th Street entrance. Before the game, kids can play interactive games, step up to the plate in batting cages and enjoy other family-friendly activities at the Family Pavilion. For general stadium information phone (314) 345-9600.

Across the street from Busch Stadium, the first phase of **Ballpark Village** opened in spring 2014. The retail and entertainment complex features shops, restaurants, live music stages and nightlife venues. The four-level Cardinals Nation Restaurant & Bar includes the **Cardinals Hall of Fame and Museum,** where true fans can immerse themselves in the team's history.

The Frontier League Western Division's **River City Rascals** play minor league baseball at

Gateway Motorsports Park

CarShield Field in O'Fallon, about 35 miles west of downtown St. Louis; phone (636) 240-2287.

The **St. Louis Blues** of the National **Hockey** League take to the ice October through April at the **Enterprise Center,** 14th and Clark streets; phone (314) 622-2500.

Gateway Motorsports Park in nearby Madison, Ill., offers marquee motorsports events, including NHRA National, Indy Car Championship, stock and sports car events; phone (618) 215-8888. **Fairmount Park** in nearby Collinsville, Ill., offers **Thoroughbred racing** April through September; phone (618) 345-4300.

Note: Policies concerning admittance of children to pari-mutuel betting facilities vary. Phone for information.

There are many **golf** courses throughout the area, including a public course at **Ruth Park,** 8211 Groby Rd., and three public courses at Forest Park.

Horseback riding is available at **A.P. Greensfelder Park,** north of I-44 on Allenton Road in nearby Pacific. The **Wayne C. Kennedy Recreation Complex,** on Wells Road, and Edgar M. Queeny Park, between Mason and Weidman roads, offer **ice-skating** and tennis. The complex also offers **swimming.** Ice skating is popular at the **Steinberg Skating Rink** in Forest Park.

The **St. Louis Riverfront Trail,** originating at Laclede's Landing, is an 11-mile **bike** path running along the Mississippi River. Bike trails also wind through Forest Park. Rentals and guided park bike tours are provided by City Cycling Tours; for information phone (314) 616-5724.

Bird-watching opportunities are plentiful during spring and fall at **Confluence Point State Park** in West Alton; a short interpretive trail leads to the point where the Missouri and Mississippi rivers merge.

Performing Arts

The **St. Louis Symphony,** founded in 1880 and one of the oldest symphony orchestras in the nation, performs from mid-September to mid-May in **Powell Hall,** 718 N. Grand Blvd. This stately building has an elegant foyer resembling the royal chapel at Versailles. Free tours are available by appointment in-season; phone (314) 286-4104. The symphony also presents a series of concerts geared to ages 5 through 12; phone (314) 534-1700 for ticket and schedule information.

Acoustically renowned **Sheldon Concert Hall,** 3648 Washington Blvd., presents a variety of concerts; phone (314) 533-9900.

There's no better place to see a musical under the stars on a warm summer evening than **The Muny,** the city's beloved outdoor theater in Forest Park. The Muny's first performances—of William Shakespeare's "As You Like It"—were given in June 1916 on a grassy hillside between two large oaks. Today this 11,000-seat outdoor amphitheater offers a 7-week summer season of Broadway classics, musical adaptations of hit movies and other entertainment. Stroll the Walk of Fame dedicated to venerable Broadway stars and composers. Free seats at the top of the house are available on a first-come, first-served basis beginning at 7 p.m. For show and ticket information phone The Muny box office at (314) 361-1900, ext. 550, or MetroTix, (314) 534-1111.

Opera Theatre of St. Louis

Traveling Broadway shows, concerts and head-lining entertainers are presented at the **Fabulous Fox Theatre,** 527 N. Grand Blvd. Public tours of the ornate interior are offered Tuesday, Thursday and Saturday at 10:30 a.m.; phone (314) 534-1678 for additional information. For ticket information phone MetroTix at (314) 534-1111.

The **Tivoli Theatre** (6350 Delmar Blvd.) dates from the era of grand old movie palaces and includes independent and foreign-language movies as well as the latest Hollywood offerings on its three screens; display cases are filled with movie memorabilia, vintage posters line the walls and yes, there's an orchestra pit and a plush burgundy curtain.

During its heyday, everyone from Rex Harrison to Twisted Sister appeared at the grand old Kiel Opera House, downtown at 14th and Market streets. Two decades after closing in 1991—and following a thorough renovation and refurbishment—this Art Deco landmark reopened in 2011 with a new face and a new name: the **Peabody Opera House.** The venue hosts theatrical performances, pop music and comedy stars, and sports and special events. For event information phone (314) 622-5435.

The Hollywood Casino Amphitheater, on Riverport Drive in Maryland Heights, is a 20,000-seat venue where concerts are scheduled April through September; phone (314) 298-9944.

The **Repertory Theatre of St. Louis** ("The Rep") is the city's leading professional theater company; phone (314) 968-4925. They give performances in the **Loretto-Hilton Center for the Performing Arts,** 130 Edgar Rd. on the Webster University campus, which also is the home of the university's **Conservatory of Theatre Arts,** (314) 968-7128, and the **Opera Theatre of St. Louis,** (314) 961-0644. The Opera Theatre's pre-opera informal picnic dinners on the scenic grounds are especially popular; guests may bring their own picnic baskets or purchase a boxed supper.

Dance St. Louis, (314) 534-5000, regularly gives performances September through April at the Fabulous Fox Theatre, the Grandel Theatre and the Touhill Performing Arts Center. Dance, music and drama are presented at the **Edison Theatre** on the campus of Washington University; phone (314) 935-6543. **Stages St. Louis** offers musical theater productions June through October at the **Robert G. Reim Theatre,** at the Kirkwood Community Center; phone (314) 821-2407.

The **Touhill Performing Arts Center,** on the campus of the University of Missouri-St. Louis, offers concerts, opera, comedy and dance year-round; phone (314) 516-4949 or (866) 516-4949. **Chaifetz Arena,** on the campus of St. Louis University, is a multipurpose arena featuring concerts, family shows and sporting events; phone (314) 977-5000.

The St. Louis **Black Repertory Company** offers theater and dance presentations December through April in the Emerson Performance Center at Harris-Stowe State University and the Edison Theatre at Washington University; phone (314) 534-3810.

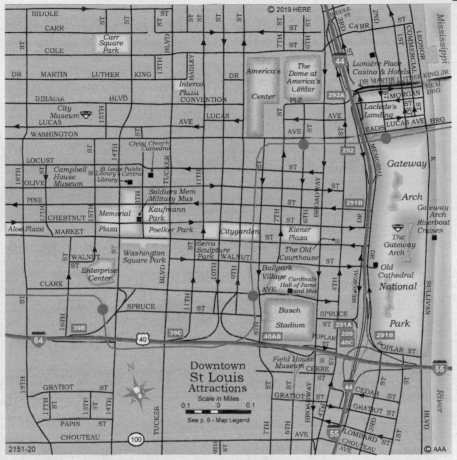

America's Center

The Dome at America's Center

Downtown St Louis Attractions
Scale in Miles
0.1   0   0.1
See p. 6 - Map Legend

At the Ivory Theater, **St. Louis Shakespeare** features classic works by the bard August through October, plus a spring production; phone (314) 361-5664. During the month of June, **Circus Flora** captivates audiences during its one-ring circus performances with a theatrical flair in a red big top tent; for information phone (314) 289-4040.

ATTRACTIONS

For a complete list of attractions, visit AAA.com/travelguides/attractions

BALLPARK VILLAGE is at exit 40B from I-64 onto 6th St. Exit left at 39C toward 11th St./Stadium. The first phase of this dining, shopping and entertainment district adjacent to Busch Stadium opened in 2014. It includes the 34,000-square-foot, four-story restaurant and bar called Cardinals Nation, the Cardinals Hall of Fame and Museum, a retail store and the 330-seat Cardinals Nation AT&T Rooftop seating deck.

Nightlife and restaurant options include Howl at the Moon, Drunken Fish, PBR St. Louis, The Lounge, Fox Sports Midwest Live!, Budweiser Brew House and The Barn at PBR. Concerts, events and summer yoga sessions also take place; check the website for schedule details. **Hours:** Hours vary by venue. **Parking:** $5-$40 on game days. Free on non-game days for 3 hours from 6 a.m.-9 p.m. (with validation from village businesses); $5 after 9 p.m. **Phone:** (314) 345-9481. 🍽

Cardinals Hall of Fame and Museum is in Ballpark Village; take exit 40B off I-64 onto 6th St., then exit left at 39C toward 11th St./Stadium. Cardinals fans can hold a game bat used by one of the team's famous players, and can trace the history of the club through the seven display galleries. The championship gallery in the center houses the trophies, rings and jerseys from the team's World Series victories. **Time:** Allow 1 hour minimum. **Hours:** Daily 10-6, or through the end of the 7th inning during evening home games. **Cost:** $12; $10 (60+ and military with ID); $8 (ages 4-15). Free admission with AT&T Rooftop Ticket. **Phone:** (314) 345-9880. 🍽

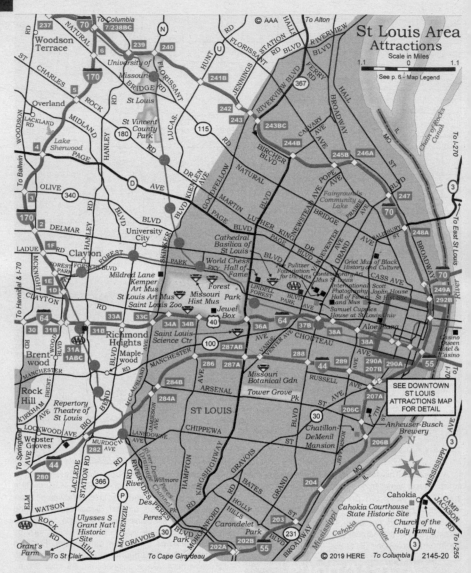

St Louis Area Attractions

BUSCH STADIUM is at 700 Clark Ave.; the Tour Ticket window is at Gate 3 on 8th St. The St. Louis Cardinals' home ballpark accommodates nearly 44,000 fans and offers views of the downtown skyline. Outside the park are historical plaques as well as statues depicting baseball legends like Stan Musial, Enos Slaughter and Rogers Hornsby. Highlights of the guided stadium tour, which lasts approximately 1 hour, include the broadcast booth and the Cardinals dugout.

Hours: Tours are given daily at 9:30, 11, 12:30 and 2, Apr.-Sept. (no tour at 2 when there is a home game starting at 6:15 p.m.); at 11 and 12:30, rest of year. Closed Jan. 1, Thanksgiving, Christmas Eve,

Christmas, Dec. 31, on game days and during special events. Phone ahead to confirm schedule. **Cost:** Tour Apr.-Oct. $18; $16 (ages 60+ and active duty military with ID); $14 (ages 4-15). Tour rest of year $15; $13 (ages 60+ and active duty military with ID); $11 (ages 4-15). **Phone:** (314) 345-9000. GT

CATHEDRAL BASILICA OF SAINT LOUIS is at 4431 Lindell Blvd. at jct. Newstead Ave. in the Central West End. Begun in 1907 and completed in 1914, this commanding Romanesque structure is a prominent St. Louis landmark with its ornately decorated exterior granite walls, massive twin towers and distinctive green-tiled dome.

Entering through the imposing oak doors is like stepping back in time. True to Byzantine tradition, the interior layout is a series of soaring domes and arches, with every square inch of the walls and columns adorned with intricate mosaics. Covering 83,000 square feet, they took more than 75 years to complete.

Millions of pieces of glass tessera depict biblical scenes from the Old and New Testaments, archdiocesan events and the life of King Louis IX of France, the cathedral's—and city's—namesake. Red and gold are the prevailing colors, executed in thousands of different shades. The baldachino over the main altar and the Italian-style mosaic work in the chapels and arcades on the church's west side were installed by different companies (more than 20 artists collaborated on the art), but everything blends into one breathtaking whole.

The museum on the lower level offers a detailed timeline of the installation process. Exhibits show the difference between Byzantine and Italian mosaic styles and explain how the stunning gold glass was created. Also on display are artifacts from Pope John Paul II's visit in 1997 and the cathedral's first pipe organ, built by the Kilgen Organ Co. in 1915. A mortuary chapel contains the crypts of former members of the city's archdiocese.

Hours: Cathedral open daily 7-5. Museum open Mon.-Sat. 10-4, Sun. noon-4. Guided tours are given Mon.-Fri. 10-3 and select Sat. and Sun. at 1. **Cost:** Cathedral by donation. Museum $2. **Phone:** (314) 373-8241, or (314) 373-8242 to schedule a tour. GT

CITYGARDEN occupies the two blocks between 8th and 10th sts. and Chestnut and Market sts. Its landscape design includes flowers, shrubs and small trees. Interspersed throughout the grounds are 24 sculpture installations, many of which are whimsical or abstract in form. Three fountains, including a spray plaza popular with children, add to the character; they operate Memorial Day-Labor Day.

Barbecue grills are not permitted in the park. **Time:** Allow 30 minutes minimum. **Hours:** Daily dawn-10 p.m. **Cost:** Free. **Phone:** (314) 241-3337 or (314) 289-5300.

CITY MUSEUM is at 750 N. 16th St. between Delmar and Washington aves. Here's a museum that truly will delight everyone from 8 to 80, not to mention those on either side of this age range. While the multitude of contraptions that invite climbing, crawling, sliding, stepping, jumping and rope climbing are geared toward kids, there are plenty of diversions for adults, too—whether it's watching their children or grandchildren have a blast or perusing exhibits about St. Louis' history and architectural heritage.

Perhaps the most fascinating thing about City Museum is that it is built entirely from recycled and found materials. Everywhere you look—the floor, the walls, columns—there are whimsical mosaics and decorated tiles. Stairways are painted bright colors.

CITYGARDEN

The museum's three mazelike floors resemble an urban phantasmagoria of tunnels, chutes and labyrinths of twisted metal.

Tables allow children to draw, paint, practice kirigami (Japanese paper cutting) or engage in interactive activities. The rooms with mounted butterflies, insects, stuffed owls and other natural history specimens are like stumbling into a taxidermist's workroom. A piano sits in another room, waiting to be played—and soon enough someone will.

Atop the Roof is a hybrid playground/jungle gym 11 stories above the street. Here are such incongruous sights as a school bus perched halfway over the edge (yes, you can go inside it), a climbing cage that looks like an airborne Slinky, a pond crisscrossed with stepping stones, a giant praying mantis and Big Eli, a working Ferris wheel. You also get a 360-degree view of downtown St. Louis.

Time: Allow 2 hours minimum. **Hours:** Mon.-Sat. 9-5 (also Fri.-Sat. 5-midnight), Sun. 11-5, Mar. 1-Labor Day; Wed.-Sat. 9-5 (also Fri.-Sat. 5-midnight), Sun. 11-5, rest of year. Atop the Roof is closed Nov.-May; phone ahead to confirm season opening and closing dates. Closed Easter, Thanksgiving and Christmas.

Cost: $16; free (ages 0-2). Atop the Roof (available only with City Museum admission) $5; free (ages 0-2). **Parking:** $10 (per vehicle). Additional pay lots and metered street parking available. **Phone:** (314) 231-2489.

CONTEMPORARY ART MUSEUM ST. LOUIS is at 3750 Washington Blvd. The museum features art exhibitions by leading contemporary artists as well as performances, lectures and special events. **Hours:** Wed.-Sun. 10-5 (also Thurs.-Fri. 5-8). **Cost:** Free. **Phone:** (314) 535-4660.

The Pulitzer Foundation for the Arts is at 3716 Washington Blvd. between Grand Blvd. and Spring Ave., on the east side of the Contemporary Art Museum St. Louis. The building was designed by Pritzker Prize-winning architect Tadao Ando. The foundation engages in a variety of programming initiatives involving the visual, literary and performing arts. Visitors can view changing exhibitions.

Time: Allow 45 minutes minimum. **Hours:** Wed.-Sat. 10-5 (also Thurs.-Fri. 5 p.m.-8 p.m.). **Cost:** Free. **Phone:** (314) 754-1850.

FOREST PARK is bounded by Lindell, Skinker and Kingshighway blvds. and Oakland Ave., covering 1,293 acres in the Central West End neighborhood, just west of downtown. Opened to the public on June 24, 1876, Forest Park is one of the country's largest urban parks. Distinguished by statues, monuments and works of art, it is home to major museums and a popular place for picnicking, jogging and bicycling.

Venetian fountains propel water up to 30 feet high at the Grand Basin, an area lined with lovely terraces. Picnickers stake out spots on the grass, while paddleboaters explore several canals and lakes. Rentals are available at the nearby Boathouse, where there is a restaurant with a large patio and a beer garden that offers entertainment on weekend evenings. Kids have fun at the Variety Wonderland Playground, which also provides play equipment for the disabled and visually impaired.

A scenic 6-mile loop trail encircles the park, providing recreational opportunities as well as access to most major attractions. One trailhead is located at the Dennis & Judith Jones Visitor and Education Center, where visitors can obtain area information. Other facilities include the Steinburg Memorial Skating Rink, with facilities for ice-skating and sand volleyball, and the 27-hole Norman K. Probstein Golf Course. **Hours:** Daily 6 a.m.-10 p.m. **Cost:** Free. **Phone:** (314) 367-7275 for the Visitor's Center at the Lindell Pavilion.

Jewel Box is at 5600 Clayton Ave. at jct. Wells and McKinley drs., within Forest Park. This Art Deco-style, glass-walled conservatory displays a collection of tropical trees, foliage plants and flowers. Seasonal floral shows take place at Easter, Mother's Day and the Christmas holidays. **Time:** Allow 30 minutes minimum. **Hours:** Mon.-Fri. 9-4, Sat. 9-11 a.m., Sun. 9-2. **Cost:** $1; free (Mon.-Tues. 9-noon). **Phone:** (314) 531-0080.

Missouri History Museum is at jct. Lindell Blvd. and DeBaliviere Ave. in Forest Park. Built at the site of the main entrance to the 1904 World's Fair, the neoclassic building honors President Thomas Jefferson's role in the Louisiana Purchase. Interactive galleries include Seeking St. Louis, which takes a look at the lives of St. Louis citizens from the city's earliest days to the present; and The 1904 World's Fair, a peek into America's future envisioned from an early 20th-century perspective; and The History Clubhouse, a hands-on gallery for kids.

Visitors can also learn more about such St. Louis traditions as breweries and baseball as well as hometown musicians like Scott Joplin and Miles Davis. Lectures, concerts and special programs are presented regularly. **Time:** Allow 1 hour minimum. **Hours:** Daily 10-5 (also Tues. 5-8). Phone ahead to confirm schedule. **Cost:** Free. **Phone:** (314) 746-4599.

Saint Louis Art Museum stands atop Art Hill at One Fine Arts Dr., within Forest Park. Built to house the Palace of Fine Arts pavilion at the 1904 World's Fair, this Beaux Arts-style building was designed by famed architect Cass Gilbert and is guarded by the heroic statue of The Apotheosis of St. Louis. The permanent collection comprises more than 30,000 works of art covering nearly every culture and time period, including Oceanic art, Pre-Columbian art, ancient Chinese bronzes, and European and American art from the late 19th through 20th centuries. There is a special emphasis on 20th-century German art and the works of Missouri artist George Caleb Bingham.

Lectures, performances, films, classes and family programs are all offered. Major touring exhibitions are presented regularly. **Time:** Allow 1 hour minimum. **Hours:** Tues.-Sun. 10-5 (also Fri. 5-9). Docent-led tours Tues.-Fri. at 10:30, Sat.-Sun. at 1:30. Closed Thanksgiving and Christmas. **Cost:** Free. Admission is charged for special exhibitions. Cash only. **Parking:** $15 daily parking garage. **Phone:** (314) 721-0072 or TTY (314) 721-4807.

Saint Louis Science Center is at 5050 Oakland Ave. in Forest Park. The center encourages hands-on exploration of such diverse topics as agriculture, aviation, cosmology, ecology, engineering, medicine and space science. Visitors can program a robot, use a radar gun to clock the speed of traffic passing under a glass bridge above I-64, conduct an experiment in the Life Science Lab and build a replica of the Gateway Arch.

The Discovery Room features imaginative science activities for ages 2-8. Nature, wildlife and adventure films from around the world are shown daily in the four-story OMNIMAX Theater. The James S. McDonnell Planetarium features a space station experience and a high-tech view of 9,000 stars in the night sky.

Time: Allow 4 hours minimum. **Hours:** Mon.-Sat. 9:30-5:30 (also Thurs. 5:30-8, early June-early Aug.), Sun. 11:30-5:30, Memorial Day-Labor Day; Mon.-Sat. 9:30-4:30, Sun. 11:30-4:30, rest of year. Hours may be extended for special exhibitions. Phone for OMNIMAX show times. **Cost:** Exhibits gallery free. A fee may be charged for special exhibitions. Planetarium $6; $5 (ages 2-12 and 60+); $4 (military with ID). OMNIMAX Theater $10; $9 (ages 2-12 and 60+). Discovery Room $4 (ages 1+); $3 (military with ID). Tickets should be purchased early in the day. Advance tickets are available. **Parking:** $12, Memorial Day-Labor Day; $10, rest of year. **Phone:** (314) 289-4400 or (800) 456-7572.

![GEM] **Saint Louis Zoo** is at 1 Government Dr. in Forest Park. More than 17,000 animals representing more than 581 species from around the world live in this zoo's scenic, natural settings. Highlights include the lushly landscaped Donn and Marilyn Lipton Fragile Forest, an outdoor compound home to separate habitats for chimpanzees, orangutans and western lowland gorillas. At Red Rocks, lions and tigers coexist peacefully with zebras, giraffes and antelope in natural settings.

Grab your pith helmet for a trek to River's Edge, a 10-acre habitat inhabited by Asian elephants, cheetahs, giant anteaters and viewing areas that provide an opportunity to observe hippos underwater. The Bayer Insectarium has 100 species of insects and a walk-through butterfly dome.

Penguin & Puffin Coast offers a close-up look at these birds, while the Andean Bear Range and Sun Bear Forest habitats are home to Andean and Malayan sun bears. The Centene Grizzly Ridge is home to two grizzly bears where visitors can view the bears through 22 glass-panel windows. At the state-of-the-art habitat McDonnell Polar Bear Point, a cave room with a glass viewing wall allows visitors to observe the bear as he swims in a dive pool. Keepers interact with and train the bear in a grassy "tundra" area.

The Judy and Jerry Kent Family Sea Lion Sound habitat replicates a Pacific Northwest coast landscape complete with a 35-foot-long underwater viewing tunnel, a see-through pool and an 800-seat amphitheater for sea lion shows. Guests can touch stingrays at Stingrays at Caribbean Cove presented by SSM Health.

At the Emerson Children's Zoo kids can touch animals and play at the playground. The Mary Ann Lee Conservation Carousel features 64 hand-carved wooden animals, each one representing a protected or endangered species. The 1.5-mile Emerson Zooline Railroad, a miniature railroad, traverses the grounds.

Time: Allow 2 hours minimum. **Hours:** Mon.-Thurs. 8-5, Fri.-Sun. 8-7, late May-early Sept.; daily 9-5, rest of year. Train rides are offered Mon.-Thurs. 9-5, Fri.-Sun. 9-7, late May-early Sept.; daily 9:30-5, rest of year. Sea lion shows are presented at 11, 1 and 2:30 (also Sat.-Sun. and holidays at 4), late May-mid-Aug.; Sat.-Sun. at 11, 1 and 2:30, mid-Aug. to late Oct.; Sat.-Sun. at 1 and 2:30, late Oct.-late Nov. Closes at 3 on Thanksgiving and Christmas Eve. Phone for schedule during Boo at the Zoo in Oct. and Wild Lights in Nov. and Dec. Closed Jan. 1 and Christmas. **Cost:** Free. Train ride $7.95; free (ages 0-1). Children's Zoo $3.95; free (ages 0-1 and

the first hour the zoo is open). Stingray exhibit $3.95; free (ages 0-1 and the first hour the zoo is open). Sea lion show $3.95; free (ages 0-1). Carousel $2.95; free (first hour the zoo is open). All-day Adventure Pass $12.95. **Parking:** $15 peak season; $10 off-season. **Phone:** (314) 781-0900 or (800) 966-8877.

GRANT'S FARM is on Gravois Rd. (at Grant Rd.). Ulysses S. Grant built a cabin here in 1856 on land he once farmed. The 281-acre tract, operated by Anheuser-Busch, is a home for some 900 animals, including goats, camels and elephants. Also on site is a Clydesdale stable and breeding farm. A show starring birds of prey invites participation from members of the audience. Visitors can ride a carousel or go for a swan paddleboat ride on Mirror Lake, and there are other lakes on the grounds stocked with goldfish and Japanese koi.

The Bauernhof, a 19th-century Bavarian-style building, houses the Busch family's carriage collection, including coaches, carts and sleighs from Europe and Asia. Trophy and tack rooms display harnesses, saddles and other gear. A tram ride offers the opportunity to observe such animals as bison, longhorn cattle, antelope, wild mustangs, zebras and red deer.

Guests 21 years of age and older are invited to enjoy complimentary samples of Anheuser-Busch products as they are walking through the park or relaxing in the Bauernhof area. **Time:** Allow 1 hour, 30 minutes minimum. **Hours:** Entrance open Tues.-Sat. 9-3:30 (also Fri. 3:30-8, Memorial Day-late Aug.), Sun. 9:30-3:30, late Apr.-late Aug.; Fri. 9:30-2:30,

Grant's Farm

Sat.-Sun. (also Labor Day) 9:30-3:30, early Sept.-late Oct. (also open 5:30-9 on select dates in Oct.; phone for schedule); Sat. 9-3:30, Sun. 9:30-3:30, mid- to late Apr. Entrance closes 90 minutes before the farm. **Cost:** Free. Pony and Camel rides $6; Carousel ride $2; Goat and Parakeet feeding $1.50; Camel feeding 50c. **Parking:** $12. **Phone:** (314) 843-1700. ⏹

HOLOCAUST MUSEUM AND LEARNING CENTER is at 12 Millstone Campus Dr. in the Kopolow Building. The museum offers a chronological history of the Holocaust. Exhibits revisit personal accounts and memories of survivors who later came to St. Louis. Jewish life in prewar Europe, the rise of Nazism, and events that occurred during the 1933-45 Holocaust and following World War II are depicted through artifacts, audiovisual presentations, photographs and text panels.

Time: Allow 1 hour minimum. **Hours:** Mon.-Thurs. 9:30-4:30, Fri. 9:30-4, Sun. 10-4. Closed Jan. 1, Memorial Day, Labor Day, Thanksgiving, Christmas and all major Jewish holidays. Advance reservations are necessary for guided tours. **Cost:** Free. **Phone:** (314) 432-0020 or (314) 442-3711.

JEFFERSON BARRACKS HISTORIC PARK is at jct. Grant Rd. and Kingston Dr., about 10 mi. s. of downtown via the I-55 S. Broadway exit; the visitor center is at 345 North Rd. Established in 1826, the site was a supply post for troops in the West. A museum in the 1857 powder magazine depicts the history of the barracks, and the Ordnance Building presents changing exhibits. The laborers' house and a stable dating from 1851 are restored. An overlook offers a view of the Mississippi River. More than 70,000 servicemen are buried in the park, one of the largest national cemeteries in the country.

Time: Allow 1 hour minimum. **Hours:** Park grounds open daily 8 a.m.-30 minutes after dusk. House and museum open Wed.-Sun. noon-4. **Cost:** Free. A fee may be charged for special events. Suggested donation to see the Ordnance Room is $3. **Phone:** (314) 615-8800. 🅰

Jefferson Barracks Telephone Museum is at 12 Hancock Ave., at the southern end of Jefferson Barracks Historic Park. Housed in a restored building dating from 1896, it features a collection of telephones—from vintage late 19th-century examples to contemporary phones—as well as telephone-related memorabilia and military telephones used from World War II through the Vietnam War. Hands-on displays encourage visitors to explore the engineering aspects of telephone operation. **Hours:** Wed.-Sun. 9-2. **Cost:** $5; $4 (ages 60+); $3 (ages 5-12). **Phone:** (314) 416-8004.

Missouri Civil War Museum is at 222 Worth Rd. near the jct. with Sherman Ave., adjacent to Jefferson Barracks Historic Park. Housed in a turn-of-the-20th-century building, it contains more than 1,500 historical items, including uniforms, medical equipment, swords, muskets and official documents from the period leading up to, through and following the Civil War. **Time:** Allow 1 hour minimum. **Hours:** Daily 9-5. **Cost:** $7; $6 (ages 60+); $5 (students with ID and veterans); free (ages 0-5 and active duty military). **Phone:** (314) 845-1861.

GATEWAY ARCH NATIONAL PARK is on the riverfront at Market St. This 91-acre national park, which covers the site of the original St. Louis settlement, was established in 1935 to commemorate St. Louis' role in the 19th-century westward expansion. The site includes The Gateway Arch, the Museum of Westward Expansion and the Old Courthouse. **Hours:** Park grounds open daily 6 a.m.-11 p.m. Hours for individual sites vary. **Cost:** Park grounds, museum and courthouse free. Admission is charged at the Gateway Arch. **Phone:** (314) 655-1600.

◤GEM **The Gateway Arch** is at Memorial Dr. and Market St. within Gateway Arch National Park. Soaring sculpture, symbolic gateway to the West, America's tallest monument—the Arch is all of these things. Standing 630 feet above the site of French fur trader Pierre Laclede's 18th-century trading post, this inverted catenary curve (the same shape that a free-hanging chain takes when held at both ends) commemorates St. Louis' role in the westward expansion of the United States.

Designed by Finnish-American architect Eero Saarinen, this gleaming stainless steel icon is ingenious in its simplicity, despite taking 2 years and 8 months to build (it opened to the public in 1967). The span of the two legs at ground level is the same as the height. Construction of the Arch required specially designed equipment; each leg needed to align precisely, and the margin of error for the failure of either one to do so was 1/64 of an inch.

The Tram Ride to the Top takes you on a trip through history en route to the small observation room at the top of the Arch. Instead of a standard elevator, passengers step aboard a unique tram system with egg-shaped compartments, each compartment containing five seats. The observation room has narrow windows with views of downtown St. Louis and the Mississippi; visibility is up to 30 miles on clear days.

The round-trip takes about an hour. Timed tickets are issued every 5 to 10 minutes throughout the day. A movie theater in the underground complex beneath the Arch shows "Monument to the Dream" a 35-minute film about its construction.

Pets on leash allowed on grounds. Service animals only allowed in the facility (call for restrictions/fees). **Hours:** Arch tram departures daily 8 a.m.-10 p.m., Memorial Day weekend-Labor Day; 9-6, rest of year. Closed Jan. 1, Thanksgiving and Christmas. Phone ahead to confirm schedule. **Cost:** Tram Ride to the Top $12-$16; $8-$12 (ages 3-15). "Monument to the Dream" film $7; $3 (ages 3-15). Combination tickets available for Tram Ride to the Top, "Monument to the Dream" film and Gateway Arch Riverboat Cruises. **Phone:** (314) 982-1410 or (877) 982-1410.

Museum of Westward Expansion is within the Gateway Arch National Park, on Market St. at Riverfront (beneath The Gateway Arch). An extensive collection of artifacts is displayed in conjunction with exhibits relating to the Lewis and Clark expedition and the social and cultural history of territories west of the Mississippi River. **Phone:** (877) 982-1410.

The Old Courthouse is at 11 N. 4th St., within the Gateway Arch National Park. Completed in 1862, the courthouse was the site of the Dred Scott slavery trial. Galleries and dioramas depict St. Louis history from its French and Spanish occupations through the westward expansion years to the present, and chronicle the era of slavery and the Scott family's struggle to gain freedom. **Hours:** Daily 7:30 a.m.-8 p.m., Memorial Day weekend-Labor Day; 8-5, rest of year. **Cost:** Free. **Phone:** (314) 655-1700 or (877) 982-1410.

LAUMEIER SCULPTURE PARK is s. of I-44 via the Lindbergh Blvd. exit at 12580 Rott Rd. The 105-acre park displays contemporary sculpture. Works by such celebrated artists as Vito Acconci, Sol LeWitt, Mary Miss, Robert Stackhouse and Tony Tasset grace the expansive lawns, which are surrounded by trees and a natural woodland with hiking trails. The Adam Aronson Fine Arts Center serves as a gallery, reception and conservation space. An annual art fair is held on Mother's Day weekend and concerts are presented during the summer. Dogs on leashes are permitted in the park.

Time: Allow 1 hour minimum. **Hours:** Park open daily 8 a.m.-30 minutes after dusk. Museum open daily 10-6 (also Thurs. 6-8 p.m.), Memorial Day-Labor Day; 10-4, rest of year. Walking tours depart the first Sun. of the month at 2; stroller tours depart the third Thurs. of the month at 10 a.m., May-Oct. Evening stroller tours and tours for visitors with memory loss also are offered; phone for details. Phone ahead to confirm schedule. **Cost:** Free. A fee may be charged for special exhibitions. **Phone:** (314) 615-5278. GT

THE MAGIC HOUSE, ST. LOUIS CHILDREN'S MUSEUM is at 516 S. Kirkwood Rd. The museum's hands-on learning experiences allow children to experiment, build creativity and develop problem solving skills. Families can explore communications, mathematics and science concepts through a variety of activities. Exhibits let kids become immersed in a giant bubble, stock grocery store shelves in the Children's Village and climb the three-story Jack and the Beanstalk structure.

Other areas include a three-story slide; an open-air plant science exhibit; a water playground; Kids Construction Zone; Solve the Mystery; and Star-Spangled Center, which includes a replica of the Oval Office. The electrically charged ball that makes visitors' hair stand on end is always a favorite.

For Baby and Me is a discovery area for children under 2, and Wonder Works is a special play area for children ages 2-8.

Time: Allow 2 hours minimum. **Hours:** Mon.-Sat. 9:30-5:30 (also Fri. 5:30-8), Sun. 11-5:30, Memorial Day-Labor Day; Tues.-Fri. noon-5:30 (also Fri. 5:30-8), Sat. 9:30-5:30, Sun. 11-5:30, rest of year. Hours may be extended during school breaks; phone to confirm schedule. Closed Thanksgiving and Christmas. **Cost:** $12; free (ages 0-1). **Phone:** (314) 822-8900. ⬤ ⬤

MILDRED LANE KEMPER ART MUSEUM is near the corner of Skinker and Forsyth blvds. at One Brookings Dr., on the Danforth Campus at Washington University. This architecturally impressive building holds an equally impressive collection of 19th-, 20th- and 21st-century art and sculpture. Highlights include paintings by Willem de Kooning, Thomas Eakins, Marsden Hartley, Henri Matisse, Joan Miró and Pablo Picasso. Computers, video and digital installations are among the various technologies incorporated into the multimedia works. Cutting-edge special exhibitions are presented regularly.

The Newman Money Museum, on the building's lower level, explores the history of money and displays rare coins and currency. **Note:** The museum will be closing in May 2018 for a year-long expansion; phone for updates. **Time:** Allow 45 minutes minimum. **Hours:** Wed.-Mon. 11-5 (also first Fri. of the month 5-8). Closed Jan. 1, Martin Luther King Jr. Day, Memorial Day, July 4, Labor Day, Thanksgiving, day after Thanksgiving and Christmas (also closes early on Christmas Eve and Dec. 31). The museum also may close during exhibit changes; phone ahead to confirm schedule. **Cost:** Free. **Phone:** (314) 935-4523 for the Kemper Art Museum, or (314) 935-9595 for the Newman Money Museum.

MISSOURI BOTANICAL GARDEN (MOBOT) is at 4344 Shaw Blvd., just s. of I-44 exit 287B near the jct. of Vandeventer and Kingshighway. St. Louisans affectionately refer to it as "Shaw's Garden"—a tribute to the British-born businessman who sold cutlery out of a rented room in St. Louis at age 18, subsequently made a fortune in hardware, retired at 40, traveled the world, found inspiration in Europe's great botanical gardens and opened one of his own in his adopted city.

MOBOT offers outdoor display gardens and several conservatories featuring tropical and non-native plants. Historic buildings include the Spink Pavilion, a private event facility, and the Tower Grove House, Shaw's country home. This mid-19th-century residence is restored and furnished in period style.

Highlights? There are many, starting with the Climatron, a geodesic dome with a lovely assortment of tropical trees, plants and flowers that luxuriate in the damp, climate-controlled environment. The Shoenberg Temperate House displays biblical and other plants from regions of the world with a Mediterranean climate. The Linnean House—named for famed botanist Carl Linnaeus—was originally used as a greenhouse to overwinter palms, tree ferns, citrus trees and other cold-sensitive plants; today its northern half houses camellias and its southern half has been returned to its original use as an orangery. The camellias begin blooming in mid-December and reach their peak in mid- to late February, providing a display of floriferous beauty for winter-weary visitors.

MOBOT's 14-acre Japanese Garden is the perfect place for a leisurely stroll. In the garden's central axis, a reflecting pool features a trio of angel musicians (bronze sculptures by Swedish artist Carl Milles). Floating in the pool from April through October are "Walla Wallas," whimsical glass sculptures by another renowned artist, Dale Chihuly (and don't miss Chihuly's Blue Chandelier hanging in the Ridgway Visitor Center).

The Kemper Center for Home Gardening encompasses 23 thematic display gardens. Next to the center, a path through the George Washington Carver Garden, planted with hydrangeas and sweet potato vines, leads to a fountain and life-size statue of the "plant scientist" and native Missourian—an appropriate tribute, since in addition to being a horticultural showplace MOBOT is known for its science and conservation efforts.

Labor Day weekend brings the Japanese Festival to the garden with drumming, dancing, martial arts, food and candlelight walks.

Hours: Grounds and facilities open daily 9-5. Tower Grove House open Wed.-Sun. 10-4, Apr.-Dec. Narrated tram tours depart on the hour Mon.-Fri. 10-4, every 40 minutes Sat.-Sun. 9:30-4:10, Apr.-Oct. Guided walking tours depart daily at 11 and 1, Apr.-Oct.; daily at 11, rest of year. **Cost:** (includes Tower Grove House) $12; free (ages 0-12). Admission for St. Louis County residents with ID $6; $4 (ages 65+); free ages 0-12. Tram tours $4; free (ages 0-2 on lap). Special rates apply for some events. **Phone:** (314) 577-5100 or (800) 642-8842. 📧 GT 🍴

Doris I. Schnuck Children's Garden: A Missouri Adventure, 4344 Shaw Blvd. at Missouri Botanical Garden, offers an interactive play space with rope swings and bridges, a man-made cave, a tree house and a re-created 19th-century town square complete with a general store, village hall and riverboat. Children also can play in the splash area. **Time:** Allow 1 hour minimum. **Hours:** Daily 9-4, Apr.-Oct. **Cost:** $5 (ages 3-12); free (ages 13+ with botanical garden admission). **Phone:** (314) 577-5100.

SIX FLAGS ST. LOUIS—see Eureka p. 189.

GAMBLING ESTABLISHMENTS

- **Lumière Place Casino & Hotels** is at 999 N. 2nd St. **Hours:** Daily 24 hours. **Phone:** (314) 881-7777 or (877) 450-7711.

Sightseeing
Boat Tours

GATEWAY ARCH RIVERBOAT CRUISES depart from the base of the Gateway Arch. Narrated 1-hour trips on the Mississippi River are offered aboard replicas of 19th-century steamboats. Dinner and specialty cruises also are available; phone for schedule and reservations. **Hours:** Sightseeing cruises depart daily at 10:30, noon, 1:30, 3 and 4:30, Mar.-Nov. (weather permitting). Departure times vary rest of year; phone ahead to confirm schedule. **Cost:** $22; $11 (ages 3-15). Combination tickets available for Tram Ride to the Top, "Monument to the Dream" movie and Gateway Arch Riverboat Cruises. **Phone:** (314) 621-4040 or (877) 982-1410.

Carriage Tours

The St. Louis Carriage Co., 1000 Cerre St., offers 15-minute, half-hour and 1-hour horse-drawn carriage tours of the downtown area nightly (weather permitting). Carriages depart from the Gateway Arch, The Old Spaghetti Factory at Laclede's Landing and the Hyatt hotel on Chestnut Street. Pickups from downtown hotels and restaurants also can be arranged. Phone (314) 621-3334 for a complete list of pickup locations. Brookdale Farms also provides nightly carriage tours of the downtown area; phone (636) 938-1005.

Driving Tours

"Day Tours from St. Louis," a 44-page booklet detailing 10 trips within a day's drive, and a St. Louis points of interest map are available to AAA/CAA members free at any AAA service office in the St. Louis area. *See AAA Offices.*

Helicopter Tours

Fostaire Helicopter Tours, based at the St. Louis Downtown Airport in Sauget, Illinois, covers various sections of St. Louis, focusing on major industries, waterways and other points of interest; phone (314) 421-5440 or (618) 337-4440.

Industrial Tours

ANHEUSER-BUSCH BREWERY is at jct. Lynch and 12th sts. Guided 45-minute complimentary tours provide an overview of the facility and include the Clydesdale stables, Beechwood Aging Cellar and the Historic Brew House. The tour concludes in the Biergarten. The Beermaster tour is a behind-the-scenes tour featuring all the stops on the complimentary tour plus viewing the full packaging line in the packaging building, the tack room in the stables and the finishing cellar, where guests 21 and older can quaff a sample from the finishing tank. Gifts are also provided on this tour. The Beer School exhibit provides background information on beer's finer points, from ingredients to pouring, and samples are available to taste. Other tours are offered; phone for details.

Note: Closed-toe shoes are required on the Beermaster tour, and access to behind-the-scenes areas may vary based on production schedule. Both tours involve outside walking and six flights of escalators.

Hours: Tours offered Mon.-Thurs. 9-5, Fri.-Sat. 9-5:30 (also 5:30-7 on July 4 weekend), Sun. 11:30-7, June-Aug.; Mon.-Sat. 10-5 (also 5-7 on Memorial Day and Labor Day weekends), Sun. 11-5, rest of year. Beermaster tour (maximum 10 guests per tour) and Beer School offered several times a day. Schedule varies with the season; phone for details. Closed Jan.

1, Martin Luther King Jr. Day, Presidents Day, Easter, Thanksgiving, Christmas Eve and Christmas. **Cost:** Complimentary tour free. Beermaster tour $35; $15 (ages 13-20). Beer School $15. Under 18 must be with an adult on overview tour. Under 21 not permitted at Beer School. Advance reservations (recommended several weeks in advance) are required for the Beermaster tour; ages 0-12 are not permitted. **Phone:** (314) 577-2626, or (314) 577-2153 for reservations. 🍴

Walking Tours

The St. Louis Walk of Fame preserves the city's historical and cultural legacy by honoring the accomplishments of individuals with St. Louis connections. A brass star is engraved with the person's name, and an accompanying bronze plaque provides a brief biographical summary. More than 150 sets of stars and plaques are embedded in the sidewalks of The Loop, an area of shops, galleries and cafés along Delmar Boulevard. Among the honorees are Maya Angelou, Josephine Baker, Chuck Berry, William Burroughs, Miles Davis, the 5th Dimension, Redd Foxx, Joe Garagiola, John Goodman, Betty Grable, Ulysses S. Grant, Kevin Kline, Charles Lindbergh, Agnes Moorehead, Nelly, Marlin Perkins, Joseph Pulitzer and Shelley Winters.

© 2019 HERE

© AAA

Downtown
St Louis
Hotels & Restaurants

Scale in Miles
0.2   0   0.2

See p. 6 - Map Legend

1820-20

Downtown St. Louis

This index helps you "spot" where hotels and restaurants are located on the corresponding detailed maps. Restaurant price range is a combination of lunch and/or dinner. Turn to the listing page for more information and consult display ads for special promotions.

For more details, rates and reservations: AAA.com/travelguides/hotels

DOWNTOWN ST. LOUIS

Map Page	Hotels	Designation	Member Savings	Page
1 this page	**Four Seasons Hotel St. Louis**	FOUR DIAMOND	✔	281
2 this page	Holiday Inn St. Louis-Downtown Convention Center	THREE DIAMOND		282
3 this page	The Last Hotel	THREE DIAMOND		282
4 this page	Drury Inn & Suites-St. Louis-Convention Center	THREE DIAMOND		281
5 this page	Courtyard by Marriott St. Louis Downtown Convention Center	THREE DIAMOND	✔	281
6 this page	**Embassy Suites by Hilton St. Louis-Downtown**	THREE DIAMOND	✔	281
7 this page	**Marriott St. Louis Grand**	THREE DIAMOND	✔	282
8 this page	Hampton Inn by Hilton St. Louis-Downtown	THREE DIAMOND	✔	282
9 this page	**Magnolia Hotel St. Louis, a Tribute Portfolio Hotel**	FOUR DIAMOND	✔	282
10 this page	Pear Tree Inn Union Station	THREE DIAMOND		282

DOWNTOWN ST. LOUIS (cont'd)

Map Page	Hotels (cont'd)	Designation	Member Savings	Page
11 p. 269	**Courtyard by Marriott Downtown West**	THREE DIAMOND	✔	281
12 p. 269	**Hotel Saint Louis, Autograph Collection**	FOUR DIAMOND	✔	282
13 p. 269	**St. Louis Union Station Hotel, Curio Collection by Hilton** *(See ad p. 283, p. 265.)*	FOUR DIAMOND	✔	284
14 p. 269	The Hotel Majestic St. Louis	fyi		282
15 p. 269	Hilton-St. Louis Downtown at the Arch	THREE DIAMOND	✔	282
16 p. 269	Drury Inn-St. Louis/Union Station	THREE DIAMOND		281
17 p. 269	**Hyatt Regency St. Louis at The Arch**	THREE DIAMOND	✔	282
18 p. 269	**Hilton St. Louis at the Ballpark**	THREE DIAMOND	✔	282
19 p. 269	Residence Inn by Marriott St. Louis Downtown	THREE DIAMOND	✔	284
20 p. 269	Drury Plaza Hotel-St. Louis at the Arch	THREE DIAMOND		281
21 p. 269	The Westin St. Louis	FOUR DIAMOND	✔	284

Map Page	Restaurants	Designation	Cuisine	Price Range	Page
1 p. 269	Al's Restaurant	THREE DIAMOND	Steak Seafood	$28-$80	284
2 p. 269	Cinder House	THREE DIAMOND	Brazilian Small Plates	$12-$78	284
3 p. 269	The Schlafly Tap Room	APPROVED	American	$10-$21	284
4 p. 269	Mango	APPROVED	Peruvian Fusion	$10-$33	284
5 p. 269	BLT's - Breakfast, Lunch and Tacos	APPROVED	Breakfast	$4-$14	284
6 p. 269	Sugarfire Smoke House	APPROVED	Barbecue	$5-$23	284
7 p. 269	Rooster	APPROVED	Breakfast	$6-$15	284
8 p. 269	Bridge Tap House & Wine Bar	APPROVED	American	$11-$28	284
9 p. 269	Bailey's Range	APPROVED	Burgers	$5-$13	284
10 p. 269	Station Grille	THREE DIAMOND	American	$8-$26	284
11 p. 269	Charlie Gitto's Downtown	APPROVED	Italian	$9-$35	284
12 p. 269	Lombardo's Trattoria	THREE DIAMOND	Italian	$11-$40	284
13 p. 269	Caleco's Bar and Grill	APPROVED	American	$8-$28	284
14 p. 269	Hard Rock Cafe	APPROVED	American	$8-$27 SAVE	284
15 p. 269	Ruth's Chris Steak House	THREE DIAMOND	Steak	$21-$50	284
16 p. 269	Imo's Pizza	APPROVED	Pizza	$6-$24	284
17 p. 269	Tony's	FOUR DIAMOND	Italian	$28-$52	284
18 p. 269	Carmine's Steak House	THREE DIAMOND	Steak	$18-$74	284
19 p. 269	Broadway Oyster Bar	APPROVED	Cajun	$8-$19	284
20 p. 269	Eleven Eleven Mississippi	APPROVED	New American	$9-$32	284
21 p. 269	Polite Society	THREE DIAMOND	New American	$11-$34	284
22 p. 269	Bogart's Smokehouse	APPROVED	Barbecue	$11-$30	284
23 p. 269	Twisted Ranch	APPROVED	American	$8-$15	284
24 p. 269	Chava's Mexican Restaurant	APPROVED	Mexican	$7-$11	284
25 p. 269	Hodak's Restaurant & Bar	APPROVED	American	$5-$17	284

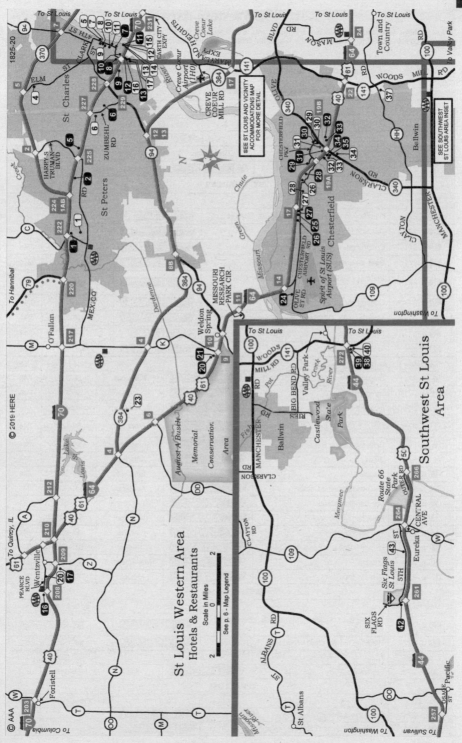

St Louis Western Area
Hotels & Restaurants

Scale in Miles

0   2

See p. 6 - Map Legend

Southwest St Louis
Area

© 2019 HERE

© AAA

St. Louis Western Area

This index helps you "spot" where hotels and restaurants are located on the corresponding detailed maps. Restaurant price range is a combination of lunch and/or dinner. Turn to the listing page for more information and consult display ads for special promotions.

 For more details, rates and reservations: AAA.com/travelguides/hotels

ST. PETERS

Map Page	Hotels	Designation	Member Savings	Page
1 p. 271	Drury Inn & Suites St. Peters	◈ THREE DIAMOND		292
2 p. 271	Courtyard by Marriott St. Peters	◈ THREE DIAMOND	✔	291

Map Page	Restaurant	Designation	Cuisine	Price Range	Page
① p. 271	Copper Chimney	◈ APPROVED	Indian	$10-$18	292

ST. CHARLES

Map Page	Hotels	Designation	Member Savings	Page
5 p. 271	Hampton Inn by Hilton - St. Louis/St. Charles	◈ THREE DIAMOND	✔	244
6 p. 271	TownePlace Suites by Marriott	◈ THREE DIAMOND	✔	244
7 p. 271	Country Inn & Suites by Radisson	◈ THREE DIAMOND		244
8 p. 271	**Best Western Plus The Charles Hotel**	◈ THREE DIAMOND	✔	244
9 p. 271	Embassy Suites by Hilton St. Louis-St. Charles Hotel	◈ THREE DIAMOND	✔	244
10 p. 271	Comfort Suites-St. Charles	◈ THREE DIAMOND		244
11 p. 271	**Ameristar St. Charles Casino Resort & Spa**	◈ FOUR DIAMOND	✔	244
12 p. 271	Drury Plaza St. Louis St. Charles	◈ THREE DIAMOND		244
13 p. 271	Tru by Hilton St. Charles St. Louis	◈ APPROVED	✔	244

Map Page	Restaurants	Designation	Cuisine	Price Range	Page
④ p. 271	Sugarfire Smoke House	◈ APPROVED	Barbecue	$6-$16	245
⑤ p. 271	Llywelyn's Pub	◈ APPROVED	Irish	$6-$19	244
⑥ p. 271	Fratelli's Ristorante	◈ APPROVED	Italian	$11-$30	244
⑦ p. 271	Lewis and Clark's An American Restaurant & Public House	◈ APPROVED	American	$9-$29	244
⑧ p. 271	Bella Vino Wine Bar & Tapas	◈ APPROVED	Small Plates	$8-$17	244
⑨ p. 271	Braddens Restaurant	◈ APPROVED	American	$7-$29	244
⑩ p. 271	Magpie's	◈ APPROVED	American	$6-$25	244
⑪ p. 271	Trailhead Brewing Company	◈ APPROVED	American	$10-$27	245
⑫ p. 271	The Landmark Buffet	◈ APPROVED	International	$16-$26	244
⑬ p. 271	Amerisports Bar & Grill	◈ APPROVED	American	$12-$27	244
⑭ p. 271	The Falcon Diner	◈ APPROVED	American	$7-$18	244
⑮ p. 271	Bugatti's Steak & Pasta	◈ THREE DIAMOND	Steak	$18-$55	244
⑯ p. 271	Prasino	◈ THREE DIAMOND	New American	$10-$35	245
⑰ p. 271	Mission Taco Joint	◈ APPROVED	Mexican	$3-$12	245

WENTZVILLE

Map Page	Hotels	Designation	Member Savings	Page
16 p. 271	Fairfield Inn & Suites by Marriott St. Louis West/Wentzville	◈ THREE DIAMOND	✔	302
17 p. 271	Hampton Inn St. Louis Wentzville	◈ THREE DIAMOND	✔	302

Map Page	Restaurant	Designation	Cuisine	Price Range	Page
⑳ p. 271	Stefanina's	◈ APPROVED	Italian	$5-$18	302

O'FALLON

Map Page	Hotels	Designation	Member Savings	Page
20 p. 271	Sleep Inn & Suites	◈ THREE DIAMOND		239
21 p. 271	Staybridge Suites O'Fallon	◈ THREE DIAMOND		239

Map Page	Restaurant	Designation	Cuisine	Price Range	Page
㉓ p. 271	Sugarfire Smoke House	◆ APPROVED	Barbecue	$6-$16	239

CHESTERFIELD

Map Page	Hotels	Designation	Member Savings	Page
㉔ p. 271	TownePlace Suites St. Louis Chesterfield	◈ THREE DIAMOND	✔	184
㉕ p. 271	Courtyard by Marriott St. Louis-Chesterfield	◈ THREE DIAMOND	✔	184
㉖ p. 271	Holiday Inn Express & Suites St. Louis-Chesterfield	◈ THREE DIAMOND		184
㉗ p. 271	Hampton Inn & Suites by Hilton-Chesterfield	◈ THREE DIAMOND	✔	184
㉘ p. 271	Hilton Garden Inn St. Louis/Chesterfield	◈ THREE DIAMOND	✔	184
㉙ p. 271	DoubleTree by Hilton Hotel St. Louis - Chesterfield	◈ THREE DIAMOND	✔	184
㉚ p. 271	Homewood Suites by Hilton St. Louis - Chesterfield	◈ THREE DIAMOND	✔	184
㉛ p. 271	Hampton Inn by Hilton St. Louis/Chesterfield	◈ THREE DIAMOND	✔	184
㉜ p. 271	SpringHill Suites by Marriott St. Louis/Chesterfield	◈ THREE DIAMOND	✔	184
㉝ p. 271	Sonesta ES Suites St. Louis - Chesterfield	◈ THREE DIAMOND		184
㉞ p. 271	Drury Plaza Hotel-Chesterfield	◈ THREE DIAMOND		184
㉟ p. 271	Hyatt Place St. Louis/Chesterfield	◈ THREE DIAMOND	✔	184

Map Page	Restaurants	Designation	Cuisine	Price Range	Page
㉖ p. 271	Annie Gunn's	◈ THREE DIAMOND	Regional American	$12-$60	185
㉗ p. 271	East Coast Pizza	◆ APPROVED	Pizza	$7-$19	185
㉘ p. 271	Taj Palace	◆ APPROVED	Indian	$10-$18	185
㉙ p. 271	Gianfabio's Italian Cafe	◆ APPROVED	Italian	$9-$32	185
㉚ p. 271	Charlie Gittos from the Hill	◈ THREE DIAMOND	Italian	$16-$36	185
㉛ p. 271	YaYa's Euro Bistro	◈ THREE DIAMOND	European	$9-$36	185
㉜ p. 271	EdgeWild Restaurant & Winery	◆ APPROVED	American	$11-$32	185
㉝ p. 271	The Cheesecake Factory	◈ THREE DIAMOND	International	$9-$30	185
㉞ p. 271	P.F. Chang's China Bistro	◈ THREE DIAMOND	Chinese	$10-$28	185

VALLEY PARK

Map Page	Hotels	Designation	Member Savings	Page
㊳ p. 271	Drury Inn & Suites-St. Louis Southwest	◈ THREE DIAMOND		301
㊴ p. 271	Hampton Inn by Hilton-St. Louis Southwest near Six Flags	◈ THREE DIAMOND	✔	301

Map Page	Restaurant	Designation	Cuisine	Price Range	Page
㊵ p. 271	Sugarfire Smokehouse	◆ APPROVED	Barbecue	$8-$24	301

EUREKA

Map Page	Hotel	Designation	Member Savings	Page
㊷ p. 271	Holiday Inn at Six Flags	◈ THREE DIAMOND		190

Map Page	Restaurant	Designation	Cuisine	Price Range	Page
㊸ p. 271	Poor Richard's	◆ APPROVED	American	$6-$15	190

TOWN AND COUNTRY

Map Page	Restaurant	Designation	Cuisine	Price Range	Page
㊲ p. 271	Cooper's Hawk Winery & Restaurant	◈ THREE DIAMOND	American	$10-$35	301

For highways, byways and more:

AAA.com/maps

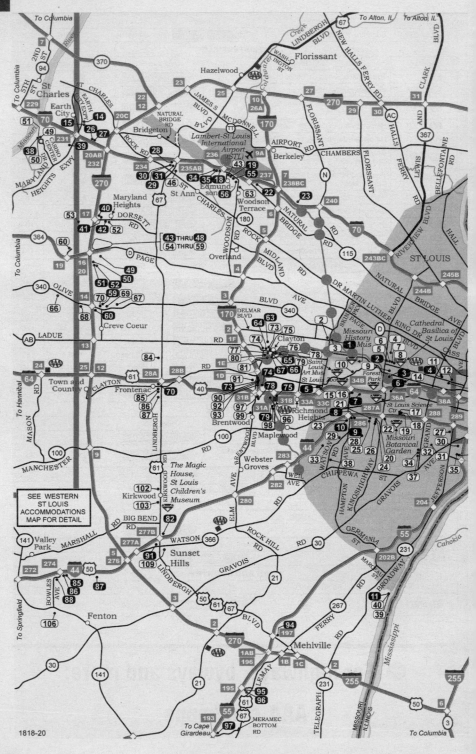

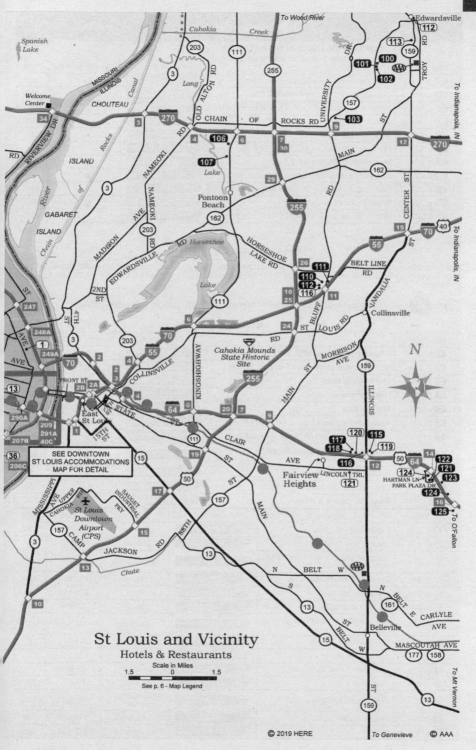

St Louis and Vicinity
Hotels & Restaurants

Scale in Miles
1.5   0   1.5

See p. 6 - Map Legend

© 2019 HERE   © AAA

SEE DOWNTOWN
ST LOUIS ACCOMMODATIONS
MAP FOR DETAIL

✈ Airport Hotels

Map Page	LAMBERT-ST. LOUIS INTERNATIONAL (Maximum driving distance from airport: 2.4 mi)	Designation	Member Savings	Page
22 p. 274	Renaissance St. Louis Airport Hotel, 1.9 mi	◈ THREE DIAMOND	✔	148
31 p. 274	**Crowne Plaza St. Louis Airport, 2.2 mi**	◈ THREE DIAMOND	✔	181
28 p. 274	Embassy Suites by Hilton St. Louis Airport, 2.4 mi	◈ THREE DIAMOND	✔	181
30 p. 274	MainStay Suites, 2.3 mi	◈ THREE DIAMOND		181
29 p. 274	Sleep Inn, 2.3 mi	◈ THREE DIAMOND		181
19 p. 274	Drury Inn & Suites St. Louis Airport, 0.8 mi	◈ THREE DIAMOND		189
18 p. 274	**Marriott-St. Louis Airport, 2.1 mi**	◈ THREE DIAMOND	✔	189
34 p. 274	Hampton Inn by Hilton - St. Louis Airport, 0.8 mi	◈ THREE DIAMOND	✔	243
35 p. 274	Pear Tree Inn by Drury-St. Louis Airport, 0.8 mi	◈ APPROVED		243
55 p. 274	**Hilton St. Louis Airport, 1.0 mi**	◈ THREE DIAMOND	✔	303
56 p. 274	Holiday Inn St. Louis Airport, 1.3 mi	◈ THREE DIAMOND		303

St. Louis and Vicinity

This index helps you "spot" where hotels and restaurants are located on the corresponding detailed maps. Restaurant price range is a combination of lunch and/or dinner. Turn to the listing page for more information and consult display ads for special promotions.

🔗 **For more details, rates and reservations: AAA.com/travelguides/hotels**

ST. LOUIS

Map Page	Hotels	Designation	Member Savings	Page
1 p. 274	**Moonrise Hotel (See ad p. 286.)**	◈ FOUR DIAMOND	✔	286
2 p. 274	**Royal Sonesta Chase Park Plaza St. Louis**	◈ FOUR DIAMOND	✔	287
3 p. 274	**The Parkway Hotel**	◈ THREE DIAMOND	✔	286
4 p. 274	**Hotel Ignacio**	◈ THREE DIAMOND	✔	285
5 p. 274	**The Cheshire**	◈ THREE DIAMOND	✔	285
6 p. 274	Home2 Suites by Hilton St. Louis/Forest Park	◈ THREE DIAMOND	✔	285
7 p. 274	Hampton Inn & Suites-St. Louis at Forest Park	◈ THREE DIAMOND	✔	285
8 p. 274	**Red Roof PLUS+ St. Louis-Forest Park/Hampton Ave.**	◈ APPROVED	✔	286
9 p. 274	**Holiday Inn Forest Park**	◈ THREE DIAMOND	✔	285
10 p. 274	Drury Inn & Suites Near Forest Park	◈ THREE DIAMOND		285
11 p. 274	**River City Casino & Hotel**	◈ FOUR DIAMOND	✔	286

Map Page	Restaurants	Designation	Cuisine	Price Range	Page
1 p. 274	Crown Candy Kitchen	◈ APPROVED	American	$5-$10	287
2 p. 274	Mission Taco Joint	◈ APPROVED	Mexican	$6-$15	287
3 p. 274	Eclipse Restaurant at the Moonrise Hotel (See ad p. 286.)	◈ APPROVED	New American	$8-$27	287
4 p. 274	Dressel's Public House	◈ APPROVED	English	$10-$19	287
5 p. 274	The Tenderloin Room	◈ THREE DIAMOND	Steak	$28-$65	288
6 p. 274	Bar Italia Ristorante	◈ APPROVED	Italian	$7-$36	287
7 p. 274	The Drunken Fish Sushi Bar & Lounge	◈ APPROVED	Asian Sushi	$11-$33	287
8 p. 274	Gamlin Whiskey House	◈ APPROVED	American	$14-$71	287
9 p. 274	Brasserie by Niche	◈ THREE DIAMOND	French	$15-$45	287
10 p. 274	Boathouse Forest Park	◈ APPROVED	American	$9-$24	287
11 p. 274	Triumph Grill	◈ APPROVED	American	$9-$35	288
12 p. 274	The Fountain on Locust	◈ APPROVED	Sandwiches Soup	$6-$11	287
13 p. 274	Pappy's Smokehouse	◈ APPROVED	Barbecue	$10-$26	288
14 p. 274	Vicia	◈ FOUR DIAMOND	New American	$12-$40	288

Map Page	Restaurants (cont'd)	Designation	Cuisine	Price Range	Page
15 p. 274	Boundary	THREE DIAMOND	American	$11-$32	287
16 p. 274	Imo's Pizza	APPROVED	Italian Pizza	$6-$24	287
17 p. 274	Nixta	THREE DIAMOND	New Mexican	$10-$22	288
18 p. 274	ELAIA	FOUR DIAMOND	New Mediterranean	$15-$70	287
19 p. 274	Olio	APPROVED	Mediterranean Small Plates	$10-$34	288
20 p. 274	Adriana's on the Hill	APPROVED	Italian Sandwiches Pizza	$7-$11	287
21 p. 274	Charlie Gitto's on the Hill	THREE DIAMOND	Italian	$16-$36	287
22 p. 274	O'Connell's Pub	APPROVED	American	$5-$10	288
23 p. 274	Bartolino's Osteria	APPROVED	Italian	$10-$39	287
24 p. 274	J. Devoti Trattoria	THREE DIAMOND	New American	$14-$32	287
25 p. 274	Zia's	APPROVED	Italian	$9-$29	288
26 p. 274	Dominic's	THREE DIAMOND	Italian	$22-$45	287
27 p. 274	Savage Restaurant	FOUR DIAMOND	New American	$25-$75	288
28 p. 274	Cunetto House of Pasta	APPROVED	Italian	$8-$25	287
29 p. 274	Brazie's Ristorante	THREE DIAMOND	Southern Italian	$12-$30	287
30 p. 274	Sidney Street Cafe	FOUR DIAMOND	New American	$23-$38	288
31 p. 274	The Shaved Duck	APPROVED	Barbecue	$10-$25	288
32 p. 274	Mangia Italiano	APPROVED	Italian	$9-$20	287
33 p. 274	Farmhaus	THREE DIAMOND	American	$19-$39	287
34 p. 274	King & I Restaurant	APPROVED	Thai	$8-$22	287
35 p. 274	Benton Park Cafe & Coffee Bar	APPROVED	Breakfast Sandwiches	$8-$17	287
36 p. 274	Frazer's	APPROVED	American	$9-$39	287
37 p. 274	Pho Grand Vietnamese Restaurant	APPROVED	Vietnamese	$7-$16	288
38 p. 274	Trattoria Marcella	THREE DIAMOND	Italian	$14-$24	288
39 p. 274	1904 Steakhouse	THREE DIAMOND	Steak	$25-$60	287
40 p. 274	The Great Food Exposition	APPROVED	American	$14-$33	287

EARTH CITY

Map Page	Hotels	Designation	Member Savings	Page
14 p. 274	Residence Inn by Marriott St. Louis Airport/Earth City	THREE DIAMOND	✔	189
15 p. 274	Candlewood Suites St. Louis	APPROVED		189

EDMUNDSON

Map Page	Hotels	Designation	Member Savings	Page
18 p. 274	Marriott-St. Louis Airport	THREE DIAMOND	✔	189
19 p. 274	Drury Inn & Suites St. Louis Airport	THREE DIAMOND		189

Map Page	Restaurant	Designation	Cuisine	Price Range	Page
43 p. 274	Lombardo's Restaurant	THREE DIAMOND	Italian	$8-$34	189

BERKELEY

Map Page	Hotels	Designation	Member Savings	Page
22 p. 274	Renaissance St. Louis Airport Hotel	THREE DIAMOND	✔	148
23 p. 274	Hilton Garden Inn St. Louis Airport	THREE DIAMOND	✔	148

BRIDGETON

Map Page	Hotels	Designation	Member Savings	Page
26 p. 274	Courtyard by Marriott-Airport/Earth City	THREE DIAMOND	✔	181
27 p. 274	SpringHill Suites by Marriott-St. Louis Airport/Earth City	THREE DIAMOND	✔	181
28 p. 274	Embassy Suites by Hilton St. Louis Airport	THREE DIAMOND	✔	181
29 p. 274	Sleep Inn	THREE DIAMOND		181
30 p. 274	MainStay Suites	THREE DIAMOND		181

BRIDGETON (cont'd)

Map Page	Hotels (cont'd)	Designation	Member Savings	Page
31 p. 274	**Crowne Plaza St. Louis Airport**	THREE DIAMOND	✔	181

Map Page	Restaurant	Designation	Cuisine	Price Range	Page
46 p. 274	Massa's	APPROVED	Italian	$10-$32	181

ST. ANN

Map Page	Hotels	Designation	Member Savings	Page
34 p. 274	Hampton Inn by Hilton - St. Louis Airport	THREE DIAMOND	✔	243
35 p. 274	Pear Tree Inn by Drury-St. Louis Airport	APPROVED		243

MARYLAND HEIGHTS

Map Page	Hotels	Designation	Member Savings	Page
38 p. 274	Hollywood Casino & Hotel	THREE DIAMOND		236
39 p. 274	Homewood Suites by Hilton St. Louis Riverport - Airport West	THREE DIAMOND	✔	236
40 p. 274	Hampton Inn by Hilton St. Louis/Westport	THREE DIAMOND	✔	236
41 p. 274	**Homewood Suites by Hilton St. Louis Westport**	THREE DIAMOND	✔	236
42 p. 274	Drury Inn & Suites-St. Louis-Westport	THREE DIAMOND		236
43 p. 274	Staybridge Suites St. Louis - Westport	THREE DIAMOND		237
44 p. 274	Courtyard by Marriott-Westport	THREE DIAMOND	✔	236
45 p. 274	**Sheraton Westport Lakeside Chalet**	THREE DIAMOND	✔	236
46 p. 274	Residence Inn by Marriott St. Louis Westport	THREE DIAMOND	✔	236
47 p. 274	Fairfield Inn & Suites by Marriott St. Louis Westport	THREE DIAMOND	✔	236
48 p. 274	**Sheraton Westport Plaza Tower**	THREE DIAMOND	✔	236
49 p. 274	Comfort Inn St. Louis - Westport	THREE DIAMOND		236
50 p. 274	**DoubleTree by Hilton Hotel St. Louis-Westport**	THREE DIAMOND	✔	236
51 p. 274	Hawthorn Suites by Wyndham St. Louis Westport Plaza	THREE DIAMOND		236
52 p. 274	**Sonesta ES Suites St. Louis Westport**	THREE DIAMOND	✔	237

Map Page	Restaurants	Designation	Cuisine	Price Range	Page
49 p. 274	The Final Cut Steakhouse	THREE DIAMOND	Steak	$24-$72	237
50 p. 274	Eat UP! Buffet	APPROVED	International	$20-$28	237
51 p. 274	Charlie Gitto's at Hollywood Casino	THREE DIAMOND	Italian	$16-$36	237
52 p. 274	DD Mau Vietnamese Eatery	APPROVED	Vietnamese	$6-$12	237
53 p. 274	Casa Juárez	APPROVED	Mexican	$8-$22	237
54 p. 274	Kemoll's Chophouse	THREE DIAMOND	Italian Steak	$35-$60	237
55 p. 274	Imo's Pizza	APPROVED	Pizza Sandwiches	$6-$24	237
56 p. 274	The Drunken Fish Sushi Bar and Lounge	APPROVED	Japanese Sushi	$8-$30	237
57 p. 274	Kobe Steak House of Japan	APPROVED	Japanese	$9-$39	237
58 p. 274	Trainwreck Saloon Westport	APPROVED	American	$9-$20	237
59 p. 274	Westport Social	APPROVED	American	$7-$13	237
60 p. 274	Balducci's Winefest Restaurant & Bar	APPROVED	Italian	$11-$16	237

WOODSON TERRACE

Map Page	Hotels	Designation	Member Savings	Page
55 p. 274	**Hilton St. Louis Airport**	THREE DIAMOND	✔	303
56 p. 274	Holiday Inn St. Louis Airport	THREE DIAMOND		303

Map Page	Restaurant	Designation	Cuisine	Price Range	Page
63 p. 274	Erio's Pizza and Restaurant	APPROVED	Italian	$8-$19	303

CREVE COEUR

Map Page	Hotels	Designation	Member Savings	Page
59 p. 274	Courtyard by Marriott-Creve Coeur	THREE DIAMOND	✔	188

CREVE COEUR (cont'd)

Map Page	Hotels (cont'd)	Designation	Member Savings	Page
60 p. 274	Drury Inn & Suites-Creve Coeur	THREE DIAMOND		188

Map Page	Restaurants	Designation	Cuisine	Price Range	Page
66 p. 274	Houlihan's	THREE DIAMOND	American	$10-$25	188
67 p. 274	Nudo House STL	APPROVED	Asian Noodles	00-$13	188
68 p. 274	La Bonne Bouchée	APPROVED	French	$9-$15	188
69 p. 274	Il Bel Lago	THREE DIAMOND	Italian	$10-$39	188
70 p. 274	Bristol Bar & Seafood Grill	THREE DIAMOND	Seafood	$12-$65	188

CLAYTON

Map Page	Hotels	Designation	Member Savings	Page
63 p. 274	Hampton Inn & Suites Clayton/Brentwood-Galleria Area	THREE DIAMOND	✔	185
64 p. 274	Seven Gables Inn	THREE DIAMOND		185
65 p. 274	The Ritz-Carlton, St. Louis	FOUR DIAMOND	✔	185
66 p. 274	Clayton Plaza Hotel	THREE DIAMOND		185
67 p. 274	**Sheraton Clayton Plaza Hotel**	fyi	✔	185

Map Page	Restaurants	Designation	Cuisine	Price Range	Page
73 p. 274	BARcelona Tapas Restaurant	APPROVED	Spanish Small Plates	$5-$23	185
74 p. 274	Ruth's Chris Steak House	THREE DIAMOND	Steak	$21-$50	185
75 p. 274	The Crossing	THREE DIAMOND	New American	$13-$42	185
76 p. 274	Pastaria	APPROVED	New Italian Pizza	$12-$20	185
77 p. 274	Café Napoli	APPROVED	Italian	$10-$41	185
78 p. 274	Sardella	THREE DIAMOND	New Italian	$18-$29	185
79 p. 274	The Grill	FOUR DIAMOND	American	$25-$42	185
80 p. 274	Dominic's Trattoria	THREE DIAMOND	Italian	$12-$37	185
81 p. 274	Morton's The Steakhouse	THREE DIAMOND	Steak	$20-$55	185

FRONTENAC

Map Page	Hotel	Designation	Member Savings	Page
70 p. 274	Hilton St. Louis Frontenac	THREE DIAMOND	✔	191

Map Page	Restaurants	Designation	Cuisine	Price Range	Page
84 p. 274	**Kreis' Steakhouse & Bar**	THREE DIAMOND	Steak	$13-$68	191
85 p. 274	Brio Tuscan Grille	THREE DIAMOND	Italian	$12-$30	191
86 p. 274	Canyon Cafe	APPROVED	Southwestern	$12-$20	191
87 p. 274	Fleming's Prime Steakhouse & Wine Bar	THREE DIAMOND	Steak	$38-$84	191

RICHMOND HEIGHTS

Map Page	Hotels	Designation	Member Savings	Page
73 p. 274	Homewood Suites by Hilton St. Louis Galleria	THREE DIAMOND	✔	241
74 p. 274	Residence Inn by Marriott-St. Louis Galleria	THREE DIAMOND	✔	241
75 p. 274	**Courtyard by Marriott St. Louis Brentwood**	THREE DIAMOND	✔	241

Map Page	Restaurants	Designation	Cuisine	Price Range	Page
90 p. 274	Blue Sky Tower Grill	APPROVED	American	$9-$12	241
91 p. 274	The Cheesecake Factory	THREE DIAMOND	International	$9-$30	241
92 p. 274	Maggiano's Little Italy	THREE DIAMOND	Italian	$13-$40	241
93 p. 274	P.F. Chang's China Bistro	THREE DIAMOND	Chinese	$10-$28	241

BRENTWOOD

Map Page	Hotels	Designation	Member Savings	Page
78 p. 274	Drury Inn & Suites Brentwood	THREE DIAMOND		181
79 p. 274	SpringHill Suites by Marriott Brentwood	THREE DIAMOND	✔	181

Map Page	Restaurants	Designation	Cuisine	Price Range	Page
96 p. 274	Mai Lee Restaurant	APPROVED	Asian	$5-$35	181
97 p. 274	Bonefish Grill	THREE DIAMOND	Seafood	$15-$32	181
98 p. 274	Houlihan's	THREE DIAMOND	American	$10-$25	181
99 p. 274	Frank Papa's Ristorante	APPROVED	Italian	$17-$40	181

KIRKWOOD

Map Page	Hotel	Designation	Member Savings	Page
82 p. 274	**Best Western Kirkwood Inn**	APPROVED	✔	233

Map Page	Restaurants	Designation	Cuisine	Price Range	Page
102 p. 274	Sunset 44	APPROVED	American	$11-$30	233
103 p. 274	Citizen Kane's Steak House	APPROVED	Steak	$30-$45	233

FENTON

Map Page	Hotels	Designation	Member Savings	Page
85 p. 274	Drury Inn & Suites-Fenton	THREE DIAMOND		190
86 p. 274	Pear Tree Inn by Drury-Fenton	APPROVED		190
87 p. 274	TownePlace Suites by Marriott	APPROVED	✔	190
88 p. 274	Holiday Inn Express Hotel & Suites	APPROVED		190

Map Page	Restaurant	Designation	Cuisine	Price Range	Page
106 p. 274	Poor Richard's	APPROVED	Wings Burgers	$6-$20	191

SUNSET HILLS

Map Page	Hotel	Designation	Member Savings	Page
91 p. 274	**Holiday Inn St. Louis SW-Route 66**	THREE DIAMOND	✔	301

Map Page	Restaurant	Designation	Cuisine	Price Range	Page
109 p. 274	Sesame Chinese Restaurant	APPROVED	Chinese	$8-$13	301

MEHLVILLE

Map Page	Hotels	Designation	Member Savings	Page
94 p. 274	Holiday Inn South County Center	THREE DIAMOND		237
95 p. 274	Hampton Inn & Suites by Hilton, St. Louis South I-55	THREE DIAMOND	✔	237
96 p. 274	Holiday Inn Express & Suites St. Louis South-I-55	THREE DIAMOND		237
97 p. 274	**Best Western St. Louis Inn**	APPROVED	✔	237

EDWARDSVILLE, IL

Map Page	Hotels	Designation	Member Savings	Page
100 p. 274	Holiday Inn Express & Suites Edwardsville	THREE DIAMOND		290
101 p. 274	**Country Hearth Inn & Suites**	APPROVED	✔	290
102 p. 274	TownePlace Suites by Marriott St. Louis Edwardsville, IL	THREE DIAMOND	✔	290
103 p. 274	Comfort Inn	THREE DIAMOND		290

Map Page	Restaurants	Designation	Cuisine	Price Range	Page
112 p. 274	Cleveland-Heath	THREE DIAMOND	American	$11-$28	290
113 p. 274	Peel Wood Fired Pizza	APPROVED	Pizza	$15	291

PONTOON BEACH, IL

Map Page	Hotels	Designation	Member Savings	Page
106 p. 274	Fairfield Inn & Suites by Marriott	THREE DIAMOND	✔	291
107 p. 274	**Best Western Plus Pontoon Beach**	THREE DIAMOND	✔	291

COLLINSVILLE, IL

Map Page	Hotels	Designation	Member Savings	Page
110 p. 274	Comfort Inn	THREE DIAMOND		290
111 p. 274	Drury Inn Collinsville-St. Louis	APPROVED		290
112 p. 274	Super 8-Collinsville	APPROVED		290

Map Page	Restaurant	Designation	Cuisine	Price Range	Page
(116) p. 274	Zapata's Mexican Restaurant & Cantina	◊◊ APPROVED	Mexican	$6-$15	290

FAIRVIEW HEIGHTS, IL

Map Page	Hotels	Designation		Member Savings	Page
(115) p. 274	Econo Lodge Inn & Suites	◊◊ APPROVED			291
(116) p. 274	Drury Inn & Suites-Fairview Heights	◊◊ THREE DIAMOND			291
(117) p. 274	Comfort Suites	◊◊ THREE DIAMOND			291
(118) p. 274	Hampton Inn by Hilton	◊◊ APPROVED		✔	291

Map Page	Restaurants	Designation	Cuisine	Price Range	Page
(119) p. 274	Lotawata Creek Southern Grill	◊◊ APPROVED	Regional American	$13-$27	291
(120) p. 274	Agostino's Italian Restaurant	◊◊ APPROVED	Italian	$9-$13	291
(121) p. 274	Lilly's Gyros	◊◊ APPROVED	Greek Sandwiches	$6-$10	291

O'FALLON, IL

Map Page	Hotels	Designation		Member Savings	Page
(121) p. 274	Baymont by Wyndham	◊◊ APPROVED			291
(122) p. 274	Candlewood Suites	◊◊ APPROVED			291
(123) p. 274	Extended Stay America-St. Louis-O'Fallon	◊◊ APPROVED			291
(124) p. 274	Hilton Garden Inn St. Louis Shiloh/O'Fallon	◊◊ THREE DIAMOND		✔	291
(125) p. 274	Drury Inn & Suites-O'Fallon	◊◊ THREE DIAMOND			291

Map Page	Restaurant	Designation	Cuisine	Price Range	Page
(124) p. 274	Mungo's Italian Eatery	◊◊ APPROVED	Italian	$11-$38	291

DOWNTOWN ST. LOUIS

- Restaurants p. 284
- Hotels & Restaurants map & index p. 269

COURTYARD BY MARRIOTT DOWNTOWN WEST
314/241-9111 (11)

◊◊ THREE DIAMOND
Hotel

COURTYARD **AAA Benefit:** Members save 5% or more!

Address: 2340 Market St 63103 **Location:** I-64/US 40 exit 39 westbound (Market St at 21st St), just n, then just w; exit 38A eastbound, just n on Jefferson Ave, then just e. **Facility:** 151 units. 4 stories, interior corridors. **Parking:** on-site (fee). **Pool:** heated indoor. **Activities:** exercise room. **Guest Services:** valet and coin laundry, boarding pass kiosk.

SAVE ECO ⊪ ⊻ CALL ♿ ⊇ ⊕ BIZ 🛜 ✕ ⊟ ⊡ /SOME UNITS ⊟

COURTYARD BY MARRIOTT ST. LOUIS DOWNTOWN CONVENTION CENTER
314/231-7560 (5)

◊◊ THREE DIAMOND SAVE Historic Hotel. **Address:** 827 Washington Ave 63101

AAA Benefit: Members save 5% or more!

DRURY INN & SUITES-ST. LOUIS-CONVENTION CENTER
314/231-8100 (4)

◊◊ THREE DIAMOND Hotel. **Address:** 711 N Broadway 63102

DRURY INN-ST. LOUIS/UNION STATION
314/231-3900 (16)

◊◊ THREE DIAMOND Hotel. **Address:** 201 S 20th St 63103

DRURY PLAZA HOTEL-ST. LOUIS AT THE ARCH
314/231-3003 (20)

◊◊ THREE DIAMOND Historic Hotel. **Address:** 2 S 4th St 63102

EMBASSY SUITES BY HILTON ST. LOUIS-DOWNTOWN
314/269-5900 (6)

◊◊ THREE DIAMOND
Historic Hotel

E **AAA Benefit:** Members save up to 15%!

Address: 610 N 7th St 63101 **Location:** Jct Washington Ave. Adjacent to America's Center Convention Complex. **Facility:** This 1920s downtown building was once a department store, and the spacious one-bedroom suites retain the high ceilings and tall windows of its original incarnation. 212 units. 2-5 stories, interior corridors. **Parking:** valet only. **Terms:** check-in 4 pm. **Amenities:** safes. **Pool:** heated indoor. **Activities:** hot tub, exercise room. **Guest Services:** valet and coin laundry. **Featured Amenity:** full hot breakfast.

SAVE ⊪ ⊻ ⊻ CALL ♿ ⊇ ⊕ BIZ SHS 🛜 ✕ ⊟ ⊡ ⊡

FOUR SEASONS HOTEL ST. LOUIS   314/881-5800 (1)

◊◊ FOUR DIAMOND
Hotel

Address: 999 N 2nd St 63102 **Location:** Jct Washington Ave, just n on 4th St, just e on Cole St, just e on Carr St, then just s. Connected through breezeway to Lumiere Place Casino. **Facility:** A spectacular view of the Gateway Arch serves as a backdrop for the 8th floor restaurant and public spaces at this property. Luxurious appointments can be found in both the guest rooms and baths. 200 units. 19 stories, interior corridors. **Parking:** on-site and valet. **Terms:** check-in 4 pm. **Amenities:** safes. **Dining:** Cinder House, see separate listing. **Pool:** heated indoor. **Activities:** hot tub, cabanas, health club, spa. **Guest Services:** valet laundry, area transportation.

SAVE ⊪ ⊻ ⊻ CALL ♿ ⊇ ⊕ BIZ HS 🛜 ⊡ ⊡ /SOME UNITS ⊟

(See map & index p. 269.)

HAMPTON INN BY HILTON ST. LOUIS-DOWNTOWN
314/621-7900 **8**

THREE DIAMOND **SAVE** Hotel. **Address:** 333 Washington Ave 63102

AAA Benefit: Members save up to 15%!

HILTON ST. LOUIS AT THE BALLPARK
314/421-1776 **18**

THREE DIAMOND
Hotel

AAA Benefit: Members save up to 15%!

Address: 1 S Broadway 63102 **Location:** Between Walnut and Market sts. **Facility:** 671 units, some two bedrooms. 22-25 stories, interior corridors. **Parking:** on-site (fee) and valet. **Terms:** check-in 4 pm. **Amenities:** safes. **Dining:** 3 restaurants, nightclub. **Pool:** heated indoor. **Activities:** sauna, hot tub, exercise room. **Guest Services:** valet laundry, boarding pass kiosk.

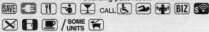

HILTON-ST. LOUIS DOWNTOWN AT THE ARCH
314/436-0002 **15**

THREE DIAMOND **SAVE** Historic Hotel. **Address:** 400 Olive St 63102

AAA Benefit: Members save up to 15%!

HOLIDAY INN ST. LOUIS-DOWNTOWN CONVENTION CENTER
314/421-4000 **2**

THREE DIAMOND Hotel. **Address:** 811 N 9th St 63101

THE HOTEL MAJESTIC ST. LOUIS
314/436-2355 **14**

fyi Historic Hotel. Under major renovation, call for details. **Last Designation:** Three Diamond. **Address:** 1019 Pine St 63101

HOTEL SAINT LOUIS, AUTOGRAPH COLLECTION
314/241-4300 **12**

FOUR DIAMOND
Boutique Contemporary Hotel

AUTOGRAPH COLLECTION' HOTELS **AAA Benefit:** Members save 5% or more!

Address: 705 Olive St 63101 **Location:** Jct N 7th St. **Facility:** This self-proclaimed "Hip-storic" hotel features an impressive two-story lobby with modern furnishings and thoughtfully crafted details including a recreation of the original stained glass roof. 140 units. 2-12 stories, interior corridors. **Parking:** on-site (fee) and valet. **Amenities:** safes. **Pool:** heated outdoor. **Activities:** exercise room, spa. **Guest Services:** valet laundry.

HYATT REGENCY ST. LOUIS AT THE ARCH
314/655-1234 **17**

THREE DIAMOND
Hotel

HYATT REGENCY' **AAA Benefit:** Members save up to 10%!

Address: 315 Chestnut St 63102 **Location:** Jct 4th St; across from Gateway Arch. **Facility:** 910 units. 18 stories, interior corridors. **Parking:** on-site (fee) and valet. **Terms:** check-in 4 pm. **Amenities:** safes. **Dining:** 2 restaurants, also, Ruth's Chris Steak House, see separate listing. **Activities:** exercise room. **Guest Services:** valet laundry, boarding pass kiosk.

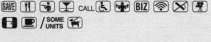

THE LAST HOTEL
314/390-2500 **3**

THREE DIAMOND Historic Boutique Hotel. **Address:** 1501 Washington Ave 63103

MAGNOLIA HOTEL ST. LOUIS, A TRIBUTE PORTFOLIO HOTEL
314/436-9000 **9**

FOUR DIAMOND
Historic Boutique Hotel

TRIBUTE PORTFOLIO **AAA Benefit:** Members save 5% or more!

Address: 421 N 8th St 63101 **Location:** Just s of convention center. **Facility:** This restored upscale boutique hotel boasts impressive architecture throughout the public areas. Many complimentary extras are offered, such as an evening reception with beer, wine and soft drinks. 182 units. 18 stories, interior corridors. **Parking:** valet only. **Terms:** check-in 4 pm. **Amenities:** safes. **Activities:** exercise room. **Guest Services:** valet laundry.

MARRIOTT ST. LOUIS GRAND
314/621-9600 **7**

THREE DIAMOND
Hotel

MARRIOTT **AAA Benefit:** Members save 5% or more!

Address: 800 Washington Ave 63101 **Location:** Jct N Broadway, just w; jct 8th St. Across from America's Center Convention Complex. **Facility:** 917 units. 21 stories, interior corridors. **Parking:** on-site (fee) and valet. **Terms:** check-in 4 pm. **Amenities:** safes. **Activities:** exercise room. **Guest Services:** valet laundry, boarding pass kiosk, rental car service.

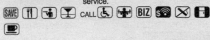

PEAR TREE INN UNION STATION
314/241-3200 **10**

THREE DIAMOND Hotel. **Address:** 2211 Market St 63103

(See map & index p. 269.)

RESIDENCE INN BY MARRIOTT ST. LOUIS DOWNTOWN
314/289-7500 **19**
▽ THREE DIAMOND [SAVE] Extended
Stay Hotel. **Address:** 525 S Jefferson
Ave 63103

AAA Benefit:
Members save 5%
or more!

**ST. LOUIS UNION STATION HOTEL, CURIO
COLLECTION BY HILTON**   314/231-1234 **13**
▽ FOUR DIAMOND

Classic Hotel

CURIO
A COLLECTION BY HILTON™

AAA Benefit:
Members save up
to 15%!

Address: 1820 Market St 63103 **Location:** I-64/US 40 exit 39 westbound (Market St at 21st St), just n, then just e; exit 38A eastbound, just n on Jefferson Ave, then 0.5 mi e. **Facility:** The hotel is located in a 100-year-old restored train station with a lobby that boasts a six-story, barrel-vaulted ceiling and beautiful architectural details. 567 units. 5-6 stories, interior corridors. **Parking:** on-site (fee) and valet. **Terms:** check-in 4 pm. **Amenities:** safes. **Dining:** Station Grille, see separate listing. **Pool:** heated outdoor. **Activities:** exercise room. **Guest Services:** valet laundry. *(See ad p. 283, p. 265.)*

[SAVE] [icons] CALL [icons] BIZ [icons]
[icons] / SOME UNITS [icon]

THE WESTIN ST. LOUIS   314/621-2000 **21**
▽ FOUR DIAMOND [SAVE] Historic
Hotel. **Address:** 811 Spruce St 63102

AAA Benefit:
Members save 5%
or more!

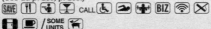

WHERE TO EAT

AL'S RESTAURANT   314/421-6399 **1**
▽ THREE DIAMOND Steak Seafood. Fine Dining. **Address:** 1200 N 1st St 63102

BAILEY'S RANGE   314/241-8121 **9**
▽ APPROVED Burgers. Casual Dining. **Address:** 920 Olive St 63101

BLT'S - BREAKFAST, LUNCH AND TACOS 314/925-8505 **5**
▽ APPROVED Breakfast. Quick Serve. **Address:** 626 N 6th St 63101

BOGART'S SMOKEHOUSE   314/621-3107 **22**
▽ APPROVED Barbecue. Quick Serve. **Address:** 1627 S 9th St 63104

BRIDGE TAP HOUSE & WINE BAR   314/241-8141 **8**
▽ APPROVED American. Gastropub. **Address:** 1004 Locust St 63101

BROADWAY OYSTER BAR   314/621-8811 **19**
▽ APPROVED Cajun. Casual Dining. **Address:** 736 S Broadway 63102

CALECO'S BAR AND GRILL   314/421-0708 **13**
▽ APPROVED American. Casual Dining. **Address:** 101 N Broadway 63102

CARMINE'S STEAK HOUSE   314/241-1631 **18**
▽ THREE DIAMOND Steak. Fine Dining. **Address:** 20 S 4th St 63102

CHARLIE GITTO'S DOWNTOWN   314/436-2828 **11**
▽ APPROVED Italian. Casual Dining. **Address:** 207 N 6th St 63101

CHAVA'S MEXICAN RESTAURANT   314/241-5503 **24**
▽ APPROVED Mexican. Casual Dining. **Address:** 925 Geyer Ave 63104

CINDER HOUSE   314/881-5759 **2**
▽ THREE DIAMOND Brazilian Small Plates. Fine Dining. **Address:** 999 N 2nd St 63102

ELEVEN ELEVEN MISSISSIPPI   314/241-9999 **20**
▽ APPROVED New American. Casual Dining. **Address:** 1111 Mississippi Ave 63104

HARD ROCK CAFE   314/621-7625 **14**
▽ APPROVED [SAVE] American. Casual Dining. **Address:** 1820 Market St, Suite 450 63103

HODAK'S RESTAURANT & BAR   314/776-7292 **25**
▽ APPROVED American. Casual Dining. **Address:** 2100 Gravois Ave 63104

IMO'S PIZZA   314/641-8899 **16**
▽ APPROVED Pizza. Casual Dining. **Address:** 1 S Broadway St 63102

LOMBARDO'S TRATTORIA   314/621-0666 **12**
▽ THREE DIAMOND Italian. Casual Dining. **Address:** 201 S 20th St 63103

MANGO   314/621-6001 **4**
▽ APPROVED Peruvian Fusion. Casual Dining. **Address:** 1001 Washington Ave 63101

POLITE SOCIETY   314/325-2553 **21**
▽ THREE DIAMOND New American. Casual Dining. **Address:** 1923 Park Ave 63104

ROOSTER   314/241-8118 **7**
▽ APPROVED Breakfast. Casual Dining. **Address:** 1104 Locust St 63101

RUTH'S CHRIS STEAK HOUSE   314/259-3200 **15**
▽ THREE DIAMOND Steak. Fine Dining. **Address:** 315 Chestnut St 63102

THE SCHLAFLY TAP ROOM   314/241-2337 **3**
▽ APPROVED American. Gastropub. **Address:** 2100 Locust St 63103

STATION GRILLE   314/802-3460 **10**
▽ THREE DIAMOND American. Fine Dining. **Address:** 1820 Market St 63103

SUGARFIRE SMOKE HOUSE   314/394-1720 **6**
▽ APPROVED Barbecue. Quick Serve. **Address:** 605 Washington Ave 63101

TONY'S   314/231-7007 **17**
▽ FOUR DIAMOND Italian. Fine Dining. **Address:** 410 Market St 63102

TWISTED RANCH   314/833-3450 **23**
▽ APPROVED American. Casual Dining. **Address:** 1731 S 7th St 63104

ST. LOUIS

- Restaurants p. 287
- Hotels & Restaurants map & index p. 274

THE CHESHIRE

314/647-7300 **5**

THREE DIAMOND

Historic Boutique Hotel

Address: 6300 Clayton Rd 63117 **Location:** I-64/US 40 exit 33C (McCausland Ave/Skinker Blvd), just n on Skinker Blvd, then just w. **Facility:** A literary theme is carried throughout this quaint, Tudor-style hotel with rooms dedicated to various authors. The lobby and Fox and Hound Pub are impressive with their old world charm. 108 units. 4 stories, interior corridors. **Parking:** on-site (fee) and valet. **Dining:** 2 restaurants, also, Boundary, see separate listing. **Pool:** outdoor. **Activities:** bicycles, exercise room. **Guest Services:** valet laundry.

Featured Amenity: continental breakfast.

SAVE 🍴 🕬 🍸 CALL ♿ 🌊 🛟 BIZ 🛜 ✕
🖥 / SOME UNITS 🐾 🔋 🖼

DRURY INN & SUITES NEAR FOREST PARK

314/646-0770 **10**

THREE DIAMOND Hotel. **Address:** 2111 Sulphur Ave 63139

HAMPTON INN & SUITES-ST. LOUIS AT FOREST PARK

314/655 3900 **7**

THREE DIAMOND SAVE Hotel. **Address:** 5650 Oakland Ave 63110

AAA Benefit: Members save up to 15%!

HOLIDAY INN FOREST PARK

314/645-0700 **9**

THREE DIAMOND

Hotel

Address: 5915 Wilson Ave 63110 **Location:** I-44 exit 286, just s on Hampton Ave. **Facility:** 119 units. 7 stories, interior corridors. **Pool:** outdoor. **Activities:** exercise room. **Guest Services:** valet and coin laundry.

SAVE 🍴 🕬 🍸 CALL ♿ 🌊
🛟 BIZ 🛜 ✕ 🖥
/ SOME UNITS 🐾 🔋 🖼

HOME2 SUITES BY HILTON ST. LOUIS/FOREST PARK

314/531-4446 **6**

THREE DIAMOND SAVE Extended Stay Hotel. **Address:** 920 S Taylor Ave 63110

AAA Benefit: Members save up to 15%!

HOTEL IGNACIO

314/977-4411 **4**

THREE DIAMOND

Historic Boutique Hotel

Address: 3411 Olive St 63103 **Location:** I-64/US 40 exit 38A westbound, just w on Forest Park Ave, just n on Grand Blvd, then just e on Lindell Blvd; exit 37B eastbound, 0.4 mi n on Grand Blvd, then just e on Lindell Blvd. **Facility:** This unique hotel houses an impressive artwork collection from the nearby university and does an excellent job of mixing art, technology and classic touches for an all-around great guest experience. 51 units. 5 stories, interior corridors. **Parking:** on-site (fee). **Terms:** check-in 4 pm. **Amenities:** safes. **Dining:** Triumph Grill, see separate listing. **Activities:** bicycles, exercise room. **Guest Services:** valet laundry.

SAVE 🍴 🕬 🍸 CALL ♿ 🛟 BIZ HS 🛜 ✕
🔋 / SOME UNITS 🐾 🖥

(See map & index p. 274.)

MOONRISE HOTEL
314/721-1111 **1**

FOUR DIAMOND

Boutique Hotel

Address: 6177 Delmar Blvd 63112 **Location:** I-64/US 40 exit 33C (McCausland Ave/Skinker Blvd), 1.7 mi n on Skinker Blvd, then just e; in The Loop. **Facility:** This intimate and attractive hotel, located in the heart of a funky shopping and dining district, features a lunar theme that starts in the lobby with upscale artwork and space-themed collectibles. 125 units. 8 stories, interior corridors. **Parking:** on-site and valet. **Amenities:** safes. **Dining:** Eclipse Restaurant at the Moonrise Hotel, see separate listing. **Activities:** exercise room. **Guest Services:** valet laundry. *(See ad this page.)*

SAVE ⊕ ¶¶ 🍴 🍷 CALL ♿ 🏃 BIZ 🛜 ✕ 🎭 📶 / SOME UNITS 🐾

THE PARKWAY HOTEL
314/256-7777 **3**

THREE DIAMOND

Hotel

Address: 4550 Forest Park Ave 63108 **Location:** I-64/US 40 exit 36A (Kingshighway Blvd), 0.6 mi n, then just e. Adjacent to Barnes-Jewish Hospital. **Facility:** 217 units. 8 stories, interior corridors. **Parking:** on-site (fee). **Terms:** check-in 4 pm. **Activities:** exercise room. **Guest Services:** valet and coin laundry, area transportation. **Featured Amenity:** breakfast buffet.

SAVE ¶¶ 🍷 CALL ♿ 🏃 BIZ HS 🛜 ✕ 🎭 📶 📶

RED ROOF PLUS+ ST. LOUIS-FOREST PARK/HAMPTON AVE.
314/645-0101 **8**

APPROVED

Hotel

Address: 5823 Wilson Ave 63110 **Location:** I-44 exit 286, 0.3 mi se. **Facility:** 110 units. 3 stories (no elevator), exterior corridors. **Amenities:** safes.

SAVE 📶 BIZ 🛜 ✕ 📶 / SOME UNITS 🐾 🎭 📶

RIVER CITY CASINO & HOTEL
314/388-7777 **11**

FOUR DIAMOND

Hotel

Address: 777 River City Casino Blvd 63125 **Location:** I-55 exit 202A, 1.6 mi s. **Facility:** Stay and play at this luxurious casino hotel where you can gamble, dine and get a peaceful night's sleep in a plush bed. 200 units. 7 stories, interior corridors. **Parking:** on-site and valet. **Terms:** check-in 4 pm. **Amenities:** safes. **Dining:** 4 restaurants, also, 1904 Steakhouse, The Great Food Exposition, see separate listings. **Activities:** exercise room. **Guest Services:** valet laundry.

SAVE 🎰 ¶¶ 🍴 🍷 CALL ♿ 🏃 BIZ 🛜 🎥 📶 📶

▼ *See AAA listing this page* ▼

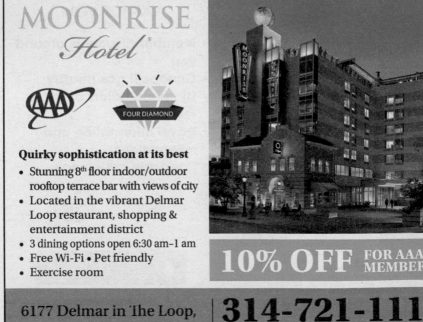

(See map & index p. 274.)

ROYAL SONESTA CHASE PARK PLAZA ST. LOUIS
314/633-3000 **2**

FOUR DIAMOND
Historic Hotel

Address: 212 N Kingshighway Blvd 63108 **Location:** I-64/US 40 exit 36A (Kingshighway Blvd), 0.8 mi n. **Facility:** The legendary, popular hotel offers a contemporary blend of charm, sophistication, and stately grandeur. All rooms are classically styled with luxurious bedding and large desks. 398 units, some two bedrooms and kitchens. 8-11 stories, interior corridors. **Parking:** on-site (fee) and valet. **Terms:** check-in 4 pm. **Amenities:** safes. **Dining:** 2 restaurants, also, The Tenderloin Room, see separate listing **Pool:** heated outdoor. **Activities:** health club. **Guest Services:** complimentary and valet laundry.

WHERE TO EAT

1904 STEAKHOUSE 314/388-7630 **39**
THREE DIAMOND Steak. Casual Dining. **Address:** 777 River City Casino Blvd 63125

ADRIANA'S ON THE HILL 314/773-3833 **20**
APPROVED Italian Sandwiches Pizza. Quick Serve. **Address:** 5101 Shaw Ave 63110

BAR ITALIA RISTORANTE 314/361-7010 **6**
APPROVED Italian. Casual Dining. **Address:** 13 Maryland Plaza 63108

BARTOLINO'S OSTERIA 314/644-2266 **23**
APPROVED Italian. Casual Dining. **Address:** 2103 Sulphur Ave 63139

BENTON PARK CAFE & COFFEE BAR 314/771-7200 **35**
APPROVED Breakfast Sandwiches. Casual Dining. **Address:** 2901 Salena St 63118

BOATHOUSE FOREST PARK 314/367-2224 **10**
APPROVED American. Casual Dining. **Address:** 6101 Government Dr 63110

BOUNDARY 314/932-7818 **15**
THREE DIAMOND American. Casual Dining. **Address:** 7036 Clayton Ave 63117

BRASSERIE BY NICHE 314/454-0600 **9**
THREE DIAMOND French. Casual Dining. **Address:** 4580 Laclede Ave 63108

BRAZIE'S RISTORANTE 314/481-5464 **29**
THREE DIAMOND Southern Italian. Casual Dining. **Address:** 3073 Watson Rd 63139

CANTINA LAREDO 314/725-2447
APPROVED Mexican. Casual Dining. **Address:** 7710 Forsyth Ave 63105

CHARLIE GITTO'S ON THE HILL 314/772-8898 **21**
THREE DIAMOND Italian. Fine Dining. **Address:** 5226 Shaw Ave 63110

CROWN CANDY KITCHEN 314/621-9650 **1**
APPROVED American. Casual Dining. **Address:** 1401 St. Louis Ave 63106

CUNETTO HOUSE OF PASTA 314/781-1135 **28**

APPROVED
Italian
Casual Dining
$8-$25

AAA Inspector Notes: Since 1972 this casual, family-run eatery has served a lengthy list of Italian favorites in generous portions. The menu includes pasta, chicken, veal, seafood and beef selections. Reservations are not accepted for dinner, and it's not unusual to have quite a wait at peak hours. **Features:** full bar. **Address:** 5453 Magnolia Ave 63139 **Location:** I-44 exit 286, 0.7 mi s on Hampton Ave, 0.4 mi e on Columbia Ave, just s on Sublette Ave, then just e.

DOMINIC'S 314/771-1632 **26**
THREE DIAMOND Italian. Fine Dining. **Address:** 5101 Wilson Ave 63110

DRESSEL'S PUBLIC HOUSE 314/361-1060 **4**
APPROVED English. Gastropub. **Address:** 419 N Euclid Ave 63108

THE DRUNKEN FISH SUSHI BAR & LOUNGE
314/367-4222 **7**
APPROVED Asian Sushi. Casual Dining. **Address:** 1 Maryland Plaza Dr 63108

ECLIPSE RESTAURANT AT THE MOONRISE HOTEL
314/726-2222 **3**
APPROVED New American. Casual Dining. **Address:** 6177 Delmar Blvd 63112 *(See ad p. 286.)*

ELAIA 314/932-1088 **18**
FOUR DIAMOND New Mediterranean. Fine Dining. **Address:** 1634 Tower Grove Ave 63101

FARMHAUS 314/647-3800 **33**
THREE DIAMOND American. Casual Dining. **Address:** 3257 Ivanhoe Ave 63139

THE FOUNTAIN ON LOCUST 314/535-7800 **12**
APPROVED Sandwiches Soup. Casual Dining. **Address:** 3037 Locust St 63103

FRAZER'S 314/773-8646 **36**
APPROVED American. Casual Dining. **Address:** 1811 Pestalozzi St 63118

GAMLIN WHISKEY HOUSE 314/875-9500 **8**
APPROVED American. Gastropub. **Address:** 236 N Euclid Ave 63108

THE GREAT FOOD EXPOSITION 314/388-7673 **40**
APPROVED American. Buffet Style. **Address:** 777 River City Blvd 63125

IMO'S PIZZA 314/644-5480 **16**
APPROVED Italian Pizza. Casual Dining. **Address:** 1000 Hampton Ave 63139

J. DEVOTI TRATTORIA 314/773-5553 **24**
THREE DIAMOND New American. Fine Dining. **Address:** 5100 Daggett Ave 63110

KING & I RESTAURANT 314/771-1777 **34**
APPROVED Thai. Casual Dining. **Address:** 3157 S Grand Blvd 63118

MANGIA ITALIANO 314/664-8585 **32**
APPROVED Italian. Casual Dining. **Address:** 3145 S Grand Blvd 63118

MISSION TACO JOINT 314/932-5430 **2**
APPROVED Mexican. Casual Dining. **Address:** 6235 Delmar Blvd 63130

(See map & index p. 274.)

NIXTA   314/899-9000   17
★★★ THREE DIAMOND New Mexican. Casual Dining. **Address:** 1621 Tower Grove Ave 63110

O'CONNELL'S PUB   314/773-6600   22
★★★ APPROVED American. Casual Dining. **Address:** 4652 Shaw Ave 63110

OLIO   314/932-1088   19
★★★ APPROVED Mediterranean Small Plates. Casual Dining. **Address:** 1634 Tower Grove Ave 63110

PAPPY'S SMOKEHOUSE   314/535-4340   13
★★★ APPROVED Barbecue. Quick Serve. **Address:** 3106 Olive St 63103

PHO GRAND VIETNAMESE RESTAURANT
314/664-7435   37
★★★ APPROVED Vietnamese. Casual Dining. **Address:** 3195 S Grand Blvd 63118

SAVAGE RESTAURANT   314/354-8488   27
★★★★ FOUR DIAMOND New American. Fine Dining. **Address:** 2655 Ann Ave 63104

THE SHAVED DUCK   314/776-1407   31
★★★ APPROVED Barbecue. Casual Dining. **Address:** 2900 Virginia Ave 63118

SIDNEY STREET CAFE   314/771-5777   30
★★★★ FOUR DIAMOND New American. Fine Dining. **Address:** 2000 Sidney St 63104

THE TENDERLOIN ROOM   314/361-0900   5
★★★ THREE DIAMOND Steak. Fine Dining. **Address:** 232 N Kingshighway Blvd 63108

TRATTORIA MARCELLA   314/352-7706   38
★★★ THREE DIAMOND Italian. Casual Dining. **Address:** 3600 Watson Rd 63109

TRIUMPH GRILL   314/446-1801   11
★★★ APPROVED American. Casual Dining. **Address:** 3419 Olive St 63103

VICIA   314/553-9239   14
★★★★ FOUR DIAMOND New American. Fine Dining. **Address:** 4260 Forest Park Ave 63108

ZIA'S   314/776-0020   25
★★★ APPROVED
**Italian
Casual Dining
$9-$29**
AAA Inspector Notes: This busy corner trattoria has served hearty classic Italian fare for more than 30 years and offers friendly service in a cozy setting. Pasta with house-made sauces, chicken, beef, veal and seafood compose the menu. Favorites include chicken spiedini, charbroiled with a lemon butter sauce and linguine carbonara. Toasted ravioli, a St. Louis staple, is a popular start to any meal. **Features:** full bar, patio dining. **Address:** 5256 Wilson Ave 63110 **Location:** I-44 exit 287 (Kingshighway Blvd), just s, 0.4 mi w on Shaw Ave, then just s on Edwards St. **Parking:** street only. L D

Nearby Illinois

ALTON pop. 27,865, elev. 450'
• Part of St. Louis area — see map p. 248

Just north of the confluence of the Mississippi and Missouri rivers, Alton was founded in the early 19th century. Col. Rufus Easton obtained the land and named the town for his son. The Eagle Packet line of boats, once built in Alton, contributed to local river traffic on the Mississippi. Riverfront Park offers a vantage point for viewing the river.

The issue of slavery found volatile expression in Alton when abolitionist editor Elijah Lovejoy was killed by a proslavery mob in 1837. The Alton Cemetery on Monument Avenue contains Lovejoy's tomb and a monument in his honor. In 1858 the last Lincoln-Douglas debate took place in town. The city's history and river heritage are among themes addressed at the Alton Museum of History and Art, 2809 College Ave.; phone (618) 462-2763.

Perhaps Alton's most renowned native son was Robert Pershing Wadlow; at 8 feet, 11.1 inches he remains the world's tallest known person. A life-size statue of Wadlow can be seen on the campus of Southern Illinois University School of Dental Medicine across the street from the Alton Museum of History and Art. Near the intersection of Broadway and William are the remnants of Alton Prison, where more than 1,300 Confederate soldiers died of various diseases. A portion of the cellblock wall remains.

Alton's Victorian, Federal and Greek Revival 19th-century houses draw attention, particularly in autumn when the trees cloaking the surrounding bluffs are ablaze with fall foliage colors. The Great River Road, which runs north along the Mississippi River, has a bicycle path offering views of the river and bluffs.

Alton Regional Convention & Visitors Bureau: 200 Piasa St., Alton, IL 62002. **Phone:** (618) 465-6676 or (800) 258-6645.

Self-guiding tours: Brochures and information about walking and driving tours can be obtained at the convention and visitors bureau.

Shopping: Alton's historic downtown antique district, along Broadway between Langdon and Alton streets, contains more than 20 shops housed in buildings dating from the 1800s.

For complete hotel, dining and attraction listings: AAA.com/travelguides

BEST WESTERN PLUS PARKWAY HOTEL   618/433-9900

THREE DIAMOND

Hotel

Best Western PLUS

AAA Benefit: Members save up to 15% and earn bonus points!

Address: 1900 Homer M Adams Pkwy 62002 **Location:** On SR 111, 1.8 mi e of jct US 67. **Facility:** 72 units. 2 stories, interior corridors. **Parking:** winter plug-ins. **Terms:** check-in 4 pm. **Pool:** outdoor. **Activities:** exercise room. **Guest Services:** coin laundry. **Featured Amenity:** full hot breakfast.

BEST WESTERN PREMIER ALTON-ST LOUIS AREA HOTEL   618/462-1220

THREE DIAMOND

Hotel

PREMIER BEST WESTERN

AAA Benefit: Members save up to 15% and earn bonus points!

Address: 3559 College Ave 62002 **Location:** Jct SR 3, just w on SR 140. **Facility:** 135 units. 4 stories, interior corridors. **Amenities:** safes. **Pool:** heated indoor. **Activities:** hot tub, exercise room, in-room exercise equipment. **Guest Services:** complimentary and valet laundry, area transportation. **Featured Amenity:** breakfast buffet.

COMFORT INN   618/465-9999

THREE DIAMOND Hotel. **Address:** 11 Crossroads Ct 62002

HAMPTON INN & SUITES   618/433-8999

THREE DIAMOND [SAVE] Hotel. **Address:** 1904 Homer Adams Pkwy 62002

AAA Benefit: Members save up to 15%!

SUPER 8   618/465-8885

APPROVED Hotel. **Address:** 1800 Homer Adams Pkwy 62002

WHERE TO EAT

BLUFF CITY GRILL RESTAURANT & BAR   618/433-8288

APPROVED American. Casual Dining. **Address:** 424 E Broadway 62002

THE BROWN BAG BISTRO   618/433-9933

APPROVED Sandwiches Soup. Quick Serve. **Address:** 318 E Broadway St 62002

CASTELLI'S RESTAURANT AT 255   618/462-4620

APPROVED Italian. Casual Dining. **Address:** 3400 Fosterburg Rd 62002

TONY'S RESTAURANT & THIRD ST. CAFE   618/462-8384

APPROVED Italian. Casual Dining. **Address:** 312 Piasa St 62002

BELLEVILLE pop. 44,478, elev. 500'
Part of St. Louis area — see map p. 248

Founded in 1814, Belleville was named by its early French settlers. The discovery of coal in 1828 attracted many German miners. The town retains much of the Teutonic influence in language, song, festivals and architecture. Manufacturers produce a variety of goods and Scott Air Force Base is nearby.

The Emma Kunz House, 602 Fulton St., is an 1830 German street house furnished in period. The house is open for tours by appointment; phone (618) 234-0600.

Greater Belleville Chamber of Commerce: 216 E. A St., Belleville, IL 62220. **Phone:** (618) 233-2015 or (800) 677-9255.

Self-guiding tours: Brochures and walking tour maps of the historic district are available from the chamber.

WILLIAM & FLORENCE SCHMIDT ART CENTER is on Southwestern Illinois College's Belleville campus at 2500 Carlyle Ave. The center houses changing exhibitions of photographs, paintings and sculptures by regional, national and international artists as well as samplings from its approximately 900-piece permanent collection. Outdoors, visitors will find several sculptures in a variety of materials strategically placed within the immaculately landscaped gardens, which feature colorful flower beds, container gardens and rock beds.

Educational programs are offered. **Time:** Allow 1 hour minimum. **Hours:** Tues.-Fri. 10-4, Sat. noon-4. Closed college holidays and between exhibitions. **Cost:** Free. **Phone:** (618) 222-5278.

COLLINSVILLE pop. 25,579, elev. 561'
- **Hotels p. 290 • Restaurants p. 290**
- **Hotels & Restaurants map & index p. 274**
- **Part of St. Louis area — see map p. 248**

Horseradishes, log cabins and coal all are a part of Collinsville's heritage, which began when the town's first inhabitant built a log cabin overlooking the Mississippi basin in 1810. The city's name changed from Downing Station to Collinsville in 1825, and it soon became a bustling coal town. Today the area around Collinsville produces most of the world's supply of horseradishes.

CAHOKIA MOUNDS STATE HISTORIC SITE is off I-255 exit 24 (Collinsville Rd.), then w. 1.5 mi. This 2,200-acre site preserves 70 Native American mounds. Monks Mound, the site's centerpiece, covers more than 14 acres at its base and is 100 feet tall. Evidence of a once-flourishing Mississippian civilization—the center of the Mississippian culture, distinguished by complex social, ritual and political activity—spans the years A.D. 900-1400. At its peak the site is said to have supported an estimated 10,000-20,000 inhabitants.

An interpretive center houses exhibits about the people who once lived in the region; a 15-minute film documenting the history of Cahokia; and a life-size, re-created Native American village. One-hour guided tours are available seasonally, as are self-guiding iPod and audio tours, a 17-minute video tour of the grounds

(See map & index p. 274.)

for the disabled and hiking trails. There are reconstructions of the woodhenge sun calendar and the stockade wall.

Hours: Grounds daily 8 a.m.-dusk. Interpretive center Wed.-Sun. 9-5. Guided tours are given Wed.-Sat. at 10:30 and 2:30, Sun. at 12:30 and 2:30, June-Aug.; Sat.-Sun. at 2:30, Apr.-May and Sept.-Oct. Closed major holidays. Phone ahead to confirm schedule and holiday hours. **Cost:** Donations. **Phone:** (618) 346-5160. GT 7&

COMFORT INN   618/346-4900 110
▼THREE DIAMOND Hotel. **Address:** 8 Commerce Dr 62234

DRURY INN COLLINSVILLE-ST. LOUIS   618/345-7700 111
▼ APPROVED Hotel. **Address:** 602 N Bluff Rd 62234

SUPER 8-COLLINSVILLE   618/345-8008 112
▼ APPROVED Hotel. **Address:** 2 Gateway Dr 62234

WHERE TO EAT

BANDANA'S BAR-B-Q   618/344-4476
▼ APPROVED Barbecue. Casual Dining. **Address:** 4 Commerce Dr 62234

ZAPATA'S MEXICAN RESTAURANT & CANTINA
                                   618/343-1337 116
▼ APPROVED Mexican. Casual Dining. **Address:** 8 Eastport Plaza Dr 62234

EAST ALTON pop. 6,301, elev. 436'
• Part of St. Louis area — see map p. 248

NATIONAL GREAT RIVERS MUSEUM is at #2 Lock and Dam Way. Next to the Mississippi River, the museum houses interactive exhibits that describe the river's natural history and its commercial importance. Visitors can view a room-size model of river bluffs that highlights area wildlife and an aquarium that is home to Mississippi River fish species.

The Pilot House simulator enables visitors to experience what it is like to steer barges through a lock. **Time:** Allow 1 hour minimum. **Hours:** Daily 9-5. Closed Jan. 1, Thanksgiving, Christmas Eve, Christmas and Dec. 31. **Cost:** Free. **Phone:** (618) 462-6979 or (877) 462-6979. 7&

Melvin Price Locks and Dam is at #1 Lock and Dam Way, at the National Great Rivers Museum. Part of the Upper Mississippi's flood control and navigation system, the Melvin Price Locks and Dam features two locks through which billions of dollars of goods pass each year.

Guided tours of the locks and dam depart from the adjacent museum, where visitors also can see a video about the project. Nearby Riverlands Migratory Bird Sanctuary has bird-watching platforms. Bald eagles inhabit the area and can often be seen in flight or resting in the treetops from various places along the levee. **Hours:** Tours are given daily (weather permitting) at 10, 1 and 3. Closed Jan. 1,

Thanksgiving, Christmas Eve, Christmas and Dec. 31. **Cost:** Free. **Phone:** (618) 462-6979 or (877) 462-6979. GT

EDWARDSVILLE pop. 24,293, elev. 433'
• Hotels & Restaurants map & index p. 274
• Part of St. Louis area — see map p. 248

Edwardsville has four historic areas that provide a glimpse of its past: the St. Louis Street Historic District, the LeClaire Historic District, the Brick Street Landmark District and the Downtown Historic District. Southern Illinois University at Edwardsville encompasses a picturesque 2,660-acre campus.

Edwardsville/Glen Carbon Chamber of Commerce: 1 N. Research Dr., Edwardsville, IL 62025. **Phone:** (618) 656-7600.

MADISON COUNTY HISTORICAL MUSEUM AND ARCHIVAL LIBRARY is at 715 N. Main St. Housed in a restored Federal-style residence built in 1836, the museum contains period furnishings, Native American and pioneer artifacts, antiques and a variety of changing seasonal exhibits that include quilts, needlework and historic costumes. A history and genealogy reference library is adjacent to the museum. **Note:** The museum will be undergoing renovations until early 2018; phone ahead for updates. **Time:** Allow 1 hour minimum. **Hours:** Wed.-Fri. 9-4, Sun. 1-4. **Cost:** Donations. **Phone:** (618) 656-7562 for the museum, or (618) 656-7569 for the library.

COMFORT INN   618/656-4900 103
▼THREE DIAMOND Hotel. **Address:** 3080 S SR 157 62025

COUNTRY HEARTH INN & SUITES 618/656-7829 101
▼ APPROVED

Hotel

Address: 1013 Plummer Dr 62025 **Location:** I-270 exit 9, 3 mi n on SR 157. **Facility:** 39 units. 3 stories, interior corridors. **Activities:** exercise room. **Guest Services:** coin laundry. **Featured Amenity:** breakfast buffet.

SAVE ⊪ CALL ✆ ♨ BIZ 🛜 ✕ 🛗 🖥 🖨

HOLIDAY INN EXPRESS & SUITES EDWARDSVILLE
                                   618/692-7255 100
▼THREE DIAMOND Hotel. **Address:** 1000 Plummer Dr 62025

TOWNEPLACE SUITES BY MARRIOTT ST. LOUIS EDWARDSVILLE, IL   618/655-3001 102
▼THREE DIAMOND SAVE Extended Stay Hotel. **Address:** 6101 Center Grove Rd 62025

AAA Benefit: Members save 5% or more!

WHERE TO EAT

CLEVELAND-HEATH   618/307-4830 112
▼THREE DIAMOND American. Casual Dining. **Address:** 106 Main St 62025

(See map & index p. 274.)

PEEL WOOD FIRED PIZZA 618/659-8561 (113)
⬥ APPROVED Pizza. Casual Dining. **Address:** 921 S Arbor Vitae 62025

FAIRVIEW HEIGHTS pop. 17,078
- **Hotels & Restaurants map & index p. 274**
- **Part of St. Louis area — see map p. 248**

COMFORT SUITES 618/394-0202 (117)
⬥ THREE DIAMOND Hotel. **Address:** 137 Ludwig Dr 62208

DRURY INN & SUITES-FAIRVIEW HEIGHTS
618/398-8530 (116)
⬥ THREE DIAMOND Hotel. **Address:** 12 Ludwig Dr 62208

ECONO LODGE INN & SUITES 618/624-3636 (115)
⬥ APPROVED Hotel. **Address:** 305 Salem Pl 62208

HAMPTON INN BY HILTON 618/397-9705 (118)
⬥ APPROVED (SAVE) Hotel. **Address:** 150 Ludwig Dr 62208

AAA Benefit: Members save up to 15%!

WHERE TO EAT

AGOSTINO'S ITALIAN RESTAURANT 618/394-1800 (120)
⬥ APPROVED Italian. Casual Dining. **Address:** 130 Ludwig Dr 62208

LILLY'S GYROS 618/398-5455 (121)
⬥ APPROVED Greek Sandwiches. Quick Serve. **Address:** 10600 Lincoln Tr 62208

LOTAWATA CREEK SOUTHERN GRILL 618/628-7373 (119)
⬥ APPROVED Regional American. Casual Dining. **Address:** 311 Salem Pl 62208

O'FALLON pop. 28,281
- **Hotels & Restaurants map & index p. 274**
- **Part of St. Louis area — see map p. 248**

BAYMONT BY WYNDHAM 618/628-9700 (121)
⬥ APPROVED Hotel. **Address:** 1320 Park Plaza Dr 62269

CANDLEWOOD SUITES 618/622-9555 (122)
⬥ APPROVED Extended Stay Hotel. **Address:** 1332 Park Plaza Dr 62269

DRURY INN & SUITES-O'FALLON 618/624-2211 (125)
⬥ THREE DIAMOND Hotel. **Address:** 1118 Central Park Dr 62269

EXTENDED STAY AMERICA-ST. LOUIS-O'FALLON
618/624-1757 (123)
⬥ APPROVED Extended Stay Hotel. **Address:** 154 Regency Park Dr 62269

HILTON GARDEN INN ST. LOUIS SHILOH/O'FALLON
618/624-4499 (124)
⬥ THREE DIAMOND (SAVE) Hotel. **Address:** 360 Regency Park Dr 62269

AAA Benefit: Members save up to 15%!

SUPER 8 O'FALLON/ SCOTT AIR FORCE BASE
618/624-6060
⬥ APPROVED
Hotel

Address: 1100 Eastgate Dr 62269 **Location:** I-64 exit 19B (SR 158), 0.5 mi n, then just sw. **Facility:** 96 units. 2 stories (no elevator), interior corridors. **Amenities:** safes. **Pool:** outdoor. **Activities:** exercise room. **Guest Services:** coin laundry. **Featured Amenity:** continental breakfast.

WHERE TO EAT

MUNGO'S ITALIAN EATERY 618/632-6864 (124)
⬥ APPROVED Italian. Casual Dining. **Address:** 1334 Central Park Dr 62269

PEEL WOOD FIRED PIZZA 618/726-2244
⬥ APPROVED Pizza. Casual Dining. **Address:** 104 S Cherry St 62269

THIP'S THAI CUISINE 618/632-8500
⬥ APPROVED Thai. Casual Dining. **Address:** 701 W US Hwy 50 62269

PONTOON BEACH pop. 5,836
- **Hotels & Restaurants map & index p. 274**
- **Part of St. Louis area — see map p. 248**

BEST WESTERN PLUS PONTOON BEACH
618/512-1314 (107)
⬥ THREE DIAMOND
Hotel
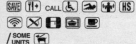
AAA Benefit: Members save up to 15% and earn bonus points!

Address: 4 Regency Pkwy 62040 **Location:** I-270 exit 6A (SR 11), just s. **Facility:** 66 units. 1-3 stories, interior corridors. **Terms:** check-in 4 pm. **Pool:** heated indoor. **Activities:** exercise room. **Guest Services:** coin laundry.

FAIRFIELD INN & SUITES BY MARRIOTT
618/709-7933 (106)
⬥ THREE DIAMOND (SAVE) Hotel. **Address:** 5224 Commerce Pkwy 62040

AAA Benefit: Members save 5% or more!

This ends the St. Louis section and resumes the alphabetical city listings for Missouri.

ST. PETERS pop. 52,575
- **Restaurants p. 292**
- **Hotels & Restaurants map & index p. 271**
- **Part of St. Louis area — see map p. 248**

COURTYARD BY MARRIOTT ST. PETERS 636/477-6900 (2)
⬥ THREE DIAMOND (SAVE) Hotel. **Address:** 4341 Veterans Memorial Pkwy 63376

AAA Benefit: Members save 5% or more!

(See map & index p. 271.)

DRURY INN & SUITES ST. PETERS   636/397-9700   **1**
THREE DIAMOND Hotel. **Address:** 170 Mid Rivers Mall Cir 63376

WHERE TO EAT

BANDANA'S BAR-B-Q   636/441-4483
APPROVED Barbecue. Casual Dining. **Address:** 4155 Veterans Memorial Pkwy 63376

COPPER CHIMNEY   636/278-1833   **1**
APPROVED Indian. Casual Dining. **Address:** 200 Mid Rivers Center 63376

ST. ROBERT (C-4) pop. 4,340, elev. 1,040'

Nestled at the foothills of the Ozarks in south-central Missouri, St. Robert is a gateway community to nearby Fort Leonard Wood, a U.S. Army installation that trains up to 90,000 military and civilians each year. It offers easy access to nearby recreational areas offering fishing, spelunking, canoeing and river floating. Historic Route 66 runs through the center of town.

Pulaski County Tourism Bureau and Visitor Center: 137 St. Robert Blvd., Suite A, St. Robert, MO 65584. **Phone:** (573) 336-6355 or (877) 858-8687.

BEST WESTERN MONTIS INN   573/336-4299
APPROVED
Hotel

BW Best Western. **AAA Benefit:** Members save up to 15% and earn bonus points!

Address: 14086 Hwy Z 65584 **Location:** I-44 exit 163, just s. **Facility:** 41 units. 2 stories (no elevator), exterior corridors. **Parking:** winter plug-ins. **Pool:** outdoor. **Guest Services:** coin laundry. **Featured Amenity: full hot breakfast.**

COMFORT INN   573/336-3553
THREE DIAMOND Hotel. **Address:** 103 St. Robert Blvd 65584

FAIRFIELD BY MARRIOTT ST. ROBERT/FORT LEONARD WOOD MO   573/336-8600
THREE DIAMOND **SAVE** Hotel. **Address:** 131 St. Robert Blvd 65584

AAA Benefit: Members save 5% or more!

HAMPTON INN BY HILTON ST. ROBERT/FT. LEONARD WOOD   573/336-3355
THREE DIAMOND **SAVE** Hotel. **Address:** 103 St. Robert Plaza Dr 65584

AAA Benefit: Members save up to 15%!

HAWTHORN SUITES BY WYNDHAM ST. ROBERT-FT. LEONARDWOOD   573/451-3535
APPROVED Hotel. **Address:** 239 St. Robert Blvd 65584

HOLIDAY INN EXPRESS HOTEL & SUITES   573/336-2299
THREE DIAMOND Hotel. **Address:** 605 Hwy Z 65584

MAINSTAY SUITES   573/451-2700
THREE DIAMOND Extended Stay Hotel. **Address:** 227 St. Robert Blvd 65584

WHERE TO EAT

EL CABRITO MEXICAN RESTAURANT   573/336-4373
APPROVED Mexican. Casual Dining. **Address:** 560 Old Route 66 65584

GLASSICO SUSHI   573/336-3877
APPROVED Japanese. Casual Dining. **Address:** 198 Old Route 66 65584

ICHIBAN JAPANESE STEAK HOUSE & SUSHI BAR   573/336-5036
APPROVED Japanese. Casual Dining. **Address:** 240 Marshall Dr 65584

SWEETWATER BAR-B-QUE   573/336-8830
APPROVED Barbecue. Quick Serve. **Address:** 14076 Hwy Z 65584

ZLOFT BAR & GRILL   573/336-7829
APPROVED American. Casual Dining. **Address:** 127 Vickie Lynn Ln 65584

STE. GENEVIEVE (C-6) pop. 4,410, elev. 397'

The first permanent settlement in Missouri, founded between 1725 and 1750, Ste. Genevieve is in the region that was once part of Upper Louisiana. French traditions are still evident in the festivals and the residential architecture of a town that once rivaled St. Louis in size and importance.

The town's historic and shopping district centers around the blocks of Market, Merchant, Third and Main streets. There, you can find antique and handmade craft shops, art galleries, home décor boutiques and restaurants.

City of Ste. Genevieve Welcome Center: 66 S. Main St., Ste. Genevieve, MO 63670. **Phone:** (573) 883-7097 or (800) 373-7007.

Self-guiding tours: Information about self-guiding walking tours is available from the welcome center.

BOLDUC HOUSE is at 125 S. Main St. The complex consists of three historic houses: the Bolduc House (circa 1792), the Bolduc-LeMeilleur House (circa 1815) and the Linden House (circa 1820). The Bolduc House, built by well-to-do French-Canadian merchant and trader Louis Bolduc, is restored in authentic French Colonial style. Visitors can see where the Bolduc family gathered for meals, hosted balls and learned the news that Louis XVI had been beheaded.

The Bolduc-LeMeilleur House, originally occupied by Bolduc's granddaughter and her husband, is an example of local architecture that incorporated French influences. Furnished in period, it contains a Hands-On History Room for children and an art gallery. The Linden House also features displays of art.

Hours: Mon.-Fri. 10-4, Sat. 10-5, Sun. noon-4. Last guided tour departs 30 minutes before closing. Closed Jan. 1, Easter, Thanksgiving, Christmas Eve, Christmas and Dec. 31. **Cost:** $8; $6 (ages 65+ and college students with ID); $4 (ages 5-18); free (active duty military with ID). **Phone:** (573) 883-3105. GT

FELIX VALLÉ HOUSE STATE HISTORIC SITE is at Second and Merchant sts. In contrast to the vertical log houses erected by French and Spanish colonists, this 1818 house was constructed from stone in the American Federal style. Two entrances enabled the building to serve as both a store and home for its owners. The house is furnished in period. **Hours:** Mon.-Sat. 10-4, Sun. noon-5, Apr.-Oct.; Thurs.-Sat. 10-4, Sun. noon-5, rest of year. **Cost:** (includes Amoureux House) $4; $3 (ages 6-17). **Phone:** (573) 883-7102 or (800) 334-6946.

The Bauvais-Amoureux House is .25 mi. s. on Main St. to 327 St. Mary's Rd., within Felix Vallé House State Historic Site. This French Colonial vertical log home, built in 1792, is one of three in the United States constructed using only vertical logs for its foundation. An exhibit room with information about the community's architectural history and a diorama room with a model of Ste. Genevieve circa 1832 are highlights.

Time: Allow 30 minutes minimum. **Hours:** Open seasonally; phone for schedule. **Cost:** (includes Felix Vallé House) $4; $3 (ages 6-17). **Phone:** (573) 883-7102 or (800) 334-6946. GT

HOTEL AUDUBON   573/883-2479
▼ THREE DIAMOND Boutique Hotel. **Address:** 9 N Main 63670

MICROTEL INN & SUITES BY WYNDHAM SAINTE GENEVIEVE   573/883-8884
▼ APPROVED   **Address:** 21958 Hwy 32 63670 **Location:** I-55 exit 150 (SR 32), 3.9 mi e. **Facility:** 48 units. 2 stories, interior corridors. **Guest Services:** coin laundry. **Featured Amenity:** continental breakfast.

Hotel

SAVE ⫿⊹ CALL ⬥ BIZ 🛜 ✕
🔲 🖨 / SOME UNITS 🐾 ▣

WHERE TO EAT

ANVIL RESTAURANT & SALOON   573/883-7323
▼ APPROVED   American. Casual Dining. **Address:** 46 3rd St 63670

OLD BRICK HOUSE   573/883-2724
▼ APPROVED   American. Casual Dining. **Address:** 90 S 3rd St 63670

SEDALIA (C-3) pop. 21,387, elev. 909'
• Restaurants p. 294

Gen. George R. Smith bought 1,000 acres along the Pacific Railroad right of way for $13 per acre in 1857, and named the town he platted Sedville in honor of his daughter Sarah, whom he affectionately referred to as Sed. Three years later Smith filed a larger plat that included Sedville and named the new town Sedalia.

In June one of the best-known ragtime composers is saluted at the Scott Joplin Ragtime Festival. The products of Missouri's fields and factories are showcased at the State Fair, held in August.

A trailhead leading to Katy Trail State Park is just east of town.

Sedalia Area Chamber of Commerce: 600 E. Third St., Sedalia, MO 65301-4499. **Phone:** (660) 826-2222.

Self-guiding tours: Walking tour brochures of the downtown historic district are available from the chamber of commerce.

KATY DEPOT HISTORIC SITE is at 600 E. Third St., 1.6 mi. e. of US 65. The Katy Depot is a reminder of the industry and prosperity that the railroad brought to Sedalia as well as rural central Missouri. The re-created buildings on the site, including a ticket office, lunch room, dining room and women's waiting room, contain original furniture and flooring. In the women's waiting room, speaking mannequins activated by motion sensors portray two people who worked at and traveled through the depot. Several railroad-themed works of art are on the grounds.

Reservations for guided tours are required at least 2 weeks in advance. **Time:** Allow 1 hour minimum. **Hours:** Mon.-Sat. 9-4, Apr.-Dec.; Mon.-Fri. 9-4, rest of year. Closed major holidays. **Cost:** Site $1. Thirty-minute guided tour $3; 1-hour guided tour $5. **Phone:** (660) 826-2932. GT

BEST WESTERN STATE FAIR INN   660/826-6100
▼ APPROVED
Hotel

BW Best Western.   **AAA Benefit:** Members save up to 15% and earn bonus points!

Address: 3120 S Limit Ave 65301 **Location:** Jct US 50, 1.5 mi s on US 65. **Facility:** 117 units. 2 stories (no elevator), interior/exterior corridors. **Pool:** heated indoor. **Activities:** hot tub. **Guest Services:** valet and coin laundry. **Featured Amenity:** breakfast buffet.

SAVE ⫿⊹ 🍸 🏊 BIZ 🛜 🔲
🖨 ▣ / SOME UNITS 🐾 HS

COMFORT INN SEDALIA STATION   660/829-5050
▼ APPROVED   Hotel. **Address:** 3600 W Broadway 65301

HAMPTON INN SEDALIA   660/951-1163
▼ THREE DIAMOND SAVE Hotel. **Address:** 3909 W 9th St 65301

AAA Benefit: Members save up to 15%!

HOLIDAY INN EXPRESS & SUITES   660/826-4000
▼ THREE DIAMOND Hotel. **Address:** 4001 W Broadway 65301

WHERE TO EAT

EL TAPATIO AUTHENTIC MEXICAN   660/827-5553
♦♦♦ APPROVED   Mexican. Casual Dining. **Address:** 3000
S Limit Ave 65301

KEHDE'S BARBEQUE   660/826-2267
♦♦♦ APPROVED   Barbecue. Casual Dining. **Address:** 1915
S Limit Ave 65301

SIKESTON pop. 16,318

COMFORT INN & SUITES   573/472-0197
♦♦♦ THREE DIAMOND   **Address:** 109 Matthews Ln 63801 **Lo-**
       Hotel   **cation:** I-55 exit 67, just sw. **Facility:** 64
                   units. 3 stories, interior corridors. **Pool:**
                   heated indoor. **Activities:** hot tub, exer-
                   cise room. **Guest Services:** coin
                   laundry. **Featured Amenity:** breakfast
                   buffet.

[SAVE] [Y+] [≈] [♦] [BIZ] [HS] [≈]
[X] [🔒] [🖼] [💻] /SOME UNITS [🐾]

HAMPTON INN SIKESTON   573/621-4100
♦♦♦ THREE DIAMOND [SAVE] Hotel. **Ad-**   **AAA Benefit:**
dress: 1240 Commerce Dr 63801   Members save up to
                                           15%!

HOLIDAY INN EXPRESS & SUITES SIKESTON 573/475-9522
♦♦♦ THREE DIAMOND   Hotel. **Address:** 115 Hospitality Dr 63801

WHERE TO EAT

EL TAPATIO   573/472-3888
♦♦♦ APPROVED   Mexican. Casual Dining. **Address:** 2113
E Malone Ave 63801

JEREMIAH'S RESTAURANT & LOUNGE   573/472-4412
♦♦♦ APPROVED   American. Casual Dining. **Address:** 102
N Kingshighway St 63801

SPRINGFIELD (D-3) pop. 159,498, elev. 1,292'
• Hotels p. 298 • Restaurants p. 299
• Hotels & Restaurants map & index p. 296

Springfield's future location was designated by
John Polk Campbell in 1829 when he carved his ini-
tials into an ash tree near the site of four springs.
Strategically located at the junction of two important
roads, the town flourished during the 1850s westward migration. This key location also made it a
target during the Civil War in a battle that took place
at what is now Wilson's Creek National Battlefield
(see place listing p. 302).

Union spy/scout James Butler Hickok, better
known as Wild Bill Hickok, stayed in Springfield after
the war. He achieved fame as a gunfighter and
made national news in 1865, when he returned fire
and killed Dave Tutt in Springfield's public square;
Hickok was later acquitted.

In 1926 plans for the first paved transcontinental
highway in the United States were drafted.
Stretching from the Great Lakes to the Pacific
Coast, Route 66 earned the nickname Main Street
USA. Traces of the original route are visible along
Kearney, Glenstone, College and St. Louis streets.

The past also is evident in the historic houses and
buildings along Walnut Street and in the Midtown
district. Christ Episcopal Church, 601 E. Walnut St.,
was built in 1870 and features stained-glass windows and ecclesiastical Gothic architecture.

The Pythian Castle, 1451 E. Pythian St., was built
as an orphanage by the Knights of Pythias in 1913
and was later used by the U.S. military. A local
legend, this 55-room, castle-like structure is said to
be haunted. It is the scene of special holiday events
and may also be toured; for information phone (417)
865-1464.

In addition to sightseeing, Springfield offers
fishing, boating and picnicking at Fellows, McDaniel
and Springfield lakes. Table Rock and Bull Shoals
reservoirs also are nearby.

The Frisco Highline Trail, Missouri's second-
longest rail trail, connects Springfield and Bolivar
along the path of a former railroad line traveled by
Harry S. Truman as a precursor to his famous
"Whistle Stop Campaign" in 1948. This 36-mile-long
bicycling trail winds through the scenic forest and
pasture lands of La Petite Gemme Prairie Natural
Area, crossing over 16 trestles along the way.
Horseback riding is permitted between Willard and
Walnut Grove. Trailheads are located in Springfield,
Willard, Walnut Grove, Wishart and Bolivar. For
more information contact Ozark Greenways, P.O.
Box 50733, Springfield, MO 65805; phone (417)
864-2015.

The Springfield Cardinals AA minor league team
is a big regional draw during baseball season.
Games are played at Hammons Field, 955 E. Trafficway; phone (417) 863-2143.

Route 66 Tourist Information Center: 815 E. St.
Louis St., Suite 100, Springfield, MO 65806. **Phone:**
(417) 881-5300 or (800) 678-8767.

Self-guiding tours: Contact the tourist information
center for pamphlets describing attractions and
driving tours of the historic downtown area.

Shopping: Antique and craft shops abound in
Springfield. Ozark Treasures, 2510 S. Campbell St.,
features more than 100 dealers. The Commercial
Street Historical District offers antiques, collectibles
and vintage clothing. Battlefield Mall, Battlefield
Road and Glenstone Avenue, has more than 170
stores, including Dillard's, Macy's and Sears.

Bass Pro Shops Outdoor World, 1935 S. Campbell St., caters to outdoor enthusiasts with features
like a 140,000-gallon game fish aquarium and waterfall, wildlife exhibits and sporting demonstrations.

**BOTANICAL GARDENS AT NATHANAEL
GREENE/CLOSE MEMORIAL PARK** is n. of jct.
Battlefield St. at 2400 S. Scenic. Hundreds of varieties of plants are displayed in outdoor gardens and
horticultural collections covering more than 100

(See map & index p. 296.)

acres. Visitors can explore an arboretum, the historic Gray-Campbell Farmstead, the South Creek Greenway Trail and a 12,700-square-foot botanical center.

At the Native Butterfly House, open from mid-May through September, visitors can view host plants and witness the stages of a butterfly's life. Specialty gardens include the Mizumoto Japanese Stroll Garden and the Master Gardener demonstration gardens. **Time:** Allow 1 hour minimum. **Hours:** Gardens and park open daily dawn-dusk. Botanical center Mon.-Sat. 8-8, Sun. 11-6, Apr.-Oct.; Mon.-Sat. 8-5, Sun. 11-5, rest of year. **Cost:** Free. **Phone:** (417) 891-1515.

Mizumoto Japanese Stroll Garden is at 2400 S. Scenic at the Botanical Gardens. A tea house and moon bridge are centerpieces of this landscaped 7.5-acre garden, which features bonsai trees and three small lakes with feeding stations for fish and ducks. **Time:** Allow 1 hour minimum. **Hours:** Daily 10-7, Apr.-Oct.; 10-6, rest of year. **Cost:** $3; free (ages 0-12). **Phone:** (417) 891-1515.

DICKERSON PARK ZOO is off I-44 exit 77, then 1 blk. n. to Norton Rd., following signs to 1401 W. Norton Rd. The zoo is home to more than 550 mammals, birds, reptiles and amphibians. Tropical Asia features Asian elephants, primates and tigers, while gray wolves, river otters and mountain lions are among the animals in the Missouri Habitats exhibits.

Visitors can also interact with animals at the petting zoo, feed the giraffe and listen to daily keeper chats (summer season only). The Titus Express train travels around the zoo grounds. A children's water play area and playground are also on site.

Time: Allow 2 hours minimum. **Hours:** Daily 9-5, Apr.-Sept.; 10-4, rest of year (weather permitting). Train operates Mon.-Fri. 10-4, Sat.-Sun. 10-4:30, Apr.-Sept.; daily 11-3, in Mar. and Oct. **Cost:** $12; $8 (ages 3-12 and 60+). Train ride $2; free (ages 0-2). **Phone:** (417) 864-1800. 🍴

FANTASTIC CAVERNS is 1.5 mi. n. of jct. I-44 and SR 13, then 3 mi. w. on W. Farm Rd. 94. Visitors experience the cave on a 1-mile, Jeep-drawn tram tour, where geological formations like columns, flowstones, stalactites and stalagmites can be seen. Guides offer background information about how the cave, one of Missouri's largest, was formed. At one of the stops along the route, a video of a hydrogeologist explaining the connections between cave life, groundwater and people is shown. The temperature in this natural limestone cave is a constant 60 F.

Fantastic Caverns has a varied history, beginning with its exploration by 12 women in 1867. The cave was equipped with a dance floor, gambling tables and a bar in the 1920s to function as a speakeasy. It served as a meeting place in the 1930s and was the site of a country music theater in the 1960s and early '70s.

Last tour departs one hour before closing. **Time:** Allow 1 hour minimum. **Hours:** Daily 8-9, mid-May to mid-Aug.; 8-8, early Apr.-mid-May and mid-Aug. to early Sept.; 8-7, mid-Mar.-early Apr. and early Sept.-Oct. 31; 8-5, rest of year. Tours depart every 20-30 minutes. Closed Thanksgiving, Christmas Eve and Christmas. **Cost:** $26; $17 (ages 6-12); free (ages 0-5 with paid adult). **Phone:** (417) 833-2010. GT 🍴

MISSOURI SPORTS HALL OF FAME is at 3861 E. Stan Musial Dr. (US 60). Displays of sports memorabilia evoke the memory of legendary Missouri teams and players. Interactive opportunities include a broadcast booth and a display where visitors stand behind home plate as major league pitches come in at 100-plus miles per hour. **Hours:** Mon.-Sat. 10-4, Sun. noon-4. **Cost:** $5; $4 (ages 55+); $3 (ages 6-15); $14 (family). **Phone:** (417) 889-3100 or (800) 498-5678.

WONDERS OF WILDLIFE NATIONAL MUSEUM & AQUARIUM is at 500 W. Sunshine St., adjacent to Bass Pro Shops Outdoor World. The expansive museum's focus is on the importance of conservation and does a thorough job of exploring the nation's hunting and fishing heritage. Some 35,000 living creatures inhabit the space. More than 800 species of live amphibians, birds, fish, mammals and reptiles as well as aquariums totaling 1.5 million gallons of water illustrate our relationship with our natural surroundings.

Wildlife Galleries bring the world to you as you journey through exotic locations including the African Savanna, Alps and North American woodlands. Immersive dioramas of wildlife in their native environment feature special effects including temperature-controlled climate, lighting intensity and painted murals as well as the smells and sounds experienced in those habitats. Get an up-close view of magnificent beasts such as crocodiles, elephants, giraffes, wolves and zebras. Not all the animals are taxidermy specimens; some live animals include a bald eagle, bats, crocodiles, owls, river otters, snakes and tree frogs.

Your journey through the Aquarium Adventure brings you face-to-face with an impressive display of eels, fish, jellies, rays and sharks. Great Oceans Hall is a 300,000-gallon ocean habitat that surrounds you from floor to ceiling with tanks of sea life including game fish, rays, sea turtles and sharks. Pop-up viewing bubbles and a walk-through tunnel provide an underwater perspective of ocean and freshwater river inhabitants. Daring guests can touch horseshoe crabs, rays, sharks and starfish in two touch tanks.

Other exhibits explain the role hunting and fishing play in the preservation of outdoor resources. **Note:** General admission is by timed entry. **Time:** Allow 3 hours, 30 minutes minimum. **Hours:** Daily 10-8. Phone ahead to confirm schedule. **Cost:** $45.95; $17.95 (ages 4-11). **Phone:** (417) 890-9453. 🍴 🅰

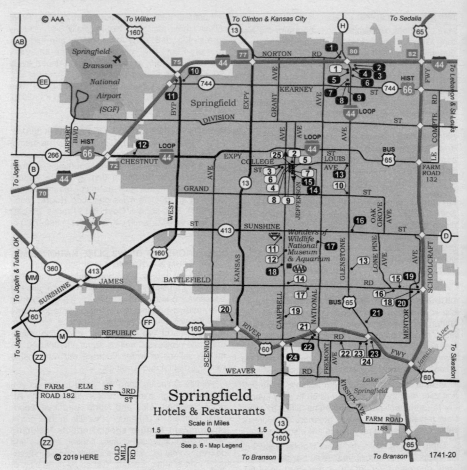

Springfield
Hotels & Restaurants

Scale in Miles

1.5   0   1.5

See p. 6 - Map Legend

© 2019 HERE

1741-20

✈ Airport Hotels

Map Page	SPRINGFIELD-BRANSON REGIONAL (Maximum driving distance from airport: 5.0 mi)	Designation	Member Savings	Page
12 this page	**Best Western Plus Springfield Airport Inn, 3.9 mi**	💎 APPROVED	✔	298
11 this page	Courtyard by Marriott Airport, 4.6 mi	◈ THREE DIAMOND	✔	298
10 this page	La Quinta Inn & Suites Springfield Airport Plaza, 5.0 mi	◈ THREE DIAMOND		299

Springfield

This index helps you "spot" where hotels and restaurants are located on the corresponding detailed maps. Restaurant price range is a combination of lunch and/or dinner. Turn to the listing page for more information and consult display ads for special promotions.

🔗 **For more details, rates and reservations: AAA.com/travelguides/hotels**

SPRINGFIELD

Map Page	Hotels	Designation	Member Savings	Page
1 this page	**Holiday Inn Express & Suites Springfield**	◈ THREE DIAMOND	✔	299
2 this page	Candlewood Suites Springfield I-44	◈ THREE DIAMOND		298

SPRINGFIELD (cont'd)

Map Page	Hotels (cont'd)	Designation	Member Savings	Page
3 p. 296	Home2 Suites by Hilton	THREE DIAMOND	✔	299
4 p. 296	Hampton Inn & Suites by Hilton	THREE DIAMOND	✔	298
5 p. 296	Drury Inn & Suites-Springfield	THREE DIAMOND		298
6 p. 296	**Oasis Hotel & Convention Center, an Ascend Hotel Collection Member**	THREE DIAMOND	✔	299
7 p. 296	**Best Western Plus Coach House**	THREE DIAMOND	✔	298
8 p. 296	Fairfield Inn & Suites by Marriott Springfield North	THREE DIAMOND	✔	298
9 p. 296	**DoubleTree by Hilton Springfield**	THREE DIAMOND	✔	298
10 p. 296	La Quinta Inn & Suites Springfield Airport Plaza	THREE DIAMOND		299
11 p. 296	Courtyard by Marriott Airport	THREE DIAMOND	✔	298
12 p. 296	**Best Western Plus Springfield Airport Inn**	APPROVED	✔	298
13 p. 296	**Best Western Route 66 Rail Haven**	APPROVED	✔	298
14 p. 296	**University Plaza Hotel and Convention Center**	THREE DIAMOND	✔	299
15 p. 296	**Hotel Vandivort**	FOUR DIAMOND	✔	299
16 p. 296	**Vib Springfield by Best Western**	THREE DIAMOND	✔	299
17 p. 296	TownePlace Suites by Marriott Springfield	THREE DIAMOND	✔	299
18 p. 296	**La Quinta Inn & Suites Springfield South**	THREE DIAMOND	✔	299
19 p. 296	Baymont Inn & Suites	APPROVED		298
20 p. 296	Clarion Inn & Suites	THREE DIAMOND		298
21 p. 296	Comfort Inn South	THREE DIAMOND		298
22 p. 296	Candlewood Suites South	THREE DIAMOND		298
23 p. 296	Hilton Garden Inn Springfield	THREE DIAMOND	✔	298
24 p. 296	Holiday Inn Express & Suites Medical District	THREE DIAMOND		298

Map Page	Restaurants	Designation	Cuisine	Price Range	Page
1 p. 296	Whole Hog Cafe	APPROVED	Barbecue	$6-$13	300
2 p. 296	Dublin's Pass Irish Pub & Restaurant	APPROVED	Irish	$9-$20	300
3 p. 296	Lost Signal Brewing Company	APPROVED	Barbecue	$5-$12	300
4 p. 296	Nonna's Italian American Cafe	APPROVED	Italian	$6-$16	300
5 p. 296	Zayka Indian Cuisine	APPROVED	Indian	$12-$19	300
6 p. 296	Springfield Brewing Company	APPROVED	American	$8-$22	300
7 p. 296	The Order	THREE DIAMOND	New American	$18-$34	300
8 p. 296	Black Sheep Burgers & Shakes	APPROVED	Burgers	$10-$16	299
9 p. 296	Maria's Mexican Restaurant	APPROVED	Mexican	$8-$14	300
10 p. 296	Anton's Coffee Shop	APPROVED	Breakfast Sandwiches	$5-$12	299
11 p. 296	Hemingway's Blue Water Cafe	APPROVED	American	$7-$20	300
12 p. 296	Springfield Family Restaurant	APPROVED	American	$7-$15	300
13 p. 296	Farmers Gastropub	APPROVED	British	$6-$19	300
14 p. 296	The Grotto	APPROVED	American	$6-$13	300
15 p. 296	Metropolitan Grill	THREE DIAMOND	New American	$8-$24	300
16 p. 296	Bambinos Cafe on Battlefield	APPROVED	Italian	$6-$11	299
17 p. 296	PaPPo's Pizzeria South	APPROVED	Pizza	$7-$25	300
18 p. 296	Pasta Express	APPROVED	Italian	$7-$12	300
19 p. 296	City Butcher and Barbecue	APPROVED	Barbecue	$7-$22	299
20 p. 296	Garbo's Pizzeria	APPROVED	Italian Pizza Sandwiches	$6-$16	300
21 p. 296	Ocean Zen	THREE DIAMOND	Pacific Rim	$12-$36	300
22 p. 296	Touch	THREE DIAMOND	New Fusion Small Plates	$8-$33	300
23 p. 296	Houlihan's	THREE DIAMOND	American	$4-$21	300
24 p. 296	Aviary Cafe	APPROVED	American	$7-$17	299
25 p. 296	Civil Kitchen	APPROVED	American	$10-$25	299

(See map & index p. 296.)

BAYMONT INN & SUITES   417/887-2323   **19**
▽▽ APPROVED   Hotel. **Address:** 3343 E Battlefield Rd 65804

BEST WESTERN PLUS COACH HOUSE
417/862-0701   **7**

▽▽ THREE DIAMOND   Hotel

BW Best Western **PLUS**   **AAA Benefit:** Members save up to 15% and earn bonus points!

Address: 2535 N Glenstone Ave 65803 **Location:** I-44 exit 80, just s. **Facility:** 126 units. 1 story, exterior corridors. **Pool:** outdoor. **Activities:** playground, exercise room. **Guest Services:** complimentary and valet laundry.

BEST WESTERN PLUS SPRINGFIELD AIRPORT INN
417/799-2200   **12**

▽▽ APPROVED   Hotel

BW Best Western **PLUS**   **AAA Benefit:** Members save up to 15% and earn bonus points!

Address: 4445 W Chestnut Expwy 65802 **Location:** I-44 exit 72, 0.8 mi s. **Facility:** 54 units. 2 stories, interior corridors. **Pool:** heated indoor. **Activities:** exercise room. **Guest Services:** coin laundry. **Featured Amenity: full hot breakfast.**

BEST WESTERN ROUTE 66 RAIL HAVEN
417/866-1963   **13**

▽▽ APPROVED   Classic Historic Motel

BW Best Western.   **AAA Benefit:** Members save up to 15% and earn bonus points!

Address: 203 S Glenstone Ave 65802 **Location:** I-44 exit 80, 3 mi s. **Facility:** This hotel offers nostalgia for the Route 66 lover with theme rooms and classic cars on the front drive. Most rooms are trendy in décor, so request a 1950s-style theme room for a unique experience. 91 units. 1 story, exterior corridors. **Terms:** check-in 4 pm. **Pool:** outdoor. **Activities:** hot tub.

CANDLEWOOD SUITES SOUTH   417/881-8500   **22**
▽▽ THREE DIAMOND   Extended Stay Hotel. **Address:** 1035 E Republic Rd 65807

CANDLEWOOD SUITES SPRINGFIELD I-44
417/866-4242   **2**
▽▽ THREE DIAMOND   Extended Stay Hotel. **Address:** 1920 E Kerr St 65803

CLARION INN & SUITES   417/520-6200   **20**
▽▽ THREE DIAMOND   Hotel. **Address:** 3370 E Battlefield Rd 65804

COMFORT INN SOUTH   417/889-8188   **21**
▽▽ THREE DIAMOND   Hotel. **Address:** 3776 S Glenstone Ave 65804

COURTYARD BY MARRIOTT AIRPORT   417/869-6700   **11**
▽▽ THREE DIAMOND **SAVE** Hotel. **Address:** 3527 W Kearney St 65803   **AAA Benefit:** Members save 5% or more!

DOUBLETREE BY HILTON SPRINGFIELD
417/831-3131   **9**

▽▽ THREE DIAMOND   Hotel

DOUBLETREE   **AAA Benefit:** Members save up to 15%!

Address: 2431 N Glenstone Ave 65803 **Location:** I-44 exit 80, just s. **Facility:** 201 units. 10 stories, interior corridors. **Amenities:** safes. **Pool:** heated outdoor, heated indoor. **Activities:** hot tub, exercise room. **Guest Services:** valet and coin laundry.

DRURY INN & SUITES-SPRINGFIELD   417/863-8400   **5**
▽▽ THREE DIAMOND   Hotel. **Address:** 2715 N Glenstone Ave 65803

FAIRFIELD INN & SUITES BY MARRIOTT SPRINGFIELD NORTH   417/833-9599   **8**
▽▽ THREE DIAMOND **SAVE** Hotel. **Address:** 2455 N Glenstone Ave 65803   **AAA Benefit:** Members save 5% or more!

HAMPTON INN & SUITES BY HILTON   417/869-5548   **4**
▽▽ THREE DIAMOND **SAVE** Hotel. **Address:** 2750 N Glenstone Ave 65803   **AAA Benefit:** Members save up to 15%!

HILTON GARDEN INN SPRINGFIELD   417/875-8800   **23**
▽▽ THREE DIAMOND **SAVE** Hotel. **Address:** 4155 S Nature Center Way 65804   **AAA Benefit:** Members save up to 15%!

HOLIDAY INN EXPRESS & SUITES MEDICAL DISTRICT
417/887-8500   **24**
▽▽ THREE DIAMOND   Hotel. **Address:** 310 E Monastery St 65810

(See map & index p. 296.)

HOLIDAY INN EXPRESS & SUITES SPRINGFIELD
417/708-4699 **1**

THREE DIAMOND
Hotel

Address: 3050 N Kentwood Ave 65803 **Location:** I-44 exit 80, just n. **Facility:** 111 units. 4 stories, interior corridors. **Amenities:** safes. **Pool:** heated indoor. **Activities:** exercise room. **Guest Services:** coin laundry.

[SAVE] CALL [&] [≈] [♦] [BIZ] [HS]
[≈] [X] [🛏] [🖨] [💻]
/ SOME UNITS [🐾]

HOME2 SUITES BY HILTON   417/864-6632 **3**

THREE DIAMOND [SAVE] Extended Stay Hotel. **Address:** 2756 N Glenstone Ave 65803

AAA Benefit:
Members save up to 15%!

HOTEL VANDIVORT
417/832-1515 **15**

FOUR DIAMOND

Boutique Contemporary Hotel

Address: 305 E Walnut St 65806 **Location:** Jct E Walnut St and S Robertson Ave; downtown. **Facility:** This swanky downtown hotel offers an open concept lobby that revolves around the restaurant and bar. Rooms are large and beautifully appointed with high ceilings and unique design details. 50 units, some efficiencies. 4 stories, interior corridors. **Parking:** valet only. **Terms:** check-in 4 pm. **Dining:** The Order, see separate listing. **Activities:** exercise room. **Guest Services:** valet laundry.

[SAVE] [←] [†↑] [≈] [Y] CALL [&]
[♦] [BIZ] [≈] [X] [🛏] [🖨] [💻]
/ SOME UNITS [🐾]

LA QUINTA INN & SUITES SPRINGFIELD AIRPORT PLAZA
417/447-4466 **10**

THREE DIAMOND Hotel. **Address:** 2445 N Airport Plaza Ave 65803

LA QUINTA INN & SUITES SPRINGFIELD SOUTH
417/890-6060 **18**

THREE DIAMOND
Hotel

Address: 2535 S Campbell Ave 65807 **Location:** Jct Battlefield Rd and Campbell Ave, 0.5 mi n. **Facility:** 61 units. 3 stories, interior corridors. **Amenities:** safes. **Pool:** heated indoor. **Activities:** exercise room. **Guest Services:** valet and coin laundry. **Featured Amenity:** full hot breakfast.

[SAVE] [†↑] [≈] [♦] [BIZ] [HS] [≈]
[X] [🐾] [🛏] [🖨] [💻]
/ SOME UNITS [🐾]

OASIS HOTEL & CONVENTION CENTER, AN ASCEND HOTEL COLLECTION MEMBER
417/866-5253 **6**

THREE DIAMOND
Hotel

Address: 2546 N Glenstone Ave 65803 **Location:** I-44 exit 80, just s. **Facility:** 173 units. 2 stories, interior corridors. **Terms:** check-in 4 pm. **Amenities:** safes. **Pool:** heated outdoor, heated indoor. **Activities:** hot tub, exercise room. **Guest Services:** valet and coin laundry, area transportation. **Featured Amenity:** breakfast buffet.

[SAVE] [←] [†↑] [↑] [Y] [≈] [♦]
[BIZ] [≈] [X] [🛏] [🖨] [💻]

TOWNEPLACE SUITES BY MARRIOTT SPRINGFIELD
417/881-8118 **17**

THREE DIAMOND [SAVE] Extended Stay Hotel. **Address:** 2009 S National Ave 65804

AAA Benefit:
Members save 5% or more!

UNIVERSITY PLAZA HOTEL AND CONVENTION CENTER
417/864-7333 **14**

THREE DIAMOND
Hotel

Address: 333 John Q Hammons Pkwy 65806 **Location:** 0.5 mi e on St. Louis St. **Facility:** 267 units. 9 stories, interior corridors. **Amenities:** *Some:* safes. **Dining:** 2 restaurants. **Pool:** outdoor, heated indoor. **Activities:** hot tub, exercise room, spa. **Guest Services:** valet and coin laundry, area transportation.

[SAVE] [†↑] [↑] [Y] CALL [&]
[≈] [♦] [BIZ] [≈] [X] [🐾] [💻]
/ SOME UNITS [🐾] [🛏] [🖨]

VIB SPRINGFIELD BY BEST WESTERN
417/881-9100 **16**

THREE DIAMOND

Boutique Contemporary Hotel

AAA Benefit:
Members save up to 15% and earn bonus points!

Address: 1845 E Sunshine St 65804 **Location:** Jct US Business Rt 65 and E Sunshine St. **Facility:** This unique hotel has socially motivated public areas with a popular restaurant and bar. The rooms are on the small side, but smartly designed. Baths feature a semi-exposed frosted glass shower. 92 units. 5 stories, interior corridors. *Bath:* shower only. **Amenities:** safes. **Activities:** exercise room. **Guest Services:** valet laundry.

[SAVE] [†↑] [≈] [Y] [♦] [BIZ] [HS] [≈] [X] [💻]
/ SOME UNITS [🛏]

WHERE TO EAT

ANTON'S COFFEE SHOP   417/869-7681 **10**
APPROVED Breakfast Sandwiches. Casual Dining. **Address:** 937 S Glenstone Ave 65802

AVIARY CAFE   417/881-9736 **24**
APPROVED American. Casual Dining. **Address:** 2144 E Republic Rd 65804

BAMBINOS CAFE ON BATTLEFIELD   417/881-4442 **16**
APPROVED Italian. Casual Dining. **Address:** 2810 E Battlefield Rd 65804

BLACK SHEEP BURGERS & SHAKES   417/319-5905 **8**
APPROVED Burgers. Casual Dining. **Address:** 209 E Walnut 65806

CITY BUTCHER AND BARBECUE   417/720-1113 **19**
APPROVED Barbecue. Quick Serve. **Address:** 3650 S Campbell Ave 65807

CIVIL KITCHEN   417/501-8486 **25**
APPROVED American. Casual Dining. **Address:** 107 Park Central Square 65806

COLTON'S STEAKHOUSE & GRILL   417/823-9909
APPROVED Steak. Casual Dining. **Address:** 2020 E Independence St 65804

(See map & index p. 296.)

DUBLIN'S PASS IRISH PUB & RESTAURANT
417/862-7625 (2)
⬦ APPROVED Irish. Casual Dining. **Address:** 317 Park
Central E 65806

FARMERS GASTROPUB 417/864-6994 (13)
⬦ APPROVED British. Gastropub. **Address:** 2620 S
Glenstone Ave 65804

GARBO'S PIZZERIA 417/883-9010 (20)
⬦ APPROVED Italian Pizza Sandwiches. Casual Dining.
Address: 2101 W Chesterfield Blvd, Bldg C 65807

THE GROTTO 417/886-9600 (14)
⬦ APPROVED American. Quick Serve. **Address:** 301 E
Battlefield Rd 65807

HEMINGWAY'S BLUE WATER CAFE 417/891-5100 (11)
⬦ APPROVED American. Casual Dining. **Address:** 1935
S Campbell Ave 65807

HOULIHAN'S 417/883-3434 (23)
⬦ THREE DIAMOND American. Casual Dining. **Address:** 2110
E Republic Rd 65804

LOST SIGNAL BREWING COMPANY 417/869-4755 (3)
⬦ APPROVED Barbecue. Casual Dining. **Address:** 610
W College St 65806

MARIA'S MEXICAN RESTAURANT 417/831-9339 (9)
⬦ APPROVED Mexican. Casual Dining. **Address:** 406
South St 65806

METROPOLITAN GRILL 417/889-4951 (15)
⬦ THREE DIAMOND New American. Casual Dining. **Address:**
2931 E Battlefield Rd 65804

NONNA'S ITALIAN AMERICAN CAFE 417/831-1222 (4)
⬦ APPROVED Italian. Casual Dining. **Address:** 306
South Ave 65806

OCEAN ZEN 417/889-9596 (21)
⬦ THREE DIAMOND Pacific Rim. Casual Dining. **Address:**
4117 S National Ave 65807

THE ORDER 417/832-1515 (7)
⬦ THREE DIAMOND New American. Fine Dining. **Address:**
305 E Walnut St 65806

PAPPO'S PIZZERIA SOUTH 417/306-9091 (17)
⬦ APPROVED Pizza. Casual Dining. **Address:** 900 E
Battlefield Rd 65807

PASTA EXPRESS 417/890-1345 (18)
⬦ APPROVED Italian. Quick Serve. **Address:** 3250 E
Battlefield Rd, Unit H 65804

RIB CRIB BBQ AND GRILL 417/866-6677
⬦ APPROVED Barbecue. Casual Dining. **Address:** 1640
N Glenstone Ave 65804

SPRINGFIELD BREWING COMPANY 417/832-8277 (6)
⬦ APPROVED American. Casual Dining. **Address:** 305
S Market Ave 65806

SPRINGFIELD FAMILY RESTAURANT 417/883-0900 (12)
⬦ APPROVED American. Casual Dining. **Address:** 2222
S Campbell St 65807

TOUCH 417/823-8383 (22)
⬦ THREE DIAMOND New Fusion Small Plates. Casual Dining.
Address: 1620 E Republic Rd 65804

WHOLE HOG CAFE 417/720-4759 (1)
⬦ APPROVED Barbecue. Quick Serve. **Address:** 2731
N Glenstone Ave 65803

ZAYKA INDIAN CUISINE 417/351-4400 (5)
⬦ APPROVED Indian. Casual Dining. **Address:** 311 S
Jefferson Ave 65806

STANTON (C-5) elev. 871'

⬦ **MERAMEC CAVERNS** is off I-44 exit 230,
then 3 mi. s. on SR W. Discovered in 1716,
the caverns accommodated powder kilns and
leaching vats for Union forces during the Civil War.

In 1864 the outlaw band of Confederate William
Quantrill's irregulars, of which Jesse James was a
member, seized the gunpowder mill. James was so
impressed with the cave that he and his gang later
used it as a hideout. This colorful history suitably
came to a close when a man avowed to be Jesse
James held an outlaw reunion in the cave on James'
102nd birthday in 1949.

The caverns feature five floors of colorful mineral
formations. At the entrance are a mineral and crystal
collection and an ultraviolet rock display. Gold panning, riverboat rides and ziplines also are offered.
Guided tours take visitors along a mile of lighted
concrete walkways; the cave maintains a constant
temperature of 60 F. *See Recreation Areas Chart.*
Hours: Tours depart daily every 20-30 minutes
8:30-7:30, July 1-Labor Day; 9-7, May-June; 9-6 in
Apr. and day after Labor Day-Sept. 30; 9-5 in Mar.
and Oct.; 9-4, rest of year. Phone ahead to confirm
schedule. **Cost:** $22; $12 (ages 5-11). **Phone:** (573)
468-3166 or (800) 676-6105. GT 🍴 ✂

SULLIVAN pop. 7,081, elev. 970'

BAYMONT INN & SUITES 573/860-3333
⬦ APPROVED Hotel. **Address:** 275 N Service Rd W
63080

COMFORT INN 573/468-7800
⬦ THREE DIAMOND **Address:** 736 S Service Rd W 63080
Hotel **Location:** I-44 exit 225, just sw. **Facility:** 59 units. 3 stories, interior corridors. **Pool:** heated indoor. **Activities:**
hot tub, exercise room. **Guest Services:**
coin laundry. **Featured Amenity: full
hot breakfast.**

SAVE 🏊 ♿ BIZ HS 📶 ✕
🔲 🔳 🔲 / SOME UNITS 🐾

■ **WHERE TO EAT** ■

EL NOPAL 573/860-5214
⬦ APPROVED Mexican. Casual Dining. **Address:** 148 S
Service Rd 63080

🔗 **AAA.com/campgrounds—**

For overnights under the stars ·

SUNSET HILLS pop. 8,496

- **Hotels & Restaurants map & index p. 274**
- **Part of St. Louis area — see map p. 248**

HOLIDAY INN ST. LOUIS SW-ROUTE 66

314/821-6600 **91**

THREE DIAMOND

Hotel

Address: 10709 Watson Rd 63127 **Location:** I-44 exit 277B (Lindbergh Blvd), just s on US 61/67. **Facility:** 213 units. 4 stories, interior corridors. **Terms:** check-in 4 pm. **Pool:** outdoor, heated indoor. **Activities:** hot tub, exercise room. **Guest Services:** valet and coin laundry, rental car service.

[SAVE] [icons] CALL [icons] / SOME UNITS [icon]

WHERE TO EAT

BANDANA'S BAR-B-Q   314/849-1162
APPROVED Barbecue. Casual Dining. **Address:** 11750 Gravois Rd 63127

SESAME CHINESE RESTAURANT   314/821-5038 **109**
APPROVED Chinese. Casual Dining. **Address:** 10500 Watson Rd 63127

TOWN AND COUNTRY pop. 10,815

- **Hotels & Restaurants map & index p. 271, 274**
- **Part of St. Louis area — see map p. 248**

COOPER'S HAWK WINERY & RESTAURANT   636/489-0059 **37**
THREE DIAMOND American. Fine Dining. **Address:** 1146 Town and Country Crossing Dr 63017

VALLEY PARK pop. 6,942

- **Hotels & Restaurants map & index p. 271**
- **Part of St. Louis area — see map p. 248**

DRURY INN & SUITES-ST. LOUIS SOUTHWEST
636/861-8300 **38**
THREE DIAMOND Hotel. **Address:** 5 Lambert Drury Dr 63088

HAMPTON INN BY HILTON-ST. LOUIS SOUTHWEST NEAR SIX FLAGS   636/529-9020 **39**
THREE DIAMOND [SAVE] Hotel. **Address:** 9 Lambert Drury Dr 63088

AAA Benefit:
Members save up to 15%!

WHERE TO EAT

SUGARFIRE SMOKEHOUSE   636/825-1400 **40**
APPROVED Barbecue. Quick Serve. **Address:** 932 Meramec Station Rd 63088

WARRENSBURG (C-2) pop. 18,838, elev. 863'

Warrensburg was named for Martin Warren, a blacksmith whose shop along a busy Osage Indian trail was a gathering place for frontier farmers. The town gained fame in 1870 as the site of the "Old Drum" trial, in which Leonidas Hornsby was accused of shooting a hunting dog owned by his brother-in-law, Charles Burden. In his appeal to the jury, Senator G.G. Vest coined the term "man's best friend" to describe the noble dog Drum.

Warrensburg is the home of University of Central Missouri, the third-largest state school in Missouri with an enrollment of 14,000 students.

Greater Warrensburg Area Chamber of Commerce and Visitors Center: 100 S. Holden St., Warrensburg, MO 64093. **Phone:** (660) 747-3168 or (877) 653-3786.

BEST WESTERN WARRENSBURG INN   660/747-3000

THREE DIAMOND

Hotel

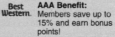

Best Western

AAA Benefit: Members save up to 15% and earn bonus points!

Address: 626 E Russell Ave 64093 **Location:** Jct US 50 and SR 13, just s to Russell Ave, then 0.8 mi e. **Facility:** 82 units. 3 stories, interior corridors. **Pool:** heated indoor. **Activities:** game room, exercise room. **Guest Services:** coin laundry.

[SAVE] [icons] CALL [icons] BIZ / SOME UNITS [HS]

COMFORT INN WARRENSBURG STATION   660/429-4848
APPROVED Hotel. **Address:** 609 E Russell Ave 64093

FAIRFIELD INN & SUITES BY MARRIOTT WARRENSBURG
660/422-3540
THREE DIAMOND [SAVE] Hotel. **Address:** 355 E Russell Ave 64093

AAA Benefit: Members save 5% or more!

WHERE TO EAT

HERO'S RESTAURANT & PUB   660/747-3162
APPROVED American. Casual Dining. **Address:** 107 W Pine St 64093

PLAYER'S RESTAURANT & LOUNGE   660/747-2115
APPROVED American. Casual Dining. **Address:** 627 E Russell Ave 64093

WARSAW (C-3) pop. 2,127, elev. 708'

Warsaw is a vacation center at the head of Lake of the Ozarks. Parts of the Butterfield Overland Trail, an early stagecoach route, can be hiked within town and the immediate environs. Harry S. Truman State Park *(see Recreation Areas Chart)* offers developed recreational facilities on Truman Dam's reservoir, formed by the Osage River.

Warsaw Area Chamber of Commerce: 109 E. Main St., P.O. Box 264, Warsaw, MO 65355. **Phone:** (660) 438-5922 or (800) 927-7294.

PARKFIELD INN   660/438-2474
APPROVED Hotel. **Address:** 151 N Dam Access Rd 65355

WASHINGTON (C-5) pop. 13,982, elev. 554'

Settled in 1839, Washington is the self-proclaimed "Corncob Pipe Capital of the World"; the nation's only corncob pipe factory is located here. Restored buildings along the riverfront and downtown house restaurants, specialty shops and bed and breakfast inns. James W. Rennick Riverfront Park, at Lafayette and Front streets, is a nice spot to relax and take in views of the Missouri River. Washington is also at the center of a wine-producing area, with some two dozen wineries within an hour's drive.

Fort Charrette Historic Village and Museum (charrette is French for "little cart"), 2 miles east off Old SR 100 at 966 Charrette Ln., is a re-creation of a late 17th-century trading post and village. Buildings are furnished with antiques, and there are flower and herb gardens on the grounds. There's also an expansive vista of the Missouri River from this elevated perspective. Guided 2-hour tours are given by appointment; phone (636) 239-4202.

Washington Visitor Center: 301 W. Main St., Washington, MO 63090. **Phone:** (636) 239-7575 or (888) 792-7466.

Self-guiding tours: A brochure for the self-guiding walking tour of the historic area is available from the visitor center at 301 W. Front St.

BEST WESTERN PLUS WASHINGTON HOTEL
636/390-8877

▼▼THREE DIAMOND   Hotel

AAA Benefit: Members save up to 15% and earn bonus points!

Address: 2621 E 5th St 63090 **Location:** I-44 exit 251, 8.5 mi w on SR 100. **Facility:** 73 units. 4 stories, interior corridors. **Pool:** heated indoor. **Activities:** hot tub, exercise room. **Guest Services:** coin laundry.

SUPER 8 WASHINGTON   636/390-0088
▼▼ APPROVED   Hotel. **Address:** 2081 Eckelkamp Ct 63090

WHERE TO EAT

SUGARFIRE SMOKEHOUSE   636/432-5550
▼▼ APPROVED   Barbecue. Quick Serve. **Address:** 512 W Front St 63090

WENTZVILLE pop. 29,070

- Hotels & Restaurants map & index p. 271
- Part of St. Louis area — see map p. 248

FAIRFIELD INN & SUITES BY MARRIOTT ST. LOUIS WEST/WENTZVILLE   636/332-5000   **16**
▼▼THREE DIAMOND SAVE Hotel. **Address:** 130 Crossroads South Dr 63385

AAA Benefit: Members save 5% or more!

HAMPTON INN ST. LOUIS WENTZVILLE   636/445-3780   **17**
▼▼THREE DIAMOND SAVE Hotel. **Address:** 150 Wentzville Bluffs Dr 63385

AAA Benefit: Members save up to 15%!

WHERE TO EAT

STEFANINA'S   636/327-5800   **20**
▼▼ APPROVED   Italian. Casual Dining. **Address:** 762 W Pearce Blvd 63385

WEST PLAINS pop. 11,986

HAMPTON INN BY HILTON WEST PLAINS   417/255-0442
▼▼THREE DIAMOND SAVE Hotel. **Address:** 1064 London Ln 65775

AAA Benefit: Members save up to 15%!

QUALITY INN WEST PLAINS   417/257-2711
▼▼ APPROVED   Hotel. **Address:** 220 Jan Howard Expwy 65775

WHERE TO EAT

COLTON'S STEAKHOUSE & GRILL   417/255-9090
▼▼ APPROVED   Steak. Casual Dining. **Address:** 1421 Preacher Roe Blvd 65775

WILSON'S CREEK NATIONAL BATTLEFIELD (D-2)

The battle of Wilson's Creek took place Aug. 10, 1861. Brig. Gen. Nathaniel Lyon was the first Union general to die in battle during the Civil War. A 5-mile, self-guiding driving tour passes eight wayside exhibits and 12 displays. A .6-mile hiking trail leads to Bloody Hill, the major battle site. The Ray House and Ray Springhouse have been restored to their 1861 appearance. Living-history programs are presented regularly on weekends from Memorial Day through Labor Day.

Allow 2 hours minimum. Park open daily 7 a.m.-8 p.m., mid-May to mid-Aug.; 7-7, mid-Aug. to mid-Oct.; 8-7, mid-Apr. to mid-May; 9-5, rest of year. Closed Jan. 1, Thanksgiving and Christmas. Admission $7 (per person); maximum charge $15 (per private vehicle with more than one adult); free (ages 0-15). For more information write the Superintendent, Wilson's Creek National Battlefield, 6424 W. Farm Rd. 182, Republic, MO 65738-0403. Phone (417) 732-2662.

WILSON'S CREEK NATIONAL BATTLEFIELD VISITOR CENTER is 10 mi. s.w. of Springfield; from I-44 exit 70, take SR MM south about 4 miles to US 60 and proceed through the intersection, continuing half a mile to County Road ZZ. Turn right on County Road ZZ and continue south 1.5 miles to Farm Road 182 (Elm Street). Turn left onto Farm Road; the battlefield entrance is on the right at 6424 W. Farm Road 182.

A film and a fiber optic map both detail the history of the battle. Exhibits include Medals of Honor earned by soldiers who fought at Wilson's Creek, John Brown's rifles fired during battle and Sterling Price's hand-carved revolver. A collection of Civil War memorabilia features flags, uniforms, weapons and other artifacts. A 5-mile, self-guided driving audio tour has eight stops that show battle locations. **Time:** Allow 30 minutes minimum. **Hours:** Daily 8-5, early Apr. to mid-Oct.; 9-5, rest of year. **Cost:** Free. Park admission $7 (per person); $15 (per private vehicle); free (ages 0-15). **Phone:** (417) 732-2662.

WINONA (D-4) elev. 932'

TWIN PINES CONSERVATION EDUCATION CENTER is 1.3 mi. e. of jct. SR 19N and US 60. Historic buildings include a log cabin and a schoolhouse. On the grounds are four trails, including a tree ID trail and a nature hike; an archery range; and a small fishing pond. The education center contains exhibits about regional animal and plant life, a display depicting the history of local logging and an interior waterfall. A section of the grounds is landscaped with native plants, with demonstration plots illustrating land management techniques. **Time:** Allow 30 minutes minimum. **Hours:** Tues.-Sat. 8-5. Closed major holidays. **Cost:** Free. **Phone:** (573) 325-1381.

WOODSON TERRACE pop. 4,063
• **Hotels & Restaurants map & index p. 274**
• **Part of St. Louis area — see map p. 248**

HILTON ST. LOUIS AIRPORT   314/426-5500 **55**
THREE DIAMOND

Hotel

AAA Benefit: Members save up to 15%!

Address: 10330 Natural Bridge Rd 63134 **Location:** I-70 exit 236 (Lambert Airport), 0.5 mi se. **Facility:** 397 units. 4-9 stories, interior corridors. **Parking:** on-site (fee). **Amenities:** safes. **Pool:** heated indoor. **Activities:** exercise room. **Guest Services:** valet laundry, area transportation.

HOLIDAY INN ST. LOUIS AIRPORT   314/427-4700 **56**
THREE DIAMOND Hotel. **Address:** 4505 Woodson Rd 63134

WHERE TO EAT

ERIO'S PIZZA AND RESTAURANT   314/423-1555 **63**
APPROVED   Italian. Casual Dining. **Address:** 4434 Woodson Rd 63134

State Capitol, Oklahoma City

Oklahoma

Whether dispossessed Native Americans moving in, destitute Dust Bowl farmers moving on or cattle-driving cowboys passing through, the comings and goings of diverse groups of people helped mold the character of Oklahoma. Highway-loving travelers can just take it all in, discovering that the state's position at the nation's crossroads makes it difficult to categorize.

Is it a Southern state? The southeastern corner, with its pine-covered hills and distinctly Southern sensibility, is often called "Little Dixie." On the other hand, undulating acres of wheat and grain elevators thrusting to the sky give northern Oklahoma a Midwestern feel.

Yet the loudest singer in a chorus of voices is that of the great American West. Rodeos both test and show off skills that have been vital to cowboys since the days of the Chisholm Trail. Powwows celebrate and preserve

Turner Falls Park

Native American heritage with traditional singing, dancing, drumming and the tales of ancestors driven west along the "Trail of Tears."

Oklahoma's Route 66

Before America's interstate system made driving cross-country a simple matter of zipping between points A and B—before the pleasure of savoring local flavor was sacrificed in the name of progress and expediency—there was Route 66. Affectionately called "The Main Street of America," this 2,400-mile-long ribbon of pavement connected Chicago and Los Angeles on a meandering path through the heart of the nation.

Nowhere is this historic road better preserved than in Oklahoma. Small towns awaiting their first traffic light, neon-lit truck stop cafes, old-fashioned filling stations and vintage motels advertising "air-cooled rooms" still line the remaining stretches of the great highway here.

Since then US 66, as it was officially labeled, has become intimately connected with the history and character of the state. John Steinbeck dubbed it the "Mother Road" in his opus "The Grapes of Wrath," a novel which dramatized the very real plight of thousands of Depression-era "Okies" who fled the Dust Bowl for California's fertile valleys.

Cowboys and Indians

Route 66 enters the state's northeast corner, an area where the river-laced Ozark foothills meet the prairies, at the town of Quapaw. Here the route intersects with a much older and sadder byway: the "Trail of Tears." Beginning in 1830, native peoples of the southeastern United States were forced to move to the newly created Indian Territory that would later become Oklahoma. Today Oklahoma has one of the largest Native American populations in the country.

Near El Reno Route 66 encounters the Chisholm Trail, a historic passage inseparably tied to cowboy legend roughly paralleling modern US 81. In the late 1800s, thousands of Texas cattlemen drove their herds along the trail to railheads in Kansas for shipment to Eastern markets. Those paid to move the cattle north were called cowboys, and they came to symbolize the rugged, often romanticized image of life in the West.

In 1952, Route 66 was renamed the Will Rogers Memorial Highway after Oklahoma's cowboy humorist and favorite son. It passes through Claremore, where the Will Rogers Memorial Museum overflows with the entertainer's personal items and memorabilia. Claremore also was home to Lynn Riggs, the playwright who penned "Green Grow the Lilacs," upon which the classic musical "Oklahoma!" was based.

Route 66 connects Oklahoma's two biggest cities as well. In Tulsa the highway winds within sight of the Art Deco skyscrapers built during the city's oil boom years. Once known as "The Oil Capital of the World," Tulsa has preserved many of its 1920s and '30s architectural gems.

West of Tulsa, Route 66 rolls through farmland and quaint towns on its way to Oklahoma City, the state capital. Literally built in a day, "OKC" materialized on the prairie April 22, 1889, during the most famous in a series of land rushes. Route 66 continues west, passing through the arid, high plains of the west to Texola, near the Texas border.

Recreation

A dry Western state evoking images of the Dust Bowl shouldn't have as much water as Oklahoma does. Though the state is naturally blessed with a multitude of rivers, the more than 200 lakes seen today are all products of human ingenuity. Dams built to control flooding have created rambling reservoirs which are perfect for outdoor fun.

At Turner Falls Park near Davis, Honey Creek cascades down a 77-foot waterfall into a natural pool. Swimmers flock to Arcadia Lake near Edmond and to lakes Ellsworth and Lawtonka near Lawton, both fed by streams from the Wichita Mountains.

Built to control flooding on the Red River, Denison Dam impounds the vast reservoir of Lake Texoma on the Texas-Oklahoma border. The lake's shoreline is sprinkled with secluded coves perfect for boating, sailing, swimming and wind surfing.

Lake Altus-Lugert, in Quartz Mountain Nature Park, is great for boating. A 3,600-acre public hunting area on the north shore supports quails, turkeys and waterfowl. In the Ozark foothills, the clear blue water of Grand Lake O' the Cherokees draws migrating white pelicans in the fall.

Oklahoma's lakes also support a variety of fish, giving anglers a reason to smile. Lakes Hugo, Sardis, Eufaula, John Wells and Clayton, all in the southeast, offer some of the best bass and bluegill catches. The crystal waters of Broken Bow Reservoir teem with trout; Lone Chimney Lake, in central Oklahoma, is home to bass, catfish and crappie.

In the western panhandle, hikers can tackle the rugged landscape of canyons and mesas. Colorful gypsum formations distinguish Alabaster Caverns State Park; natural springs, old-growth forests and venerable hills characterize the Arbuckle Mountains.

Wichita Mountains

Historic Timeline

500	Moundbuilders inhabit eastern Oklahoma.
1541	Spanish explorer Francisco Vásquez de Coronado ventures through the area searching for a city of gold.
1817	The federal government begins to forcibly relocate the Five Civilized Tribes from their homes in the Southeast to Oklahoma.
1866	Texas ranchers begin to move their cattle along the Chisholm Trail through Oklahoma to reach the railroads in Kansas.
1879	Humorist Will Rogers is born in Oologah.
1889	The unassigned prairie land of the Oklahoma Territory opens for settlement.
1897	The first commercial oil well in Oklahoma Territory is drilled in Bartlesville.
1930s	Years of plowing and sustained drought dry up farmland forcing hundreds of thousands of people to leave their homes.
1933	Oklahoman Wiley Post makes the first successful solo flight around the world.
2000	A memorial and museum are dedicated to the 168 people killed in the 1995 bombing of the Alfred. P. Murrah Federal Building.
2007	Oklahoma celebrates 100 years of statehood.

What To Pack

Temperature Averages Maximum/Minimum	JANUARY	FEBRUARY	MARCH	APRIL	MAY	JUNE	JULY	AUGUST	SEPTEMBER	OCTOBER	NOVEMBER	DECEMBER
Frederick	52/26	57/30	65/37	75/47	83/57	92/67	97/71	96/70	88/61	76/49	64/37	52/27
Goodwell	49/20	52/23	61/30	70/39	79/49	89/59	94/64	92/63	84/54	73/42	60/30	49/21
Oklahoma City	50/29	55/33	63/41	72/50	80/60	88/68	94/72	93/71	85/63	73/52	62/40	51/31
Tishomingo	53/28	58/32	68/42	76/52	83/60	90/68	95/71	94/69	86/62	76/51	65/40	54/30
Tulsa	48/27	53/31	62/40	72/49	79/59	88/68	93/73	93/71	84/62	73/51	61/40	49/30
Woodward	49/22	54/27	64/36	74/46	82/56	91/65	95/69	93/67	85/58	74/46	60/34	50/24

From the records of The Weather Channel Interactive, Inc.

Good Facts To Know

ABOUT THE STATE

POPULATION: 3,751,351.

AREA: 69,899 square miles; ranks 20th.

CAPITAL: Oklahoma City.

HIGHEST POINT: 4,973 ft., Black Mesa.

LOWEST POINT: 287 ft., Little River.

TIME ZONE(S): Central. DST.

GAMBLING

MINIMUM AGE FOR GAMBLING: 21; 18 for some casinos.

REGULATIONS

TEEN DRIVING LAWS: Teens are not allowed to transport more than one passenger, with the exception of parents, guardians and licensed drivers over 21, Driving is not permitted 10 p.m.-5 a.m., unless the teen is going to school, work or church. The minimum age for an unrestricted license is 16 years, 6 months (with driver's education courses); 17 years (without). Phone (405) 425-2300 for more information about Oklahoma driver's license regulations.

SEAT BELT/CHILD RESTRAINT LAWS: Seat belts are required for driver and front-seat passengers ages 9 and over. Children age 8 or taller than 4'9" are required to use a seat belt; booster seats are required for children ages 4-7 who are under 4'9"; child restraints are required for children ages 2-3; rear-facing child seats are required for children under age 2. AAA recommends the use of seat belts and appropriate child restraints for the driver and all passengers.

CELLPHONE RESTRICTIONS: All drivers are prohibited from texting while driving. Law enforcement may issue a citation for not devoting full time and attention to driving if an officer observes driving in such a manner that poses a danger to other persons on the roadway or if the driver is involved in an accident. Learner's permit and intermediate license holders may not use a handheld electronic device while driving.

HELMETS FOR MOTORCYCLISTS: Required for riders under 18.

RADAR DETECTORS: Permitted. Prohibited for use by commercial vehicles.

MOVE OVER LAW: State law requires drivers approaching a stationary emergency vehicle displaying flashing lights, including wreckers, traveling in the same direction, to vacate the lane closest if safe and possible to do. Or slow to a speed safe for road, weather and traffic conditions. Also included in the law are road maintenance vehicles and any stationary vehicle displaying flashing lights.

FIREARMS LAWS: Vary by state and/or county. Contact the Oklahoma State Bureau of Investigation, 6600 N. Harvey, Oklahoma City, OK 73116; phone (405) 848-6724.

HOLIDAYS

HOLIDAYS: Jan. 1 ▪ Martin Luther King Jr. Day, Jan. (3rd Mon.) ▪ Washington's Birthday/Presidents Day, Feb. (3rd Mon.) ▪ Memorial Day, May (last Mon.) ▪ July 4 ▪ Labor Day, Sept. (1st Mon.) ▪ Veterans Day, Nov. 11 ▪ Thanksgiving, Nov. (4th Thurs.) and following Fri. ▪ Christmas, Dec. 25 ▪ day after Christmas, Dec. 26.

MONEY

TAXES: Oklahoma's statewide sales tax is 4.5 percent, with local options for additional increments to be levied by cities and counties. A Tourism Promotion Tax of 0.1 percent is levied on lodgings, restaurants, tour vehicles and amusement admissions.

VISITOR INFORMATION

INFORMATION CENTERS: State welcome centers are near the Oklahoma-Kansas line at I-35 exit 222 in Blackwell ▪ east of Miami at I-44/Will Rogers Turnpike exit 313 ▪ at I-44 exit 238 east of Tulsa ▪ near the Oklahoma-Arkansas border at I-40 exit 311 at Sallisaw ▪ near the Oklahoma-Texas border on US 69/75 at Colbert ▪ at the Oklahoma-Texas border on I-35 exit 5 at Thackerville ▪ east of the Oklahoma-Texas border near Erick at I-40 exit 11 ▪ on US 412/Cherokee Turnpike just west of the Oklahoma-Arkansas border and east of Kansas, OK ▪ north of the Oklahoma-Texas border at I-44 exit 20 near Walters ▪ at I-40 exit 157 at Midwest City ▪ at I-35 exit 137 (N.E. 122nd Street) in Oklahoma City ▪ and in the Oklahoma Capitol Building at N.E. 23rd Street and Lincoln Boulevard in Oklahoma City.

With the exception of the center in the Oklahoma Capitol Building, which is open Mon.-Fri 8-4:30 year-round, state information centers are open daily 8:30-5. Closed Thanksgiving and Christmas.

FURTHER INFORMATION FOR VISITORS:
Oklahoma Tourism & Recreation Department
900 N. Stiles Ave.
Oklahoma City, OK 73104
(405) 230-8400
(800) 652-6552

NATIONAL FOREST INFORMATION:
U.S. Forest Service
Southern Regional Office
1720 Peachtree St. N.W., Suite 700B
Atlanta, GA 30309
(404) 347-4177
(877) 444-6777 (reservations)

FISHING AND HUNTING REGULATIONS:
Oklahoma Department of Wildlife Conservation
2145 N.E. 36th St.
Oklahoma City, OK 73111
(405) 521-3851

RESORT & PARK RESERVATIONS:
For reservations for lodge or cabin accommodations phone (800) 654-8240.

Oklahoma Annual Events

Please call ahead to confirm event details.

Visit **AAA.com/travelguides/events** to find
AAA-listed events for every day of the year

WINTER

Dec. - Territorial Christmas and Victorian
Walk Evenings / Guthrie
405-282-1947

Jan. - Ultimate Eagle Watch / Ponca
City / 580-762-9494
- Holidays at the Gardens / Oklahoma
City / 405-517-3303
- International Finals Rodeo
Oklahoma City / 405-235-6540

Feb. - Oklahoma Horse Fair / Duncan
580-255-3231
- Tulsa Indian Art Festival / Glenpool
918-298-2300
- National Rod and Custom Car Show
Tulsa / 918-257-4234

SPRING

Mar. - Cinch Timed Event Championship
Guthrie / 405-282-7433
- Oklahoma Youth Livestock Expo
Oklahoma City / 405-235-0404
- Taste of Yukon / Yukon
405-354-8442

Apr. - Azalea Festival / Muskogee
918-684-6302
- 89er Celebration / Guthrie
405-282-2589

May - Pioneer Days Rodeo / Guymon
580-338-3376
- Rooster Days Festival / Broken
Arrow / 918-251-1518
- Fried Onion Burger Day Festival / El
Reno / 405-262-8888

SUMMER

June - SunFest / Bartlesville / 918-331-0456
- LibertyFest / Edmond / 405-340-2527

July - Whole Hawg Days / Eufaula
918-689-2791
- Tulsa FreedomFest / Tulsa
918-596-2001

Aug. - Will Rogers Memorial Rodeo / Vinita
918-244-0265
- Okmulgee Invitational Rodeo &
Festival / Okmulgee / 918-756-0761

FALL

Sept. - Oklahoma State Fair / Oklahoma
City / 405-948-6700
- Scotfest / Tulsa / 918-740-7738

Oct. - Halloween Festival / Muskogee
918-687-3625
- Linde Oktoberfest / Tulsa
918-596-2007
- Grand National and World
Championship Morgan Horse Show
Oklahoma City / 505-867-4379

Nov. - Midwest City Holiday Lights
Spectacular / Midwest
City / 405-739-1293
- Dickens on the Boulevard
Claremore / 918-341-5881
- Dia De Los Muertos (Day of the
Dead) Arts Festival / Tulsa
918-585-1234

Get the scoop from AAA inspectors:

AAA.com/travelguides/restaurants

WE COME HERE TO REMEMBER
KILLED, THOSE WHO SURVIVED AND TH[
WHO LEAVE HERE KNOW THE IMPACT
RIAL OFFER COMFORT, STRENGTH, PEACE

Oklahoma City National
Memorial & Museum

Azalea Festival, Muskogee

Chickasaw Bricktown
Ballpark, Oklahoma City

Tulsa Indian Art Festival, Glenpool

Oklahoma State Fair, Oklahoma City

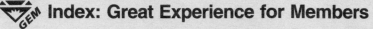

Index: Great Experience for Members

AAA editor's picks of exceptional note

Chickasaw National
Recreation Area

Will Rogers Memorial
Museum

Tulsa Zoo

Oklahoma Aquarium

See Orientation map on p. 316 for corresponding grid coordinates, if applicable.
* Indicates the GEM is temporarily closed.

Bartlesville (B-10)
Woolaroc Ranch, Museum and Wildlife
Preserve *(See p. 325.)*

Chickasaw National Recreation Area (F-9)
Chickasaw National Recreation Area
(See p. 327.)

Claremore (E-3)
J.M. Davis Arms & Historical Museum
(See p. 328.)
Will Rogers Memorial Museum *(See p. 328.)*

Duncan (F-7)
Chisholm Trail Heritage Center *(See p. 329.)*

Fort Sill (E-7)
Fort Sill National Historic Landmark and
Museum *(See p. 333.)*

Grove (B-12)
Har-Ber Village Museum *(See p. 334.)*

Jenks (F-2)
Oklahoma Aquarium *(See p. 335.)*

Norman (I-2)
Sam Noble Oklahoma Museum of Natural
History *(See p. 340.)*

Oklahoma City (D-8)
Museum of Osteology *(See p. 350.)*
Myriad Botanical Gardens and Crystal Bridge
Tropical Conservatory *(See p. 350.)*
National Cowboy & Western Heritage
Museum *(See p. 351.)*
Oklahoma City National Memorial & Museum
(See p. 352.)
Oklahoma City Zoo & Botanical Garden
(See p. 353.)
Oklahoma Hall of Fame at the
Gaylord-Pickens Museum *(See p. 353.)*
Oklahoma History Center *(See p. 353.)*
Science Museum Oklahoma *(See p. 353.)*

Tulsa (E-2)
Gilcrease Museum *(See p. 382.)*
Oral Roberts University *(See p. 382.)*
Philbrook Museum of Art *(See p. 382.)*
Tulsa Zoo *(See p. 385.)*

Hit the Road
with a Prepaid Card

Stay on budget during travel and use again
to save for the next adventure.

Visit your local AAA office or
AAA.com/MemberPay to learn more.

Oklahoma
Atlas Section

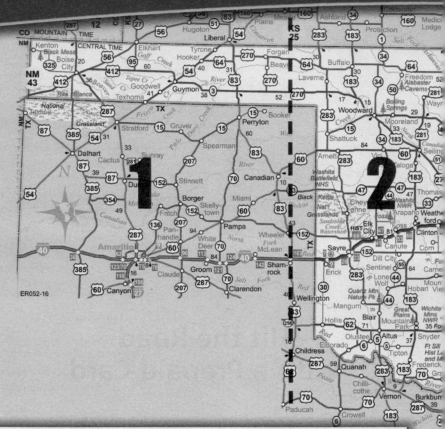

CO MOUNTAIN | 12 | KS | Coldwater
NM TIME | 25 | Medicine Lodge

ER052-16

ROADS/HIGHWAYS

▬▬▬	INTERSTATE
▬▬▬	CONTROLLED ACCESS
▬▬▬	CONTROLLED ACCESS TOLL
▬▬▬	TOLL ROAD
▬▬▬	PRIMARY DIVIDED
▬▬▬	PRIMARY UNDIVIDED
▬▬▬	SECONDARY DIVIDED
▬▬▬	SECONDARY UNDIVIDED
▬▬▬	LOCAL DIVIDED
▬▬▬	LOCAL UNDIVIDED
▬▬▬	UNPAVED ROAD
- - - -	UNDER CONSTRUCTION
▦▦▦▦	TUNNEL
▪▪▪▪▪	PEDESTRIAN ONLY
•••••	AUTO FERRY
•••••	PASSENGER FERRY
•••••	SCENIC BYWAY
10	DISTANCE BETWEEN MARKERS
	EXIT NUMBER-FREE/TOLL
◇ ◆	INTERCHANGE FULL/PARTIAL
?	WELCOME/INFORMATION CENTER
	REST AREA/ SERVICE CENTER

BOUNDARIES

▬▬▬	INTERNATIONAL
▬▬▬	STATE
▬▬▬	COUNTY
┼┼┼┼	TIME ZONE
>>>>>	CONTINENTAL DIVIDE

ROAD SHIELDS

95 95	INTERSTATE/BUSINESS
22 22 22	U.S./STATE/COUNTY
22 22	FOREST/INDIAN
⬡	TRANS- CANADA
1	PROVINCIAL AUTOROUTE/ KING'S HIGHWAY
1	MEXICO
66	HISTORIC ROUTE 66
VT 41	REFERENCE PAGE INDICATOR

AREAS OF INTEREST

	INDIAN
	MILITARY
	PARK
	FOREST
	GRASSLANDS
	HISTORIC
✈	INT'L/REGIONAL AIRPORT
	INCORPORATED CITY

POINTS OF INTEREST

○	TOWN
✪	NATIONAL CAPITAL
✪	STATE/PROVINCIAL CAPITAL
■	AAA/CAA CLUB LOCATION
■	FEATURE OF INTEREST
🎓	COLLEGE/UNIVERSITY
⊗	CUSTOMS STATION
⊞	HISTORIC
⚐	LIGHTHOUSE
⛫	MONUMENT/MEMORIAL
⚑	STATE/PROVINCIAL PARK
⛺	NATIONAL WILDLIFE REFUGE
⛷	SKI AREA
⊙	SPORTS COMPLEX
▬	DAM

CITIES/TOWNS are color-coded by size, showing where to find AAA Inspected and Approved lodgings or restaurants listed in the AAA TourBook guides and on AAA.com:

- ● **Red** - major destinations and capitals; many listings
- ● **Black** - destinations; some listings
- ● **Grey** - no listings

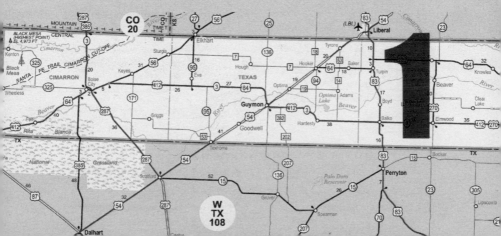

OKLAHOMA

1:1,552,320
Scale in Miles
25   0   25

Scale in Kilometers
25   0   25

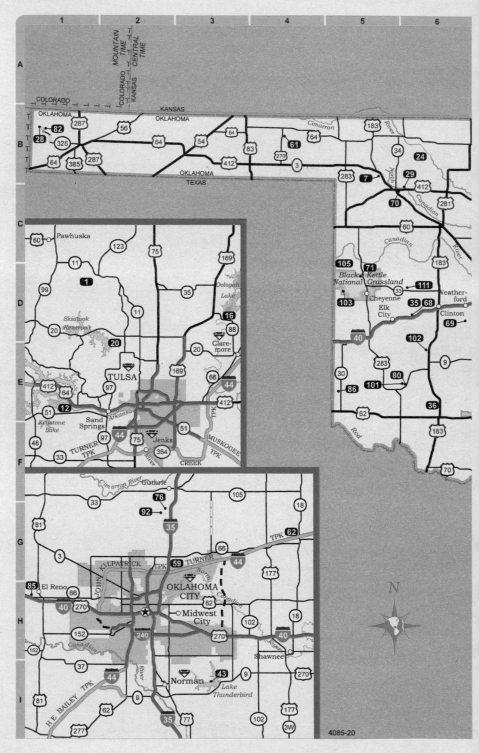

4085-20

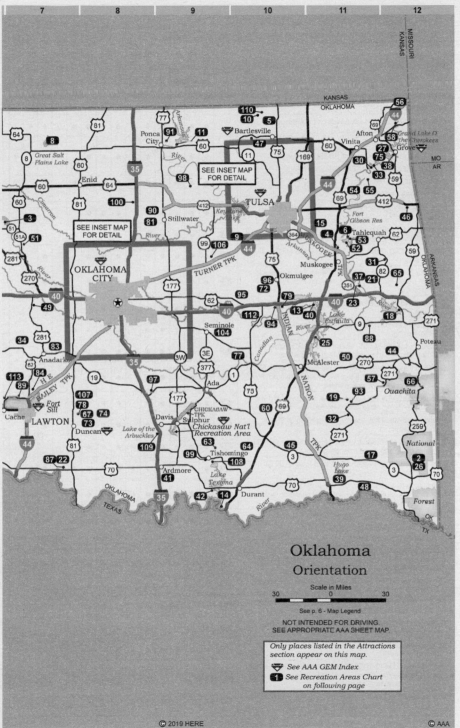

Oklahoma
Orientation

Scale in Miles

30   0   30

See p. 6 - Map Legend

NOT INTENDED FOR DRIVING.
SEE APPROPRIATE AAA SHEET MAP.

Only places listed in the Attractions section appear on this map.

☗ *See AAA GEM Index*

■1 *See Recreation Areas Chart on following page*

© 2019 HERE

© AAA

Recreation Areas Chart

The map location numerals in column 2 show an area's location on the preceding map.

Find thousands of places to camp at AAA.com/campgrounds

	MAP LOCATION	CAMPING	PICNICKING	HIKING TRAILS	BOATING	BOAT RAMP	BOAT RENTAL	FISHING	SWIMMING	PET FRIENDLY	BICYCLE TRAILS	WINTER SPORTS	VISITOR CENTER	LODGE/CABINS	FOOD SERVICE
NATIONAL FORESTS															
Ouachita (E-12) 1.8 million acres. West-central Arkansas and southeastern Oklahoma. Horse trails.		•	•	•	•	•	•	•	•	•	•	•	•	•	
NATIONAL GRASSLANDS															
Black Kettle (D-5) 30,724 acres off SR 283 in Cheyenne.		•	•	•	•	•	•		•	•	•				•
NATIONAL RECREATION AREAS *(See place listings.)*															
Chickasaw (F-9) 10,000 acres.		•	•	•	•	•	•	•	•	•	•		•		•
ARMY CORPS OF ENGINEERS															
Birch Lake (D-1) 3,278 acres 17 mi. s.e. of Pawhuska via SRs 99 and 11. Water skiing; playground.	1	•	•	•	•	•	•		•	•					
Broken Bow Lake (F-12) 28,113 acres 12 mi. n. of Broken Bow off US 259. Canoeing, kayaking, scuba diving.	2	•	•	•	•	•	•		•	•	•		•	•	
Canton Lake (C-7) 18,901 acres 2 mi. n. of Canton on SR 58A. Water skiing.	3	•	•	•	•	•		•	•	•			•		
Chouteau Lock and Dam (C-11) 7,151 acres 7 mi. n. of Muskogee on US 69, then 3 mi. s.e. on an access road. Hunting; playground.	4	•	•		•	•		•		•			•		
Copan Lake (B-10) 15,952 acres 2 mi. s.w. of Copan off US 75. Hunting.	5	•	•	•	•	•		•	•	•				•	
Fort Gibson Lake (C-11) 52,654 acres 15 mi. w. of Tahlequah off SR 51. Hunting.	6	•	•	•	•	•		•	•	•			•		
Fort Supply Lake (B-5) 8,039 acres 2 mi. s. of Fort Supply via US 270 and SR 3. Hunting, water skiing; playground.	7	•	•		•	•		•	•	•					
Great Salt Plains Lake (B-7) 8,690 acres 3 mi. n. of Jet on SR 38. Canoeing, hunting, kayaking; horse trails, playground. Personal watercraft are not recommended.	8	•	•	•	•	•		•	•	•					
Heyburn Lake (C-10) 6,344 acres 4 mi. w. of Kellyville off 151st St. S. Water skiing; horse trails, playground.	9	•	•	•	•	•		•	•	•					
Hulah Lake (B-10) 21,505 acres 2 mi. w. of Hulah on SR 10. Hunting; playground.	10	•	•		•	•		•	•	•					
Kaw Lake (B-9) 49,963 acres 9 mi. e. of Ponca City on Lake Rd. Equestrian camping; horse trails, playground.	11	•	•	•	•	•		•	•	•			•		
Keystone Lake (E-1) 714 acres 16 mi. w. of Tulsa off US 64. Hunting; horse trails, playground.	12	•	•	•	•	•		•	•	•			•	•	•
Lake Eufaula (D-10) 102,200 acres 6 mi. n. of McAlester on US 69. Historic. Canoeing, golf, hunting, kayaking, rafting, water skiing; all-terrain vehicle trails, horse trails, playground.	13	•	•	•	•	•	•	•	•	•			•	•	
Lake Texoma (G-9) 202,300 acres on Oklahoma-Texas border off US 75. Golf; horse trails, marinas, playground.	14	•	•	•	•	•	•	•	•	•			•		
Newt Graham Lock and Dam (C-11) 3,787 acres 8 mi. s.w. of Inola on CR 420.	15	•	•		•	•		•		•					
Oologah Lake (D-3) 50,150 acres 8 mi. n. of Claremore via SR 88. Canoeing, sailing; horse trail, playground.	16	•	•	•	•	•		•	•	•			•		
Pine Creek Lake (F-11) 26,179 acres 10 mi. n. of Valliant on Pine Creek Rd. Hunting, water skiing; playground.	17	•	•	•	•	•		•	•	•					
Robert S. Kerr Lock, Dam and Reservoir (D-12) 56,720 acres 9 mi. s. of Sallisaw off US 59. Hunting, sailing; playground.	18	•	•		•	•		•		•					
Sardis Lake (E-11) 21,564 acres 3 mi. n. of Clayton off SR 2. Hunting; playground.	19	•	•	•	•	•		•	•	•					
Skiatook Lake (E-2) 18,911 acres 5 mi. w. of Skiatook off SR 20. Hunting, water skiing.	20	•			•	•		•		•			•		•
Tenkiller Ferry Lake (D-11) 30,524 acres 21 mi. s.e. of Muskogee on SR 10, then 7 mi. e. on SR 10A. Golf, hunting, scuba diving; playground, recreational complex.	21	•	•	•	•	•	•	•	•	•	•		•		•
Waurika Lake (F-7) 21,500 acres 6 mi. n.w. of Waurika off SR 5. Hunting, water skiing; horse trail, playground.	22	•	•	•	•	•	•	•	•	•			•	•	

Recreation Areas Chart

The map location numerals in column 2 show an area's location on the preceding map.

🔗 Find thousands of places to camp at AAA.com/campgrounds

	MAP LOCATION	CAMPING	PICNICKING	HIKING TRAILS	BOATING	BOAT RAMP	BOAT RENTAL	FISHING	SWIMMING	PET FRIENDLY	BICYCLE TRAILS	WINTER SPORTS	VISITOR CENTER	LODGE/CABINS	FOOD SERVICE
Webbers Falls Lock and Dam (D-11) 15,953 acres 3 mi. n.w. of Gore off SR 10. Hunting.	23	•	•	•	•	•		•	•	•			•		
STATE															
Alabaster Caverns (B-6) 200 acres 6 mi. s. of Freedom on SR 50, then .5 mi. e. on SR 50A. Scenic. Volleyball; cave tours, horseshoe pit, playground.	24	•	•	•						•			•		
Arrowhead (E-11) 2,200 acres 15 mi. n. of McAlester off US 69. Equestrian camping, golf, water skiing; airstrip, horse rental trails, marina, playground.	25	•	•	•	•	•	•	•	•	•	•			•	•
Beavers Bend (F-12) 3,522 acres 10 mi. n.e. of Broken Bow on US 259A. Golf, tennis, volleyball, water skiing; horse rental, miniature golf, museum, nature center, playground.	26	•	•	•	•	•	•	•	•	•	•		•	•	•
Bernice (B-12) 88 acres .5 mi. e. of Bernice off SR 85A. Water skiing; nature center, playground.	27	•	•	•	•	•		•	•	•					
Black Mesa (B-1) 349 acres 27 mi. n.w. of Boise City off CR 325. Playground.	28	•	•	•	•	•		•		•					
Boiling Springs (B-6) 820 acres 6 mi. n.e. of Woodward on SR 34C. Interpretive center. Golf, volleyball; playground, swimming pool.	29	•	•	•				•	•	•	•		•		
Cherokee Area at Grand Lake (B-11) 43 acres e. of Langley on SR 20. Golf (nine holes), water skiing; playground.	30	•	•		•	•		•	•	•					
Cherokee Landing (D-11) 146 acres about 12 mi. s. of Tahlequah off SR 82. Disc golf, volleyball, water skiing; playground, softball field, swimming beach.	31	•	•	•	•	•		•	•	•	•				
Clayton Lake (F-11) 510 acres 30 mi. n.e. of Antlers on US 271. All-terrain vehicle trails, playground.	32	•	•	•	•	•		•	•	•			•		
Disney/Little Blue (C-11) 32 acres e. of Disney on SR 28. Playground.	33	•	•		•	•		•	•	•					
Fort Cobb (E-7) 1,872 acres 5 mi. n.w. of Fort Cobb off SR 9. Golf, water skiing; jet ski, pontoon and tube rentals, marina, playground.	34	•	•		•	•	•	•	•	•			•	•	•
Foss (D-6) 1,749 acres 15 mi. n.w. of Clinton via SRs 73 and 44. Disc golf, equestrian camping, horseback riding, water skiing; playground.	35	•	•	•	•	•	•	•	•	•					•
Great Plains (E-6) 487 acres 6 mi. n. of Snyder on US 183. Mountain climbing, water skiing; playground.	36	•	•	•	•	•		•	•	•					
Greenleaf (D-11) 565 acres 3 mi. s. of Braggs on SR 10A. Volleyball; basketball courts, children's fishing pond, marina, miniature golf, nature center, playground, swimming beach, swimming pool, watercraft rentals (canoe, kayak and paddleboat). Personal watercraft not permitted.	37	•	•	•	•	•	•	•	•	•			•	•	•
Honey Creek (B-12) 30 acres 2 mi. s.w. of Grove on SR 10. Water skiing; playground, swimming pool.	38	•	•		•	•		•	•	•					
Hugo Lake (F-11) 300 acres 8 mi. e. of Hugo on US 70. Archery, water skiing; horse trails, playground, pontoon boat rental.	39	•	•	•	•	•		•		•			•	•	
Lake Eufaula (D-11) 2,853 acres 14 mi. s.w. of Checotah via I-40 and SR 150. Archery, disc golf, golf, tennis, volleyball, water skiing; airstrip, horse rental, marina, playground. Yurts available.	40	•	•	•	•	•	•	•	•	•	•		•	•	•
Lake Murray (F-9) 12,496 acres 6 mi. s.e. of Ardmore off US 77. Golf (nine holes), tennis, water skiing; airstrip, horse rental, marina, miniature golf, nature center, playground, swimming pool, watercraft (canoe, kayak, jet ski, paddleboat, pontoon boat) rentals.	41	•	•	•	•	•	•	•	•	•	•		•	•	•
Lake Texoma (G-9) 1,882 acres 5 mi. e. of Kingston on US 70. Golf, volleyball, water skiing; canoe and pontoon boat rentals, marina, nature center.	42	•	•	•	•	•	•	•	•	•			•	•	•
Lake Thunderbird (I-3) 1,834 acres 13 mi. e. of Norman on SR 9. Archery, canoeing, hunting, kayaking, rafting, water skiing; canoe, paddleboat and tube rentals, horse trails, marina, nature trails, playground, swimming beach.	43	•	•	•	•	•	•	•	•	•	•				•

Recreation Areas Chart

The map location numerals in column 2 show an area's location on the preceding map.

Find thousands of places to camp at AAA.com/campgrounds

	MAP LOCATION	CAMPING	PICNICKING	HIKING TRAILS	BOATING	BOAT RAMP	BOAT RENTAL	FISHING	SWIMMING	PET FRIENDLY	BICYCLE TRAILS	WINTER SPORTS	VISITOR CENTER	LODGE/CABINS	FOOD SERVICE
Lake Wister (E-12) 3,428 acres 2 mi. s. of Wister on US 270. Canoeing, water skiing; horse trails, miniature golf, playground, water spray park.	44	•	•	•	•	•	•	•	•	•	•			•	•
McGee Creek (F-10) 15,100 acres 18 mi. s.e. of Atoka off US 69. Canoeing, jet skiing, kayaking, rafting, water skiing; horse trails, playground, swimming beach.	45	•	•	•	•	•	•	•	•	•	•				•
Natural Falls (C-12) 120 acres 3 mi. w. of West Siloam Springs off US 412. Disc golf, volleyball; basketball court, horseshoe pits, observation deck, playground.	46	•	•	•				•	•	•	•		•		
Osage Hills (B-10) 1,199 acres 11 mi. w. of Bartlesville off US 60. Tennis; ball field, playground, swimming pool.	47	•	•	•	•	•	•	•		•				•	
Raymond Gary (F-11) 64 acres 16 mi. e. of Hugo on US 70. Canoeing, kayaking, rafting; canoe and paddleboat rentals, playground.	48	•	•	•	•	•		•	•	•					
Red Rock Canyon (D-7) 310 acres s. of Hinton on SR 8. Scenic. Rappelling; playground, swimming pool.	49	•	•	•				•	•	•				•	•
Robbers Cave (E-11) 8,246 acres 4 mi. n. of Wilburton on SR 2. Historic. Rappelling; all-terrain vehicle trails, bicycle rental, canoe and paddleboat rentals, horse trails, miniature golf, playground, swimming beach, swimming pool.	50	•	•	•	•	•	•	•	•	•	•		•	•	•
Roman Nose (C-7) 515 acres 8 mi. n.w. of Watonga via SRs 8 and 8A. Golf, horseback riding, tennis; canoe, kayak and paddleboat rentals, fishing gear rental, horse rental, mountain bike rental, playground, swimming pool.	51	•	•	•	•	•	•	•	•	•	•		•	•	•
Sequoyah Bay (C-11) 303 acres 5 mi. s. of Wagoner on SR 16, then 5 mi. e. on Grey Oaks Rd. Horseback riding, tennis, volleyball, water skiing; ball field, basketball court, fishing and pontoon boat rentals, horse rental, playground, swimming pool.	52	•	•	•	•	•	•	•	•	•					
Sequoyah (C-11) 2,876 acres 8 mi. e. of Wagoner on SR 51. Disc golf, golf, tennis, water skiing; horse rental, marina, nature center, pontoon boat rental.	53	•	•	•	•	•	•	•	•	•	•		•	•	•
Snowdale (C-11) 15 acres 2 mi. w. of Salina on SR 20. Volleyball; playground, swimming beach.	54	•	•		•	•	•	•	•	•					
Spavinaw (C-11) 35 acres in Spavinaw on SR 20. Hunting; playground.	55	•	•	•	•			•	•	•					
Spring River Canoe Trails (B-12) 35 acres 3 mi. n. of Quapaw off I-44. Canoeing, kayaking. Primitive camping only.	56	•	•	•	•			•							
Talimena (E-11) 20 acres 6 mi. n. of Talihina on US 271. All-terrain vehicle trails, playground.	57	•	•	•						•	•				
Twin Bridges (B-12) 63 acres 6 mi. n.e. of Fairland on US 60. Volleyball; fishing center, horseshoe pits, playground.	58	•	•	•	•			•	•	•				•	
OTHER															
Arcadia Lake (G-3) 5,078 acres 1.5 mi. w. of Arcadia on US 66. Disc golf, water skiing; horse trails, playground.	59	•	•	•	•	•	•	•	•	•	•			•	
Atoka Reservoir (E-10) 6,000 acres 3 mi. n.e. of Atoka on US 69. Water skiing; playgrounds.	60	•	•	•	•	•	•	•	•						
Beaver Dunes (B-4) 520 acres 1 mi. n. of Beaver on US 270. Dune buggy riding; playground.	61	•	•	•				•		•					•
Bell Cow Lake (G-4) 1,079 acres about 3 mi. n. of Chandler on SR 18. Horse trails, swimming beach.	62	•	•	•	•	•		•	•	•					
Blue River Public Hunting and Fishing Area (F-9) 3 mi. n.e. of Tishomingo on SR 99. Canoeing, hunting, kayaking.	63	•	•		•			•	•	•	•				
Boggy Depot (F-10) 630 acres 11 mi. w. of Atoka on SR 7, then 4 mi. s. Ball field, nature trail, playground.	64	•	•	•				•		•			•		
Brushy Lake (D-12) 90 acres 8 mi. n. of Sallisaw on US 64. Playground.	65	•	•		•	•		•		•					

Recreation Areas Chart

The map location numerals in column 2 show an area's location on the preceding map.

Find thousands of places to camp at AAA.com/campgrounds

	MAP LOCATION	CAMPING	PICNICKING	HIKING TRAILS	BOATING	BOAT RAMP	BOAT RENTAL	FISHING	SWIMMING	PET FRIENDLY	BICYCLE TRAILS	WINTER SPORTS	VISITOR CENTER	LODGE/CABINS	FOOD SERVICE
Cedar Lake (E-12) 90 acres 10 mi. s. of Heavener on US 270, 3 mi. w. on Holson Valley Rd., then 1 mi. n. on FR 269. Canoeing, equestrian camping, volleyball; horse trails, nature trail, playground.	66	•	•	•	•	•	•		•	•	•	•		•	
Clear Creek Lake (F-8) 560 acres 13 mi. n.e. of Duncan. Hunting; playground.	67	•	•		•	•		•	•	•					•
Clinton Lake (D-6) 355 acres 14 mi. w. of Clinton on I-40.	68		•		•	•		•		•					
Crowder Lake University Park (D-6) 22 acres 8 mi. s. of Weatherford on SR 54. Canoeing, kayaking, rafting; canoe rental, interpretive nature trail, rappelling tower, rock climbing wall, ropes course.	69	•	•	•	•	•	•	•	•	•	•		•		
Crystal Beach Park & Lake (C-5) 20 acres on the s.e. edge of Woodward. Golf (nine holes), tennis; miniature golf, playgrounds, pool with water slide, train ride.	70		•	•				•	•	•	•				•
Dead Warrior Lake (D-5) 80 acres 10 mi. n. of Cheyenne on US 283. Hunting; playground.	71	•	•	•	•	•		•	•	•					
Dripping Springs Lake (D-10) 420 acres 6 mi. w. of Okmulgee on SR 56. Playground.	72	•	•		•	•		•	•	•					
Duncan Lake (F-8) 400 acres 9 mi. n.e. of Duncan on Plato Rd., then .5 mi. s. on Duncan Lake Rd. Disc golf, sailing, water skiing; horse rentals, horse trails.	73	•	•	•	•	•		•	•	•					•
Fuqua Lake (F-8) 1,500 acres 21 mi. n.e. of Duncan off SR 29, then 1 mi. s.	74	•	•	•	•	•		•	•	•					•
Grand Lake O' the Cherokees (B-11) 59,200 acres off I-44 at Vinita or Afton. Hunting, sailing, water skiing; all-terrain vehicle trails, horse trails, playground, swimming pool.	75	•	•	•	•	•	•	•	•	•	•		•	•	•
Guthrie Lake (F-2) 230 acres 4 mi. s. of Guthrie on US 77, then 1 mi. w. Playground.	76	•	•	•	•	•		•		•	•				
Holdenville City Lake (E-10) 550 acres 3 mi. s. of Holdenville off SH 48. Horseback riding, water skiing.	77	•	•	•	•	•		•	•	•					•
Humphreys Lake (E-8) 882 acres 8 mi. n.e. of Duncan off SR 29. Hunting.	78	•	•		•	•		•		•					
Jim Hall Lake (D-10) 616 acres 4 mi. e. of Henryetta on New Lake Rd. Water skiing.	79	•	•		•	•		•		•					
Lake Altus-Lugert (E-5) 17 mi. n. of Altus via US 283. Golf; playground, swimming beach, swimming pool.	80	•	•	•	•	•		•	•	•			•	•	•
Lake Carl Blackwell (C-8) 3,300 acres 8 mi. w. of Stillwater on SR 51. Canoeing, jet skiing, kayaking, rafting, sailing, water skiing; canoe, kayak and paddleboat rentals, horse trails.	81	•	•	•	•	•	•	•	•	•	•			•	•
Lake Carl Etling (B-1) 260 acres 26 mi. n.w. of Boise City on SR 325. Playground.	82	•	•	•	•	•		•		•					
Lake Chickasha (E-7) 1,900 acres 15 mi. n.w. of Chickasha via US 62. Hunting, water skiing; playground.	83	•	•		•	•		•	•	•					
Lake Ellsworth (E-7) 5,600 acres 14 mi. n.e. of Lawton via I-44. Hunting, jet skiing, water skiing; marina.	84	•	•		•	•		•	•	•					•
Lake El Reno (H-1) 175 acres at El Reno. Golf, water skiing; motorcycle dirt track, playground, remote-controlled airplane field, skate park.	85	•	•		•	•		•	•	•					•
Lake Hall (E-5) 50 acres 13 mi. n. of Hollis off SR 30. Hunting.	86		•		•	•		•	•						
Lake Jap Beaver (F-7) 213 acres 4.5 mi. n.w. of Waurika off SR 5. Hunting.	87		•	•	•		•	•		•					
Lake John Wells (E-11) 160 acres 1 mi. e. of Stigler on SR 9, then 1 mi. s. Water skiing; playground.	88	•	•		•	•		•	•	•					
Lake Lawtonka (E-7) 1,900 acres 10 mi. n.w. of Lawton via I-44, SR 49 and SR 58. Hunting, jet skiing, water skiing; swimming beach.	89	•	•		•	•		•	•	•					•
Lake McMurtry (C-8) 6 mi. n. of Stillwater on US 177. Canoeing, disc golf, hunting, kayaking; kayak rental, swimming beach.	90	•	•	•	•	•	•	•	•	•	•				

Recreation Areas Chart

The map location numerals in column 2 show an area's location on the preceding map.

Find thousands of places to camp at AAA.com/campgrounds

	MAP LOCATION	CAMPING	PICNICKING	HIKING TRAILS	BOATING	BOAT RAMP	BOAT RENTAL	FISHING	SWIMMING	PET FRIENDLY	BICYCLE TRAILS	WINTER SPORTS	VISITOR CENTER	LODGE/CABINS	FOOD SERVICE
Lake Ponca (B-9) 900 acres 3 mi. n. of Ponca City via SR 11. Disc golf, golf, water skiing; children's fishing pond, nature trail, playground, swimming pool.	91	•	•	•	•	•	•	•	•	•	•		•	•	•
Liberty Lake (G-2) 250 acres 5 mi. s. of Guthrie on US 77, then 2 mi. w. Duck hunting (in season), horseback riding, water skiing.	92	•	•	•	•	•		•		•					•
Nanih Waiya Lake (E-11) 349 acres 1.5 mi. n.w. of Tuskahoma off US 271. Hunting nearby; fishing jetties.	93	•	•		•	•		•		•					
Nichols Lake (D-10) 600 acres 2 mi. s. of Henryetta off Indian Nation Tpke.	94	•	•		•	•		•	•	•					
Okemah Lake (D-10) 730 acres 6 mi. n. of Okemah. Hunting; playground.	95	•	•		•	•		•						•	•
Okmulgee Lake (D-10) 535 acres 5 mi. w. of Okmulgee on SR 56. Water skiing; playground.	96	•	•		•	•		•	•	•			•		
Pauls Valley City Lake (E-8) 750 acres 3 mi. e. of Pauls Valley off SR 19. Hunting, jet skiing.	97	•	•		•	•		•		•					
Pawnee City Lake (C-9) 257 acres 1 mi. n. of Pawnee on SR 18. Golf (nine holes), water skiing; beach, swimming pool.	98	•	•		•	•		•	•	•					
Pennington Creek (F-9) 15 acres in Tishomingo on the 300 block of S. Capitol St.	99	•	•					•	•	•					
Perry Lake (C-8) 614 acres 1.5 mi. s.w. of Perry on Perry Lake Rd. Water skiing; playground.	100	•	•		•	•		•		•					
Quartz Mountain (E-5) 4,284 acres 10 mi. s. of Lone Wolf on SR 44, then 1.5 mi. n. on SR 44A. Golf, water skiing; ATV trails, fishing dock, playground, swimming pool, train ride.	101	•	•	•	•	•	•	•	•	•	•	•	•	•	•
Rocky Lake (D-6) 1,205 acres .5 mi. w. and 1 mi. n. of Rocky via US 183.	102	•	•	•	•	•		•		•					
Skipout Lake (D-5) 60 acres 10 mi. w. of Cheyenne on SR 47.	103	•	•	•	•	•		•	•						
Sportsman Lake (D-9) 350 acres 3 mi. e. of Seminole on US 270, then 2 mi. n. and 1.5 mi. e. on county roads. Equestrian camping; horse trails, playground.	104	•	•	•	•	•	•	•	•	•	•				
Spring Creek Lake (C-5) 50 acres 21 mi. n.w. of Cheyenne on US 283, then 6 mi. w. on a gravel road.	105	•	•	•	•	•		•	•	•					
Stroud Lake (C-9) 17,600 acres 3 mi. n. of Stroud off SR 99, then 3 mi. e. Water skiing; horse trails, playground, ropes course, swimming beach.	106	•	•		•	•		•	•						
Taylor Lake (E-8) 227 acres 7 mi. n. of Marlow on US 81, then 2 mi. e. Playground.	107	•	•	•	•	•		•	•	•					
Tishomingo National Wildlife Refuge (F-10) 16,464 acres 3 mi. s. of Tishomingo via an access road off SR 78.	108	•	•	•	•			•		•					
Turner Falls (F-8) 1,500 acres 5.2 mi. s. of Davis on US 77. Playground.	109	•	•	•				•	•	•				•	•
Wah-Sha-She (B-10) 266 acres 4 mi. w. of Hulah on SR 10. Hunting, water skiing; playground, swimming beach.	110	•	•		•	•		•	•	•					
Washita National Wildlife Refuge (D-6) 8,000 acres 11 mi. w. of Clinton on SR 73, 9 mi. n. on SR 44, 4 mi. w. on SR 33, then .5 mi. n.w. on a county road. Hunting.	111	•	•	•	•			•					•		
Weleetka Lake (D-10) 30 acres 1 mi. w. of Weleetka.	112		•		•	•		•		•					
Wichita Mountains National Wildlife Refuge (E-7) 59,020 acres 3 mi. n. of Cache on SR 115.	113	•	•	•	•			•		•					

ADA (E-9) pop. 16,810, elev. 1,010'

Ada is the seat of Pontotoc County, an area known for oil and gas production as well as cattle raising. Byrd's Mill Spring, south on Cradduck Road following signs to Fittstown, is a popular picnicking site. Opportunities for water skiing and boating are available at Konawa Lake.

Wintersmith Park, on E. 18th Street, has walking trails, a small zoo, a miniature golf course, children's rides, horseshoe pits and a swimming pool. The park contains a restored one-room schoolhouse built in 1907; it is furnished with such items as a pot-bellied stove and desks that have inkwells.

Ada Area Chamber of Commerce: 209 W. Main St., Ada, OK 74821. **Phone:** (580) 332-2506.

Self-guiding tours: A brochure describing a walking tour of the historic district is available at the chamber of commerce.

HAMPTON INN & SUITES ADA   580/436-4040
THREE DIAMOND SAVE Hotel. **Ad-**   **AAA Benefit:**
dress: 1220 Lonnie Abbott Blvd 74820   Members save up to
                                            15%!

RAINTREE INN   580/332-6262
APPROVED Hotel. **Address:** 1100 N Mississippi Ave 74820

WHERE TO EAT

JD'S CAFE & CAFETERIA   580/332-9750
APPROVED American. Casual Dining. **Address:** 911 N Broadway 74820

RIB CRIB BBQ AND GRILL   580/436-1170
APPROVED Barbecue. Casual Dining. **Address:** 1004 Lonnie Abbott Blvd 74820

AFTON (B-11) pop. 1,049, elev. 784'

NATIONAL ROD & CUSTOM CAR HALL OF FAME MUSEUM is 5.3 mi. s.w. on US 60/69, 2 mi. s.e. on SR 85, then 5 mi. e. to 55251 E. SR 85A. Well-known custom car designer and builder Darryl Starbird established this museum to display classic hot rods and custom cars, and to honor the imagination and craftsmanship of the men like Barris, Roth, Posies and Titus, who created them. More than 50 of these exotic, one-of-a-kind cars are exhibited, and about half of the vehicles were designed and built by Starbird himself.

Thousands of photos and memorabilia related to these vehicles and builders cover the walls of the museum. **Time:** Allow 45 minutes minimum. **Hours:** Wed.-Mon. 10-5, Mar.-Nov.; by appointment rest of year. **Cost:** $15; $14 (ages 65+); $10 (ages 8-12). **Phone:** (918) 257-4234 or (918) 519-9562.

🔗 Booth or table?
AAA.com/travelguides/restaurants

ALTUS pop. 19,813, elev. 1,388'

DAYS INN ALTUS   580/482-9300
APPROVED Hotel. **Address:** 2804 N Main St 73521

HAMPTON INN & SUITES ALTUS   580/482-1273
THREE DIAMOND SAVE Hotel. **Ad-**   **AAA Benefit:**
dress: 3601 N Main St 73521   Members save up to
                                            15%!

HOLIDAY INN EXPRESS & SUITES ALTUS   580/480-1212
THREE DIAMOND Hotel. **Address:** 2812 E Broadway 73521

WHERE TO EAT

FRED'S STEAKHOUSE & SALOON   580/480-0555
APPROVED Steak. Casual Dining. **Address:** 2021 N Main St 73521

ANADARKO (E-7) pop. 6,762, elev. 1,164'

The area in and around Anadarko traditionally served as hunting grounds for three major Native American tribes. The town was founded in 1901 by white settlers claiming land used by the Kiowa, Comanche and Wichita reservations. Farming and stock raising were the major livelihoods until oil was discovered in 1920 and drilling ensued. Agriculture and oil remain the leading industries.

Local Native American tribes include the Apache, Caddo, Delaware, Fort Sill Apache, Kiowa and Wichita. A Bureau of Indian Affairs office is in Anadarko, servicing western Oklahoma and Horton, Kan. Representative of regional Native American heritage are the striking murals by Kiowa artists in the Federal Building at 120 S. First St.

Colorful sandstone canyons and lakes skirt US 281, which travels 16 miles north of Anadarko to Binger. From Binger a scenic portion of SR 37/152 runs 20 miles east to Minco, where US 81 begins a scenic course through the Canadian River Valley to El Reno at I-40. The Wichita Mountains are southwest of the city.

Anadarko Chamber of Commerce: 501 W. Virginia Ave., Anadarko, OK 73005. **Phone:** (405) 247-6651.

ARDMORE (F-9) pop. 24,283, elev. 868'
• Hotels p. 324 • Restaurants p. 324

Ardmore was the site of a track-side tent city, which Santa Fe Railroad officials selected as a permanent townsite in 1887. Named after one official's hometown in Pennsylvania, the land was part of the Roff Brothers' 700 Ranch. The Roffs were the first homeowners in Ardmore. A replica of the ranch house was moved from Fair Park to the Carter County Historical Museum. Ranching is still an important industry, along with oil drilling and refining and tire manufacturing.

Art exhibits and music, dance and theater performances are offered at the Charles B. Goddard

Center for the Visual and Performing Arts, First Avenue and D Street S.W., and at The Brass Ring Performing Arts Center, 120 A St. N.E. Two miles east of Ardmore on SR 199, the Samuel Roberts Noble Foundation specializes in medical and agricultural research.

Four municipal lakes—Ardmore City Lake, Lake Jean Neustadt, Mountain Lake and Rock Creek Reservoir—offer fishing, boating and picnicking opportunities. Southeast of the city, Lake Murray State Park *(see Recreation Areas Chart)*, Oklahoma's largest state park, offers extensive recreational facilities. The Arbuckle Mountains, about 20 miles north of Ardmore, provide another popular recreation area. Ardmore Regional Park has walking and biking trails, a large family picnic area and a softball complex.

Ardmore Chamber of Commerce: 410 W. Main St., Ardmore, OK 73402. **Phone:** (580) 223-7765.

Self-guiding tours: A brochure describing two tours—a self-guiding walking tour of downtown Ardmore's historic sites as well as a driving tour covering sites throughout the city—is available at the chamber of commerce.

An MP3 player is provided for use with the 26-page Historic Downtown Walking Tour booklet. The booklet is available for $12 at the Ardmore Main Street Authority, 251 E. Main St.

GREATER SOUTHWEST HISTORICAL MUSEUM is at 35 Sunset Dr. The museum's main hall features an original 1895 log cabin along with reproductions of a courtroom, law office, school, post office, dentist's office, blacksmith shop and doctor's office. One wing exhibits military memorabilia from the American Revolution through Operation Iraqi Freedom. The From the Ashes exhibit in the south wing recounts the city's great fire of 1895. Another wing houses carriages, an early electric car and a working model of an oil field. **Hours:** Tues.-Sat. 10-5. Closed major holidays. **Cost:** Free. **Phone:** (580) 226-3857.

BEST WESTERN PLUS ARDMORE INN & SUITES
580/223-3200
▼▼ THREE DIAMOND
Hotel

AAA Benefit:
Members save up to 15% and earn bonus points!

Address: 2600 W Broadway 73401 **Location:** I-35 exit 31A, just e. **Facility:** 66 units, some efficiencies. 3 stories, interior corridors. **Pool:** heated indoor. **Activities:** exercise room. **Guest Services:** coin laundry.

BOARDERS INN & SUITES OF ARDMORE   580/223-7525
◆ APPROVED Hotel. **Address:** 136 Holiday Dr 73401

COURTYARD BY MARRIOTT ARDMORE   580/224-2764
▼▼ THREE DIAMOND [SAVE] Hotel. **Address:** 2025 N Rockford Rd 73401

AAA Benefit:
Members save 5% or more!

HAMPTON INN & SUITES BY HILTON   580/490-9011
▼▼ THREE DIAMOND
Hotel

Hampton
AAA Benefit:
Members save up to 15%!

Address: 526 Railway Express St 73401 **Location:** I-35 exit 31A, just se. **Facility:** 73 units. 4 stories, interior corridors. **Pool:** heated indoor. **Activities:** exercise room. **Guest Services:** valet and coin laundry.

[SAVE] [TI+] CALL [symbols] BIZ
[wifi symbols]

HILTON GARDEN INN ARDMORE   580/226-2223
▼▼ THREE DIAMOND [SAVE] Hotel. **Address:** 710 Premier Pkwy 73401

AAA Benefit:
Members save up to 15%!

HOLIDAY INN ARDMORE- I-35   580/226-3333
▼▼ THREE DIAMOND Hotel. **Address:** 2207 N Rockford Rd 73401

QUALITY HOTEL   580/223-7130
◆ APPROVED Hotel. **Address:** 2705 W Broadway 73401

SPRINGHILL SUITES BY MARRIOTT   580/226-7100
▼▼ THREE DIAMOND [SAVE] Hotel. **Address:** 2501 Centennial Dr N 73402

AAA Benefit:
Members save 5% or more!

WHERE TO EAT

CAFE ALLEY   580/223-6413
◆ APPROVED American. Casual Dining. **Address:** 126 Caddo St 73401

EL CHICO   580/226-3343
◆ APPROVED Tex-Mex. Casual Dining. **Address:** 124 Holiday Dr 73401

SIRLOIN STOCKADE   580/226-6281
◆ APPROVED Steak. Quick Serve. **Address:** 1217 N Commerce 73401

TWO FROGS GRILL   580/226-3764
◆ APPROVED American. Casual Dining. **Address:** 2646 W Broadway 73401

ATOKA pop. 3,107, elev. 583'

COMFORT INN & SUITES   580/889-8999
▼▼ THREE DIAMOND
Hotel

Address: 1502 S Mississippi Ave 74525 **Location:** Just s of center. **Facility:** 52 units. 3 stories, interior corridors. **Activities:** exercise room. **Guest Services:** coin laundry. **Featured Amenity:** breakfast buffet.

[SAVE] [TI+] [symbols] BIZ [wifi] [symbols] / SOME UNITS

SUPER 8 ATOKA 580/889-7381
APPROVED Hotel. **Address:** 2421 S Mississippi Ave 74525

BARTLESVILLE (B-10) pop. 35,750, elev. 695'

A working replica of the first oil well of commercial importance drilled in Oklahoma is in Johnstone Park, which adjoins the Bartlesville city limits. The original well, Nellie Johnstone No. 1, has been reproduced as a memorial to oilmen and features gushing water.

Bartlesville Area Convention and Visitors Bureau: 201 S.W. Keeler Ave., Bartlesville, OK 74003. **Phone:** (918) 336-8709 or (800) 364-8708.

GEM SAVE **WOOLAROC RANCH, MUSEUM AND WILDLIFE PRESERVE** is 12 mi. s.w. on SR 123 to 1925 Woolaroc Ranch Rd. Covering 3,700 acres of rugged timberland, oilman Frank Phillips' Woolaroc Ranch depicts the culture and legacy of the American West.

Woolaroc (the name comes from the *woo*ds, *la*kes and *ro*cks that are part of the Osage Hills area) was designed as a retreat for Phillips, a place where he could get back to nature. What began as a small cabin became an elaborate log lodge with nine bedrooms. Completed in 1927, the house is decorated in a rustic lodge style.

The 50,000-square-foot museum is highlighted by works by Frederic Remington, Charles M. Russell and other Western artists; artifacts from 40 Native American tribes that lived in Oklahoma; a collection of Colt firearms; and exhibits of Western gear.

More than 800 animals, including bison, elk, deer and water buffalo, can often be seen on a driving tour through the wildlife preserve. Phillips wanted the preserve to retain the feel of the West as he recalled it prior to the turn of the 20th century. Nature trails allow visitors to explore the grounds, and an animal barn is available in summer and on weekends in fall. Mountain Man Camp is a re-creation of an 1830s trading post, and is open Memorial Day through Labor Day. Films showing the history of Woolaroc are presented in the Heritage Center.

Time: Allow 3 hours minimum. **Hours:** Tues.-Sun. 10-5, Memorial Day-Labor Day; Wed.-Sun. 10-5, rest of year. Animal barn open mid-Mar. to late Dec. Mountain Man Camp open mid-Mar. to early Sept. **Cost:** $12; $10 (ages 65+); free (ages 0-11). **Phone:** (918) 336-0307 or (888) 966-5276.

CANDLEWOOD SUITES 918/766-0044
APPROVED Extended Stay Hotel. **Address:** 3812 SE Washington Pl 74006

HAMPTON INN BY HILTON 918/333-4051
THREE DIAMOND SAVE Hotel. **Address:** 130 SE Washington Blvd 74006
AAA Benefit: Members save up to 15%!

HILTON GARDEN INN BARTLESVILLE 918/336-0808
THREE DIAMOND SAVE Hotel. **Address:** 205 SW Frank Phillips Blvd 74003
AAA Benefit: Members save up to 15%!

HOLIDAY INN EXPRESS & SUITES 918/766-0020
THREE DIAMOND Hotel. **Address:** 4016 SE Price Rd 74006

WHERE TO EAT

HIDEAWAY PIZZA 918/214-8777
APPROVED Pizza. Casual Dining. **Address:** 100 SW Frank Phillips Blvd 74003

LA FIESTA MEXICAN RESTAURANT 918/333-0032
APPROVED Mexican. Casual Dining. **Address:** 3800 Washington Blvd 74006

MONTANA MIKE'S 918/333-2666
APPROVED Steak. Casual Dining. **Address:** 3825 SE Adams Rd 74006

RIB CRIB BBQ AND GRILL 918/333-6200
APPROVED Barbecue. Casual Dining. **Address:** 2077 SE Washington Blvd 74006

BLACKWELL pop. 7,092

BEST WESTERN BLACKWELL INN 580/363-1300
THREE DIAMOND Hotel Best Western. **AAA Benefit:** Members save up to 15% and earn bonus points!

Address: 4545 W White Ave 74631 **Location:** I-35 exit 222, just ne. **Facility:** 122 units. 3 stories, interior corridors. **Pool:** heated indoor. **Activities:** exercise room. **Guest Services:** coin laundry.
SAVE CALL BIZ HS SOME UNITS

BROKEN ARROW pop. 98,850, elev. 755'
- Restaurants p. 326
- Hotels & Restaurants map & index p. 386
- Part of Tulsa area — see map p. 375

BEST WESTERN KENOSHA INN 918/251-2795 62
THREE DIAMOND Hotel Best Western. **AAA Benefit:** Members save up to 15% and earn bonus points!

Address: 1200 E Lansing St 74012 **Location:** 0.4 mi nw of jct SR 51 and Kenosha/71st sts. **Facility:** 44 units. 2 stories (no elevator), interior corridors. **Pool:** outdoor. **Activities:** exercise room. **Featured Amenity:** full hot breakfast.
SAVE BIZ

CLARION HOTEL 918/258-7085 56
APPROVED Hotel. **Address:** 2600 N Aspen Ave 74012

(See map & index p. 386.)

HAMPTON INN BY HILTON-TULSA/BROKEN ARROW
918/251-6060 **57**
THREE DIAMOND [SAVE] Hotel. **Address:** 2300 W Albany St 74012
AAA Benefit: Members save up to 15%!

HILTON GARDEN INN BROKEN ARROW 918/940-8444 **58**
THREE DIAMOND [SAVE] Hotel. **Address:** 420 W Albany St 74012
AAA Benefit: Members save up to 15%!

HOLIDAY INN EXPRESS & SUITES 918/355-3200 **60**
THREE DIAMOND Hotel. **Address:** 2201 N Stone Wood Cir 74012

HOMEWOOD SUITES BY HILTON TULSA SOUTH
918/392-7700 **61**
THREE DIAMOND [SAVE] Extended Stay Hotel. **Address:** 4900 W Madison Pl 74012
AAA Benefit: Members save up to 15%!

TOWNEPLACE SUITES BY MARRIOTT 918/355-9600 **59**
THREE DIAMOND [SAVE] Extended Stay Hotel. **Address:** 2251 N Stonewood Cir 74012
AAA Benefit: Members save 5% or more!

WHERE TO EAT

CHARLESTON'S RESTAURANT 918/355-9177
APPROVED American. Casual Dining. **Address:** 251 E Hillside Dr 74012

DUFFY'S RESTAURANT 918/251-3285 **42**
APPROVED American. Casual Dining. **Address:** 706 S Elm Pl 74012

EL VIEJO'S 918/251-4175 **40**
APPROVED Mexican. Casual Dining. **Address:** 600 S Aspen Ave 74012

FIESTA MAMBO DOWNTOWN 918/455-0356 **39**
APPROVED Mexican. Casual Dining. **Address:** 219 S Main St 74012

GOLDIES PATIO GRILL 918/455-6128
APPROVED American. Casual Dining. **Address:** 1912 S Elm Pl 74012

HIDEAWAY PIZZA 918/286-1777
APPROVED Pizza. Casual Dining. **Address:** 1150 N 9th St 74012

IN THE RAW SUSHI 918/893-6111 **38**
APPROVED Asian Sushi. Casual Dining. **Address:** 216 S Main St 74012

JAKE'S CAFE 918/258-7710 **41**
APPROVED American. Casual Dining. **Address:** 626 S Aspen Ave 74012

LOS CABOS MEXICAN GRILL & CANTINA 918/355-8877 **33**
APPROVED Mexican. Casual Dining. **Address:** 151 E Bass Pro Dr 74012

LOUIE'S GRILL & BAR 918/355-0421 **35**
APPROVED American. Casual Dining. **Address:** 1640 N 9th St 74013

MEXICO LINDO 918/294-0987 **36**
APPROVED Mexican. Casual Dining. **Address:** 4950 W Kenosha St 74012

MR MAMBO 918/994-7300 **43**
APPROVED Mexican. Casual Dining. **Address:** 3326 S Elm Pl 74012

OKLAHOMA JOE'S BAR-B-CUE 918/355-0000 **32**
APPROVED Barbecue. Quick Serve. **Address:** 333 W Albany St 74012

RIB CRIB BBQ AND GRILL 918/258-1559
APPROVED Barbecue. Casual Dining. **Address:** 121 W Kenosha St 74012

RON'S HAMBURGERS & CHILI 918/451-7667
APPROVED American. Casual Dining. **Address:** 1913 E Elm Pl 74012

STONE MILL BBQ AND STEAKHOUSE 918/258-4227 **34**
APPROVED Barbecue. Casual Dining. **Address:** 2000 W Reno Ave 74012

TED'S CAFE ESCONDIDO 918/254-8337 **37**
APPROVED Mexican. Casual Dining. **Address:** 3202 W Kenosha St 74012

CACHE (E-6) pop. 2,796, elev. 1,271'

WICHITA MOUNTAINS NATIONAL WILDLIFE REFUGE visitor center is 3 mi. n. to 20539 SR 115 at jct. SR 49; the refuge headquarters is 6 mi. w. of the visitor center. The 59,020-acre refuge protects bison, longhorn cattle, elk, deer and turkeys. The strangely eroded, often vividly colored mountains form one of the nation's oldest ranges. The Charon's Garden Wilderness Area preserves rugged portions of these mountains.

A paved road leads to Mount Scott's summit, and a scenic stretch of SR 49 passes through the refuge. The visitor center has exhibits and a video presentation. Fishing, camping, picnicking and boating are permitted in designated areas. More than 15 miles of hiking trails wind through scrub oak forests, boulder-strewn mountains and prairie grasslands. Phone for information about interpretive programs and guided tours. *See Recreation Areas Chart.*

Hours: Refuge open daily dawn-dusk. Visitor center daily 9-5. Phone ahead to confirm visitor center hours. Closed major holidays. **Cost:** Free. **Phone:** (580) 429-3222. [GT] [▲] [⊠] [🏠] [⛽]

CATOOSA pop. 7,151, elev. 605'
• Part of Tulsa area — see map p. 375

HAMPTON INN & SUITES BY HILTON-CATOOSA
918/739-3939
THREE DIAMOND [SAVE] Hotel. **Address:** 100 McNabb Field Rd 74015
AAA Benefit: Members save up to 15%!

Love the great outdoors? Find places to camp at AAA.com/campgrounds

HARD ROCK HOTEL & CASINO TULSA   918/384-7800

FOUR DIAMOND
Resort Hotel

Address: 777 W Cherokee St 74015 **Location:** I-44 exit 240A, just nw. **Facility:** The property features shopping, gaming and an attractively furnished pool area. Three towers offer varying levels of luxury. TV view seating, honor bars and granite accents are featured in all rooms. 454 units. 7-19 stories, interior corridors. **Parking:** on-site and valet. **Terms:** check-in 4:30 pm. **Amenities:** safes. **Dining:** 7 restaurants, also, McGill's, Wild Potato Buffet, see separate listings. **Pool:** heated outdoor. **Activities:** hot tub, cabanas, regulation golf, exercise room, in-room exercise equipment, spa. **Guest Services:** valet laundry, area transportation. *(See ad p. 391.)*

🆂🅰🆅🅴 🕱 🕂 🍽 🏊 🍸 CALL 🚹 🛍 🌊 BIZ
HS 📶 ✕ 🧑 🔌 ▭ 💻

LA QUINTA INN & SUITES BY WYNDHAM TULSA - CATOOSA ROUTE 66   918/739-4600

THREE DIAMOND
Hotel

Address: 2009 S Cherokee St 74015 **Location:** I-44 exit 240A, just n. **Facility:** 67 units. 4 stories, interior corridors. **Pool:** heated indoor. **Activities:** hot tub, par 3 golf, exercise room. **Guest Services:** valet and coin laundry, area transportation. **Featured Amenity:** full hot breakfast.

🆂🅰🆅🅴 🕂 🍸 CALL 🚹 🌊 🕂
BIZ 📶 ✕ 🔌 ▭ 💻
/ SOME UNITS 🍽

WHERE TO EAT

MCGILL'S   918/384-7500
THREE DIAMOND Steak. Fine Dining. **Address:** 777 W Cherokee St 74015

MOLLY'S   918/266-7853
APPROVED American. Casual Dining. **Address:** 3700 N Hwy 66 74015

WILD POTATO BUFFET   918/384-7800
APPROVED American. Casual Dining. **Address:** 777 W Cherokee St 74015

CHEYENNE   (D-5) pop. 801, elev. 1,968'

Cheyenne was site of the 1868 Battle of the Washita, in which Lt. Col. George A. Custer initiated an attack upon Chief Black Kettle and his people. This was the first attack in a campaign to quell uprisings by the Cheyenne and Arapaho, who felt the government had broken promises made at the 1867 peace treaty signing in Medicine Lodge, Kan. Also in Cheyenne is Black Kettle National Grassland *(see Recreation Areas Chart).*

Cheyenne—Roger Mills Chamber of Commerce & Tourism: 101 S. L.L. Males Ave., Cheyenne, OK 73628. **Phone:** (580) 497-3318 or (877) 497-3318.

WASHITA BATTLEFIELD NATIONAL HISTORIC SITE, 2 mi. w. on SR 47A, is the site of Lt. Col. George A. Custer's 1868 charge on the sleeping Cheyenne village of Chief Black Kettle, the first attack in an attempt to halt rebellious acts by the Cheyenne and Arapaho on Kansas settlers. Custer's attack set the stage for his defeat 8 years later at Little Big Horn.

The visitor center, .9 mile west on SR 47A, also serves as the headquarters for Black Kettle National Grassland. The center has panoramic views of the Washita River Valley and features exhibits and a 27-minute film "Destiny at Dawn: Loss and Victory on the Washita," detailing the events leading to Custer's charge.

Self-guiding tours are available. An overlook pavilion at the battlefield site on SR 47A is the beginning of a 1.5-mile self-guiding loop trail. **Hours:** Historic site daily dawn-dusk. Visitor center daily 8-5; closed Jan. 1, Thanksgiving and Christmas. **Cost:** Free. **Phone:** (580) 497-2742. 🅿

⚜ CHICKASAW NATIONAL RECREATION AREA   (F-9)

Near Sulphur on US 177 and SR 7, the Chickasaw National Recreation Area encompasses 10,000 acres in south-central Oklahoma. Woods and streams with small waterfalls characterize this region, which is known for its mineral waters. Springs within the area have been classified as sulphur, freshwater and bromide.

A small herd of American bison in a natural setting recalls the vast herds that once roamed the territory. Campfire talks, children's programs and nature walks are summer features. Arbuckle Dam impounds the Lake of the Arbuckles at the confluence of Buckhorn, Guy Sandy and Rock creeks.

Various recreational facilities are offered at specified sites, including six campgrounds. There are several picnic areas, and other facilities are in nearby Sulphur. The 2,350-acre Lake of the Arbuckles offers swimming and boating; a safety inspection for boats is available at launch ramps. A state license is required for fishing; hunting is permitted in season.

The recreation area is split into two districts: The Lake District includes Lake of the Arbuckles, and the Platt District includes Travertine Nature Center and 67-acre Veteran's Lake. Pets are permitted but must be restricted at all times; they are not allowed in swimming areas.

Note: Due to extended periods of drought, swimming areas and boat launches may be closed when water levels are too low. Check online for current park alerts or phone (580) 622-7234 or (580) 622-3165. *See Recreation Areas Chart.*

TRAVERTINE NATURE CENTER is 2 mi. from the Chickasaw National Recreation Area headquarters at jct. US 177 and Broadway Rd. Straddling Travertine Creek, the interpretive center exhibits live animals and reptiles native to the surrounding woods, plains and streams. Rangers sometimes carry a live snake for visitors to handle; slides, movies and demonstrations provide further insight into man's relationship with nature.

Hours: Nature center daily 9-5:30, Memorial Day-Labor Day; 9-4:30, rest of year. Ranger programs and nature walks Fri.-Sun. at 9 a.m., 2, and 9 p.m., Memorial Day-Labor Day; Sat.-Sun. at 3, rest of year. Phone ahead to confirm ranger program schedule. **Cost:** Free. **Phone:** (580) 622-3165.

CHICKASHA pop. 16,036

HAMPTON INN   405/320-5955

▼▼**THREE DIAMOND** SAVE Hotel. **Address:** 3004 S 4th St 73018

AAA Benefit: Members save up to 15%!

QUALITY INN CHICKASHA   405/224-4890

▼▼ APPROVED
Hotel

Address: 2101 S 4th St 73018 **Location:** I-44 exit 80, just nw. **Facility:** 150 units. 2 stories (no elevator), interior/exterior corridors. **Pool:** heated indoor. **Activities:** limited exercise equipment. **Guest Services:** valet and coin laundry. **Featured Amenity:** breakfast buffet.

SAVE ▼ ≈ BIZ 🖧 📱 🍽 🖥 / SOME UNITS 🐾

CLAREMORE (E-3) pop. 18,581, elev. 608'
• Part of Tulsa area — see map p. 375

Claremore was the home of Lynn Riggs, author of "Green Grow the Lilacs," the play that inspired the musical "Oklahoma!" Northeast of town on SR 28A near Foyil stands what is said to be the world's largest totem pole. Carved of stone and concrete, this 90-foot by 18-foot monument to Native American tribes is the center of Totem Pole Park. The park also has a museum and picnic area.

Claremore Expo & Tourism Development: 400 Veterans Pkwy., Claremore, OK 74017. **Phone:** (918) 341-8688 or (877) 341-8688.

J.M. DAVIS ARMS & HISTORICAL MUSEUM, 330 N. J.M. Davis Blvd., houses a diverse collection of firearms, swords and knives; Western, Civil War-era and Native American artifacts; music boxes and musical instruments; steins; political buttons; statues; and World War I posters. More than 50,000 items are on display. A library provides reference works.

The area's Western heritage is remembered through displays of saddles, Stetsons, cattle brands and lariats as well as Native American pottery and arrowheads.

Antique musical instruments such as Victrolas and banjos are displayed as are 1,200 German beer steins and more than 600 World War I posters. A group of statuary art by late 19th-century sculptor John Rogers depicts vignettes of everyday life. **Hours:** Tues.-Sat. 10-5. **Cost:** Donations. **Phone:** (918) 341-5707.

WILL ROGERS MEMORIAL MUSEUM, 1720 W. Will Rogers Blvd., is a ranch-style museum overlooking Claremore on the site where Will Rogers planned to build a home. In the foyer is a well-known bronze sculpture of Rogers by Jo Davidson. Among personal items exhibited are an international saddle collection, miniature saddles, riding whips and ropes, and an extensive collection of movie posters.

Dioramas highlight Rogers' life and stints as a rodeo performer, vaudeville sensation, columnist, author and star of some 70 films. Documentaries and several of Will Rogers' movies are shown continuously; a hands-on children's area specializes in Native American life. A library and archives are included; the Rogers' family tomb is in a sunken garden; the Heritage Gallery showcases Rogers' Cherokee roots. **Time:** Allow 1 hour minimum. **Hours:** Daily 10-5, Mar. 1 to Nov. 11; Wed.-Sun. 10-5, rest of year. Phone ahead to confirm schedule. **Cost:** $7; $5 (ages 62+ and active military with ID); $3 (ages 6-17).

HAMPTON INN & SUITES BY HILTON CLAREMORE
918/965-1360

▼▼**THREE DIAMOND** SAVE Hotel. **Address:** 1811 S Scissortail Ave 74017

AAA Benefit: Members save up to 15%!

MOTEL 6   918/343-3297

▼▼ APPROVED Hotel. **Address:** 1720 S Lynn Riggs Blvd 74017

WHERE TO EAT

HAMMETT HOUSE RESTAURANT   918/341-7333

▼▼ APPROVED
American
Casual Dining
$7-$24

AAA Inspector Notes: This casual family-friendly restaurant offers daily specials and a great variety of home-style American dishes. They also serve homemade pie and freshly baked rolls. The serving staff is attentive and efficient. It's regionally known and has been in business for more than 30 years. **Features:** beer only. **Address:** 1616 W Will Rogers Blvd 74017 **Location:** On SR 88; adjacent to Will Rogers Memorial Park. L D

RIB CRIB BBQ AND GRILL   918/283-4600

▼▼ APPROVED Barbecue. Casual Dining. **Address:** 1736 S Lynn Riggs Blvd 74017

CLINTON (D-6) pop. 9,033, elev. 1,564'

Clinton is a major shipping center for the area's cotton, wheat and cattle industries. Recreational opportunities are offered at the Washita River. Foss State Park *(see Recreation Areas Chart)* covers 1,749 acres northwest of town, and the Clinton Dam creates a 700-acre lake along the city limits. The nearby 8,000-acre Washita National Wildlife Refuge offers opportunities for wildlife observation and limited hunting and fishing *(see Recreation Areas Chart)*.

Clinton Chamber of Commerce: 101 S. 4th St., Frisco Center, Clinton, OK 73601. **Phone:** (580) 323-2222.

OKLAHOMA ROUTE 66 MUSEUM is off I-40 exit 65; take I-40 Bus. Rte. w. to 2229 W. Gary Blvd. The museum tells the story of Route 66 and the history of transportation, reflecting American life from the opening of the road in the 1920s through its closing in the 1970s. Notable are vintage automobiles and a replica of a 1950s roadside diner.

Time: Allow 30 minutes minimum. **Hours:** Mon.-Sat. 9-7, Sun. 1-6, May-Aug.; Mon.-Sat. 9-5, Sun. 1-5, Feb.-Apr. and Sept.-Nov.; Tues.-Sat. 9-5, rest of year. Closed state holidays and first week in Jan. **Cost:** $5; $4 (ages 65+); $1 (ages 6-18). **Phone:** (580) 323-7866.

HAMPTON INN   580/323-4267
THREE DIAMOND **SAVE** Hotel. **Ad-dress:** 2000 Lexington Ave 73601

AAA Benefit: Members save up to 15%!

HOLIDAY INN EXPRESS   580/323-1950
THREE DIAMOND Hotel. **Address:** 2000 Boulevard of Champions 73601

LA QUINTA INN & SUITES   580/547-4128
THREE DIAMOND Hotel. **Address:** 2715 Chapman Rd 73601

WHERE TO EAT

MONTANA MIKE'S   580/323-3333
APPROVED Steak. Casual Dining. **Address:** 2020 Lexington Ave 73601

COWETA pop. 9,943
• Part of Tulsa area — see map p. 375

BEST WESTERN PLUS COWETA'S 1ST HOTEL
                                                      918/279-6644
THREE DIAMOND
Hotel

Best Western PLUS. **AAA Benefit:** Members save up to 15% and earn bonus points!

Address: 13593 SR 51 S 74429 **Location:** 1 mi n of Jct 141st St. **Facility:** 53 units. 3 stories, interior corridors. **Pool:** heated indoor. **Activities:** exercise room. **Guest Services:** complimentary laundry. **Featured Amenity: full hot breakfast.**

SAVE CALL

CUSHING pop. 7,826

BEST WESTERN PLUS CUSHING INN & SUITES
                                                      918/306-4299
THREE DIAMOND
Hotel

Best Western PLUS. **AAA Benefit:** Members save up to 15% and earn bonus points!

Address: 508 E Main St 74023 **Location:** Jct SR 33 and 18. **Facility:** 52 units, some cottages. 3 stories, interior corridors. **Pool:** heated indoor. **Activities:** exercise room. **Guest Services:** coin laundry.

SAVE CALL

DAVIS (F-9) pop. 2,683, elev. 843'

Near Davis in the Arbuckle Mountains is 1,500-acre Turner Falls Park, 5.25 miles south on US 77. The scenic park has a 77-foot waterfall that has created several natural swimming pools. The park also features streams and ponds cutting through rock and hills, camp sites, cabins, caves (too small to enter) and hiking trails. Phone (580) 369-2988 for additional information. *See Recreation Areas Chart.*

Davis Chamber of Commerce : 100 E. Main St., Davis, OK 73030. **Phone:** (580) 369-2402.

THE INN AT TREASURE VALLEY CASINO   580/369-3223
APPROVED Hotel. **Address:** 12252 Ruppe Rd 73030

DUNCAN (F-7) pop. 23,431, elev. 1,125'
• Hotels p. 329

GEM **SAVE** CHISHOLM TRAIL HERITAGE CENTER is at 1000 Chisholm Trail Pkwy. The history of the Chisholm Trail—the route used to move an estimated 5 million head of cattle between Texas ranches and Kansas railroads—is recounted through a multisensory experiential theater, animatronic Jesse Chisholm conversation, paintings, sculptures and a 245-foot Chisholm Trail walkway. Interactive displays allow visitors to make trail drive decisions, rope a steer, learn about early settlers and visit the historic Duncan store. A life-size bronze statue depicting a cattle drive is a museum highlight.

The Garis Gallery of the American West houses a rotating collection of bronzes, drawings and paintings depicting frontier- and trail-era life created by national and local artists, including Frederic Remington and Charles M. Russell. Docent-led and self-guiding tours are provided.

Time: Allow 1 hour minimum. **Hours:** Mon.-Sat. 10-5, Sun. 1-5 or by appointment. **Cost:** $6; $5 (ages 55+); $4 (ages 5-17 and military with ID); $17 (family, two adults and four children). **Phone:** (580) 252-6692. **GT**

HAMPTON INN   580/255-1700
THREE DIAMOND **SAVE** Hotel. **Ad-dress:** 2301 N Hwy 81 73533

AAA Benefit: Members save up to 15%!

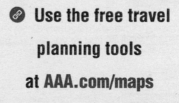

Use the free travel planning tools at AAA.com/maps

DURANT (F-10) pop. 15,856, elev. 643'

The capital of the Choctaw Nation was moved to Durant after Oklahoma became a state in 1907. The Choctaw Nation Tribal Headquarters is at the intersection of 16th and Locust.

An unusual statue stands on the front lawn of the Durant City Hall. Known as the World's Largest Peanut, the monument is a tribute to Bryan County peanut growers and processors.

Durant Area Chamber of Commerce: 215 N. 4th Ave., Durant, OK 74701. **Phone:** (580) 924-0848.

BEST WESTERN MARKITA INN   580/924-7676

 APPROVED
Hotel

Best Western. **AAA Benefit:** Members save up to 15% and earn bonus points!

Address: 2401 W Main St 74701 **Location:** Just w of jct US 69/75 and 70. **Facility:** 62 units. 2 stories (no elevator), exterior corridors. **Pool:** outdoor. **Activities:** exercise room. **Guest Services:** coin laundry.

CHOCTAW CASINO/RESORT   580/920-0160

FOUR DIAMOND
Contemporary Resort Hotel

Address: 4216 S Hwy 69/75 74701 **Location:** US 75 exit Choctaw Rd, just e. **Facility:** You may get lucky in the casino, but it's a sure thing you'll be pleased spending your time enjoying the hopping aquatic oasis surrounded by lush palm trees or being pampered at the full-service spa. 717 units. 12-13 stories, interior corridors. **Parking:** on-site and valet. **Amenities:** safes. **Dining:** 12 restaurants, also, 1832 Steakhouse, see separate listing. **Pool:** heated outdoor, heated indoor. **Activities:** hot tub, steamroom, cabanas, game room, exercise room, spa. **Guest Services:** coin laundry. *(See ad starting on p. 38.)*

CHOCTAW INN   580/920-0160

APPROVED
Hotel

Address: 4202 S Hwy 69/75 74701 **Location:** US 75 exit Choctaw Rd, just e. **Facility:** 101 units. 2 stories, interior corridors. **Amenities:** safes. **Pool:** heated outdoor, heated indoor. **Activities:** hot tub, cabanas, game room, exercise room. **Guest Services:** coin laundry, area transportation. *(See ad starting on p. 38.)*

HAMPTON INN & SUITES BY HILTON DURANT   580/924-0300
THREE DIAMOND SAVE Hotel. **Address:** 3199 Shamrock Ln 74701

AAA Benefit: Members save up to 15%!

HOLIDAY INN EXPRESS & SUITES DURANT   580/924-9777
THREE DIAMOND Hotel. **Address:** 613 University Pl 74701

WHERE TO EAT

1832 STEAKHOUSE   580/920-0160
THREE DIAMOND Steak. Fine Dining. **Address:** 4216 S Hwy 69/75 74701

MAIN STREET BARBECUE   580/745-9120
APPROVED American. Casual Dining. **Address:** 42 W Main St 74701

EDMOND pop. 81,405, elev. 1,204'
- **Hotels & Restaurants map & index p. 356**
- **Part of Oklahoma City area — see map p. 343**

BEST WESTERN EDMOND INN & SUITES   405/216-0300 66

APPROVED
Hotel

Best Western. **AAA Benefit:** Members save up to 15% and earn bonus points!

Address: 2700 E 2nd St 73034 **Location:** I-35 exit 141, 1.1 mi w. Located in a quiet area. **Facility:** 60 units. 2 stories (no elevator), interior corridors. **Pool:** heated indoor. **Activities:** exercise room. **Guest Services:** coin laundry.

FAIRFIELD INN & SUITES BY MARRIOTT   405/341-4818 69
THREE DIAMOND SAVE Hotel. **Address:** 301 Meline Dr 73034

AAA Benefit: Members save 5% or more!

HAMPTON INN BY HILTON   405/844-3037 70
THREE DIAMOND
Hotel

 **AAA Benefit:** Members save up to 15%!

Address: 300 Meline Dr 73034 **Location:** I-35 exit 141, just w. **Facility:** 70 units. 3 stories, interior corridors. **Pool:** heated indoor. **Activities:** exercise room. **Guest Services:** valet and coin laundry. **Featured Amenity:** breakfast buffet.

HILTON GARDEN INN & EDMOND CONFERENCE CENTER   405/285-0900
THREE DIAMOND SAVE Hotel. **Address:** 2833 Conference Dr 73034

AAA Benefit: Members save up to 15%!

HOLIDAY INN EXPRESS HOTEL & SUITES   405/844-3700 67
THREE DIAMOND Hotel. **Address:** 3840 E 2nd St 73034

LA QUINTA INN & SUITES EDMOND   405/513-5353 68
THREE DIAMOND Hotel. **Address:** 200 Meline Dr 73034

SLEEP INN & SUITES   405/844-3000 71
APPROVED Hotel. **Address:** 3608 S Broadway Extension 73013

(See map & index p. 356.)

WHERE TO EAT

BOULEVARD STEAKHOUSE   405/715-2333   (27)
THREE DIAMOND Steak Seafood. Fine Dining. **Address:**
505 S Boulevard St 73034

CHARLESTON'S RESTAURANT   405/478-4949
APPROVED American. Casual Dining. **Address:** 3409
3 Broadway, Suite 400 73013

RIB CRIB BBQ AND GRILL   405/513-5883
APPROVED Barbecue. Casual Dining. **Address:** 2601
S Broadway 73013

TED'S CAFE ESCONDIDO   405/810-8337   (24)
APPROVED Mexican. Casual Dining. **Address:** 801 E
Danforth Rd 73034

WICH PHO   405/285-2038   (26)
APPROVED Vietnamese. Quick Serve. **Address:**
1822 F 2nd St 73034

ELK CITY (D-5) pop. 11,693, elev. 1,912'

In the late 1800s Elk City was a rest stop for cattlemen driving herds along the Great Western Trail from Texas to Kansas. Oil was discovered in 1947, and the "black gold" flowed until reserves were depleted in the late 1960s. Interests then turned to deep gas exploration in Elk City and the surrounding Anadarko Basin. The town is on historic Route 66.

The quarter horse, which is notable as both a racehorse and the cowboy's mount of choice, is raised in and around Elk City. The breed almost disappeared with the cowboy era but was reintroduced in the 1940s.

Elk City Chamber of Commerce: 1016 E. Airport Industrial Rd., Elk City, OK 73648. **Phone:** (580) 225-0207 or (800) 280-0207.

ELK CITY OLD TOWN MUSEUM COMPLEX, 2717 W. 3rd St., is a continuous restoration project that re-creates an early Western town. A museum in a late 19th-century Victorian frame house contains detailed period furnishings. Upstairs is the Beutler Brothers Rodeo Hall. The complex also features the Farm and Ranch Museum, the Transportation Museum, the National Route 66 Museum, a pioneer doctor's office, the Pioneer Memorial Chapel, a railroad station, a blacksmith shop, a Native American teepee, a schoolhouse and a wagon yard.

Hours: Mon.-Sat. 9-5, Memorial Day-Labor Day (also Sun. 1-5, mid-Mar. through early Nov.). **Cost:** (includes all museums and other sites within the complex) $5; $4 (ages 6-16 and 60+); free (active military with ID on Memorial Day and Veterans Day). **Phone:** (580) 225-6266.

National Route 66 Museum, at the Elk City Old Town Museum Complex, 2717 W. 3rd St., takes visitors on a trip through the famous route's history with photographs, old signs and vintage automobiles. **Hours:** Mon.-Sat. 9-5 (also Sun. 2-5, mid-Mar.

through early Nov. and Mon.-Sat. 5-7, Memorial Day-Labor Day). **Cost:** (includes all sites within Elk City Old Town Museum Complex) $5; $4 (ages 6-16 and 60+); free (active military with ID on Memorial Day and Veterans Day). **Phone:** (580) 225-6266.

BEST WESTERN PLUS EXECUTIVE RESIDENCY ELK
CITY   580/303-4851

THREE DIAMOND

Extended Stay Hotel

Best Western PLUS **AAA Benefit:** Members save up to 15% and earn bonus points!

Address: 105 Meadow Ridge Dr 73644 **Location:** I-40 exit 38, just sw. **Facility:** 70 units, some efficiencies. 3 stories, interior corridors. **Pool:** outdoor. **Activities:** exercise room. **Guest Services:** coin laundry. **Featured Amenity:** full hot breakfast.

SAVE CALL 🔒 🛗 🏋 BIZ HS
🛜 ✕ 🛏 🖨 📶
/ SOME UNITS 🐾

HAMPTON INN & SUITES ELK CITY   580/225-2553
THREE DIAMOND SAVE Hotel. **Address:** 102 Regional Dr 73644

AAA Benefit: Members save up to 15%!

HOLIDAY INN EXPRESS & SUITES   580/303-4556
THREE DIAMOND Hotel. **Address:** 2101 E 3rd St 73644

EL RENO (H-1) pop. 16,749, elev. 1,360'

• Restaurants p. 332
• Part of Oklahoma City area — see map p. 343

El Reno was established in June 1889 when the Rock Island Railroad picked a site on the south bank of the North Canadian River for a depot. Angry citizens of nearby Reno City decided they did not want to be left out of any future railroad riches. They packed their belongings and loaded their houses, stores and even a hotel onto log rollers, forded the river and resettled in the new town of El Reno.

The Heritage Express Trolley transports riders Wednesday through Sunday from Heritage Park through the downtown area. A scenic portion of US 81 runs 12 miles south from El Reno through the Canadian River Valley to Minco.

El Reno Chamber of Commerce: 206 N. Bickford, El Reno, OK 73036. **Phone:** (405) 262-1188.

BAYMONT INN & SUITES EL RENO   405/262-3050
APPROVED Hotel. **Address:** 1707 SW 27th St 73036

⊘ For complete hotel, dining and attraction listings:
AAA.com/travelguides

BEST WESTERN EL RENO   405/262-6490

🔷 APPROVED

Hotel

Best Western. **AAA Benefit:** Members save up to 15% and earn bonus points!

Address: 2701 S Country Club Rd 73036 **Location:** I-40 exit 123, just s. **Facility:** 60 units. 2 stories (no elevator), exterior corridors. **Pool:** outdoor. **Activities:** playground. **Guest Services:** coin laundry. **Featured Amenity: full hot breakfast.**

[SAVE] [🍽] [🏊] [BIZ] [📶] [📱] [📺]
[💻] / SOME UNITS [🐾] [HS]

FAIRFIELD INN & SUITES BY MARRIOTT OKLAHOMA CITY EL RENO   405/295-1811

🔷🔷🔷 THREE DIAMOND [SAVE] Hotel. **Address:** 1501 Domino Dr 73036

AAA Benefit: Members save 5% or more!

HAMPTON INN BY HILTON   405/702-9200

🔷🔷🔷 THREE DIAMOND [SAVE] Hotel. **Address:** 1530 SW 27th St 73036

AAA Benefit: Members save up to 15%!

MOTEL 6 EL RENO #4267   405/262-6060

🔷 APPROVED

Hotel

Address: 1506 Domino Dr 73036 **Location:** I-40 exit 123, just ne. **Facility:** 64 units. 3 stories, interior corridors. **Pool:** outdoor. **Guest Services:** coin laundry.

[SAVE] [🍽] [🏊] [BIZ] [HS] [📶] [📱]
[📺] / SOME UNITS [🐾]

WHERE TO EAT

MONTANA MIKE'S   405/422-1100

🔷 APPROVED   Steak. Casual Dining. **Address:** 1609 SW 27th St 73036

ENID (C-7) pop. 49,379, elev. 1,246'

Although some sources hold that the town's name came from Alfred, Lord Tennyson's "Idylls of the King," more colorful stories credit the naming of Enid to cattle drovers who turned the "Dine" sign on the cook's tent upside down.

In an effort to encourage the Rock Island Railroad to stop at Enid rather than its rival North Enid, an unknown party sawed through the supports on a railroad trestle southeast of town. While attempting to pass through Enid on its usual route, the train fell into a gully, thereby making its first official "stop" at Enid. Enid later was included on the route.

Greater Enid Chamber of Commerce: 210 Kenwood Blvd., Enid, OK 73702. **Phone:** (580) 237-2494.

Shopping: More than 40 specialty stores and eateries as well as anchor stores Dillard's and JCPenney

comprise Oakwood Mall, at W. Owen K. Garriott and S. Oakwood roads.

[SAVE] **CHEROKEE STRIP REGIONAL HERITAGE CENTER,** 507 S. 4th St., exhibits 1893 Cherokee Strip Land Run and pioneer artifacts depicting the settlement of the area from 1893 to the present. On the museum grounds is the Humphrey Heritage Village, a living history area which includes four historic buildings: a one-room schoolhouse, a church, a Victorian house and the original Enid land office. The 24,000-square-foot facility features five galleries that chronicle the history and the development of the Cherokee Strip Outlet. Temporary exhibits also are offered.

Time: Allow 1 hour minimum. **Hours:** Tues.-Sat. 10-5. Guided tours of Humphrey Heritage Village are given at 11:30, 1:30 and 3 (weather permitting). **Cost:** $6; $4 (ages 65+ and students ages 6-18 with ID); $15 (family, four people); free (active military and veterans with ID). **Phone:** (580) 237-1907. [GT]

RAILROAD MUSEUM OF OKLAHOMA, 702 N. Washington, has a collection of train cars and objects that were used on local trains. China and silver services, steam engine bells, line maps and postcards are among the memorabilia on display; train buffs can peruse a library of railroading books. A room is devoted to model railroads. Rail excursions are offered twice annually. **Hours:** Tues.-Fri. 1-4, Sat. 9-4. Closed major holidays. **Cost:** $5. **Phone:** (580) 233-3051. [GT]

BAYMONT INN & SUITES-ENID   580/234-6800

🔷 APPROVED   Hotel. **Address:** 3614 W Owen K Garriott Rd 73703

HAMPTON INN & SUITES   580/234-4600

🔷🔷🔷 THREE DIAMOND [SAVE] Hotel. **Address:** 511 Demla Ct 73701

AAA Benefit: Members save up to 15%!

HOLIDAY INN EXPRESS HOTEL & SUITES   580/237-7722

🔷🔷🔷 THREE DIAMOND Hotel. **Address:** 4702 W Owen K Garriott Rd 73703

OYO ENID   580/242-7110

🔷 APPROVED   Hotel. **Address:** 2818 S Van Buren St 73703

RAMADA ENID   580/234-0440

🔷 APPROVED   Hotel. **Address:** 3005 W Owen K Garriott Rd 73703

SPRINGHILL SUITES BY MARRIOTT ENID   580/540-4256

🔷🔷🔷 THREE DIAMOND [SAVE] Contemporary Hotel. **Address:** 5815 KL Dr 73703

AAA Benefit: Members save 5% or more!

WHERE TO EAT

RIB CRIB BBQ AND GRILL   580/237-7333

🔷 APPROVED   Barbecue. Casual Dining. **Address:** 4901 W Owen K Garriott Rd 73703

EUFAULA pop. 2,813

BEST WESTERN EUFAULA INN
918/689-5553

APPROVED

Hotel

Best Western. **AAA Benefit:** Members save up to 15% and earn bonus points!

Address: 1300 Birkes Rd 74432 **Location:** 0.7 mi ne of jct US 69 and SR 9. **Facility:** 50 units. 2 stories, interior corridors. **Pool:** heated indoor. **Activities:** exercise room. **Guest Services:** coin laundry.

FAIRVIEW pop. 2,579

BEST WESTERN PLUS FAIRVIEW INN & SUITES
580/227-2880

THREE DIAMOND

Hotel

Best Western PLUS. **AAA Benefit:** Members save up to 15% and earn bonus points!

Address: 802 N Main St 73737 **Location:** Center. **Facility:** 52 units, some efficiencies. 3 stories, interior corridors. **Pool:** heated indoor. **Activities:** hot tub, exercise room. **Guest Services:** coin laundry. **Featured Amenity:** full hot breakfast.

FORT SILL (E-7)

FORT SILL NATIONAL HISTORIC LANDMARK AND MUSEUM is at 435 Quanah Rd.; visitors must stop at the Visitor Control Center, 6701 Sheridan Rd., jct. Sheridan Rd. and US 62 to present identification and obtain a pass. The interpretive center is in Building 435. The fort, which consists of more than 38 buildings from the original 19th-century military outpost, retains its frontier atmosphere. It was established in 1869 by Gen. Philip Sheridan to control the Southern Plains tribes and, at the same time, protect their lands from encroachment.

Since the fort has been in continuous use since the Indian Wars period, it is virtually unchanged. The site remains an active Army post, with many of the original family living quarters still being used for that purpose.

The museum interprets early cavalry and infantry history (including Col. George Custer's 7th Cavalry and the famous 10th Cavalry Buffalo Soldiers); the Apache, Comanche and Kiowa tribes; the settlement of early Oklahoma; and the history of the area's early military and law enforcement divisions.

Among the graves in seven Native American cemeteries are those of Geronimo and Quanah Parker, the last chief of the Comanche. Visitors can see barracks restored to resemble those used by cavalry soldiers in 1875 and the stone Quartermaster Corral, which has been returned to its original appearance. The Post Guardhouse has exhibits focusing on the early law enforcement mission of the Army and the Indian police. The Warrior's Journey gallery addresses the Native American collections in the museum.

Living-history presentations, which take place on a regular basis, include such activities as the firing of Civil War-era muzzle-loading cannons, 19th-century baseball and programs about the Army's Buffalo Soldiers.

Note: A government-issued photo ID is required. **Time:** Allow 1 hour, 30 minutes minimum. **Hours:** Tues.-Sat. 9-5. Closed Jan. 1-2, Thanksgiving, Christmas and day after Christmas. **Cost:** Free. **Phone:** (580) 442-5123.

U.S. Army Air Defense Artillery Museum is at 1506 Bateman Rd; visitors must stop at the Visitor Control Center, 6701 Sheridan Rd., jct. Sheridan Rd. and US 62, to present identification and obtain a pass to enter Fort Sill. On the grounds of Fort Sill National Historic Landmark and Museum, the museum contains anti-aircraft weapons that trace the history of air defense from World War I to current operations. **Note:** A government-issued photo ID is required for entry to Fort Sill. **Time:** Allow 45 minutes minimum. **Hours:** Tues.-Sat. 9-5. Closed Jan. 1-2, Thanksgiving, Christmas and day after Christmas. **Cost:** Free. **Phone:** (580) 442-0424.

U.S. Army Field Artillery Museum is at 238 Randolph Rd.; visitors must stop at the Visitor Control Center, 6701 Sheridan Rd., jct. Sheridan Rd. and US 62 to present identification and obtain a pass to enter Fort Sill. On the grounds of Fort Sill National Historic Landmark and Museum, the museum's large collection of artillery pieces, uniforms, small arms and equipment relates the history of American artillery from 1775 to the present. Exhibits trace the development of artillery from cannons that could be broken down and carried on mules to the latest technology that uses computers for aiming.

The newly completed Artillery Park next to the museum contains more than 80 artillery weapons and vehicles from World War I to the present in an outdoor exhibit. Included are "Atomic Annie," the 280-millimeter cannon that fired the first atomic artillery round, U.S. artillery, rockets and missiles and captured German, Italian, Japanese, Soviet and Iraqi artillery. **Note:** A government-issued photo ID is required for entry to Fort Sill. **Time:** Allow 45 minutes minimum. **Hours:** Tues.-Sat. 9-5. Closed Jan. 1-2, Thanksgiving, Christmas and day after Christmas. **Cost:** Free. **Phone:** (580) 442-1819.

GLENPOOL pop. 10,808
• Part of Tulsa area — see map p. 375

COMFORT INN & SUITES GLENPOOL   918/995-2225
THREE DIAMOND Hotel. **Address:** 12119 N Casper St 74033

QUALITY INN   918/322-5201
APPROVED Hotel. **Address:** 14831 S Casper St 74033

GRANT

CHOCTAW CASINO HOTEL   580/317-8500

THREE DIAMOND
Hotel

Address: 1516 Hwy 271 S 74738 **Location:** Center. **Facility:** These good-size guest rooms include enhanced bedding and comfy seating. The area around the swimming pool is decorated with stone accents, attractive landscaping and a variety of furniture. 156 units. 3 stories, interior corridors. **Parking:** on-site and valet. **Amenities:** safes. **Dining:** 4 restaurants. **Pool:** heated outdoor. **Activities:** hot tub, cabanas. *(See ad starting on p. 38.)*

[SAVE] [icon] [icon] [icon] CALL [icon] [icon]

[BIZ] [HS] [icon] [icon] [icon]

GROVE (B-12) pop. 6,623, elev. 774'

Grove Area Chamber of Commerce: 9630 US 59, Grove, OK 74344. **Phone:** (918) 786-9079.

HAR-BER VILLAGE MUSEUM, 3.5 mi. w. on Har-Ber Rd. to 4404 W. 20th Rd., is on the shores of Grand Lake O' the Cherokees. Created by Harvey and Bernice Jones, the founders of Jones Truck Lines, this reconstructed 19th-century pioneer village includes more than 100 exhibits featuring glassware, dolls, china, furniture and farm machinery. Other exhibits include primitives (Native American pottery or artifacts made before the advent of a spoken language).

Included among the village buildings are a bank, a beauty shop, a courthouse, a dentist's office, a drug store, a one-room schoolhouse, a post office and log cabins. A visitor center contains displays. A nature trail, an heirloom garden and an herb garden also are on the grounds.

Time: Allow 3 hours minimum. **Hours:** Thurs.-Mon. 9-4:30, mid-Mar. to early Nov.; last admission 1 hour before closing. Holiday hours are offered 3 weekends late Nov.-early Dec.; phone ahead to confirm schedule. **Cost:** $10; $7.50 (ages 63+); $5 (ages 6-13); $30 (family, two adults and up to 10 children ages 6-13). **Phone:** (918) 786-6446 for the visitor center. [icon] [icon]

LENDONWOOD GARDENS is 1 mi. w. of US 59 at 1308 W. 13th St. (Har-Ber Rd.). The garden features seven areas, each with a distinct look. The Display Garden features daylilies, Japanese maples and other plants that thrive in Oklahoma. The Oriental Garden contains dogwoods and rhododendrons and the Azalea Garden abounds with the spring-blooming shrub. The Japanese Pavilion overlooks a koi pond.

The Angel of Hope Garden, with its bronze angel statue, offers a quiet setting for remembering lost loved ones. The American Backyard features drought-resistant plants, and an English Terrace Garden accented by tree peonies complements the other areas. **Time:** Allow 30 minutes minimum. **Hours:** Daily dawn-dusk. **Cost:** $5; $3 (students with ID); free (ages 0-12). **Phone:** (918) 786-2938.

BEST WESTERN TIMBERRIDGE INN   918/786-6900

APPROVED
Hotel

[BW] **Best Western.** **AAA Benefit:** Members save up to 15% and earn bonus points!

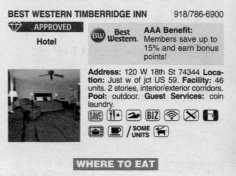

Address: 120 W 18th St 74344 **Location:** Just w of jct US 59. **Facility:** 46 units. 2 stories, interior/exterior corridors. **Pool:** outdoor. **Guest Services:** coin laundry.

[SAVE] [icon] [icon] [BIZ] [icon] [icon] [icon]
[icon] [icon] / SOME UNITS [icon]

WHERE TO EAT

RIB CRIB BBQ AND GRILL   918/786-5400
APPROVED Barbecue. Casual Dining. **Address:** 1801 Main St 74344

GUTHRIE (F-2) pop. 10,191, elev. 961'
• Part of Oklahoma City area — see map p. 343

As the focal point of the 1889 Oklahoma land rush, Guthrie became a tent city of 15,000 residents by nightfall on April 22, 1889, the day the Unassigned Lands of Oklahoma were officially opened for settlement. Oklahoma was admitted to the Union in 1907, and Guthrie became the first capital of the state. At some point in their lives, Lon Chaney, Tom Mix, Carry Nation and Will Rogers all lived in Guthrie.

Ninety percent of Guthrie's original buildings remain intact; the city has one of the largest districts on the National Register of Historic Places. Belgian-born architect Joseph Foucart designed most of the town's eclectic Victorian structures.

The Pollard Theater, a renovated early 20th-century opera house at 120 W. Harrison Ave., presents productions performed by Guthrie's resident theater company. Houses dating from Guthrie's territorial and early statehood days line E. Harrison, Oklahoma, Cleveland, Noble and Warner streets. Trolley tours of the historic district depart from the intersection of 2nd and Harrison on Saturdays at noon and 2; phone (405) 282-6000.

Guthrie Convention and Visitors Bureau: 101 N. 2nd St., Guthrie, OK 73044. **Phone:** (405) 282-0197.

TERRITORIAL CAPITAL SPORTS MUSEUM is at 315 W. Oklahoma Ave. The museum houses a collection of memorabilia honoring athletes, coaches and sports teams with connections to Oklahoma. Sports celebrities and champions highlighted include Troy Aikman, Mickey Mantle, Shannon Miller and Jim Thorpe. The Basketball Gallery focuses on the Oklahoma City Thunder NBA team. **Time:** Allow 1 hour minimum. **Hours:** Tues.-Sat. 10-4. Closed major holidays. **Cost:** Donations. **Phone:** (405) 260-1342.

HAMPTON INN & SUITES GUTHRIE   405/293-9595
THREE DIAMOND SAVE Hotel. **Ad-** **AAA Benefit:** **dress:** 401 Cimarron Blvd 73044   Members save up to 15%!

HOLIDAY INN EXPRESS   405/293-6464
THREE DIAMOND Hotel. **Address:** 2227 E Oklahoma Ave 73044

STAY EXPRESS INN - GUTHRIE   405/282-2100
APPROVED Hotel. **Address:** 2323 Territorial Tr 73044

WHERE TO EAT

STABLES CAFE   405/282-0893
APPROVED Barbecue. Casual Dining. **Address:** 223 N Division St 73044

GUYMON pop. 11,442

BEST WESTERN PLUS GUYMON HOTEL & SUITES
580/338-0800

THREE DIAMOND
Hotel

Best Western PLUS

AAA Benefit: Members save up to 15% and earn bonus points!

Address: 1102 NE 6th St 73942 **Location:** Just s of jct US 64. **Facility:** 70 units, some efficiencies. 3 stories, interior corridors. **Pool:** heated indoor. **Activities:** sauna, hot tub, exercise room. **Guest Services:** valet and coin laundry.

SAVE YI CALL [icons] BIZ
HS [icons] / SOME UNITS

HOLIDAY INN EXPRESS HOTEL & SUITES GUYMON
580/338-4208
THREE DIAMOND Hotel. **Address:** 701 SE Hwy 3 73942

QUALITY INN & SUITES   580/338-0831
APPROVED Hotel. **Address:** 501 Hwy 54 E 73942

WHERE TO EAT

PUB ON THE BRICKS   580/338-3463
APPROVED American. Casual Dining. **Address:** 120 NW 5th St 73942

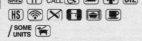

🔗 **Where Diamonds**

make the difference:

AAA.com/travelguides/hotels

JENKS (F-2) pop. 16,924, elev. 617'
• **Hotels p. 336** • **Restaurants p. 336**
• **Hotels & Restaurants map & index p. 386**
• **Part of Tulsa area — see map p. 375**

What do a river, a railroad, oil, farming, antiques and an aquarium have in common? They all played a major role in the evolution of Jenks, a vibrant community on the Arkansas River just southwest of Tulsa.

Although its location on the river was advantageous, it was the Midland Valley Railroad that put Jenks on the map. The town was established in 1905 as a weigh station for the railroad. It wasn't long, however, before oil was discovered nearby, and Jenks became the site of "tank farms" to store the black gold.

The oil fields eventually played out, and farming became the area's economic mainstay; cotton, vegetables, dairy cattle and livestock production were prominent players.

Two more recent developments, though, are responsible for luring visitors to the city. The early 20th-century brick buildings on Main Street began to be filled with antique stores, adding to downtown's turn-of-the-century, country-style charm. The town claims to be known as the Antique Capital of Oklahoma.

The second development, the decision to build the Oklahoma Aquarium *(see attraction listing)* in Jenks, though, was a major coup. The attraction, on the west bank of the Arkansas River, draws close to a half-million visitors to the city each year.

If you want to do some shopping, grab a bite or just plain relax after your aquarium visit, head to Riverwalk Crossing, a trendy entertainment district overlooking the river. You might even be able to catch some live music at the outdoor amphitheater.

OKLAHOMA AQUARIUM is at 300 Aquarium Dr. Home to thousands of animals from around the world, the aquarium is divided into galleries that include the Siegfried Families Shark Adventure, where visitors can walk through a clear acrylic tunnel surrounded by 500,000 gallons of water and schools of sharks. Marvels & Mysteries houses seahorses, moon jellies and piranhas. Other unusual sea creatures can be found in the Amazing Invertebrates gallery, which includes sea stars, urchins and sponges. The Aquatic Oklahoma gallery contains native species such as alligator gar and turtles, while the Hayes Family Ozark Stream has otters, beavers and smallmouth bass.

The Extreme Fishes gallery illustrates how animals have adapted to their habitats. A variety of coastal environments are re-created in the EcoZone and Coral Reef gallery, which also features touch tanks. Children can crawl through tunnels under water at Extreme Amazon. Visitors can watch daily feeding shows; schedules are posted at the information desk.

Time: Allow 2 hours minimum. **Hours:** Daily 10-6, also Tues. 6-9; Last admission 1 hour before

(See map & index p. 386.)

closing. **Cost:** $17.95; $13.95 (ages 62+ and military with ID, ages 3-12). **Phone:** (918) 296-3474. ⓘ

HOLIDAY INN EXPRESS HOTEL & SUITES
918/296-7300 ⑥⑤
⬥ **THREE DIAMOND** Hotel. **Address:** 150 Aquarium Dr 74037

WHERE TO EAT

LOS CABOS MEXICAN GRILL & CANTINA 918/298-2226 ㊻
⬥ **APPROVED** Mexican. Casual Dining. **Address:** 300 Riverwalk Terr 74037

WATERFRONT GRILL 918/518-6300 ㊼
⬥ **THREE DIAMOND** Seafood. Fine Dining. **Address:** 120 Aquarium Dr 74037

LAWTON (F-7) pop. 96,867, elev. 1,111'

On the morning of Aug. 6, 1901, Lawton was merely a tumbleweed connection on a vast Native American reservation. By evening it had blossomed into a town of 10,000, the last of the Oklahoma cities to spring up overnight. Lawton was created by a land lottery, in which successful bidders without the cash for immediate payment were allowed 30 minutes to get the money before the lot was put up for sale again.

The town celebrates all things art at the ⬥ Arts for All Festival, held in early May at Shepler Park. The 2-day festival features a juried art show, children's art area, live entertainment, multicultural food vendors and a wine garden.

Lawton Fort Sill Chamber of Commerce: 302 W. Gore Blvd., Lawton, OK 73501. **Phone:** (580) 355-3541 or (800) 872-4540.

Shopping: Central Mall, just off I-44 on C Avenue, has Dillard's and JCPenney as its anchor stores.

⬥ **FORT SILL NATIONAL HISTORIC LANDMARK AND MUSEUM**—see Fort Sill p. 333.

THE HISTORIC MATTIE BEAL HOME is at 1008 S.W. 5th St. at jct. Summit Ave. The house was built 1907-09 for Mattie Beal, a young Kansan who won a 160-acre plot in the 1901 Oklahoma land lottery. The 14-room house was, for many years, one of the finest in Lawton.

A philanthropist, Ms. Beal donated land for parks, a church and a school. She also subdivided her property into affordable lots for new settlers. The house has been restored to how it appeared in 1923. Highlights include the original grand staircase, curved front door, the second floor ballroom, stained glass windows and an Italian marble mantle. **Hours:** Thurs.-Sun. noon-3, Feb.-Dec. **Cost:** $4; $3 (ages 60+); $2 (students grades K-12). **Phone:** (580) 678-3156.

APACHE CASINO HOTEL 580/248-5905

⬥ **THREE DIAMOND**
Contemporary Hotel

Address: 2325 E Gore Blvd 73501 **Location:** I-44 exit 37, 1 mi e. **Facility:** Guests here enjoy multiple dining options, gaming, and if the timing is right, maybe a concert! Rooms have spacious bathrooms and comfortable seating. 132 units. 5 stories, interior corridors. **Parking:** on-site and valet. **Terms:** check-in 4 pm. **Amenities:** safes. **Dining:** 2 restaurants. **Pool:** heated outdoor. **Activities:** hot tub, exercise room. **Guest Services:** valet laundry.

⬥ / SOME UNITS ⬥

BEST WESTERN PLUS LAWTON HOTEL 580/353-0200

⬥ **THREE DIAMOND**
Hotel

Best Western PLUS.

AAA Benefit: Members save up to 15% and earn bonus points!

Address: 1125 E Gore Blvd 73501 **Location:** I-44 exit 37, just e. **Facility:** 148 units. 2 stories, interior/exterior corridors. **Pool:** outdoor, heated indoor. **Activities:** exercise room. **Guest Services:** coin laundry.

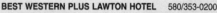

FAIRFIELD INN & SUITES BY MARRIOTT 580/248-5500
⬥ **THREE DIAMOND** ⬥ Hotel. **Address:** 201 SE 7th St 73501

AAA Benefit: Members save 5% or more!

HAMPTON INN & SUITES 580/355-8200
⬥ **THREE DIAMOND** ⬥ Hotel. **Address:** 2610 NW Cache Rd 73505

AAA Benefit: Members save up to 15%!

HILTON GARDEN INN 580/280-2100
⬥ **THREE DIAMOND** ⬥ Hotel. **Address:** 135 NW 2nd St 73501

AAA Benefit: Members save up to 15%!

HOLIDAY INN EXPRESS HOTEL & SUITES 580/248-4446
⬥ **THREE DIAMOND** Hotel. **Address:** 209 SE Interstate Dr 73501

HOMEWOOD SUITES BY HILTON 580/357-9800
⬥ **THREE DIAMOND** ⬥ Extended Stay Hotel. **Address:** 415 SE Interstate Dr 73501

AAA Benefit: Members save up to 15%!

SLEEP INN & SUITES 580/353-5555
⬥ **THREE DIAMOND** Hotel. **Address:** 421 SE Interstate Dr 73501

SPRINGHILL SUITES BY MARRIOTT 580/248-8500
⬥ **THREE DIAMOND** ⬥ Hotel. **Address:** 3 SE Interstate Dr 73501

AAA Benefit: Members save 5% or more!

WHERE TO EAT

EL CHICO   580/357-9006
 APPROVED   Tex-Mex. Casual Dining. **Address:** 83 Central Mall 73501

FIRO FIRE-KISSED PIZZA   580/699-3476
APPROVED   Pizza. Quick Serve. **Address:** 3902 NW Cache Dt 73503

THE SILVER SPOON   580/357-6800
APPROVED   American. Casual Dining. **Address:** 529 SW C Ave 73501

LINDSAY pop. 2,840

BEST WESTERN LINDSAY INN & SUITES   405/756-3988

THREE DIAMOND   Hotel

Best Western. **AAA Benefit:** Members save up to 15% and earn bonus points!

Address: 14114 US Hwy 19 73052 **Location:** Center. **Facility:** 57 units. 3 stories, interior corridors. **Pool:** heated indoor. **Activities:** exercise room. **Guest Services:** coin laundry.

SAVE CALL ♿ ✈ BIZ HS 📶 ✕ 🍴 🛗 💻

LOCUST GROVE pop. 1,423

BEST WESTERN LOCUST GROVE INN & SUITES
918/479-8082

APPROVED   Hotel

Best Western. **AAA Benefit:** Members save up to 15% and earn bonus points!

Address: 106 Holiday Ln 74352 **Location:** Just nw of jct US 412 and SR 82. **Facility:** 60 units. 2 stories, interior corridors. **Pool:** outdoor. **Activities:** hot tub, exercise room. **Guest Services:** coin laundry.

SAVE 🍴 ✈ BIZ HS 📶 ✕ 🛗 💻 / SOME UNITS

MADILL pop. 3,770, elev. 791'

BEST WESTERN PLUS SAND BASS INN & SUITES
580/677-9890

THREE DIAMOND   Hotel

Best Western PLUS. **AAA Benefit:** Members save up to 15% and earn bonus points!

Address: 827 S 1st St 73446 **Location:** Just s on US 70 from jct US 377. **Facility:** 63 units. 3 stories, interior corridors. **Pool:** outdoor. **Activities:** hot tub, exercise room. **Guest Services:** coin laundry. **Featured Amenity: full hot breakfast.**

SAVE 🍴 CALL ♿ ✈ BIZ HS 📶 ✕ 🛗 💻 / SOME UNITS

MCALESTER (E-10) pop. 18,383, elev. 734'
• Restaurants p. 338

McAlester began as a tent store owned by J.J. McAlester at the crossroads of the old California Trail and the Texas Road. He later discovered and mined coal in the area.

Because McAlester had married a Choctaw Indian, which made him a member of the Choctaw Nation, the Native Americans claimed rights to his newly found wealth. When McAlester protested, the tribal court ruled in his favor; however, the Choctaw chief sentenced him to death in spite of this decision. McAlester made a dramatic escape and later served the state as lieutenant governor.

McAlester Scottish Rite Temple, 2nd and Adams streets, has an auditorium with Egyptian decor. Guided tours are available by reservation; phone (918) 423-6360.

Six miles north is Lake Eufaula *(see Recreation Areas Chart)*, a huge reservoir on the Canadian River with more than 600 miles of shoreline. Boating, swimming, water skiing, hiking and horseback riding are just a few of the activities that make the lake a popular destination. Anglers come from miles around in pursuit of bass, crappie and catfish, and lakeside Arrowhead and Lake Eufaula state parks offer campsites and numerous recreational activities.

McAlester Area Chamber of Commerce and Agriculture: 119 E. Choctaw St., Suite 103, McAlester, OK 74501. **Phone:** (918) 423-2550.

AMERICINN LODGE & SUITES OF MCALESTER
918/426-1300
APPROVED   Hotel. **Address:** 609 S George Nigh Expwy 74501

BEST WESTERN INN OF MCALESTER   918/426-0115

APPROVED   Hotel

Best Western. **AAA Benefit:** Members save up to 15% and earn bonus points!

Address: 1215 George Nigh Expwy 74502 **Location:** 3 mi s on US 69. **Facility:** 61 units. 2 stories (no elevator), exterior corridors. **Pool:** outdoor. **Guest Services:** valet laundry.

SAVE 🍴 ✈ BIZ 📶 🛗 💻 / SOME UNITS

CANDLEWOOD SUITES   918/426-4171
APPROVED   Extended Stay Hotel. **Address:** 425 S George Nigh Expwy 74501

DAYS INN AND SUITES MCALESTER   918/426-1111
APPROVED   Hotel. **Address:** 400 S George Nigh Expwy 74501

ECONO LODGE   918/426-4420
APPROVED   Motel. **Address:** 731 S George Nigh Expwy 74501

HAMPTON INN & SUITES BY HILTON   918/302-3882
THREE DIAMOND SAVE Hotel. **Address:** 711 S George Nigh Expwy 74501

AAA Benefit: Members save up to 15%!

HAPPY DAYS HOTEL   918/429-0910
APPROVED   Hotel. **Address:** 1400 S George Nigh Expwy 74501

HOLIDAY INN EXPRESS & SUITES   918/423-1118
THREE DIAMOND Hotel. **Address:** 1811 S Peaceable Rd 74501

TRAVELODGE BY WYNDHAM MCALESTER   918/420-5002
APPROVED   Hotel. **Address:** 2200 E South Ave 74501

WHERE TO EAT

ADELITA'S MEXICAN RESTAURANT   918/423-7311
APPROVED   Mexican. Casual Dining. **Address:** 1710 E Carl Albert Pkwy 74501

ANGEL'S DINER   918/423-2633
APPROVED   American. Casual Dining. **Address:** 1402 S George Nigh Expwy 74501

GIA COMO'S RESTAURANT   918/423-2662
APPROVED   Italian. Casual Dining. **Address:** 501 S George Nigh Expwy 74501

SAKE JAPANESE RESTAURANT   918/558-5381
APPROVED   Japanese. Casual Dining. **Address:** 1702 E Carl Albert Parkway 74501

MIAMI   pop. 13,570, elev. 798'

HAMPTON INN BY HILTON   918/541-1500
THREE DIAMOND SAVE Hotel. **Address:** 115 S Deacon Turner Rd 74354

AAA Benefit: Members save up to 15%!

HOLIDAY INN EXPRESS & SUITES   918/542-7424
THREE DIAMOND   **Address:** 509 Henley St 74354 **Location:** I-44 exit 313, just w. **Facility:** 75 units. 3 stories, interior corridors. **Amenities:** safes. **Pool:** heated indoor. **Activities:** hot tub, exercise room. **Guest Services:** coin laundry. **Featured Amenity: full hot breakfast.**
Hotel

SAVE CALL ♿ ➿ ✈ BIZ HS ⊚ ✕ 🛢 📠 🍽 / SOME UNITS 🐾

WHERE TO EAT

MONTANA MIKE'S   918/542-8808
APPROVED   Steak. Casual Dining. **Address:** 840 NE Main St 74354

STONEHILL GRILL   918/542-3463
APPROVED   American. Casual Dining. **Address:** 1220 N Main St 74354

MIDWEST CITY   (H-3) pop. 54,371, elev. 1,253'
• **Hotels & Restaurants map & index p. 356**
• **Part of Oklahoma City area — see map p. 343**

Only 8 miles from Oklahoma City, the suburb of Midwest City is the home of Tinker Air Force Base. Eleven shopping areas, including national chains and local merchants, are fun alternatives to mall shopping. Dining choices, from Buffalo wings and burgers to Asian, Italian and Mexican cuisine, is offered. More than 30 parks, several golf courses and a water park provide opportunities for outdoor activities.

Midwest City Convention & Visitors Bureau: 7200 S.E. 29th St., Midwest City, OK 73110. **Phone:** (405) 739-8239.

BEST WESTERN PLUS MIDWEST CITY INN & SUITES
          405/737-6060   78
THREE DIAMOND
Hotel

Best Western PLUS.

AAA Benefit: Members save up to 15% and earn bonus points!

Address: 6701 Tinker Diagonal 73110 **Location:** I-40 exit 157A, just nw. **Facility:** 69 units. 3 stories, interior corridors. **Pool:** heated indoor. **Activities:** exercise room. **Guest Services:** coin laundry. **Featured Amenity: full hot breakfast.**

SAVE CALL ♿ ➿ 💼 BIZ HS ⊚ ✕ 🛢 📠 🍽

HAMPTON INN BY HILTON   405/732-5500   76
THREE DIAMOND SAVE Hotel. **Address:** 1833 Center Dr 73110

AAA Benefit: Members save up to 15%!

HOLIDAY INN EXPRESS HOTEL & SUITES
          405/736-1000   74
THREE DIAMOND Hotel. **Address:** 1700 S Sooner Rd 73110

LA QUINTA INN & SUITES OKLAHOMA CITY-MIDWEST CITY   405/733-1339   77
THREE DIAMOND   **Address:** 5653 Tinker Diagonal 73110 **Location:** I-40 exit 156A (Sooner Rd), just n. **Facility:** 78 units. 4 stories, interior corridors. **Pool:** heated indoor. **Activities:** exercise room. **Guest Services:** valet and coin laundry. **Featured Amenity: full hot breakfast.**
Hotel

SAVE 🍽 ➿ 💼 BIZ ⊚ 🛢 📠 🍽 / SOME UNITS 🐾

🔗 **Get member rates and reservations**

at AAA.com/hertz

(See map & index p. 356.)

SHERATON MIDWEST CITY HOTEL AT THE REED CONFERENCE CENTER   405/455-1800   75

THREE DIAMOND   **Hotel**   SHERATON

AAA Benefit: Members save 5% or more!

Address: 5750 Will Rogers Rd 73110 **Location:** I-40 exit 156A (Sooner Rd), just ne. **Facility:** 151 units. 5 stories, interior corridors. **Amenities:** safes. **Pool:** heated indoor. **Activities:** hot tub, exercise room. **Guest Services:** valet and coin laundry. *(See ad p. 367.)*

WHERE TO EAT

RIB CRIB BBQ AND GRILL   405/737-4500
APPROVED   Barbecue. Casual Dining. **Address:** 1821 S Douglas Blvd 73130

RON'S HAMBURGERS & CHILI   405/733-7667
APPROVED   American. Casual Dining. **Address:** 351 N Air Depot, Suite A 73110

MOORE pop. 55,081
• Hotels & Restaurants map & index p. 356
• Part of Oklahoma City area — see map p. 343

BEST WESTERN GREENTREE INN & SUITES
405/912-8800   81

THREE DIAMOND   **Hotel**   Best Western.

AAA Benefit: Members save up to 15% and earn bonus points!

Address: 1811 N Moore Ave 73160 **Location:** I-35 exit 118, just n on west frontage road. **Facility:** 63 units, some efficiencies. 3 stories, interior corridors. **Pool:** heated indoor. **Activities:** exercise room. **Guest Services:** coin laundry. **Featured Amenity:** continental breakfast.

HAMPTON INN & SUITES BY HILTON MOORE
405/735-6821   85
THREE DIAMOND Hotel. **Address:** 614 NW 8th St 73160

AAA Benefit: Members save up to 15%!

HOLIDAY INN EXPRESS & SUITES   405/735-9400   84
THREE DIAMOND Hotel. **Address:** 621 NW 8th St 73160

QUALITY INN   405/912-1400   82
APPROVED Hotel. **Address:** 1809 N Moore Ave 73160

SPRINGHILL SUITES BY MARRIOTT   405/759-2600   83
THREE DIAMOND Hotel. **Address:** 613 NW 8th St 73160

AAA Benefit: Members save 5% or more!

WHERE TO EAT

THE CATCH   405/735-5559   30
APPROVED   Seafood. Casual Dining. **Address:** 1301 S I 35 Service Rd 73160

RICKY'S CAFE   405/793-7999   31
APPROVED   Mexican. Casual Dining. **Address:** 2160 S I-35 Service Rd 73160

ROYAL BAVARIA RESTAURANT & BREWERY
405/799-7666   32
APPROVED   German. Casual Dining. **Address:** 3401 S Sooner Rd 73165

MUSKOGEE (D-11) pop. 39,223, elev. 601'
• Hotels p. 340 • Restaurants p. 340

The town takes its name from the Muscogee tribe of the Creek Nation who moved to Oklahoma in the 1830s. Muskogee also was the home of notable Oklahoma historians Grant and Carolyn Foreman, who wrote a number of books about the Five Civilized Tribes. The couple's residence, the Thomas-Foreman Historic Home at 1419 W. Okmulgee, contains their original furniture and is open for tours Fri.-Sat. 10-5, in summer; otherwise by request; phone (918) 686-6624.

Honor Heights Park, at 40th Street and Park Boulevard, is a 132-acre park with extensive plantings of azaleas, roses and irises surrounding lakes, lily ponds and picnic grounds.

Greater Muskogee Area Chamber of Commerce and Tourism: 310 W. Broadway, Muskogee, OK 74401. **Phone:** (918) 682-2401 or (866) 381-6540.

Shopping: Arrowhead Mall, 501 N. Main, has Dillard's and JCPenney as its anchor stores.

USS *BATFISH* WAR MEMORIAL PARK MUSEUM, Port of Muskogee exit off the Muskogee Tpke. at 3500 Batfish Rd., offers self-guiding tours of the USS *Batfish*, a World War II submarine that sank three enemy submarines in 76 hours and 11 other enemy vessels during battle. Tours include the torpedo room and crew cabins. The museum also contains monuments to other submarines lost during the war, a 45-foot mast section from the USS *Oklahoma* BB37, and a Walk of Honor that pays tribute to all veterans.

Hours: Wed.-Sat. 10-6, Sun. 1-6, Mar. 15-Oct. 15 (weather permitting); Thurs.-Sat. 10-5, Sun. 1-5, rest of year. **Cost:** $7; $5 (ages 13-18 and 61+); $4 (ages 7-12). **Phone:** (918) 682-6294.

Booth or table?

AAA.com/travelguides/restaurants

BEST WESTERN PLUS INN & SUITES MUSKOGEE
918/910-5060

THREE DIAMOND
Hotel

Best Western PLUS

AAA Benefit: Members save up to 15% and earn bonus points!

Address: 2701 Military Blvd 74401 **Location:** Just se of jct US 62 and 69. **Facility:** 66 units, some efficiencies. 3 stories, interior corridors. **Pool:** heated indoor. **Activities:** exercise room. **Guest Services:** valet and coin laundry.

SAVE 📶 CALL 📶 📶 📶 BIZ HS 📶 📶 📶 📶 📶

COMFORT INN
918/682-3724
APPROVED Hotel. **Address:** 3133 Azalea Park Dr 74401

FAIRFIELD INN & SUITES BY MARRIOTT
918/683-6700
THREE DIAMOND SAVE Hotel. **Address:** 1650 N 32nd St 74401

AAA Benefit: Members save 5% or more!

HAMPTON INN
918/682-2587
THREE DIAMOND SAVE Hotel. **Address:** 3101 Military Blvd 74401

AAA Benefit: Members save up to 15%!

HOLIDAY INN EXPRESS & SUITES
918/687-4224
THREE DIAMOND Hotel. **Address:** 2701 W Shawnee St 74401

HOME2 SUITES BY HILTON MUSKOGEE
918/910-5444
THREE DIAMOND SAVE Extended Stay Contemporary Hotel. **Address:** 2819 Military Blvd 74401

AAA Benefit: Members save up to 15%!

WHERE TO EAT

EL CHICO
918/682-3442
APPROVED Tex-Mex. Casual Dining. **Address:** 204 W Shawnee St 74401

GINO'S ITALIAN RISTORANTE
918/686-7773
APPROVED Italian. Casual Dining. **Address:** 139 W Shawnee St 74401

MAHYLON'S
918/686-7427
APPROVED Barbecue. Casual Dining. **Address:** 3301 Chandler Rd 74403

RIB CRIB BBQ AND GRILL
918/686-0991
APPROVED Barbecue. Casual Dining. **Address:** 150 W Shawnee St 74401

NORMAN (I-2) pop. 110,925, elev. 1,168'
• Part of Oklahoma City area — see map p. 343

Shortly after its 1889 beginnings and with a population of 500, Norman boasted four churches, two newspapers and 29 businesses. A year later the University of Oklahoma was established.

The Moore-Lindsay Historical House Museum, 508 N. Peters Ave., is in a 1900 Queen Anne-style house once owned by William S. Moore, a Norman businessman. Tours of the house are available; phone (405) 321-0156.

Recreational opportunities in the Norman vicinity are available at Lake Thunderbird State Park, 13 miles east on SR 9. *See Recreation Areas Chart.*

Visit Norman: 309 E. Main St., Norman, OK 73069. **Phone:** (405) 366-8095 or (800) 767-7260.

Shopping: Dillard's, JCPenney and Sears are the anchor stores at Sooner Mall, 3301 W. Main St.

UNIVERSITY OF OKLAHOMA is off I-35 Lindsey St. exit. The educational and research institution houses 21 colleges on its 3,000-acre campus. Sooners' campus tours can be arranged at the visitor center in Jacobson Hall, 550 Parrington Oval. **Time:** Allow 2 hours minimum. **Hours:** Tours are available Mon.-Fri. and select Sat.; phone for tour times and to confirm schedule. Closed holidays and holiday weekends. **Cost:** Free. **Phone:** (405) 325-2151 or (800) 234-6868. GT

Fred Jones Jr. Museum of Art, 555 Elm Ave. on the University of Oklahoma campus, includes French Impressionism works, Native American art, Southwestern art and contemporary American pieces from its permanent collection as well as rotating exhibitions throughout the year. Special events and programs are held weekly. **Time:** Allow 1 hour, 30 minutes minimum. **Hours:** Tues.-Sat. 10-5 (also Thurs. 5-9), Sun. 1-5. Closed university holidays. **Cost:** Free. **Phone:** (405) 325-4938.

GEM **Sam Noble Oklahoma Museum of Natural History,** 2401 Chautauqua Ave. on the University of Oklahoma campus, offers a look back 300 million years at the state's natural history. Visitors can walk through realistic dioramas that depict Oklahoma's natural landscapes, as well as view dinosaur skeletons, including the world's largest Apatosaurus and a 10.5-foot-tall Pentaceratops skull. Also displayed are artifacts from native Oklahomans and exhibits about modern-day activities of the western tribes.

A Discovery Room engages young visitors with hands-on science activities. **Time:** Allow 1 hour, 30 minutes minimum. **Hours:** Mon.-Sat. 10-5, Sun. 1-5. **Cost:** $8; $7 (active military with ID;) $6 (ages 65+); $5 (ages 4-17); free Memorial Day-Labor Day (active military with ID); free (first Mon. of the month ages 4-17). **Phone:** (405) 325-4712. 📶

W.B. Bizzell Memorial Library is at 401 W. Brooks St. on the University of Oklahoma campus. There are four special collections: the History of Science Collection, featuring Bibles and works by Charles Darwin, Galileo and others; the Bass Business History Collection; the John and Mary Nichols Rare Books and Special Collections whlch contains first editions of Charles Dickens' works; and the Bizzell Bible Collection.

Time: Allow 30 minutes minimum. **Hours:** Library open Mon.-Sat. at 7:30, Sun. at noon; closing times vary. Closed major holidays. Phone ahead to confirm schedule. **Cost:** Free. **Phone:** (405) 325-4142.

BEST WESTERN PLUS NORMAN   405/801-2100

⬥THREE DIAMOND
Hotel

BW Best Western PLUS.
AAA Benefit: Members save up to 15% and earn bonus points!

Address: 3100 Medical Park Pl 73072 **Location:** I-35 exit 112, just sw. **Facility:** 116 units. 4 stories, interior corridors. **Pool:** heated outdoor. **Activities:** exercise room. **Guest Services:** valet and coin laundry.
[SAVE] CALL [symbols] [BIZ] [HS]
[symbols]
/ SOME UNITS

COMFORT INN & SUITES NORMAN   405/701-5200
⬥THREE DIAMOND Hotel. **Address:** 840 Copperfield Dr 73019

COURTYARD BY MARRIOTT NORMAN   405/701-8900
⬥THREE DIAMOND [SAVE] Hotel. **Address:** 770 Copperfield Dr 73072
AAA Benefit: Members save 5% or more!

DAYS INN NORMAN   405/360-1234
⬥ APPROVED Motel. **Address:** 2543 W Main St 73069

EMBASSY SUITES BY HILTON NORMAN-HOTEL & CONFERENCE CENTER   405/364-8040
⬥THREE DIAMOND [SAVE] Hotel. **Address:** 2501 Conference Dr 73069
AAA Benefit: Members save up to 15%!

FAIRFIELD INN & SUITES BY MARRIOTT NORMAN   405/447-1661
⬥THREE DIAMOND [SAVE] Hotel. **Address:** 301 Norman Center Ct 73072
AAA Benefit: Members save 5% or more!

HILTON GARDEN INN   405/579-0100
⬥THREE DIAMOND [SAVE] Hotel. **Address:** 700 Copperfield Dr 73072
AAA Benefit: Members save up to 15%!

LA QUINTA INN & SUITES NORMAN   405/579-4000
⬥THREE DIAMOND Hotel. **Address:** 930 Ed Noble Dr 73072

MONTFORD INN & COTTAGES   405/321-2200
⬥THREE DIAMOND Bed & Breakfast. **Address:** 322 W Tonhawa 73069

QUALITY INN & SUITES   405/701-4011
⬥ APPROVED Hotel. **Address:** 2841 S Classen Blvd 73071

SLEEP INN & SUITES   405/307-0919
⬥THREE DIAMOND Hotel. **Address:** 2601 Bankers Ave 73072

SUPER 8 NORMAN   405/329-1624
⬥ APPROVED Hotel. **Address:** 2600 W Main St 73069

WHERE TO EAT

CHARLESTON'S RESTAURANT   405/360-0900
⬥ APPROVED American. Casual Dining. **Address:** 300 Ed Noble Pkwy 73072

EL CHICO   405/360-2146
⬥ APPROVED Tex-Mex. Casual Dining. **Address:** 3439 W Main St 73072

LEGEND'S RESTAURANT   405/329-8888
⬥ APPROVED Continental. Casual Dining. **Address:** 1313 W Lindsey St 73069

MISAL OF INDIA BISTRO   405/579-5600
⬥ APPROVED Indian. Casual Dining. **Address:** 580 Ed Noble Pkwy 73072

RIB CRIB BBQ AND GRILL   405/573-7900
⬥ APPROVED Barbecue. Casual Dining. **Address:** 1131 Rambling Oaks Dr 73072

TED'S CAFE ESCONDIDO   405/307-8337
⬥ APPROVED Mexican. Casual Dining. **Address:** 700 N Interstate Dr 73070

VAN'S PIG STANDS   405/364-0600
⬥ APPROVED Barbecue. Quick Serve. **Address:** 320 N Porter Ave 73069

Oklahoma City

Then & Now

Born in an afternoon, built over a field of black gold, and redesigned by architect I.M. Pei, Oklahoma City has a history with few plateaus. Between noon and sundown on April 22, 1889, the unassigned prairie lands of the Oklahoma Territory were opened for settlement, and 10,000 land claims surrounding a Santa Fe Railroad station site were made in one afternoon. Oklahoma City blossomed overnight.

Established as state capital in 1910, Oklahoma City welcomed thousands of government employees, whose arrival swelled its population to the largest in the state. Manufacturing concerns were established along with the development of natural resources.

On Dec. 4, 1928, what would become a major force in Oklahoma City's economic future surfaced: The first oil well within the city limits struck a gusher. It changed not only the economy but the scenery. Oil derricks sprouted throughout town, adding a familiar silhouette to the city's rapidly changing skyline. Producing wells still are found on the Capitol grounds, and more than 2,000 wells are either within or adjacent to the city limits. The pool on which Oklahoma City rests is considered among the richest ever developed in the United States.

Along with the discovery of oil, drilling equipment and petroleum refining industries flourished. Aviation remains a major industry, with the FAA Mike Monroney Aeronautical Center and the Civil Aeromedical Institute making their home at Will Rogers World Airport. "OKC," as the city is affectionately called by its residents, also ranks among the eight primary livestock markets in the country.

AAA.com/travelguides—
more ways to look, book and save

A large bronze sculpture of a cowboy and his steed marks the entrance to the Oklahoma National Stockyards, 2501 Exchange Ave., founded in 1910 and said to be the world's largest cattle market. Visitors can watch the cattle auctions on Monday and Tuesday mornings.

To complement the city's successful commercial growth, local leaders recommended a new look for downtown. In 1964 well-known urban architect I.M. Pei created a master redevelopment plan. Inspired by Copenhagen's Tivoli Gardens, the rejuvenated area includes lakes, water concourses, landscaped hills, an amphitheater and a striking glass and steel botanical bridge containing a greenhouse with exotic plants. Another innovative addition is the Underground, a system of tunnels and skywalks which connects hotels, office buildings, conference areas, restaurants and stores.

Oklahoma State Capitol

(Continued on p. 344.)

Destination Oklahoma City

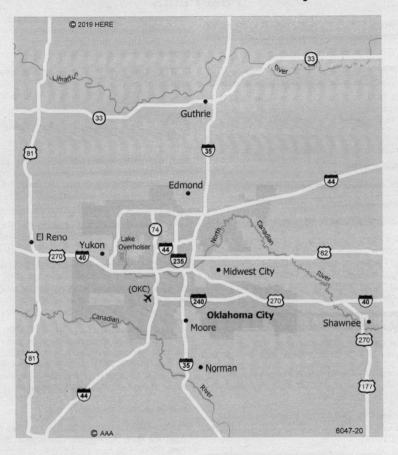

This map shows cities in the Oklahoma City vicinity where you will find attractions, hotels and restaurants. Cities are listed alphabetically in this book on the following pages.

Fast Facts

ABOUT THE CITY

POP: 579,999 ■ **ELEV:** 1,201 ft.

MONEY

SALES TAX: Oklahoma City levies a sales tax of 8.38 percent, a lodging tax of 13.87 percent and a rental car tax of 14.37 percent.

WHOM TO CALL

EMERGENCY: 911

POLICE (non-emergency): (405) 297-1000

FIRE (non-emergency): (405) 297-3439

TIME AND TEMPERATURE: (405) 599-1234

HOSPITALS: AllianceHealth Deaconess, (405) 604-6000 ■ Integris Baptist Medical Center, (405) 949-3011 ■ Integris Southwest Medical Center, (405) 636-7000 ■ Mercy Hospital, (405) 755-1515 ■ OU Medical Center, (405) 271-4700 ■ St. Anthony Hospital, (405) 272-7000.

VISITOR INFORMATION

Greater Oklahoma City Chamber: 123 Park Ave., Oklahoma City, OK 73102. **Phone:** (405) 297-8900.

Oklahoma City Convention & Visitors Bureau: 123 Park Ave., Oklahoma City, OK 73102. **Phone:** (405) 297-8912 or (800) 225-5652.

Oklahoma City CVB Visitor Information Center: 1 Myriad Gardens, Oklahoma City, OK 73102. **Phone:** (405) 602-5141.

TRANSPORTATION

AIR TRAVEL: Will Rogers World Airport (OKC) is 10 miles southwest of downtown. Airport parking is $4-$24 per day. Cabs average 10-20 minutes to the downtown area; the average cost is $25-$26. Airport vans depart frequently and provide shuttle service between the airport and downtown for $17-$22 per person.

RENTAL CARS: Several rental car agencies serve the Oklahoma City area. Hertz, (405) 681-2341 or (800) 654-3080, offers discounts to AAA members.

 Book and save at AAA.com/hertz

RAIL SERVICE: Amtrak's Heartland Flyer provides daily train service between Oklahoma City and Fort Worth, Texas. The station is at 100 South E.K. Gaylord Blvd. Phone (800) 872-7245.

BUSES: Greyhound Lines Inc. and Jefferson Lines are the major bus lines that serve the city. They both operate out of the same terminal at 1938 E. Reno Ave. Phone (405) 606-4382.

TAXIS: Cab companies include A1 Taxi Service, (405) 321-3111 ■ and Yellow Cab, (405) 232-6161. Taxis are metered and charge $2.75 per call for the first 1/8 mile and an additional $.25 per 1/8 mile. There is a $1 charge for each additional passenger ages 12+.

PUBLIC TRANSPORTATION: EMBARK, (405) 235-7433, operates throughout the metropolitan area. The main terminal/transit center is at 420 N.W. 5th St. Bus fare is $1.75; 75c (ages 7-17 and 60+). A 1-day pass is $4; $2 (ages 7-17 and 60+). Downtown Discovery shuttle buses traverse the downtown area between the Oklahoma City National Memorial & Museum and Bricktown; fare is free.

BOATS: Oklahoma River Cruises operates on the Oklahoma River April through December. Boarding points for the 1.25-hour trip are at Regatta Park, 701 S. Lincoln Blvd.; Meridian Landing, 4345 S.W. 15th St.; Exchange Landing, 1503 Exchange Ave.; and Bricktown Landing, at 334 Centennial Dr. Fare is $6 per stop, $15 maximum; $3 per stop, $7.50 maximum (ages 7-12 and 60+). Phone (405) 702-7755.

(Continued from p. 342.)

Among Oklahoma City's main public buildings is the Civic Center Music Hall, a performing arts facility. The Art Deco-style building anchors the west end of the downtown Arts District. The Spring Festival of the Arts is held nearby at Bicentennial Park, and Myriad Botanical Gardens hosts a holiday light display and other seasonal events.

Despite a sleek and sophisticated appearance, Oklahoma City has not forgotten its pervasive Western and Native American heritage. It sprang from Indian Territory, and the 39 Native American tribes still represented in the state hold regular tribal activities in and around the city. Their artwork decorates building interiors and is displayed in local galleries and museums.

The skills of horses and cowboys are revered at many rodeos and horse shows as well as at the National Cowboy & Western Heritage Museum *(see attraction listing p. 351)*, and cowboys still practice their trade at horse and cattle ranches in the surrounding region.

Must Do: AAA Editor's Picks

- Spend some quiet time at the ⚡ **Oklahoma City National Memorial & Museum** (620 N. Harvey Ave.). Enter through the bronze Gates of Time and visit the Field of Empty Chairs, where handcrafted chairs stand as a somber reminder of the 168 lives lost during the Oklahoma City bombing on April 19, 1995. Listen to an audio recording of the blast and read Oklahomans' stories of hope and survival at the nearby museum.

- Brush up on Sooner state history at the ⚡ **National Cowboy & Western Heritage Museum** (1700 N.E. 63rd St.), where you'll find an extensive collection of Native American art, Western movie props and the Rodeo Hall of Fame. Journey back to the Wild West with a tour of Prosperity Junction, a replica of a circa 1900 cattle town complete with a full-size saloon.

- Discover a tropical oasis at ⚡ **Myriad Botanical Gardens and Crystal Bridge Tropical Conservatory** (301 W. Reno Ave.), a 17-acre garden in the center of downtown. Wander the tree-shaded paths and marvel at the Tropical Bridge, a 7-story cylindrical conservatory suspended over a sunken lake.

- Check out the action in Bricktown—OKC's entertainment district on the eastern edge of downtown. This revitalized warehouse area offers live music and plenty of places to eat. Try **Jazmo'z Bourbon Street Café** (100 E. California Ave.) or **Bricktown Brewery** (1 N. Oklahoma Ave.). If you eat too much, don't worry—the walk along Bricktown Canal is the perfect place to work off a meal. At the south end of the canal is the **Centennial Land Run Monument,** an impressive grouping of bronze statues that's worth a look.

- Catch a baseball game at **Chickasaw Bricktown Ballpark** (2 S. Mickey Mantle Dr.). Street names around "The Brick" pay homage to hometown heroes. Snap a photo in front of the "History of Bricktown" mosaic murals located outside the stadium; the panels are made of 158,000 brightly colored porcelain tiles.

- Hunt for treasures while browsing art galleries and boutique shops in the bohemian **Paseo Arts District**, where brightly colored buildings and clay-tile roofs create the feel of a Spanish village just north of downtown. Die-hard shoppers will love the antique shops and retail stores along **Western Avenue** (between N.W. 36th Street and Wilshire Boulevard).

- Witness a live cattle auction (Monday and Tuesday mornings) in **Stockyards City** (1305 S. Agnew Ave.), where the Oklahoma National Stockyards Company has been in operation since 1910. If you don't make it in time for an early-morning auction, browse the shops on South Agnew and Exchange avenues for cowboy-approved boots, custom-fitted hats and authentic Western wear. Grab dinner at **Cattlemen's Steakhouse** (1309 S. Agnew Ave.), an Oklahoma favorite and purveyor of award-winning T-bone steaks.

- Ooh and aah over the 55-foot tall, multi-colored tower of glass by sculptor Dale Chihuly inside the **Oklahoma City Museum of Art** (415 Couch Dr.). In addition to a large Chihuly collection, the museum touts numerous galleries of European and American art.

- See the command module simulator used by Apollo astronauts at the ⚡ **Science Museum Oklahoma** (2100 N.E. 52nd St.). A Smithsonian affiliate, the museum also includes the Oklahoma Aviation and Space Hall of Fame and the International Gymnastics Hall of Fame.

- If you're looking for fun things to do with kids, Get up close and personal with gorillas, elephants, grizzly bears and thousands of other native and exotic creatures at the ⚡ **Oklahoma City Zoo & Botanical Garden** (2000 Remington Pl.). A narrated ride on the Elephant Express Tram is a good way to scope out the lay of the land before your hooves get too tired.

- Snap a photo of the giant milk bottle that sits atop the wedge-shaped building at 2426 N. Classen Blvd. It's an iconic photo spot along the original path of Route 66.

Myriad Botanical Gardens and Crystal Bridge Tropical Conservatory

Oklahoma City 1-day Itinerary

AAA editors suggest these activities for a great short vacation experience.

Morning

- Start your morning in OKC a little southwest of downtown in Stockyards City, where the Wild West is still alive and kicking. If you arrive hungry, make a pit stop at **Cattlemen's Steakhouse** (1309 S. Agnew Ave.) for a cowboy-approved breakfast of steak, eggs and coffee (or try the calf brains and eggs if you're feeling adventurous). Browse the shops on South Agnew and Exchange avenues for authentic Western wear and custom-fitted cowboy hats. If you arrive early on a Monday or Tuesday (before 8 a.m.) you can watch a live cattle auction at the Oklahoma National Stockyards Co. (2501 Exchange Ave.).

- Hitch up the wagon and make your way to the **Oklahoma City Museum of Art** (415 Couch Dr.), where you can marvel at one of the world's largest collections of Dale Chihuly blown-glass art. As you enter the atrium, gaze up at the museum's signature piece—the 55-foot-tall sculpture made up of 2,100 blown glass parts in beautiful yellows, oranges, blues and greens.

- For blues and greens of the more natural type, travel a few blocks south to **Myriad Botanical Gardens and Crystal Bridge Tropical Conservatory** (301 W. Reno Ave.), a 17-acre tropical oasis in the middle of downtown. Built with Copenhagen's Tivoli Gardens in mind, Myriad Gardens features tree-shaded paths and plenty of photo opportunities. The real jewel is the Crystal Bridge Conservatory, a 224-foot-long cylindrical jungle bursting with plant life.

Afternoon

- For lunch, try **Cheever's Cafe** (2409 N. Hudson Ave.). The menu includes chicken fried steak, an Oklahoma staple that is served here with mashed potatoes and jalapeño cream gravy.

- No visit to Oklahoma City is complete without a trip to the **National Cowboy & Western Heritage Museum** (1700 N.E. 63rd St.). You'll need at least a few hours to explore the museum's extensive collection of pioneer artifacts and memorabilia, but be sure to check out the Rodeo Hall of Fame (complete with portraits and saddles from legendary riders) and Prosperity Junction, a replica of a turn-of-the-20th-century cattle town, before you leave.

- As you make your way back downtown, stop at the **Oklahoma City National Memorial & Museum** (620 N. Harvey Ave.), another OKC must-see. Enter through the bronze Gates of Time—marked 9:01 and 9:03 to signify the moments before and after the bombing—and visit the museum for a self-guiding tour that

Cattlemen's Steakhouse

takes you through the story of April 19, 1995. Pine trees planted around the memorial grounds outline the footprint of the fallen Alfred P. Murrah Federal Building. Stay until dusk and you'll see the Field of Empty Chairs glowing with light—one for each victim of the bombing.

Evening

- To begin your evening, head to **Bricktown,** the city's entertainment hotspot on the eastern edge of downtown. Once a dilapidated warehouse district, Bricktown is now home to bustling restaurants, live music venues and late-night watering holes.

- Stroll along the mile-long Bricktown Canal (a man-made waterway built one floor below street level) or take a water taxi to **Chickasaw Bricktown Ballpark** (2 S. Mickey Mantle Dr.). If the home team is playing, catch a game and a ballpark hot dog at this famed minor league stadium. The ballpark's three entrances display statues of baseball legends Johnny Bench, Warren Spahn and hometown hero Mickey Mantle.

- If you'd prefer a sit-down dinner over a ballpark hot dog, reserve a table at **Mantel Wine Bar & Bistro** (201 E. Sheridan Ave.), an upscale restaurant well worth the splurge. Also within walking distance is **Mickey Mantle's Steakhouse** (7 S. Mickey Mantle Blvd.).

- For a sweet end to the night, pop in to local-favorite **Pinkitzel Cupcakes & Candy** (in the train depot at 150 N. E.K. Gaylord Blvd.) for a homemade cupcake and a sweet-tooth-satisfying pink hot chocolate.

Top Picks for Kids

Under 13

- Escape into nature during your vacation with a visit to  **Myriad Botanical Gardens and Crystal Bridge Tropical Conservatory**, a 15-acre oasis of gardens, water features, and walking and jogging paths right in the heart of downtown. Little ones will love exploring the children's garden, playground and splash fountains. The 13,000-square-foot conservatory is filled with thousands of tropical and desert plants, a waterfall and a sky bridge offering a birds-eye view of the tropical forest.

- When it comes to fun things to do outdoors, you can't go wrong with a zoo, and the **Oklahoma City Zoo & Botanical Garden** offers lots of attractions for young children such as the Children's Zoo Barnyard, the Children's Zoo Water Stream and a one-of-a-kind, handcrafted carousel featuring 42 endangered animals. If you're feeling adventurous, how about an elephant ride? When it's time for a break, take a ride around the park on the Centennial Choo Choo.

- If your trip to Oklahoma City includes the first or third Saturday during the spring and summer months, don't miss the chance to hop aboard an old-fashioned passenger train at the **Oklahoma Railway Museum**. Vintage trains depart from the historic Oakwood Depot throughout the day for 40 minute rides. Kids will also enjoy seeing the museum's collection of railroad cars and memorabilia.

- When it's time for a break from sightseeing, head to **Roxy's Ice Cream Social** and cool off with a frozen treat. Enjoy a variety of classic and seasonal ice cream flavors along with floats, cookie sandwiches and sundaes.

Teens

- Teens and tweens will love **Frontier City**, which offers breathtaking roller coasters, water rides and other thrilling attractions, along with shows and tons of dining options. On select dates, the park offers concerts in its Starlight Amphitheater.

- **Hideaway Pizza** has been serving up its award-winning pies since 1957. Get adventurous with a specialty pizza such as "Maui Magic"—red sauce, mozzarella, Canadian bacon, pineapple and mandarin orange—or choose your own toppings. Sandwiches, salads and deep-dish baked pastas round out the menu.

- The **Museum of Osteology** exhibits more than 300 animal skeletons from around the world, from invertebrates to a 40-foot humpback whale, and some museum rarities. See what they have in common and how they've adapted to fly, climb, swim or jump. Aspiring detectives should check out the forensic pathology exhibit.

All Ages

- Experience the culture of the American West with a visit to the **National Cowboy & Western Heritage Museum**, which features more than 28,000 Western and Native American artifacts and artworks. View paintings, sculptures and historical artifacts, and take a walk through an authentic turn-of-the-century prairie town. Little buckaroos can put on chaps and spurs, sit around a campfire and listen to a cowboy sing in the Children's Cowboy Corral.

- Stop in for a tasty treat at **Pie Junkie**, where you'll find all your favorites plus some new flavors to try. Whether you're tempted by a traditional Apple Crumble or Coconut Cream, or up for digging into something new such as S'more or "Drunken Turtle," there's something to please every pie palate here.

- With 350,000 square feet of exhibits, **Science Museum Oklahoma** is filled with activities for kids of all ages. Tiny tots are introduced to science in KidSpace, while younger children can play and learn in the neighborhoods of CurioCity. Teens can drive Segways and engage in hundreds of other activities on the Science Floor, and movies and live shows in the Kirkpatrick Planetarium will entertain everyone in the family.

- For some splashy summer fun, head to **White Water Bay**. Brave older kids can race down the Acapulco Cliff Dive, a giant high-speed "free-fall" slide, While the whole family can ride a tube down to asplash landing on the Big Kahuna. Younger children will have a blast in Barefootin' Bay'swater play area.

National Cowboy & Western Heritage Museum

Arriving
By Car

Transcontinental I-40 is the primary east-west route through the area; it traverses the heart of the city, offering easy interchanges with main streets and other through routes. I-44, a shorter east-west corridor, angles in from the northeast and the southwest, skirting the western side of the city and offering frequent interchanges.

Except for its path through the city, I-44 is a toll highway throughout most of Oklahoma; its various segments are known as the Will Rogers Turnpike, Turner Turnpike and H.E. Bailey Turnpike. Other east-west routes serving the area mainly accommodate local traffic and include US 62, US 270 and old US 66, which parallels I-44 from the northeast and I-40 from the west.

I-35 bisects both the nation and Oklahoma City, bringing travelers from Lake Superior to the north and from the Mexican border to the south. It courses along the city's east side with frequent interchanges. US 77 closely parallels I-35 and serves mostly local traffic. Also of importance is SR 3, which provides access to Will Rogers and Wiley Post airports as it skirts the city's west side.

I-240 (the Southwest Expressway) combines with I-44 and I-35 to form a loop around Oklahoma City, providing a bypass of the downtown area.

Getting Around
Street System

Except for the area around the Capitol and state office buildings, Oklahoma City is laid out in a grid pattern with streets either running north-south or

Langston's Western Wear

east-west. The numbered streets run east-west both north and south of Main Street; named north-south streets intersect them. East-west address numbers start at Grand Avenue, and north-south numbers begin at Broadway.

Unless otherwise posted, the speed limit on most streets is 25 to 30 mph. Rush hour traffic, 7:30-9 a.m. and 4-6 p.m., should be avoided.

Parking

Ample parking is available downtown. There are many commercial garages, and most hotels provide parking for guests. Rates are $1-$2 per hour, or $10 per day.

Shopping

Whether you are looking for Western wear or the latest in high fashion, you can find it in Oklahoma City's department stores and specialty shops.

Establishments that sell cowboy hats, boots and belts are **Langston's Western Wear,** 2224 Exchange Ave.; **Sheplers Western Wear,** 812 S. Meridian; and **Tener's,** 4320 W. Reno. Other characteristic Oklahoma City purchases are Native American art and jewelry.

Several enclosed malls are convenient for one-stop shopping. To the north is **Penn Square Mall,** 1901 Northwest Expwy., one of the largest malls in the area, where Dillard's, JCPenney and Macy's are the anchor stores. Also north of the city is **Quail Springs Mall,** Memorial Road at Pennsylvania Avenue, with anchors Dillard's, JCPenney and Von Maur. The **Outlet Shoppes at Oklahoma City,** off I-40 at 7624 W. Reno Ave., features more than 90 shops and eateries.

Shops, nightclubs and restaurants crowd the historic commercial area known as **Bricktown,** named for its many turn-of-the-20th-century red brick warehouses. A canal lined with eateries offering outdoor seating winds through Bricktown and links downtown OKC with parks and the Oklahoma River.

Big Events

Home of the National Cowboy & Western Heritage Museum, Oklahoma City also pays tribute to the cowboy's trusted companion, the horse. Several national and international horse shows and at least 20 state and regional competitions are held throughout the year. The major shows take place at the arena in **State Fair Park** at 3001 General Pershing Blvd.

The **Grand National and World Championship Morgan Horse Show** is held in October at State Fair Park. The **World Championship Quarter Horse Show** is in November. The season ends in early December with the **National Reining Futurity** and the **Barrel Racing Futurity.** In a similar Western vein, the 🏆 **Chuck Wagon Gathering and Children's Cowboy Festival,** held in late May, is a family event featuring chuck wagon cooks from across the country as well as entertainment, pony rides, square dancing and an Old West Medicine Show.

With a large Native American population, Oklahoma is rich with Native American culture and tradition. One such tradition is the powwow, when tribe members in full costume gather for days filled with traditional competitions, dance, music and food. These powwows take place throughout the summer, and many are held in Oklahoma City. One of the largest powwows is the **Red Earth Native American Cultural Festival;** representatives from more than 100 tribes gather in June to celebrate and share their heritage.

The city celebrates the visual and performing arts during April and September with art festivals held in area parks; the events feature singers and musicians performing throughout the day as well as artists displaying their works. The activity is enhanced by food stands serving international cuisines. **An Affair of the Heart** takes place in February and October and includes more than 400 arts and crafts exhibitors.

In September the **Oklahoma State Fair** transforms the 435-acre fairgrounds into a lively happening. One of the largest state fairs in the country, the 11-day event features ice shows, car races, a rodeo and livestock and cooking contests. Closing out the year, the ❧ **Holidays at the Gardens** celebration, held around Thanksgiving through the end of the year at **Myriad Botanical Gardens and Crystal Bridge Tropical Conservatory,** glows with thousands of twinkling lights among the trees and trails.

Sports & Rec

Oklahoma City's parks offer the setting for almost any activity. **Tennis, swimming** and **picnicking** facilities are plentiful at **Will Rogers Park,** 36th Street and N. Portland. **Boating** and **fishing** are popular at lakes Hefner, Draper and Overholser. **Lake Hefner** is particularly known for its good **sailing. Water skiing** can be enjoyed at **Draper Lake.**

Kayaking is possible from the Chesapeake Boathouse, 725 S. Lincoln Blvd., and Route 66 Boathouse, 3115 E. Overholser Dr.; phone (405) 552-4040. White-water rafting, paddleboarding, a zipline course and other outdoor adventure activities are available.

Additionally, **jogging** trails are available at **Earlywine Park,** S.W. 119th and May; Lake Hefner, N. Grand Boulevard between May and Portland; and **Memorial Park,** 34th and Classen. Thirteen miles of paved trails run along the north and south banks of the **Oklahoma River,** with access points at **River Park,** 800 S. Agnew Ave.; **Wheeler Park,** 1120 S. Western Ave.; and **Wiley Post Park,** 2021 S. Robinson Ave. The Oklahoma City Parks and Recreation Department offers information about all of their facilities; phone (405) 297-2211.

Daily **bicycle** rentals are available with **Spokies,** Oklahoma City's bicycle-sharing system. Two-wheelers may be rented and returned at any of eight kiosks scattered throughout the city. Kiosk locations include the Cox Convention Center, Oklahoma City

Oklahoma State Fair

National Memorial, Chickasaw Bricktown Ballpark, Ronald J. Norick Downtown Library and others. A 1-day pass costs $5 and includes all rides under 30 minutes; longer rides incur an additional fee of $2 per half-hour. Phone (405) 606-4008 for more information.

Golf courses are readily available. Public links include nine-hole courses such as **Brookside Golf Course,** 9016 S. Shields Blvd.; **Lakeside Golf Course,** 3400 N. Eastern Ave.; and **The Links Golf & Athletic Club,** 700 N.E. 122nd St. For 18-hole courses offerings include **Earlywine Golf Course,** 11600 S. Portland Ave; **Lake Hefner Golf Course,** 4491 S. Lake Hefner Dr.; **Lincoln Park Golf Course,** 4001 N.E. Grand Blvd.; and **Trosper Golf Club,** 2301 S.E. 29th St.

Spectator sports also are favorite pastimes. The **Oklahoma City Dodgers,** the Triple-A **baseball** affiliate of the Los Angeles Dodgers, draw fans every spring to **Chickasaw Bricktown Ballpark,** 2 S. Mickey Mantle Dr.; phone (405) 218-1000. Fall welcomes college **football** as the **University of Oklahoma Sooners,** members of the Big 12 Conference, begin their season at the **Gaylord Family Oklahoma Memorial Stadium at Owen Field** in Norman; phone (405) 325-2424 or (800) 456-4668. The city also plays host to a number of **rodeos** and **horse shows** throughout the year *(see Big Events)*.

Basketball rounds out the sports year. The National Basketball Association's **Oklahoma City Thunder**—formerly the Seattle SuperSonics—plays at **Chesapeake Energy Arena,** 100 W. Reno Ave. The team is in action from late October to mid-April;

phone (405) 602-8700. The **Oklahoma City University Stars** play at the **Freede Center,** N.W. 27th and Florida streets; phone (800) 633-7242. The Sooners from the University of Oklahoma compete at **Lloyd Noble Center** in Norman; phone (405) 325-2424.

Performing Arts

Oklahoma City offers a diverse palette of cultural entertainment. **Oklahoma City Ballet,** (405) 848-8637, stages elaborate productions at the **Civic Center Music Hall,** 201 N. Walker Ave. The music hall also is the home of the **Oklahoma City Philharmonic,** (405) 842-5387, which performs both classical and pop music. Their seasons run concurrently from September or October through April or May. The **Chamber Music Series of Oklahoma City,** (405) 974-2415, complements the symphony's season with its concerts at Christ the King Catholic Church, 8005 Dorset Dr., from October to early April.

Oklahoma City University's music school also contributes to the performing arts scene with six musical performances and vocal and instrumental performances scheduled throughout the year; phone (405) 208-5227 or (800) 633-7242. The **Canterbury Voices,** (405) 232-7464, performs October through April at the Civic Center Music Hall.

In summer the great outdoors provides a showcase for pop and rock concerts at the amphitheater at **Frontier City.** Plenty of guitar playin', banjo pickin' and foot stompin' goes on at Del City's **Oklahoma Country-Western Museum and Hall of Fame,** 3925 S.E. 29th St., during **Bluegrass Music Society** performances on the second Saturday of each month and during gospel bluegrass music performances on the fifth Saturday of the month; phone (405) 308-3595 or (405) 677-7515.

Oklahoma City's theater scene offers several choices. The productions of the **Black Liberated Arts Center** focus on African American culture and are held at various locations throughout the city; phone (405) 524-3800. A professional summer stock company, the **Lyric Theatre,** performs musicals from June through August at the Civic Center Music Hall; for ticket information phone (405) 297-2264.

Locals show their talent in a six-play season of musicals and dramas at the **Jewel Box Theatre,** 3700 N. Walker; phone (405) 521-1786.

ATTRACTIONS

For a complete list of attractions, visit AAA.com/travelguides/attractions

45TH INFANTRY DIVISION MUSEUM, .7 mi. w. off I-35 at 2145 N.E. 36th St., traces Oklahoma's military history from 1541 to the present. Exhibits include a collection of Adolf Hitler's personal items from his Munich office, uniforms and what is said to be the world's largest collection of Bill Mauldin's "Willie and Joe" cartoons. A military weapons collection illustrates the development of American military arms from the American Revolution to current operations.

More than 70 military vehicles, aircraft and artillery are outdoors. **Time:** Allow 1 hour minimum. **Hours:** Museum Tues.-Fri. 9-4:15, Sat. 10-4:15, Sun. 1-4:15. Outdoor military park closes no later than 5. **Cost:** Free. **Phone:** (405) 424-5313.

FRONTIER CITY, off I-35 exit 136 (Hefner Rd.) to 11501 N. I-35 Service Rd., is both a re-created 1880s Oklahoma town and an amusement park. Featured are steel and wooden roller coasters, bumper cars, a carousel and Wild West Water Works, a water play area with some 10 slides and a 1,000-gallon tipping bucket. Gunfights, live shows and musical reviews are staged daily.

Additional entertainment includes a concert series April-Aug., FrightFest in October and Holiday in the Park in December.

Time: Allow 1 hour minimum. **Hours:** Mon.-Fri. 10:30-8, Sat. 10:30-10, Sun. noon-8, early June-mid-Aug.; Sat. 10:30-8, Sun. noon-8, April-May; Sat. 10:30-10, Sun. noon-8, mid-Aug.-Sept; Fri. 6 p.m.-11 p.m., Sat. noon-11, Sun. noon-10, Oct.; Fri.-Sat. 5 p.m.-10 p.m., Sun. 5 p.m.-9 p.m., late Nov.-Dec. Hours vary. Phone ahead or check website to confirm schedule. **Cost:** $41.99; $31.99 (under 48 inches tall and ages 62+); free (ages 0-2). **Parking:** $20. **Phone:** (405) 478-2140. [T]

JIM THORPE MUSEUM AND OKLAHOMA SPORTS HALL OF FAME is at 20 S. Mickey Mantle Dr. The 13,000-square-foot museum honors Olympic gold medalist Jim Thorpe and other celebrated Oklahoma athletes. The permanent collection houses more than 4,000 items with displays of photographs, videos, uniforms, equipment, trophies and other sports memorabilia. Oklahoma Sports Hall of Fame inductees also are featured. **Time:** Allow 1 hour minimum. **Hours:** Tues.-Sat. 10-5. Guided tours are available by appointment. Closed major holidays. **Cost:** Free. **Phone:** (405) 427-1400. [GT]

MUSEUM OF OSTEOLOGY, 10301 S. Sunnylane Rd., displays nearly 400 skulls and skeletons from a variety of animals including apes, cats, elephants, giraffes, horses, humans, rhinoceroses and whales. Many skeletons may be touched. Explorer's Corner allows visitors to handle and examine North American animal skulls. A 40-foot, 2,500-pound skeleton of a humpback whale is suspended from the ceiling. **Time:** Allow 1 hour, 30 minutes minimum. **Hours:** Mon.-Fri. 9-5, Sat. 11-5, Sun. 1-5. **Cost:** $10; $8 (ages 3-12); free (ages 0-2). **Phone:** (405) 814-0006.

MYRIAD BOTANICAL GARDENS AND CRYSTAL BRIDGE TROPICAL CONSERVATORY, 301 W. Reno Ave., contains both an outdoor garden and an enclosed tropical conservatory. Set on 15 acres surrounding a lake in the downtown central business district, the gardens were the vision of the late oil and gas magnate Dean A. McGee,

Oklahoma City Attractions

© 2019 HERE

To Enid

© AAA

To Tulsa & Guthrie

2146-20

founder of Kerr-McGee Corp. Architect I.M. Pei was commissioned to create McGee's dream, based on the Tivoli Gardens.

The gardens' serene landscape includes a lake, winding paths, innovative water features, hundreds of trees and an assortment of colorful plantings that bloom from winter through fall. Sculptures add to the enchanting scene, and a bridge across the lake provides views of the city skyline. Among the flowers that blossom throughout the year are pansies, wisteria, daylilies, peonies, daffodils, tulips, chrysanthemums and black-eyed Susans.

The 224-foot-long, seven-story-high conservatory is a cylinder 70 feet in diameter made of more than 3,000 translucent acrylic panels. You know you're in a tropical environment as soon as you enter and the warm, humid air envelops you.

The Crystal Bridge Tropical Conservatory is home to more than 2,000 types of plants and is divided into two areas: the Tropical Rain Forest Zone (known as the Wet Mountain) and the Dry Tropical Zone (Dry Mountain). The lush wet zone is where you'll find a 35-foot waterfall and a skywalk across

the center of the conservatory that offers panoramic views. The dry zone, which is only watered in summer, can reach a temperature of 95 F. More than 100 types of palms, cycads, gingers, funnel-shaped bromeliads, dozens of varieties of orchids, spiny plants known as euphorbias and more than 100 varieties of begonias are among the exotic plantings in the conservatory.

A variety of programming and special events are held throughout the year. **Time:** Allow 30 minutes minimum. **Hours:** Grounds daily 6 a.m.-11 p.m. Water features daily 10-8, in summer. Conservatory Mon.-Sat. 9-5, Sun. 11-5. **Cost:** Grounds free. Conservatory $8; $7 (ages 62+, active military with ID and students ages 13+ with ID); $5 (ages 4-12). **Phone:** (405) 445-7080. 🍴 🛍

NATIONAL COWBOY & WESTERN HERITAGE MUSEUM is .5 mi. w. of I-35 via I-44 at 1700 N.E. 63rd St. This 32-acre memorial to our Western pioneers has an extensive collection of art, historic artifacts and exhibits about Native American and pioneer life in realistic settings. James Earle

Fraser's 18-foot statue "The End of the Trail" and a 33-foot statue of Buffalo Bill are featured.

The Rodeo Hall of Fame has legendary performers' portraits, trophies, saddles and memorabilia. A Western art collection features works by Albert Bierstadt, Frederic Remington and Charles M. Russell as well as contemporary pieces depicting both the historical and the new West.

The Western Performers Gallery shows the idealized West portrayed in motion pictures. Prosperity Junction replicates a circa 1900 western cattle town at dusk with full-size structures, including a saloon, school and church. **Time:** Allow 2 hours minimum. **Hours:** Mon.-Sat. 10-5, Sun. noon-5. **Cost:** $12.50; $9.75 (students with ID); $5.75 (ages 6-12). **Phone:** (405) 478-2250.

NINETY-NINES MUSEUM OF WOMEN PILOTS is at 4300 Amelia Earhart Dr. at the entrance to Will Rogers World Airport. The Ninety-Nines were founded in 1929 by a group of female pilots that included Amelia Earhart. The museum chronicles the history of women in aviation with displays that cover more than 5,000 square feet of the spacious facility. Featured highlights include exhibits about Earhart, the 1929 Women's Air Derby, World War II, air racing, the first female commercial and military pilots and the Women of Mercury 13. The group is named for the number of women who formed the original membership.

Time: Allow 1 hour minimum. **Hours:** Mon.-Fri. 10-4, Sat. by appointment. Guided tours are available by appointment. Closed major holidays. Phone ahead to confirm schedule. **Cost:** $5; $4 (ages 60+

Oklahoma City Zoo & Botanical Garden

and military with ID); $3 (grades K-12). **Phone:** (405) 685-9990. GT

OKLAHOMA CITY MUSEUM OF ART is at 415 Couch Dr. The three-level structure offers visitors a collection that covers a period of five centuries, with highlights including American and European art, contemporary art and a comprehensive group of glass sculptures by Dale Chihuly. The museum also hosts special exhibitions drawn from throughout the world.

Galleries feature portraits, landscapes, modern art, photography, sculpture, abstract art and decorative and fine arts. A repertory cinema presents international, independent and classic films.

Educational programs and art camps are offered. **Time:** Allow 1 hour, 30 minutes minimum. **Hours:** Museum Tues.-Sat. 10-5 (also Thurs. 5-9), Sun. noon-5. Films are shown Thurs.-Sun.; phone ahead for schedule. **Cost:** Museum $12; $10 (ages 6-18, 62+ and college students with ID); $5 (military with ID). Films $9; $7 (ages 13-18, ages 62+ and college students with ID); $5 (ages 0-12). **Phone:** (405) 236-3100 or (800) 579-9278. TI

OKLAHOMA CITY NATIONAL MEMORIAL & MUSEUM, is at 620 Harvey Ave. The site includes a museum and an outdoor symbolic memorial built in remembrance of the victims, survivors and rescuers of the Alfred P. Murrah Federal Building bombing on Apr. 19, 1995.

Twin gates, marking the east and west entrances to the memorial, represent 9:01 and 9:03, the minutes before and after the tragedy. Each of the 168 lives lost is represented by a chair made of bronze, stone and glass. The plot used for the field of chairs is the same size and configuration as the blueprint of the destroyed building. The memorial also has a reflecting pool; a special area for children; and the Survivor Tree, an American elm dating back to 1927 that miraculously withstood the blast.

The memorial museum is housed in the former Journal Record Building that also withstood the bombing. Interactive galleries serve as a timeline of the event, from the first exhibit depicting everyday morning activities in Oklahoma City through the last exhibit about hope for the future. Audio from a hearing being conducted across the street provides the sounds of the explosion and the resulting panic and confusion. Media coverage of the event is shown, as the story moves from rescue and recovery to investigation and capture. The Gallery of Honor is a tribute to the 168 lives lost. A glass overlook provides a view of the downtown skyline and the outdoor memorial.

Time: Allow 1 hour, 30 minutes minimum. **Hours:** Outdoor memorial open daily 24 hours. Rangers are on-site 9-5. Museum open Mon.-Sat. 9-6, Sun. noon-6; last admission 1 hour before closing. Museum closed Jan. 1, Easter, Thanksgiving, Christmas Eve and Christmas. **Cost:** Outdoor memorial free. Museum $15; $12 (ages 6-17, ages

62+, college students and military with ID). **Phone:** (405) 235-3313 or (888) 542-4673.

OKLAHOMA CITY ZOO & BOTANICAL GARDEN,

at 2000 Remington Pl., is home to nearly 1,600 animals, including several endangered or threatened species and acres of lush gardens. Great EscApe features gorillas, orangutans and chimpanzees in a rain forest environment. Cat Forest and Lion Overlook are naturalistic habitats for large and small wild cats. The Oklahoma Trails exhibit is home to more than 800 animals native to Oklahoma, including grizzly and black bears, mountain lions, bobcats, alligators and bison. The Elephant Habitat is home to a herd of Asian elephants.

The Children's Zoo is a 2.5-acre exhibit featuring flamingos, goats, monkeys and lorikeets. The sea lion show at the Noble Aquatic Center Performance Arena features sea lions performing in 15- to 20-minute shows. Wild Encounters behind-the-scenes programs take place daily; schedule and fees are posted near the main entrance. Rides are available on the Endangered Species Carousel, Centennial Choo Choo and Elephant Express tram for additional fees.

Time: Allow 2 hours minimum. **Hours:** Daily 9-5. Exhibit buildings close 15 minutes before park closing. **Cost:** $11; $8 (ages 3-11 and 65+); $5.50 (military with ID). **Phone:** (405) 424-3344.

OKLAHOMA HALL OF FAME AT THE GAYLORD-PICKENS MUSEUM

is at jct. N.W. 13th St. and Shartel Ave. at 1400 Classen Dr. The museum's Chickasaw Nation Oklahoma Through Its People gallery includes five interactive exhibits focusing on the state's heritage and its effect on the achievements and contributions of revered Oklahomans. The Tulsa World-Lorton Family Gallery features the works of Oklahoma artists in temporary exhibits. Built in 1927, the building was formerly home to the Mid-Continent Life Insurance Co.; a tour of the president's office as furnished in the 1920s is offered.

The museum site houses the Oklahoma Hall of Fame, which honors the accomplishments of nearly 700 individuals inducted since 1928, including Gene Autry, Reba McEntire, Mickey Mantle, Will Rogers and Jim Thorpe. **Time:** Allow 1 hour minimum. **Hours:** Tues.-Fri. 9-5, Sat. 10-5. **Cost:** $7; $5 (ages 6-17 and 62+). **Phone:** (405) 235-4458 or (888) 501-2059.

OKLAHOMA HISTORY CENTER, 800

Nazih Zuhdi Dr., showcases the state's history with its thousands of artifacts and more than 200 interactive exhibits in five galleries. Topics include aviation, commerce, culture, geology, heritage, the oil and gas industry and transportation. Major exhibits depict the history of Native American tribes living in the state and settler life during the Oklahoma land runs. Items from the 1838 steamship *Heroine,* excavated from the Red River, also are on display.

Outdoor sculptures, oil derricks and the .25-mile Red River Journey walking tour, which replicates the river valley and its plant life, adorn the grounds. Extensive archives and research materials, including genealogy records and newspapers, are available.

Time: Allow 2 hours minimum: **Hours:** Mon.-Sat. 10-5. **Cost:** $7; $5 (ages 62+); $4 (students with ID); free (ages 0-5 and active military and veterans with ID); $18 (family, up to six people). **Phone:** (405) 522-0765.

SCIENCE MUSEUM OKLAHOMA

is at 2020 Remington Pl. This science museum, a Smithsonian affiliate, features more than 350,000 square feet of interactive exhibits; space, aviation and cultural artifacts; and the Kirkpatrick Planetarium.

Science Live is a daily, live entertainment performance that engages the audience in scientific fun. A Segway course lets visitors ride one of these self-balancing vehicles and navigate an obstacle course. GadgetTrees is a gigantic tree house with one of the longest spiral slides in the country. Destination Space looks at the challenges of manned space exploration, while the Tinkering Garage lets visitors be creative and build imaginative structures. In Big Game Theory play larger-than-life versions of your favorite board games.

The 20,000-square-foot CurioCity exhibit features eight neighborhoods and more than 85 custom activities, including a walk-in kaleidoscope, an oversized music box and a human-powered carousel. Rotating art gallery displays are located in smART Space. Traveling exhibits may also be offered.

Time: Allow 2 hours minimum. **Hours:** Mon.-Fri. 9-5, Sat. 9-6, Sun. 11-6. **Cost:** (includes all permanent exhibits, Science Live and Kirkpatrick Planetarium) $15.95; $12.95 (ages 3-12 and 65+). An additional fee may be charged for traveling exhibits. **Phone:** (405) 602-6664.

WHITE WATER BAY, off I-40 exit 145 (Meridian Ave.) at 3908 W. Reno Ave., is a 20-acre water park with more than 35 water rides, including a giant wave pool, waterslides, body flumes and activity pools as well as Barefootin' Bay, a children's pool. Enjoy Late Night Wednesdays in June and July, plus Dive-In Movies on Fridays in July.

Time: Allow 1 hour minimum. **Hours:** Daily 10:30-7, (also Wed. 7 p.m.-9 p.m.), early June to mid-Aug; Sat.-Sun. 10:30-6, mid-May to early June and mid-Aug. to mid-Sept. Phone ahead to confirm schedule. **Cost:** $41.99; $31.99 (under 48 inches tall and ages 62+); free (ages 0-2). **Parking:** $20. **Phone:** (405) 943-9687.

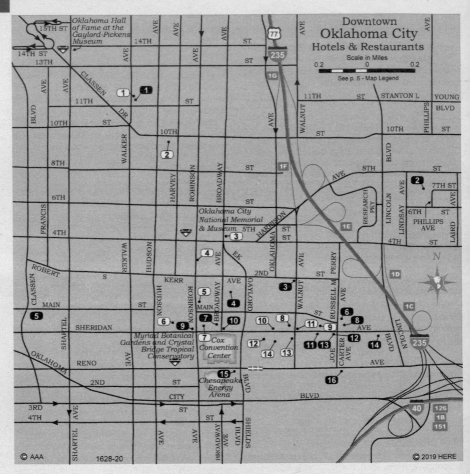

Downtown Oklahoma City

This index helps you "spot" where hotels and restaurants are located on the corresponding detailed maps. Restaurant price range is a combination of lunch and/or dinner. Turn to the listing page for more information and consult display ads for special promotions.

For more details, rates and reservations: **AAA.com/travelguides/hotels**

DOWNTOWN OKLAHOMA CITY

Map Page	Hotels	Designation	Member Savings	Page
1 this page	**Ambassador Oklahoma City, Autograph Collection**	FOUR DIAMOND	✔	361
2 this page	Embassy Suites by Hilton Oklahoma City Downtown/Medical Center	THREE DIAMOND	✔	361
3 this page	Aloft Oklahoma City Downtown-Bricktown	THREE DIAMOND	✔	361
4 this page	**Skirvin Hilton**	FOUR DIAMOND	✔	362
5 this page	21c Museum Hotel Oklahoma City	FOUR DIAMOND	✔	361
6 this page	**Hyatt Place Oklahoma City Bricktown**	THREE DIAMOND	✔	362
7 this page	**Sheraton Oklahoma City Downtown Hotel**	THREE DIAMOND	✔	362
8 this page	**AC Hotel by Marriott Oklahoma City Bricktown**	THREE DIAMOND	✔	361
9 this page	**Colcord Hotel**	FOUR DIAMOND	✔	361
10 this page	**Renaissance Oklahoma City Convention Center, Hotel & Spa**	THREE DIAMOND	✔	362

DOWNTOWN OKLAHOMA CITY (cont'd)

Map Page	Hotels (cont'd)	Designation	Member Savings	Page
11 p. 354	Hampton Inn & Suites Oklahoma City-Bricktown	THREE DIAMOND	✔	361
12 p. 354	Homewood Suites by Hilton Oklahoma City-Bricktown	THREE DIAMOND	✔	362
13 p. 354	Hilton Garden Inn Oklahoma City-Bricktown	THREE DIAMOND	✔	361
14 p. 354	SpringHill Suites by Marriott Oklahoma City/Bricktown	THREE DIAMOND	✔	362
15 p. 354	Courtyard by Marriott Oklahoma City Downtown	THREE DIAMOND	✔	361
16 p. 354	Residence Inn by Marriott Bricktown	THREE DIAMOND	✔	362

Map Page	Restaurants	Designation	Cuisine	Price Range	Page
1 p. 354	Waffle Champion	APPROVED	Breakfast	$6-$12	363
2 p. 354	Ludivine	THREE DIAMOND	New American	$22-$36	362
3 p. 354	Red PrimeSteak	THREE DIAMOND	Steak	$10-$38	362
4 p. 354	Kitchen No. 324	APPROVED	American	$8-$26	362
5 p. 354	The Urban Taco Shop	APPROVED	Mexican	$3-$8	363
6 p. 354	Vast	FOUR DIAMOND	American	$24-$85	363
7 p. 354	Mahogany Prime Steakhouse	THREE DIAMOND	Steak	$15-$70	362
8 p. 354	Tapwerks	APPROVED	American	$9-$12	363
9 p. 354	Pearl's Crabtown	APPROVED	Cajun Seafood	$10-$46	362
10 p. 354	Bricktown Brewery	APPROVED	American	$6-$16	362
11 p. 354	Mantel Wine Bar & Bistro	APPROVED	American	$10-$40	362
12 p. 354	Chelino's Mexican Restaurant	APPROVED	Mexican	$6-$13	362
13 p. 354	Mickey Mantle's Steakhouse	THREE DIAMOND	Steak	$20-$57	362
14 p. 354	Jazmo'z Bourbon Street Cafe	APPROVED	Cajun	$10-$49	362

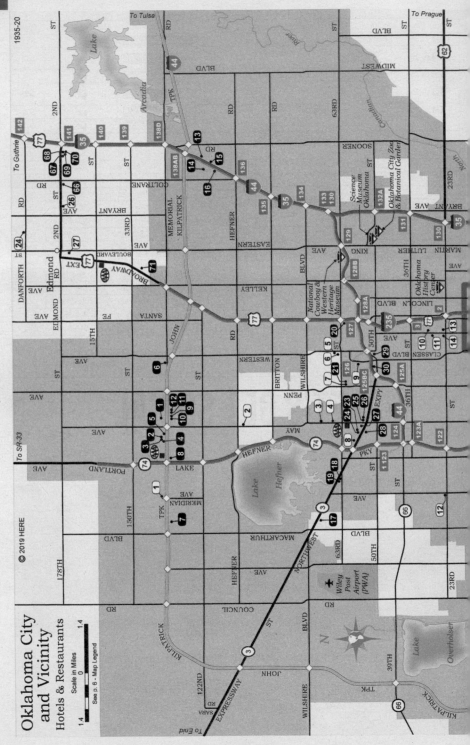

Oklahoma City and Vicinity
Hotels & Restaurants

See p. 6 - Map Legend

Scale in Miles

© 2019 HERE

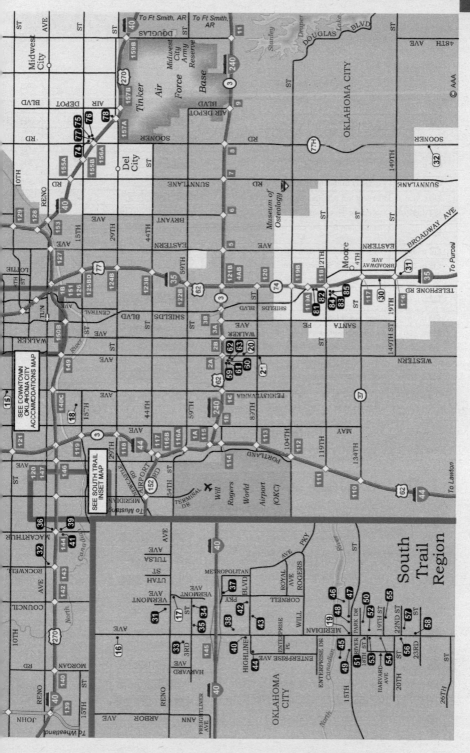

✈ Airport Hotels

Map Page	WILL ROGERS WORLD (Maximum driving distance from airport: 4.8 mi)	Designation	Member Savings	Page
53 p. 356	AmericInn Hotel & Suites Oklahoma City Airport, 3.8 mi	◈ THREE DIAMOND		363
50 p. 356	Candlewood Suites Hotel, 3.8 mi	◈ APPROVED		363
43 p. 356	Clarion Inn & Suites, 4.5 mi	◈ THREE DIAMOND		363
42 p. 356	**Courtyard by Marriott Oklahoma City Airport, 4.8 mi**	◈ THREE DIAMOND	✔	364
55 p. 356	DoubleTree by Hilton Oklahoma City Airport, 3.7 mi	◈ THREE DIAMOND	✔	364
51 p. 356	**Embassy Suites by Hilton, 3.7 mi**	◈ THREE DIAMOND	✔	364
49 p. 356	**Fairfield Inn & Suites by Marriott, 3.8 mi**	◈ THREE DIAMOND	✔	365
58 p. 356	Governors Suites Hotel, 3.4 mi	◈ THREE DIAMOND		365
46 p. 356	Hampton Inn & Suites Oklahoma City Airport, 4.1 mi	◈ THREE DIAMOND	✔	365
40 p. 356	Hilton Garden Inn Oklahoma City Airport, 4.4 mi	◈ THREE DIAMOND	✔	365
47 p. 356	**Holiday Inn & Suites, 3.9 mi**	◈ THREE DIAMOND	✔	365
52 p. 356	**Hyatt Place Oklahoma City Airport, 3.7 mi**	◈ THREE DIAMOND	✔	366
57 p. 356	Ramada by Wyndham Oklahoma City Airport North, 3.5 mi	◈ APPROVED		366
44 p. 356	**Sleep Inn, 4.5 mi**	◈ APPROVED	✔	366
48 p. 356	**Staybridge Suites, 3.8 mi**	◈ THREE DIAMOND	✔	367
45 p. 356	TownePlace Suites by Marriott, 4.0 mi	◈ THREE DIAMOND	✔	367
38 p. 356	Tru by Hilton Oklahoma City Airport, 4.5 mi	◈ APPROVED	✔	367
54 p. 356	**Wingate by Wyndham, 3.6 mi**	◈ THREE DIAMOND		367
56 p. 356	Wyndham Garden Hotel Oklahoma City Airport, 3.4 mi	◈ THREE DIAMOND		368

Oklahoma City and Vicinity

This index helps you "spot" where hotels and restaurants are located on the corresponding detailed maps. Restaurant price range is a combination of lunch and/or dinner. Turn to the listing page for more information and consult display ads for special promotions.

 For more details, rates and reservations: AAA.com/travelguides/hotels

OKLAHOMA CITY

Map Page	Hotels	Designation	Member Savings	Page
1 p. 356	Avid Hotel Oklahoma City Quail Springs	◈ APPROVED		363
2 p. 356	Four Points by Sheraton Quail Springs Oklahoma City	◈ THREE DIAMOND	✔	365
3 p. 356	Hilton Garden Inn Oklahoma City North/Quail Springs	◈ THREE DIAMOND	✔	365
4 p. 356	SpringHill Suites by Marriott	◈ THREE DIAMOND	✔	367
5 p. 356	La Quinta Inn & Suites OKC North-Quail Springs	◈ THREE DIAMOND		366
6 p. 356	**Best Western Plus Memorial Inn & Suites**	◈ THREE DIAMOND	✔	363
7 p. 356	Home2 Suites by Hilton Oklahoma City Quail Springs	◈ THREE DIAMOND	✔	365
8 p. 356	Country Inn & Suites by Radisson	◈ THREE DIAMOND		363
9 p. 356	Fairfield Inn & Suites by Marriott Oklahoma City Quail Springs North	◈ APPROVED	✔	365
10 p. 356	Baymont Inn & Suites Oklahoma City	◈ APPROVED		363
11 p. 356	Comfort Inn & Suites Quail Springs	◈ THREE DIAMOND		363
12 p. 356	Courtyard by Marriott	◈ THREE DIAMOND	✔	364

OKLAHOMA CITY (cont'd)

Map Page	Hotels (cont'd)	Designation	Member Savings	Page
13 p. 356	Sleep Inn & Suites	◆◆ APPROVED		366
14 p. 356	Baymont Inn & Suites Oklahoma City Edmond	◆◆ APPROVED		363
15 p. 356	Hampton Inn Oklahoma City Northeast	◆◆ THREE DIAMOND	✔	365
16 p. 356	Americas Best Value Inn-Oklahoma City/I-35 North	◆◆ APPROVED		363
17 p. 356	Fairfield Inn & Suites by Marriott	◆◆ THREE DIAMOND	✔	365
18 p. 356	Tru by Hilton Oklahoma City NW Expressway	◆◆ APPROVED	✔	367
19 p. 356	Home2 Suites by Hilton Oklahoma City NW Expressway	◆◆ THREE DIAMOND	✔	365
20 p. 356	Holiday Inn Hotel & Suites Oklahoma City North	◆◆ THREE DIAMOND		365
21 p. 356	**Renaissance Waterford Oklahoma City Hotel**	◆◆ FOUR DIAMOND	✔	366
23 p. 356	Comfort Inn at Founders Tower	◆◆ APPROVED		363
24 p. 356	Country Inn & Suites by Radisson, Oklahoma City-NW Expressway	◆◆ THREE DIAMOND		364
25 p. 356	Holiday Inn Express Hotel & Suites Penn Square	◆◆ THREE DIAMOND		365
26 p. 356	Hilton Garden Inn Oklahoma City/Midtown	◆◆ THREE DIAMOND	✔	365
28 p. 356	Hampton Inn by Hilton NW	◆◆ THREE DIAMOND	✔	365
29 p. 356	Sleep Inn & Suites	◆◆ APPROVED		366
30 p. 356	Courtyard by Marriott Oklahoma City Northwest	◆◆ THREE DIAMOND	✔	364
31 p. 356	**Sonesta ES Suites Oklahoma City**	◆◆ THREE DIAMOND	✔	367
32 p. 356	Homewood Suites by Hilton Oklahoma City-West	◆◆ THREE DIAMOND	✔	365
33 p. 356	Super 8 by Wyndham Oklahoma Airport Fairgrounds West	◆◆ APPROVED		367
34 p. 356	**Best Western Plus Saddleback Inn & Conference Center**	◆◆ THREE DIAMOND	✔	363
35 p. 356	Howard Johnson by Wyndham Oklahoma City	◆◆ APPROVED		365
36 p. 356	SpringHill Suites by Marriott	◆◆ THREE DIAMOND	✔	367
37 p. 356	Baymont Inn & Suites	◆◆ APPROVED		363
38 p. 356	Tru by Hilton Oklahoma City Airport	◆◆ APPROVED	✔	367
39 p. 356	Microtel Inn & Suites by Wyndham Oklahoma City Airport	◆◆ APPROVED		366
40 p. 356	Hilton Garden Inn Oklahoma City Airport	◆◆ THREE DIAMOND	✔	365
41 p. 356	**Comfort Inn & Suites**	◆◆ THREE DIAMOND	✔	363
42 p. 356	**Courtyard by Marriott Oklahoma City Airport** *(See ad p. 364.)*	◆◆ THREE DIAMOND	✔	364
43 p. 356	Clarion Inn & Suites	◆◆ THREE DIAMOND		363
44 p. 356	**Sleep Inn**	◆◆ APPROVED	✔	366
45 p. 356	TownePlace Suites by Marriott	◆◆ THREE DIAMOND	✔	367
46 p. 356	Hampton Inn & Suites Oklahoma City Airport	◆◆ THREE DIAMOND	✔	365
47 p. 356	**Holiday Inn & Suites**	◆◆ THREE DIAMOND	✔	365
48 p. 356	**Staybridge Suites**	◆◆ THREE DIAMOND	✔	367
49 p. 356	**Fairfield Inn & Suites by Marriott**	◆◆ THREE DIAMOND	✔	365
50 p. 356	Candlewood Suites Hotel	◆◆ APPROVED		363
51 p. 356	**Embassy Suites by Hilton**	◆◆ THREE DIAMOND	✔	364
52 p. 356	**Hyatt Place Oklahoma City Airport** *(See ad p. 366.)*	◆◆ THREE DIAMOND	✔	366
53 p. 356	AmericInn Hotel & Suites Oklahoma City Airport	◆◆ THREE DIAMOND		363
54 p. 356	Wingate by Wyndham	◆◆ THREE DIAMOND		367
55 p. 356	DoubleTree by Hilton Oklahoma City Airport	◆◆ THREE DIAMOND	✔	364
56 p. 356	Wyndham Garden Hotel Oklahoma City Airport	◆◆ THREE DIAMOND		368

OKLAHOMA CITY (cont'd)

Map Page	Hotels (cont'd)	Designation	Member Savings	Page
57 p. 356	Ramada by Wyndham Oklahoma City Airport North	APPROVED		366
58 p. 356	Governors Suites Hotel	THREE DIAMOND		365
59 p. 356	Comfort Inn	THREE DIAMOND		363
60 p. 356	Red Roof Inn & Suites Oklahoma City	APPROVED		366
61 p. 356	**Best Western Plus Barsana Hotel & Suites**	THREE DIAMOND	✔	363
62 p. 356	Hampton Inn & Suites by Hilton-Oklahoma City South	THREE DIAMOND	✔	365
63 p. 356	Home2 Suites by Hilton Oklahoma City South	THREE DIAMOND	✔	365

Map Page	Restaurants	Designation	Cuisine	Price Range	Page
1 p. 356	Gopuram Taste Of India	APPROVED	Indian	$8-$15	368
2 p. 356	Papa Dio's Italian Restaurant & Wine Bar	APPROVED	Italian	$9-$28	368
3 p. 356	La Baguette Bistro Casual Restaurant & Bakery	APPROVED	French	$9-$45	368
4 p. 356	Ted's Cafe Escondido	APPROVED	Mexican	$8-$14	368
5 p. 356	Osteria	THREE DIAMOND	Italian	$16-$34	368
6 p. 356	The Hutch on Avondale	THREE DIAMOND	American	$16-$32	368
7 p. 356	Bellini's Ristorante & Grill	THREE DIAMOND	Italian	$9-$32	368
8 p. 356	Beverly's Pancake House	APPROVED	American	$5-$12	368
9 p. 356	Pearl's Oyster Bar	APPROVED	Seafood	$9-$27	368
10 p. 356	El Fogoncito	APPROVED	Mexican	$9-$17	368
11 p. 356	Paseo Grill	THREE DIAMOND	American	$8-$30	368
12 p. 356	Gopuram, Taste of India	APPROVED	Indian	$8-$15	368
13 p. 356	Cheever's Cafe	THREE DIAMOND	Regional Southwestern	$14-$36	368
14 p. 356	The Drake	THREE DIAMOND	Seafood	$14-$39	368
15 p. 356	Nic's Grill	APPROVED	Burgers	$6-$8	368
16 p. 356	Cimarron Steak House	APPROVED	Steak	$6-$22	368
17 p. 356	Trapper's Fishcamp & Grill	APPROVED	Seafood	$7-$23	368
18 p. 356	Cattlemen's Steakhouse	APPROVED	Steak	$8-$32	368
19 p. 356	Golden Palace	APPROVED	Chinese	$8-$12	368
20 p. 356	Ted's Cafe Escondido	APPROVED	Mexican	$8-$14	368
21 p. 356	Louie's Grill and Bar	APPROVED	American	$6-$10	368

EDMOND

Map Page	Hotels	Designation	Member Savings	Page
66 p. 356	**Best Western Edmond Inn & Suites**	APPROVED	✔	330
67 p. 356	Holiday Inn Express Hotel & Suites	THREE DIAMOND		330
68 p. 356	La Quinta Inn & Suites Edmond	THREE DIAMOND		330
69 p. 356	Fairfield Inn & Suites by Marriott	THREE DIAMOND	✔	330
70 p. 356	**Hampton Inn by Hilton**	THREE DIAMOND	✔	330
71 p. 356	Sleep Inn & Suites	APPROVED		330

Map Page	Restaurants	Designation	Cuisine	Price Range	Page
24 p. 356	Ted's Cafe Escondido	APPROVED	Mexican	$9-$16	331
26 p. 356	Wich Pho	APPROVED	Vietnamese	$5-$10	331
27 p. 356	Boulevard Steakhouse	THREE DIAMOND	Steak Seafood	$27-$52	331

MIDWEST CITY

Map Page	Hotels	Designation	Member Savings	Page
74 p. 356	Holiday Inn Express Hotel & Suites	THREE DIAMOND		338

MIDWEST CITY (cont'd)

Map Page	Hotels (cont'd)	Designation	Member Savings	Page
75 p. 356	**Sheraton Midwest City Hotel at the Reed Conference Center** *(See ad p. 367.)*	◈ THREE DIAMOND	✔	339
76 p. 356	Hampton Inn by Hilton	◈ THREE DIAMOND	✔	338
77 p. 356	**La Quinta Inn & Suites Oklahoma City-Midwest City**	◈ THREE DIAMOND	✔	338
78 p. 356	**Best Western Plus Midwest City Inn & Suites**	◈ THREE DIAMOND	✔	338

MOORE

Map Page	Hotels	Designation	Member Savings	Page
81 p. 356	**Best Western Greentree Inn & Suites**	◈ THREE DIAMOND	✔	339
82 p. 356	Quality Inn	◈ APPROVED		339
83 p. 356	SpringHill Suites by Marriott	◈ THREE DIAMOND		339
84 p. 356	Holiday Inn Express & Suites	◈ THREE DIAMOND		339
85 p. 356	Hampton Inn & Suites by Hilton Moore	◈ THREE DIAMOND	✔	339

Map Page	Restaurants	Designation	Cuisine	Price Range	Page
30 p. 356	The Catch	◈ APPROVED	Seafood	$4-$14	339
31 p. 356	Ricky's Cafe	◈ APPROVED	Mexican	$7-$12	339
32 p. 356	Royal Bavaria Restaurant & Brewery	◈ APPROVED	German	$12-$28	339

DOWNTOWN OKLAHOMA CITY

- Restaurants p. 362
- Hotels & Restaurants map & index p. 354

21C MUSEUM HOTEL OKLAHOMA CITY   405/982-6900 **5**
◈ **FOUR DIAMOND** Historic Boutique Hotel. **Address:** 900 W Main St 73106

AC HOTEL BY MARRIOTT OKLAHOMA CITY BRICKTOWN
405/605-1555 **8**

◈ THREE DIAMOND [SAVE] Hotel. **Address:** 411 E Sheridan Ave 73104

AAA Benefit:
Members save 5% or more!

ALOFT OKLAHOMA CITY DOWNTOWN-BRICKTOWN
405/605-2100 **3**

◈ THREE DIAMOND [SAVE]
Contemporary Hotel. **Address:** 209 N Walnut Ave 73104

AAA Benefit:
Members save 5% or more!

AMBASSADOR OKLAHOMA CITY, AUTOGRAPH COLLECTION   405/600-6200 **1**
◈ FOUR DIAMOND

Boutique Hotel

AUTOGRAPH COLLECTION® HOTELS

AAA Benefit:
Members save 5% or more!

Address: 1200 N Walker Ave 73103 **Location:** Jct 12th St. **Facility:** This beautifully restored 1929 hotel features luxuriously decorated rooms and modern, spa-like bathrooms with huge showers. An outdoor pool and lounging patio are very enticing on warm days. 54 units. 7 stories, interior corridors. **Parking:** on-site (fee) and valet. **Amenities:** safes. **Pool:** outdoor. **Activities:** exercise room. **Guest Services:** valet laundry, area transportation.

[SAVE] [icons] / SOME UNITS

COLCORD HOTEL   405/601-4300 **9**
◈ FOUR DIAMOND
Historic Boutique Hotel

Address: 15 N Robinson Ave 73102 **Location:** Jct Sheridan and Robinson aves. **Facility:** This property does a wonderful job of mixing historical architecture with the needs of the modern traveler. Guest rooms feature some luxury decor enhancements, varying styles and sizes. 108 units. 12 stories, interior corridors. **Parking:** valet only. **Amenities:** safes. **Activities:** exercise room. **Guest Services:** valet laundry, area transportation.

[SAVE] [ECO] [icons] CALL [icons]
[icons] [BIZ] [icons]

/ SOME UNITS

COURTYARD BY MARRIOTT OKLAHOMA CITY DOWNTOWN
405/232-2290 **15**

◈ THREE DIAMOND [SAVE] Hotel. **Address:** 2 W Reno Ave 73102

AAA Benefit:
Members save 5% or more!

EMBASSY SUITES BY HILTON OKLAHOMA CITY DOWNTOWN/MEDICAL CENTER   405/239-3900 **2**
◈ THREE DIAMOND [SAVE] Hotel. **Address:** 741 N Phillips Ave 73104

AAA Benefit:
Members save up to 15%!

HAMPTON INN & SUITES OKLAHOMA CITY-BRICKTOWN
405/232-3600 **11**

◈ THREE DIAMOND [SAVE] Hotel. **Address:** 300 E Sheridan Ave 73102

AAA Benefit:
Members save up to 15%!

HILTON GARDEN INN OKLAHOMA CITY-BRICKTOWN
405/270-0588 **13**

◈ THREE DIAMOND [SAVE] Hotel. **Address:** 328 E Sheridan Ave 73104

AAA Benefit:
Members save up to 15%!

(See map & index p. 354.)

HOMEWOOD SUITES BY HILTON OKLAHOMA CITY-BRICKTOWN
405/232-3200 **12**

THREE DIAMOND [SAVE] Extended Stay Hotel. **Address:** 328 E Sheridan Ave 73104

AAA Benefit: Members save up to 15%!

HYATT PLACE OKLAHOMA CITY BRICKTOWN
405/702-4028 **6**

THREE DIAMOND
Hotel

 HYATT PLACE

AAA Benefit: Members save up to 10%!

Address: 20 Russell M. Perry Ave 73104 **Location:** Just n of jct E Sheridan and Russell M Perry aves. **Facility:** 134 units. 5 stories, interior corridors. **Parking:** on-site (fee). **Pool:** heated indoor. **Activities:** exercise room. **Guest Services:** valet and coin laundry. **Featured Amenity:** breakfast buffet.

RENAISSANCE OKLAHOMA CITY CONVENTION CENTER, HOTEL & SPA
405/228-8000 **10**

THREE DIAMOND
Hotel

R RENAISSANCE HOTELS

AAA Benefit: Members save 5% or more!

Address: 10 N Broadway Ave 73102 **Location:** Jct Sheridan and Broadway aves. **Facility:** 311 units. 15 stories, interior corridors. **Parking:** valet only. **Terms:** check-in 4 pm. **Pool:** heated indoor. **Activities:** sauna, hot tub, exercise room, spa. **Guest Services:** valet and coin laundry.

RESIDENCE INN BY MARRIOTT BRICKTOWN
405/601-1700 **16**

THREE DIAMOND [SAVE] Extended Stay Hotel. **Address:** 400 E Reno Ave 73104

AAA Benefit: Members save 5% or more!

SHERATON OKLAHOMA CITY DOWNTOWN HOTEL
405/235-2780 **7**

THREE DIAMOND
Hotel

 SHERATON

AAA Benefit: Members save 5% or more!

Address: 1 N Broadway Ave 73102 **Location:** Jct Sheridan and Broadway aves. **Facility:** 396 units. 15 stories, interior corridors. **Parking:** on-site (fee) and valet. **Pool:** outdoor. **Activities:** exercise room. **Guest Services:** valet laundry.

SKIRVIN HILTON
405/272-3040 **4**

FOUR DIAMOND
Historic Hotel

 Hilton HOTELS & RESORTS

AAA Benefit: Members save up to 15%!

Address: 1 Park Ave 73102 **Location:** Corner of N Broadway and Park aves. **Facility:** Modern conveniences are plentiful throughout the three architecturally impressive towers built in 1911. Guest rooms feature upgraded bedding and upscale furnishings to maximize your comfort. 225 units. 14 stories, interior corridors. **Parking:** on-site (fee) and valet. **Amenities:** safes. **Dining:** 2 restaurants. **Pool:** heated indoor. **Activities:** hot tub, exercise room. **Guest Services:** valet laundry.

SPRINGHILL SUITES BY MARRIOTT OKLAHOMA CITY/BRICKTOWN
405/601-6206 **14**

THREE DIAMOND [SAVE] Hotel. **Address:** 600 E Sheridan Ave 73104

AAA Benefit: Members save 5% or more!

WHERE TO EAT

BRICKTOWN BREWERY   405/232-2739 **10**
APPROVED American. Casual Dining. **Address:** 1 N Oklahoma Ave 73104

CHELINO'S MEXICAN RESTAURANT   405/235-3533 **12**
APPROVED Mexican. Casual Dining. **Address:** 15 E California Ave 73104

JAZMO'Z BOURBON STREET CAFE   405/232-6666 **14**
APPROVED Cajun. Casual Dining. **Address:** 100 E California Ave 73104

KITCHEN NO. 324   405/763-5911 **4**
APPROVED American. Casual Dining. **Address:** 324 N Robinson Ave 73102

LUDIVINE   405/778-6800 **2**
THREE DIAMOND New American. Fine Dining. **Address:** 805 N Hudson Ave 73102

MAHOGANY PRIME STEAKHOUSE   405/208-8800 **7**
THREE DIAMOND Steak. Fine Dining. **Address:** 145 W Sheridan Ave 73102

MANTEL WINE BAR & BISTRO   405/236-8040 **11**
APPROVED American. Casual Dining. **Address:** 201 E Sheridan Ave 73104

MICKEY MANTLE'S STEAKHOUSE   405/272-0777 **13**
THREE DIAMOND Steak. Fine Dining. **Address:** 7 S Mickey Mantle Dr 73104

PEARL'S CRABTOWN   405/232-7227 **9**
APPROVED Cajun Seafood. Casual Dining. **Address:** 303 E Sheridan Ave 73104

RED PRIMESTEAK   405/232-2626 **3**
THREE DIAMOND Steak. Fine Dining. **Address:** 504 N Broadway Ave 73102

(See map & index p. 354.)

TAPWERKS   405/319-9599   (8)
▼ APPROVED   American. Brewpub. **Address:** 121 E Sheridan Ave 73104

THE URBAN TACO SHOP   405/270-7825   (5)
▼ APPROVED   Mexican. Quick Serve. **Address:** 110 N Robinson Ave 73102

VAST   405/702-7262   (6)
▼ FOUR DIAMOND   **American Fine Dining** **$24-$85**   **AAA Inspector Notes:** You'll find yourself surrounded by a remarkable view of the city from this 49th-floor location in the Devon tower. Dishes like crispy-skinned duck breast and seared rack of lamb burst with flavor. Come early for a craft cocktail in the stylish airy lounge. **Features:** full bar. **Reservations:** suggested. **Address:** 333 W Sheridan Ave 73102 **Location:** Jct Sheridan and Hudson aves. **Parking:** valet and street only. [L] [D] CALL [&]

WAFFLE CHAMPION   405/525-9235   (1)
▼ APPROVED   Breakfast. Quick Serve. **Address:** 1212 N Walker Ave 73103

OKLAHOMA CITY elev. 1,201'
- Restaurants p. 368
- Hotels & Restaurants map & index p. 356

AMERICAS BEST VALUE INN-OKLAHOMA CITY/I-35 NORTH   405/478-0400   (16)
▼ APPROVED   Hotel. **Address:** 12001 N I-35 Service Rd 73131

AMERICINN HOTEL & SUITES OKLAHOMA CITY AIRPORT   405/682-2080   (53)
▼ THREE DIAMOND   Hotel. **Address:** 1905 S Meridian Ave 73108

AVID HOTEL OKLAHOMA CITY QUAIL SPRINGS   405/608-0900   (1)
▼ APPROVED   Hotel. **Address:** 2700 NW 138th St 73134

BAYMONT INN & SUITES   405/943-4400   (37)
▼ APPROVED   Hotel. **Address:** 4240 W I-40 Service Rd 73108

BAYMONT INN & SUITES OKLAHOMA CITY   405/752-7070   (10)
▼ APPROVED   Hotel. **Address:** 13500 Plaza Terr 73120

BAYMONT INN & SUITES OKLAHOMA CITY EDMOND   405/478-7282   (14)
▼ APPROVED   Hotel. **Address:** 4625 NE 120th St 73131

BEST WESTERN PLUS BARSANA HOTEL & SUITES   405/601-1200   (61)
▼ THREE DIAMOND   **Hotel**

Best Western PLUS   **AAA Benefit:** Members save up to 15% and earn bonus points!

Address: 7701 CA Henderson Blvd 73139 **Location:** I-240 exit 2A, just sw. **Facility:** 64 units. 3 stories, interior/exterior corridors. **Pool:** heated indoor. **Activities:** exercise room. **Guest Services:** coin laundry.
SAVE [Y•] CALL [&] [⇌] [♿] [BIZ] [HS] [⌃] [✕] [☎] [🖶] [▭]

BEST WESTERN PLUS MEMORIAL INN & SUITES   405/286-5199   (6)
▼ THREE DIAMOND   **Hotel**   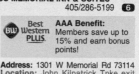 Best Western PLUS   **AAA Benefit:** Members save up to 15% and earn bonus points!

Address: 1301 W Memorial Rd 73114 **Location:** John Kilpatrick Tpke exit Western Ave, just nw. **Facility:** 60 units. 3 stories, interior corridors. **Pool:** heated indoor. **Activities:** exercise room. **Guest Services:** coin laundry.
SAVE [Y•] [⇌] [♿] [BIZ] [⌃] [✕] [☎] [🖶] [▭]

BEST WESTERN PLUS SADDLEBACK INN & CONFERENCE CENTER   405/947-7000   (34)
▼ THREE DIAMOND   **Hotel**    Best Western PLUS   **AAA Benefit:** Members save up to 15% and earn bonus points!

Address: 4300 SW 3rd St 73108 **Location:** I-40 exit 145 (Meridian Ave), just ne. **Facility:** 218 units. 3 stories, interior/exterior corridors. **Amenities:** safes. **Pool:** outdoor. **Activities:** sauna, hot tub, exercise room. **Guest Services:** valet and coin laundry, area transportation. **Featured Amenity:** full hot breakfast.
SAVE [⇥] [Y•] [↕] [Y] CALL [&]

[⇌] [♿] [BIZ] [⌃] [✕] [☎] [🖶] [▭] /SOME UNITS [🐾]

CANDLEWOOD SUITES HOTEL   405/680-8770   (50)
▼ APPROVED   Extended Stay Hotel. **Address:** 4400 W River Park Dr 73108

CLARION INN & SUITES   405/948-3366   (13)
▼ THREE DIAMOND   Hotel. **Address:** 4400 Highline Blvd 73108

COMFORT INN   405/631-3111   (59)
▼ THREE DIAMOND   Hotel. **Address:** 7601 CA Henderson Blvd 73139

COMFORT INN & SUITES   405/470-7676   (41)
▼ THREE DIAMOND   **Hotel**   **Address:** 5921 SW 8th St 73128 **Location:** I-40 exit 144, just sw. **Facility:** 89 units. 4 stories, interior corridors. **Pool:** heated indoor. **Activities:** exercise room. **Guest Services:** coin laundry. **Featured Amenity:** full hot breakfast.
SAVE [Y•] [⇌] [♿] [BIZ] [HS] [⌃]

[✕] [☎] [🖶] [▭]

COMFORT INN & SUITES QUAIL SPRINGS   405/286-2700   (11)
▼ THREE DIAMOND   Hotel. **Address:** 13501 N Highland Park Blvd 73120

COMFORT INN AT FOUNDERS TOWER   405/810-1100   (23)
▼ APPROVED   Hotel. **Address:** 5704 Mosteller Dr 73112

COUNTRY INN & SUITES BY RADISSON   405/286-3555   (8)
▼ THREE DIAMOND   Hotel. **Address:** 13501 Memorial Park Dr 73120

(See map & index p. 356.)

COUNTRY INN & SUITES BY RADISSON, OKLAHOMA CITY-NW EXPRESSWAY   405/843-2002   24
THREE DIAMOND Hotel. **Address:** 3141 Northwest Expwy 73112

COURTYARD BY MARRIOTT   405/418-4000   12
THREE DIAMOND SAVE Hotel. **Address:** 13511 Highland Park Blvd 73120

AAA Benefit:
Members save 5% or more!

COURTYARD BY MARRIOTT OKLAHOMA CITY AIRPORT   405/946-6500   42
THREE DIAMOND
Hotel

 COURTYARD

AAA Benefit:
Members save 5% or more!

Address: 4301 Highline Blvd 73108 **Location:** I-40 exit 145 (Meridian Ave), just e on south frontage road. **Facility:** 149 units. 3 stories, interior corridors. **Pool:** heated outdoor. **Activities:** exercise room. **Guest Services:** valet and coin laundry, boarding pass kiosk. *(See ad this page.)*

SAVE ECO 🛏 🍴 🏊 ⚕ BIZ
📶 ✕ 🔌 ☕ / SOME UNITS 📷

COURTYARD BY MARRIOTT OKLAHOMA CITY NORTHWEST   405/848-0808   30
THREE DIAMOND SAVE Hotel. **Address:** 1515 Northwest Expwy 73118

AAA Benefit:
Members save 5% or more!

DOUBLETREE BY HILTON OKLAHOMA CITY AIRPORT   405/688-3300   55
THREE DIAMOND SAVE Hotel. **Address:** 4410 SW 19th St 73108

AAA Benefit:
Members save up to 15%!

EMBASSY SUITES BY HILTON   405/682-6000   51
THREE DIAMOND
Hotel

EMBASSY SUITES
AAA Benefit:
Members save up to 15%!

Address: 1815 S Meridian Ave 73108 **Location:** I-40 exit 145 (Meridian Ave), 1 mi s. **Facility:** 236 units. 6 stories, interior corridors. **Amenities:** safes. **Pool:** heated indoor. **Activities:** exercise room. **Guest Services:** valet and coin laundry. **Featured Amenity:** breakfast buffet.

SAVE 🛏 🍴 🏃 🍽 🏊 ⚕
BIZ 📶 ✕ 🔌 📷 💻

/ SOME UNITS 🐾

🔗 **Discover member savings around the world: AAA.com/discounts**

(See map & index p. 356.)

FAIRFIELD INN & SUITES BY MARRIOTT
405/604-3223 **49**

THREE DIAMOND
Hotel

Fairfield

AAA Benefit: Members save 5% or more!

Address: 4521 SW 15th St 73128 **Location:** I-40 exit 145 (Meridian Ave), 1 mi sw. **Facility:** 110 units. 5 stories, interior corridors. **Pool:** heated indoor. **Activities:** exercise room. **Guest Services:** valet and coin laundry, area transportation. **Featured Amenity:** continental breakfast.

SAVE ✈ ❤ CALL ♿ ✈ 🛄
BIZ HS 🛜 ✕ 🔌 🛏 💻

FAIRFIELD INN & SUITES BY MARRIOTT
405/470-8484 **17**

THREE DIAMOND SAVE Hotel. **Address:** 5700 Northwest Expwy 73132

AAA Benefit: Members save 5% or more!

FAIRFIELD INN & SUITES BY MARRIOTT OKLAHOMA CITY QUAIL SPRINGS NORTH
405/755-8686 **9**

APPROVED SAVE Hotel. **Address:** 13520 Plaza Terr 73120

AAA Benefit: Members save 5% or more!

FOUR POINTS BY SHERATON QUAIL SPRINGS OKLAHOMA CITY
405/418-8448 **2**

THREE DIAMOND SAVE Hotel. **Address:** 3117 NW 137th St 73134

AAA Benefit: Members save 5% or more!

GOVERNORS SUITES HOTEL
405/682-5299 **58**

THREE DIAMOND Hotel. **Address:** 2308 S Meridian Ave 73108

HAMPTON INN & SUITES BY HILTON-OKLAHOMA CITY SOUTH
405/602-3400 **62**

THREE DIAMOND SAVE Hotel. **Address:** 920 SW 77th St 73139

AAA Benefit: Members save up to 15%!

HAMPTON INN & SUITES OKLAHOMA CITY AIRPORT
405/604-8000 **46**

THREE DIAMOND SAVE Hotel. **Address:** 4333 SW 15th St 73108

AAA Benefit: Members save up to 15%!

HAMPTON INN BY HILTON NW
405/947-0953 **28**

THREE DIAMOND SAVE Hotel. **Address:** 3022 Northwest Expwy 73112

AAA Benefit: Members save up to 15%!

HAMPTON INN OKLAHOMA CITY NORTHEAST
405/608-2744 **15**

THREE DIAMOND SAVE Hotel. **Address:** 11820 N I-35 Service Rd 73131

AAA Benefit: Members save up to 15%!

🌀 **Save on travel, shopping and more:**
AAA.com/discounts

HILTON GARDEN INN OKLAHOMA CITY AIRPORT
405/942-1400 **40**

THREE DIAMOND SAVE Hotel. **Address:** 801 S Meridian Ave 73108

AAA Benefit: Members save up to 15%!

HILTON GARDEN INN OKLAHOMA CITY/MIDTOWN
405/607-4000 **26**

THREE DIAMOND SAVE Hotel. **Address:** 2809 Northwest Expwy 73112

AAA Benefit: Members save up to 15%!

HILTON GARDEN INN OKLAHOMA CITY NORTH/QUAIL SPRINGS
405/752-5200 **3**

THREE DIAMOND SAVE Hotel. **Address:** 3201 NW 137th St 73134

AAA Benefit: Members save up to 15%!

HOLIDAY INN & SUITES
405/601-7272 **47**

THREE DIAMOND
Hotel

Address: 4401 SW 15th St 73108 **Location:** I-40 exit 145 (Meridian Ave), 1 mi se. **Facility:** 147 units. 6 stories, interior corridors. **Amenities:** safes. **Pool:** heated indoor. **Activities:** hot tub, exercise room. **Guest Services:** valet and coin laundry.

SAVE ✈ ❤ ♿ 🍴 CALL ♿
✈ 🛄 BIZ HS 🛜 ✕ 🔌
🛏 💻

HOLIDAY INN EXPRESS HOTEL & SUITES PENN SQUARE
405/848-1500 **25**

THREE DIAMOND Hotel. **Address:** 2811 Northwest Expwy 73112

HOLIDAY INN HOTEL & SUITES OKLAHOMA CITY NORTH
405/286-4777 **20**

THREE DIAMOND Hotel. **Address:** 6200 N Robinson Ave 73118

HOME2 SUITES BY HILTON OKLAHOMA CITY NW EXPRESSWAY
405/608-6094 **19**

THREE DIAMOND SAVE Extended Stay Hotel. **Address:** 4110 NW Expwy 73116

AAA Benefit: Members save up to 15%!

HOME2 SUITES BY HILTON OKLAHOMA CITY QUAIL SPRINGS
405/792-2420 **7**

THREE DIAMOND SAVE Extended Stay Contemporary Hotel. **Address:** 5500 NW 135th St 73142

AAA Benefit: Members save up to 15%!

HOME2 SUITES BY HILTON OKLAHOMA CITY SOUTH
405/536-4663 **63**

THREE DIAMOND SAVE Extended Stay Hotel. **Address:** 1001 Straka Terrace 73139

AAA Benefit: Members save up to 15%!

HOMEWOOD SUITES BY HILTON OKLAHOMA CITY-WEST
405/789-3600 **32**

THREE DIAMOND SAVE Extended Stay Hotel. **Address:** 6920 W Reno Ave 73127

AAA Benefit: Members save up to 15%!

HOWARD JOHNSON BY WYNDHAM OKLAHOMA CITY
405/896-8493 **35**

APPROVED Motel. **Address:** 400 S Meridian Ave 73108

(See map & index p. 356.)

HYATT PLACE OKLAHOMA CITY AIRPORT
405/682-3900 **52**

THREE DIAMOND HYATT PLACE'
Hotel

AAA Benefit: Members save up to 10%!

Address: 1818 S Meridian Ave 73108 **Location:** I-40 exit 145 (Meridian Ave), 1 mi s. **Facility:** 126 units. 6 stories, interior corridors. **Amenities:** *Some:* safes. **Pool:** heated outdoor. **Activities:** exercise room. **Guest Services:** valet laundry, area transportation. **Featured Amenity:** breakfast buffet. *(See ad this page.)*

LA QUINTA INN & SUITES OKC NORTH-QUAIL SPRINGS
405/755-7000 **5**

THREE DIAMOND Hotel. **Address:** 3003 W Memorial Rd 73134

MICROTEL INN & SUITES BY WYNDHAM OKLAHOMA CITY AIRPORT
405/942-0011 **39**

APPROVED Hotel. **Address:** 624 S MacArthur Blvd 73128

RAMADA BY WYNDHAM OKLAHOMA CITY AIRPORT NORTH
405/681-9000 **57**

APPROVED Hotel. **Address:** 2200 S Meridian Ave 73108

🔗 **Get an expert view from**

AAA inspectors:

AAA.com/travelguides/hotels

RED ROOF INN & SUITES OKLAHOMA CITY
405/632-6666 **60**

APPROVED Hotel. **Address:** 7800 CA Henderson Blvd 73139

RENAISSANCE WATERFORD OKLAHOMA CITY HOTEL
405/848-4782 **21**

FOUR DIAMOND
Hotel

R
RENAISSANCE'
HOTELS

AAA Benefit: Members save 5% or more!

Address: 6300 Waterford Blvd 73118 **Location:** I-44 exit 125A, 1.4 mi n. Located in a corporate/residential area. **Facility:** The beautifully landscaped grounds, courtyard and pool area offer carefree spaces in which to relax. Guest rooms feature sophisticated comfort and décor. 196 units. 9 stories, interior corridors. **Parking:** on-site and valet. **Amenities:** safes. **Pool:** outdoor. **Activities:** sauna, hot tub, health club. **Guest Services:** valet and coin laundry, boarding pass kiosk.

SLEEP INN
405/946-1600 **44**

APPROVED
Hotel

Address: 4620 Enterprise Way 73128 **Location:** I-40 exit 145 (Meridian Ave), just sw. **Facility:** 56 units. 3 stories, interior corridors. **Pool:** heated indoor. **Activities:** exercise room. **Guest Services:** valet and coin laundry. **Featured Amenity:** continental breakfast.

SLEEP INN & SUITES
405/478-9898 **13**

APPROVED Hotel. **Address:** 12024 N I-35 Service Rd 73131

SLEEP INN & SUITES
405/286-5400 **29**

APPROVED Hotel. **Address:** 5200 N Classen Cir 73118

(See map & index p. 356.)

SONESTA ES SUITES OKLAHOMA CITY
405/942-4500 **31**

THREE DIAMOND
Extended Stay Hotel

Address: 4361 W Reno Ave 73107 **Location:** I-40 exit 145 (Meridian Ave), 0.3 mi n, then just e. **Facility:** 136 kitchen units. 2 stories (no elevator), exterior corridors. **Pool:** outdoor. **Activities:** exercise room. **Guest Services:** valet and coin laundry. **Featured Amenity:** breakfast buffet.

[SAVE] [TI+] [icons] [BIZ] [icons] / SOME UNITS

SPRINGHILL SUITES BY MARRIOTT
405/749-1595 **4**

THREE DIAMOND [SAVE] Hotel. **Address:** 3201 W Memorial Rd 73134

AAA Benefit:
Members save 5% or more!

SPRINGHILL SUITES BY MARRIOTT
405/604-0200 **36**

THREE DIAMOND [SAVE] Hotel. **Address:** 510 S MacArthur Blvd 73128

AAA Benefit:
Members save 5% or more!

STAYBRIDGE SUITES
405/429-4400 **48**

THREE DIAMOND
Extended Stay Hotel

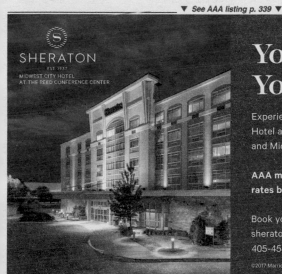

Address: 4411 SW 15th St 73108 **Location:** I-40 exit 145 (Meridian Ave), 1 mi se. **Facility:** 103 efficiencies. 4 stories, interior corridors. **Amenities:** safes. **Pool:** heated indoor. **Activities:** hot tub, exercise room. **Guest Services:** complimentary and valet laundry, area transportation. **Featured Amenity:** breakfast buffet.

[SAVE] [icons] [TI+] CALL [icons] / SOME UNITS

SUPER 8 BY WYNDHAM OKLAHOMA AIRPORT FAIRGROUNDS WEST
405/947-7801 **33**

APPROVED Hotel. **Address:** 311 S Meridian Ave 73108

TOWNEPLACE SUITES BY MARRIOTT
405/600-9988 **45**

THREE DIAMOND [SAVE] Extended Stay Contemporary Hotel. **Address:** 4601 SW 15th St 73128

AAA Benefit:
Members save 5% or more!

TRU BY HILTON OKLAHOMA CITY AIRPORT
405/609-3955 **38**

APPROVED [SAVE] Contemporary Hotel. **Address:** 802 S Meridian Ave 73108

Members save up to 15%!

TRU BY HILTON OKLAHOMA CITY NW EXPRESSWAY
405/286-0407 **18**

APPROVED [SAVE] Hotel. **Address:** 4100 NW Expwy 73116

Members save up to 15%!

WINGATE BY WYNDHAM
405/682-3600 **54**

THREE DIAMOND Hotel. **Address:** 2001 S Meridian Ave 73108

▼ See AAA listing p. 339 ▼

(See map & index p. 356.)

WYNDHAM GARDEN HOTEL OKLAHOMA CITY AIRPORT
405/685-4000 56
THREE DIAMOND Hotel. **Address:** 2101 S Meridian Ave
73108

WHERE TO EAT

BELLINI'S RISTORANTE & GRILL   405/848-1065 7
THREE DIAMOND Italian. Fine Dining. **Address:** 6305
Waterford Blvd 73118

BEVERLY'S PANCAKE HOUSE   405/848-5050 8
APPROVED American. Casual Dining. **Address:** 3315
Northwest Expwy 73112

CATTLEMEN'S STEAKHOUSE   405/236-0416 18
APPROVED Steak. Casual Dining. **Address:** 1309 S
Agnew Ave 73108

CHARLESTON'S RESTAURANT
APPROVED American. Casual Dining.
LOCATIONS:
Address: 2000 S Meridian Ave 73102 **Phone:** 405/681-6686
Address: 5907 Northwest Expwy 73132 **Phone:** 405/721-0060
Address: 1429 SW 74th St 73159 **Phone:** 405/681-0055
Address: 5608 W Memorial Rd 73142 **Phone:** 405/470-8169

CHEEVER'S CAFE   405/525-7007 13
THREE DIAMOND Regional Southwestern. Casual Dining.
Address: 2409 N Hudson Ave 73103

CIMARRON STEAK HOUSE   405/948-7778 16
APPROVED Steak. Casual Dining. **Address:** 201 N
Meridian Ave 73107

THE DRAKE   405/605-3399 14
THREE DIAMOND Seafood. Casual Dining. **Address:** 519
NW 23rd St 73103

EL CHICO   405/752-0677
APPROVED Tex-Mex. Casual Dining. **Address:** 2501
W Memorial Rd, Space 101 73134

EL FOGONCITO   405/225-1583 10
APPROVED Mexican. Casual Dining. **Address:** 3020
N. Walker Ave Suite A 73103

GOLDEN PALACE   405/686-1511 19
APPROVED Chinese. Casual Dining. **Address:** 1500
S Meridian Ave 73108

GOPURAM, TASTE OF INDIA   405/948-7373 12
APPROVED Indian. Casual Dining. **Address:** 4559
NW 23rd St 73127

GOPURAM TASTE OF INDIA   405/286-2865 1
APPROVED Indian. Casual Dining. **Address:** 4401 W
Memorial Rd 73134

HIDEAWAY PIZZA   405/796-7777
APPROVED Pizza. Casual Dining. **Address:** 901 N
Broadway Ave 73102

THE HUTCH ON AVONDALE   405/842-1000 6
THREE DIAMOND American. Fine Dining. **Address:** 6437
Avondale Dr 73116

LA BAGUETTE BISTRO CASUAL RESTAURANT & BAKERY
405/840-3047 3
APPROVED French. Casual Dining. **Address:** 7408 N
May Ave 73116

LOUIE'S GRILL AND BAR   405/691-4400 21
APPROVED American. Casual Dining. **Address:** 9101
S Western Ave 73139

NIC'S GRILL   405/524-0999 15
APPROVED Burgers. Quick Serve. **Address:** 1201 N
Pennsylvania Ave 73107

OSTERIA   405/254-5058 5
THREE DIAMOND Italian. Casual Dining. **Address:** 6430
Avondale Dr 73116

PAPA DIO'S ITALIAN RESTAURANT & WINE BAR
405/755-2255 2
APPROVED Italian. Casual Dining. **Address:** 10712 N
May Ave 73120

PASEO GRILL   405/601-1079 11
THREE DIAMOND American. Casual Dining. **Address:** 2909
Paseo Dr, Suite A 73103

PEARL'S OYSTER BAR   405/848-8008 9
APPROVED Seafood. Casual Dining. **Address:** 5641
N Classen Blvd 73118

RIB CRIB BBQ AND GRILL   405/616-7800
APPROVED Barbecue. Casual Dining. **Address:** 401
W Interstate 240 Service Rd 73139

RON'S HAMBURGERS & CHILI   405/943-7667
APPROVED American. Casual Dining. **Address:** 4723
N May Ave 73112

SHORTY SMALL'S   405/947-0779
APPROVED Barbecue. Casual Dining. **Address:** 2037
S Meridian Ave 73127

TED'S CAFE ESCONDIDO   405/848-8337 4
APPROVED Mexican. Casual Dining. **Address:** 2836
NW 68th St 73116

TED'S CAFE ESCONDIDO   405/635-8337 20
APPROVED Mexican. Casual Dining. **Address:** 8324
S Western Ave 73159

TRAPPER'S FISHCAMP & GRILL   405/943-9111 17
APPROVED Seafood. Casual Dining. **Address:** 4300
W Reno Ave 73107

ZIO'S ITALIAN KITCHEN   405/680-9999
APPROVED Italian. Casual Dining. **Address:** 2035 S
Meridian Ave 73108

OKMULGEE (D-10) pop. 12,321, elev. 678'

Okmulgee, a Creek word meaning "bubbling
water," was capital of the Muscogee Creek Nation a
half century before Oklahoma became a state, and
it remains the capital.

Dripping Springs Lake & Recreation Area, 6 miles
west of town on SR 56 to 16830 Dripping Springs
Rd., offers camping, swimming, fishing and boating;
phone (918) 756-5971. *See Recreation Areas Chart.*

Okmulgee Tourism: 112 N. Morton, Okmulgee, OK
74447. **Phone:** (918) 758-1015.

BEST WESTERN OKMULGEE   918/756-9200

Hotel

BW Best Western.

AAA Benefit: Members save up to 15% and earn bonus points!

Address: 3499 N Wood Dr 74447 **Location:** Just n of jct US 75 and SR 56. **Facility:** 50 units. 2 stories, interior corridors. **Parking:** winter plug-ins. **Pool:** outdoor. **Activities:** exercise room. **Guest Services:** coin laundry. **Featured Amenity:** full hot breakfast.

SAVE 🏊 🛁 BIZ HS 🛜 🖥
📷 🖨 / SOME UNITS 🐾

HOLIDAY INN EXPRESS   918/756-0100
◆ THREE DIAMOND Hotel. **Address:** 2780 N Wood Dr 74447

WHERE TO EAT

SIRLOIN STOCKADE   918/756-4440
◆ APPROVED Steak. Quick Serve. **Address:** 130 S Wood Dr 74447

OUACHITA NATIONAL FOREST—See Arkansas p. 60

OWASSO pop. 28,915
• Part of Tulsa area — see map p. 375

CANDLEWOOD SUITES   918/272-4334
◆ APPROVED Extended Stay Hotel. **Address:** 11699 E 96th St N 74055

HAMPTON INN & SUITES BY HILTON TULSA NORTH OWASSO   918/609-0700
◆ THREE DIAMOND SAVE Hotel. **Address:** 9009 N 121st E Ave 74055

AAA Benefit: Members save up to 15%!

LA QUINTA INN & SUITES OWASSO   918/376-4447
◆ THREE DIAMOND Hotel. **Address:** 8949 N Garnett 74055

QUALITY INN & SUITES   918/272-2000
◆ APPROVED Hotel. **Address:** 7653 N Owasso Expwy 74055

TOWNEPLACE SUITES BY MARRIOTT TULSA NORTH/OWASSO   918/376-4400
◆ THREE DIAMOND SAVE Extended Stay Hotel. **Address:** 9355 N Owasso Expwy 74055

AAA Benefit: Members save 5% or more!

WHERE TO EAT

ANDOLINI'S PIZZERIA   918/272-9328
◆ APPROVED Italian. Casual Dining. **Address:** 12140 E 96th St N 74055

HIDEAWAY PIZZA   918/928-4777
◆ APPROVED Pizza. Casual Dining. **Address:** 12903 96th St N 74055

LOS CABOS MEXICAN GRILL & CANTINA   918/609-8671
◆ APPROVED Mexican. Casual Dining. **Address:** 9455 N Owasso Expwy 74055

RIB CRIB BBQ AND GRILL   918/376-2600
◆ APPROVED Barbecue. Casual Dining. **Address:** 8551 N 129th E Ave 74055

RON'S HAMBURGERS & CHILI   918/272-6996
◆ APPROVED American. Casual Dining. **Address:** 9100 N Garnett Rd 74055

PAULS VALLEY pop. 6,187, elev. 873'

BEST WESTERN PLUS PAULS VALLEY   405/444-6035

Hotel

BW Best Western PLUS.

AAA Benefit: Members save up to 15% and earn bonus points!

Address: 2509 W Grant Ave 73075 **Location:** I-35 exit 72, just e. **Facility:** 63 units. 3 stories, interior corridors. **Pool:** outdoor. **Activities:** exercise room. **Guest Services:** coin laundry.

SAVE 🍴 CALL ♿ 🛁 🛜 BIZ
🛜 ✕ 🖥 📷 🖨

COMFORT INN & SUITES   405/207-9730
◆ THREE DIAMOND Hotel. **Address:** 103 S Humphrey Blvd 73075

HAMPTON INN & SUITES PAULS VALLEY   405/238-7700
◆ THREE DIAMOND SAVE Contemporary Hotel. **Address:** 105 S Humphrey Blvd 73075

AAA Benefit: Members save up to 15%!

HOLIDAY INN EXPRESS & SUITES   405/207-9434
◆ THREE DIAMOND Hotel. **Address:** 2412 W Grant Ave 73075

PAWHUSKA (C-1) pop. 3,584, elev. 847'
• Part of Tulsa area — see map p. 375

Pawhuska is capital of the Osage Nation, the wealthiest Native American tribe in America. The town was named after Pahuiska, chief of the Osage Tribe at the beginning of the 19th century. Pawhuska was later the home of the first Boy Scout troop in America, organized by Rev. John Mitchell in May 1909.

The architectural diversity of Pawhuska's downtown historic district stems from the prosperity that came with the oil strike on Osage land in 1921. Buildings of note include the 1887 Gothic-style Immaculate Conception Catholic Church; the Constantine Theatre and the 1894 City Hall, originally the Osage Agency house.

Pawhuska Chamber of Commerce: 210 W. Main St., Pawhuska, OK 74056. **Phone:** (918) 287-1208.

PERRY pop. 5,126, elev. 989'

HOLIDAY INN EXPRESS   580/336-5050
◆ THREE DIAMOND Hotel. **Address:** 3002 W Fir St 73077

MICROTEL INN & SUITES BY WYNDHAM PERRY
580/336-2666

APPROVED
Hotel

Address: 410 32nd St 73077 **Location:** I-35 exit 186, just w. **Facility:** 63 units. 4 stories, interior corridors. **Pool:** heated indoor. **Activities:** hot tub, exercise room. **Guest Services:** coin laundry. **Featured Amenity:** full hot breakfast.

SAVE CALL 🚹 🛼 🛏 BIZ 🛜
✕ 🖥 📷 💻 / SOME UNITS 🐾

POCOLA

CHOCTAW CASINO HOTEL   918/436-7761
THREE DIAMOND Hotel. **Address:** 3400 Choctaw Rd 74902
(See ad starting on p. 38.)

PONCA CITY (B-9) pop. 25,387, elev. 1,003'

Ponca City was created in true Oklahoma fashion during the land runs of the late 1800s. On Sept. 16, 1893, homesteaders lined up for a race to claim one of the 160-acre lots in the area surrounding what would soon be Ponca City. Certificates for lots in the business section were sold for $2 each.

Ponca City was built in the midst of the Cherokee Strip, a narrow section of land 58 miles wide that had been reserved for the Native Americans as bison hunting grounds. President Grover Cleveland instead opened the land to settlement. When oil was discovered in 1910, E.W. Marland, who later became governor of Oklahoma, established Marland Oil, thereby propelling Ponca City into the age of industrialization.

Ponca City Tourism: 420 E. Grand Ave., Ponca City, OK 74601. **Phone:** (580) 763-8092 or (866) 763-8092.

PIONEER WOMAN STATUE AND MUSEUM, 701 Monument Rd., is a tribute to the women who settled new territory with their families. Exhibits showcase tools, clothing, furniture and personal items that belonged to pioneers. A 17-foot-tall bronze statue, commissioned by oilman and 10th governor of Oklahoma E.W. Marland, depicts a pioneer woman and her son. **Time:** Allow 1 hour minimum. **Hours:** Tues.-Sat. 10-5. Closed major holidays. **Cost:** $6; $3 (ages 6-18, ages 62+ and students with ID); free (military with ID). **Phone:** (580) 765-6108.

COMFORT INN & SUITES   580/765-2322
THREE DIAMOND
Hotel

Address: 3101 N 14th St 74604 **Location:** I-35 exit 214, 3 mi n on US 77. **Facility:** 59 units. 3 stories, interior corridors. **Amenities:** safes. **Pool:** heated indoor. **Activities:** hot tub, limited exercise equipment. **Guest Services:** valet and coin laundry. **Featured Amenity:** full hot breakfast.

SAVE 📶 CALL 🚹 🛼 BIZ HS
🛜 ✕ 🖥 📷 💻 / SOME UNITS 🐾

FAIRFIELD INN & SUITES BY MARRIOTT   580/765-3000
THREE DIAMOND SAVE Hotel. **Address:** 3405 N 14th St 74601

| AAA Benefit: Members save 5% or more! |

HAMPTON INN & SUITES PONCA CITY   580/765-3700
THREE DIAMOND SAVE Motel. **Address:** 2805 N 14th St 74601

| AAA Benefit: Members save up to 15%! |

WHERE TO EAT

HUNAN CHINESE RESTAURANT   580/765-6716
APPROVED   Chinese. Casual Dining. **Address:** 2800 N 5th St 74601

POTEAU (E-12) pop. 8,520, elev. 489'

Poteau, situated on the banks of the Poteau River, is almost entirely surrounded by mountains. The Winding Stair and Kiamichi mountains are on the southwest horizon, while the Poteau Range dominates the view to the south. Cavanal, said to be the world's highest hill, provides a splendid view of Sugar Loaf Mountain.

The town is an outfitting center for recreation in nearby Ouachita National Forest *(see place listing in Arkansas p. 60)*. A scenic stretch of US 59/270 extends 25 miles south to the US 259 intersection before the town of Page.

Poteau Chamber of Commerce: 501 S. Broadway, Poteau, OK 74953. **Phone:** (918) 647-9178.

DAYS INN & SUITES   918/647-3510
APPROVED   Hotel. **Address:** 1702 N Broadway 74953

HOLIDAY INN EXPRESS & SUITES-POTEAU   918/649-0123
THREE DIAMOND Hotel. **Address:** 201 Hillview Pkwy 74953

SURESTAY PLUS HOTEL BY BEST WESTERN POTEAU
918/647-4001
APPROVED   Hotel. **Address:** 3111 N Broadway 74953

PRYOR pop. 9,539

HOLIDAY INN EXPRESS & SUITES   918/476-5400
THREE DIAMOND Hotel. **Address:** 271 Mid America Dr 74361

ROLAND pop. 3,169, elev. 482'

CHEROKEE HOTEL-CASINO ROLAND   918/427-1000
THREE DIAMOND Hotel. **Address:** 109 W Cherokee Blvd 74954 *(See ad p. 37.)*

SAND SPRINGS (E-2) pop. 18,906, elev. 676'
• Part of Tulsa area — see map p. 375

West of downtown Tulsa, Sand Springs is nestled in the steep and wooded hills overlooking the Arkansas River, providing a setting often used as a backdrop in movies. Boating and sailing are available at Keystone Lake *(see Recreation Areas Chart)*.

Sand Springs Chamber of Commerce: 1 W. 1st St., Sand Springs, OK 74063. **Phone:** (918) 245-3221.

HAMPTON INN-TULSA/SAND SPRINGS   918/245-8500

▼▼ THREE DIAMOND (SAVE) Hotel. **Address:** 7852 W Parkway Blvd 74127

AAA Benefit: Members save up to 15%!

HOLIDAY INN EXPRESS HOTEL & SUITES TULSA WEST-SAND SPRINGS   918/419-2700

▼▼ THREE DIAMOND Contemporary Hotel. **Address:** 101 W Morrow Rd 74063

MAGNUSON HOTEL SAND SPRINGS   918/245-4999

▼▼ APPROVED Hotel. **Address:** 211 S Lake Dr 74063

WHERE TO EAT

RIB CRIB BBQ AND GRILL   918/241-5200

▼▼ APPROVED Barbecue. Casual Dining. **Address:** 450 W Wekiwa Rd 74063

RON'S HAMBURGERS & CHILI   918/245-6010

▼▼ APPROVED American. Casual Dining. **Address:** 233 S Adams Rd 74063

SEMINOLE (D-9) pop. 7,488, elev. 892'

Named after the Seminole Indians who previously settled the site, the town reached its peak in 1926 when a large oil pool was tapped. Thousands rushed to the site, and the Seminole post office is reported to have received mail for more than 100,000 people.

Seminole Chamber of Commerce: 326 E. Evans Ave., Seminole, OK 74868. **Phone:** (405) 382-3640.

JASMINE MORAN CHILDREN'S MUSEUM is 1 mi. w. of jct. SR 9/US 377 at 1714 W. Wrangler Blvd. (SR 9W). This hands-on museum is in the form of a child-size town complete with street signs. A courthouse, grocery store, fire station, hospital, television studio and other settings are incorporated into a community just for children.

Exhibits are designed to stimulate the imagination. A child can assume various roles in a community by donning a grocer's apron, dentist's jacket or firefighter's uniform. Other highlights include model airplanes, an aquarium, a soap bubble factory, ScienceWorks and Tinkering in the Park, an area where visitors can create projects.

A 1936 fire truck, 1921 Model T and 1927 caboose can be explored. Children can practice street safety in Safety Town, ride the SuperSONIC Express train or explore the 12,000-square-foot outdoor castle maze. **Time:** Allow 1 hour minimum. **Hours:** Tues.-Sat. 10-5, Sun. 1-5; closed major holidays and 2 weeks following Labor Day. **Cost:** $10;

$9 (ages 60+); free (ages 0-2 with parent). **Phone:** (405) 382-0950. 〔¶〕

BEST WESTERN SEMINOLE INN & SUITES   405/382-3139

▼▼ THREE DIAMOND Hotel

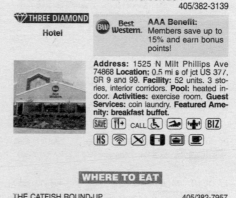

(BW) Best Western. **AAA Benefit:** Members save up to 15% and earn bonus points!

Address: 1525 N Milt Phillips Ave 74868 **Location:** 0.5 mi s of jct US 377, SR 9 and 99. **Facility:** 52 units. 3 stories, interior corridors. **Pool:** heated indoor. **Activities:** exercise room. **Guest Services:** coin laundry. **Featured Amenity:** breakfast buffet.

(SAVE) (¶+) CALL (&) (⊒) (♦) (BIZ) (HS) (📶) (✕) (🗎) (⊟) (⊡)

WHERE TO EAT

THE CATFISH ROUND-UP   405/382-7957

▼▼ APPROVED American. Casual Dining. **Address:** I-40 & Hwy 99 74868

SHAWNEE (H-4) pop. 29,857, elev. 1,043'
- **Restaurants p. 372**
- **Part of Oklahoma City area — see map p. 343**

Shawnee was settled in a matter of minutes after the American Indian Territory of which it was a part was opened to pioneer settlement. Emerging as a bustling railroad town, Shawnee made a bid to become the capital of Oklahoma in 1910 but lost the honor to Oklahoma City. The town's fortunes turned, however, with the discovery of oil in 1926. Since then Shawnee's industry has diversified to include the manufacture of electronic equipment, aircraft parts, clothing and hair dryers.

Visit Shawnee: 231 N. Bell Ave., Shawnee, OK 74801. **Phone:** (405) 275-9780 or (888) 404-9633.

POTTAWATOMIE COUNTY MUSEUM, 614 E. Main St., is in a building that was once the town's train depot. The museum chronicles Pottawatomie County history with antique automobiles, dolls, furniture, clothing, tools and pump organs. Also on the grounds is the first house built in Shawnee. **Time:** Allow 1 hour minimum. **Hours:** Tues.-Sat. 10-4. Closed major holidays. **Cost:** $2; $1 (children and students with ID). **Phone:** (405) 275-8412.

COMFORT INN & SUITES   405/273-8667

▼▼ THREE DIAMOND Hotel

Address: 5400 Enterprise Ct 74804 **Location:** I-40 exit 186, just ne. **Facility:** 72 units. 3 stories, interior corridors. **Pool:** heated indoor. **Activities:** exercise room. **Guest Services:** coin laundry. **Featured Amenity:** full hot breakfast.

(SAVE) CALL (&) (⊒) (♦) (BIZ) (HS) (📶) (✕) (🗎) (⊟) (⊡)

DAYS INN-SHAWNEE
405/275-6720

APPROVED

Motel

Address: 5107 N Harrison St 74804 **Location:** I-40 exit 186, just n. **Facility:** 51 units. 2 stories (no elevator), interior corridors. **Parking:** winter plug-ins. **Activities:** limited exercise equipment. **Guest Services:** coin laundry. **Featured Amenity: continental breakfast.**

HAMPTON INN BY HILTON
405/275-1540

THREE DIAMOND **SAVE** Hotel. **Address:** 4851 N Kickapoo Ave 74801

AAA Benefit: Members save up to 15%!

HOLIDAY INN EXPRESS HOTEL & SUITES
405/275-8880

THREE DIAMOND Hotel. **Address:** 4909 N Union Ave 74804

LA QUINTA INN & SUITES SHAWNEE
405/275-7930

THREE DIAMOND

Hotel

Address: 5401 Enterprise Ct 74804 **Location:** I-40 exit 186, just ne. **Facility:** 79 units. 3 stories, interior corridors. **Pool:** heated indoor. **Activities:** hot tub, exercise room. **Guest Services:** coin laundry. **Featured Amenity: full hot breakfast.**

SUPER 8 SHAWNEE
405/275-0089

APPROVED Motel. **Address:** 5104 N Harrison St 74804

WHERE TO EAT

BILLY BOY BBQ
405/275-2040

APPROVED Barbecue. Quick Serve. **Address:** 120 W MacArthur St 74801

VAN'S PIG STANDS
405/273-0000

APPROVED Barbecue. Quick Serve. **Address:** 3815 N Harrison St 74804

STILLWATER (C-9) pop. 45,688, elev. 870'

On April 22, 1889, the town of Stillwater was born with a population of 300. A year later the Oklahoma Agricultural and Mechanical College, now Oklahoma State University, was founded, and Stillwater became one of the Southwest's major educational centers. The city also is known as a center for agribusiness, medical services and industry. Experimental farms can be seen along highways leading into town.

Stillwater is the home of the Sheerar Cultural and Heritage Center Museum, 702 S. Duncan St., (405) 377-0359.

Visit Stillwater: 2617 W. 6th Ave., Stillwater, OK 74074. **Phone:** (405) 743-3697 or (800) 991-6717.

BEST WESTERN PLUS CIMARRON HOTEL & SUITES
405/372-2878

THREE DIAMOND

Hotel

AAA Benefit: Members save up to 15% and earn bonus points!

Address: 315 N Husband St 74074 **Location:** Just w of jct Hall of Fame Ave and Main St. **Facility:** 76 units. 4 stories, interior corridors. **Amenities:** safes. **Pool:** heated indoor. **Activities:** hot tub, exercise room. **Guest Services:** valet and coin laundry.

FAIRFIELD INN & SUITES BY MARRIOTT STILLWATER
405/372-6300

THREE DIAMOND **SAVE** Hotel. **Address:** 418 E Hall of Fame Ave 74075

AAA Benefit: Members save 5% or more!

HAMPTON INN & SUITES BY HILTON
405/743-1306

THREE DIAMOND

Hotel

AAA Benefit: Members save up to 15%!

Address: 717 E Hall of Fame Ave 74075 **Location:** Just e of jct US 177 (Perkins Rd). **Facility:** 81 units. 3 stories, interior corridors. **Pool:** heated outdoor. **Activities:** hot tub, exercise room. **Guest Services:** valet and coin laundry.

HAMPTON INN & SUITES BY HILTON STILLWATER WEST/ AIRPORT
405/332-5575

THREE DIAMOND **SAVE** Hotel. **Address:** 615 S Country Club Rd 74074

AAA Benefit: Members save up to 15%!

HOLIDAY INN & SUITES
405/372-2445

THREE DIAMOND Hotel. **Address:** 715 S Country Club Rd 74074

HOME2 SUITES BY HILTON
405/372-2550

THREE DIAMOND **SAVE** Extended Stay Contemporary Hotel. **Address:** 306 E Hall of Fame Ave 74075

AAA Benefit: Members save up to 15%!

MICROTEL INN AND SUITES BY WYNDHAM STILLWATER
405/372-7100

APPROVED Hotel. **Address:** 423 E Hall of Fame Ave 74075

RESIDENCE INN BY MARRIOTT
405/707-0588

THREE DIAMOND **SAVE** Extended Stay Hotel. **Address:** 800 S Murphy St 74074

AAA Benefit: Members save 5% or more!

⌁ **For complete hotel, dining and attraction listings: AAA.com/travelguides**

SPRINGHILL SUITES BY MARRIOTT   405/564-7173
THREE DIAMOND **SAVE** Hotel. **Ad-**
dress: 315 S C-Star Blvd 74074

> **AAA Benefit:**
> Members save 5%
> or more!

WYNDHAM GARDEN STILLWATER   405/377-7010
THREE DIAMOND Hotel. **Address:** 600 E McElroy Rd 74075

WHERE TO EAT

ESKIMO JOE'S   405/372-8896
APPROVED American. Casual Dining. **Address:** 501
W Elm Ave 74074

MEXICO JOE'S   405/372-1169
APPROVED Mexican. Casual Dining. **Address:** 311 W
Hall of Fame Ave 74075

RIB CRIB BBQ AND GRILL   405/372-1900
APPROVED Barbecue. Casual Dining. **Address:** 103
S Perkins Rd 74074

THAI LOCO   405/332-4343
APPROVED Thai. Casual Dining. **Address:** 2223 W
6th Ave 74074

SULPHUR (F-9) pop. 4,929, elev. 1,001'

CHICKASAW CULTURAL CENTER, 867 Cooper
Memorial Dr., celebrates the history and culture of
the Chickasaw Nation and other Native American
tribes in the southeastern U.S. An exhibit center features interactive displays, stomp dance performances and an orientation film. An outdoor traditional
village re-creates 18th-century Chickasaw life with a
council house, a stickball field, cooking demonstrations, archery and blowgun demonstrations and
other activities.

Also on the grounds is a 40-foot-tall pavilion with an
overlook, a research/genealogy center, a garden and
a large-format theater with daily showings of films focused on or made by Chickasaw citizens. **Hours:**
Grounds and exhibit center Mon.-Sat. 10-5, Sun.
noon-5. Traditional village (weather permitting) Sat.
10-4:30, Sun. noon-4:30. Closed major holidays.
Cost: Exhibit center or large-format theater film $6; $5
(ages 55+ and students and military with ID); free
(ages 0-12). Combination exhibit center and theater
film $10; $8 (ages 55+ and students and military with
ID); $3 (ages 0-12). **Phone:** (580) 622-7130. **GT** **榊**

TAHLEQUAH pop. 15,753, elev. 861'

In a region of lakes within the foothills of the
Ozark Mountains, Tahlequah has been the capital of
the Cherokee Indian Nation since 1839. Old
Cherokee government buildings still standing are
the 1844 Supreme Court Building, the 1867
Cherokee Capitol Building and the 1844 Cherokee
National Prison.

Designated a scenic highway, SR 10 winds 30
miles northeast from Tahlequah, intersecting with
US 412 and US 59 in the town of Kansas. Two miles
north of the junction of US 62 and SR 10, Elephant

Rock Nature Park offers 120 acres with nature and
hiking trails and access to the Illinois River for
fishing, swimming and float trips.

Tour Tahlequah: 123 E. Delaware St., Tahlequah,
OK 74464-2817. **Phone:** (918) 456-3742.

Self-guiding tours: City maps, announcements of
community activities and brochures outlining self-
guiding tours of Tahlequah's historic homes and
sites are available at the Tour Tahlequah office.

HOLIDAY INN EXPRESS & SUITES TAHLEQUAH
          918/506-4545
THREE DIAMOND Contemporary Hotel. **Address:** 2142 Mah-
aney Ave 74464

WHERE TO EAT

EL ZARAPE   918/456-0708
APPROVED Mexican. Casual Dining. **Address:** 701 E
Downing St 74464

SAM AND ELLA'S CHICKEN PALACE   918/456-1411
APPROVED Pizza. Casual Dining. **Address:** 419 N
Muskogee Ave 74464

THACKERVILLE pop. 445

BEST WESTERN RED RIVER INN & SUITES
          580/276-5001
APPROVED
Hotel

BW Best Western. **AAA Benefit:** Members save up to
15% and earn bonus
points!

Address: 22106 Blackjack Rd 73459
Location: I-35 exit 1, 1.1 mi n on E Service Rd. **Facility:** 60 units. 3 stories, interior corridors. **Pool:** outdoor.
Activities: exercise room. **Guest Ser-**
vices: coin laundry. **Featured Amenity:**
full hot breakfast.
SAVE **▤** CALL **⚅** **⊇** **◈** **BIZ**
⧈ **⊠** **▤** **◲** **▣**

THE INN AT WINSTAR   580/276-4487
APPROVED Hotel. **Address:** 21943 Red River Rd
73459

TISHOMINGO (F-9) pop. 3,034, elev. 673'

Historically significant as the capital of the
Chickasaw Nation, Tishomingo is on Lake Texoma.
After serving as the last Chickasaw National Capitol,
the granite Victorian Gothic building at N. Capitol Avenue and W. 9th Street housed the Johnston County
Courthouse 1907-89. Guided tours of the building
are available; phone (580) 371-9835. The restored
1902 Indian Territory Bank of the Chickasaw Nation,
a block from Court House Square, houses the Johnston County Museum of History.

Johnston County Chamber of Commerce: 106 W.
Main St., Tishomingo, OK 73460. **Phone:** (580)
371-2175.

Tulsa

Then & Now

As Oklahoma's second largest city, Tulsa is the product of an unlikely mixture of oil and water; the development of these two liquid resources spurred the city's rapid economic growth and made Tulsa into the vibrant, bustling community it is today.

Tulsa's beginnings date to 1836 when a band of displaced Creek Indians from Alabama built a council fire under a sturdy oak tree (near S. Cheyenne Avenue and W. 18th Street), ending a long, harsh journey over the "Trail of Tears." The name Tulsa is derived from the Creek word "Tullahassee" or "Tallahassee," meaning "old town."

While early settlers were attracted to the lush banks of the Arkansas River, the area remained largely undeveloped until a trading post opened in 1846, signaling the beginning of organized commerce in the area. Tulsa became the official name of the town with the creation of the first post office in 1879.

The arrival of the St. Louis-San Francisco Railway provided further impetus for growth. Farmers, ranchers and traders were attracted to the area's increasingly stable system of transportation. One of the first organized groups, a union Sunday school, held class in a tent belonging to a railroad carpenter. By the time Tulsa was incorporated on Jan. 8, 1898, cattle shipping had become the principal industry.

AAA.com/travelguides—
more ways to look, book and save

Tulsa skyline

On June 25, 1901, the pace of the town's development quickened. Drillers operating a rig known as Sue Bland #1 struck black gold, creating the state's first commercially important oil well. Eager prospectors swarmed the area, repeating the frenzy of land rushes a few years prior. A second major strike tapped into large reserves at the Ida Glenn farm in 1905. Oil prices began to climb after pipelines were established to the Gulf of Mexico.

As oil fortunes were literally being made overnight, enterprising Tulsans began an aggressive campaign to attract oilmen to establish themselves in the community. The result was a building boom that also created hotels, office buildings, paved roads, bridges and more railroad links.

Train trips organized by civic leaders to promote Tulsa were common at the turn of the 20th century, and humorist Will Rogers was known to accompany these early business boosters. Their vision helped to elevate Tulsa from a

(Continued on p. 376.)

Destination Tulsa

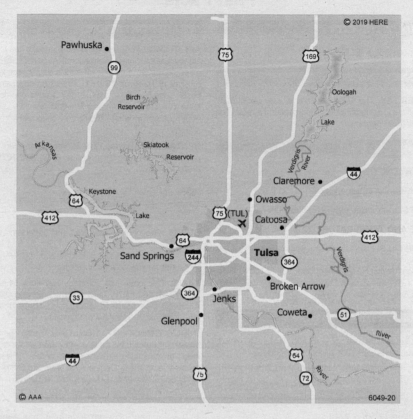

This map shows cities in the Tulsa vicinity where you will find attractions, hotels and restaurants. Cities are listed alphabetically in this book on the following pages.

Fast Facts

ABOUT THE CITY

POP: 391,906 ▪ **ELEV:** 689 ft.

MONEY

SALES TAX: The Tulsa area has a sales tax of 8.52 percent, a lodging tax of 13.52 percent and a rental car tax of 14.51 percent.

WHOM TO CALL

EMERGENCY: 911

POLICE (non-emergency): (918) 596-9222

FIRE (non-emergency): (918) 596-9444

TIME AND TEMPERATURE: (918) 743-3311

HOSPITALS: Hillcrest Hospital South, (918) 294-4000 ▪ Hillcrest Medical Center, (918) 579-1000 ▪ OSU Medical Center, (918) 599-1000 ▪ Saint Francis Hospital, (918) 494-2200 ▪ St. John Medical Center, (918) 744-2345.

VISITOR INFORMATION

Visit Tulsa: 1 W. 3rd St., Suite 100, Tulsa, OK 74103. **Phone:** (918) 585-1201 or (800) 558-3311.

Maps and visitor information are available Mon.-Fri. 8-5.

TRANSPORTATION

AIR TRAVEL: With service to most major cities in the United States, Tulsa International Airport (TUL) is 8 miles northeast of downtown and is easily accessible by way of I-244 or US 169. Airport on-site parking costs range from $6 to $16 per day. Taxi fare to downtown Tulsa is approximately $20-$30 one way. Many area hotels provide free shuttle service to and from the airport.

RENTAL CARS: Hertz, 7727 E. Young Pl., offers discounts to AAA members; phone (918) 838-1015 or (800) 654-3080.

 Book and save at AAA.com/hertz

BUSES: Greyhound Lines Inc. and Jefferson Lines are the major bus lines serving the city. Both operate out of the terminal at 317 S. Detroit Ave.; phone (918) 584-4428 for schedule information.

TAXIS: The major cab company is Yellow Checker Cab, (918) 582-6161. Taxis are metered and charge $1.50-$2 plus $1.90 for each mile. There is a $1 charge for each additional passenger.

PUBLIC TRANSPORTATION: Tulsa Transit operates buses throughout the metropolitan area and includes stops at attractions and shopping centers. The main terminal is at 319 S. Denver Ave. at W. 3rd St.; phone (918) 582-2100 for schedules and information.

(Continued from p. 374.)

dusty cow town in Native American territory to a dynamic urban center with a vigorous economy.

While at one time everyone in Tulsa seemed to be involved in some way with the oil business, the city now has a more diversified economy. Although hundreds of area firms are still associated with the petroleum business, current industries include aviation, computer technology, financial services, health care, manufacturing and mining.

Tulsans place a heavy importance on culture—from museums to performing arts organizations to public art around the city. One of the most beautiful aspects of the destination is its architecture. You may be surprised to learn that Tulsa has one of the largest collections of Art Deco buildings in the country; there are several dozen examples of the style. The design was all the rage in the 1920s and '30s, which is when much of Tulsa's construction occurred. A walking tour through Tulsa's historical business district will take you past more than 30 Art Deco sites. The Tulsa Arts District is where you'll find museums, studios and monthly art walks.

Development of water resources has enabled Tulsa to boast the largest number of man-made lakes in the nation. Barge traffic between the Tulsa Port of Catoosa and New Orleans qualifies Tulsa as a major inland harbor. This 445-mile navigation system links Oklahoma with domestic ports in the surrounding five-state area through a complex system of dams, lakes, reservoirs and locks.

The area earns its nickname "Green Country" from an abundance of parks and gardens that enhance the city's urban appearance. Many acres of parkland have been preserved despite Tulsa's numerous industries. River Parks, the scene of several festivals, includes a lake with a floating stage as well as a lengthy trail system on the east and west banks of the Arkansas River. Woodward Park offers a peaceful escape from the city with a rose garden, rock gardens, a Shakespeare monument, a conservatory and more than 15,000 azaleas.

Tulsa is an ideal destination for fans of equestrian events. Tulsa's Expo Square, which includes several venues, hosts many horse shows and competitions throughout the year, showcasing a variety of breeds and events.

Must Do: AAA Editor's Picks

- The ⫷ **Gilcrease Museum** (1400 N. Gilcrease Museum Rd.) is a must-see for any aficionado of Western and Native American art. Virtually every item in the museum's vast collection relates to the discovery, expansion and settlement of North America. The Western-themed works by masters like Albert Bierstadt, George Catlin and John Singer Sargent are noteworthy.

- The ⫷ **Philbrook Museum of Art** (2727 S. Rockford Rd.), Tulsa's other outstanding art museum, occupies an expansive Italian Renaissance villa built for city oilman Waite Phillips. Today it's a repository for the museum's collections, which range from Italian Renaissance paintings and European sculpture to African, Asian and Native American art. The gardens feature a variety of native Oklahoma plants.

- "My ancestors didn't come over on the Mayflower, but they met the boat." That's one of many memorable lines attributed to William Penn Adair "Will" Rogers, the vaudevillian, humorist, movie star and social commentator who was one of the world's best-known celebrities during the 1920s and '30s. The ⫷ **Will Rogers Memorial Museum** (1720 W. Will Rogers Blvd.) in nearby Claremore pays tribute to the legacy and accomplishments of an Oklahoma native son.

- Guns, guns and more guns—but also saddles, spurs, German beer steins and Native American artifacts—are on display at the ⫷ **J.M. Davis Arms & Historical Museum** (330 N. J.M. Davis Blvd.) in Claremore. The extensive collection of firearms includes Davis' first weapon, a muzzle-loading shotgun given to him by his father. But Davis also collected everything from political buttons to music boxes, and they're all on display.

- Stop and smell the roses at the **Tulsa Garden Center** (2435 S. Peoria Ave.) in Woodward Park. The lovingly tended rose garden, created by the WPA in the 1930s, encompasses five terraces. Ivy-covered stone walls, fountains and magnolia trees accent the many varieties of hybrid tea roses, which are at peak bloom from mid-May through June and again in October.

- Australian stonefish and Giant Pacific octopi in Oklahoma? You can find them at the ⫷ **Oklahoma Aquarium** (300 Aquarium Dr.) in Jenks. The aquarium also spotlights the diversified marine life—alligator snapping turtles, gars, sunfish and more—inhabiting the Sooner State's lakes, rivers and streams.

- If you're looking for fun things to do with kids, head to the ⫷ **Tulsa Zoo** (6421 E. 36th St. N.). One of the most impressive exhibits is The Rainforest, an enclosure where free-flying bats and birds flit about and visitors can see jungle dwellers like dwarf caimans, black howler monkeys, sloths and jewel-colored poison dart frogs.

- Named for a Route 66 gas station's fanciful blue dome, the **Blue Dome District** along E. 2nd Street is the center of downtown Tulsa's nightlife scene. Partiers congregate at laid-back nightspots like Woody's Corner Bar (325 E. 2nd St.), the unofficial after-game gathering place of the Tulsa Oilers ice hockey team. Other hotspots? The arcade games at Max Retropub, German beer and live music at Fassler Hall, and the rooftop bar at El Guapo's Cantina (332 E. 1st St.).

- More than a quarter of a million people gather to ring in **Tulsa International Mayfest,** one of Oklahoma's biggest festivals held downtown (400 S. Main St.). This celebration of live music and the visual arts offers everything from powwow dances and drum circles to body artists and a youth art gallery.

- A carnival midway, prize-winning livestock, corn dogs and funnel cakes—there's no finer family entertainment in town than the **Tulsa State Fair,** which takes place at Expo Square (4145 E. 21st St.) in late September and early October.

Oklahoma Aquarium

Tulsa 1-day Itinerary

AAA editors suggest these activities for a great short vacation experience.

Morning

- Get your wake-up jolt of caffeine at The Coffee House on Cherry Street (1502 E. 15th St.). It's roomy but cozy, with a random collection of sofas, chairs and tables that offers a living-room feel. There's also a front porch if you'd rather sit outside (and it's equipped with a fire pit for nippy fall and winter days). The lattes are strong and frothy, the blueberry and pumpkin muffins are tasty and Wi-Fi is free and fast.

- Spend an hour exploring the stretch of 15th Street known as Cherry Street. Just north of downtown, Tulsa's midtown is the location of several historic neighborhoods. Antique shops, galleries and funky stores like Cheap Thrills Vintage (3018 E. 15th St.) occupy old 1920s and '30s storefronts. The Cherry Street Farmers Market sets up between Quaker and Rockford avenues on Saturdays from April to October. It's a fun place to browse.

- Depart Cherry Street and head to nearby **Woodward Park** (21st Street and Peoria Avenue). This charming green space has plenty of trees, ponds and the occasional statue. There also are lovely gardens; azaleas put on a show in the spring, and the rose garden at the **Tulsa Garden Center** (2435 S. Peoria Ave.) is a riot of color and fragrance in summer.

Afternoon

- There are more gardens on the grounds of the ₹ **Philbrook Museum of Art** (2727 S. Rockford Rd.), a grand Italianate villa that was once home to a Tulsa oil baron. The museum's works span the globe from Europe to Asia to Africa, and include a collection of 19th-century American paintings and sculpture emphasizing the theme of westward exploration and expansion. Don't miss the exhibits of Native American jewelry and pottery, and in particular "The Brilliant Prayer" by Allan C. Houser, a Chiricahua Indian and native Oklahoman.

- You'll also want to visit the ₹ **Gilcrease Museum** (1400 N. Gilcrease Museum Rd.). Exhibiting what has been called the world's foremost collection of art and artifacts representing the American West, the Gilcrease has paintings by artists Charles M. Russell and Frederic Remington, panoramic landscapes by Thomas Moran and Albert Bierstadt, and works by non-Western masters like Winslow Homer. Not to be missed is Bierstadt's majestically serene "Sierra Nevada Morning." The grounds are beautified by 11 themed gardens.

- If it's a nice day, stop at the **Oxley Nature Center** (6700 Mohawk Blvd.). The center has nearly 9 miles of hiking trails that wind through forests, fields and wetlands; pick up a map at the Interpretive Building.

Woodward Park

Evening

- **Andolini's Pizzeria** (1552 E. 15th St.) is a Tulsa favorite for great pizza. Freshly prepared ingredients are used throughout the menu, which includes everything from a "Maccheroni" pizza topped with penne pasta and cream to a specialty pie made with brie, toasted walnuts, honey glaze and Granny Smith apples. Be sure to get an order of the garlic knots—if you have room.

- If it's Saturday night, attend a performance of "The Drunkard," billed as "America's longest-running play," at **Tulsa Spotlight Theatre** (1381 Riverside Dr.). This old-fashioned melodrama has a good guy to cheer for, a villain to hiss at and plenty of participatory sing-a-long moments. It's followed by "The Olio," a showcase for local talent. Curtain time is 7:30 p.m.

- Everybody from Hank Williams to the Sex Pistols has played **Cain's Ballroom** (423 N. Main St.). Built in 1924 and famous in the 1930s for popularizing Western swing, a musical offshoot blending jazz, blues, big band and even mariachi, the ballroom's maple-wood dance floor is illuminated by a silver disco ball.

- The **Mercury Lounge** (1747 S. Boston Ave.) was once a Sinclair service station; its current incarnation is a dive bar with local and regional bands that tend to play rowdy rockabilly. There's plenty of beer on tap, a pool table, two patios and an old-school jukebox.

Top Picks for Kids

Under 13

- Get your wake-up jolt of caffeine at The Coffee House on Cherry Street (1502 E. 15th St.). It's roomy but cozy, with a living-room feel. There's also a front porch if you'd rather sit outside (and it's equipped with a fire pit for nippy days). The lattes are strong and frothy, the blueberry and pumpkin muffins are tasty and Wi-Fi is free and fast.

- Spend an hour exploring the stretch of 15th Street known as Cherry Street. Just north of downtown, Tulsa's midtown is the location of several historic neighborhoods. Antique shops, galleries and funky stores like Cheap Thrills Vintage (3018 E. 15th St.) occupy old 1920s and '30s storefronts. The Cherry Street Farmers Market sets up between Quaker and Rockford avenues on Saturdays from April to October.

- Depart Cherry Street and head to nearby **Woodward Park** (21st Street and Peoria Avenue). This charming green space has plenty of trees, ponds and the occasional statue. There also are lovely gardens; azaleas put on a show in the spring, and the rose garden at the **Tulsa Garden Center** (2435 S. Peoria Ave.) is a riot of color and fragrance in summer.

Teens

- Colorful Oklahoma artworks add to the festive atmosphere at **Hideaway Pizza** (7549 S. Olympia Ave.). Specialty pizzas here include the "Maui Magic" with red sauce, mozzarella, Canadian bacon, pineapple and Mandarin

orange. Be adventurous or order your favorite toppings, then watch the pros make your pie. A variety of salads, baked pastas and sandwiches also are available. No matter what you choose for your main course, follow it up with a cool, refreshing slice of frozen lemonade pie.

- No matter when you're on your Tulsa vacation, it's shark week at the ☲ **Oklahoma Aquarium** (300 Aquarium Dr., Jenks), where you'll find yourself surrounded by a school of 10 bull sharks in the Shark Adventure exhibit. Don't worry; you'll be safely inside a plexiglass tunnel as these large predators swirl overhead. Other things to see include river otters splashing in the Ozark Stream and a feeding show featuring an electric eel and piranhas.

- Serious shoppers will want to hit **Woodland Hills Mall** (7021 S. Memorial Dr.), which has more than 165 stores including some 120 trendy specialty shops and restaurants, anchored by large department stores offering something for everyone in the family.

All Ages

- The ☲ **Gilcrease Museum** (1400 Gilcrease Museum Rd.) houses the world's largest collection of art of the American West, along with Native American artifacts and artworks. The museum has three interactive spaces including the Kids Site-Animal Influences, where kids can learn about animals found in Oklahoma while enjoying activities including creating art, playing computer games, examining the stamp station and paddling a birch bark canoe. • The ☲ **Philbrook Museum of Art** (2727 S. Rockford Rd.) features collections from around the world along with Native American art. Though there's a satellite location downtown, the main museum is a 1927 Italian Renaissance villa surrounded by 25 acres of formal and informal gardens with bridges, a creek, pathways and a sculpture walk. Kids will love exploring the gardens to see if they can spot the museum's three "garden cats," Acer, Perilla and Cleome.

- If you're planning to travel to Tulsa in mid-May, don't miss **Tulsa International Mayfest** (North Main Street and East Pine Street), the city's annual celebration of visual and performing arts. You'll see works by national and regional juried artists and free shows by local dancers, musicians and other performers. Plenty of festival fare, including food truck offerings, is available and the Kidzone offers entertainment and activities for children.

- IdWhite River Fish Market (1708 N. Sheridan Rd.) is both a fish market and a restaurant. You'll find everything on the menu here from alligator to walleye, available broiled, fried or grilled to please everyone in the family. If you love lobster, be sure to dine here on a Tuesday or Wednesday when it's available.

Hideaway Pizza

Arriving
By Car

Several major highways lead to and from Tulsa. One of the most important is I-44, which approaches the city from the northeast as the Will Rogers Turnpike and from the southwest as the Turner Turnpike. Although I-44 bypasses the downtown area, the city's center is accessible from I-44 by way of numerous interchanges. Martin Luther King Jr. Memorial Expressway (I-244/US 412) is a major access route from I-44 to the heart of Tulsa.

US 75 leads into downtown Tulsa from both the north and the south; the southern segment is known as the Okmulgee Expressway, which becomes the Indian Nation Turnpike farther south.

US 64/412 approaches the city from the west as the Cimarron Turnpike, but becomes the Keystone Expressway before entering the city limits. The Muskogee Turnpike is a major access highway from the southeast. Converging with SR 51, it enters Tulsa as the Broken Arrow Expressway.

East of the city, the Mingo Valley Expressway (US 169) approaches from the north; it is connected to downtown via I-244. Historic Route 66, which at one time carried traffic from Chicago to Southern California, passes through downtown as 11th Street.

Getting Around
Street System

The east-west dividing line is Main Street, while Admiral Boulevard is the city's north-south bisector. Numbered streets run east and west beginning 1 block south of Admiral, unless otherwise designated.

Tulsa Indian Art Festival

A right turn on red is permitted after a complete stop, unless otherwise posted.

Parking

Ample parking is available downtown. There are many commercial garages and lots, and most hotels provide free parking for guests. Rates in the commercial garages range $2-$5 for the first hour or $4-$10 per day.

Shopping

From small, exclusive boutiques to large, bargain-packed malls, Tulsa's shopping centers provide visitors with a wide range of choices. With more than one million square feet of retail floor space, **Woodland Hills Mall,** E. 71st Street and S. Memorial Drive, is said to be the largest in the state. The mall comprises more than 160 stores including Dillard's, JCPenney, Macy's and Sears.

Utica Square, 21st Street S. and Utica Avenue, caters to upscale tastes and also serves as the backdrop for live performances in summer. Centered about a rustic, restored barn at 51st Street S. and Sheridan Avenue, **The Farm** offers a variety of boutiques in a setting that is reminiscent of a village square.

Among the retailers at **Tulsa Promenade,** E. 41st Street and S. Yale Avenue, are Dillard's and JCPenney.

Nightlife

Feeling lucky? Head to **Hard Rock Hotel & Casino Tulsa** (111 W. Cherokee St., Catoosa), which has more than 2,600 popular electronic games, 40 table games and poker. Entertainment options include comedy shows, concerts and a dance club. Choose from blackjack, roulette, table games and more than 1,600 electronic games at the **Osage Casino Hotel** (951 W. 36th St. N.). The casino offers several dining options along with live music and events at the Skyline Event Center. **River Spirit Casino Resort** (8330 Riverside Pkwy.) is a AAA Four Diamond resort with a casino featuring poker, table games, more than 3,100 electronic games and Jimmy Buffett's Caribbean-themed Margaritaville Casino & Restaurant.

If you're craving a well-crafted cocktail, try one of the inventive offerings at the **R Bar & Grill** (3421 South Peoria Ave.), where drinks are designed to highlight fresh seasonal ingredients. **Valkyrie** (13 E. Mathew B. Brady St.) is a laid-back bar in the Arts District with an extensive menu of craft cocktails as well as a large selection of spirits and craft beers.

In the mood for a laugh? Giggles are guaranteed from the improv, sketch and stand-up shows at the **Loony Bin** (6808 S. Memorial Dr., Ste. 234). A dinner menu includes appetizers, sandwiches, fish and chips and fried shrimp, and beer, wine and cocktails are available.

Craft brew fans will find a lengthy list of beers to sample at **McNellie's Public House** (409 E. 1st

St.). The menu, which changes monthly, includes awide selection of draught and bottled beers from Oklahoma and around the world. Look for beer-related events and specials happening during your visit. **Prairie Brewpub** (223 N. Main St.) features beers brewed on site with unique offerings such as the "Birthday Bomb!," a stout with flavors of caramel sauce, chili peppers, coffee, cocoa nibs, toffee and vanilla bean.

Experience a little of Tulsa's music history at **Cain's Ballroom** (423 N. Main St.). Built in 1924 as a garage, it was later a dance hall and academy until 1935, when Bob Wills and the Texas Playboys popularized a style of music here known as Western Swing. It's now a popular concert venue for country, rock and other genres. The wide-open ballroom offers limited seating, a full bar and barbecue during most concerts. For a more intimate live music experience, head to the **Duet Jazz Club** (108 N. Detroit Ave.) in the Arts District, featuring performances Wednesday through Saturday and a restaurant serving modern American cuisine. **Soundpony** (409 N. Main St.) is a live music venue featuring indie bands, DJs, hip-hop, jazz and punk soul music, along with trivia nights and fashion shows.

Big Events

Several events keep Tulsans in touch with their heritage. The **Tulsa Indian Art Festival** is held in February in nearby Glenpool with Native American tribes participating from across the country. The city celebrates the arts in mid-May with **Tulsa International Mayfest,** held in the **Main Mall** downtown.

The **Pinto World Championship Horse Show** in June features more than 2,000 colorful horses and riders; the event is held at **Expo Square.**

More than 400 independent artists and retailers display arts, crafts, antiques and collectibles during **An Affair of the Heart,** held in mid-July at Expo Square. The event returns to Expo Square in mid-November.

The **Intertribal Indian Club of Tulsa Powwow of Champions** held in mid-August attracts dancers from throughout the United States to participate in contests and other cultural activities.

Scotfest is held in mid-September at **River West Festival Park.** The festival includes a Scottish athletic competition for both men and women plus Scottish entertainment, whisky tastings and dance workshops. Tents are set up by Scottish clans, food vendors and various Celtic merchants.

The **Brush Creek Bazaar** held in the fall features more than 80 arts and crafts exhibitors, live music and youth activities, as well as clogging and other dance performances.

The **Tulsa State Fair** is held at Expo Square starting in late September or early October. The fall season also brings **Linde Oktoberfest,** with German folk bands, European food, arts and crafts, a dachshund race and a carnival.

Tulsa Ballet

Sports & Rec

With hundreds of miles of lakeshore within a 2-hour drive of their city, Tulsans enjoy a variety of water sports. **Fishing, boating** and **water skiing** are popular on any one of the 40 lakes in the Tulsa vicinity including **Birch, Eufaula, Fort Gibson, Fountainhead, Greenleaf, Keystone, Skiatook** and **Tenkiller.** Provisions for **swimming** and **picnicking** are plentiful.

Hikers have their choice of trails at nearby **Chandler Park** and **Heyburn, Okmulgee** and **Oologah** lakes, to name a few. A recreation area on one of the largest bodies of water in Oklahoma, **Grand Lake O' the Cherokees,** is home to 36 holes of year-round **golf.** LaFortune Park in southern Tulsa has a popular three-mile **jogging** track around two 18-hole golf courses and a public swimming pool.

City and county parks are numerous. Among them is **Mohawk Park** on 36th Street N., one of the largest municipal parks in the nation. Near downtown, the **River Parks** system offers miles of jogging, walking and **bicycling** trails along the banks of the Arkansas River. Many area parks feature lighted **softball** diamonds.

The **Tulsa Drillers,** the Double-A farm team of **baseball**'s Los Angeles Dodgers, play in **ONEOK Field** in downtown's Greenwood district; phone (918) 744-5901 for schedule information. **Ice hockey** fans flock to the **BOK Center** to watch the **Tulsa Oilers;** phone (918) 632-7825.

At the college level the **University of Tulsa Golden Hurricanes** and the **Oral Roberts University Golden Eagles** both field competitive baseball and **basketball** teams. Fans of **football** find plenty of gridiron action every fall at the University of Tulsa's **Skelly Field at H. A. Chapman Stadium;** phone (918) 631-4688.

Those who enjoy the thrill of "playing the ponies" can visit **Fair Meadows** at **Expo Square** for pari-mutuel Thoroughbred and quarter **horse racing** at various dates during the year; phone (918) 743-7223.

Note: Policies concerning admittance of children to pari-mutuel betting facilities vary. Phone for information.

Performing Arts

Early Tulsa settlers included cultured people who brought their appreciation of music with them, thus sowing the seeds for future growth of the arts.

The **Tulsa Opera** presents a season of internationally renowned productions. The **Performing Arts Center** (PAC), E. 2nd Street and Cincinnati Avenue in downtown Tulsa, was built with a combination of public and private funds. It serves as the hub of the arts entertainment community in the city. For ticket information phone (918) 596-7111. In addition, **Tulsa Ballet** performs in **Chapman Music Hall** at the Tulsa Performing Arts Center; for ticket information phone (918) 749-6006.

The **Tulsa Spotlighters** present "The Drunkard," a 19th-century melodrama that has been in regular production since 1953. The play, which encourages audience participation, is followed by "The Olio," an old-fashioned variety show. The landmark **Spotlight Theatre,** 1381 Riverside Dr., serves as the play's venue; phone (918) 587-5030.

The **Jazz Depot** at the **Oklahoma Jazz Hall of Fame,** 5 S. Boston Ave., features jazz, gospel and blues concerts on Sunday afternoons. On Tuesday evenings the public is invited to drop in to hear local jazz musicians during "Depot Jams." The Hall of Fame also hosts live jazz music on Friday mornings. For schedules and ticket information phone (918) 928-5299.

ATTRACTIONS

For a complete list of attractions, visit AAA.com/travelguides/attractions

GILCREASE MUSEUM is off US 64/SR 51 at 1400 N. Gilcrease Museum Rd. The museum is known for its comprehensive collection of art of the American West, including works by Albert Bierstadt, Thomas Moran, Frederic Remington and Charles Russell. The Helmerich Center for American Research at Gilcrease Museum houses the Gilcrease Library and Archive containing more than 100,000 rare books, documents, maps and unpublished works.

Paintings, drawings, prints and sculpture by more than 400 artists from the 18th century to the present are included in the museum's collection. Artists include John James Audubon, John Singleton Copley, Winslow Homer, John Singer Sargent, James McNeill Whistler and N.C. Wyeth. A collection of Native American art and artifacts, along with historical manuscripts, documents and maps also is featured. Anthropological and archeological collections feature artifacts from North, Central and South American cultures.

Time: Allow 3 hours minimum. **Hours:** Tues.-Sun. 10-5. Guided 45-minute tours are given at 2. **Cost:** (includes The Gardens at Gilcrease Museum) $8; $6 (ages 62+ and active military with ID); $5 (college students with ID); free (ages 0-18 and to all first Tues. of the month and third Sun. of the month). An additional fee may be charged for special exhibitions. **Phone:** (918) 596-2700, or (918) 596-2782 for tour information. GT

The Gardens at Gilcrease Museum, on the grounds of the Gilcrease Museum at 1400 N. Gilcrease Museum Rd., comprises 23 acres of thematic formal gardens, including Victorian, Colonial, pre-Columbian and pioneer styles. Paved walking trails allow for exploration, and guided tours are available. **Hours:** Tues.-Sun. 10-5. Guided 45-minute docent-led garden tours are given Sat. at 11, May-June and Sept.-Oct. **Cost:** (includes Gilcrease Museum) $8; $6 (ages 62+ and active military with ID); $5 (college students with ID); free (ages 0-18 and to all first Tues. of the month and third Sun. of the month). **Phone:** (918) 596-2700. GT

ORAL ROBERTS UNIVERSITY, 7777 S. Lewis Ave., has a 200-foot glass and steel prayer tower, a seven-story diamond-shaped library and graduate center complex, a sports center, symphony hall, chapel, carillon and television production studio. The Prayer Tower Visitor Center offers views of the campus from its observation deck. Campus tours are available.

Time: Allow 2 hours minimum. **Hours:** Welcome center Mon.-Sat. noon-5; Campus tours Mon.-Fri. at 10 and 2:15; reservations are required. Closed during spring and fall breaks. Phone ahead to confirm schedule. **Cost:** Free. **Phone:** (918) 495-6165. GT

PHILBROOK MUSEUM OF ART is at 2727 S. Rockford Rd., 1 blk. e. of Peoria Ave. at 27th Pl. This elaborate Italian Renaissance-style villa set on 25 acres of formal and informal gardens was the palatial home of oilman Waite Phillips and his wife Genevieve. Built in the late 1920s, it now houses permanent collections of African, American, Asian, European, Native American and contemporary art.

Changing exhibitions, lectures, films, performances and special events are scheduled throughout the year. **Time:** Allow 2 hours minimum. **Hours:** Wed.-Thurs., Sat-Sun. 9-5; Fri. 9-9. Guided tours Tues.-Sun. at 2. Tour times vary; phone ahead. Closed major holidays. **Cost:** $9; $7 (ages 62+, students with ID); free (ages 0-17 and to all second

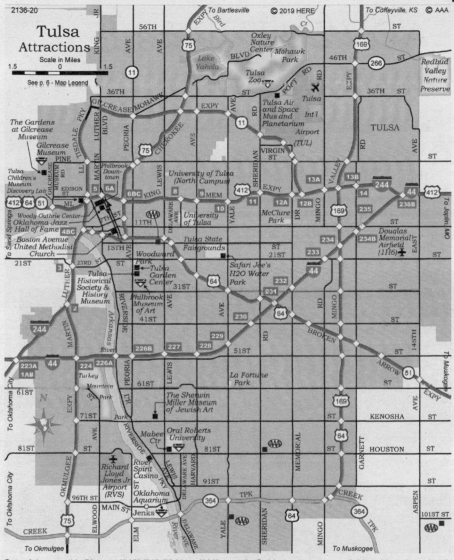

Tulsa Attractions

Scale in Miles

1.5   0   1.5

See p. 6 - Map Legend

Sat. of the month). **Phone:** (918) 749-7941 or (800) 324-7941. GT [✶]

THE SHERWIN MILLER MUSEUM OF JEWISH ART is on the Zarrow Campus at 2021 E. 71st St. The museum houses ancient artifacts; Jewish ritual objects and items used in rites of passage; displays comparing a range of societies and their influence on Jewish culture; history exhibits, including accounts of the Jewish experience in Oklahoma; and displays of fine art.

An area dedicated to the Holocaust features videotaped interviews with survivors. Another part of the museum contains changing exhibitions. **Time:** Allow 1 hour minimum. **Hours:** Mon.-Fri. 10-5, Sun.

1-5. Guided tours are available with a 2-week advance reservation. Closed Jewish holidays and federal holidays. **Cost:** $6.50; $5.50 (ages 55+); $3.50 (ages 6-21). **Phone:** (918) 492-1818. GT

SAVE **TULSA AIR AND SPACE MUSEUM AND PLANETARIUM** is just n. of the Tulsa International Airport at 3624 N. 74th E. Ave. The museum features several aircraft, historic aviation displays and hands-on exhibits. Flight simulator stations offer jet flight experiences. Stars and planets can be identified at the planetarium. Visitors can enjoy an airline flight experience in the MD-80 Flight Theater.

Time: Allow 1 hour minimum. **Hours:** Mon.-Sat. 10-4. Planetarium and MD-80 Flight Theater shows

CHEROKEE
ADVENTURE
AWAITS

DISCOVER A NATION. ENRICH YOUR WORLD.

Cherokee Nation offers unparalleled insight into the largest tribe in the United States. With many unique sites across northeast Oklahoma, including the brand new **Cherokee National History Museum**, we invite you to experience the culture and history of the Cherokee people like never before.

— PLAN YOUR ADVENTURE AT —
VisitCherokeeNation.com

begin at 11; last show begins at 3. Closed major holidays. **Cost:** Museum and one planetarium show $15; $12 (ages 62+ and active military with ID); $10 (ages 5-17 and students with ID). Individual planetarium show $7. Flight Theater show $5. **Phone:** (918) 834-9900.

TULSA CHILDREN'S MUSEUM DISCOVERY LAB is at 560 N. Maybelle Ave. Discovery Lab provides learning experiences for children through interactive exibits designed to enhance skills such as creativity, problem solving and communication. Exhibits include a 30-foot slide and tunnels made of packing tape; a workshop where children and their families can play and create things using a variety of materials; and a toddler play area featuring activities for small children. **Hours:** Mon.-Sat. 9:30-5, Sun. 11:30-5. Closed Thanksgiving and Christmas. **Cost:** $8; free (ages 0-2 and teachers with current staff ID). **Phone:** (918) 295-8144.

TULSA ZOO, 6 mi. n.e. off Sheridan Rd. in Mohawk Park at 6421 E. 36th St. N., houses more than 3,000 animals representing more than 400 species, including many that are rare or endangered. The zoo's 84 acres feature outdoor exhibit areas as well as indoor eco-themed buildings with animals from around the world in habitats similar to their native homes.

The Rainforest exhibit highlights tropical rain forests and includes howler monkeys, reptiles and sloths, among other animals. The Mary K. Chapman Rhino Reserve is a 3-acre habitat housing white rhinoceroses, antelopes and several bird species. A miniature train operates daily, and children can ride in a parade of animal figures on the ARVEST Wildlife Carousel as well as enjoy a playground. Seasonal camel tours, animal chats and demonstrations also are available.

Time: Allow 2 hours minimum. **Hours:** Zoo daily 9-5. Closed third Fri. in June and Christmas. Train and carousel operate when the temperature is between 50 degrees Fahrenheit and a heat index of 100 degrees Fahrenheit; phone ahead for schedule. **Cost:** $12; $10 (ages 65+); $8 (ages 3-11). **Parking:** $2 weekends and holidays, Apr.-Oct. **Phone:** (918) 669-6600. GT

WOODWARD PARK, 21st St. and Peoria Ave., is a 34-acre city park containing the Tulsa Garden Center and the Tulsa Historical Society & History Museum in addition to other areas of horticultural interest, including rock gardens, an herb garden, a conservatory and more than 15,000 azaleas. **Hours:** Daily 5 a.m.-11 p.m. Garden center Tues.-Sat. 9-4. **Cost:** Free. **Phone:** (918) 746-5125. 🅵🆃

Tulsa Garden Center, 1.5 mi. s. of SR 51 at 2435 S. Peoria Ave. in Woodward Park, is the former 1919 home of wealthy oilman David Travis. Included on the grounds are the Linnaeus Teaching Garden, a demonstration space for home gardeners; the Tulsa Rose Garden, created by the Works Progress

Administration (WPA) 1934-35, with nearly 250 varieties of roses on five terraced levels enhanced by stone walls and fountains; and the 3-acre Tulsa Arboretum.

Docent-led tours of the Linnaeus Teaching Garden are offered. **Hours:** Tues.-Sat. 9-4. Closed Jan 1, Memorial Day, July 4, Labor Day, Thanksgiving and Dec. 24-31. **Cost:** Donations. **Phone:** (918) 746-5125. GT

Tulsa Historical Society & History Museum, 2445 S. Peoria Ave. near Woodward Park, offers eight exhibit galleries that change frequently with themes covering a wide range of Tulsa-related topics and a variety of time periods.

The Vintage Gardens, on the grounds, have paved walkways; outdoor statues, including the Five Moons, life-size depictions of Native American ballerinas from Oklahoma; and cornerstones and other architectural elements from former Tulsa buildings. **Time:** Allow 30 minutes minimum. **Hours:** Tues.-Sat. 10-4. Guided tours are available by appointment. Closed major holidays. **Cost:** $5; $3 (ages 65+); free (ages 0-18 and students with ID). **Phone:** (918) 712-9484. GT

WOODY GUTHRIE CENTER, 102 E. M.B. Brady St., features items and memorabilia from the archives of American folk singer and songwriter Woodrow Wilson "Woody" Guthrie. Included in the collection are personal journals, drawings, paintings, instruments, musical recordings and Guthrie's original handwritten lyrics to "This Land is Your Land." **Time:** Allow 45 minutes minimum. **Hours:** Tues.-Sun. 10-6 (also first Fri. of the month 6-9 p.m.). **Cost:** $8; $7 (ages 55+ and college students with ID); $6 (ages 5-17 and military with ID). **Phone:** (918) 574-2710.

Sightseeing

Walking Tours

Tulsa's historical business district mirrors the wealth of the oil industry through its opulent Art Deco architecture. Some of the finest examples of zigzag skyscrapers, the streamline style of the 1930s and the classical style popular during the Great Depression are displayed.

Visitors may choose to explore the area on foot; between 2nd and 6th streets and Cincinnati and Cheyenne avenues there are approximately 40 Art Deco sites. The Tulsa Union Depot, built in 1931, is on 1st Street; the Philtower, known as the "Queen of the Tulsa skyline," can be found on 5th Street near Boston Avenue; the Mincks-Adams Hotel, with its terra cotta facade, is at 4th Street and Cheyenne Avenue; and the 320 South Boston Building, formerly the National Bank of Tulsa, containing a lavish lobby, is at 320 S. Boston Ave.

Visit Tulsa has maps detailing a walking tour of the Art Deco District; check online or phone (918) 585-1201 or (800) 558-3311.

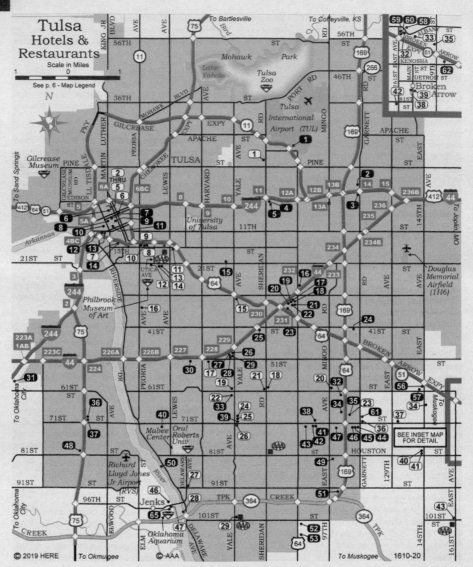

Tulsa
Hotels & Restaurants

Scale in Miles

See p. 6 - Map Legend

N

© 2019 HERE   To Okmulgee   © AAA   To Muskogee   1610-20

✈ Airport Hotels				
TULSA INTERNATIONAL (Maximum driving distance from airport: 4.6 mi)				
Map Page		Designation	Member Savings	Page
❸ this page	Best Western-Airport, 4.6 mi	💎 APPROVED	✔	390
❷ this page	Country Inn & Suites by Radisson, 4.1 mi	💎 APPROVED		390
❶ this page	Hilton Garden Inn Tulsa Airport, 0.9 mi	💎💎 THREE DIAMOND	✔	392
❺ this page	La Quinta Inn & Suites Tulsa Airport/Expo Square, 3.0 mi	💎💎 THREE DIAMOND		393
❹ this page	Super 8 Tulsa Airport, 2.9 mi	💎 APPROVED		394

Tulsa and Vicinity

This index helps you "spot" where hotels and restaurants are located on the corresponding detailed maps. Restaurant price range is a combination of lunch and/or dinner. Turn to the listing page for more information and consult display ads for special promotions.

 For more details, rates and reservations: AAA.com/travelguides/hotels

TULSA

Map Page	Hotels	Designation	Member Savings	Page
1 p. 386	Hilton Garden Inn Tulsa Airport	THREE DIAMOND	✔	392
2 p. 386	Country Inn & Suites by Radisson	APPROVED		390
3 p. 386	**Best Western-Airport**	APPROVED	✔	390
4 p. 386	Super 8 Tulsa Airport	APPROVED		394
5 p. 386	La Quinta Inn & Suites Tulsa Airport/Expo Square	THREE DIAMOND		393
6 p. 386	Fairfield Inn & Suites by Marriott Tulsa Downtown	THREE DIAMOND	✔	392
7 p. 386	Hyatt Regency Tulsa *(See ad p. 393.)*	FOUR DIAMOND	✔	393
8 p. 386	Hampton Inn & Suites by Hilton Tulsa Downtown	THREE DIAMOND	✔	392
9 p. 386	Courtyard by Marriott-Tulsa Downtown	THREE DIAMOND	✔	390
10 p. 386	Aloft-Tulsa Downtown	THREE DIAMOND	✔	390
11 p. 386	**Holiday Inn Tulsa City Center**	THREE DIAMOND	✔	392
12 p. 386	**Best Western Plus Downtown Tulsa**	THREE DIAMOND	✔	390
13 p. 386	DoubleTree by Hilton Tulsa Downtown	THREE DIAMOND	✔	392
14 p. 386	**Ambassador Hotel Tulsa, Autograph Collection**	FOUR DIAMOND	✔	390
15 p. 386	Expo Inn Hotel	APPROVED		392
16 p. 386	Ramada	THREE DIAMOND		393
17 p. 386	**Best Western Plus Tulsa Inn & Suites**	THREE DIAMOND	✔	390
18 p. 386	Clarion Inn & Suites	APPROVED		390
19 p. 386	Days Inn Tulsa Central	THREE DIAMOND		390
20 p. 386	Embassy Suites by Hilton Hotel	THREE DIAMOND	✔	392
21 p. 386	Comfort Suites	THREE DIAMOND		390
22 p. 386	Sleep Inn & Suites Tulsa Central	APPROVED		394
23 p. 386	Hampton Inn & Suites Tulsa/Central	THREE DIAMOND	✔	392
24 p. 386	Wyndham Tulsa	THREE DIAMOND		394
25 p. 386	La Quinta Inn & Suites Tulsa Central	fyi		393
26 p. 386	Comfort Inn Midtown	APPROVED		390
27 p. 386	Holiday Inn Express & Suites Tulsa Midtown	THREE DIAMOND		392
28 p. 386	Hilton Garden Inn Tulsa Midtown	THREE DIAMOND	✔	392
29 p. 386	Residence Inn by Marriott Tulsa Midtown	THREE DIAMOND	✔	393
30 p. 386	Wingate by Wyndham Tulsa	THREE DIAMOND		394
31 p. 386	Super 8 Tulsa	APPROVED		394
32 p. 386	**Best Western Plus Woodland Hills Hotel & Suites**	THREE DIAMOND	✔	390
33 p. 386	DoubleTree by Hilton Hotel Tulsa-Warren Place	THREE DIAMOND	✔	392
34 p. 386	Aloft Tulsa	THREE DIAMOND	✔	390
35 p. 386	**Renaissance Tulsa Hotel & Convention Center**	FOUR DIAMOND	✔	393
36 p. 386	Home2 Suites by Hilton Tulsa Hills	THREE DIAMOND	✔	392
37 p. 386	Hampton Inn & Suites by Hilton Tulsa/Tulsa Hills	THREE DIAMOND	✔	392
38 p. 386	Courtyard by Marriott Woodland Hills	THREE DIAMOND	✔	390
39 p. 386	**Hyatt Place Tulsa/South Medical District**	THREE DIAMOND	✔	392
40 p. 386	Tulsa Marriott Southern Hills	THREE DIAMOND	✔	394
41 p. 386	Baymont Inn & Suites by Wyndham Tulsa	APPROVED		390

TULSA (cont'd)

Map Page	Hotels (cont'd)	Designation	Member Savings	Page
42 p. 386	Comfort Inn	THREE DIAMOND		390
43 p. 386	Hampton Inn & Suites by Hilton-Woodland Hills	THREE DIAMOND	✔	392
44 p. 386	Staybridge Suites	THREE DIAMOND		394
45 p. 386	Residence Inn by Marriott	THREE DIAMOND	✔	393
46 p. 386	SpringHill Suites by Marriott	THREE DIAMOND	✔	394
47 p. 386	Candlewood Suites	APPROVED		390
48 p. 386	SpringHill Suites by Marriott Tulsa at Tulsa Hills	THREE DIAMOND	✔	394
49 p. 386	Hilton Garden Inn Tulsa South	THREE DIAMOND	✔	392
50 p. 386	**River Spirit Casino Resort**	FOUR DIAMOND	✔	394
51 p. 386	Fairfield Inn & Suites by Marriott Tulsa Southeast Crossroads Village	THREE DIAMOND	✔	392
52 p. 386	Holiday Inn Express & Suites	THREE DIAMOND		392
53 p. 386	**Hampton Inn & Suites by Hilton Tulsa South-Bixby**	THREE DIAMOND	✔	392

Map Page	Restaurants	Designation	Cuisine	Price Range	Page
1 p. 386	White River Fish Market	APPROVED	Seafood	$7-$23	395
2 p. 386	Prairie Brewpub	APPROVED	American	$9-$16	395
3 p. 386	The Tavern	THREE DIAMOND	American	$11-$33	395
4 p. 386	Caz's Chowhouse	APPROVED	American	$6-$17	394
5 p. 386	PRHYME: Downtown Steakhouse	THREE DIAMOND	Steak	$23-$70	395
6 p. 386	El Guapo's Cantina	APPROVED	Mexican	$6-$13	394
7 p. 386	The Chalkboard	THREE DIAMOND	Mediterranean	$10-$34	394
8 p. 386	Society Burger	APPROVED	American	$6-$11	395
9 p. 386	Palace Cafe	THREE DIAMOND	New American	$18-$30	395
10 p. 386	Kilkenny's Irish Pub	APPROVED	Irish	$8-$20	394
11 p. 386	Brothers Houligan	APPROVED	American	$5-$15	394
12 p. 386	McGill's	THREE DIAMOND	Steak	$12-$38	395
13 p. 386	Polo Grill	FOUR DIAMOND	Steak	$11-$55	395
14 p. 386	Fleming's Prime Steakhouse & Wine Bar	THREE DIAMOND	Steak	$28-$65	394
15 p. 386	Celebrity Restaurant	APPROVED	Steak	$7-$60	394
16 p. 386	Virgola	THREE DIAMOND	Seafood	$10-$36	395
17 p. 386	Bodeans Seafood Restaurant	THREE DIAMOND	Seafood	$9-$42	394
18 p. 386	La Roma Pizza	APPROVED	Pizza	$5-$10	394
19 p. 386	McGill's	THREE DIAMOND	Steak	$10-$36	395
20 p. 386	The Gnarley Dawg	APPROVED	Hot Dogs	$3-$7	394
21 p. 386	Ti Amo Ristorante	THREE DIAMOND	Italian	$8-$27	395
22 p. 386	Warren Duck Club	THREE DIAMOND	American	$10-$40	395
23 p. 386	Cyprus Grille	THREE DIAMOND	Mediterranean	$10-$38	394
24 p. 386	Mahogany Prime Steakhouse	THREE DIAMOND	Steak	$17-$40	394
25 p. 386	McNellie's Public House	APPROVED	Irish	$7-$18	395
26 p. 386	The French Hen	THREE DIAMOND	Continental	$7-$45	394
27 p. 386	Pepper's Grill	APPROVED	Tex-Mex	$6-$16	395
28 p. 386	Redrock Canyon Grill	THREE DIAMOND	American	$12-$29	395
29 p. 386	The Bistro At Seville	THREE DIAMOND	American	$10-$31	394

BROKEN ARROW

Map Page	Hotels	Designation	Member Savings	Page
56 p. 386	Clarion Hotel	APPROVED		325
57 p. 386	Hampton Inn by Hilton-Tulsa/Broken Arrow	THREE DIAMOND	✔	326
58 p. 386	Hilton Garden Inn Broken Arrow	THREE DIAMOND	✔	326

BROKEN ARROW (cont'd)

Map Page	Hotels (cont'd)	Designation	Member Savings	Page
59 p. 386	TownePlace Suites by Marriott	◈ THREE DIAMOND	✔	326
60 p. 386	Holiday Inn Express & Suites	◈ THREE DIAMOND		326
61 p. 386	Homewood Suites by Hilton Tulsa South	◈ THREE DIAMOND	✔	326
62 p. 386	**Best Western Kenosha Inn**	◈ THREE DIAMOND	✔	325

Map Page	Restaurants	Designation	Cuisine	Price Range	Page
32 p. 386	Oklahoma Joe's Bar-B-Cue	◈ APPROVED	Barbecue	$5-$22	326
33 p. 386	Los Cabos Mexican Grill & Cantina	◈ APPROVED	Mexican	$8-$20	326
34 p. 386	Stone Mill BBQ and Steakhouse	◈ APPROVED	Barbecue	$7-$21	326
35 p. 386	Louie's Grill & Bar	◈ APPROVED	American	$6-$10	326
36 p. 386	Mexico Lindo	◈ APPROVED	Mexican	$5-$10	326
37 p. 386	Ted's Cafe Escondido	◈ APPROVED	Mexican	$7-$14	326
38 p. 386	In The Raw Sushi	◈ APPROVED	Asian Sushi	$8-$45	326
39 p. 386	Fiesta Mambo Downtown	◈ APPROVED	Mexican	$7-$12	326
40 p. 386	El Viejo's	◈ APPROVED	Mexican	$5-$11	326
41 p. 386	Jake's Cafe	◈ APPROVED	American	$5-$9	326
42 p. 386	Duffy's Restaurant	◈ APPROVED	American	$5-$9	326
43 p. 386	Mr Mambo	◈ APPROVED	Mexican	$5-$14	326

JENKS

Map Page	Hotel	Designation	Member Savings	Page
65 p. 386	Holiday Inn Express Hotel & Suites	◈ THREE DIAMOND		336

Map Page	Restaurants	Designation	Cuisine	Price Range	Page
46 p. 386	Los Cabos Mexican Grill & Cantina	◈ APPROVED	Mexican	$8-$20	336
47 p. 386	Waterfront Grill	◈ THREE DIAMOND	Seafood	$10-$29	336

TULSA
- Restaurants p. 394
- Hotels & Restaurants map & index p. 386

ALOFT TULSA   918/949-9000 **34**
THREE DIAMOND **SAVE** Hotel. **Address: 6716 S 104th E Ave 74133**

> **AAA Benefit:** Members save 5% or more!

ALOFT-TULSA DOWNTOWN   918/947-8200 **10**
THREE DIAMOND **SAVE** Hotel. **Address: 200 Civic Center 74103**

> **AAA Benefit:** Members save 5% or more!

AMBASSADOR HOTEL TULSA, AUTOGRAPH COLLECTION   918/587-8200 **14**
FOUR DIAMOND
Historic Hotel

AUTOGRAPH COLLECTION® HOTELS

> **AAA Benefit:** Members save 5% or more!

Address: 1324 S Main St 74119 **Location:** Jct 14th St. **Facility:** Public areas are tastefully furnished and very well appointed. Although this property has a historic background, the guest rooms are spacious with upscale features. 55 units. 9 stories, interior corridors. **Parking:** on-site and valet. **Amenities:** safes. **Dining:** The Chalkboard, see separate listing. **Activities:** exercise room. **Guest Services:** valet laundry, area transportation.

BAYMONT INN & SUITES BY WYNDHAM TULSA
918/252-7754 **41**
APPROVED Hotel. **Address: 9020 E 71st St 74133**

BEST WESTERN-AIRPORT   918/438-0780 **3**
APPROVED
Hotel

Best Western.

> **AAA Benefit:** Members save up to 15% and earn bonus points!

Address: 222 N Garnett Rd 74116 **Location:** I-244 exit 14 (Garnett Rd), just s. **Facility:** 106 units. 2 stories (no elevator), exterior corridors. **Pool:** outdoor. **Activities:** exercise room. **Guest Services:** coin laundry. **Featured Amenity:** full hot breakfast.

BEST WESTERN PLUS DOWNTOWN TULSA
918/794-6000 **12**
THREE DIAMOND
Hotel

Best Western PLUS.

> **AAA Benefit:** Members save up to 15% and earn bonus points!

Address: 707 S Houston Ave 74127 **Location:** Just s of jct 7th St. **Facility:** 79 units. 5 stories, interior corridors. **Activities:** exercise room. **Guest Services:** valet and coin laundry.

BEST WESTERN PLUS TULSA INN & SUITES
918/858-2100 **17**
THREE DIAMOND
Hotel

Best Western PLUS.

> **AAA Benefit:** Members save up to 15% and earn bonus points!

Address: 3212 S 79th E Ave 74145 **Location:** I-44 exit 231 (31st St) eastbound; exit 232 (Memorial Dr) westbound, just sw. **Facility:** 62 units. 3 stories, interior corridors. **Pool:** heated indoor. **Activities:** exercise room. **Guest Services:** valet and coin laundry.

BEST WESTERN PLUS WOODLAND HILLS HOTEL & SUITES   918/249-8100 **32**
THREE DIAMOND
Hotel

Best Western PLUS.

> **AAA Benefit:** Members save up to 15% and earn bonus points!

Address: 10143 E 62nd St S 74133 **Location:** Just w of jct US 169 and 61st St. **Facility:** 65 units. 3 stories, interior corridors. **Amenities:** safes. **Pool:** heated indoor. **Activities:** hot tub, exercise room. **Guest Services:** coin laundry. **Featured Amenity:** full hot breakfast.

CANDLEWOOD SUITES   918/294-9000 **47**
APPROVED Extended Stay Hotel. **Address: 10008 E 73rd St S 74133**

CLARION INN & SUITES   918/663-1000 **18**
APPROVED Hotel. **Address: 3209 S 79th E Ave 74145**

COMFORT INN   918/459-5321 **42**
THREE DIAMOND Hotel. **Address: 9010 E 71st St 74133**

COMFORT INN MIDTOWN   918/488-8777 **26**
APPROVED Hotel. **Address: 4530 E Skelly Dr 74135**

COMFORT SUITES   918/622-6300 **21**
THREE DIAMOND Hotel. **Address: 8039 E 33rd St S 74145**

COUNTRY INN & SUITES BY RADISSON 918/234-3535 **2**
APPROVED Hotel. **Address: 1034 N Garnett Rd 74116**

COURTYARD BY MARRIOTT-TULSA DOWNTOWN
918/508-7400 **9**
THREE DIAMOND **SAVE** Hotel. **Address: 415 S Boston Ave 74103**

> **AAA Benefit:** Members save 5% or more!

COURTYARD BY MARRIOTT WOODLAND HILLS
918/994-4500 **38**
THREE DIAMOND **SAVE** Hotel. **Address: 9041 E 71st St 74133**

> **AAA Benefit:** Members save 5% or more!

DAYS INN TULSA CENTRAL   918/665-4242 **19**
THREE DIAMOND Hotel. **Address: 3215 S 79th E Ave 74145**

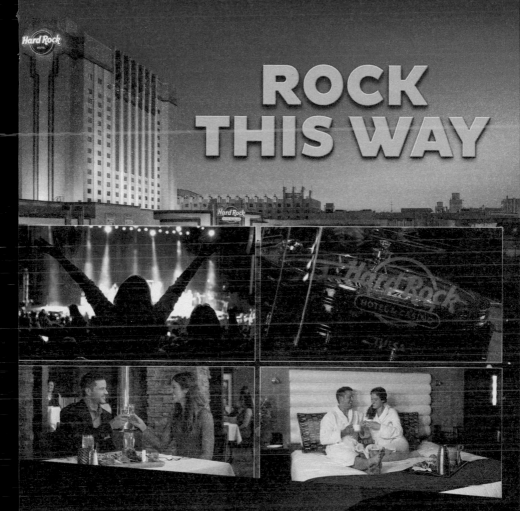

ROCK THIS WAY

At Hard Rock Hotel & Casino Tulsa, you can do it all. Rock the roof off at
The Joint: Tulsa, unwind at The Spa and relax in one of our rooms or suites. Enjoy the
delicious fare at any of our various restaurants or play one of the over 2,400 games on
our massive casino floor. Any gamer is sure to find a new favorite or enjoy an old classic.

Often Imitated. Never Duplicated.

Hard Rock
HOTEL & CASINO

TULSA

AAA
FOUR DIAMOND

1-44 Exit 240 | 800.760.6700 | HARDROCKCASINOTULSA.COM

ONE★STAR

Know your limits. Gambling problem? Call 800.522.4700.

(See map & index p. 386.)

DOUBLETREE BY HILTON HOTEL TULSA-WARREN PLACE
918/495-1000 **33**
THREE DIAMOND **SAVE** Hotel. **Address:** 6110 S Yale Ave 74136

AAA Benefit: Members save up to 15%!

DOUBLETREE BY HILTON TULSA DOWNTOWN
918/587-8000 **13**
THREE DIAMOND **SAVE** Hotel. **Address:** 616 W 7th St 74127

AAA Benefit: Members save up to 15%!

EMBASSY SUITES BY HILTON HOTEL 918/622-4000 **20**
THREE DIAMOND **SAVE** Hotel. **Address:** 3332 S 79th E Ave 74145

AAA Benefit: Members save up to 15%!

EXPO INN HOTEL 918/858-3775 **15**
APPROVED Hotel. **Address:** 4531 E 21st St 74114

FAIRFIELD INN & SUITES BY MARRIOTT TULSA DOWNTOWN
918/879-1800 **6**
THREE DIAMOND **SAVE** Hotel. **Address:** 111 N Main St 74103

AAA Benefit: Members save 5% or more!

FAIRFIELD INN & SUITES BY MARRIOTT TULSA SOUTHEAST CROSSROADS VILLAGE 918/994-4700 **51**
THREE DIAMOND **SAVE** Hotel. **Address:** 9150 S 102nd E Ave 74133

AAA Benefit: Members save 5% or more!

HAMPTON INN & SUITES BY HILTON TULSA DOWNTOWN
918/949-6900 **8**
THREE DIAMOND **SAVE** Hotel. **Address:** 211 W 3rd St 74103

AAA Benefit: Members save up to 15%!

HAMPTON INN & SUITES BY HILTON TULSA SOUTH-BIXBY 918/394-2000 **53**
THREE DIAMOND
Hotel

AAA Benefit: Members save up to 15%!

Address: 8220 E Regal Pl 74133 **Location:** Just e of jct Memorial Dr. **Facility:** 102 units. 4 stories, interior corridors. **Pool:** heated indoor. **Activities:** exercise room. **Guest Services:** valet and coin laundry.

HAMPTON INN & SUITES BY HILTON TULSA/TULSA HILLS
918/340-5000 **37**
THREE DIAMOND **SAVE** Hotel. **Address:** 7004 S Olympia Ave 74132

AAA Benefit: Members save up to 15%!

HAMPTON INN & SUITES BY HILTON-WOODLAND HILLS
918/294-3300 **43**
THREE DIAMOND **SAVE** Hotel. **Address:** 7141 S 85th E Ave 74133

AAA Benefit: Members save up to 15%!

HAMPTON INN & SUITES TULSA/CENTRAL
918/779-4000 **23**
THREE DIAMOND **SAVE** Hotel. **Address:** 3418 S 79th E Ave 74145

AAA Benefit: Members save up to 15%!

HILTON GARDEN INN TULSA AIRPORT 918/838-1444 **1**
THREE DIAMOND **SAVE** Hotel. **Address:** 7728 E Virgin Ct 74115

AAA Benefit: Members save up to 15%!

HILTON GARDEN INN TULSA MIDTOWN 918/878-7777 **28**
THREE DIAMOND **SAVE** Hotel. **Address:** 4518 E Skelly Dr 74135

AAA Benefit: Members save up to 15%!

HILTON GARDEN INN TULSA SOUTH 918/392-2000 **49**
THREE DIAMOND **SAVE** Hotel. **Address:** 8202 S 100th E Ave 74133

AAA Benefit: Members save up to 15%!

HOLIDAY INN EXPRESS & SUITES 918/970-6000 **52**
THREE DIAMOND Hotel. **Address:** 8405 E 102nd St 74133

HOLIDAY INN EXPRESS & SUITES TULSA MIDTOWN
918/986-8200 **27**
THREE DIAMOND Hotel. **Address:** 4680 E Skelly Dr 74135

HOLIDAY INN TULSA CITY CENTER 918/585-5898 **11**
THREE DIAMOND
Hotel

Address: 17 W 7th St 74119 **Location:** Jct Boulder Ave. **Facility:** 220 units. 15 stories, interior corridors. **Parking:** on-site (fee). **Amenities:** safes. **Pool:** heated indoor. **Amenities:** hot tub, exercise room. **Guest Services:** valet and coin laundry, area transportation.

HOME2 SUITES BY HILTON TULSA HILLS
918/970-6800 **36**
THREE DIAMOND **SAVE** Extended Stay Contemporary Hotel. **Address:** 6910 S Olympia Ave 74132

AAA Benefit: Members save up to 15%!

HYATT PLACE TULSA/SOUTH MEDICAL DISTRICT
918/491-4010 **39**
THREE DIAMOND
Hotel

HYATT PLACE **AAA Benefit:** Members save up to 10%!

Address: 7037 S Zurich Ave 74136 **Location:** I-44 exit 229 (Yale Ave), 3 mi s to 71st St, then just e. **Facility:** 126 units. 6 stories, interior corridors. **Pool:** outdoor. **Activities:** exercise room. **Guest Services:** valet laundry. **Featured Amenity:** breakfast buffet.

(See map & index p. 386.)

HYATT REGENCY TULSA   918/234-1234   **7**

FOUR DIAMOND   **HYATT REGENCY**   **AAA Benefit:** Members save up to 10%!
Hotel

Address: 100 E 2nd St 74103 **Location:** Jct 2nd St and Boston Ave; downtown. **Facility:** This hotel has a great location near the BOK Center, restaurants and museums The recently renovated, upscale rooms feature large desks and enhanced bedding. 444 units. 14 stories, interior corridors. **Parking:** on-site (fee) and valet. **Terms:** check-in 4 pm. **Amenities:** safes. **Pool:** heated outdoor, heated indoor. **Activities:** exercise room. **Guest Services:** valet and coin laundry, area transportation. (See ad this page.)

[SAVE] [icons] CALL [icons] [BIZ] [icons] / SOME UNITS [icons]

GET THE APP
Download today.
Connect every day.
AAA.com/mobile
CAA.ca/mobile

[AAA logo] [CAA logo]

LA QUINTA INN & SUITES TULSA AIRPORT/EXPO SQUARE
918/949-3600   **5**
THREE DIAMOND Hotel. **Address:** 23 N 67th E Ave 74115

LA QUINTA INN & SUITES TULSA CENTRAL
918/665-2630   **25**
[fyi] Hotel. Under major renovation, call for details. Last Designation Approved. **Address:** 6030 E Skelly Dr 74135

RAMADA   918/828-9128   **16**
THREE DIAMOND Hotel. **Address:** 8175 E Skelly Dr 74129

RENAISSANCE TULSA HOTEL & CONVENTION CENTER   918/307-2600   **35**
FOUR DIAMOND   **R RENAISSANCE HOTELS**   **AAA Benefit:** Members save 5% or more!
Hotel

Address: 6808 S 107th E Ave 74133 **Location:** Just ne of jct US 169 and 71st St. **Facility:** Water cascading over a rock wall and a stream winding through the lobby create a scenic and serene ambience at this upscale hotel. Guest rooms feature upgraded bedding and comfy seating. 300 units. 9 stories, interior corridors. **Terms:** check-in 4 pm. **Amenities:** safes. **Dining:** Cyprus Grille, see separate listing. **Pool:** heated indoor. **Activities:** sauna, exercise room. **Guest Services:** valet and coin laundry, boarding pass kiosk, area transportation.

[SAVE] [icons] CALL [icons] [BIZ] [SHS] [icons] / SOME UNITS [icons]

RESIDENCE INN BY MARRIOTT   918/250-4850   **45**
THREE DIAMOND [SAVE] Extended Stay Hotel. **Address:** 11025 E 73rd St 74133
AAA Benefit: Members save 5% or more!

RESIDENCE INN BY MARRIOTT TULSA MIDTOWN
918/984-3600   **29**
THREE DIAMOND [SAVE] Extended Stay Hotel. **Address:** 4522 E Skelly Dr 74135
AAA Benefit: Members save 5% or more!

▼ See AAA listing this page ▼

(See map & index p. 386.)

RIVER SPIRIT CASINO RESORT 918/995-8581 **50**
FOUR DIAMOND
Hotel

Address: 8330 Riverside Pkwy 74137 **Location:** Waterfront. Just s of jct 81st St. **Facility:** Upscale furnishings, quality and comfort are the hallmarks of this spacious and colorful property. When you step into the pool area, you'll feel like you've been transported to a tropical paradise. 483 units. 26 stories, interior corridors. **Parking:** on-site and valet. **Terms:** check-in 4 pm. **Amenities:** safes. **Dining:** 5 restaurants. **Pool:** heated outdoor. **Activities:** cabanas, exercise room, spa. **Guest Services:** valet laundry. **Featured Amenity: full hot breakfast.**

SLEEP INN & SUITES TULSA CENTRAL 918/663-2777 **22**
APPROVED Hotel. **Address:** 8021 E 33rd St S 74145

SPRINGHILL SUITES BY MARRIOTT 918/254-1777 **46**
THREE DIAMOND SAVE Hotel. **Address:** 11015 E 73rd St S 74133

AAA Benefit: Members save 5% or more!

SPRINGHILL SUITES BY MARRIOTT TULSA AT TULSA HILLS
918/392-8100 **48**
THREE DIAMOND SAVE Hotel. **Address:** 1521 W 80th St S 74132

AAA Benefit: Members save 5% or more!

STAYBRIDGE SUITES 918/461-2100 **44**
THREE DIAMOND Extended Stay Hotel. **Address:** 11111 E 73rd St 74133

SUPER 8 TULSA 918/446-6000 **31**
APPROVED Motel. **Address:** 5811 S 49th W Ave 74107

SUPER 8 TULSA AIRPORT 918/836-1981 **4**
APPROVED Hotel. **Address:** 6616 E Archer 74115

TULSA MARRIOTT SOUTHERN HILLS 918/493-7000 **40**
THREE DIAMOND SAVE Hotel. **Address:** 1902 E 71st St 74136

AAA Benefit: Members save 5% or more!

WINGATE BY WYNDHAM TULSA 918/392-5116 **30**
THREE DIAMOND Hotel. **Address:** 2854 E 51st St 74105

WYNDHAM TULSA 918/627-5000 **24**
THREE DIAMOND Hotel. **Address:** 10918 E 41st St 74146

WHERE TO EAT

ANDOLINI'S PIZZERIA 918/728-6111
APPROVED Pizza. Casual Dining. **Address:** 1552 E 15th St 74120

THE BISTRO AT SEVILLE 918/296-3000 **29**
THREE DIAMOND American. Fine Dining. **Address:** 10021 S Yale Ave 74145

BODEANS SEAFOOD RESTAURANT 918/749-1407 **17**
THREE DIAMOND Seafood. Fine Dining. **Address:** 3376 E 51st St 74105

BROTHERS HOULIGAN 918/747-1086 **11**
APPROVED American. Casual Dining. **Address:** 2508 E 15th St 74104

CAZ'S CHOWHOUSE 918/588-2469 **4**
APPROVED American. Casual Dining. **Address:** 18 E Brady St 74103

CELEBRITY RESTAURANT 918/743-1800 **15**
APPROVED Steak. Casual Dining. **Address:** 3109 S Yale Ave 74135

THE CHALKBOARD 918/582-1964 **7**
THREE DIAMOND Mediterranean. Fine Dining. **Address:** 1324 S Main St 74119

CHARLESTON'S RESTAURANT
APPROVED American. Casual Dining.
LOCATIONS:
Address: 6839 S Yale Ave 74136 **Phone:** 918/495-3511
Address: 3726 S Peoria Ave 74136 **Phone:** 918/749-3287

CYPRUS GRILLE 918/307-2600 **23**
THREE DIAMOND Mediterranean. Fine Dining. **Address:** 6808 S 107th E Ave 74133

EL CHICO
APPROVED Tex-Mex. Casual Dining.
LOCATIONS:
Address: 9705 E 71st St 74133 **Phone:** 918/252-9442
Address: 9825 E 21st St 74129 **Phone:** 918/663-7755
Address: 4107 S Yale Ave, Suite DL401 74135 **Phone:** 918/665-6519

EL GUAPO'S CANTINA 918/382-7482 **6**
APPROVED Mexican. Casual Dining. **Address:** 332 E 1st St 74120

FLEMING'S PRIME STEAKHOUSE & WINE BAR
918/712-7500 **14**
THREE DIAMOND Steak. Fine Dining. **Address:** 1976 Utica Square 74114

THE FRENCH HEN 918/492-2596 **26**
THREE DIAMOND Continental. Fine Dining. **Address:** 7143 S Yale Ave 74136

THE GNARLEY DAWG 918/893-4663 **20**
APPROVED Hot Dogs. Quick Serve. **Address:** 6011 S Mingo Ave 74146

GOLDIES PATIO GRILL 918/494-0330
APPROVED American. Casual Dining. **Address:** 6121 E 61st St 74136

HIDEAWAY PIZZA
APPROVED Pizza. Casual Dining.
LOCATIONS:
Address: 7877 E 51st St 74145 **Phone:** 918/270-4777
Address: 8222 E 103rd St 74133 **Phone:** 918/366-4777
Address: 7549 S Olympia Ave 74132 **Phone:** 918/609-6777

KILKENNY'S IRISH PUB 918/582-8282 **10**
APPROVED Irish. Gastropub. **Address:** 1413 E 15th St 74120

LA ROMA PIZZA 918/491-6436 **18**
APPROVED Pizza. Quick Serve. **Address:** 6027 S Sheridan Rd 74145

MAHOGANY PRIME STEAKHOUSE 918/494-4043 **24**
THREE DIAMOND Steak. Fine Dining. **Address:** 6823 S Yale Ave 74136

(See map & index p. 386.)

MCGILL'S   918/388-8080 (19)
◆◆ THREE DIAMOND Steak. Fine Dining. **Address:** 6058 S
Yale Ave 74136

MCGILL'S   918/742-8080 (12)
◆◆ THREE DIAMOND Steak. Fine Dining. **Address:** 1560 E
21st St 74114

MCNELLIE'S PUBLIC HOUSE   918/933-5250 (25)
◆◆ APPROVED Irish. Casual Dining. **Address:** 7031 S
Zurich St 74136

PALACE CAFE   918/582-4321 (9)
◆◆ THREE DIAMOND New American. Fine Dining. **Address:**
1301 E 15th St 74120

PEPPER'S GRILL   918/296-0592 (27)
◆◆ APPROVED Tex-Mex. Casual Dining. **Address:** 2809
E 91st St 74137

POLO GRILL   918/744-4280 (13)
◆◆ FOUR DIAMOND Steak. Fine Dining. **Address:** 2038 Utica
Square 74114

PRAIRIE BREWPUB   918/936-4395 (2)
◆◆ APPROVED American. Brewpub. **Address:** 223 N
Main St 74103

PRHYME: DOWNTOWN STEAKHOUSE   918/794-7700 (5)
◆◆ THREE DIAMOND Steak. Fine Dining. **Address:** 111 N Main
St 74103

REDROCK CANYON GRILL   918/394-7625 (28)
◆◆ THREE DIAMOND American. Casual Dining. **Address:** 9916
Riverside Pkwy 74137

RIB CRIB BBQ AND GRILL
◆◆ APPROVED Barbecue. Casual Dining.
LOCATIONS:
Address: 5025 S Sheridan Rd 74145 **Phone:** 918/663-4295
Address: 8040 S Yale Ave 74136 **Phone:** 918/492-8627
Address: 1601 S Harvard Ave 74112 **Phone:** 918/742-2742
Address: 3232 W Skelly Dr 74104 **Phone:** 918/447-1400

RON'S HAMBURGERS & CHILI
◆◆ APPROVED American. Casual Dining.
LOCATIONS:
Address: 7119 S Mingo Rd 74133 **Phone:** 918/250-7667
Address: 8201 S Harvard Ave 74105 **Phone:** 918/496-4328

SOCIETY BURGER   918/392-7667 (8)
◆◆ APPROVED American. Casual Dining. **Address:** 1419
E 15th St 74120

THE TAVERN   918/949-9801 (3)
◆◆ THREE DIAMOND American. Gastropub. **Address:** 201 N
Main 74103

TI AMO RISTORANTE   918/499-1919 (21)
◆◆ THREE DIAMOND Italian. Fine Dining. **Address:** 6024A S
Sheridan Rd 74145

VIRGOLA   918/345-0680 (16)
◆◆ THREE DIAMOND Seafood. Casual Dining. **Address:** 1326
E 35th St 74105

WARREN DUCK CLUB   918/497-2158 (22)
◆◆ THREE DIAMOND American. Fine Dining. **Address:** 6110 S
Yale Ave 74136

WHITE RIVER FISH MARKET   918/835-1910 (1)
◆◆ APPROVED Seafood. Quick Serve. **Address:** 1708 N
Sheridan Rd 74115

ZIO'S ITALIAN KITCHEN   918/250-5999
◆◆ APPROVED Italian. Casual Dining. **Address:** 7111 S
Mingo Rd 74133

VINITA (B-11) pop. 5,743, elev. 702'

Vinita was named by a Cherokee Indian, Col. Elias C. Boudinot, after sculptress Vinnie Ream, whose most renowned work is the pensive statue of Abraham Lincoln at the U.S. Capitol. Boudinot fell in love with the young artist while she was in Washington, D.C., on a commission to create the statue. The first woman to be granted such a federal art commission, Ream's sculpture was unveiled in 1871, the same year Vinita was founded.

Since the days of the longhorn cattle drives from Texas, ranching has been an important industry in Vinita. Early cattlemen, however, would hardly recognize the Brangus, which is a hardy combination of purebred Brahman and Aberdeen-Angus cattle. The breed was created by Raymond Pope, a rancher who lived in the area.

The Eastern Trails Museum, inside the Vinita Public Library at 215 W. Illinois Ave., outlines Oklahoma history through displays of regional Native American and pioneer artifacts, Route 66 relics, a re-created post office and general store and memorabilia from the Civil War and World Wars I and II. The museum is open Mon.-Fri. 11-4, Sat. 11-3; phone (018) 323 1300.

Vinita is an access point for the recreational opportunities on the western shore of Grand Lake O' the Cherokees, created in 1941 with the completion of the Pensacola Dam on the Grand River. *See Recreation Areas Chart.*

Vinita Area Chamber of Commerce: 105 W. Delaware Ave., Vinita, OK 74301. **Phone:** (918) 256-7133.

HOLIDAY INN EXPRESS HOTEL & SUITES   918/256-4900
◆◆ APPROVED Hotel. **Address:** 232 S 7th St 74301

WHERE TO EAT

CLANTON'S CAFE   918/256-9053
◆◆ APPROVED American. Casual Dining. **Address:** 319
E Illinois Ave 74301

WEATHERFORD (D-6) pop. 10,833, elev. 1,647'
• Hotels p. 396 • Restaurants p. 396

On the afternoon of April 18, 1892, Oklahoma began its third land run; throngs of men and women gathered at the border of Cheyenne and Arapaho country, waiting for a chance at land ownership. The next morning they rose early, arriving by wagon and on foot to establish the town of Weatherford.

Once a stop on historic Route 66, Weatherford is home to Southwestern Oklahoma State University, known for its school of pharmacy.

Weatherford Chamber of Commerce: 210 W. Main St., Weatherford, OK 73096. **Phone:** (580) 772-7744.

HEARTLAND OF AMERICA MUSEUM is off I-40 exit 84 westbound or exit 82 eastbound at 1600 S. Frontage Rd. The museum, which features a wide variety of items from the late 19th century through the middle of the 20th, houses displays about agriculture, Route 66, vintage cars and tractors, Native Americans and the petroleum industry.

Areas of the museum re-create a general store, a pharmacy, a funeral home and a doctor's office while outside the main building stands a replica of a blacksmith shop and a little redbrick schoolhouse. An exhibit about famous Oklahomans describes Weatherford native, astronaut Thomas P. Stafford. An exterior feature is an original, refurbished Route 66 diner, which in its heyday is said to have had a few famous names drop in, including Elvis Presley. Rotating exhibits also are offered. **Time:** Allow 45 minutes minimum. **Hours:** Tues.-Fri. 9-5, Sat. 1-5, during DST; Tues.-Fri. 9-4, Sat. 1-4, rest of year. Closed major holidays. **Cost:** $6; $2 (ages 6-18 and college students with ID). **Phone:** (580) 774-2212. GT

STAFFORD AIR & SPACE MUSEUM, 3000 Logan Rd. at the Stafford Airport, is a Smithsonian affiliate and tribute to Weatherford native Lt. Gen. Thomas P. Stafford's military and aeronautical career. Exhibits showcase the evolution of aviation and spaceflight.

On display is a 10-story-high Titan II rocket, an Apollo command and service module, NASA space suits (including an Apollo 10 pressure suit worn by Stafford) and a space shuttle solid rocket booster through which visitors can walk.

Hours: Mon.-Sat. 9-5, Sun. 1-5. **Cost:** $7; $5 (ages 55+, veterans and active military with ID); $2 (ages 6-18 and students with ID). **Phone:** (580) 772-5871.

BEST WESTERN PLUS - WEATHERFORD 580/772-3325

THREE DIAMOND

Hotel

Best Western PLUS. **AAA Benefit:** Members save up to 15% and earn bonus points!

Address: 525 E Main St 73096 **Location:** I-40 exit 82, 0.5 mi n. **Facility:** 63 units, some two bedrooms and kitchens. 2 stories, exterior corridors. **Pool:** outdoor. **Activities:** exercise room. **Guest Services:** coin laundry. **Featured Amenity:** full hot breakfast.

SAVE CALL BIZ / SOME UNITS

COMFORT INN & SUITES 580/772-9100
THREE DIAMOND Hotel. **Address:** 1311 E Main St 73096

FAIRFIELD INN & SUITES BY MARRIOTT 580/774-0800
THREE DIAMOND SAVE Hotel. **Address:** 201 N Nevada 73096

AAA Benefit: Members save 5% or more!

HOLIDAY INN EXPRESS HOTEL & SUITES 580/774-0400
THREE DIAMOND Hotel. **Address:** 3825 E Main St 73096

WHERE TO EAT

EL PATIO MEXICAN GRILL AND CANTINA 580/774-5336
APPROVED Mexican. Casual Dining. **Address:** 310 W Washington St 73096

LUIGI'S ITALIAN RESTAURANT 580/774-2502
APPROVED Italian. Casual Dining. **Address:** 111 W Main St 73096

WEST SILOAM SPRINGS pop. 846, elev. 1,142'
• Hotels p. 396

BEST WESTERN STATELINE LODGE 918/422-4444

APPROVED

Hotel

Best Western. **AAA Benefit:** Members save up to 15% and earn bonus points!

Address: 273 S Hwy 59 74338 **Location:** Jct US 59 and 412. **Facility:** 50 units. 2 stories, interior corridors. **Pool:** heated indoor. **Activities:** exercise room. **Guest Services:** coin laundry.

SAVE BIZ HS

CHEROKEE CASINO & HOTEL WEST SILOAM SPRINGS 918/422-6301
THREE DIAMOND Hotel. **Address:** 2416 Hwy 412 74338 *(See ad p. 66.)*

WEWOKA pop. 3,430, elev. 804'

BEST WESTERN PLUS WEWOKA INN & SUITES
405/257-6777

THREE DIAMOND
Hotel

Best Western PLUS.

AAA Benefit: Members save up to 15% and earn bonus points!

Address: 201 Commerce Dr 74884 **Location:** Jct US 270 and SR 56. **Facility:** 52 units. 3 stories, interior corridors. **Pool:** heated indoor. **Activities:** hot tub, exercise room. **Guest Services:** coin laundry. **Featured Amenity: full hot breakfast.**

SAVE CALL

WOODWARD pop. 12,051, elev. 1,893'

HAMPTON INN & SUITES WOODWARD
580/254-5050

THREE DIAMOND SAVE Hotel. **Address:** 2814 Williams Ave 73801

AAA Benefit: Members save up to 15%!

HOLIDAY INN EXPRESS HOTEL & SUITES
580/256-5200

THREE DIAMOND Hotel. **Address:** 3333 Williams Ave 73801

NORTHWEST INN
580/256-7600

THREE DIAMOND
Hotel

Address: 3202 1st St 73801 **Location:** 1.4 mi s of jct US 183, 270 and 412. **Facility:** 125 units. 2 stories (no elevator), interior/exterior corridors. **Pool:** heated indoor. **Activities:** miniature golf, game room, exercise room. **Guest Services:** valet and coin laundry. **Featured Amenity:** full hot breakfast.

SAVE

Make the Connection

Find this symbol for places to look, book and save on AAA.com.

YUKON pop. 22,709

• Part of Oklahoma City area — see map p. 343

BEST WESTERN PLUS YUKON
405/265-2995

THREE DIAMOND
Hotel

Best Western PLUS.

AAA Benefit: Members save up to 15% and earn bonus points!

Address: 11440 W I-40 Service Rd 73099 **Location:** I-40 exit 138, just sw. **Facility:** 69 units. 2 stories, interior/exterior corridors. **Pool:** heated indoor. **Activities:** hot tub, exercise room. **Guest Services:** coin laundry. **Featured Amenity: full hot breakfast.**

SAVE

COMFORT SUITES
405/577-6500

THREE DIAMOND Hotel. **Address:** 11424 NW 4th St 73099

HAMPTON INN BY HILTON
405/350-6400

THREE DIAMOND
Hotel

Hampton

AAA Benefit: Members save up to 15%!

Address: 1351 Canadian Ct 73099 **Location:** I-40 exit 136, just ne. **Facility:** 73 units. 3 stories, interior corridors. **Pool:** heated indoor. **Activities:** exercise room. **Guest Services:** valet and coin laundry. **Featured Amenity:** full hot breakfast.

SAVE

HOLIDAY INN EXPRESS & SUITES
405/494-7171

THREE DIAMOND Hotel. **Address:** 700 Shedeck Pkwy 73099

HOME2 SUITES BY HILTON OKLAHOMA CITY YUKON
405/265-0999

THREE DIAMOND SAVE Extended Stay Contemporary Hotel. **Address:** 11510 W I-40 Service Rd 73099

AAA Benefit: Members save up to 15%!

LA QUINTA INN & SUITES OKLAHOMA CITY-YUKON
405/494-7600

THREE DIAMOND Hotel. **Address:** 11500 W I-40 73099

SLEEP INN & SUITES
405/265-4945

THREE DIAMOND Hotel. **Address:** 12520 NW 10th St 73099

WHERE TO EAT

ALFREDO'S MEXICAN CAFE
405/354-4343

APPROVED Mexican. Casual Dining. **Address:** 1751 Garth Brooks Blvd, Suite 110 73099

HIDEAWAY PIZZA
405/231-4777

APPROVED Italian Pizza. Casual Dining. **Address:** 1701 Shedeck Pkwy 73099

PRIMO'S D'ITALIA
405/350-9090

APPROVED Italian. Casual Dining. **Address:** 1215 Garth Brooks Blvd, Suite C 73099

RIB CRIB BBQ AND GRILL
405/354-2828

APPROVED Barbecue. Casual Dining. **Address:** 1750 Garth Brooks Blvd 73099

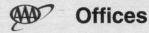 **Offices**

Main office listings are shown in **BOLD TYPE** and toll-free member service numbers appear in *ITALIC TYPE*.
All are closed Saturdays, Sundays and holidays unless otherwise indicated.
The addresses, phone numbers and hours for any AAA/CAA office are subject to change.
The type of service provided is designated below the name of the city where the office is located:

✛ Auto travel services, including books and maps, and on-demand TripTik® routings.
● Auto travel services, including selected books and maps, and on-demand TripTik® routings.
■ Books/maps only, no marked maps or on-demand TripTik® routings.
▲ Travel Agency Services, cruise, tour, air, car and rail reservations; domestic and international hotel reservations; passport photo services; international and domestic travel guides and maps; travel money products; and International Driving Permits. In addition, assistance with travel related insurance products including trip cancellation, travel accident, lost luggage, trip delay and assistance products.
✪ Insurance services provided. If only this icon appears, only insurance services are provided at that office.
⚡ Car Care Plus Facility provides car care services.
🔌 Electric vehicle charging station on premises.

AAA NATIONAL OFFICE: 1000 AAA DRIVE, HEATHROW, FLORIDA 32746-5063, (407) 444-7000

ARKANSAS

BENTONVILLE—AAA MISSOURI, 1501 SE WALTON BLVD #111, 72712. WEEKDAYS (M-F) 9:00-5:30, SAT 9:00-1:00. (479) 254-9223 ✛ ▲ ✪

CONWAY—AAA MISSOURI, 603 COURT ST # 2, 72032. WEEKDAYS (M-F) 9:00-5:30 (SAT BY APPOINTMENT ONLY). (501) 327-9222 ✪

FAYETTEVILLE—AAA MISSOURI, 3595-6 N SHILOH DR, 72703. WEEKDAYS (M-F) 9:00-5:30, SAT 9:00-1:00. (479) 444-9222 ✛ ▲ ✪

FORT SMITH—AAA MISSOURI, 1401 S WALDRON RD #103, 72903. WEEKDAYS (M-F) 9:00-5:30, SAT 9:00-1:00. (479) 452-2010 ✪

HOT SPRINGS—AAA MISSOURI, 227 HOBSON AVE, 71913. WEEKDAYS (M-F) 9:00-5:30 (SAT BY APPOINTMENT ONLY). (501) 624-1222 ✪

LITTLE ROCK—AAA MISSOURI, 9116 RODNEY PARHAM RD, 72205. WEEKDAYS (M-F) 9:00-5:30, SAT 9:00-1:00. (501) 223-9222 ✛ ▲ ✪

NORTH LITTLE ROCK—AAA MISSOURI, 4505 JFK BLVD STE 1, 72116. WEEKDAYS (M-F) 9:00-5:30 (SAT BY APPOINTMENT ONLY). (501) 771-9100 ✪

KANSAS

ANDOVER—AAA CLUB ALLIANCE INC, 321 S ANDOVER RD STE 300, 67002. WEEKDAYS (M-F) 8:30-5:30 (SAT BY APPOINTMENT). (316) 733-1720 ■ ✪

LAWRENCE—AAA CLUB ALLIANCE INC, 3514 CLINTON PKWY #L, 66047. WEEKDAYS (M-F) 9:00-6:00, SAT 9:00-3:00. (785) 843-1600, *(800) 234-1442.* ✛ ▲ ✪

MANHATTAN—AAA CLUB ALLIANCE INC, 321 SOUTHWIND RD, 66503. WEEKDAYS (M-F) 9:00-6:00, SAT 9:00-3:00. (785) 776-3131, *(800) 579-9470.* ✛ ▲ ✪

MISSION—AAA MISSOURI, 5421 JOHNSON DR, 66205. WEEKDAYS (M-F) 9:00-5:30 (SAT BY APPOINTMENT ONLY). (913) 236-5678 ✪

OLATHE—AAA MISSOURI, 113 S MUR LEN RD, 66062. WEEKDAYS (M-F) 9:00-5:30 (SAT BY APPOINTMENT ONLY). (913) 764-5300 ✪

OVERLAND PARK—AAA MISSOURI, 10600 METCALF, 66212. WEEKDAYS (M-F) 9:00-5:30, SAT 9:00-1:00. (913) 649-2280 ✛ ▲ ✪

OVERLAND PARK—AAA MISSOURI, 8260 W 151ST ST, 66223. WEEKDAYS (M-F) 9:00-5:30 (SAT BY APPOINTMENT ONLY). (913) 851-8383 ✪

SHAWNEE—AAA MISSOURI, 15810 B SHAWNEE MSN PKWY, 66217. WEEKDAYS (M-F) 9:00-5:30, SAT 9:00-1:00. (913) 248-1627 ✛ ▲ ✪

TOPEKA—AAA CLUB ALLIANCE INC, 1223 SW WANAMAKER, 66604. WEEKDAYS (M-F) 9:00-6:00. (785) 233-0222, *(866) 245-6222.* ✛ ▲ ✪

TOPEKA—AAA CLUB ALLIANCE INC, 1940 SW GAGE STE B, 66604. WEEKDAYS (M-F) 9:00-5:00 (SAT BY APPT ONLY). (785) 439-2820 ■ ✪

WICHITA—AAA CLUB ALLIANCE INC, 2110 N MAIZE RD STE 400, 67212. WEEKDAYS (M-F) 9:00-6:00, SAT 9:00-3:00. (316) 942-0008, *(800) 789-4222.* ✛ ▲ ✪

WICHITA—AAA CLUB ALLIANCE INC, 4425 WEST ZOO BLVD STE #5, 67212. WEEKDAYS (M-F) 9:00-5:00. (316) 636-7744 ■ ✪

WICHITA—AAA CLUB ALLIANCE INC, 7730 E CENTRAL AVE, 67206. WEEKDAYS (M-F) 9:00-6:00, SAT 9:00-3:00. (316) 685-5241, *(800) 759-7222.* ✛ ▲ ✪

MISSOURI

ARNOLD—AAA MISSOURI, 3510 JEFFCO BLVD STE 103, 63010. WEEKDAYS (M-F) 9:00-5:30 (SAT BY APPOINTMENT ONLY). (636) 464-6222 ✪

ARNOLD—AAA MISSOURI, 3904 VOGEL RD, 63010. WEEKDAYS (M-F) 9:00-5:30 (SAT BY APPOINTMENT ONLY). (636) 287-9222 ✪

BALLWIN—AAA MISSOURI, 477 LAFAYETTE CENTER, 63011. WEEKDAYS (M-F) 9:00-5:30, SAT 9:00-1:00. (636) 394-0052 ✛ ▲ ✪

BRENTWOOD—AAA MISSOURI, 8308 EAGER RD, 63144. WEEKDAYS (M-F) 9:00-5:30, SAT 9:00-1:00. (314) 862-8021 ✛ ▲ ✪

CAPE GIRARDEAU—AAA MISSOURI, 1903 BROADWAY, 63701. WEEKDAYS (M-F) 9:00-5:30, SAT 9:00-1:00. (573) 334-3038 ✛ ▲ ✪

CHESTERFIELD—AAA MISSOURI, 15510 OLIVE BLVD STE 202, 63017. WEEKDAYS (M-F) 9:00-5:30 (SAT BY APPOINTMENT ONLY). (636) 532-9229 ✪

COLUMBIA—AAA MISSOURI, 1205 GRINDSTONE PKY #117, 65201. WEEKDAYS (M-F) 9:00-5:30, SAT 9:00-1:00. (573) 445-8426 ✛ ▲ ✪

COLUMBIA—AAA MISSOURI, 313 S PROVIDENCE RD, 65203. WEEKDAYS (M-F) 8:30-5:30 (SAT BY APPOINTMENT ONLY). (573) 874-1909 ✪

CREVE COEUR—AAA MISSOURI, 11441 OLIVE BLVD, 63141. WEEKDAYS (M-F) 9:00-5:30, SAT 9:00-1:00. (314) 989-0793 ✪

CREVE COEUR—AAA MISSOURI, 13035 OLIVE BLVD STE 101, 63141. WEEKDAYS (M-F) 9:00-5:30 (SAT BY APPOINTMENT ONLY). (314) 434-5555 ✪

FARMINGTON—AAA MISSOURI, 725B MAPLE VALLEY DR, 63640. WEEKDAYS (M-F) 9:00-5:30, SAT 9:00-1:00. (573) 756-4299 ✪

FLORISSANT—AAA MISSOURI, 8194 N LINDBERGH BLVD, 63031. WEEKDAYS (M-F) 9:00-5:30, SAT 9:00-1:00. (314) 838-9900 ✚▲✪

INDEPENDENCE—AAA MISSOURI, 19210 E 39TH ST STE B, 64057. WEEKDAYS (M-F) 9:00-5:30, SAT 9:00-1:00. (816) 373-1717 ✚▲✪

JEFFERSON CITY—AAA MISSOURI, 757A W STADIUM BLVD, 65109 WEEKDAYS (M-F) 9:00-5:30, SAT 9:00-1:00. (573) 634-3322 ✚✪

JOPLIN—AAA MISSOURI, 2639 E 32ND ST #D, 64804. WEEKDAYS (M-F) 9:00-5:30, SAT 9:00-1:00. (417) 624-2000 ✪

KANSAS CITY—AAA MISSOURI, 3245 BROADWAY, 64111. WEEKDAYS (M-F) 9:00-5:30, SAT 9:00-1:00. (816) 931-5252 ✚✪

KANSAS CITY—AAA MISSOURI, 9194 NORTH SKYVIEW AVE, 64154. WEEKDAYS (M-F) 9:00-5:30, SAT 9:00-1:00. (816) 455-4900 ✚▲✪

KANSAS CITY—AAA MISSOURI, 9205 NE HWY 152, 64158. WEEKDAYS (M-F) 9:00-5:30, SAT 9:00-12:00. (816) 781-4222 ✪

LEE'S SUMMIT—AAA MISSOURI, 621 NW MURRAY RD, 64081. WEEKDAYS (M-F) 9:00-5:30, SAT 9:00-1:00. (816) 623-3369 ✚▲✪

LIBERTY—AAA MISSOURI, 810 W LIBERTY DR, 64068. WEEKDAYS (M-F) 9:00-5:30 (SAT BY APPOINTMENT ONLY). (816) 781-9999 ✪

MOBERLY—AAA MISSOURI, 213 N WILLIAMS, 65270. WEEKDAYS (M-F) 8:30-5:30 (SAT BY APPOINTMENT ONLY). (660) 263-8844 ✪

O'FALLON—AAA MISSOURI, 2277 HWY K, 63368. WEEKDAYS (M-F) 9:00-5:30, SAT 9:00-1:00. (636) 272-2362 ✚▲✪

O'FALLON—AAA MISSOURI, 844 BRYAN RD, 63366. WEEKDAYS (M-F) 9:00-5:30 (SAT BY APPOINTMENT ONLY). (636) 272-1365 ✪

SEDALIA—AAA MISSOURI, 1204 WINCHESTER, 65301. WEEKDAYS (M-F) 9:00-5:30, SAT 9:00-1:00. (660) 826-1800 ✪

SPRINGFIELD—AAA MISSOURI, 2552 S CAMPBELL #B, 65807. WEEKDAYS (M-F) 9:00-5:30, SAT 9:00-1:00. (417) 882-8040 ✚▲✪

ST. CHARLES—AAA MISSOURI, 1046 COUNTRY CLUB RD, 63303. WEEKDAYS (M-F) 9:00-5:30 (SAT BY APPOINTMENT ONLY). (636) 946-2229 ✪

ST. JOSEPH—AAA MISSOURI, 3823 FREDERICK BLVD, 64506. WEEKDAYS (M-F) 9:00-5:30, SAT 9:00-1:00. (816) 233-1377 ✪

ST. LOUIS—AAA MISSOURI, 12901 N FORTY DR, 63141. WEEKDAYS (M-F) 9:00-5:30, SAT 9:00-1:00. (314) 514-7888 ✚▲✪

ST. LOUIS—AAA MISSOURI, 3917 LINDELL BLVD, 63108. WEEKDAYS (M-F) 9:00-5:30, SAT 9:00-1:00. (314) 531-0700 ✚✪

ST. LOUIS—AAA MISSOURI, 9005 WATSON RD, 63126. WEEKDAYS (M-F) 9:00-5:30, SAT 9:00-1:00. (314) 962-2282 ✚▲✪

ST. LOUIS—AAA MISSOURI, 9960 KENNERLY CTR PLZ, 63128. WEEKDAYS (M-F) 9:00-5:30, SAT 9:00-1:00. (314) 849-6663 ✚▲✪

ST. PETERS—AAA MISSOURI, 591 MID RIVERS MALL DR, 63376. WEEKDAYS (M-F) 9:00-5:30, SAT 9:00-1:00. (636) 279-2299 ✚▲✪

WASHINGTON—AAA MISSOURI, 2000 WASHINGTON CROSSING, 63090. WEEKDAYS (M-F) 9:00-5:30, SAT 9:00-1:00. (636) 239-6791 ✚▲✪

WENTZVILLE—AAA MISSOURI, 1126 W PEARCE BLVD #100, 63385. WEEKDAYS (M-F) 9:00-5:30, SAT 9:00-1:00. (636) 327-0570 ✪

OKLAHOMA

ADA—AAA CLUB ALLIANCE INC, 1306 ARLINGTON ST, 74820. WEEKDAYS (M-F) 9:00-5:00 (SAT BY APPOINTMENT ONLY), FRI 9:00-4:00. (580) 332-4222 ✪

ARDMORE—AAA CLUB ALLIANCE INC, 604 GRAND AVE, 73401. WEEKDAYS (M-F) 9:00-5:00 (SAT BY APPOINTMENT ONLY). (580) 223-0222 ✪

ATOKA—AAA CLUB ALLIANCE INC, 151 S MISSISSIPPI, 74525. WEEKDAYS (M-F) 9:00-5:00 (SAT BY APPOINTMENT ONLY). (580) 889-7571 ✪

BARTLESVILLE—AAA CLUB ALLIANCE INC, 112 SE FRANK PHILLIPS BLV, 74003. WEEKDAYS (M-F) 8:30-5:00. (918) 337-3737, (800) 688-2701. ✚▲✪

BETHANY—AAA CLUB ALLIANCE INC, 6901 NW 23RD ST, 73008. WEEKDAYS (M-F) 8:30-5:30 (SAT BY APPOINTMENT ONLY). (405) 787-9595 ✪

BIXBY—AAA CLUB ALLIANCE INC, 8222 E 103RD ST S STE 110, 74133. WEEKDAYS (M-F) 8:30-5:00 (SAT BY APPOINTMENT ONLY). (918) 364-8222 ✪

BROKEN ARROW—AAA CLUB ALLIANCE INC, 1103 N KALANCHOE AVE, 74012. WEEKDAYS (M-F) 9:00-5:00 (SAT BY APPOINTMENT ONLY). (918) 251-8877 ✪

BROKEN ARROW—AAA CLUB ALLIANCE INC, 3746 S ELM PL, 74011. WEEKDAYS (M-F) 8:30-5:30. (918) 455-4764, (800) 380-6443. ✚▲✪

BROKEN ARROW—AAA CLUB ALLIANCE INC, 721 W QUEENS STREET, 74012. WEEKDAYS (M-F) 9:00-5:00 (SAT BY APPOINTMENT ONLY). (918) 872-8105 ✪

CATOOSA—AAA CLUB ALLIANCE INC, 750 CHEROKEE ST STE F, 74015. WEEKDAYS (M-F) 9:00-5:00. (918) 213-4443 ✪

CHOCTAW—AAA CLUB ALLIANCE INC, 14855 BYPASS ST STE 105, 73020. WEEKDAYS (M-F) 8:30-5:00 (SAT BY APPT ONLY). (405) 602-1512 ●✪

CLAREMORE—AAA CLUB ALLIANCE INC, 445 S BRADY, 74017. WEEKDAYS (M-F) 8:30-5:30 (SAT BY APPOINTMENT ONLY). (918) 341-2100 ✪

COLLINSVILLE—AAA CLUB ALLIANCE INC, 11519 N GARNETT RD STE A, 74055. WEEKDAYS (M-F) 8:30-5:00 (SAT BY APPOINTMENT ONLY). (918) 371-7800 ✪

EDMOND—AAA CLUB ALLIANCE INC, 1312 N KELLY AVE, 73003. WEEKDAYS (M-F) 9:00-5:00 (SAT BY APPOINTMENT ONLY). (405) 513-6500 ✪

EDMOND—AAA CLUB ALLIANCE INC, 16620 N WESTERN AVE, 73012. WEEKDAYS (M-F) 9:00-5:00 (SAT BY APPOINTMENT ONLY). (405) 340-5222 ✪

EDMOND—AAA CLUB ALLIANCE INC, 1701 S BROADWAY AVE, 73013. WEEKDAYS (M-F) 7:30-6:00, SAT 8:00-5:00. (405) 348-8281, (888) 841-9127. ✚▲✪🄲

ENID—AAA CLUB ALLIANCE INC, 215 W OWEN GARRIOTT # 1B, 73701. WEEKDAYS (M-F) 8:30-5:30 (SAT BY APPOINTMENT ONLY). (580) 242-7100 ✪

GROVE—AAA CLUB ALLIANCE INC, 1006 S MAIN ST, 74344. WEEKDAYS (M-F) 9:00-5:00 (SAT BY APPOINTMENT ONLY). (918) 786-4500 ✪

GUTHRIE—AAA CLUB ALLIANCE INC, 622 S DIVISION ST, 73044. WEEKDAYS (M-F) 9:00-5:00 (SAT BY APPOINTMENT ONLY). (405) 293-6633 ✪

LANGLEY—AAA CLUB ALLIANCE INC, 445800 HWY 28, 74350. MON 9:00-4:00, TUE 9:00-4:00, WED 9:00-4:00, THU 9:00-4:00, FRI 9:00-3:00. (918) 782-4240 ✪

LAWTON—AAA CLUB ALLIANCE INC, 1924 NW CACHE RD STE 3, 73507. WEEKDAYS (M-F) 9:00-5:00 (SAT BY APPOINTMENT ONLY). (580) 536-9100 ✪

MCALESTER—AAA CLUB ALLIANCE INC, 319 S 6TH ST, 74501. WEEKDAYS (M-F) 9:00-5:00, FRI 9:00-4:00. (918) 426-1104 ✪

MIDWEST CITY—AAA CLUB ALLIANCE INC, 101 N DOUGLAS BLVD STE Y, 73130. WEEKDAYS (M-F) 8:30-5:30. (405) 670-1474 ✪

MOORE—AAA CLUB ALLIANCE INC, 420 S BROADWAY STE A, 73160. WEEKDAYS (M-F) 8:30-5:30 (SAT BY APPOINTMENT ONLY), FRI 8:00-5:00. (405) 799-2870 ✪

MUSKOGEE—AAA CLUB ALLIANCE INC, 1021 W OKMULGEE ST, 74401. WEEKDAYS (M-F) 8:30-5:30. (918) 683-0341, *(800) 259-9299.* ✚▲✪

NEWCASTLE—AAA CLUB ALLIANCE INC, 216 N MAIN ST, 73065. WEEKDAYS (M-F) 8:30-5:00. (405) 387-2318 ■✪

NORMAN—AAA CLUB ALLIANCE INC, 1017 24TH AVE NW, 73069. WEEKDAYS (M-F) 8:30-5:30. (405) 360-7771, *(877) 314-3489.* ✚▲✪

NORMAN—AAA CLUB ALLIANCE INC, 430 W MAIN ST, 73069. WEEKDAYS (M-F) 8:30-5:00 (SAT BY APPOINTMENT ONLY). (405) 801-3353 ✪

OKLAHOMA CITY—AAA CLUB ALLIANCE INC, 3549 W MEMORIAL RD, 73134. WEEKDAYS (M-F) 8:30-5:30. (405) 753-9777, *(888) 434-2270.* ✚▲✪

OKLAHOMA CITY—AAA CLUB ALLIANCE INC, 6163 N MAY AVE, 73112. WEEKDAYS (M-F) 7:30-6:00, SAT 8:00-5:00. (405) 717-8200, *(800) 926-9922.* ✚▲✪€

OKLAHOMA CITY—AAA CLUB ALLIANCE INC, 8503 S WESTERN AVE, 73139. WEEKDAYS (M-F) 9:00-5:00 (SAT BY APPOINTMENT ONLY). (405) 604-5600 ✪

OWASSO—AAA CLUB ALLIANCE INC, 8506 N 128 E AVE, 74055. WEEKDAYS (M-F) 8:30-5:30 (SAT BY APPOINTMENT ONLY). (918) 272-4700 ✪

PURCELL—AAA CLUB ALLIANCE INC, 104 S GREEN, 73080. WEEKDAYS (M-F) 9:00-5:30 (SAT BY APPOINTMENT ONLY). (405) 527-1200 ✪

SALLISAW—AAA CLUB ALLIANCE INC, 116 CHEROKEE AVE, 74955. WEEKDAYS (M-F) 9:00-5:00 (SAT BY APPOINTMENT ONLY). (918) 208-0146 ✪

SAND SPRINGS—AAA CLUB ALLIANCE INC, 401 E BROADWAY STE B2, 74063. WEEKDAYS (M-F) 8:30-5:30 (SAT BY APPOINTMENT ONLY). (918) 245-8884 ✪

SAPULPA—AAA CLUB ALLIANCE INC, 114-B W TAFT AVE, 74066. WEEKDAYS (M-F) 9:00-5:30. (918) 512-6565 ✪

SHAWNEE—AAA CLUB ALLIANCE INC, 1146 N HARRISON, 74801. WEEKDAYS (M-F) 9:00-5:30 (SAT BY APPOINTMENT ONLY). (405) 275-4222 ✪

SKIATOOK—AAA CLUB ALLIANCE INC, 518 W ROGERS BLVD, 74070. WEEKDAYS (M-F) 9:00-5:00. (918) 396-7542 ✪

STILLWATER—AAA CLUB ALLIANCE INC, 106 W MILLER AVE, 74075. WEEKDAYS (M-F) 8:30-5:30. (405) 372-7448 ✪

TAHLEQUAH—AAA CLUB ALLIANCE INC, 1409 S MUSKOGEE AVE STE 1, 74464. WEEKDAYS (M-F) 8:00-5:00 (SAT BY APPOINTMENT ONLY). (918) 456-5835 ✪

TULSA—AAA CLUB ALLIANCE INC, 10051 S YALE STE 106, 74137. WEEKDAYS (M-F) 8:30-5:30. (918) 296-9600, *(888) 222-7611.* ✚▲✪

TULSA—AAA CLUB ALLIANCE INC, 11609 E 31ST ST, 74146. WEEKDAYS (M-F) 9:00-5:30 (SAT BY APPOINTMENT ONLY). (918) 949-4080 ✪

TULSA—AAA CLUB ALLIANCE INC, 2121 E 15TH ST, 74104. WEEKDAYS (M-F) 8:30-6:00. (918) 748-1000, *(800) 222-2582.* ✚▲✪

TULSA—AAA CLUB ALLIANCE INC, 3856 SOUTHWEST BLVD, 74107. WEEKDAYS (M-F) 8:30-5:00 (SAT BY APPOINTMENT ONLY). (918) 960-2700 ✪

TULSA—AAA CLUB ALLIANCE INC, 4103 E 31ST ST, 74135. WEEKDAYS (M-F) 9:00-5:00 (SAT BY APPOINTMENT ONLY), FRI 9:00-3:00. (918) 712-8003 ✪

TULSA—AAA CLUB ALLIANCE INC, 4924 S MEMORIAL DR, 74145. WEEKDAYS (M-F) 8:30-5:30 (SAT BY APPOINTMENT ONLY). (918) 663-7600 ✪

TULSA—AAA CLUB ALLIANCE INC, 5920 S LEWIS AVE, 74105. WEEKDAYS (M-F) 8:30-5:30. (918) 748-1230 ✪

TULSA—AAA CLUB ALLIANCE INC, 6808 S MEMORIAL STE 208, 74133. WEEKDAYS (M-F) 8:30-5:30 (SAT BY APPOINTMENT ONLY). (910) 872-7100 ✪

TULSA—AAA CLUB ALLIANCE INC, 8013 S SHERIDAN RD, 74133. WEEKDAYS (M-F) 8:30-5:30, SAT 9:00-1:00. (918) 496-0496, *(800) 745-5222.* ✚▲✪

WOODWARD—AAA CLUB ALLIANCE INC, 1915 OKLAHOMA AVE STE # 1, 73801. WEEKDAYS (M-F) 9:00-5:00 (SAT BY APPOINTMENT ONLY). (580) 256-7200 ✪

YUKON—AAA CLUB ALLIANCE INC, 1817 COMMONS CIRCLE STE B, 73099. WEEKDAYS (M-F) 9:00-5:00. (405) 494-6550 ✪

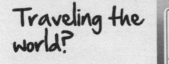

Photo Credits

Page numbers are in bold type. Picture credit abbreviations are as follows:
- (i) numeric sequence from top to bottom, left to right ▪ (AAA) AAA Travel library.

- (Cover) The Gateway Arch, St. Louis, MO / © iStockphoto.com / Davel5957
- **8** (i) © iStockphoto.com / Sean Pavone
- **8** (ii) © iStockphoto.com / zrfphoto
- **9** © iStockphoto.com / zrfphoto
- **10** (i) Courtesy of Wikimedia Commons
- **10** (ii) © Walmart Corporate / flickr / CC BY
- **13** (i) © iStockphoto.com / Diane Helentjaris
- **13** (ii) © iStockphoto.com / MindStorm-inc
- **13** (iii) © iStockphoto.com / SteveClever
- **13** (iv) © iStockphoto.com / traveler1116
- **13** (v) © iStockphoto.com / Foxys_forest_manufacture
- **14** (i) © iStockphoto.com / jcrader
- **14** (ii) © iStockphoto.com / zrfphoto
- **14** (iii) © iStockphoto.com / Lukasok
- **14** (iv) © iStockphoto.com / zrfphoto
- **70** (i) © iStockphoto.com / tomofbluesprings
- **70** (ii) © iStockphoto.com / lfistand
- **71** © iStockphoto.com / Timurpix
- **72** (i) Courtesy of Wikimedia Commons
- **72** (ii) Courtesy of Wikimedia Commons
- **75** (i) © iStockphoto.com / ale_rizzo
- **75** (ii) Dan Leeth / Alamy Stock Photo
- **75** (iii) Ian Dagnall / Alamy Stock Photo
- **75** (iv) © iStockphoto.com / snipes213
- **75** (v) © iStockphoto.com / sjlayne
- **76** (i) © Jim Bowen / flickr / CC BY
- **76** (ii) © iStockphoto.com / NEALITPMCCLIMON
- **76** (iii) © iStockphoto.com / hfrankWI
- **76** (iv) © iStockphoto.com / sframephoto
- **130** (i) © iStockphoto.com / snipes213
- **130** (ii) © iStockphoto.com / traveler1116
- **131** © iStockphoto.com / alejandrophotography
- **132** (i) Courtesy of Wikimedia Commons
- **132** (ii) Courtesy of Wikimedia Commons
- **135** (i) © iStockphoto.com / MikeVanSchoonderwalt
- **135** (ii) © iStockphoto.com / ANDREYGUDKOV
- **135** (iii) © iStockphoto.com / Scott Gross
- **135** (iv) © iStockphoto.com/ Stephen Emlund
- **135** (v) © iStockphoto.com / stevanovicigor
- **136** (i) © Don Kasak / Wikimedia Commons / CC BY
- **136** (ii) © iStockphoto.com / RobFranklin
- **136** (iii) © IStockphoto.com / Stephen Emlund
- **136** (iv) © iStockphoto.com / SondraP
- **150** Courtesy of Titanic Branson
- **153** Courtesy of Silver Dollar City Attractions
- **154** Courtesy of Chateau on the Lake Resort and Spa
- **155** © iStockphoto.com / LauriPatterson
- **156** © iStockphoto.com / boggy22
- **157** © iStockphoto.com / sergeyryzhov
- **158** © iStockphoto.com / artisteer
- **159** © iStockphoto.com / P_Wei
- **160** Courtesy of Silver Dollar City
- **161** © iStockphoto.com / kali9
- **162** © iStockphoto.com / alexsokolov
- **164** © iStockphoto.com / akaplummer
- **198** © iStockphoto.com / SharonDay

(cont'd)

Safe Travels
We've Got You Covered

AAA Insurance

From vacations to recreation, downtime should be worry free. Trust your knowledgeable AAA insurance representative to help you get the right coverage for every phase of life.
Enjoy quality products at competitive rates.

Stop by your local AAA office
or visit us online.
AAA.com/Insurance

Auto • Home • Life & Other Insurance Products

Hit the Road
with Foreign Currency

A treasure trove of artisan masterpieces awaits.

Visit your local AAA office or
AAA.com/ForeignCurrency
to learn more.

Get INVOLVED and Keep Teens Safe

Exploring the countryside or visiting nearby cities can be perfect opportunities to teach your teens good habits and rules of the road — before and after they learn to drive.

TeenDriving.AAA.com
DriveRight.CAA.ca